Shakespeare's Sonnets

Sunil Kumar Sarker

ATLANTIC

PUBLISHERS & DISTRIBUTORS (P) LTD

Published by

ATLANTIC

PUBLISHERS & DISTRIBUTORS (P) LTD

7/22, Ansari Road, Darya Ganj,
New Delhi-110002
Phones : +91-11-40775252, 23273880, 23275880, 23280451
Fax : +91-11-23285873
Web : www.atlanticbooks.com
E-mail : orders@atlanticbooks.com

Branch Office
5, Nallathambi Street, Wallajah Road,
Chennai-600002
Phones : +91-44-64611085, 32413319
E-mail : chennai@atlanticbooks.com

Printed in India at Glorious Printers, A-13, D.S.I.D.C.,
Jhilmil Industrial Area, Delhi-110095

TO

THE MEMORY OF MY FATHER-IN-LAW

LATE MOTILAL DAS

TO

THE MEMORY OF MY FATHER-IN-LAW

LATE MOTILAL DAS

Preface

By consensus, Shakespeare is the greatest sonneteer of the Elizabethan period of English literature, and further, one of the greatest sonneteers of the world. A.C. Ward was not amiss when he wrote : "If Shakespeare had written nothing but his *Sonnets* he would still have a secure place among the great poets." But, unfortunately, Shakespeare, the dramatist, has over-shadowed Shakespeare, the sonneteer. Perhaps we should re-adjudicate : we should change the situation — we should place the 'dramatist Shakespeare' and the 'poet Shakespeare' side by side, and then have a full view of him as a great literary genius. And that will not be possible, if we do not take into account the sonnets of the poet. This is one reason why we should allocate more leisure to Shakespeare's sonnets. The sweet-sounding words, the sonorous alliterations, the appropriate rhythms, the beautiful images, and, to cap all these, the unalloyed sincerity and overwhelming intensity of passions, of the sonnets, will always appeal to sonnet-lovers.

In literature, we generally first admire the works of the author, and then seek for the author, the man behind the works himself, so that we can love him, and so that we can try to find out the equation between the works of the author and the author himself. As regards Shakespeare, we certainly admire his works, but, unfortunately, we have not yet been able to find out the man, Shakespeare — the man with all his individual likes and dislikes, his weals and woes, his aspirations and frustrations, his intellectual merits and moral faults, etc. If we sincerely want to understand this mysterious man, his plays will not help us much, but perhaps, his sonnets will do a lot. Who is not interested in the man, Shakespeare ? And if one really is, let him read the sonnets of the man, between the lines. This is the second reason. There is an over-lapping, an interface, between Shakespeare's sonnets, on the one hand, and his plays, particularly his early plays, on the other. The cross-reference between the two are very interesting : they show us the same mind working behind, from two different perspectives, and thus help advance our knowledge of Shakespeare and his great genius. If we do not want to multiply the reasons of reading the sonnets of Shakespeare, let us content ourselves with this third reason.

The principal purpose of this book is to explain all the 154 sonnets of Shakespeare, and discuss about some of the topical questions regarding them. Generally, sonnets, as they are song-like, are simple poems, easy to follow. But Shakespeare's sonnets are not of the common ilk. W.G. Ingram and Theodore Redpath very rightly wrote : "We believe that most honest and intelligent readers of these poems [the sonnets of Shakespeare] admit that many of them are far from easy to understand." Therefore, while discussing the topical problems of the sonnets, I have taken helps of a number of authors; and while explaining the sonnets themselves, I admit, three great commentators have been my constant guides : Ingram and Redpath, and John Kerrigan.

Nevertheless, I have, certainly, preferred to explain the sonnets, to a great extent, from my own point of view. I have tried to make the explanations as plain and easy-to-understand as possible, so that even initiates may not find any cumbrance.

I very sincerely thank Dr. K.R. Gupta, Ph.D., Managing Director, M/s Atlantic Publishers and Distributors, New Delhi for publishing this book. His interest in my manuscripts has greatly inspired me to write on. The helps of my wife, Smt. Manju Sarker, and my two sons, Suman and Sutanu, in preparing the manuscript of this book, were auxiliary. They all deserve my affectionate thanks.

SUNIL KUMAR SARKER

Contents

I

Shakespeare : Life and Works

It is curious that we know very little about the man who is the greatest dramatist, and one of the greatest poets and sonneteers, of the world : William Shakespeare. The cause of this our ignorance is not far to seek. Over four hundred years ago, when one unknown Stratford-born man, one almost uncouth villager, Shakespeare, staged his dramas in the famous Globe and other theatre-houses, the poeple of London, from all walks of life, enjoyed his plays being spell-bound and immobile in their seats; but almost as soon as he left his 'mortal coil', the same people forgot him almost forthwith, for, to them the play was the thing and the dramatist nothing. This was true not only about Shakespeare, but also about his contemporary playwrights and poets. For, how much do we know of Ben Jonson, or of Marlowe, or of Spenser? Generally, people then were not interested in biography; that is why we do not find any biography, worth the term, in the Elizabethan age. Moreover, the playwrights then were not held in high esteeem.

Even most of his contemporary and immediately succeeding poets and playwrights failed to correctly assess the greatness of Shakespeare. The University Wits thought him to be simply a poetaster. Robert Green, for instance, wrote about Shakespeare, in his *Groatsworth of Wit* : "An upstart crow beautified with our feathers". Shakespeare's contemporary dramatist, Ben Jonson, with whom he had many points of biographical similitude — both of them starting their career as virtual knaves and reaching the height of literary fame within very short periods, and both of them being great dramatists, poets, and actors — had a great opinion about him as a dramatist, and saw him as the " 'Soul of the Age, the applause, delight, the wonder of our stage' " (Raleigh, 2), but has not left for us any biographical sketch of him. Others simply failed to understand the depth and the height of Shakespeare. Even as great a poet as Milton could not well gauge the greatness of Shakespeare's genius, otherwise he would not consider him "Simply as the author of a marvellous book'' (Raleigh, 2). The situation did not improve in the 17th and the 18th centuries, because in these two centuries, for unsatisfactory reasons, or rather for uncanny reasons, Shakespeare was very sparingly read and hardly staged. However, it was principally due to the insoucience of the Elizabethans about biography that we lost the personal data of the poet. Not that the Elizabethans were only interested in the action and not in the actor, but that they were interested only in the actions and personalities of great men, such as Kings and Queens and their strappling courtiers, which the playwrights certainly were not. Nor could the Sonnets of Shakespeare bring him wide and immediate eminence, because these were only privately printed and circulated as pirated copies. Therefore, his sonnets and other poems also could not save him from the doom of partial anonymity. And so when since the beginning of the 19th century, he came back to abiding eminence, all the traces of his memory well went to the limbo beyond retrieval.

There is yet another difficulty in understanding the man William Shakespeare. There are 'disintegrators' of Shakespeare who hold that there was no such person called William Shakespeare who wrote the plays and the poems generally known to have been written by a person of that name, but that those works actually belong to Christopher Marlowe (1564-1593) or to Francis Bacon (1561-1626) or to somebody else. The 'distintegrators' bank their assumptions on the outcrops of other writers to be sparingly found in Shakespeare's works. The Shakespeare-Marlowe theory contends that Marlowe was not actually fatally stabbed and killed on 30 May, 1593, by the hired assasin Ingram Frizer, in a Deptford inn, but he went underground after recovering from the stabbing, for fear of being persecuted for reasons of his atheistic persuasion and publications, and that he, from his hide-out, poured forth in a continual stream the dramatic and poetic works generally known to be written by Shakespeare.

On the other hand, the Shakespeare-Bacon theory holds that ''the Stratford Peasant'' (Carlyle) who was ''self-schooled'' (Arnold) cannot be expected to be such a great master of thoughts, histories, philosophy, psychology and all that are strewn throughout the works known to be Shakespeare's, but that the presence of these prove that the works known to be Shakespeare's must have been done by the great contemporary master of all these profounder regions of knowledge, Francis Bacon (1561-1626). Francis, or Lord, Bacon was a great philosopher and scientist, and an author of a number of books, such as

Novum Organum, The Advancement of Learning, History of Henry VII, etc. He was, in his later life, accused of 'corruption and neglect', but his intellectual pre-eminence was not completely overcast thereby. That was why Alexander Pope called him the "wisest, brightest, meanest of mankind", and Macaulay described him as "the supreme example of shining intellect conjoined to a base and abject moral nature". The Shakespeare-Bacon theorists try to find out parallels between Bacon's works and Shakespeare's, regarding style, wisdom, and even phraseology. Some of the Shakespeare-Bacon theorists are : Delia Bacon, W.H. Smith, Mrs. Henry Pott, Mrs. E.W. Gallup and Sir Edwin Dunning-Lawrence. The last named scholar found a cryptographic word at *Love's Labour's Lost*, V, i, 38, to 'conclusively' prove that all the works of Shakespeare actually belong to Francis Bacon. "This (word) is 'honorificabilitudinitatibus' the 27 letters of which form the anagram, "Hi ludi F Baconis nati tuiti orbi' : 'These plays, F. Bacon's offspring, are preserved for the world.' " (Halliday, 48).

The move to 'distintegrate' Shakespeare continued till the first half of the 20th century. In Germany and Belgium, some critics thought that the works of Shakespeare actually belonged to Roger Manners, the 5th Earl of Rutland. In France, some of the 'distintegrators' claimed William Stanley, the 6th Earl of Derby, to be the real name behind the *nom de plume* William Shakespeare. But the movement of the 'distintegrators' has now stopped, perhaps for ever. Today the plea of the 'distintegrators' is taken only as too fantastical.

Today we know for certain that there was a real William Shakespeare who was born to John Shakespeare and Mary Arden (Shakespeare) of Stratford-upon-Avon on 23 or 26 April, 1564, as the third among the seven issues of his parents. The surname 'Shakespeare' is of great antiquity, and it originated in the county of Warwick from where the Shakespeares branched out in all directions, one branch establishing itself at Stratford, a village on the bank of the narrow river Avon. Shakespeare's paternal grandfather, Richard Shakespeare, farmed in two manors at Snitterfield. One of these manors belonged to Robert Arden, the maternal grandfather of our poet. Richard Shakespeare had two sons — Henry and John, the father of William Shakespeare. Richard died about three years before the birth of our poet, *i.e.* in 1561. John Shakespeare moved from Snitterfield to Henley Street, and became a 'glover' and also traded in barley, timber, wool, etc. When John was in his teens, the family could hardly make the two ends meet; but by dint of devotion and perseverance he soon prospered in business and could provide his family with a modest living. In 1565, when our poet was only about one year old, John Shakespeare became an Alderman, and in 1568 the Bailiff or Mayor of the town. John married Mary Arden, daughter of his father's landlord at Snitterfield, in 1577. It may be mentioned here that there was another John Shakespeare (c. 1584-95) at Stratford, who was a shoemaker. These two 'John Shakespeares' must not be confused. Mary Arden came from the Arden family that resided at Wilmcote, a village about three miles north-west of Startford.

Our poet, Shakespeare, went to Stratford Grammar School which provided liberal education to boys upto the age of sixteen. Whether he was a "whining school-boy" we do not know, but what Jaques says in *As You Like It* (II, vii, 145-47) about a school-boy may be his self-portraiture: "Then the whining school-boy, with his satchel/And shining morning face, creeping like snail/Unwilling to school." To the school he went with his 'horn book' ("a first book for children, which consisted of a single leaf set in a frame, with thin plate of transparent horn in front to preserve it", and in course of time picked up some French, Italian and Latin (but not Greek) along with smacks of other subjects, and also acquainted himself with Caesar, Cicero, Virgil, Horace, Ovid, Plautus, Terence and Seneca. Probably when Shakespeare was in the last grade in the Grammar School, or just before that, his father's business suffered a great set back for unknown reasons. This is apparent from the fact that in 1578 or 1579, John Shakespeare mortgaged his wife's property at Wilmcote, and also sold her share in the Snitterfield estate. This fiancially straitened condition of the family compelled young Shakespeare to leave the Grammar School, and henceforth he was being taught in the universal school of the world.

It was also from this time that John Shakespeare had been going through a critical and distressing social situation. In 1580, he was fined £ 40 for failing to keep the peace; in 1586, he lost his Aldermanship; in 1587, he was sued for debt; and in 1592, his name was listed " 'for not comminge monethlie to the churche...It is sayed... for fear of process for debtte'." (Halliday, 442). Perhaps this despondency of the family compelled the poet to leave Stratford for London in search of fortune. But tradition has an adscititious reason also : it is said that the young and passionate Shakespeare was caught red-handed while poaching deer in the garden of Sir Thomas Lucy of Charlecote, and he flew the country in order to escape the trial and punishment thereof. But, perhaps, the principal reason was his family's financial hardship. By this time, *i.e.* on 27 November, 1582, he was hastily married to Ann Hathaway, daughter of Richard Hathaway and grand-daughter of John Hathaway. Ann was born in 1555 or 1556, and so was elder than Shakespeare by about 8 years. They say that Shakespeare was forced into the wedlock with Anna, because then she had been carrying a child by him. This may be confirmed by the fact that Anna gave birth to her eldest girl child Susanna on 26 May, 1583. Next, a twin — Hamnet and Judith — was born to her on 2 February, 1585. This increase in the number of family members and consequent increase in expenditure coupled with decrease in the income of his father forced Shakespeare to seek some job in the township of London.

An opportunity of visiting London, and if luck would have it, to find a job there, soon arrived. In those days, travelling performing companies would stage Morality plays and Interludes even outside London. Upto his teens, Shakespeare witnessed and enjoyed such performances at least twice. At one time, he picked up acquaintance with the men of one of such companies, and from such acquaintance he might have dreamt of some fortune should he joined one of the performing companies of London. He was then only marking time, and at one fortunate moment left Stratford for London. A grand decision indeed! For, otherwise, the world would have lost its greatest play-wright. The London of Shakespeare's time was small and semicircular, having only two main thoroughfares running through the city. It had about 200,000 strong population, and was the home for merchants, craftsmen and journeymen. It was also the hub of dramatic performances. Secular plays were used to be staged in such theatre-houses of London as Curtain, Theatre, Fortune, Red Bull, Rose, Swan, Globe, Hope, Newington, Butts, and Blackfriars. At one time or another Shakespeare was associated with Curtain, Theatre, Rose, Swan, Globe and Blackfriars.

In which year, exactly, Shakespeare moved to London, we do not know. But, perhaps, it was 1585 or 1586, *i.e.* after the birth of Hamnet and Judith. He had only these three issues : Susanna (d. 1649), Hamnet (d. 1596) and Judith (d. 1662) — two daughters and only one son. We also do not know if Shakespeare had any job in Stratford. Some say that before moving to London, he worked as a school-teacher for a stint at Stratford. Again, we do not know for certain what exactly Shakespeare first did to eke out a living, in London. Many conjectures have been hazarded. Some say that at first he worked as a stable boy looking after the horses of coaches in which fashionable ladies and gentlemen would come to see performances of plays. Then he was inducted as a spot-boy or as a proxy actor in plays. Ifor Brown writes: "The certain record of Shakespeare's career as an actor occurs only at the end of 1594'' (Brown, 172). Next, he would be asked to taste the drudgery of an amanuensis copying out prompt-books or individual roles. And then, when by fluke some managers of companies had glimpses of the genius of Shakespeare, they invited him to occasionally amend or tailor set speeches to suit particular occasions or particular actors. And only after this Shakespeare began his original works.

Critics do not agree as to which works Shakespeare wrote or published first, nor do they agree as to the exact chronology of all his works. But we definitely know that before 1590, he composed a set of 25 sonnets and an Envoy (Sonnet 26), and, perhaps, *Henry VI,* Part I. Shakespeare dedicated this short sonnet-sequence to a young Earl. The poet was influenced by the craze in vogue for sonneteering, and especially by the fashion of his briefless lawyer-friends of writing sub-standard sonnets, and doing merry-making over them. Besides the 26 Sonnets, Shakespeare probably wrote some other sonnets, for instance Sonnets 107, 123 and 124; and, according to some scholars, all the 126 'Fair Youth Sonnets'. This point may be emphasised here: Shakespeare began his literary career with sonneteering. The Sonnets, therefore, may be taken to be the prolegomenon to his plays. And actually this is so; for, if we closely analyse the core themes of the plays, then we will find that the plays are, as if, extended metaphors of the Sonnets.

Immediately after successfully trying his hand at sonneteering, Shakespeare embarked upon the profession of a dramatist. He began this new profession with *Henry VI,* Part I which was followed by *Henry VI,* Part II and Part III, *Richard III* and *Titus Andronicus.* All these are historical plays, and all these he completed by 1593. This shows that Shakespeare began his career as a dramatist with historical plays. The next two or three years he spent in writing comedies, such as *Comdey of Errors, Taming of the Shrew, Two Gentlemen of Verona, Love's Labour's Lost* and *Rameo and Juliet.* If the 'Fair Youth Sonnets' were not completed by 1590 as some scholars claim, and this is very implausable, then we must say that Shakespeare wrote many of the Sonnets in between his engagements with the above-mentioned plays. And this is why we find so many parallels between these plays and the Sonnets, particularly the 'Fair Youth Sonnets'. Meanwhile, Shakespeare published two long poems : *Venus and Adonis* and *The Rape of Lucrece,* which were written between 1592 and 1593, and both of the poems were dedicated to Henry Wriothesley, the Earl of Southampton, his patron. It is on this fact that some critics depend to conjecture that the mysterious Mr. W.H. is none else than Henry Wriothesley.

This little amount of literary production that was received with wide acclaim by the public, evoked the boundless jealousy of some of Shakespeare's coeval dramatists and poets: Robert Green (c. 1558-92), George Peele (1556-96), Thomas Nashe (c.1567-1601), John Lyly (c. 1554-1606) and Thomas Lodge (c. 1558-1625). These dramatists were known as University Wits as most of them studied in universities. Many of these dramatists mounted literary attacks on Shakespeare, because they could not bear with the idea that Shakespeare who was a man of little learning could write plays that could challenge theirs. Greene's jealousy was the bitterest. In the Epilogue to his *Groatsworth of Wit* (1592), he expressed his savage ire against Shakespeare by writing of him : "There is an upstart crow, beautified with our feathers, that with his Tygers heart in a Plyers hyde, supposes he is as well able to bombast out a blank verse as the best of you; and being an absolute *Iohannes factotum,* is in his own conceit the only Shak-scene in a countrey." (Here is praise indeed shrøuded in vituperations!) Such attacks were mounted on Shakespeare probably during the period from 1590 to 1594. Greene's invective has nothing in it, for he was by nature quarrelsome and was of profligate character. Nonetheless, such attacks certainly made Shakespeare depressed, and he felt estranged, sequestered, forlorn. His temperament of this period is reflected in some of the Sonnets. Sonnet 29, for instance, expresses his dejection :

> When, in disgrace with fortune and men's eyes,
> I all along beweep my outcast state,
> And trouble deaf heaven with my bootless cries,
> And look upon myself, and curse my fate,...

Gentle by nature, well-spoken, and affable in demeanor, Shakespeare suffered very much in the inner regard of his heart from the jeerings, tauntings and belittling comments of most of the University Wits, regarding himself. On the other hand, he himself was feeling jealous of those poets and dramatists, because he lacked in social status, literary eminence, and all that they enjoyed. In Sonnet 29, again, he writes:

> Wishing me like to one more rich in hope,
> Featur'd like him, like him with friends possess'd,
> Desiring this man's art, and that man's scope,
> With what I most enjoy contented least;

And yet agian, in Sonnet 30, he writes: "I sigh the lack of many a thing

I sought''. But Shakespeare never returned the ill-behaviour of the University Wits, rather he accused his own fate for his crest-fallen state. In Sonnet 37, he says : ''So, I, made lame by fortune's dearest spite''. Whether Shakespeare was introverted in nature, psychologists may decide.

But, though dejected, undaunted he was; and continued producing plays — only plays, since about 1598 or even before that — at the rate of two plays a year. He was certainly a fast writer. And as he continued turning out plays incessantly — plays that entertrained large audiences for centuries of nights — the jealousy of the ill-meaning dramatists was buried under the applause that those plays received from the public. The jealousy, now, rather, was converted into admiration. However, all his contemporary playwrights and poets were not hostile to him, or looked down upon him. There were Ben Jonson (1572-1637), the dramatist, and Michael Drayton (1563-1631), the poet, who were constant to Shakespeare in friendship and admiration. And there was Christopher Marlowe (1564-93) who never had any animosity against Shakespeare.

Shakespeare's literary life can be divided into four periods : the first period from 1585 or 1586, when he arrived in London, to 1594; the second from 1594 to 1600; the third from 1600 to 1608; and the fourth from 1608 to 1612. Four years before his death in 1616, the poet's pen ceased moving. In the first period, Shakespeare produced at least 26 sonnets and an Envoy, and at least seven plays (*Henry VI,* Part I, II, and III, *Richard III, Titus Andronicus, Comedy of Errors* and *Taming of the Shrew),* and two long poems (*Venus and Adonis* and *The Rape of Lucrece*). Even in this period Shakespeare could carve out a prominent piace in the literary world of London, though, to him, it was a period of literary exercises.

In the second period, he produced 15 plays, comprising comedies, such as *Love's Labour's Lost, As You Like It, Twelfth Night;* tragedies, such as *Romeo and Juliet;* and mostly histories, such as *Richard II, King John, Henry IV,* Part I and II, and *Julius Caesar.* It was probably in this period that Shakespeare wrote the Sonnets 28-154. The Italian sonnet form was then in vogue, where only one theme prevailed : love. But instead of the Italian form, he adotped the English form perfected by Wyatt and Surrey. The previous 27 Sonnets were also composed in this English form. Instesad of the Italian octave and sestet, Shakespeare adopted three quartrains and a concluding couplet or envoy. This form of sonnet is also known as the Shakespearean form. Shakespeare also introduced new themes in the sonnet, besides the universal theme of love: personal state of the poet, thoughts on the destructiveness of Time, etc. It may be mentioned here that about half a century later, Milton also changed the form and the contents of the sonnet. But we must say that it was Shakespeare who for the first time conceived of new themes for the sonnet.

The central figures of the sonnets of Shakespeare are a beautiful youth, the Fair Youth, and a brunette of doubtful character. Who are actually the beautiful youth and the brunette we do not know for certain: their identities are till now shrouded in mystery. But the general trend is to believe that the beautiful youth is the Earl of Southampton, Henry Wriothesley, and the brunette is Mrs. Mary Fitton. One of the befuddling question regarding the Sonnets is : did Shakespeare unlock his heart in the Sonnets? Some commentators answer this question in the positive, but others in the negative. The other vexing question about the Sonnets relates to the quality of these, and here also critics are polarised.

However, in the third period of his literary career, Shakespeare produced mostly tragedies and a few romances dipped in the fluid of tragedy. Some of the tragedies of this period are : *Hamlet, Othello, King Lear, Macbeth* and *Antony and Cleopatra.* And some of the tragic romances or dark comedies are : *All's Well that Ends Well, Measure for Measure* and *Troilus and Cressida.* In this period, Shakespeare reached the height of his poetic and dramatic power. Some of the plays that Shakespeare wrote in the fourth period are : *Antony and Cleopatra, Pericles, Coriolanus* and *Henry VIII.* All these are weak tragedies compared to the tragedies of the third period, but the plays are ripe regarding characterisation. In the last period of his literary career — the eventide of his poetic life — Shakespeare once again turned to the theme of love; but this time love was commingled with mystery. He wrote three such plays at the fag end of his life : *Cymbeline, The Winter's Tale* and *The Tempest.*

Most of all these plays were staged in different theatre houses of London for days on end, and were well received by the assorted audience. As a result, Shakespeare financially profited immensely and bought a considerable property, including one of the best houses at Stratford, called *New Place,* and also a share of the Globe Theatre where most of his plays were staged. Thus, Shakespeare who once been a despicable immigrant villager in London, became a gentleman of status and withal a playwright of eminence. While in London, the poet would put up in lodging houses near theatre houses in which his plays were staged.

Shakespeare was then, in 1614, fifty-two. His health gradually waned. He was then at the apex of his fame. His plays continued to be in constant demand : no Court festivities were thought to be complete without a performance of a play of Shakespeare. But, as ill luck would have it, for the past two years, the facile pen of the poet ceased moving. Maybe the poet thought what was to be written was already written, and nothing remained unsaid. He thought that he was well relieved of his 'poetic burden' : he had shown man, sufficiently well, the ways of man and the ways of the world. By then, he had tasted all sorts of pains and griefs : his father died in 1601 and his mother in 1608. In 1603, a bolt from the blue fell on his head and transfixed his heart for a long time : Hannet, his only son, died at the very young age of about 18. His two brothers also died recently: Gilbert, aged 45, in 1612; and Richard, aged 39, in 1613. For the last four years of his life, the poet had been permanently residing at Stratford, and only occasionally would go to London to meet his old friends or to oversee the performances of his plays there. He had his last glimpse of his dear London in 1615, the year in which his dear Globe theatre was gutted by a huge fire caused by fire-works to add extra reality to the performance of some one of his plays.

In the second half of April 1616, Shakespeare contracted a fatal fever from which he never came round, and he died on Tuesday, the 23rd of April, 1616. Tradition has it that Shakespeare died of a drinking bout. One evening Ben Jonson and Drayton — the two close friends of the poet — and the poet himself had a merry meeting in which the three drank too hard. It was then that Shakespeare contracted that fatal fever. But we are not sure how actually Shakespeare died. *The Statesman* (India) of 20.10.1995 reports that "William Shakespeare may have died of eye cancer, according to a study of a death mask found in Germany, the British *Daily Telegraph* reported today, reports AFP. "It said the mask, which has been traced back to 1775 when a German nobleman bought it in London, has been accepted as true likeness by comparing it to a limestone bust and an engraving of him which are considered genuine. "Citing the *New Scientist Magazine,* the paper said a swelling above the left eye on the mask indicated that he could have suffered a potentially fatal lymphoma of the tear glands."

Shakespeare's mortal remains were buried, two days later, at Stratford, and not at the Westminster Abbey where most of the great English poets lie buried. Stratford may not seem to be the befitting burial ground for the great bard to some Shakespeare-lovers who would like him lying at the Westminster Abbey with the other great poets of the English language, but William Basse in a sonnet beautifully justify the bard's burial at the place where he is lying (Brown, 202):

> Under this carved marble of thine own,
> Sleep, brave tragedian, Shakespeare, sleep alone.

A man of medium height, Shakespeare, with a bald pate, was, perhaps, of endomorphic constitution. He was sociable, generous and affable. His literary activities might have created, at the beginning of his life in London, a few jealous competitors, but, nevertheless, as a man as well as as a poet and dramatist he was loved by all and sundry. He was a keen observer of life in all its aspects; and though he could not traverse all the walks of life, he could pick up the essences of all the diverse walks of life, if he could have taken just glimpses of them. It is for this reason that his characters of all denominations are so true to reality: kings, queens, knaves, soldiers — all. No one has perceived this quality of Shakespeare better than Dr. Samuel Johnson (1709-84). Johnson wrote in his *Preface to Shakespeare* (Preface to his 'volume edition of Shakespeare's works of 1765) : ''Shakespeare is above all writers, at least above all modern writers, the poet of nature; the poet that holds up to his readers a faithful mirror of manners and of life.'' Shakespeare could be deeply meditative, and he could be as light as anything; again, he could be profoundly moralist, and, immediately after, he could draw a profligate character. So great was his range of keen observation, and so skilled was his brush. A daguerreotyped picture of the man Shakespeare and the poet Shakespeare can be found at *Love's Labour's Lost*, II, i. 66-76, where Rosaline says of Berowne who may be compared with Shakespeare :

> Berowne they call him; but a merrior man,
> Within the limit of becoming mirth,
> I never spent an hour's talk withal.
> His eye begets occasion for his wit,
> For every object that the one doth catch
> The other turns to a mirth-moving jest,
> Which his fair tongue, conceit's expositor,
> Delivers in such apt and gracious words
> That aged ears play truant at his tales,
> And young hearings are quite ravished;
> So sweet and voluble is his discourse.

Thomas Carlyle (1795-1881), in his *On Heroes and Hero-Worship,* wrote : ''Of this Shakespeare of ours, perhaps the opinion one sometimes hears a little idolatrously expressed is, in fact, the right one; I think the best judgement not of this country only, but of Europe at large, is slowly pointing to the conclusion, that Shakespeare is the chief of all Poets hitherto; the greatest intellect who, in our recorded world, has left record of himself in the way of Literature. On the whole, I know not such a power of vision, such a faculty of thought, if we take all of characters of it, in any other man. Such a calmness of depth; placid joyous strength; all things imaged in that great soul of his so true and clear, as in a tranquil unfathomable sea!'' (Tennyson, 396). And, comparing Shakespeare with Dante, Carlyle concludes : "Two fit men: Dente, deep, fierce as the central fire of the world; Shakespeare, wide, placid, far-seeing, as the Sun, the upper light of the world. Italy produced the one world-voice; we English had the honour of producing the other'' (Tennyson, 395).

These are praises about two hundred years after his death. But how was the praise of his contemporary poet and dramatist Ben Jonson (1573-1673)? Yes, Jonson was no less full-throated than Carlyle, in his praise of Shakespeare : Jonson wrote about Shakespeare :

Soul of the Age!
The applause! delight! the wonder of our Stage!
My *Shakespeare,* rise; I will not lodge thee by
Chaucer, or *Spenser,* or bid *Beaumont* lye
A little further, to make thee a roome:
Thou art a Moniment, without a tombe,
And art alive still, while thy Booke doth live,
And we have wits to read, and praise to give.
That I not mixe thee so, my brain excuses;
I meane with great, but disproportion'd *Muses*:
For, if I thought my judgement were of yeeres,
I should commit thee surely with thy peeres,
And tell, how farre thou didst our *Lily* out-shine,
Or sporting *Kid,* or *Morlowes* mighty line.
And though thou hadst small Latine, and lesse *Greeke,*
From thence to honour thee, I would not seeke
For names; but call forth thund'ring *Aeschilus,*
Euripides, and *Sophocles* to us,
Paccuvius, Accius, him of *Cordova* dead,
To life againe, to hear thy Buskin tread,
And shake a Stage: Or, when they Sockes were on,
Leave thee alone, for the comparison

Of all, that insolent *Greece,* or haughtie *Rome*
Sent forth, or since did from their ashes come.
Triumph, my *Britaine,* thou hast one to showe,
To whom all Scenes of *Europe* homage owe.
He was not of an age, but for all time!
And all the Muses still were in their prime
When like *Apollo* he came forth to warme
Our eares, or like a *Mercury* to charme!
Nature her selfe was proud of his designes,
And joy'd to weare the dressing of his lines!
Which were so rightly spun, and woven so fit,
As, since, she will vouchsafe no other Wit.

The merry *Greeke,* tart *Aristophanes,*
Neat *Terrence,* witty *Plautus,* now not please;
But antiquated, and deserted lye
As they were not of Natures family.
Yet must I give nature all: Thy Art,
My gentle *Shakespeare,* must enjoy a part.
For though the Poets matter, *Nature* be,
His Art doth give the fashion. And, that he,
Who casts to write a living line, must sweat,
(Such as thine are) and strike the second heat
Upon the Muses anvile: turne the same,
(And himselfe with it) that he thinkes to frame;
Or for the lawrell, he may gaine a scorne,
For a good Poet's made, as well as borne.
And such wert thou. Looke how the fathers face
Lives in his issue, even so, the race
Of *Shakespeare* minde, and manners brightly shines
In his well torned, and true-filed lines:
In each of which, he seemes to shake a Lance,
As brandish't at the eyes of Ignorance.
Sweet Swan of *Avon!* what a sight it were
To see thee in our waters yet appeare,
And make those flights upon the bankes of *Thames,*
That so did take *Eliza,* and our *James!*
But stay, I see in the *Hemisphere*
Advanc'd, and made a constellation there!
Shine forth, thou Starre of *Poets,* and with rage,

Or influence, chide, or cheere the drooping Stage;
Which, since thy flight from hence, hath mourn'd the night,
And despaires day, but for thy Volumes light.

How much more praise can a poet and dramatist deserve, or wish? How much more? And when Jonson thus praised Shakespeare, perhaps, he had in his view not only the plays of Shakespeare, but also his sonnet-sequences, for all were written by the same soul : Shakespeare.

❑

II

What is a Sonnet?

The term 'sonnet', perhaps, cannot be better designated by anything than by pointing out its form which, of all the features of it, has remained throughout ages, more or less unchanged, constant: it is a fourteen-line poem in iambic pentameter. The term has been derived from the Italian word 'sonnetto' which means a 'little sound' or 'little song'. In Italy, at first, the term used to refer to any short poem; but, in course of time, it came to be restricted to a particular form of poem, to a lyrical poem of 14 lines, generally in iambic pentameter. But in further course of time, this feature of the sonnet has also undergone several mutations; for instance, in France, the sonnet is usually written in iambic hexameter. This is because the sonnet has had to adjust itself with the features and structure of particular languages and their ideosyncracies. Apart from its specificity of being a 14-line poem, we can say that the sonnet is a lyric poem, being true to the etymology of its originary term, with musicality and song-like rhythm. Like the lyric, which is also fairly short, the sonnet revolves round a single core emotion. Therefore, we can say that the sonnet differs from the lyric only in form. Compton Rickett beautifully distinguishes between the lyric and the sonnet by highlighting the principal features of the latter: "The tilt and abandonment of the lyric are replaced (in the sonnet) by a more deliberate manner, a more austere treatment. There may be the some intensity of feeling, and an equal scope for fancy, but in one case (*i.e.* that of the lyric) it affects one like the scent of a wayside flower, in the other (*i.e.* in the sonnet) like the fragrance of a well-ordered garden" (Compton Rickett, 124).

The difficulty of defining the sonnet still persists, because, sometimes, the sonnet assumed some other denominations; for instance, Francesco Petrarch (1304-1374) called his sonnets *canzoni.* Again, if we say that the sonnet is a sort of lyric, or that it is a kind of song, yet the difficulty will not be removed. Ronald Peacock rightly says: "The history of the nomenclature within lyric poetry (also) shows changes and mutations, sometimes hidden or arbitrary, sometimes gradual or natural, in the use of forms. Horace called his 'odes' *carmina,* or, as we should say, songs. Petrarch's sonnets to Laura were called *canzoni*; the term sonnet thus assimilates the Provencal term and indicates in effect a genre of love songs'' (Peacock, 102). Can the sonnet then be boiled down to a love song? No, because in course of time newer and yet newer themes, besides the love-theme, accrued to the sonnet. Again, there are other forms of poem on the same theme of love on which the sonnet is built. Take, for instance, the German *Minnesinger* whose universal theme is love and is, like the sonnet in most cases, composed as ''homage to a lady''. But, regarding form, the *Minnesinger* differs from the sonnet very widely.

Should we then identify the sonnet by its length, and say that it is a poem of 14 lines? That will also be unprofitable, because, for instance, the *quatorzain* is also a poem of exactly 14 lines. But whereas any poem of 14 lines is a *quatorzain,* all *quartorzains* are not sonnets. Further, as we shall soon see, all sonnets are not of 14 lines. There are sonnets of more than or less than 14 lines. To get out of this pedantic labyrinth, we may simply say that the sonnet is a short poem. But that will also not help us. Because, for instance, in Japan, there is a kind of short poem, known as *hokku* or *haiku,* which can certainly not claim to be sonnets. The *haiku* is a verse form consisting of only seventeen syllables, distributed in three lines: the first line consists of 5 syllables, the second 7 and the third, again, 5. Like the sonnet, the *haiku* also expresses a single concentrated idea or thought. Many English poets have imitated the *haiku* form, for diverse themes, such as Ezra Pound, Robert Frost, Conrad Aiken, W.B. Yeats and James Kirkup. An example of *haiku* from Kirkup's *Haiku on the Inland Sea* is being given below (Cuddon, 300) :

> In the amber dusk
> Each island dreams its own night.
> The sea swarms with gold.

This is a short, rather very short, poem; but it is in no sense a sonnet. Therefore, the length of a poem is not the only determinant of a sonnet.

There is another kind of sonnet, invented by Gerard Manley Hopkins (1844-89). In the Preface to his *Poems* (1918), he presented a sort of curtailed sonnets, and called these curtal sonnets. The curtal sonnet consists of only 10 lines, instead of usual 14. Hopkins divided these 10 lines into two stanzas: the first comprising of 6 lines, and the second 4. In addition, there is a short tail-piece which is not longer than half of the length of a line. An example of the curtal sonnet is being given below, from Hopkins' *Poems* (Cuddon, 170-71) :

Glory be to God for dappling things —
For skies of couple-colour as a brinded cow;
For rose-moles all in stipple upon trout that swim;
Fresh-firecoal chestnut-falls; finches' wings;
Landscape plotted and pieced — fold, fallow, and plough;
And áll trádes, their gear and tackle and trim.

All things counter, original, spare, strange;
Whatever is fickle, freckled (who knows how?)
With swift, slow; sweet, sour; adazzle, dim;
He fathers-forth whose beauty is past change:
Praise him.

On the other hand, sonnets may be longer than the usual 14-line sonnets. Thomas Watson (c. 1557-92), for instance, in his *Hecatompathia* or *Passionate Century of Sonnets* (1582), wrote poems of 18 lines, in the rhyme scheme a b a b c c, repeated twice, which he called sonnets. For an instance, the 7th poem of *Hecatompathia* is being cited below (Kerrigan, 19-20) :

Hark you that list to hear what saint I serve:
Her yellow locks exceed the beaten gold;
Her sparkling eyes in heaven a place deserve;
Her forehead high and fair of comely mould;
Her words are music all of silver sound;
Her wit so sharp as like can scarce be found;
Each eyebrow hangs like Iris in the skies;
Her Eagle's nose is straight of stately frame;
On either cheek a Rose and Lily lies;
Her breath is sweet perfume, or holy flame;
Her lips are more red than any coral stone;
Her neck more white than aged swans can moan;
Her breast transparent is, like crystal rock;
Her figners long, fit for Apollo's lute;
Her slipper such as Momus dare not mock;
Her virtues all so great as make me mute;
What other parts she hath I need not say,
Whose face alone is cause of my deacy.

Watson's junior contemporary, John Donne (1572-1631), the metaphysical poet, also wrote some poems of 18 lines and claimed them to be sonnets.

Donne did not follow Watson's rhyme scheme but invented one for himself: a b a b, c d c d, e f e f, g h g h, i i. For an example, his 'Sonnet : The Token' which is comprised in his collection of poems, *Songs and Sonnets,* is being cited below:

Send me some token, that my hope may live,
    Or that my easelesse thoughts may sleep and rest;
Send me some honey to make sweet my hive,
    That in my passion I may hope the best.
I beg noe ribbond wrought with thine owne hands,
    To knit our loves in the fantastick straine
Of new-toucht youth; nor Ring to shew the stands
    Of our affection, that as that's round and plaine,
So should our loves meet in simplicity;
    No, nor the Coralls which thy wrist infold,
Lac'd up together in congruity,
    To shew our thoughts should rest in the seame hold
No, nor the picture, though most gracious,
    And most desir'd, because best like the best;
Nor witty Lines, which are most copious,
    Within the Writings which thou hast addrest.

    Send me nor this, nor that, t' increase my store,
    But swear thou thinkst I love thee, and no more.

There is a peculiar type of sonnets, or rather sonnet sequence, where the main sonnet sequence is preceded by another sonnet sequence, known as 'crown of sonnets'. Donne's sonnet sequence, *Holy Sonnets,* for instance, is preceded by such a 'crown of sonnets' which consists of seven sonnets. These 'crown sonnets' are usually linked together in a peculiar way. In Donne's case, the last line of the first sonnet of the 'crown of sonnets' is the first line of the second sonnet; the last line of the second sonnet is the first line of the third sonnet; and so on. And, further, the first line of the first sonnet is also the last line of the last line of the last sonnet.

Sonnets can be of diverse types, as we have so far seen, but the three pincipal types are the following :

1. *The Italian, or the Petrarchan, Sonnet :* The sonnet originated in Italy in the 14th century, and was perfected by Francesco Petrarca Petrarch (1304-74). He called his poems, now generally known as sonnets, *canzoniere.* The Petrarchan or Italian sonnet consists of two parts : the octave or octet, rhyming a b b a a b b a; and the sestet, rhyming c d e c

d e, or c d c d c d, or "a similar combination that avoids the closing couplet". The first eight lines, the octave, develops one single thought or idea. But, at the beginning of the sestet, there is a *volta* or 'turn'. Nevertheless, the sestet actually grows out of the octave, though in a different way, and completes the single thought of the whole poem. "The effect of the a b b a a b b a octave is truly remarkable. It is actually a blend of 3 brace-rhyme quatrains, since the middle 4 verses, whose sounds overlap the others and echo their pattern, impress the reader with a similar rhyme pattern, thus, a b b a a b b a. Normally, too, a definite pause is made in thought development at the end of the eighth verse, serving to increase the independent unit of an octave that has already progressed with the greatest economy in rhyme sounds. Certainly it would be difficult to conceive a more artistically compact and phonologically effective pattern. The sestet, in turn, leads out of the octave and, if the closing couplet is avoided, assures a commendable variety within uniformity to the poem as a whole" (Preminger, 781).

Petrarch wrote both in vernacular Italian and in the highly polished Latin. His nearly four hundred *canzoniere* or sonnets were written in Italian. Keeping aside the point of rhyming, the following two sonnets of his, in translation, may help us understand his style in the sonnet (Artz, 36-37) :

I

Oft as in pensive mood I sit and write,
'Mid plaint of birds and whisp'ring leafy trees,
Where betwixt flowery banks and river bright
Laughs back in ripples at the ruffling breeze,
She whom heaven hath stolen from my sight,
Whose face though mortal eye no longer sees
Earth cannot hide, in pity of my plight
Rebukes my grief with words more sweet than these —
Velestial words not breathed by mortal breath:
"Ah why consume thy strength ere yet 'tis night
In barren tears and tempest of fierce sighs?
Weep not for me, for by the boon of death
My days were made immortal, and mine eyes,
Closing, were opened on eternal light."

II

The nightingale that so forlornly weeps
    Perchance his little ones or his dear mate,
Whose fiery, tender song insatiate
With sweetness fills the air, his vigil keeps
All night with me, and never tires nor sleeps,
    Reminding me of my unhappy fate.
    For I, oh foolish, know it now too late,
    Death the divinest bloom most quickly reaps.
How blind is he who thinks to stand secure!
    Meseemed those fair lamps, than the sun more bright,
    Could ne'er be quenched, and leave us plunged in night.
Now do I know my cruel destiny
    Would have me learn in tears and agony,
    Nought that delighteth may on earth endure.

2. *The Spenserian Sonnet:* The rhyme-scheme of the Spenserian sonnet is quite different from that of the Petrarchan sonnet. Its rhyme-scheme is : a b a b, b c b c, c d c d, e e. It contains four parts: three quatrains and a concluding couplet. The Spenserian sonnet is also called 'linked sonnet', because of its peculiar rhyme-scheme where the three quatrains are linked together : the last line of the first quatrain rhymes with the first line of the second quatrain; and similarly, the last line of the second quatrain rhymes with the first line of the third quatrain. As in the Shakespearean sonnet, here also the concluding couplet summarises the argument of the foregoing lines, or binds up the sense of the foregoing lines. The following sonnet of Spenser may illustrate the rhyme-scheme as well as other features of the Spenserian sonnet :

One day I wrote her name upon the strand;
But came the waves, and washed it away;
Again I wrote it, with a second hand;
But came the tide, and made my pains his prey;
Vain man, said she, that dost in vain assay
A mortal thing so to immortalize;
For I myself shall like to this decay,
And eke my name be wiped out likewise.
Not so, quoth I, let base things devise
To die in dust, but you shall live by fame;
My verse your virtues rare shall eternize,
And in the heavens write your glorious name.
Where, when as death shall all the world subdue,
Our love shall live, and later life renew.

3. *The Shakespearean or the English Sonent* : The Shakespearean sonnet does not vary very much from the Spenserian sonnet. One difference between the Spenserian sonnet and the Shakespearean sonnet is that whereas in the former the quatrains are linked, in the latter they are not. The other difference relates to the rhyme-scheme, the Shakespearean rhyme-scheme being: a b a b, c d c d, e f e f, g g. Though both Shakespeare and Spenser did not follow the Petrarchan division of the sonnet into the octave and the sestet, yet there is an invisible division of the Shakespearean and the Spenserian sonnets into octaves and sestets, because the arguments in a great number of sonnets of both Shakespeare and Spenser have silent pauses at the eighth lines.

Unlike in the Italian form of the sonnet, in the Spenserian and the Shakespearean form, different ideas or thoughts are expressed in the three quatrains; of course each succeeding quatrain grows out of the preceding ones. The first quatrain may be called the argument which is an explanation of what is going to happen in the following verses. The second quatrain may be called the theme or the central idea which may be expressed directly or indirectly. And the third or the last quatrain may be called the dialectic or the logic or the reason, that supports the whole argument or the central argument. And the concluding couplet is the 'tie-up' which binds the arugment or the theme, and also presents a conclusion. On the other hand, in the Italian sonnet, the theme is developed in two stages. The first eight lines, or the octave, presents the theme or raise the issue, and corresponding doubt, query, etc., and the last six lines, the sestet, "answer the query, resovle the problem, drive home the point by an abstract comment." Sometimes the octave of the Italian sonnet is divided into two parts or quatrains, as the sestet is divided into two parts called tercets. "The Spenserian and Shakespearean patterns, on the other hand, offer some relief to the difficulty of rhyming in Eng. (English) and invite a division of thought into 3 quatrains and a closing or summaring couplet; and even though such arbitrary divisions are frequently ignored by the poet, the more open rhyme schemes tend to impress the fourfold structure on the reader's ear and to suggest a stepped progression toward the closing couplet. Such matters of relationship between form and content are, however, susceptible to considerable control in the hands of a skilled poet, and the ultimate effect in any given instance may override theoretical considerations in achievement of artistic integrity" (Preminger, 781-82).

Since its inception, poets have freely and continuously experimented on the pattern of the sonnet, giving rise to ramifications in the pattern. The variations in the pattern of the sonnet wre created by changing the rhyme-schemes. As a result of the innovations of the poets, a considerable number of patterns have evolved. But some of these patterns have not been able to attract the fascination of poets or that of the reading public, and so have gone to oblivion. The rest have enjoyed popularity for a considerably long time. Some of these new patterns are the following :

1. *Caudate Sonnet:* In it, in addition to the usual 14 lines, a coda or 'tail', generally in the shape of a half line, is added. Sometimes more than one codas are appended. This type of sonnet was invented by the Italian poet Francesco Berni (1497-1536). Generally sonnets of this pattern or type are used for satirical purposes. John Milton, for instance, used the caudate pattern in his satirical sonnet 'On the New Forcers of Conscience Under the Long Parliament' in which two codas occur :

Because you have thrown off your Prelate Lord,
    And with stiff vows renounced his Litergy,
    To seize the widowed whore Plurality
    From them whose sin ye envied, not abhorred,
Dare ye for this adjure the civil sword
    To force our consciences that Christ set free,
    And ride us with a classic hierarchy,
    Taught ye by mere A.S. and Rutherford?
Men whose life, learning, faith, and pure intent,
    Would have been held in high esteem with Paul,
    Must now be named and printed heretics
By shallow Edwards and Scotch What-d'ye-call!
    But we do hope to find out all your tricks,
    Your plots and packing, worse than those of Trent,
                                That so the Parliament
May with their wholesome and preventive shears
Clip your phylacteries, though baulk your ears,
                                And succour our just fears,
When they shall read this clearly in your charge :
New *Presbyter* is but old *Priest* writ large.

2. *Continuous or Iterating Sonnet:* This type of sonnet is not very different from the common types of sonnets, but varies from them in only one respect : in it one (or sometimes more than one) rhyme sound occurs throughout the sonnet. If the same-sounding word or words

occur in the rhyming for a number of times in the lines, then the sonnet may be called a continuous or iterating sonnet — it is not essential that the same-sounding word will occur in all the lines and rhyme. For instance, Shakespeare's Sonnet 135 may be called a continuous or iterating sonnet. If such a sonnet is read backward, then we may call it a retrograde sonnet.

3. *Chained or Linked Sonnet :* Here the last word of the preceding verse becomes the first word of the succeeding verse. Here, again, it is not essential for a sonnet to follow this pattern throughout to be called a chained or linked sonnet, but if most of the verses follow this pattern, then that will do.

4. *Crown of Sonnets :* "Traditionally a sequence of 7 Italian sonnets so interwoven as to form a 'crown' or panegeric for the one to whom they (*i.e.* these seven sonnets, and the other sonnets to which these seven are working as a 'crown') are addressed. The interweaving is accomplished by using the last line of each of the first 6 sonnets as the first line of the succeeding sonnets, with the last line of the seventh being a repetition of the opening line of the first. A further restriction prohibits the repetition of any given rhyme sound once it is used in the crown." (Preminger, 174). An example of the 'crown of sonnets' had already been given before.

5. *Terza Rima Sonnet :* The only differentiating feature of this type of sonnet is that its rhyme-scheme follows the terza rima pattern. The terza rima is "A verse form composed of iambic tercets rhyming a b a, b c b, etc., the seocnd line of the first tercet supplying the rhyme for the second, the second line of the second tercet supplying the rhyme for the third, and so on, thus giving an effect of linkage to the entire composition" (Preminger, 847-48).

6. *Tetrameter Sonnet :* Generally, sonnets are written in decasylabic pentameters. But in tetrameter sonnets, the verses are octosyllabic tetrameters. Shakespeare's Sonnet 145 is a tetrameter sonnet : "Those lips that Love's own hand did make... And sav'd my life, saying — 'Not you'."

Ever since its genesis, the sonnet has been a very popular form of poem. Generally, poets wrote a series of sonnets for a particular person or on a particular central theme, and called the series a 'sonnet cycle'. The "advantages of the cycle are that they eanble the poet to explore many different aspects and moods of the experience, to analyse his feelings in detail and to record the vicissitudes of the affair. At the same time each individual sonnet lives as an independent poem'' (Cuddon, 646-94). Cuddon has listed a number of sonnet cycles : ''Dante's *Vita Nouva* (1292-94) in which there are extensive prose links; Petrarch's *Canzoniere* (c. 1328-74); du Bellay's *L'Olive* (1549); Ronsard's *Amours* (1552); *Sidney's Astrophil and Stella* (1591); Spenser's *Amoretti* (1595); Shakespeare's *Sonnets* (1609); Donne's *Holy Sonnets* (1635-39); Wordsworth's *Ecclesiastical Sonnets* (1882); Rossetti's *The House of Fame* (1881); Elizabeth Barrett Browning's *Sonnets from the Portuguese* (1850); Rilke's *Sonette on Orpheus* (1923)'' (Cuddon, 647). From this list, which is certainly not exhaustive, it is clear that the sonnet has enjoyed popularity throughout centuries. And only at the beginning of the twentieth century, has the sonnet began to lose public favour.

The sonnet form has also been greatly abused, thanks, perhaps to its popularity and brevity, that have invited even unskilled hands that have drowned the sonnet in utter confusion. Curiously enough, the sonnet, again, has also had protests through another sort of sonnet, called 'anti-sonnet'. Beaty and Matchett write about the anti-sonnet: ''There is even an old tradition of the anti-sonnet, which attempts freshness through denying the usual images, as in Shakespeare's 'Sonnet 130' (''My Mistress' eyes are nothing like the Sunne''), ... through adopting supposedly shocking directness, as in Edna St. Vincent Millay's sonnet beginning 'I too beneath your moon, almighty Sex/Go forth at nightfall crying like a cat' '' (Beaty, 328-29). Nevertheless, Beaty and Matchett further write : ''The abuses should not be counted against it; when it has been well handled, the form has produced some of the finest brief poems in English'' (Beaty, 329).

III

The History of the Sonnet

The sonnet originated in Italy in the 13th century, and developed when the spirit of the *dolce stil novo* (sweet new style) in poetry was raging the country. It is generally held that it was Giacomo da Lentino (Preminger, 782) or Jacopo da Lentini (*The Penguin Companion to Literature*, vol. 2, p. 469) who flourished in the early part of the 13th century, invented the sonnet form. Lentino or Lentini was a poet and a notary at the court of Frederick II. He wrote 14-line hendecasyllabic poems rhyming a b a b a b a b, c d e c d e, thus dividing the poem into octave and sestet. The themes of his poems are Provencal, a region of France adjacent to Italy. The central theme of his poems is that he is a vassal of a lady and offers devotion to her, but receives from her only derision and disdain. As the poems are Provencal in inspiration, the love that the poet speaks of is chivalrous. His poems bear witness to his technical ingenuity and to the depth of his love. Most of his poems are now in oblivion, but that once he could influence other poets is evident from the fact that even Dante quotes him in his *De vulgari eloquentia* and mentions him in the *Divine Comedy (Purgatory,* xxiv). However, Lentini or Lentino is now remembered chiefly for his invention of the sonnet form.

We do not know for certain if Lentini had any 'rough-hewn' model for his sonnet, or whether he drew elements from some sources, for his sonnet. But scholars generally agree that the Sicilian *strambotto* may be the source of Lentini's sonnet. The *strambotto* is a one-stanza poem of eight lines, rhyming variously. But the most popular rhyming form was a b a b a b a b. The Sicilians, the Tuscans and the French used the *strambotto* for satirical purposes, but the Italians used it for amorous and sentimental themes. It may be noted here that even before Lentini, the *strambotto* was prevalent in Italy, though the poets there did not rigidly follow the eight-line canon of the *strambotto.* In Italy, poets wrote *strambottos* in more or less eight lines. However, what Lentini especially did was that he added to the 2-quatrain Sicilian *strambotto* a double refrain of six lines or 2 tercets, making the poem one of 14 lines. Thus, the Sicilian *strambotto* became the octave or octet of the later-day sonnet. The word *strambotto* derived from two Sicilian words : *strambo,* meaning 'squint-eyed' or 'sideling glancing'; and *motto,* meaning 'dictum'. But the estymology of the word *strambotto* had nothing to do with the themes of the *strambottos.* Scholars think that the extra 6 lines that Lentini added to the eight-line Sicilian *strambotto* were drawn from Tuscany where the Sicilian octave (the *strambotto* of eight lines) was transmogrified into the six-line poem. However, the 14-line hendecasyllabic *canzone* or sonnet that Lentini invented by combining the Sicilian 8-line *strambotto* (octave) and the Tuscan 6-line *strambotto* (sestet) rhymed a b a b a b a b, c d e, c d e. This pattern of the *canzone* or sonnet was also followed by Lentini's contemporary poets, such as Abbot of Tivoli, Jacopo Mostacii, Pierro delle Vigne, Monaldo d'Aquino and others.

Though Lentini invented the sonnet form, the form was perfected by another Italian poet, Guittone d'Arezzo (1230-1294) of Tuscacy. He was the most influential poet of Tuscany, and for that matter, of Italy. Guittone d'Arezzo was influenced, like Lentini before him, by the spirit of the *dolce stil novo* or, simply, *stil novo* introduced into Italian poetry by Guido Guinzelli (c. 1235-1276) in the thirteenth century. Guinizelli was a stundent of law and became a judge. After he was exiled for political reasons, he composed his *Rime* which, actually, ushered in the spirit of the *dolce stil novo* in a big way in Italy. In this sense, Guinizelli's collection of poems or sonnets called *Rime* has great importance in the history of the sonnet. The intensity and sweetness of Guinizelli's poems reach their height when he expresses his "ecstatic adoration of his lady". This aspect of his poems has certainly influenced the sonnet down the ages, the sonnet being the expression of intense love for a beautiful lady, in a specifically structured poem, Guinizelli's influence was so great that along with Lentini, Guinizelli is also mentioned in Dante's *Divine Comedy* (Purgatory or *Purgatorio,* xxvi).

To come back to Guittone d'Arezzo, at the age of about 25, he had undergone a religious conversion, and entered the order of the Knights of the Virgin Mary. Before that, he composed secular poems, but after the conversion, his poems were saturated with religious fervour. His collection of poems, *Canzoniers,* contains a number of *canzoni* or sonnets that are harsh, obscure and extravagantly artificial. Nevertheless, his concern for stylistic beauty perfected the sonnet form that was earlier invented by Lentini. Guittone d'Arezzo's most important contribution to the pattern of the sonnet was his invention of the hitherto unknown a b b a a b b a octave. Dante (1265-1321) used this rhyme-scheme in his *Vita Nuova* and *Canzoniere* or (sonnet-sequence) and Petrarch (1304-1374) followed his rhyme-scheme in his *Canzoniere.* Through Dante's an Petrarch's preferences, this pattern of the octave remained very popu for a long time. The *canzoni* or sonnets of both Dante and Petrarch ar conspicuous for their intensity of love and the artificiality of style. Dante addressed his sonnets to his lady-love Beatrice, and Petrarch to his beloved Laura. Their loves were not carnal, but purely Platonic.

Besides Dante and Petrarch, Guiodo Cavalcanti (1259-1300) of Florence also composed about 50 *canzoni* and some sonnets, following their instances. All these were written on the theme of love. Cavalcanti's works intensified the spirit of the *stil novo.* The spirit of the *stil novo* and the fashion of the sonnet continued to remain in Italy till the 16th century. F.T. Prince wrote about the influence of the sonnet in Italy and about the appreciation of it " 'The Sonnet had emerged as a new poetic force in the *dolce stil novo* of the thirteenth century. Cavalcanti and Dante had revealed in it a magic of the intellect and the senses, but in very brief compass. Petrarch completed its evolution with 300 sonnets of sustained and deeply felt beauty; in their kind they have never been equalled. The sixteenth-century Italians, led by Bembo, took up the literary effort where Petrarch had left off; they strove to enrich and elevate the form, loading their verses with reminiscences, not only of Petrarch, but of Horace and Virgil.' " (Jones, 165). However, the Italian masters used the sonnet form "for love-poetry and more particularly for that semi-Platonic and semi-religious devotion to the Lady or *Donna* which subsequently became a cliché of love poetry" (Cuddon, 643).

The Italian poets did not only write isolated or independent sonnets, but also sonnet-sequences. The sonnet-sequences of such masters as Serafino dall'Aquila (1466-1500), Pietro Bembo (1470-1547), Michelangelo (1475-1564), Baldassar Castiglione (1478-1579) and Torquato Tasso (1544-1595) and such other poets are beautiful creations, and once were very popular. Bembo's sonnet-sequence, *Gli asolani,* is a dialogue on non-Platonic love. Michelangelo's sonnet-sequence, *Rime,* contains some sonnets of beauty, in spite of the fact that they lack technical accomplishment, their beauty depending on the ideas expressed through them. These sonnet-sequences, later on, inspired poets to write similar sonnet-sequences.

In the 15th and the 16th centuries, the Italian sonnet sailed to Spain, Portugal, France, the Netherlands, Poland and England. Some time later, the sonnet moved to Germany, Scandinavia, Russia and to some other countries of the world. The sonnet has been so applauded by the people of the whole world that there have been very few languages in the world in which poets have not tried their hands at sonneteering. From Italy, the sonnet first moved to Spain, with the help of the Spanish poet Marquis de Santillana (1398-1458). But it took some time for the sonnet to establish itself in Spain. The Spanish poets and dramatists of Spain who helped the sonnet take roots in the soil of Spain were Juan Boscan (1490-1552), Garcilaso de la Vega (1503-1536) and Lope de Vega (1562-1635). From Spain, next, the sonnet travelled to Portugal with the helping hand of Antonio Ferreira (1528-1569), and there it flourished at the hands of Camoes (1524-1580) and Anthero de Quental (1842-1891). From Spain and Portugal, the sonnet now was brought to France by Clement Marot (1496-1544) and Mellin de Saint Gelais (1491-1558). It was in France, for the first time, that the Petrarchan form of the sonnet lost its hold on poets. It was Joachim du Bellay (1522-1560) who deviated from the Petrarchan form of sonnet and invented his own form of sonnet, and wrote three famous non-Italian sonnet-sequences : *L'Olive, Regrets,* and *Antiquites de Rome* (translated by Spenser as *The Ruins of Rome*). Thanks to Pierre de Ronsard (1524-1585) and Philippe Desportes (1546-1606) — both of them designated 'prince of poets' — the sonnet had a heyday in France. The former in his *Sonnets pour Hélène* and the latter in his *Amours* raised the sonnet to its perfection. Ronsard and Desportes were instrumental in transporting the spirit of the sonnet to England in the 16th century.

In France, Francois de Malherbe (1555-1628) introduced a new rhyme-scheme into the sonnet : a b b a a b b a, c c d e d e, or c c d c c d. Malherbe also introduced the alexandrine or the twelve-syllable line in the sonnet in the 16th century. The sonnet could not sustain its popularity for long in France. In the 18th century, the sonnet saw its declining popularity throughout Europe, and therefore, also in France. In the 19th century France, the sonnet had its revival, thanks to the efforts of Theophile Gautier (1811-1872) and Baudlaire (1821-1867), and once again reached its new height of popularity at the hands of such poets as Heredia, Lecomte de Lisle, Valéry, Mallarme and Rimbaud.

From France, the sonnet travelled to Germany, but the movement was slow. The German poets G.R. Weckherlin (1584-1653) and Andreas Griphius (1616-1664) were inspired by the sonnetry in France, and composed many sonnets. But their efforts to popularise the sonnet soon fell through, and for about half a century, there was no demand for sonnets in Germany. In the 18th century, Gottfried Burger (1747-1794) tried to revive sonnetry in Germany, and he was followed in his mission by some romantic poets such as Schlegel, Eichendorff, Tieck and others. In the 19th century, the sonnet reached its height of beauty at the hand of August Graf von Platen (1796-1835) whose *Sonette aus Venedig* is simply superb. Likewise, in the 20th century, the mystical sonnet sequence of Rainer Maria Rilke (1875-1926), *Sonette an orpheus* (1923), and the sonnets of R.A. Schröder have demonstrated the height of beauty that the sonnet can reach in the German language.

The sonnet was not very late to come to England : it came there in the first half of the 16th century. England was then being flushed with the spirit of the Reniassance humanism. The God-centred consciousness of the medieval England gave way to man-centred consciousness. Man now found divinity or divine qualities in man himself, as is evident in Hamlet's wondering at man : "What a piece of work is a man! How noble in reason! how infinite in faculties! in form and moving, how express and admirable! in action, how like an angel! in apprehension, how like a god! the beauty of the world! the paragon of animals!" This deification of man brought in its wake enlightened awareness about the most potent and excellent quality of man, the universal element of humanity : love, particularly the love between man and woman. And this love found its most fitting expression in the sonnet. England is geographically not far off from France, and so the verve of the sonnet soon reached the Dover beach for the waiting Englanders.

It is generally held that Henry Howard, the Earl of Surrey (1517-47) and Sir Thomas Wyatt (1503-42) were the pioneers of sonnetry in the 16th century England. But it should be borne in mind that the *dolce stil novo* of the sonnet would not be possible in England had John Skelton (1464?-1529) not paved the path of the Italian hendecasyllabic lines in English through his poetry. Skelton was a narrowly orthodox priest and tutor to Prince Henry (later Henry VIII). He was a master of metre, and is now known particularly for his 'Skeltonic verse' — a generally 3-stress line. To take an example of the Skeltonic verse from his *Cloyn Clout:* "What can is avayle/To dryve forth a snayle,/Or to make a sayle/Of an herynges tayle." Though Skelton was a priest, he did not hesitate to write beautiful verses in praise of beautiful and noble ladies. He also invented the 'pausing line', an example of which may be taken from his Morality play Magnificence :

Two faces in a hood/covertly I bear,
    Water in the one hand,/and fire in the other;
I can feed with a fool,/and lead him by the ear;
    Falsehood-in-Fellowship/is my sworn brother.

With all these, Skelton prepared the ground for sowing the seed of the sonnet. Therefore, F.T. Prince is right when he worte that "Wyatt was not wholly an innovator (of the sonnet), for his songs continued a long and flourishing tradition" (Edward, 13). Prince, here, must have had the contributions of Skelton behind his mind.

Though England borrowed the spirit of the sonnet from France, the pioneer poets of England who wrote sonnets immitated the Italian or Petrarchan form. But the Italianate form did not squarely fit into the English language, and so it had to be reconstructed or restructured to dovetail it into the natural rhythm of the English language. It may be mentioned here that the Latin and Italian langauages allow for much more diversification of the rhyming in poetry than the English language. However, in English, the rhythm of the 'pausing line' is more natural, and so the English poets had to keep this in mind while writing sonnets. F.T. Prince wrote in this regard : "If we look at Wyatt's adaptations or translations from the Italian we may see the pressure of the form (of the Italian sonnet) upon the native (English) rhythm of the 'pausing line'. In all his sonnets there are more or less self-contained, antithetically-balanced lines, in which a marriage is effected between the pausing rhythm and the pattern of the original" (Edward, 13-14).

As a diplomat, Wyatt frequented the French and Italian courts and thus got himself acquainted with the French and Italian sonnetry. But he was more attracted by the Italian and Italianate sonnets, and so he adopted the Italian or Italianate form of sonnet for the English langauge. Nevertheless, he made some variations in the Italian or Petrarchan form of the sonnet. In the Italian sonnet, there are the octave and the sestet, which are, as if, two independent poems about the same theme or idea that unites the two parts or 'poems' of the sonnet, or at the least, the two stanzas of the sonnet. Wyatt did not follow this Petrarchan scheme of two stanzas of the sonnet; he rather took the first twelve lines of the sonnet as a complete poem. Further, Petrarch did not use any final emphasis (the concluding couplet), but Wyatt "accidentally or deliberately chose to end most of his sonnets with a couplet, and thus helped to give a speical character to the Elizabethan sonnet'' (Sampson, 118). This emphasis — the summarising end-couplet — was retained even by Shakespeare.

In addition to this change in the Italianate sonnet, Wyatt's contemporary, Henry Howard, the Earl of Surrey, introduced another variation in it. Surrey did not follow the Petrarchan or Italian octave-sestet structure, but divided the first twelve lines into three quatrains, retaining the final couplet of Wyatt unchanged. Surrey had a brief life of only 30 years, as in 1547 he was arrested on a trumped-up charge of treason and executed. But within this short life, he could bestow upon the English sonnet a permanent form and elegance of beauty, for which reason, in the Elizabethan period, he was taken to be a better poet than Wyatt. The perfection of his metre, propriety of diction, rationality of syntax, and the urbanity, control, precision and clarity of his thought process gave his poems, particularly his sonnets, a permanent place in English literature. Surrey's quatrains and his rhyme-scheme were retained by Shakespeare : a b a b, c d c d, e f e f, g g. And this form was also adopted by the Elizabethan literary circle as the standard form of the sonnet. However, in this way, with the aid of Skelton, Wyatt and Surrey, the sonnet took its office in the Elizasbethan literary world. Incidentally, in 1575, George Gascoigne, the playwright and sonneteer, defined the (Elizabethan) sonnet thus : " 'Sonnets are of fourteene lynes, every lyne conteyning tenne syllables. The first twelve to ryme in staves of foure lynes by cross metre, and the last two ryming together do conclude the whole' '' (Cuddon, 644).

The Elizabethan period was the heyday of the sonnet, and most of the poets of that period tried their hands in sonnetry, and many of them composed some beautiful sonnet-sequences. Some of the famous sonneteers of the Elizabethan period were: Sir Philip Sidney (1554-86), Samuel (1562/3-1619), Thomas Lodge (1558-1625), Henry Constable (1562-1613), Michael Drayton (1563-1631), Edmund Spenser (1527-1599), and of course, William Shakespeare. We shall deal to some extent with these sonneteers (barring Shakespeare whom we will take up in Chapter 5) in the next Chapter. Again, some of these sonneteers wrote beautiful sonnet-sequences, some of which are : Sidney's *Astrophil and Stella;* Daniel's *Delia;* Lodge's *Phillis;* Constable's *Diana;* .Drayton's *Idea's Mirror;* and Spenser's *Amoretti;* but the most splendid sonnet-sequences is that of Shakespeare.

The craze of the sonnet came to a halt as the 16th century passed by. Neither the poets of the Jacobean period (1603-1625) nor those of the Caroline period (1625-49) showed interest in sonnet writing. Ben Jonson (1572-1637), the noted dramatist, for instance, was not at all interested in the sonnet. Nevertheless, some very beautiful sonnets were composed in both the periods. John Donne (1572-1631), the metaphysical poet, in his *Songs and Sonnets,* published some very beautiful sonents. He also introduced variety in the form of the sonnet. Curioiusly, Donne did not always stick to the 14-line length of the sonnet. For instance, his Sonnet 'The Token' (cited before) is a 18-line sonnet, like some of the 18-line sonnets of Thomas Watson's *Hecatompathia* (instance cited above). But the rhyme-scheme of Donne differed from that of Watson, as we have already seen.

The causes of the decline of the sonnet after the Elizabethan age are very difficult to identify. Perhaps the reasons lie in the change in the spirit of the English people and in their changed attitude toward life. The Elizabethan age was followed by the Puritan age (1620-1660). The Puritan movement wanted to reform the prevailing moral ways of the people. The Elizabethan England was essentially pagan and sensual; and so it had an atmosphere in which the sonnet found a fertile ground. On the other hand, in the Puritan age, the chivalry, the romantic love, the flirtations, the hypocrisy in love, etc. that Elizabethan age borrowed from the medieval age and nursed them, withered away. And, consequently, the sonnet starved for want of its staple food love and its concomitant chairoscuro of emotions. Further, contrary to the abundance of optimistic spirit of the people of the Elizabethan age, the people of the Puritan age (in the Stuart period) were pessimistic, suffering from an inalienable free-floating gloom. In such an atmosphere, only metaphysical poetry could thrive, and it actually did, but no sonnet. The spirit of the Puritan age can be gauged from such works as Burton's *Anatomy of Melancholy.* True, many of the major works of Shakespeare were written in the transition peiod, *i.e.,* in the period between the Elizabethan and the Puritan periods, but it must be borne in mind that these works were done in the limping Elizabethan spirit. In that rational, moralistic and pessimistic Puritan age, a tribe of metaphysical poets came up : Donne, Herbert, Vaughan, Marvell, Waller, Denham, Cowley, Crashaw, Davenant, and such others. Some of these metaphysical poets also composed a few beautiful sonnets and sonnet cycles. Not that, in the Puritan period, there was no scope at all for lighter veins. For even in that tolerable gloom of the Puritan age, the Cavalier poets, such as

Lovelace, Suckling, Carew, Harrick and such others wrote poems in lighter veins, perhaps, in protest against the prevailing puritan and gloomy spirit; but none of them, for reasons unknown, preferred the sonnet form.

Therefore, the sonnet had to hibernate for about fifty years; after which John Milton (1608-74) came up to revive the sonnet, though for a short while. But even he did not write a sonnet-sequence, but only a few sonnets, the cause of which may his non-chalance for the sonnet form. Curiously, he did never write sonnets on the theme of love, perhaps, because he himself experienced the aridity of this universal passion. Milton wrote sonnets only on special occasions — to celebrate an occasion, to memorise an event, to glorify a person, etc. — and so his sonnets may be called occasional sonnets. A sonnet of Mitlon's may be cited below, for getting a taste of his sweet-sounding sonnets:

On His Blindness

When I consider how my light is spent,
Ere half my days in this dark world and wide,
And that one talent which is death to hide
Lodged with me useless, though my soul more bent
To serve therewith my Maker, and present
My true account, lest He returning chide;
'Doth God exact day-labour, light denied?'
I fondly ask : but Patience, to prevent
That murmur, soon replies, 'God doth not need
Either man's work or his own gifts. Who best
Bear his mild yoke, they serve him best: his state
Is kingly : thousands at his bidding speed,
And post o'er land and ocean without rest;
They also serve who only stand and wait.'

Milton always used the same rhyme-scheme for the octave: a b b a, a b b a. But he used different rhyme-schemes for the sestet: c d e c d e, c d c d c d, etc. with variations even in these.

After Milton, the sonnet again went into hybernation; this time for about a hundred years, for during the whole of the 18th century, poets did not show any interest in sonnetry — maybe they thought it was too old a form of poetry — and consequently, only a few good sonnets were composed, such as Thomas Gray's 'Ode on the Death of Richard West', Thomas Warton's 'To the River London', William Bowles's 'At

Ostend', etc. The sonnet was taken up once again — this time with considerable enthusiasm — in the Romantic period, perhaps thanks to the superfluity of passions of the poets as well as of the people of that period. Most of the major poets wrote sonnets, and wrote them beautifully. Keats, Shelley and Wordsworth, amongst others, have left for us many inspiring sonnets, but those of Wordsworth are undoubtedly the best. Wordsworth wrote two sonnet cycles, entitled *The River Duddon* and *Ecclesiastical Sonnets,* but unfortunately, both have come croppers. On the other hand, some of his individual sonnets — and he wrote a good number of such sonnets — are certainly memorable, such as '(Sonnet) Composed upon Westminster Bridge, September 3, 1802', 'To Toussaint L'Ouverture', and 'On the Extinction of the Venetian Republic'. A representative sonnet of Wordsworth is being cited below :

Composed upon Westminster Bridge, September 3, 1802

Earth has not anything to show more fair:
Dull would he be of soul who could pass by
A sight so touching in its majesty:
This City now doth, like a garment wear
The beauty of the morning; silent bare,
Ships, towers, domes, theatres, and temples lie
Open unto the fields, and to the sky;
All bright and glittering in the smokeless air.
Never did sun more beautifully steep
In his first splender, valley, rock, or hill;
Ne'er saw I, never felt, a calm so deep!
The river glideth at his own sweet will:
Dear God! the very houses seem asleep;
And all that mighty heart is lying still!

Like Milton, Wordsworth had no predilection for love as the theme of the sonnet, and used the sonnet form for diverse purposes, writing only very few sonnets on the theme of love. He stuck to the 14-line sonnet form, again like Milton, but used various rhyme-schemes, the principal one being a b b a, a b b a, c d c d, c d.

Keats also wrote a large number of sonnets, at least compared with the number of his other poems. Like Wordsworth, Keats also used various themes and rhyme-schemes for the sonnet. Some of his sonnets are permanent treasure-troves of the English poesy, such as 'On First Looking into Chapman's Homer' and 'Bright Star! would I were steadfast as thou art'. He composed a sonnet on the sonnet itself, which is being cited below:

Sonnet on the Sonnet

If by dull rhymes our English must be Chain'd,
And, like Andromeda, the sonnet sweet
Fettered, in spite of pained loveliness,
Let us find out, if we must be constrain'd,
Sandals more interwoven and complete
To fit the naked foot of Poesy:
Let us inspect, the Lyre, and weight the stress
Of every chord, and see what may be gain'd
By ear industrious, and attention meet;
Misers of sound and syllable, no less
Than Midas of his coinage, let us be
Jealous of dead leaves in the bay wreath crown;
So, if we may not let the Muse be free,
She will be bound with garlands of her own.

One of the other poets of the Romantic period who wrote some sonnets is Percy Bysshe Shelley (1792-1822). Two of his splendid sonnets are 'Ozymandias' and 'England in 1819'. But Shelley was not very fond of the sonnet. His 'Ozymandias' is being quoted in full below :

Ozymandias

I met a traveller from an antique land
Who said : Two vast and trunkless legs of stone
Stand in the desert. near them on the sand,
Half sunk, a shattered visage lies, whose frown,
And wrinkled lip, and sneer of cold command.
Tell that its sculptor well those passions read
Which yet survive, stamped on these lifeless things.
The hand that mocked them and the heart that fed;
And on the pedestal these words appear:
"My name is Ozymandias, ye mighty, and despair!"
Nothing beside remains. Round the decay
Of that colossal wreck, boundless and bare,
The lone and level sands stretch far away.

During the last part of the 18th and the early part of the 19th centuries, there was a resurgence of the sonnet, not only in England (in the Romantic period) but also in almost the whole of Europe — especially in Italy, France and Germany. In Italy, Ugo Foscolo (1778-1827) and Carducci (1835-1907) composed some beautiful sonnets, as in France Gautier (1811-72) and Baudlaire (1821-67) did. Baudlaire's sonnet 'Meditation' is being quoted below (as translated by Joanna Richardson) :

Meditation

Be wise, O my Affliction, be serene.
You called upon the Evening; now it falls:
Obscurity envelops all the town,
To some brings peace, to others brings ordeals.

While the vile multitude of common men,
Whipped on by unrelenting festivals,
Lay up regrets, like servile citizens,
Come you Affliction, far from carnivals,

Give me your hand. See the dead Years lean down,
In dated dress, from balconies in heaven;
Behold Regret rise from the deep, unbowed;

The Sun sleep underneath an arch, and die,
And, trailing in the East, like a long shroud,
Listen, my dear: sweet Night walks through the sky.

Baudlaire preferred two quatrains, and a sestet, divided into two equal parts, each part consisting of three lines. The other French poets who produced outstanding sonnets were Lecomte de Lisle, Valèry, Mallarmé and Rimbaud. In Germany, the sonnet was revived by Bürger (1747-94), and there the sonnet form was much used by such romantic poets as Tieck, Eichendorff, and August Graf von Platen-Hallemünde whose *Sonette a us Venedig* reached the perfection of the sonnet form.

After yet another pause, this time of about three decades, in the Victorian period (1837-1901), the sonnet form was again preferred by some of the poets of England. Several sonnet sequences were composed in this period, and some of the major sonnet sequences of this period are : Elizabeth Barrett Browning's *Sonnets from the Portuguese* (1847-50), Robert Bridge's *The Growth of Love* (1976), D.G. Rossetti's *The House of Life* (1881) which consists of one hundred and three romantic and sensual sonnets, and George Meredith's *Modern Love* (1862) which is a sequence of 50 sonnets and which is the "tragic masterpiece" of the poet. In addition to these, Rossetti's sister, Christian, also composed some very beautiful sonnets, and a very short sonnet sequence of only three sonnets, on her unhappiness.

In the Victorian period, some experiments were done on the form of the sonnet. George Meredith did not follow the usual 14-line form of the sonnet, but used 16 lines for his sonnets. Such sort of amplification of the sonnet was not new, because, as we have seen, Milton used 18 lines in some of his sonnets, and Shakespeare wrote at least one sonnet of 15 lines. The most interesting experiment on the sonnet form, in the Victorian period, was done by Gerard Manley Hopkins (1844-89) who during his life-time had been almost anonymous. In the sonnet, he combined the alexandrine or the twelve-syllable line with his own invention of the sprung rhythm. The sprung rhythm is a peculiar form of rhythm which is quite different from the traditional patterns of rhythm. In his *Preface to Poems* (1918), Hopkins himself wrote about the sprung rhythm : " '(It) is measured by feet of from one to four syllables, regularly, and for particular effects any number of weak or slack syllables may be used. It has one stress, which falls on the only syllable, if there is only one, or, if there are more, than scanning as above, on the first, and so gives rise to four sorts of feet, a monosyllable and the so-called accentual Trochee, Dactyl, and the First Paeon (Paeon is a foot of one stressed and three unstressed syllables.) (....) And there will be four corresponding natural rhythms; but nominally the feet are mixed and any one may follow any other' " (Cuddon, 651-52). Hopkins's sonnets, such as 'Carrion Comfort', 'Justus quidem tu es Domine' are simply superb. An example of Hopkins's experiment on prosody may be taken from the first lines of four of his poems: "No worst, there is none. Pitched past pitch of grief,"; "I wake and feel the feel of dark, not day."; "Patience, hard thing ! the hard thing but to pray,"; and "My own heart let me none have pity on; let".

In the 20th century, even the lingering interest in the sonnet was left out in the cold. Very few poets have composed sonnets in this century; and those who have done, have done very scantily. Only three poets can be counted as major sonneteers of this century in the English language : Rupert Chawner Brooke (1887-1915) of England, Robert Frost (1874-1963) of the USA, and Wystan Hugh Auden (b. 1907), the English-born poet of the USA. Brooke was a 'war poet', but composed some very beautiful sonnets. Robert Frost, though he did not experiment on the form or pattern of the sonnet, wrote some novel sonnets. And Auden, who is recognised as one of the major poets of the 20th century, also wrote a number of splendid sonnets. He wrote sonnets on public affairs, and on famous men, such as A.E. Houseman, Rimbaud and Edward Lear, and not on personal affairs or on love. Besides, Dylan Thomas, Robert Lowell and George Barker also wrote sonnets, and experimented with the form of the sonnet.

But the account of the sonnet in the 20th century will not be complete without any mention of another major poet, the Irish-English poet, William Butler Yeats (1865-1939). He wrote very few sonnets (or only one?), but has left the indelible mark of his poetic skill and his experiment on the form of the sonnet in his sonnet or sonnets. His sonnet, 'The Folly of Being Comforted', is very beautiful. It has rhyming couplets and is divided into three parts : sestet, sestet, and a concluidng rhyming couplet. The sonnet which first appeared in *The Speaker* in 1902 is being cited below :

The Folly of Being Comforted

One that is ever kind said yesterday:
'Your well-beloved's hair has threads of grey,
And little shadows come about her eyes;
Time can but make it easier to be wise
Though now it seems impossible, and so
All that you need is patience.
Heart cries, 'No,
I have not a crumb of comfort, not a grain.
Time can but make her beauty over again:
Because of that great nobleness of hers
The fire that stirs about her, when she stirs,
Burns out more clearly. O she had not these ways
When all the wild summer was in her gaze.'

O heart ! O heart ! if she 'd but turn her head,
You'd know the folly of being comforted.

In the contemporary times, the sonnet is not much in demand. This is true not only of England, but also of the rest of the world. In Germany, for instance, very few sonnets have been composed after Rilke's *Sonette an Orpheus* (1925). However, to conclude this chapter, we may say that down the centuries, the sonnet has proved itself to be a very powerful form of poetic expression, and that it has undergone much experimentation so far. J.A. Cuddon very justly wrote: "During over 700 years, the 'narrow room of the sonnet' has been adapted to a remarkable variety of experiment and development and also to an astonishing range of feeling and themes" (Cuddon, 646).

IV

The Elizabethan Sonnetry

It is generally — and, perhaps, rightly — held that Sir Thomas Wyatt (1503-42) and his literary disciple and colleague, Henry Howard, the Earl of Surrey (1517-47) — "the two cheftain" in "a new company of courtly makers" of Henry VIII's reign — were the harbingers of the sonnet into the English language. But as the earliest English sonnet form was Italian or Italianate, we may say that Wyatt deserves more praise than Surrey for introducing the sonnet in England. It was actually Wyatt who brought the sonnet form from Italy, as he came across the opportunity of doing so. He was born at Allington Castle in Kent, studied at Cambridge for some time, held some court appointments, and then went on diplomatic missions to the Courts of France, Italy and Spain — the countries which were, by then, as we have seen, already influenced by the sonnet form. Though he got acquainted with the French and the Spanish sonnet as well, Wyatt was influenced by the sonnets of Italy, and held the Italian form as his model for sonnet writing.

Perhaps, Wyatt's unconsumated love-affairs, from 1526 to 1532, with Ann Boleyn whom Henry VIII ultimately married, inspired him to write sonnets on the theme of love that was the theme of all the Italian or Italianate sonnets. Besides sonnets, Wyatt wrote lyrics and satires, and also translated from Plutarch. Some of his sonnets and other poems were published in Richard Tottel's (d. 1594) *Songs and Sonnets Written by the Right Honourable Lord Henry Howard Late Earl of Surrey* and Others (1557), better known as *Tottel's Miscellany*. Though initially this book contained fewer sonnets of Wyatt, yet, as the book went through subsequent publications, the number of his sonnets and other poems increased phenomenally. In its 1587 edition, the book contained 310 poems, in all, of which 81 belonged to Wyatt, and only 36 to Surrey. This fact may vouchsafe for the superiority of Wyatt to Surrey as a poet.

Wyatt did not always write in regular metre, but sometimes in irregular metre, and yet his sonnets were very striking. But as regards arguments, ideas and themes, Wyatt showed no originality, for most of his sonnets are either translations of the sonnets of Petrarch and his followers, or imitations of their sonnets. Further, he could not introduce new themes into the sonnet, as later on, Milton and Wordsworth, for instances, did. Nevertheless, he has shown intensity of passion, subtlety of modulation of tone, and sincerity of feeling in his sonnets. "In the sonnets, whether he is translating or imitating, Wyatt is committed by his Italian models to rather more elaborate figures of speech. The effect is, sometimes, a loss of force and immediacy. But the best of the sonnets (*e.g.* 'My galey charged with forgetfulness', 'Whoso list to hunt', 'Farewell love') have all the qualities of his best lyrics, with an additional richness. The critics have, on the whole, underrated them" (Daiches, 566).

Following the Italian model, Wyatt's sonnets comprises the octave rhyming a b b a a b b a, and the sestet rhyming variously, but generally c d e c d e. In most of Wyatt's sonnets, the octave posits a question which the sestet answers; but in some, the octave expresses one aspect of the theme, and the sestet gives us another aspect of the same. Wyatt had a difficult time in following the Italian model, because the Italian sonnet demands repeated rhymes which are easy to find in the Italian langauge, but which are very difficult to find in English. It is for this reason that some of the English adopter of the Italian form introduced changes in the Italian or Petrarchan model. For instance, some sonneteers employed the rhyme-scheme a b b a a c c a for the octave. In addition, Henry Howard, the Earl of Surrey, introduced a quasi-independent and rhymed concluding or summarising couplet, as a result of which the whole rhyme-scheme of his sonnet was a b b a c d c d e f e f g g, and this very rhyme-scheme was adopted by Shakespeare.

Wyatt added yet another feature to the sonnet : he introduced the 'pausing line' as the verse. The 'pausing line' is a self-contained and antithetically balanced line, examples of which can be found in the following sonnet of Wyatt's :

I fynde no peace/ and all my warr is done;
I fere and hope,/ I burrne and freise like yse;
I fley above the wynde/ yet can I not arrise;
And nought I have/ and all the world I seson (seize on);
That loseth nor locketh/ holdeth me in prison
And holdeth me not,/ yet can I scape nowise;

Not letteth me lyve/ nor dye at my devise,
And yet of deth/ it gyveth none occasion.
Without lyen, I se;/ and withoute tong I plain;
I desire to perisshe,/ and yet I aske helthe;
I love an othre,/ and thus I hate my self;
I fede me in sorrowe/ and laugh in all my pain;
Likewise displeaseth me/ boeth deth and lyffe;
And my delite/ in causer of this stryff.

Surrey, the disciple of Wyatt, so to say, was born in a great family of England, and was educated along with the Duke of Richmond, the bastard son of King Henry VIII, in English and French courts. Afterwards Surrey married the daughter of the Earl of Oxford. In 1545, at the siege of Montreuil, he saw active service and was wounded. In the following year he was falsely charged of treason and was jugulated in 1547. In his brief life, he translated Books II and IV of Virgil's *Aeneid,* and also wrote a small number of sonnets, most of which appeared in *Tottel's Miscellany* along with Wyatt's sonnets and poems, in 1557, *i.e.* about seven years before the birth of our poet Shakespeare. True, Surrey produced fewer sonnets, but nevertheless, it was he who could influence his contemporary and succeeding sonneteers much more than Wyatt himself could. "His poetry is smoother and more graceful than Waytt's but less strong; some poems seem exercises rather than declarations of love" (Daiches, 263). Surrey's poems and sonnets are distinguished by their "urbanity, control, clarity and precision" (*loc. cit.).* Further, we should not forget that it was Surrey who actually invented the English or Shakespearean sonnet form proper, though, we must admit, before him Wyatt invented the concluding couplet of the English or Shakespearean sonnet. The following sonnet of Surrey may give us an idea about how his sonnets read :

Set me wheras the sunne doth parche the grene,
Or where his beames do not dissolve the yse:
In temperate heate where he is felt and sene:
In presence prest of people madde or wise.
Set me in hye, or yet in lowe degree:
In longest night, or in the shortest daye:
In clearest skye, or where clowdes thickest be:
In lusty youth, or when my heeres are graye.
Set me in heaven, in earth, or els in hell,
In hyll, or dale, or in the fomying flood:
Thrall, or at large, alive where so I dwell:

Sicke, or in health: in evil fame, or good.
Hers will I be, and only with this thought
Content my self, although my chaunce be nought.

After Surrey, sonnet-writing certainly continued to be in vogue, but there was no remarkable sonneteer till Edmund Spenser (1552-1599) sat down to compose sonnets. He was born in East Smithfield, London, and attended Merchant Taylor's School where the great educationist and humanist Richard Mulcaster was the headmaster, and where Thomas Kyd and Thomas Lodge once read. After taking M.A. degree of Cambridge in 1576, Spenser became secretary to John Young, Bishop of Rochester, and thus became acquainted with Sir Philip Sidney after whose death he wrote the famous pastoral elegy *Astrophel* in Sidney's memory. Spenser is remembered for his three other great works : *The Shephard's Calender, Eclogues,* and the ambitious *Faerie Queene* most of which was burnt by fire caused by the Irish insurrection of 1598. Next year, he died in distressed circumstances.

Spenser's sonnet sequence is entitled *Amoretti.* It contains eighty-nine sonnets, of which only one is in the Shakespearean form, and the rest are in the form invented by himself. His own rhyme-scheme for the sonnet is a b a b b c b c c d c d e e, whereby he mingled couplets and separate verses, and also bound the three quatrains togehter in a very subtle way. Spenser wrote the sonnets of *Amoretti* on the theme of his love and courtship with Elizabeth Boyle whom he married as his second wife. "*Amoretti* is a distinguished sonnet-sequence reflecting the various stages of the courtship, while individuality is given by Spenser's characteristic union of courtly sentiment with praise for the institution of marriage, found too in *The Faerie Queene.* The style of the sonnets is musical and decorated, and the language at times shows traces of that archaisms found more notably in *The Faerie Queene*" (Daiches, 494). The following sonnet of Spenser may illustrate the form, and show the beauty of his sonnets :

My Lady's presence makes the Roses red,
Because to see her lips they blush for shame.
The Lily's leaves, for envy, pale become;
And her white hands in them this envy bred.
The Marigold the leaves abroad doth spread;
Because the sun's and her power is the same.
The Violet of purple colour came,
Dyed in the blood she made my heart to shed.
In brief all flowers from her their virtue take;

From her sweet breath, their sweet smells do proceed.
The living heat which her eyebeams doth make
Warmeth the ground, and quickeneth the seed.
The rain, wherewith she watereth the flowers,
Falls from mine eyes, which she dissolves in showers.

That Spenser was influenced by Sir Philip Sidney (1554-86) is evident from the fact that just after Sidney's death, Spenser wrote a pastoral elegy, *Astrophel,* in his memory. Sidney, one of the finest sonneteers of the Elizabethan world, has become immortal for his sonnet-sequence *Astrophel and Stella* which contains one hundred and eight sonnets. Besides this sonnet-sequence, he also wrote a few other sonnets, but these are of lesser quality than those of *Astrophel and Stella.* Sidney was the eldest son of Sir Henry Sidney, three times Lord Deputy of Ireland. He went to Christ Church, Oxford, but left the institution without taking any degree, and travelled over Europe, and soon became a brilliant member of Queen Elizabeth's Court. For his personal beauty, sweet demeanor, brilliant conversation, sparkling wit and undaunted chivalry, he became the *beau idéal* of the young generation. Besides the sonnets, he wrote *The Lady of Mary,* a masque, in honour of the queen, and published it in 1578. After some quarrels with the Earl of Oxford, he left the Court for ever, and stayed with his dearest sister, the Countess of Pembrok, for whose amusement he wrote *Arcadia.*

Astrophel and Stella is a 'semi-autobiographical, semi-fictional story of human passion'. In the sonnets contained in it, he showed his mastery of the Petrarchan form of the sonnet. His mastery of the sonnet-form was so great that as a sonneteer he was, perhaps, second only to Shakespeare. Sidney generally followed the Italian mode, but separated the octave from the sestet, though there is seldom any distinction between the content of the octave and that of the sestet. He also introduced some interesting variations in the pattern of rhyming of the octave and the sestet. He mostly used the Petrarchan octave, rhyming a b b a, b a b a, and sometimes, ababbaba or a b a b, b a a b, etc. On the other hand, his sestet commonly rhymed c d c d e e. Sidney's sonnets are notable for their sincere passion, restraining and shaping control, and lofty inspiration. The following sonnet from *Astrophel and Stella* may illustrate the form, movement and beauty of Sidney's sonnets in general :

Stella, since thou so right a Princess art
Of all the Powers which life bestows on me,
That are by them ought undertaken be,

They first resort unto that sovereign part;
Sweet for a time give respite to my heart,
Which pants as though it still should leape to thee;
And on my thought give the Lievetenancie
To this great cause, which needs both wit and Art
And as a Queen, who from her presence sends
Whom she employs, dismis from thee my wit,
Still to have wrought that thy own will attends,
For servants shame of Masters blame doth sit.
O let not Fools in me thy works approve,
And scorning say, see what it is to love.

Barnabe Barnes (c. 1569-1609), a prolific poet, was also a sonneteer of considerable importance, in the Elizabethan period. He was greatly influenced by Sidney, particularly in his *Parthenophil and Parthenophe* — a sonnet-sequence. Barnes was the son of the Bishop of Durham. Besides the above-mentioned sonnet-sequence, he wrote a century of religious sonnets : *Divine Century of Spiritual Sonnets*. Some critics think that Barnes may be a candidate for the 'rival poet' in Shakespeare's sonnets, and this may vouchsafe for his fame as a poet and, especially, for his mastery of sonnetry. A representative sonnet of Barnes is being quoted below :

What can these wrinkles and vain tears portend,
But their hard favour and indurate heart?
What shew these sighs, which from my soul I send,
But endless smoke, raised from fiery smart?
Canst thou not frame those eyes to cast a smile?
Wilt thou with no sweet sentence make me blest?
To make amends wilt thou not sport a while?
Shall we not once with our opposed eyne
In interchange send golden darts rebated
With short reflexion, 'twixt thy brows and mine,
Whilst love with thee of my griefs hath debated?
Those eyes of love were made for love to see,
And cast regards on others, not on me!

As Barnes wrote beautiful sonnets principally on the theme of religious sentiments, so Michael Drayton (1563-1631) wrote a sonnet-sequence on the theme of his early love with Anne Goodere, the youngest daughter of Sir Henry Goodere and later wife of Sir Henry Rainsford. Drayton was a close friend of Shakespeare, like Ben Jonson. His sonnet-sequence was published in 1594 under the title *Idea's Mirror*. It shows his mastery of the sonnet form and the intensity of his love for Anne. Anne's marriage shocked him so much that he did never marry. One of Drayton's most famous sonnet begins with the line : 'Since there's no help, come let us kiss and part.' This line may remind one of Browning's poem 'The Last Ride Together':

I said — Then, Dearest, since 'tis so,
Since now at length my fate I know,
Since nothing all my love avails,
Since all, my life seemed meant for, fails,
Since this was written and needs must be —
My whole heart rises up to bless
Your name in pride and thankfulness !
Take back the hope you gave, — I claim
Only a memory of the same.

Drayton's *Idea's Mirror* was so popular that it was reprinted several times from 1594 to 1619. The sonnets of this collection are in the Shakespearean form which Drayton preferred. He used alexandrine in some of his sonnets, and also introduced other variations in the English or Shakespearean sonnet. In the skill of employing the English or Shakespearean form, he was, perhaps, second only to Shakespeare. The following sonnet of Drayton will show the form and beauty of his sonnets in general:

Taking my pen with words to cast my woe,
Duly to count the sum of my all cares,
I find my griefs innumerable grow,
The reckonings rise to millions of despairs;
And thus driving of my fatal hours.
The payments of my Love I read and cross:
Subtracting, set my sweets' units my sours;
My joy's arrange leads to my loss.
And thus mine eyes a debtor to thine eyes,
Which by extortion gaineth all their looks:
My heart hath paid such grievous usury !
That all their wealth lies in thy beauty's books,
And all is thine which hath been due to me,
And I a bankrupt, quite undone by thee !

Drayton's other works include : *The Harmony of the Church* (1591), *The Shepherd's Garland* (1593), *Endimion ad Phoebe* (1595), *Matilda* (1594), *The Legend of Great Cromwell* (1607), etc.

Samuel Daniel (1562/3-1619) was a poet and also a man of letters. He was born in Somerset and matriculated from Oxford in 1581. Daniel found Court patronage and maintained Court connection till his death. Though he was not a great poet, he sometimes wrote very well. He is best known for his sonnet-sequence, *Dalia.* His other writings include : *The Complaint of Rosamund* (1592), *The Tragedy of Cleopatra* (1594), *To the Countess of Bedford,* and *To the Countess of Cumberland* (1599), *The Queen's Arcadia* (1605), *Hymen's Triumph* (1615), etc. The following sonnet of Daniel will reveal some of his poetic qualities and the form of his sonnets in general :

> Let others sing of palladins and knights,
> In aged accents, and untimely words,
> Paint shadows in imaginary lines,
> Which well the reach of their high wit records:
> But I must sing of thee and those fair eyes.
> Authentic shall my verse, in time to come,
> When yet the unborn shall say, "Lo, where she lies !
> Whose beauty made him speak, that else was dumb."
> These are the arks, the trophies I erect,
> That fortify their name against old age;
> And these thy sacred virtues must protect,
> Against the dark, and Time's consuming rage.
> Though the error of my Youth they shall discover,
> Suffice they show I lived, and was thy lover.

Daniel preferred the English or Shakespearean rhyme-scheme : a b a b c d c d e f e f g g. His sonnets reveal appropriate emotion, well chosen words and, sometimes, beautiful images.

Henry Constable (1562-1613) was a minor sonneteer like Barnabe Barnes and Samuel Daniel. Constable was educated at St. John's college, became a Roman Catholic and settled in Paris. He wrote only one sonnet-sequence, *Diana : the Praises of His Mistress,* and published it in 1592. This sonnet-sequence consists of only 23 sonnets written in the style of Sir Philip Sidney. Constable sometimes followed the rhyme-scheme of Daniel. The following is one of his best sonents :

> To live in hell, and heaven to behold;
> To welcome life, and die a living death;
> To sweat with heat, and yet be freezing cold;
> To grasp at stars, and lie the earth beneath;
> To trade the maze that never shall have end;

To burn in sighs, and starve in daily tears;
To climb a hill, and never to descend;
Giants to kill and quake at childish fears;
To pine for food, and watch th' Hesperian tree;
To thirst for drink, and nectar still to draw;
To live accurs'd, whom men hold blest to be;
And weep those wrongs which never creature saw;
If this be love, if love in these bounded,
My heart is love, for these in it are grounded.

Besides all these sonneteers, there were some other minor sonneteers in the Elizabethan age, such as Giles Fletcher, Lodge, Flulke Greville, William Percy, Nicholas Breton, Peele, Bartholomew Griffin, and, of course, George Gascoigne. Griffin was a lawyer-sonneteer of some reputation, particularly for his collection of poems, *Fidessa.* George Gascoigne (c. 1530-77) had considerable influence in the world of Elizabethan sonnetry. In 1573, his collected sonnets — a sort of connected sonnets — was published under the title *A Hundred Sundry Flowers,* and the collection was well received by the public. This sonnet-sequence is historically very important "for anticipating, in its groups of connected sonnets, the form of the sonnet-sequence which was to become so popular in the Elizabethan period" (Daiches, 203-4).

The Elizabethan people were thirsty for music, and wanted the beauty of modulating tunes, and so the sonnet could easily find a place in their hearts. The popularity of the sonnets was so great that it became a fashion to write sonnets of all grades. And, yet, we must say that the Englishers were not as enthusiastic for the sonnet as the Italians or the French were. F.T. Prince justly wrote: " 'The sum total of sonnets in English from the sixteenth century to the present day, including those in 'Shakespearean' form or otherwise irregular, would be but a fraction of those in Italian or French' " (Jones, 164). One of the causes of this comparatively low production of sonnets in the Elizabethan period may be that the sonnet form did not well fit into the structure of the English language. To quote F.T. Prince : " 'It is clear that the extreme facility of the form in Italian is only equalled by its difficulty in English' " (Jones, 164). Prince further wrote about the facility of the sonnet form in Italian and consequent huge production of sonnets in that language : " 'Rhyme in Italian is so musical and expressive, that this intricate form proved capable of almost endless employment from its invention in the 13th century. By the late sixteenth century, there existed an enormous mass of Italian sonnets of all kinds, amorous, didactic, satiric, occasional' "

(Jones, 164). Another cause of the comparatively low production of sonnets in the Elizabethan period may be that most of the poets of that period heavily engaged themselves in drama, as the Elizabethan age was outstandingly an age of drama.

However low the production of sonnets in the Elizabethan period may be, compared to the production of that of Italy and France or of any other country, the English sonnets of that period are certainly a precious possession of the literature of the whole world. Yet, it must, at the same time, be admitted that a great amount of the Elizabethan sonnets could not touch the mark. Derek Traversi wrote about the Elizabethan sonnets : "Not all the poems are in any sense equal in interest. A high proportion clearly consist of little more than literary exercises, addressed either to a patron of letters or, specially in the case of the later numbers, to an imaginary and conventional mistress" (Ford, 186). However, the Elizabethan sonnets, in general, are distinctive for their varieties, melifluousness, sincerity of passion, etc., — particularly the sonnets of Sidney, Spenser, and, of course, Shakespeare. No genre of English poetry has been so popular, since the days of Chaucer, as the sonnet. The Elizabethan poets heavily experimented, as none else nowhere so much did, on the form and the content of the sonnet, and thus raised the sonnet to its possible perfection. They tried it on all passions; they modulated the tune of it in diverse ways; and they assayed the elasticity of the form of it; and thus they shaped the sonnet as a very pert vehicle of expressing a broad spectrum of emotions, including complex ones. And this perfection of the sonnet occurred firstly at the hand of Edmund Spenser, for which reason George Sampson says that "Spenser is the true father of the Elizabethan sonnet" (Sampson, 126). As Spenser invested the sonnet and thus perfected it with his musicality, so Shakespeare sharpened it with his wit, and beautified it with his ingenious artistry.

Again, complementarily, Shakespeare himself was perfected by the iron rules of the sonnet. The necessity of crisp expressions, unexpected turns, emotional intensity, occasional complex emotion, etc. of the sonnet contributed much to the development of Shakespeare as the greatest dramatist of the world. Derek Traversi elaborated on this point: "The very fact that the sonnet form itself is strictly limited, not merely by structural considerations but by strict conventions covering theme and expression alike, afforded the poet (Shakespeare) an opportunity of another though related kind; for the convention could be accepted in varying degrees, in attitudes ranging from simple adherence to a highly ambiguous irony. All these possibilities, thus set in a narrow and apparaently confined form, contributed greatly to extending the scope of Shakespeare's art. Above all, it is possible that the linguistic discipline associated with the sonnet form and imposed by it upon his natural Elizabethan exuberance was a decisive factor in the formation of his mature style. It encouraged the association of compression with depth of content and variety of emotional response to a degree unparalleled in English, giving simultaneous point and intensity to the expression of personal feeling. "These new tendencies in verse and rhythm were accompained in the sonnets by the exploration of fresh themes. The most important of these look forward, like so much in the parallel linguistic development, to the 'problem' plays which inaugurated the tragic period. They are concerned above all with the relationship of individual experience, and especially of the personal ties of love and friendship, as the most intimate and intense manifestations of that experience, with time. This is familiar ground in Renaissance poetry, and it is therefore not surprising that Shakespeare's first approach to the theme seems to have been through the sonnet form" (Ford, 187-88). Let us then turn to the next chapter to see how Shakespeare dealt with the sonnet, and how far he profited out of it.

❐

V

Shakespeare and the Sonnet

Around 1586, Shakespeare came to London to seek fortune there. He was perhaps constrained to leave Stratford behind and come to the metropolis, because the financial condition of his family was now straitened as a consequence of dwindling of his father's business and extension of the family by the addition of new faces — Anna and her three issues, Susanna, Hamnet and Judith. It is probable, as some scholars surmise, that before coming to London, Shakespeare served as schoolmaster for a stint, for the character of 'Master Holofernes' in *Love's Labour's Lost* can be so realistically drawn only by a person who himself has been a real schoolmaster. Mark, for instance, what Holofernes tells Nathaniel at the beginning of the second scene of the fourth Act : "The deer was, as you know, sanguis, in blood; ripe as the pomewater, who now hangeth like jewel in the ear of caelo, the sky, the welkin, the heaven; and anon falleth like a crab on the face of terra, the soil, the land, the earth." This is all extreme pedantry, very appropriate for the type of a schoolmaster. Again, some scholars suggest that before coming to London, Shakespeare joined some touring performing conpanies of the metropolis, and acted in minor roles in performances given in the country. A.C. Ward supports such a surmise. He wrote about Shakespeare : "He may have become a provincial actor, first in a travelling company associated with a Lancashire patron, and afterwards as one of Lord Strange's Man, also a travelling company before they settled in the metropolis" (Ward, 197).

Where in London Shakespeare first put up we do not know for certain, but this we know that he frequently changed his lodging. Probably, he first lived in Shoreditch near the theatre houses. Then he moved to St. Helen's Bishopgate, then to the "convenient lodging with a Huguenot family in Cripplegate on the Bankside. A.C. Ward is able to give even the dates of Shakespeare's residing at the various places : "Legal documents show that Shakespeare lived in Bishopgate in 1595, in Southwark in 1599, and in Cripplegate about 1604" (Ward, 198). However, before going to reside in Bishopgate, Shakespeare certainly either lived in the Inns of Court and Chancery or picked up friendship with the lawyer inmates of the Inns. The environment of these two Inns was intellectually very stimulating and literarily very inspiring, for, most of the briefless lawyers there, besides arranging stimulating discourses on matters of law, tried their hands in amateur sonneteering.

Sonneteering was the go of the day, and so those who could, and those who could not, shape out even a single verse, turned out sonnets, principally for private amusements. Edgar I. Fripp wrote : " 'sonneting' was in fashion in the years immediately following the defeat of the Armada — from 1588 to 1595. It reached its height after the publication of Sidney's *Astrophil and Stella* in 1591. Thousands of love poems, wherein the writers 'took upon themselves to court exactly', were circulated in manuscript. They were not intended for publication, and their appearance in print was at first an act of piracy" *(Fripp. 247).* That the lawyer-sonneteers of the Inns inspired Shakespeare regarding sonnet writing is evident from the fact that some of his connets are strewn with many legal terms. For instance, 'bar', 'right', 'plead', 'tenants', 'verdict' (Sonnet 46); 'audit', 'advis'd', 'lawful', 'strength of laws' (Sonnet 49); 'nail', 'interest', 'review' (Sonnet 74); 'confess'd', 'mortgaged', 'forfeit', 'statute', 'usurer', 'sue', 'debtor' (Sonnet 134); etc. It may be mentioned here that the laywer-sonneteers also attracted Shakespeare's facination to the province of drama. Fripp wrote in this regard: "Another link between Shakespeare and the lawyers had its effect on his (Shakespeare's) works. They (the lawyers) were keen supporters of the drama. Writers themselves, of verse and plays, they were prominent in the playhouses, as spectators and critics, appluding and hissing the actors, and the occasion of brawls" (Fripp, 255). However, Shakespeare was inspired for sonnet writing partly by the lawyer-sonneteers and partly by the craze for sonnetry in vogue. But, perhaps, he was mostly influenced to write sonnets by his coeval and established poets and dramatists, such as Spenser, Drayton, Sidney and Watson. Watson's *The Hecatompathia, or Passionate Centuries of Love* (1582) and *The Tears of Fancie, or Love Disdained* (1593) had, probably, a great influence over Shakespeare's fancy for the sonnet. Watson's *Love Disdained* "Consists of sonnets in the typical Elizabethan form, which Watson did much as anyone to establish, and in that limited respect Shakespeare's sonnets may owe something to his" (Ward, 130).

Though the Italian form of the sonnet was the order of the day,

Shakespeare chose the English form invented earlier by Wyatt. Again, Shakespeare did not like to confine the sonnet on the single theme of love, but adopted other themes too, such as time, despair grown out of unrequited love or wordly failures, beauty (of both male and female human beings), etc., and also complex and ambivalent emotions, such as love and hate for the same person. Most of the Elizabethan sonnets were not meant for publication, but were meant for private circulation among friends and admirers. Likewise, Shakespeare's sonnets were also privately circulated, and thereby the purpose of their author was abundantly served. However much criminality Thomas Thorpe may have shown by piratically publishing the sonnets of our poet, had he been too honest by not doing what he did, we would, perhaps, be the poorer for not having the precious gems of Shakespeare's sonnets, because otherwise these would, it might occur, go to oblivion, like most other Elizabethan sonnets.

When actually Shakespeare composed the sonnets we do not know. However, the period of composition was, probably, between 1592 and 1598. This dating of the sonnets is generally accepted, and is congruent with the opinion of L.C. Knight, according to whom, the sonnets were written " 'roughly from 1592 to 1597 or 1598' " (Jones, 75). But all do not agree with this dating. For instance, "Hotson, in *Shakespeare's Sonnets Dated,* argued ingeniously that Sonnets 107, 123, 124, were written by 1589, and on the assumption that the group (of sonnets) 1-126 is chronological, that 'Shakespeare completed this main group of his sonnets by 1589' " (Halliday, 461). Hotson's opinion is in keeping with that of Edgar I. Fripp who wrote "That his (Shakespeare's) sonnet-range was later than 1594 is unthinkable that it was over in 1593 is in the highest degree probable" (Fripp, I, 259).

Sir Philip Sidney's *Astrophil and Stella* was published in 1591, and this ushered in an era of sonnetry which lasted till 1598. During the period from 1591 to 1598, as many as twenty sonnet-sequences were published — a huge production indeed ! Shakespeare must have been inspired by the industry of sonnetry, right at the beginning. But he was not exclusively engaged in sonneteering, rather he composed sonnets in between, or along with, writing plays. This is evident from the fact that from 1592 to 1598 he wrote some 15 plays : *Henry VI*, Part I and Part II, *Richard III, Titus Andronicus, Comedy of Errors, Taming of the Shrew, Two Gentlemen of Verona, Love's Labour's Lost, Romeo and Juliet, Richard II, Midsummer Night's Dream, King John, Merchant of Venice,* and *Henry IV,* Part I and Part II. Among all these plays, *Love's Labour's*

Lost, Romeo and Juliet and *Richard II,* and the two long poems, *Venus and Adonis* and *The Rape of Lucrece,* have the highest number of 'parallels' with the Sonnets. These plays and poems may, therefore, serve to find out the exact date of composition of the Sonnets. Yet, as things stand today, perhaps we will never be able to ascertain the date of composition of the Sonnets. However, besides the above-mentioned guesses, Samuel Butler has yet another, and, may be, absurd, conjecture about the date of composition of the Sonnets. "In 1899 Samuel Butler dated the series 1-126 (of the Sonnets) between April 1585 and 1 December 1588" (Halliday, 461).

We knew almost nothing about the Sonnets of Shakespeare before 1609, in which year Thomas Thorpe piratically published the Sonnets, because till before that year, these were circulated only among the poet's friends (most of whom were his lawyer friends) and admirers. The little that we knew about Shakespeare's Sonnets before 1609, was from Francis Meres' (1565-1647) *Palladis Tamia: Witt's Treasury* that was published in 1598, in which there was a reference to our poet's sonnets: " 'As the soule of *Euphorbus* was thought to liue in *Pythagoras*: so the sweete wittie soule of *Ouid* liues in mellifluous and hony-tongued *Shakespeare,* witness his *Venus* and *Adonis,* his *Lucrece,* his sugred Sonnets among his priuate friends, &c.' " (Hlliday, 312). Probably, Meres referred to only the Sonnets 1-26 in his *Palladis Tamia.* If we suppose that Shakespeare wrote the Sonnets between 1592 and 1598, then we must say that he wrote them between his ages of 28 and 34 years, when he was a full-blown young man with all the vigour of his passions. By that time he must have tasted the honey of real love as well as the bitterness of adversity due to the betrayal of his fortune, and jealousy and contempt of his literary competitors, and concomitant *Katzenjammer.* All the various hues of his emotions he poured out into the Sonnets.

The Sonnets were registered in 1609, and the registration note of the Sonnets reads thus: " '20 Maij (May) Thomas Thorpe Entred for his copie vnder handes of master Wilson and master Lownes Warden a Booke called Shakespeares sonnettes' " (Halliday, 462). Edgar I. Fripp further wrote about the registration and publication of the Sonnets: "On 20 May (1609), while Shakespeare was in Kent or Sussex, a collection of his sonnets was entered at Stationer's Hall to Thomas Thorpe as 'a book called Shakespeare's Sonnettes'. It had fallen into the hands of this piratical publisher and notorious procurer of manuscript, possibly on the break-up of the Countess of Oxford's establishment at King's Place in the village of Hackney" (Fripp, 713). This collection contained all the Sonnets of Shakespeare. Shakespeare's Sonnets were again published in 1640 by Benson, and once again in 1709 by Charles Gildon (as an appendage to the first octavo edition of Shakespeare's works by Rowe).

Around about 1598, Shakespeare became averse to sonneteering. His aversion to the sonnet might have been caused, or aggravated, by the falling popularity of the sonnet during the last decade of the 16th century. Another cause of his turning away from the sonnet might be his break-neck speed of turning out a concatenation of a number of serious plays, such as *Julius Caesar, Hamlet, Troilus and Cressida, Othello, King Lear, Macbeth,* etc. interspersed with comedies and 'dark' comedies. In any case, Shakespeare "anticipated the general weariness (of the public about the sonnet), which began with the extensive publication (of sonnets) in 1593 and 1594" (Fripp, 259), and gracefully bowed out of sonnetry before doldrums set in on the sonnet. Afterwards, Shakespeare occasionally caricatured with the sonnet. Fripp wrote : "Shakespeare early made his entry into and departure from sonnetry, and was among the first to make fun of it" (Fripp, 259).

We cannot certainly be certain that Shakespeare wrote only the accepted 154 sonnets that have come down to us, and no more. It is very possible that some other sonnets of Shakespeare could not be pilferred by Meres and therefore have been lost to posterity. Again, John Dover Wilson doubts that Sonnets 153 and 154 were written by Shakespeare. Of course Wilson qualifies his doubt by saying that if these two Sonnets are at all written by the poet, then, in that case these two were his early 'essays' (Wilson, 266). On the other hand, we may add four more sonnets to the accepted 154 Sonnets, if we like:

1. Longaville reads a sonnet at *Love's Labour's Lost,* IV, iii, 56-69:

   'Did not the heavenly rhetoric of thine eye,
   'Gainst whom the world cannot hold argument,
   Persuade my heart to this false perjury?
   Vows for thee broke deserve not punishment.
   A woman I forswore; but I will prove,
   Thou being a goddess, I forswore not thee:
   My vow was earthly, thou a heavenly love;
   Thy grace being gain'd cures all disgrace in me.
   Vows are but breath, and breath a vapour is;
   Than thou, fair sun, which on my earth dost shine,

Exhal'st this vapour-vow, in thee it is.
If broken, then it is no fault of mine;
If by me broke, what fool is not so wise
To lose an oath to win a paradise?'

2. The Prologue (Chorus) to *Romeo and Juliet* is in the form of a sonnet:

Two households, both alike in dignity,
In fair Verona, where we lay our scene,
From ancient grudge break to new mutiny,
Where civil blood makes civil hands unclean.
From forth the fatal loins of these two foes
A pair of stat cross'd lovers take their life;
Whose misadventur'd piteous overthrows
Doth with their death bury their parents' strife.
The fearful passage of their death-mark'd love.
And the continuance of their parents' rage,
Which, but their children's end, nought could remove,
Is now the two hours' traffic of our stage;
The which if you with patient ears attend,
What here shall miss, our toil shall strive to mend.

3. The dialogue between Romeo and Juliet at *Rameo and Juliet*, I, v, 91-104, is in the form of a sonnet:

Rom. (*To Juliet*) If I profane with my unworthiest hand
This only shrine, the gentle fine is this:
My lips, two blushing pilgrims, ready stand
To smooth that rough touch with a tender kiss.

Jul. Good pilgrim, you do wrong your hand too much,
Which mannerly devotion shows in this :
For saints have hands that pilgrims' hands do touch,
And palm to palm is holy palmers' kiss.

Rom. Have not saints lips, and holy palmers too?

Jul. Ay, pilgrim, lips that they must use in pray'r.

Rom. O, then, dear saint, let lips do what hands do !
They pray; grant thou, lest faith turn to despair.

Jul. Saints do not move, though grant for prayers' sake.

Rom. Then move not while my prayer's effect I take.

4. The Prologue (Chorus) to the second Act of *Romeo and Juliet* is also in the form of a sonnet:

> Now old desire doth in his death-bed lie,
> And young affection gapes to be his heir;
> That fair for which love groan'd for and would die,
> With tender Juliet march'd, is now not fair.
> Now Romeo is belov'd, and loves again,
> Alike bewitched by the charm of looks;
> But to his foe suppos'd he must complain,
> And she steal love's sweet bait from fearful hooks.
> Being held a foe, he may not have access
> To breathe such vows as lovers use to swear;
> And she as much in love, her means much less
> To meet her new beloved anywhere.
> But passion lends them power, time means, to meet,
> Temp'ring extremities with extreme sweet.

We know these four are not sonnets in the true sense of the term, at least not good sonnets. But, then, can certainly count them as bad 'sonnets'. Further, Sonnets 153 and 154, are, perhaps, in no sense better than these four 'Sonnets'. Now, if we include Sonnets 153 and 154, why can we not also include these four? And if we take into account these four 'sonnets', then, the number of Shakespeare's Sonnets rises up to 158. But, however, let us stick to the generally accepted 154 Sonnets.

As we have seen, all the 154 Sonnets were published by Thomas Thorpe in '1609 in Quarto edition'. But it should be stated here that a few of the Sonnets were published earlier and elsewhere: Sonnets 138 and 144 were published in 1599 by William Jaggard and Issac Jaggard, both printers, along with *Passionate Pilgrim.* About ten years after this, *i.e.* in 1609, Thrope published the Quarto edition. The title-page of Thorpe's volume read thus: " 'Shakespeare's Sonnets. Neuer before Imprinted. At London by G. Eld for T.T. and are to be solde by Iohn Wright, dwelling at Christ Church gate. (Some copies have 'by William Aspley') 1609" (Halliday, 462). And the epigramatic dedication of Thorpe's volume read thus : "TO. THE. ONLIE. BEGETTTER. OF THESE. INSVING. SONNETS. MR W.H. ALL. HAPPINESSE. AND. THAT. ETERNITIE. PROMISED. BY. OVR. EVERLIVING. POET. WISHETH. THE. WELL. WISHING. ADVENTURER. IN. SETTING. FORTH. T.T." P.E. Halliday wrote about this edition : "The text is a fair one, but the errors suggest that Shakespeare did not see it through the press, though it is possible that the volume was not pirated" (Halliday, 462). But Robert

Gittings did not agree with Halliday. According to Gittings, Thorpe published this volume "possibly without the author's consent" (Gittings, 89).

The 154 Sonnets are generally divided into two broad groups: Sonnets 1-126 are devoted to a Fair Youth who is avowedly the poet's friend, and therefore, called the 'Fair Youth Sonnets'; and Sonnets 127-154 are devoted to a 'black mistress' to whom the poet was spiritually and, perhaps, carnally, attracted, and so these Sonnets are called the 'Dark Lady Sonnets'. But John Dover Wilson has divided the 154 Sonnets into the following groups (Wilson, 268-273) :

Section I

1. *Marriage Sonnets:* 1-17.
2. *A Glorious Morning:* 18-24.
3. *The Poet goes on a Journey:* 25-32, 36-39, 43-47, 50-56, 59-60, 62-75, 81.
4. *Liaison Sonnets:* 48, 57-58, 61, 77.
5. *The Rival Poet:* 76, 78-80, 82-86.
6. *Farewell Sonnets:* 49, 87-99, 100-126.

Section II

7. *My Mistress' Eyes*: 127, 130, 139-140, 153-154.
8. *Poet, Friend, and Mistress:* 131-136, 143-144.
9. *Perjury of Eye and Heart:* 129, 137, 141-142, 146-148, 149-152.
10. *Independent Sonnets:* 128, 138, 145.

The 154 Sonnets were differently divided by F.E. Halliday. He wrote: "The 154 sonnets, as printed in Q 1609, fall into two main groups, the first of which may be sub-divided.

1-126 : addressed mainly to a young man, described as a 'sweet boy', 'my lovely boy', with a 'woman's face'.

1-17 : an appeal to this friend to marry and reproduce his beauty in a child.

40-42 : the friend steals the poet's mistress (see also 133, 134, 144).

78-86 : a rival poet secures the favour of his friend, who also appears to be his patron.

127-52 : addressed to his mistress, a dark, married woman. This series contains the so-called 'vituperative' sonnets.

153-4 : two versions of a Greek epigram on Cupid. These may not be Shakespeare's'' (Halliday, 462).

Besides the general division of the Sonnets into 'Fair Youth Sonnets' and the 'Dark Lady Sonnets', and besides the divisions of them suggested by Wilson and Halliday, some other commentators and critics have divided the 154 Sonnets into other various groups. Some such groups tally with those suggested by Wilson and Halliday, but others do not. The Sonnets, thus, have been differently categorised by other commentators and critics under such headings as : 'Breeding Group Sonnets' (1-17), 'Travel Sonnets', 'Time Sonnets', 'Will Sonnets', etc. To such divisions, we may suggest adding some other groupings under other rubrics. For instance, Sonnet 66 may be called 'And Sonnet' (in line with the 'Will Sonnets'); Sonnets 71-74 may be called 'Death Sonnets' (71, 'when I am dead'; 72, 'After my death'; 73, 'Death's second self'; and 74, 'when that fell arrest/Without all bail shall carry me away'); Sonnet 105 may be called '' 'Fair, kind, true' Sonnet''; etc. But no ideal categorisation of the Sonnets is possible.

Critics and commentators also do not agree among themselves as to the appropriate arrangement of the Sonnets; they only agree that Thorpe's arrangement is wrong. They say that there are a few sonnets in the 'Fair Your Sonnets' group that also refer to the Dark Lady. Again, Butler ''shows good reasons why (Sonnets) 143 and 144 cannot well come after 134'' (Knight, 12). Further, D.G. Rossetti wrote about the traditional arrangement of the Sonnets : '' 'There should be an essential reform in the printing of Shakespeare's Sonnets. After Sonnet cxxv should occur the words *End of Part I.* The couplet-piece, numbered cxxvi, should be called *Epilogue to Part I.* Then before cxxvii, should be printed *Part II.* After clii, should be put *End of Part II* — and the last two Sonnets should be called *Epilogue to Part II*' '' (Jones, 51).

F.E. Halliday observes that besides the beauty of the individual Sonnets, some of the individual Sonnets or groups of Sonnets have additional importance (Halliday, 462) :

Sonnet 13 : ''The first use of the 2nd person plural instead of singular; 'you' instead of 'thou' is used in only thirty-four of the sonnets.''

Sonnet 20 : A clue to W.H.: ''A man in hew all Hews, in his controwling''.

Sonnet 26	:	''Resembles the prose dedication of Lucrece to Southampton.''
Sonnet 37	:	Shakespeare refers to himself as a lame, figuratively of course, though it has been interpreted literally (see also 89).''
Sonnet 99	:	This Sonnet has fifteen lines.
Sonnet 104	:	''States that friendship has lasted three years.''
Sonnet 107	:	This Sonnet gives a clue to the date of composition of the Sonnets. '' 'That mortall Moone hath her eclipse indur'de' may mean that Elizabeth has survived her 'grand climacteric', her 63rd year, *i.e.* 1596; or, Elizabeth is dead, *i.e.* 1603. Hotson maintains that it means that the deadly, moon-shaped Armada has been defeated, *i.e.* 1588.''
Sonnet 110-111	:	''Seem to refer to Shakespeare's profession as an actor.''
Sonnet 126	:	''Only twelve lines and written in couplets, forming an envoy to the series addressed to 'my lovely boy'.''
Sonnets 135-6	:	'' 'The Will Sonents'.''
Sonnet 145	:	''In octosyllabics.''

Besides these importances and peculiarities of some of the Sonnets, we may find some other peculiarities of some of the Sonnets :

1. Sonnets 78-86: these are the harshest Sonnets.
2. Sonnet 144: While all other Sonnets are addressed to some person, this Sonnet is addressed to none. Further, in this Sonnet the Fair Youth and the Dark Lady converge.
3. Sonnet 151: This Sonnet is full of double meanings or antithetical statements. It is also fuli of sexual implications, particularly in lines 8-12.
4. Sonnet 152: This Sonent displays Shakespeare's profligate character, and the triangle of love among the Fair Youth, the Dark Lady and the poet.
5. John Kerrigan has found that there are some paired Sonnets. For instance, Sonnets 27 and 28 are on insomnia; 44 and 45 on 'the

four elements'; 50 and 51 on 'journey on horseback'; and 57 and 58 on 'emotional slavery'.

6. In most of the Sonnets, the envoy or concluding couplet employs alliterations or repetition of words or word-play (for instance, in Sonnets 30-32, 35-36).
7. Almost all the Sonnets are panegyric, like most of the Elizabethan sonnets.
8. There are fewer references to nature in the Sonnets.
9. Only in Sonnet 99 do we come across deliberate reference to three flowers.
10. Unlike the 126 'Fair Youth Sonnets', which to Meres were 'sugred Sonnets', the 26 'Dark Lady Sonnets' are " 'full of fine things said unintentionally — in the intensity of working out conceits' " (Gittings, 89).

What were the sources or fountains of inspiration of Shakespeare's Sonnets? Leishman thinks that Horace, Ovid, Petrarch, Tasso, Ronsard, Sidney, Spenser, Daniel, Drayton and such other poets were the inspiration behind Shakespeare's Sonnets. But Dover Wilson disagrees with Leishman, and says that it is doubtful to say that Shakespeare was acquainted with the Italian masters. According to him, our poet was influenced in sonnetry rather by his preceding and contemporary sonneteers. Wilson writes : "As regards the English predecessors, we cannot doubt that he (Shakespeare) read them eagerly, without necessarily paying them the compliment of imitation" (Wilson, cix-cx). Shakespeare was certainly influenced, as regards the form and the content of the sonnet, by the convention of sonnetry in his contemporary literary milieu. For, every writer, as T.S. Eliot would like to say, must consciously or unconsciously write within the tradition of his medium, and within the convention of his age. He must take literary sustenance from his contemporary society and the preserved tradition. This is well expressed in Keats' 'Sonnet to Spenser': "The flower must drink the nature of the soii,/Before it can put forth its blossoming". So we must presume that Shakespeare at least partially got his style and themes from his preceding and contemporary sonneteers, and the rest was his own. The themes of most of his sonnets are the non-pareil beauty of the beloved Fair Youth and his love-hate relationship with the Dark Lady. All other subordinate themes grew out of these two principal ones. He got his principal themes from his contemporary poets, but the subordinate ones and their complexities he invented for himself.

One of the special features of the Sonnets of the Elizabethan period is their concern about time and eternity. The Elizabethan poet wanted to immortalise the beauty of hte beloved and his love for her. This is also particularly true of Shakespeare's Sonnets. Again, the sonnet, since its invention, has always strived to exrpess the suffering and self-pity of the lover — of the individual poet. Shakespeare's Sonnets are distinctive in the sense that they do not so much as express the suffering and self-pity of the poet himself, but, rather, they express the objective and impersonal emotions tangentially related with the poet. Joan Grundy wrote about this feature of Shakespeare's sonnets: " 'Shakespeare does not write about his own suffering, but unself-consciously and without self-pity. His love is, literally, not self-regarding; he has therefore no interest in displaying or surveying it in his verse, and no groups for equating self-portraiture with the portraying of the beloved. This introduces a fundamental change (from the Elizabethan sonnets in general): the sonnet-sequence in Shakespeare's hands loses its affinity with the love-complaint. Here there are no 'tears of fancie', no 'blackest face of woe' " (Jones, 191). In most of Shakespeare's Sonnets, there is universal *Schadenfreud,* and no individual gloom.

In this sense also Shakespeare is not Petrarchan. Actually, in the Elizabethan period there in some corners an anti-Petrarchan sentiment among some of the sonneteers. Even if Shakespeare is not anti-Petrarchan, he is not a Petrarchan also. Shakespeare widened the scope of the sonnet, like Donne and Milton, after him. He added new themes to the sonnet: despair due to adversity and frowning of fate, the destructiveness of Time, immortalising the beauty of the beloved through the poet's Sonnets, desire for increase of the beauty of the beloved through his procreation, death, ambivalence to love, etc.

Shakespeare followed the sonnet-form invented by Wyatt and Surrey. He used three quatrains and a concluding couplet, the rhyme-scheme of the whole sonnet being a b a b c d c d e f e f g g. The first quatrain posits a thesis, so to say, the second another — an antithesis, so to say, — and the third either elaborates or supports the second. And the concluding couplet or the envoy summarises the three quatrains and presents a conclusion. One striking feature of many of Shakespeare's concluding couplets is that they contain either alliteration or puns or repetition of words (and this has not, so far, been taken notice of by critics), particularly those of the sonnets beginning with Sonnet 28. For instance, the couplet of Sonnet 28 reads: "But *day doth daily* draw my sorrows longer,/And *night* doth *nightly* make grief's length seem stronger."; that of Sonnet 32 : "But since he dies, and poets better prove,/*Theirs* for *their* style I'll read, *his* for *his* love."; that of Sonnet 35 : "To that *sweet* thief which *surly* robs from me."; that of Sonnet 36 : "As, thou being *mine, mine* is thy good report."; that of Sonnet 74 : "The worth of *that* is *that* which it contains,/And *that* is *this* and *this* with thee remains."; etc. (See also Sonnets 75, 81, 84, 88, 120 and 154.) It may be mentioned that, perhaps, Shakespeare believed in the necessity of rhyming in poems, and accordingly we find that all his poems are rhymed. In *Love's Labour's Lost* (IV, iii, 54-55), Berowne lays stress on rhyming in poems : "O, rhymes are guards on wanton Cupid's hose:/ Disfigure not his slop."

During the first half of the nineties of the 16th century, while he was engaged in writing long poems, such as *Venus and Adonis, The Rape of Lucrece,* etc. and the early plays, such as *Comdey of Errors, Taming of the Shrew, Love's Labour's Lost, Romeo and Juliet,* etc., Shakespeare felt a penchant for writing sonnets. It is for this reason that we find references to the Sonnet in some of these early plays of his. In *Love's Labour's Lost,* Berowne's speech at IV, iii, 229-249, may remind one of a sonnet:

Berowne. My eyes are then no eyes, nor I Berone.
O, but for my love, day would turn to night !
Of all complexions the cull'd sovereignty
Do meet, as at a fair, in her cheek,
Where several worthies make one dignity,
Where nothing wants that want itself doth seek.
Lend me the flourish of all gentle tongues —
Fie, painted rhetoric ! O, she needs it not !
To things of sale a seller's praise belongs:
She passes praise; then praise too short doth blot.
A wither'd hermit, five-score winters worn,
Might shake off fifty, looking in her eye.
Beauty doth varnish age, as if new-born,
And gives the crutch the cradle's infancy.
O, 'tis the sun that maketh all things shine !

Again, *The Two Gentlemen of Verona* also shows Shakespeare's interest in the sonnet. The Duke at III, i, (139-149) of the same play reads a letter (" 'To Silvia'!") which resembles a sonnet:

'My thoughts do harbour with my Silvia nightly,
And slaves they are to me, that send them flying.

O, could their master come and go as lightly,
Himself would lodge where senseless,
they are lying !
My herald thoughts in thy pure bosom rest them,
While I, their king, that thither them importune,
Do curse the grace that with such grace hath blest them,
Because myself, do want my servant's fortune.
I curse myself, for they are sent by me,
That they should harbour where their lord should be.'

Most of the plays and long poems written during the time in which the Sonnets were composed have at least one thing in common : the theme of love. Shakespeare was then between 28 and 34 years of age (between 1592 and 1598). His flower of love was in full bloom, and so the common theme of love is present both in plays of that period and in the long poems and the Sonnets. But how did he conceive of the sonnet? In *The Two Gentlemen of Verona* (III, ii, 66-81), Shakespeare beautifully expresses his concept of the sonnet :

Proteus. As much as I can do I will effect.
But you, Sir Thurio, are not sharp enough;
You must lay time ot tangle her desires
By wailful *sonnets,* whosed composed rhymes,
Should be full-fraught with servicable vows.
Duke. Ay,
Much is the force of heaven-bred poesy.

Proteus. Say that upon the altar of her beauty
You sacrifice your tears, your sighs, your heart;
Write till your ink be dry, and with your tears
Moist it again, and frame some feeling line
That may discover such integrity;
For Orpheus' lute was strung with poet's sinews,
Whose golden touch could soften steel and stones,
Make tigers tame, and huge leviathans
Forsake unsounded deeps to dance on sands....

Though Shakespeare has given us a glance of his conception of the sonnet, he has never expressed his idea of a poet, and has never told us what poetry should look like — poetry in general. Nevertheless, Inga-Stina Ewbank has found at least the things Shakespeare would not like to have in a poem. For instance, she writes, Shakespeare mocked at "taffeta phrases, silken terms precise,/Three piled hyperboles, spruce affectation,/Figures pedantical'' (Berowne's speech at *Love's Lasbour's Lost,* V, ii, 406-408) (Jones, 224). Again, Shakespeare liked variations in verses. This is evident in Sonnet 76, where he is pitying himself for not being able to write better, and for not being able to introduce variations in his verses :

> Why is my verse so barren of new pride,
> So far from variation or quick change?
> Why, with the time, do I not glance aside
> To new-found methods and to compounds strange?
> Why write I still all one, ever the same,
> And keep invention in a noted weed,
> That every word doth almost tell my name,
> Showing their birth, and where they did proceed?

Certainly, here, he has used his idea of beauty of poetry, though partially. We have already seen Shakespeare's stray and light-hearted comments on poetry and prosody in general, in *Love's Labour's Lost* (IV, iii, 54-55), where Berowne comments on the rhyme of Holofernes' poetry: ''O, rhymes guard on wanton Cupid's hose:/Disfigures not his slop.'' Further, Ewbank writes about Shakespeare's notion of writing poetry as is expressed in his sonnets. His (Shakespeare's) poet's prayer is : 'O, let me, true in love, but truely write (xxvi); and to write truly means to show 'that you alone are you' (lxxxiv)' '' (Jones, 225). Again, at least regarding the sonnet, Shakespeare is putting emphasis more on the subject-matter than on the style. Ewbank writes (Jones, 225) : ''Explicitly, then, in the sonnets, Shakespeare is striving for a subordination of the style to the subject matter. Ideally, the style is the subject:

> O, know, sweet love, I always write of you,
> And you and love are still my argument;
>
> [(Sonnet) LXXVI]
>
> In other's works thou dost but mend the style,
> And arts with thy sweet graces graced be;
> But thou art all my art.
>
> [(Sonnet) LXXVIII].''

Different critics have been struck by the different aspects of the Sonnets. Some have especially appreciated the lyric of the Sonnets; some have principally praised the images of the Sonnets; and some have been engrossed by the vision of the Sonnets. But G.K. Hunter said that the dramatic element of the Sonnets out-tops all other qualities of them. Hunter wrote: ' ''The power of these poems does not reside in lyrical utterance; the vision they present is an individual's, and to that extent like lyric, but in them the reader is not concerned with solitary imaginings presented as of universal significance (as in the Odes of Keats and Shelley), but with the relation of one human heart to others. By setting up a system of tension between forces presented as persons Shakespeare's sonnets engage the reader's interest in a manner akin to the dramatist' '' (Jones, 122).

According to G.W. Knight, the main symbols used in the Sonnets are Rose, King, Sun, Gold and Jewels. He wrote about these symbols : ''They are, on the natural plane, flowers, especially the rose; on the human plane, kingship, with gold; on the universal, the Sun, with gold; on the spiritual, jewels'' (Knight, 59). Knight extensively summarised the uses of these symbols in the Sonnets, in his book *The Mutual Flame*. Let us quote Knight at some length. Regarding the symbol of the rose, used in the Sonnets, knight wrote : ''The rose as truth is contrasted with shams and vices. The youth's 'true' rose of beauty,..., is contrasted with the false beautifyings of society (67). If faults be present in him, 'roses have thorns, and silver fountains mud' (35). His beauty encloses 'sins' as the rose contains a 'canker' (95). But 'canker' may also mean wild roses, as when 'canker-blooms' are used to have colour without 'the perfumed tincture' of 'sweet roses', which survive death in distillation, even as the inmost truth of the boy's beauty is distilled by poetry (54). With the rose we may group the lily : 'Lilies that fester smell far worse than weeds' (94). The youth is the 'pattern' of both 'the lily's white' and 'the deep vermilion in the rose' (98). In one Sonnet the poet relates, point by point, violet, lily, majoram and roses, red and white, together with the 'vengeful canker' of destruction, to the separate excellences of his love's beauty (99). In contrast his mistress' cheeks have nothing of 'roses damask'd, red and white' in them (130)'' (Knight, 60).

As to the symbol of kingship, Knight worte : ''Next Kingship. Royal images recur, as in the love-poetry of Donne, some of them holding similar connotations. The poet addresses the youth as 'lord of my love', to whom he sends a 'written ambassage' (26); he is 'my sovereign' and the poet his 'servant' or 'slave' (57)....The loved one is royal, and so compared to 'a throned queen' (96). He is 'crowned' with various gifts of nature and fortune (37), especially 'all those beauties whereof now he's king' (63). Like a sovereign, he radiates worth, his eyes lending 'a double majesty' to the rival poets' 'grace' (78); if it were not for certain suspicions, he would be owning 'kingdoms of hearts' (7). This royalty is somehow shared by the lover; having found his own king, he regards all others, more common place, grandeurs as poor stuff in comparison. His astronomy, learned from those 'constant stars', his love's eyes, cannot, and clearly has no desire to, busy itself with the fortunes of 'princes'; it is a different 'art', prophesying 'truth and beauty' (14). After all, 'great princes' favourites' enjoy an insecure glory in comparison (25); time changes the 'decrees of kings', but his love is lasting (115); it is in no sense 'the child of state', and is independent of 'smiling pomp' (124); bearing 'the canopy' means nothing to him, nor does any such external 'honouring' (125). The result is that the poet, through accepted love, becomes himself royal. His mind is 'crown'd' with the wondrous youth, and is accordingly 'kingly' (114); when he is sure of him, he is a 'king', but when disillusioned, 'no such matter' (87). However depressed he may be in other ways, in so far as his love is assured, it brings such wealth, well-being and power, 'that then I scorn to change my state with kings' (29)'' (Knight, 60-61).

And regarding the symbols of kingship and gold, Knight wrote : ''Kingship is naturally golden, and golden impressions recur with similar variations in use. 'Gilded honour' may be 'shamefully misplac'd' (66); poets flatter the youth with 'golden quill' (85); his hair is contrasted with false 'golden tresses' (68); Shakespeare's poetry can make him outlive 'a gilded tomb' (101). More important is his eye 'gilding' the object on which it gazes (20) — eyes in Shakespeare's are active powers, not just passive reflections (...) — and the lovely phrase characterising youth as 'this thy golden time' (3). Stars are 'gold candles' (21).

''The Sun is nature's king, and also pre-eminently golden. Throughout Shakespeare king and sun are compared. The Dark Lady's eyes are 'nothing like the Sun' (130); they are 'mourning' because dark, eyes, and may at the best be compared to the 'morning sun' in a grey dawn, or the evening star (132). With the Fair Youth, the association 'that sun, thine eye' (49) comes easily enough. The successful lover compares himself to the morning 'lark' singing 'hymns at Heaven's gate' (29), though, when things go wrong, 'basest clouds' obscure the Sun, who now rides 'with ugly rack on his celestial face', and steals to the west disfigured (33); for 'clouds and eclipses stain both Moon and Sun' (35). In our 'transparency' sonnet (24) the Sun functions as the supernal love corresponding to Donne's prince (...). The Sun, 'daily new and old' (76), is visualised in all positions of his diurnal course, with close reference to age. Youth is a 'day' ready to decline (15), and the poet's age just such an hour 'as after sunset fadeth in the west' (73).

"We have various clusters of king, gold, and sun. King and gold come together in 'the gilded monuments of princes' (55); and sun and gold, when the Sun's 'gold complexion' is dimmed in the sonnet, 'Shall I compare thee to a summer's day?' (18), or the young man graces 'the day' and 'gilds' the evening in place of stars (28). We may have all three. so 'great princes' favourites' are compared to the marigold opening to the Sun's 'eye' (25). Man's life resembles the diurnal progress of the Sun, who first 'lifts up his burning head' from the orient, everything beneath doing 'homage' to his 'sacred majesty' as he makes his 'golden pilgrimage', till finally he 'reeleth' to his setting (7). Love resembles a 'glorious morning' seen to 'flatter the mountain tops with sovereign eye', kissing meadows with his 'golden face', and 'gilding' streams with his 'heavenly alchemy' (33)" (Knight, 60-63).

Shakespeare was influenced by Platonism then much read and talked about, and the nimbus of Platonism always hangs over the Sonnets, particularly on the theme of Time and on the theme of the 'Fair Youth Sonnets'. For instance, the Platonic theory of immortality of the soul and reminiscences of former lives in glaringly evident in Sonnet 123 (particularly in lines 4 and 8) : "They are the dressings of a former sight" and "Then think that we before have heard them told." Of course Shakespeare speaks of immortality in another sense, sometimes, — immortality in the sense of perpetuating his existence in the minds of the people through generations, through his verses. For instance, in Sonnet 107, he says : "I'll live in this poor rhyme". Though Shakespeare was certainly influenced by Platonism, he was never engrossed by that : he could shuttle with ease and facility from the Platonic height down to carnal love, and back again. For instance, in Sonnet 135 (in lines 5 and 6) the poet asks the Dark Lady : "Wilt thou, whose will is large and specious,/Not vouchsafe to hide my will in thine?"

Some critics and commetators have found a smack of homosexuality in the 'Fair Youth Sonnets'. The point is certainly debatable, and term 'homosexuality' is itself ambiguous. Does the term include carnal relationship, or does it simply mean the love of a man for a man (or of woman for a woman) that the man might have borne for a woman (or the woman for a man), for instance, the love of Socrates for Plato? Certainly Shakespeare had no homosexual relation with the Fair Youth, in the carnal sense, for othewise, he would not have felt carnal attraction towards the Dark Lady. However, regarding the point of homosexuality in the 'Fair Youth Sonnets', G.W. Knight wrote : "The love poetry of Shakespeare's contemporaries is couched for the most part in heterosexual terms; but that, among a number of sonnet sequences supposedly at least celebrating the love of a lady, we should find Shakespeare directly confessing love for a young man, is not strange. It is what, having regard to the psychology of his peers, we should expect" (Knight, 25).

Lastly, can we bring the categories of the 'Fair Youth Sonnets' and the 'Dark Lady Sonnets' under different rubrics? According to G.W. Knight, Yes. Knight has found the 'Fair Youth Sonnets' to be Apollonian and the 'Dark Lady Sonnets' to be Dionysian. He said: "Dionysus is an effeminate God, Apollo a figure of masculine beauty.... ... These are inexhaustible categories : once you understand them, you find them everywhere. "You certainly find them in the Sonnets. The Fair Youth is continually...., realised in pre-eminently *visual* terms, with much talk of 'eyes', 'image' and painting. He is exactly defined by calling him an Apollonian conception. The Dark Lady is visually repellent, but exerts a fascination and a magnatism which eludes intellectual definition (....). The youth enjoys Apollonian 'praise' of his beauty (84), and appears to have been the willing centre of a poetic cult (78); and he is blamed for mixing in a society whose 'painting' imitates the roses of his good looks (67). He is *colourfully* depicted, with metaphors from painting (101). But he significantly feels, like Jessica in *The Merchant of Venice* (V, i, 69), ill-at-ease : 'Music to hear, why hear'st thou music sadly? (8)" (Knight, 26-27).

❐

VI

The Themes of Shakespeare's Sonnets

Traditionally, the principal theme of the sonnet has been love : love between a man and his exquisitely beautiful (at least in his estimation) lady-love. From Petrarch to Wyatt and Surrey, love has dominated the genre of poetry called sonnet. Of course, other themes have also occasionally come into the sphere of the sonnet, particularly at the hands of Shakespeare and his successors. For instance, Donne's *Holy Sonnets* deal with matters spiritual. And since Donne, the sonnet has employed even such apparently implausible themes as politics, nationality, historical events, etc. Shakespeare did not principally use any new theme for his sonnets: he mostly used the same eternal theme of the sonnet: love. Oscar Wilde is not, perhaps, very wrong when he said that all the 154 sonnets of Shakespeare might be taken to be a whole drama of love. According to him, Sonnets 1-32 constitute the first Act of the drama in which the poet falls in love with a beautiful youth, Willie Hughes (according to Wilde, of course). Shakespeare asks the youth to become a player in his company, and the youth, after some vacillation, consents. In the second Act, *i.e.* in the Sonnets 32-52, 61 and 127-152, there comes a woman, dark but attractive, and she falls in love with Willie Hughes, and Hughes requites her love. Consequently, Shakespeare suffers from extreme jealousy. In the third Act, the love between Hughes and the lady cools down, and as a result, Shakespeare repossesses the youth. Meantime, Marlowe entices Hughes to the Globe Theatre to play Gaveston in *Edward II,* and Shakespeare again loses Hughes. The last Act comprises Sonnets 100-126. In it Shakespeare recovers the lost love of Hughes. Thus, Oscar Wilde interpreted the sonnet-sequence of Shakespeare as a tragi-comedy or as a dark comedy. Wilde's interpretation is doubtful and imaginary, for we are still not certain that the beautiful youth is none else than Willie Hughes. However, his interpretation of Shakespeare's sonnets as a play is, of course, amusing.

This imaginary drama discovered by Wilde in the Sonnets of Shakespeare is also enjoyed by Jan Knott who wrote : " 'The Sonnets can be interpreted as a drama. They have action and heroes. The action consists of lyrical sequences which slowly mount to a tragedy. There are three characters : a man, a youth and a woman. This trio exhaust every form of love and go through all its stages. They exhaust all the variants and forms of faithlessness, every kind of relationship, including love, friendship, jealousy. They go through the heaven and hell of love. The diction of the Sonnets, however is not Petrarchan, and another epithet would be more apt here : the characters go through Eden and through Sodom. "The fourth character of drama is time. Time which destroys and devours everything. Greedy time which has been compared to gaping jaws. It devours the fruits of human labour and man himself' " (Jones, 219).

Perhaps we need not ferret out for the themes of Shakespeare's Sonnets, for the poet himself speaks about them in Sonnet 144 :

> Two loves I have of comfort and despair,
> Which like two spirits do suggest me still:
> The better angel is a man right fair,
> The worser spirit a woman colour'd ill.

Who are this man and this woman we do not know for certain, but we know that for years together Shakespeare had an ambivalence in his love for both the young man and the dark but attractive woman. He had been undulated in his emotion of love towards these two persons, for which he smiled and shed tears, alternately. Whatever other joys he enjoyed found consummation in his love for this 'angel' and this 'spirit'; and whatever sorrows he came by were aggravated by the despair in his love for these two persons. These two persons, as if, created nights and days for him for some time. the poet looked at the world through the perspectives of his love, hate, and despair due to these two persons. The 154 Sonnets are the records in verse of the poet's love-hate relations with the man and the woman, and the consequent joys and sorrows.

That a Fair Youth occupied a niche in the heart of the poet — a youth whom he called his 'friend' — is manifest in Sonnet 110 : "to try an older friend,/A god in love, to whom I am confin'd." And the existence of a 'dark' lady by whom he was bemused is evident in, among others, Sonnet 127:

In the old age black was not counted fair,
Or if it were, it bore not beauty's name;
But now is black beauty's successive heir,
And beauty slander'd with a bastard shame;

The existence of the 'dark' lady and the poet's fascination for her may be extrapolated also from what Berowne says at *Love's Labour's Lost,* IV, iii, 244-49 :

Is ebony like her? O wood divine !
A wife of such wood were felicity.
O, who can give an oath? Where is a book?
That I may swear beauty doth beauty lack,
If that she learn not of her eye to look.
No face is fair that is not full so black.

As the Fair Youth and the Dark Lady are the two persons to whom Shakespeare addresses his Sonnets, the first and the central theme of the 154 Sonnets is Love. In the Sonnets, he has shown love in its broader perspectives and with its divergent facets. By loving the youth, he has fairly extended the traditionally circumscribed boundary of love. By love we generally mean that relationship which specially subsists between a man and a woman; and, therefore, we can say that the love between the poet and the youth is certainly a novelty, or rather, an invention. But such a love is certainly not unnatural, as some may take it to be. Shakespeare's love for the young man is manifestly Platonic, and it is never homosexual in the ordinary sense of the term — in the sense of pederasty. Such homosexual Platonic love was not very uncommon in ancient Greece, and to some extent, in the Elizabethan society. In ancient Greece, it was believed that pure love or friendship is possible only between two persons of the same sex, where there is no desire for non-spiritual gains. Thus, it is believed that such love existed between Socrates and his discipline, the 'white swan' Plato. Such homosexuality is certainly harmless, and socially permissible. Shakespeare experienced and expressed such a love in the 'Fair Youth Sonnets' (Sonnets 1-126), and thereby widened the scope of love. F.T. Prince, therefore, very justly wrote that in the Sonnets of Shakespeare " 'love has been liberated from its nominal limits' " (Jones, 182).

C.S. Lews said that some critics had seen pederasty in the Sonnets, but he swiftly brushed aside this charge against Shakespeare. He said that Shakespeare certainly did not intend pederasty. Lews wrote: " 'If he (Shakespeare) had intended in these Sonnets to be the poet of pederasty, I think he would have left us in no doubt; the lovely *paidika,* attended by a whole train of mythological perversities, would have blazed across the page' " (Wilson, xv). The love theme of the 'Fair Youth Sonnets' may be compared with the love theme of the poets of the Lyon school of the first half of the 16th century. The members of this school "were chiefly poets, and were in some cases invovled in other arts; their particular interest as a group was a theory of spiritual love based on ideals of Plato and Plutarch."(Cuddon, 371).

On the other hand, Shakespeare's love for the Dark Lady is avowedly heterosexual. While his relation with the Fair Youth is spiritual attachment, his relation with the Dark Lady is both mental and physical, though the latter might not have been consumated. Shakespeare thus have shown us both the facets of love: the physical love and the non-physical love or the Platonic love. The Sonnets on the Dark Lady are instances of physical love : "My mistress 'eyes are nothing like the sun; /Coral is far more red than her lips' red" (130); "Those lips that Love's own hand did make" (145); "My soul doth tell my body that he may/Triumph in love; flesh stays no further reason;/But, rising at thy name, doth point out thee/As his triumphant prize"(151); etc. Such instances can be multiplied, but, perhaps, these few will suffice.

The second theme of the Sonnets is grounded in Hellenism: beauty. But when we speak of Hellenism in the Sonnets, we must be on our guard, for we know that Shakespeare had "less Greek". Yet we can say that Shakespeare certainly had come in touch with Hellenism through secondary sources. J.A.K. Thomson, in his *Classical Influences on English Poetry,* showed us how Shakespeare was at least tangentially influenced by some Greek masters, poets as well as dramatists, such as Seneca (4 B.c.- 65 A.D.) and his kinsman Lucan (A.D. 39-65). Thomson wrote : "I do not suppose Shakespeare read Lucan in the original, but Marlowe had translated the first book of *Pharsalia* into blank verse, and this I do suppose Shakespeare had read" (Thomson, 44). Again, Thomson said that Shakespeare's *Hamlet* and *Titus Andronicus* were influenced by Senecan tragedies (Thomson, 110). Therefore, it is possible that our poet was quite acquainted with the Greek desire for perfect beauty, with Hellenism.

Shakespeare's Hellenism — his appetite for beauty — is evident in the Sonnets. Sonnets 1-7 express the poet's idolatrous attitude towards beauty. He is concerned because the Fair Youth is not intent upon marrying and thereby upon depleting the treasure of beauty. The poet therefore persuades the Fair Youth to marry : "From fairest creatures we desire increase,/That thereby beauty's rose might never die'' (Sonnet 1). The poet knows that though beauty is mighty enough to dominate over the hearts of men, yet it is ephemeral : ''When forty winters shall besiege thy brow,/And dig deep trances in thy beauty's field,/Thy youth's proud livery, so gazed on now,/Will be a tatter'd weed, of small worth held''. Beauty is the possession of nature, and nature bestows beauty freely, and she desires that beauty is multiplied. Beauty and love are inseparable : where there is beauty, there must be love. The poet loves the Fair Youth not for anything else but simply for his non-pareil beauty. The question of morality cannot arise in the case of beauty, because beauty is superior to morality. The poet himself is suspicious about the moral integrity of the Dark Lady, and yet he cannot but love her, because she is very attractive. Again, blondness and beauty are not the same thing. The poet says : ''In the old age black was not counted fair,/Or if it were, it bore not beauty's name;/But now is black beauty's successive heir,/And beauty slander'd with a bastard shame'' (Sonnet 127).

In Sonnet 101, Shakespeare says : ''Both truth and beauty on my love depends''. According to him, truth and beauty are complementary, and so in the same Sonnet he cries : ''O truant Muse, what shall be thy amends/For thy neglect of truth in beauty dy'd?'' Truth and beauty are not only complementary, but also interdependent : where there is beauty, there is truth, and where there is truth, perhaps, there is beauty. May be, it was from this Sonnet (Sonnet 101) that Keats derived his idea of the identity of truth and beauty : ''Truth is beauty, beauty truth''. But love is more powerful than both truth and beauty, because both of them depend on love : ''Both truth and beauty on my love depends'' (Sonnet 101). But the poet himself contradicts this statement of his in Sonnet 137, where he says that love is ''blind fool'', and so love does not always leads us to truth. In Sonnet 148, the poet dwells at length on the falsity of love:

> O, me, what eyes hath Love put in my head,
> Which have no correspondence with true sight!
> Or, if they have, where is my judgement fled,
> That censures falsely what they see aright?
>
> ....
>
> Love's eye is not so true as all men's; no,
> How can it? O, how can Love's eye be true,
> That is so vex'd with watching and with tears?

Despair due to personal frustration is another theme of the Sonnets. A streak of pain runs through almost all the Sonnets; they are overcast with a sense of gloom. But, in a few of them, the despair is clearly evident. When the young Shakespeare of around 28 years of age left Stratford and came to London, in search of fortune, he had high hopes in his breast. But, soon after, he found himself an outlandish stranger amongst the *avant garde* young poets and dramatists of London, who received Shakespeare only with jeerings and brow-beatings. Being a youth from the lower-middle class, if not worse than that, he found himself neglected in the company of the high-ups. Being humiliated by some of his fellow playwrights, and being unable to achieve what he wanted to, Shakespeare felt frustrated, felt as an outcast. The poet poured out this his feeling of this state mostly in two of his Sonnets: Sonnets 29 and 30. In Sonnet 29 he wrote:

> When, in disgrace with fortune and men's eyes,
> I all along beweep my outcast state,
> And trouble deaf heaven with my bootless cries,
> And look upon myself, and curse my fate,
> Wishing me like to one more rich in hope,
> Featur'd like him, like him with friends possess'd,
> Desiring this man's art, and that man's scope,
> With what I most enjoy contended least;...

In Sonnet 30, the poet continues his remorse:

> When to the sessions of sweet silent thought
> I summon up remembrance of things past,
> I sigh the lack of many a thing I sought,
> And with old woes new wail my dear time's waste:...

Was Shakespeare too much ambitious? Perhaps not; because, otherwise, he could not be gentle, companionable, affable and modest in behaviour, as he was described by his contemporaries. What he wanted was a modest fortune, but even that much was denied him, or rather, that much he could not fetch. And this led him to utter despair, as some of the Sonnets bear witness thereof for us.

His despair was due also to another factor : he had one or two rival poets — rival in the sense that he himself thought them to be his rivals, there, perhaps, being no real rivalry grown between them. This rival poet (or poets) is yet another theme of Sonnets 78-80, 82-86. We first come across the reference to the rival poet (or poets) in Sonnet 78:

> So oft have I invok'd thee for my muse,
> And found such fair assistance in my verse,

As every *alien pen* hath got my use,
And under thee *their* poesy disperse.

....

In *others'* works thou dost but mend the style,
And art with thy sweet graces graced be;

In sonnet 79, the poet persuades the Fair Youth not to thank the rival poet for what praise he tendered to him, because what the rival poet tendered to him was actually what he had stolen from the Fair Youth; and because it requires a 'worthier pen' than that of the rival poet to delineate the beauty of the Fair Youth :

I grant, sweet love, thy lovely argument
Deserves the travail of a worthier pen;
Yet what of thee *thy poet* doth invent
He robs thee of, and pay it thee again.
He lends thee virtue, and *he* stole that word
From thy behaviour; beauty doth *he* give,
And found it in thy cheek; he can afford
No praise to theee but what in thee doth live.

Then thank *him* not, for that which he doth say,
Since what *he* owes thee thou thyself dost pay.

In the next Sonnet, *i.e.* in Sonnet 80, Shakespeare says that he swoons in fright when he learns that there is a rival poet who also writes verses in praise of the Fair Youth. And he then feels that he is cast away by the youth :

O, how I faint when I of you do write,
Knowing a better spirit doth use your name,

....

My saucy bark, inferior to his,
On your broad main doth wilfully appear.
Your shallowest help will hold me up afloat,
While *he* upon your soundless deep doth ride;
Or, being wreck'd, I am a worthless boat,
He of tall building and of goodly pride:

Then if *he* thrive, and I be cast away,
The worst was this, — my love was my decay.

Here in this Sonnet, the poet is clearly expressing his feeling of real or imaginary inferiority, comparing himself with the rival poet. So far, the poet has spoken of the rival poet in singular number, but in the next but one Sonnet, *i.e.* in Sonnet 82, he speaks of not one rival poet but of more than one. Shakespeare says that those rival poets can only grossly paint the beauty of the Fair Youth with their 'strained touches', and that thus they are only abusing the beauty of the Fair Youth :

> ....yet when *they* have devis'd
> What strained touches rhetoric can lend,
> Thou truly fair wert truly sympathiz'd
> In true-plain words *by thy true-telling friend;*
>
> And *their* gross painting might be better us'd
> Where cheeks need blood, — in thee it is abus'd.

In the next Sonnet, the poet, as if, breaks the puzzle about the number of the rival poets, and says that there are two rival poets. He says (in Sonnet 83): "There lives more life in one of your fair eyes/ That *both your poets* can in praise devise." Sonnet 84 does not speak about the rival poet explicitly, but in innuendoses : "But he that writes of you, if he can tell/That you are you, so dignifies his story" and "Let him but copy what in you is writ". The rival poets sometimes write good verses and sometimes bad, but the thoughts of the poet, regarding the Fair Youth, are always far superior than those of the rival poets : "I think good thoughts, whilst other write good words". It may be noticed here that the poet is confusing us here regarding the number of the rival poet. In line 5 of this Sonnet (*i.e.* Sonnet 85) he speaks of the rival poet in singular number, but in line 13, he speaks of more than one rival poets ('others'). The last rival poet sonnet is Sonnet 86. In it Shakespeare is repeating his apprehension that the rival poet may possess the Fair Youth — the apprehension that he expressed earlier in Sonnet 80 : "Was it the proud full sail of *his* great verse,/Bound for the prize of all-too-precious you". In this Sonnet, the poet thinks that the rival poet is getting help from some other poets in his composing of verses addressed to the Fair Youth, and with their aid the rival poet is composing verses "Above a mortal pitch". But, nevertheless, Shakespeare is not afraid of all that :

> No, neither he, nor *his* compeers by night
> Giving *him* aid, my verse astonished.
> *He,* nor that affable familiar ghost
> Which nightly gulls *him* with intelligence,
> As visitors, of my silence cannot boast;
> I was not sick of any fear from thence:

> But when your countenance fill'd up *his* line,
> Then lacked I matter; that enfeebled mine.

Shakespeare is here again and again revealing his inferiority complex, and this is not unnatural, for, we must remember that the Sonnets were among his earlier works, or rather, his literary exercises. John Dover Wilson wrote about this inferiority complex of Shakespeare: "That he felt him (the rival poet) more learned than himself (87.7) is not surprising, since he must have been keenly conscious of that 'small Latin, and less Greek' which was all the learning a curtailed grammar school education had furnished him with" (Wilson, lxiii-lxiv).

Who was this rival poet (or poets) we do not know for certain. The question of the identity of the rival poet was (probably first) raised in 1885 by Professor Minto who thought that Chapman was the rival poet (Chapman's *The Shadow of Night* was indicated as the cause of the jealousy, or inferiority complex of Shakespeare). George Chapman (c. 1560-1634) published his philosophical poem *The Shadow of Night* in 1594, and Shakespeare may have referred to this poem in *Love's Labour's Lost* (IV, iii, 229): "O, but for my love, day would turn to night!" Shakespeare might have been jealous of Chapman for he was a much acclaimed contemporary poet and dramatist. This we say on the authority of Francis Meres who in 1598 mentioned that Chapman was "one of the best (playwright) both for tragedy and comedy." (Halliday, 96). Whether Minto is correct or not in his assumption, it is true that *The Shadow of Night* and Shakespeare's Sonnets are contemporaneous, and this, to an extent, may support the contention of Minto. On the other hand, J.A.K. Thomson believed that the rival poet referred to Homer himself from whom Chapman got direct guidance. Thomson said that Chapman could not be the rival poet : " 'As Chapman never mentions the name of Shakespeare, nor Shakespeare the name of Chapman, there can be no certainty in any discussion of their relations.' " (Gittings, 99). The third candidate for the rival poet can be Marlowe, but according to some critics, this is a wild guess. However, John Dover Willson suggested that the rival poet could be any one of the following poets : Chapman, Daniel, Constable, or Marlowe (posthumously). But, as we have said, nobody has been able to determine, beyond all doubts, the true identity of the rival poet or poets. The different theories about the rival poet is due to the fact that different critics have taken up different clusters of words or images, and at the same time ignored other groups of words or images, to identify the Fair Youth. Lastly, there is yet another theory about the rival poet. According to this theory, the rival poet is an abstraction which refers to the generality of the contemporary competing poets.

Last, but not the least, Time and its attending destructiveness have been a great theme of a good number of the Sonnets. In fact, Time, its destructiveness, and Death run through almost all the works of Shakespeare. L.C. Kinghts rightly said that " 'An essay might well be written on the Time theme in Shakespeare. Starting from an examination of *King Henry IV, Troilus and Cressida* and the Sonnets, it would illuminate some important aspects of Shakespeare's genius and of the Elizabethan mind' " (Johnes, 96). L.C. Knights further wrote: " 'Wherever we look, Shakespeare is concerned merely with the effects of time on animate and inanimate beings, on persons and personal relationships. As a poet he reports and evaluates experiences, but he does not attempt to *explain* them, nor do they arouse speculation in his mind' " (Jones, 97-98). Because, Shakespeare is not concerned with the metaphysical Time.

Shakespeare was not a peculiar poet to think so deeply over Time. If we go back to the Elizabethan age and try to analyse the consciousness of the people of that period, then we will find that Time occupied a great portion of their consciousness. "In the middle ages, time almost always was what Spenser tried to make it : an aspect of process. Candles burned to tell the time, sand seeped through tubes, water trickled from a pierced vessel, and the sun moved across the sky. Time was an abstraction from growth and decay, nothing without them. Being an aspect of process, time changed with it" Kerrigan, 34). This omnipotence of time took its roots in the consciousness of the Elizabethan people. When the mechanical clock was first invented in Italy in the middle ages, the concept of time more firmly occupied the consciousness of the people, and it continued to remain there till the end of the Renaissance. So it was only natural for the Elizabethan poets, including Shakespeare, to include Time as a theme of their poetry. And the Elizabethan poets laid relatively more emphasis on the destructiveness of Time.

The Elizabethan poet's consciousness suffered from the dichotomy of permanence and change, of eternity and mutability. As we have seen, Elizabethan mind was much influenced by the philosophy of Plato who assured it that there was a permanent and eternal Being which was the reality; on the other hand, the change, the mutability, was only phenomenal, illusory and unreal. The *daimonic* Plato told the Elizabethan poets of the permanence, but they saw only mutability all around.

Therefore, they questioned themselves : could mutable beings be made eternal? And they found the answer : only in art could beings be eternal. Thus Daniel, for instance, wrote : "And these thy sacred virtues must protect; Against the dark, and Time's consuming rage." And thus Drayton in one of his sonnets wrote : "Whilst in despite of tyranizing Times,/Medea-like, I make thee young again." Shakespeare was also certainly and morbidly aware of the destructiveness of Time. In Sonnets 12, 15-19, 39, 60, 63-65, 100, 115-116, 123-124, and 126, and some other Sonnets, he has expressed his utter concern over the corroding action of Time over the beauty of his friend, the Fair Youth.

Curiously enough, Shakespeare does not mention the destructiveness of Time, or even simply does not refer to Time, in his sonnets on the theme of the Dark Lady. What may be the reason of this? Perhaps, the reason is that when the poet was writing sonnets on the theme of the Fair Youth, he was engrossed in pure beauty, the eternal beauty, the copies of which were available on the earth, and which copies Time was intent upon destroying. His meditation on pure beauty led him to the thought of temporality, to the thought of Time. He desired to preserve pure beauty for eternity, for, to him beauty was so precious that it had to be preserved. But Time stood against pure beauty, and so the poet could not but think of Time and accost Time beard to beard. On the other hand, in the 'Dark Lady Sonnets', he was concerned with sensuality which, perhaps, he never desired to preserve, and therefore, time did not enter into his consciousness. We are not conscious about Time while we are engaged in things temporal; we are conscious about Time only when we desire something to be permanent.

In the 'Fair Youth Sonnets', Shakespeare is a Platonist, primarily in so far as he is concerned with beauty and Time. It may be mentioned here that some critics do not find any trace of Platonism in the Sonnets. Such critics may be reminded of what S.T. Coleridge wrote about Shakespeare and others : "Dryden could not have been a Platonist: Shakespeare, Milton, Dante, Michael Angelo and Raphael could not have been other than Platonists" (Coleridge, 384). Further, we may, perhaps, say that in addition to the influence of Plato, Shakespeare was influenced by Leonardo da Vinci (1452-1519), as Jan Knott suggested, regarding his conception of Time. Leonardo wrote : " 'O time, thou that consumest all things! O envious age, thou destroyest all things and devourest all things with the hard teeth of the years, little by little, in slow death! Helen, when she looked in her mirror and saw the withered wrinkles which old age had made in her face, wept, and wondered to herself why ever she had twice been carried away. O Time, thou that consumest all things! O envious age, whereby all things are consumed!' " (Jones, 220). Now, this same idea about Time is to be found in the Sonnets. In Sonnet 115, for instance, Shakespeare says : "Time, whose million'd accidents/Creep in 'twist vows, and change decrees of kings." This conception of Time is present not only in the Sonnets but also in the plays. To take an example, in *Troilus and Cressida* (III, ii, 181-185), Cressida speaks about Time:

When time is old and hath forgot itself,
When water drops have worn the stones of Troy,
And blind oblivion swallow'd cities up,
And mighty states characterless are grated
To dusty nothing —

And, to take yet another instance, Gloucestor, in *King Lear* (IV, vi, 134-135), while narrating the deranged state of Lear's mind, apostrophises about Time : "O ruin'd piece of nature! This great world/Shall so wear out to nought."

Shakespeare has aspersions ready for Time also in *The Rape of Lucrece* (lines 925-931) :

'Mis-shapen Time, copesmate of ugly Night,
Swift subtle post, carrier of grisly care,
Eater of youth, false slave to false delight,
Base watch of woes, sin's packhorse, virtue's snare;
Thou nursest all, and murd'rest all that are.
O hear me then, injurious, shifting Time!
Be guilty of my death, since of my crime.

Time was always present at the back of Shakespeare's mind, and so the concept of Time is strewn in the plays. For instance, in *Cymbeline* (II, ii, 51), Iachimo is instantly reminded of the passage of Time just as the '*Clock strikes*' : "One, two, three. Time, time!" Again, in *Love's Labour's Lost* (V, ii, 776-777), the Princess of France says: "A time, methinks, too short/To make a world-without-end bargain in." However, it is not true that the Elizabethan people, or at least the Elizabethan poets, were queer beings in the sense that they were very much concerned about Time. The mystery of Time has always thrown spell over human consciousness. For instance, the noted modern French novelist Marguerite Duras (b. 1914) was highly concerned with the phenomenon of Time and its impact in love, as is evident from her novels.

In the Sonnets, Shakespeare has shown different facets or aspects of Time. Time is a fleeting phenomenon; it is the instrument of mutability; and it covers up bright things with blankets of darkness: "brave day sunk in hideous night" (Sonnet 12). Time is a "bloody tyrant" (Sonnets 16 and 115) and is omnivorous: "Devouring Time" (Sonnets 19 and 126). It is old and yet is always intent upon doing wrong: "old Time: despite thy wrong" (Sonnet 19). Time is a deceiver of love: "thoughts of love, —/Which time and thoughts doth deceive, —" (Sonnet 39). Time's hand is injurious ("Time's injurious hand", Sonnet 63) and fell ("Time's fell hand", Sonnet 64). Time mutilates beauty, and roughs up the smoothness of beauty : "If Time have any wrinkle graven there" (Sonnet 100). Time changes vows by million accidents, besmears beauty with ugliness, cools down intentions, and diverts minds to alternative things: "But reckoning Time, whose million'd accidents/Creeps in 'twixt vows, and change decrees of kings,/Tan sacred beauty, blunt the sharp'st intents/Divert strong minds to the course of altering things" (Sonnet 115). Again, Time is deceptive, because it shows the identical thing to be different at different moments; and, further, it is destructive, and fickle: "Time's fickle glass, his sickle, hour" (Sonnet 126).

But sometimes Time is not as potent as it seems to be. In Sonnet 65, Shakespeare says that though "Nor gates of steel so strong, but Time decays", though there is none who can stall the destructive onslaught of Time on beauty ("Or who his spoil of beauty can forbid?"), yet there is at least one monument that can withstand the rage of Time, and that monument is the verse of the poet — a monument in which his love and his lady-love will live eternally in spite of the raging storm of Time: "O, none, unless this miracle have might,/ That in black ink my love may still shine bright." Again, in Sonnet 116, the poet is confident that Time is impotent to destroy true love though it can destroy beauty :

> Love's not Time's fool, though rosy lips and cheeks
> Within his bending sickle's compass come;
> Love alters not with his brief hours and weeks,
> But bears it out even to the edge of doom.

In Sonnet 123, the poet is even defiant towards Time: he swaggeringly tells Time that it will not be able to change him, *i.e.* change his fast and constant love for the Fair Youth: "No, Time, thou shall not boast that I do change:/...This I do vow, and this shall ever be,/I will be true, despite thy scythe and thee." G.W. Knight found that Time and Death are recurrent themes both of the plays and the Sonnets of Shakespeare. In his *The Mutual Flame,* Knight wrote: "The Sonnets approach time in the manner of *Troilus and Cressida,* where, ...it is a recurring concept. Throughout Shakespeare's later works, as I have emphasised in my own commentaries from *Myth and Miracle* onwards, 'time' and 'death' are central problems, pushing towards solution in *Antony and Cleopatra* and the Final Plays. This whole progress is adumbrated in the Sonnets'' (Knight, 73).

The last theme of the Sonnets, if we like to admit, is the Christian theme that John Kerrigan claimed to have discovered in Sonnets 73 and 74. Kerrigan wrote about the Christian theme of the two Sonnets: ''As the argument proceeds through Sonnets 73 and 74 it becomes increasingly Christian in tenor. The Ovidian association between man and the seasons which informs 73.1-4 (....) gives way, after the *Bare ruined echoirs* are introduced, to echoes of Job 17.11-13:

> My days are past, and my counsels and thoughts of my heart are vanished away, changing the night into day, and the light approaching into darkness. Though I tarry never so much, yet the grave is my house, and I have made my bed in the dark.

But it is not until the second quatrain of Sonnet 74 that the stark despair of Job 17.14-15 is invoked:

> I said to corruption, thou art my father, and to the worms, you are my mother and sister. Where is then now my hope? Or who hath considered the thing that I look for? These shall go down with me into the pit, and lie with me in the dust.

Compare with line 7 (of Sonnet 74) the following words in Elizabethan burial service (in the Book of Common Prayer), 'earth to earth, ashes to ashes, dust to dust', and its scriptural analogue: 'Then shall the dust be turned again unto earth from where it came, and the spirit shall return unto God who gave it' (Ecclesiastes 12.8). This suggests, in turn, 1 Corinthians 15.53-5 (also included in the burial service), with it message of hope:

> For this corruptible, must put on incorruption, and this mortal (must) put on immortality. When this corruptible hath put on incorruption, and this mortal hath put on immortality, then shall be brought to pass the saying that is written, Death is swallowed up into victory. O Death, where is thy sting?

And yet the Sonnet, by no means orthodox in its treatment of the flesh, the spirit, and immortality, harnesses Christian *contemptus mundi,* it might be said, ''for its own secular ends'' (Kerrigan, 266-67).

To conclude this chapter, all these themes are not to be found everywhere in all the Sonnets of Shakespeare, for, to be very precise, the Sonnets are not acutally a sonnet-sequence; but they include different groups of sonnets. L.C. Knights very judiciously wrote: " 'Shakespeare's Sonnets is a miscellaneous collection of poems, written at different times, for different purposes, and with very different degress of poetic intensity' " (Jones, 75).

VII

The Identity of the Fair Youth

The identity of the Fair Youth and the Dark Lady has, till today, remained a vexing question — an engima, though. The Fair Youth is the 'fair friend' (Sonnet 104) and 'an older friend' (Sonnet 110) — older because of long friendship — of the poet, and yet the poet has, perhaps deliberately, kept the identity of the Fair Youth in deep mystery. Only one vague hint about the identity of the Fair Youth is there — in the Dedication of the 'sonnet-sequence'. But the Dedication itself is puzzling to us: who is 'Mr. W.H.'? who is 'T.T.'? and, why is 'Mr. W.H.' the 'onlie begetter of these insuing sonnets' (because there are the 'Dark Lady Sonnets' too)? Generally, sonnet-sequences used to be dedicated, according to the Elizabethan custom, to the person to whom the sonnets had been addressed. Commonsensically, therefore, we may assume that the Fair Youth and 'Mr. W.H.' are the same person. But here too we should be wary, for Shakespeare is inordinate in many things: the Fair Youth and 'Mr. W.H.' may not be the same person. If the dedicator, Shakespeare, can be 'T.T.', why 'Mr. W.H.' cannot be some one else than the Fair Youth?

Things were further complicated later on by some publisher as well. In his 1640 edition of the Sonnets (the same publisher called them Poems), John Benson (d. 1667), a London book-seller and publisher, altered the pronouns of all the 'Fair Youth Sonnets' (1-126), so that the Fair Youth appeared to be a woman (Jones, 36). Further, G.W. Knight cast a sceptical look at the word 'fair' in regard to the Fair Youth. He said : "Whether the youth was what we should call 'fair' remains doubtful : Butler argues that the word means no more than 'good looking', and supports his contention with a number of quotations" (Knight, 11).

Many critics and scholars have burnt mid-night oil to reveal the mystery of the Fair Youth, but have ended their searches in surmises of different degrees of dependability. Many candidates have been suggested for the appellation of the 'Fair Youth', but none of them has been found to be credible, so far. However, before searching for the Fair Youth or 'Mr. W.H.', let us have with us a living picture of the youth as can be gleaned from the Sonnets and from other sources. Firstly, the 'fair friend' of the poet was very handsome, like (John Dover Wilson says) Rupert Brooke, for instance. In many of his Sonnets, Shakespeare has dwelt upon the description of the beauty of the youth. In Sonnet 20, he says that the beauty of the youth can be compared with the beauty of a woman: "A woman's face, with Nature's own hand painted,/ Hast thou, the master-mistress of my passion". Again, for another instance, in Sonnet 99, the poet makes a detailed comparison between the Fair Youth on the one hand, and the violet, lily and marjoram, on the other. The smell of the youth is like that of the violet, the complexion of the youth is like that of the lily, and the colour of his hair is like the colour of marjoram; but, the poet says, the youth exceeds all of them in their respective qualities.

Secondly, the youth comes of a stock higher in social status than that of Shakespeare. John Dover Wilson wrote: "Sonnets 36 and 37 (again) cannot be rightly understood unless we assume a considerable difference in rank between the two persons (the Fair Youth and Shakespeare) concerned" (Wilson, xlviii). Wilson furhter wrote: "Sonnet 101, again, claims that the Poet's praise will 'much outlive a gilded tomb', which I take to be an allusion to the painted monuments beneath which Elizabethans of distinguished families lay after death. And from 16 and 47 we learn...., that the young man (the Fair Youth) had had his portrait painted to give away to his friend as persons of fashion were wont, as young Sir Philip Sidney had his painted by Paul Veronese to give away to Hubert Languet" (Wilson, xlix). Thirdly, the Fair Youth is wanton and 'lascivous', for which reason the poet reproachingly warns him in Sonnets 14 and 84. In Sonnet 14, the poet tells him that if he diverts his eyes from so many inviting looks, only then his beauty and his 'truth' or integrity will thrive, otherwise "this I prognosticate, —/ Thy end is truth's and beauty's doom and date." And in Sonnet 84, the poet, again, sounds a warning to the youth for his wantonness and lascivousness: "You to your beautious blessings add a curse,/Being fond on praise, which makes your praises worse." Fourthly, the youth is kind, as he is fair and true. In Sonnet 105, Shakespeare says that the Fair Youth is 'Fair, kind and true', and repeats these appellations thrice, in lines 9, 10 and 13. To these four identifying marks of the Fair Youth, we may add yet another mark, being informed by the history of the Sonnets, and that is that the Fair Youth was younger to Shakespeare, may be, by seventeen years or so.

With all these descriptions of the Fair Youth, let us search for the person concerned. As already told, many candidates have been put forward, including William Hughes forwarded by Oscar Wilde. But, perhaps, only two among them have the most chance of being identified as the Fair Youth of the Sonnets: Henry Wriothesley (pronounced 'Rizzly' or 'Wreesley') (1573-1624), the thrid Earl of Southampton, and William Herbert, who succeeded his father in 1601 as the third Earl of Pembroke. The claim of Southampton was put forth by Nathan Drake in 1817. The candidature of Southampton depends on the following points. Firstly, Southampton was a man of high rank, being a distinguished Earl. Secondly, Shakespeare dedicated *Venus and Adonis* to Southampton who was the patron of the poet, in 1593; and, again, *The Rape of Lucrece* in 1594. This clearly indicate Shakespeare's admiration and fascination or infatuation for Southampton. Thirdly, many critics agree that the general drift of the arguments in Sonnets 1-17 are in consonance with the argument in *Venus and Adonis*; and, further, we know that those Sonnets preceded *Venus and Adonis*.

But, similarly, there are strong argumetns against the candidature of Henry Wriothesley. Firstly, W.H. ('Mr. W.H.') in no sense imply H.W. (Henry Wriothesley). Secondly, though there may be similarity of thought between the Sonnets and *Venus and Adonis,* the poetry in the Sonnets is, as Beeching said, much finer than that in *Venus and Adonis;* and this may suggest that the Sonnets were of a later period than that of *Venus and Adonis;* and so the dedication of *Venus and Adonis* to the "Right Honlourable Henrie Wriothesley" does not imply that the same Wriothesley should be the Fair Youth of the Sonnets. Thirdly, John Dover Wilson said that "There is no evidence, again, that Southampton had any dealings with Shakespeare after 1594, the absence of reference to him in the dedicatory material of the First Folio being particularly noticeable" (Wilson, xci). Fourthly, Wilson continued, "The *Sonnets* contains no conceivable allusions to his (Wriothesley's) courtship of Elizabeth Vernon in 1595, to his adoration of Essex in 1597, with whom he took part in the Island Voyage expedition, the war in Ireland, or his part in the rising of 1601 and subsequent imprisonment" (Wilson, xci). Fifthly, Wilson further said that "if we accept 1597-8 as the year in which Shakespeare began the *Sonnets,* he (Wriothesley) was at that date too old, being then twenty-four or twenty-five, while he (Wriothesley) must have been thirty or more when Shakespeare was writing his Envoy to his 'lovely boy' " (Wilson, xci).

Though all these points point to the rejection of the candidature of Wriothesley, the Earl of Southampton, to be the Fair Youth, yet Edgar I. Fripp pleaded for his candidature. According to Fripp, the physical features, age and personality correspond to the description of the Fair Youth as in the Sonnets. Fripp wrote that Shakespeare found his young admirer and patron Henry Wriothesley in the company of his (Shakespeare's) lawyer friends. Henry Wriothesley was born on 6 October, 1573, at Cowdray in Sussex and took M.A. by grace in 1589. Fripp wrote about Wriothesley: "The 'goodly boy' had grown into a clever, engaging, lively, stubborn, handsome, high-minded youth of sixteen when he met and, as he might, loved William Shakespeare, aged five-and-twenty" (Fripp, I., 264). Fripp further wrote in support of his contention: "There is little doubt that Shakespeare wrote Sonnets i-xxvi in the summer or autumn of 1590, some time at any rate before the youthful Earl (of Southampton) to escape the matchmaking, fled to the Continent...By declining to marry Lady Elizabeth, the Earl of Southampton, from a worldly point of veiw, threw away the chance of his life" (Fripp, I., 267). In the Sonnets 1-17, also Shakespeare persuades the Fair Youth to marry, to procreate, and thereby to increase the treasure of beauty. Circumstantially, therefore, the Sonnets 1-17 may point to the matchmaking of Wriothesley, the Earl of Southampton, and thus support his candidature for being the Fair Youth of the Sonnets. Nevertheless, we cannot, being in the present state of our knowledge about the matter under consideration, set aside the points, stated before, against the candidature of Wriothesley, the Earl of Southampton.

Now, if we cannot accept Wriopthesley as the Fair Youth of the Sonnets, let us review the claim of William Herbert to be the Fair Youth of the Sonnets — William Herbert who became the Earl of Pembroke in January, 1601, and not his first cousin, another William Herbert who became the Earl of Pembroke in 1629. The candidature of Pembroke for the title of the Fair Youth of the Sonnets was first staked by Ulric Nisbet in 1936 in his book *The Onlie Begetter*. Nisbet's claim was supported by Baldwin and Rollins. Let us take stock of the arguments in favour of the candidature of William Herbert. Firstly, Herbert was by disposition given to carnal wantoness, though he was never happy in all this as he was not happy even with his wife. This may have been innuendoed to by Shakespeare in Sonnet 40: "By wilful taste of what thy self refusest". Secondly, we know from evidences from history that Herbert was a very handsome person. Thirdly, it is a fact — and this fact has been gathered from the correspondences of

Herbert's partents — that Herbert showed disinclination towards marriage, which is actually the theme of the Sonnets 1-17. Fourthly, it has now become an established fact that Shakespeare met Herbert for the first time on 8 April, 1597.

Fifthly, Clarendon's description of William Herbert also innuendoes to the Fair Youth of the Sonnets being none else than Herbert himself: " 'William Earl of Pembroke was next, a man of another mould and making, and of another fame and reputation with all men, being the most universally loved and esteemed of any man of that age; and, having a office in the Court (he) made the Court itself better esteemed and more reverend in the country. And as he had a great number of friends of the best men, so no man had ever the wickedness to avow himself to be his enemy. He was a man very well bred, and of excellent parts, and a graceful speaker upon any subject, having a good proportion of learning, and a ready wit to apply it and enlarge upon it; of a pleasant and facetious humour, and a disposition affable, generous, and magnificent. He was a master of a great fortune from his ancestors, and had a great addition by his wife (another daughter and heir of the Earl of Shrewsbury), which he enjoyed during his life she outliving him: but all served not his expense, which was only limited by his great mind and occasions to use it nobly' " (Wilson, cxx).

The candidature of William Herbert, the Earl of Pembroke, is also dubitable. We have seen that Shakespeare met Herbert, for the first time, in 1597, the year before which most of the Sonnets (if not all) were already written. So, how can Herbert be the theme of the Sonnets? Secondly, Ivor Brown did not admit the Earl of Pembroke as a possible candidate for 'Mr. W.H.' or the Fair Youth, because, he wrote, "the dates are against him and so are some of the qualities attributed in the Sonnets, such as lack of father and brother" (Brown, 196). In this atmosphere of uncertainty, Robert Gittings has introduced yet another candidate — William Harvey — with a little bit of trepidation. In his *Shakespeare's Rival,* while discussing about the identity of the Fair Youth, Gittings, as an *obiter dictum,* innuendoed that William Harvey might be the Fair Youth. About the candidature of Harvey, Gittings wrote: "It is sufficient to underline in passing (....) — that we would be unwise to neglect the claims of a man with the correct initials and designation, a member of the Essex group, married first to Southampton's widowed mother, and secondly to a girl whose Christian name was a form of Cordelia, and who opposed her two elder sisters' claims on the person and estate of their lunatic father: a man, moreover, whose own surname Shakespeare apparently used for one of his characters in an early version of *Henry IV,* Part I'' (Gittings, 89-90). This William Harvey, Gittings cautions us, must not be confused with another William Harvey, the discoverer of the circulation of blood.

Ivor Brown also supported the candidature of William Harvey. Brown wrote : ''On the other hand there is a likely candidate for office (of 'Mr. W.H.' or of the Fair Youth) in William Harvey; admittedly he was *Sir* William Harvey, in 1609, but at least he was not an Earl who has been degraded to 'Mr.' in the ever-baffling note by Thorpe. If anybody is coming down to 'Mr.' it might be a knight who had been one in his youth not a Earl who had previously been a Lord. Dr. Stopes has put the point plainly.

> There is no objection in the use of 'Mr W.H.' 'Sir' was not a title in the same way as Earl or Baron. Lady Southampton always called her husbands in correspondence, 'Master Heneage', and 'Master Harvey,' though both of them were knights. The late Dr. Furnivall was argued into agreeing that though the Harvey theory was not absolutely certified, it was the best which had ever appeared'' (Brown, 187).

As we have seen in chapter 5, Oscsar Wilde suggested that Willie Hughes was the Fair Youth or the 'Mr. W.H.' of the Sonnets. This Willie Hughes was, as Wilde supposed, an actor. But Ivor Brown said that ''There is no trace in any records of any actor or boy-player called Will or Willie Huges'' (Brown, 187). Samuel Butler (not the other Samuel Butler, author of *Hudibras*) in his *Shakespeare's Sonnets Reconsidered and in Part Rearranged* (1899), claimed that the Sonnets were not addressed to a person of high rank, but to a man of low birth and profession — a man by the name of Willie Hughes who had been a ship's cook. This is a very wild guess of Butler, congruent with many of his cranky ideas in some of his works. The reverential tone of the Sonnets will not allow us to think that the young man of the Sonnets is of a low birth and that he is a ship's cook. Both Wilde and Butler depended for their conjectures particularly on the punning at line 7 of Sonnet 20 : ''A man in *hew* all *Hews* in his controlling''. Ivor Brown wrote about this punning: ''Of course this kind of pun on names and words is Shakespearean and the Sonnets themselves pun on the name-word Will on several occasions. But all the lines need mean was that the lovely boy was in the habit of flushing and changing colour very easily. This quick change of colour in the face is a quality of which Shakespeare spoke frequently, so much so that Dr. Caroline Spurgeon has suggested that he himself was quick to flush and blush'' (Brown, 187). Therefore, we cannot accept the suggestions of both Wilde and Butler.

Shakespeare industry will perhaps never stop, and this industry has been turning out dubitable and non-dubitable conjectures about our various questions, non-stop. But, so far, only a few conjectures have been able to satisfy our quests with some degrees of certainty. However, among other dubitable candidates for the title of 'Mr. W.H.' or the 'Fair Youth', there is one William Hall — the last candidate under our consideration. Ivor Brown wrote about this William Hall: ''There has also been hunted out a William Hall, a relative of Shakespeare's son-in-law, Dr. Hall, who acted as a printer and literary jobber in London. It has been argued that the words 'Mr. W.H. All Happinesse' include a pun on his name'' (Brown, 187-88). But Brown himself rejected the prospect of this William Hall of being the 'Mr. W.H.' of the Sonnets. But, why did the name of William Hall surfaced as a possible candidate? The reason is that some critics guessed, after long hunting, that the 'onlie begetter' might mean the procurer or the printer of the manuscript of the Sonnets, and that William Hall was a printer. However, being thus dejected in our search for the identity of the Fair Youth or the 'Mr. W.H.', let us here stop our searching, and say what Matthew Arnold said in his Sonnet 'Shakespeare':

> Others abide our questions. Thou art free.
> We ask and ask: Thou smilest and art still,
> Out-topping knowledge.

❐

VIII

The Identity of the Dark Lady

After 1598, we hear nothing from Shakespeare about the 'man right fair' or the Fair Youth of the Sonnets. In his place, we find a 'woman colour'd ill' — the 'Black Mistress' or the 'Dark Lady' — the two terms coined by modern fancy. The image of the Dark Lady haunted Shakespeare, for years together. Ivor Brown wrote about her: "For years the Dark Lady, in my opinion, kept him (Shakespeare) on edge, a figure adored and loathed, a memory that shone and scorched and tormented" (Brown, 196). According to Ivor Brown, the craze for identifying the Fair Youth and the Dark Lady is now over; but, nevertheless, he was one of the few who cared to write at some length about the identity of the two mysterious persons. Brown's contention that the Dark Lady kept Shakespeare 'on edge' for a considerable period of time is true, otherwise we would not come across the image of a 'black' and 'voluptuous' lady so frequently in the plays written during the period or thereabout in which the 'Dark Lady Sonnets' were composed.

It is generally agreed that Shakespeare wrote 28 sonnets about the Dark Lady : Sonnets 127-154. But this agreement should be qualified. Because, firstly, Sonnets 153 and 154 are rather two versions of a Greek epigram on Cupid, and, further, these two Sonnets may not have been written by Shakespeare. Or, we may also say, these two Sonnets are not concerned with the Dark Lady, but they, according to M.M. Reese, "discussed the connection between erotism and bathing" (Reese, 411). Secondly, Sonnets 127-154 are actually miscellaneous. Most of them certainly refer to the Dark Lady, but there are some which bear no reference to the lady; for instance, Sonnet 129 does not speak anything about the Dark Lady. Thirdly, it is also true that the Dark Lady "had already appeared in some of the earlier sonnets" (Reese, 411).

The Fair Youth 'sonnet-sequence' and the Dark Lady 'sonnet-sequence' were written at two different periods, having a gap of about 2/3 years between them. This is manifest in the fact that there are more parallels between the 'Fair Youth Sonnets' and such plays as were written between 1593 and 1598, particulalry the comedies, such as *Love's Labour's Lost* and *Romeo and Juliet,* than between the 'Dark Lady Sonnets' and those plays. This may, of course, prove that the 'Dark Lady Sonnets' were written either before or after the 'Fair Youth Sonnets'; but as we know that the 'Dark Lady Sonnets' were not written before the 'Fair Youth Sonnets', so these were certainly written after the 'Fair Youth Sonnets', and in no case long with the 'Fair Youth Sonnets'. Parallels to the 'Dark Lady Sonnets' are to be found mostly in *Love's Labour's Lost, Romeo and Juliet* and *Antony and Cleopatra.* For instance, Rosaline in *Love's Labour's Lost* is black-complexioned but beautiful, like the Dark Lady, and in that play (IV, iii, 244-49), Berowne describes her thus :

> Is ebony like her? O wood divine !
> A wife of such wood were felicity.
> O, who can give an oath? Where is a book?
> That I may swear beauty doth beauty lack,
> If that she learn not of her eye to look.
> No face is fair that is not full so black.

Again, in *Antony and Cleopatra,* Cleopatra is a 'tawny front', but, yet in her the great general Antonio has been 'transform'd/ Into a strumpet's fool'. This clearly reminds us of the 'Dark Lady Sonnets' where the poet is infatuated by the Dark Lady, with a 'tawny front', perhaps. Before this, in *Romeo and Juliet* (II, i, 17-20), Mercutio described the beauty of Rosaline to Romeo thus : "I conjure thee by Rosaline's bright eyes, /By her high forehead and her scarlet lip,/By her fine foot, straight leg, and quivering thigh,/And the demesnes that there adjacent lie". Afterwards Mercutio says : "poor Romeo...Stabb'd with a white wench's black eye". Rosaline of *Romeo and Juliet* therefore bears resemblances with the Dark Lady of the Sonnets. Ivor Brown says that Rosaline, in *Romeo and Juliet,* never comes upon the stage, and yet Shakespeare has a detailed description of her. Why? Brown's explanation deserves consideration. He wrote : "There is no good reason for this little flow of detail, no dramatic cause for recording the facial items, the pallor, the high forehead, the jet-black eyes, the alluring foot (...). The only explanation is that Shakespeare was himself haunted by such a mask. Rosaline never enters the play and soon fades from the mind of the audience; Romeo has to be the sad hero of another and a larger romance. It is the more astonishing, therefore, that Rosaline, who is nothing in the story compared with Juliet, should be drawn with such definition, almost with a catalogue of features. 'Stabb'd with a white wench's black eye.' That is not only the very language of the Sonnets, *it is the very Lady''* (*Italics mine*) (Brown, 201). *Romeo and Juliet* was written in 1595 which year falls within the period in which the Sonnets were written. And this provides for the reason why there are similarity between Rosaline and the Dark Lady. *Love's Labour's Lost* was written a year before *Romeo and Juliet*; and so we find elements of similarity between this play and the Sonnets. In *Love's Labour's Lost,* Berowne describes Rosaline (another Rosaline) thus :

> Who sees the heavenly Rosaline
> That, like a rude and savage man of Inde
> At the first op'ning of the gorgeous east,
> Bows not his vassal head and, strucken blind,
> Kisses the base ground with obedient breast?
> What peremptory eagle-sighted eye
> Dares look upon the heaven of her brow
> That is not blinded by her majesty?

This generally tallies with the general description of the Dark Lady of the 'Dark Lady Sonnets'.

Now, if we go beyond the period of the Sonnets, then also we will find that there are other women with whom the Dark Lady may be compared. This also proves that the image of the Dark Lady never left Shakespeare's consciousness. In *Troilus and Cressida,* Shakespeare is raging against the wantonness of Cressida. In *Hamlet,* the Prince of Denmark rebukes his mother in abject physical terms. So also he does his beloved Ophelia : ''I have heard of your paintings too, well enough; God hath given you one face, and you make *yourselves* another. You jig amble, and you lisp, and nickname God's creatures, and make your *wantonness* your ignorance.'' Here Hamlet is rebuking not only Ophelia, but women folk in general, for their 'wantonness' that is a notorious feature of the Dark Lady. Again, in *Antony and Cleopatra,* as we have seen, Cleopatra has a 'tawny front'. These features of a woman was not attractive to Shakespeare. What he like a woman to be was something different. Ivor Brown wrote that the features of a woman that continually appealed to Shakespeare were ''white skin, the veins' blue tracery, and the motion of a bosom stiring as it breathes'' (Brown, 28). And yet he was, against his will, drawn to the Dark Lady. According to Ivor Brown, the spell of the Dark Lady was gone only around 1606 or 1607 by which time the poet for the last time painted yet another portrait of the Dark Lady in *Antony and Cleopatra.* Brown wrote · ''The woman' 'colour'd ill' had achieved her worst : she had well-nigh cracked a great heart (Shakespeare's) and she had driven to wild ravings a hand unparallel'd. But the battle of the two was not over. In *Antony and Cleopatra* Shakespeare was to paint her for the last time and almost to forgive her. Why this change of mind? Because, I believe, she was by that time dead'' (Brown, 215). It may be mentioned here in passing that the word 'Dark' may be ambiguous. According to G.W. Knight, the word may not mean 'black'. He said: ''the Dark Lady may not have been so 'black' as the poetry makes her'' (Knight, 11). In the Elizabethan age, as probably even today, dark complexion was not a thing for admiration. Shakespeare also took dark complexion to be 'unfair', as is evident from what Theseus says at *A Midsummer Night's Dream* (V, i, 10-11) : ''The lover all as frantic,/Sees Helen's beauty in a brow of Egypt.''

Now, before we enter into our project of identifying the Dark Lady, we should answer a very pertinent question : was there really a 'Dark Lady'? Or, was she a phantom of Shakespeare's imagination? G.W. Knight and Arthur Compton-Rickett, among others, believe that both the Fair Youth and the Dark Lady were real persons. In his *The Mutual Flame* Knight wrote : ''The two persons appear to be real individuals....'' (Knight, 11). Compton-Rickett wrote about the 'real' Dark Lady : ''Throughout Shakespeare's plays there is curious emphasis upon a special physical type, black-eyed and pale-faced. Such is always the type of inconstancy and depravity. Romeo is stabbed by 'a white wench's black eye'; Biron is infatuated by 'a whitely wanton with a velvet brow. Recalling these allusions by the light of the fickle 'dark ladie' of the Sonnets, it is not unreasonable to imagine that here we have memories of this capricious love that serve the dramatist in his studies'' (Compton-Rickett, 133).

Before we try to identify the Dark Lady, let us have her features or characteristics garnered from the Sonnets. Edgar I. Fripp has summarised her features or traits for us : ''She is Shoreditch quean, and a Court coquette. She is a sluttish and odious harlot ('where all men ride', 'so foul a face', 'false plague', 'I have what others do abhor'), offensive to *all* the five senses —

> (In faith I do not love thee with mine *Eyes*,
> Nor are mine *Ears* with thy tongue's tune delighted,
> Nor tender feeling to base *Touches* prone,
> Nor *Taste* nor *Smell* desire to be invited
> To any sensual feast with thee alone),

and a gentlewoman ('gentle cheater', 'thy sweet self'); ungainly lumpish, ugly ('my mistress treads', than her speech 'music hath a far more pleasing sound', 'thy face hath not the power to make love groan', 'mine eyes in thee a thousand errors note', 'black as Hell', 'eyes well seeing thy foul faults find', 'I have sworn thee fair : more perjured I to swear so foul a lie') and graceful, charming ('born fair', 'so becoming every tongue says Beauty should look so', 'her pretty looks' and 'glancing eye', 'lips that Love's own hand did make'); contemptuous, full of hate ('thou art tyrannous', 'thy heart torments me with disdain', 'thou art cruel', 'my pity — wanting pain', 'O cruel ! hate on', 'thou should not abhor my state') and pitiful ('lips breath'd forth *I hate,* but when she saw my woeful state, straight in her heart did mercy come and saved my life, saying *not you*')." (Fripp, I, 261-62).

Now let us follow the Sonnets themselves to find out these features in their proper places. In the first sonnet of the Dark Lady 'sonnet-sequence' (Sonnet 127), Shakespeare describes his lady-love as a black beauty, and, further, says that beauty cannot be beauty if it is not black — as black as the Dark Lady. He says that beauty has undergone trans-valuation in course of time :

> In the old age black was not counted fair,
> Or if it were, it bore not beauty's name;
> But now is black beauty's successive heir,
> And beauty slander'd with a bastard shame:

Here the poet speaks of the *fait accopmpli* of the trans-valuation of beauty. But in Sonnet 132, he himself approves of this trans-valuation: "Then will I swear beauty herself is black,/And all they foul that thy complexion lack."

In Sonnet 137, the poet tells about the licentiousness of the Dark Lady. He says that she is "the bay where all men ride" and that she is a "false plague". From Sonnet 138, we know that the lady is a lier : "she lies" and she has a "false-speaking tongue". The lady, the poet admits, is not attractive, physically; the poet is infatuated by her only erroneously: "In faith, I do not love thee with mine eyes,/For they in thee a thousand errors note." The Dark Lady is also not well-spoken: "Nor mine ears with thy tongue's tune delighted". She is not at all a "sensual feast". She can infatuate the poet only because of his "foolish heart". In Sonnet 144, the poet, again, speaks of the dark complexion of the lady: "The worser spirit a woman colour'd ill". He adds that she is a "bad angel". But, in Sonnet 145, Shakespeare says that there is a saving grace in the Dark Lady: she is sometimes merciful, particularly when the poet is full of sorrows: "But when she saw my woeful state,/Straight in her heart did mercy come."

The Dark Lady is devoted to rich cosmetics and costly toiletry, and yet she bemoans her lack of beauty. In Sonnet 146, the poet asks her:

> Why dost thou pine within and suffer death,
> Painting thy outward walls so costly gay?
> Why so large cost, having so short a lease,
> Dost thou upon thy fading mansion spend?

The lady has grown old and so even the heavy use of cosmetics cannot save her from her dark complexion, because even with the aid of artifices she is "as black as hell, as dark as night" (Sonnet 147). In Sonnet 152, the poet says, for the last time, that the Dark Lady is certainly not fair: "For I have sworn thee fair, — more perjur'd I,/To swear, against the truth, so foul a lie!" These are, then, the features and traits of the lady. Ivor Brown summarise the physical features of the Dark Lady thus: "The Sonnets, in short, give a precise picture of a pale-skinned, red-lipped, black-haired woman, with eyes of gleaming black, witty, fond of music, alluring, maddening, magical, utterly wanton" (Brown, 200). And about the wanton character of the lady, Ivor Brown wrote: "She has broken her 'bed-vow' with her husband and betrays lovers no less lightly" (Brown, 200).

The Dark Lady is not an extract from the upper crust of society. This may be evident from Sonnet 143 where Shakespeare compares her purusance of love with the running of a housewife to catch her "feather'd creatures". K.D. Sethna wrote about the social status of the Dark Lady: "She may have been a woman of some income, but the strong probability is that her status was of no more than an ordinary London citizen" (Sethna, 133). But Sonnet 128 (line 6) may stand in contradiction to Sethna's opinion about her social status. In this sonnet, the poet speaks of the "tender inward" of the lady's hand. The inner side of the hand, or the palm, of a man or woman remains tender only if he or she does not do chores. However, the lady is full of lust as is manifest particularly in Sonnets 135 and 136 (the 'Will Sonnets'): "Wilt thou, whose will is large and specious,/ Not once vouchsafe to hide my will in thine?"(135) and "Will will fulfil the treasure of thy love,/Ay, fill it full with wills, and my will one" (136). According to Seymour-Smith, the word 'will' here means the male pudendum, as it did in the Elizabethan age, and probably, even today (Sethna, 133). Further, this bawdy woman is fond of music.

Our last question about the Dark Lady : how old is she? Tyler suggested that she might have been young. Sonnets 132, 139 and 145 support Tyler's assumption. In Sonnet 132 (line 4), Shakespeare calls her "pretty ruth". In Sonnet 139 (line 10), he again speaks of her "pretty looks". Being pretty is possible if the age is young. In Sonnet 145 (line 1), the poet marvels at the coral lips of the lady: "Those lips that Love's own hand did make". Lips show perfect shape and colour only in tender age. Is Shakespeare older than the Dark Lady, or the other way round? Sonnet 138 is a whit confusing:

> When my love swears that she is made of truth,
> I do believe her, though I know she lies,
> That she might think me some untutor'd youth,
> Unlearned in the world's false subtleties.

Why will the lady think the poet to be an "untutor'd youth" if he is not really young? But, next, the poet says : "Thus vainly thinking that she thinks me young,/Although she knows *my days are past the best*". If the poet is really young, why does he say that his "*days are past the best* "? The solution of this problem may be this : the poet is just past the prime of his youth. Probably Shakespeare came to London around 1586, just after the birth of Hamnet and Judith, when he was about 22. His acquaintance with the Dark Lady occurred probably not 6/7 years after that when Shakespeare was around 28 or 29. So the poet was certainly not old — his youth was not over. But, of course, the prime of his youth was gone: "*my days are past the best*". But, why, then, does it appear that the poet is older that the Dark Lady? It is because the lady was pretty young — may be she was around 'sweet sixteen'. And in that case, the poet was older than she. K.D. Sethna wrote about the matter: "If Shakespeare's Mistress is older than he, if her years are even more past the best, there is no reason for him to be so eager to be thought young. It is difficult to credit Brooke's conclusion from the insincerities on which rests the relation between the poet and the woman. When the poet is pictured as trying 'to affect juvenility to make her think him 'some untutor'd youth', Brooke rightly adds : "The Dark Lady, though precocious, was probably very young.' Shakespeare must have been fairly older than she" (Sethna, 126).

Now let us try to find out if there really lived a base woman of dark colour corresponding to the Dark Lady of the Sonnets. To begin with, like in the case of the Fair Youth, in the case of the Dark Lady also some critics raised the natural question: was there really such a woman or is she a creation of Shakespeare's furtile imagination? Those critics who especially doubt the real existence of the Fair Youth, bank, among other things, on Sonnet 53:

> What is your substance, whereof are you made,
> That millions of strange shadows on you tend?
> Since every one hath, every one, one shade,
> And you, but one, can every shadow lend.

So, were the Fair Youth and the Dark Lady real? This is a topical question, no doubt; but, if we understand that the 'beloveds' of most of the Elizabethan sonnets were conventionally real persons, then we have reasons to ferret out for the woman of whom the Dark Lady is the replica. To the scepticism of those who doubted the ontological reality of the Fair Youth, L.C. Knights wrote: "Indeed many of the Sonnets in which the friend is given something more than perfunctory recognition it is hard to resist the conclusion that Shakespeare is addressing *his own conscience*"*(italics mine)* (Alpers, 293). C.L. Barber also believed that the emotions of the Sonnets are real emotions. He wrote that the Sonnets "Have the additional interest that they are the only poems we have which Shakespeare wrote out of *his own life, in his own person" (italics mine)* (Alpers, 299). Barber further wrote: "The *who, where, when* (of the Sonnets) are beyond knowing, despite the tantalizing closeness of the poems to Shakespeare's personal life" (*italics mine*) (Alpers, 299). L.C. Knights also further wrote: "The most satisfying of the sonnets which deal with Shakespeare's difficulties in love are those where he is using the sonnets primarily to confront what love *reveals to him about himself*" (*italics mine)* (Alpers, 317).

Now, as in the case of the Fair Youth, so in the case of the Dark Lady also there are a number of contending candidates for the title of the Dark Lady: Lady Anon, Luce Morgan, Mary Fitton and the Italian whore 'Anastasia'. The name of Lady Anon was put forward by Frank Harris, but her candidature is so tenuous that critics had discarded it outright. Ivor Brown wrote: "She is, as I said, out of fashion and criticism now tend to pass her by as Frank Harris's fad" (Brown, 197).

The name of Luce Morgan was submitted by Hotson. Luce was in Queen Elizabeth's (reigned 1558-1603) retinue from 1579 to 1581. She was a base woman, a whore, a bawd. Davies of Hereford wrote about Luce : " 'For Luce did like a whore begin, but ended like a bawd' " (Sethna, 117). Hotson's arguments in favour of Luce being the Dark Lady are three. Firstly, J.M. Murry wrote that Luce " 'seems to have been a woman of the courtesan type, whose attraction for Shakespeare and whose hold on him was purely sensual' " (Sethna, 117). Luce came of a noble family, but she lost all her dignities through her voluptuousness. Hotson saw parallels between her character and the Sonnets 40-42 and 127-152. In both the cases the two ladies are courtesan and voluptuous. Hotson believed that the lady addressed to in the Sonnets written between 1587 and 1589 was Luce Morgan. Secondly, Hotson found cross-references between Luce's sufferings from venereal disease and Sonnet 144 (line 14) where Shakespeare says: "Till my bad angel fire my good one out." In the Elizabethan age, the phrase 'fire out' referred to venereal disease from which Shakespeare was said to have been suffering. Thirdly, and this is his most potent argument, Hotson thought that Sonnets 147 and 150 referred to the name of Luce. In Sonnet 147 (lines 13-14), the poet says:

> For I have sworn thee fair, and thought thee bright,
> Who art as black as hell, as dark as night.

And in Sonnet 150 (lines 3-4), the poet again writes:

> To make me give the lie to my true sight
> And swear that brightness doth not grace the day...

Hotson believed that the term 'Luce' was derived from Latin *Lucia* which means 'lightsome' or 'bright'. Here 'brightness' means, according to Hotson, 'wit and courage'. But Luce is dark too, because of her lack of moral rectitude or uprightness. Therefore, she is dark but bright. Hotson supports this contention of his with evidences from the Elizabethan custom and from the Sonnets themselves : "Hotson continues: "Shakespeare adds the apparent paradox : this 'bright' woman is in fact *as dark as night.* Which night was Lucy's? Consult the Calendar, Old Style. We find Lucy *on the* darkest night of the whole year: December 13, the winter solstice — 'Lucy bright, the shortest day and longest night'. And John Donne writes : 'A Nocturnall upon S. Lucies Day' — *Tis the years mid-night. Lucy* as the name of Bright-Dark Woman is clearly more than a possibility, as we look further into Shakespeare's topics.

"Hotson's next move is in connection with a theme that 'so hunts and haunts the reader that there is no escaping it: *eyes, seeing, sight, blind, blindness, eyes corrupt* (diseased) with *plague'.* Hotson quotes extensively from the Sonnets to match several associations which according to the books of reference, have especially to do with St. Lucy 'plucked out her eyes when they became a snare to her lover', but 'they were afterwards restored to her more beautiful', and she 'is regarded as the special patroness of those who suffer from diseases of the eyes'. 'Many paintings represent her bearing her eyes in her hand or on a salver. Some artists have even represented her blind.' Hotson, quoting Sonnet-phrases, writes: '*Bear thine eyes straingth...Swear to thy blind soul ... to enlighten thee, gave eyes to blindness ... eyes, corrupt ... Lucy* bearing her eyes; Lucy blind, enlightened by being given eyes even more beautiful; *Lucy invoked* by men plagued with diseased eyes — beyond question this cluster is the connotation of these sonnets. Joined with *Lucy bright,* in my mind, it leaves no room for doubt that the name Shakespeare is playing upon here, the name of the Bright-Dark Woman, is Lucy or Luce' " (Sethna, 119-20).

K.D. Sethna admitted that Luce's candidature was certainly strong: "Hotson's case is indeed the best so far. And Luce Morgan falls even within our own time-bracket. The temptation is great to regard the case not only as good in itself but also as confirmed by our chronological findings." Nevertheless, Sethna put forward some counter-arguments against Hotson's contention. Firstly, he said that the terms picked up by Hotson to prove his point — such as *eyes, seeing, sight, blind, blindness, eyes corrupt,* etc. — were not to be especially found only in the 'Dark Lady Sonnets', but they can equally be found in other Sonnets as well. To take only a few examples :

Sonnet 5 (line 2) : "Thy lovely gaze where every eye doth dwell."

Sonnet 17 (line 5) : "If I could write the beauty of thine eyes."

Sonnet 20 (lines 5-6): "An eye more bright than theirs, less false in rolling,
Gilding the object whereupon it gazeth."

Sonnet 29 (lines 9-10): "I tell the day, to please him, thou art bright
And dost him grace when clouds do blot the heaven."

Sonnet 113 (lines 1-4): "Since I left you mine eye is in my mind,
And that which governs me to go about
Doth part his function and is partly blind."

Secondly, Sethna said that the name of Luce does not indicate light or brightness : "To swear a woman fair is to affairm one's sense of her beauty or her truth (fidelity); to think her bright is to believe either that she is a creature of light, of goodness, or that she is exceedingly well-favoured. Neither act depends on a mere name (of Luce) or is guided by it" (Sethna, 123). Thirdly and lastly, Sethna did not admit that the 'black' character of the Dark Lady could be equated with the available biography of Luce Morgan : "Hotson has equated the 'black' character of the Dark Lady with Luce's history. But actually we have not the slightest evidence of this harlotry in Hotson's period for the Sonnets: 1587-9. If to read her name in these poems is arbitrary, we get a big gap between the records for 1579-81 of the Queen's Household, in which gifts to her as a Queen's-gentlewoman are mentioned, and the *Gesta Grayorum* of 1594-5 mentioning her brothel at Clerkenwell. All we know from John Davies of Hereford is that before she became a bawd she had been a whore; but it is pure guess-work that her whoring was in full swing in Hotson's Sonnet-years. We do not even know anything about the end of her connection with the Queen : Hotson confesses, 'Some day we may learn when and how Mistress Morgan was banished from Queen Elizabeth's side.' Her marriage too is practically a blank for us. Hotson chooses to put it before 1588, but he honestly informs us about her husband Parker : '... his baptismal name and the date of the marriage are still to find.' Nothing about Luce that would suit Hotson's dating of the Sonnets is in our possession" (Sethna, 124-25).

Next, Mistress Mary Fitton. Mary Fitton was claimed by Thomas Tyler (1826-1902), the biblical and Shakespearean scholar, as the Dark Lady of the Sonnets. Tyler put forward this claim in his edition of Shakespeare's Sonnets (1890). Frank Harris (alias James Thomas : 1856-1931), though at first he thought that some Lady Anon was the Dark Lady, later abandoned his own theory and believed that Tyler's claim was justified. The Lady Anon-Dark Lady theory of Frank Harris was, as we have seen, unbelievable and queer. However, Harris, an adventurer and an author, who ran away from home and served first as a cowboy and then as a war correspondent, became the editor of the *Evening News*. In his *The Women of Shakespeare* and *Shakespeare and His Love,* Harris supported the view of Tyler that Mary Fitton was the Dark Lady of the Sonnets. By the by, Harris said that Shakespeare revealed himself in the characters of Berowne, Romeo, Jaques, Hamlet and such others, and that Shakespeare was an 'embittered man, dying broken-hearted for love of the Dark Lady'.

Tyler thought that William Herbert, the Earl of Pembroke was the 'man right fair' and Mary Fitton was the 'woman colour'd ill' of the Sonnets. Tyler published his thesis in the *Pall Mall Gazette* of January 7, 1886, and thus Mary Fitton was introduced to Frank Harris. Harris was so fascinated by Tyler's suggestion that Mary Fitton was the Dark Lady that he wrote a play about Mary Fitton and also made the temptress, the principal character of his book *The Man Shakespeare and His Tragic Life Story*. Mary Fitton, a maid of honour to Elizabeth, was the wife of William Herbert, the Earl of Pembroke. Mary Fitton's canditure was not accepted, among others, by G.B. Shaw. Shaw said that contrary to the assumed dark complexion of the Dark Lady, Mary Fitton was a blonde. According to him, Southampton, and not Pembroke, was Mr. W.H., and this was another reason why he rejected the Dark Lady-Mary Fitton theory of Tyler and Harris. K.D. Sethna here added that Mary Fitton did not fit into the accepted chronology of the Sonnets : "And she suffers exclusion also by coming on the scene too late for our chronology" (Sethna, 115).

Jane Davenant is yet another candidate for the appellation of the 'Dark Lady'. Her claim rests on the tradition according to which Sir William Davenant (or D'Avenant) (1606-68) was the illegitimate son of Shakespeare. Jane Davenant was the wife of John Davenant, a vinter of Oxford, and later on the Mayor of Oxford. Sir William Davenant was the fourth and youngest child of John Davenant. William Davenant was a dramatist of some importance, and he wrote four plays — *Albovine,The Cruel Brother, The Just Italian* and *Siege of Rhode* — and three masques and an epic, *Gondibert*. According to tradition, first recorded by John Aubrey (1626-97) in c. 1680, " 'Mr. William Shakespeare was wont to goe into Warwickshire once a yeare, and commonly in his journey lye at this house (the house of John Davenant) in Oxon : where he was exceedingly respected. I have heard parson Robert D. (William's elder brother) say that Mr. Wm. Shakespeare here gave him (William Davenant) a hundred kisses. Now Sr Wm would sometimes when he was pleasant over a glass of wine with his most intimate friends, *e.g.* Sam: Butler (author of *Hudibras*) &c. say, that it seemed to him that he (Sir William Davenant) writt with the very spirit that Shakespeare (*sic.),* and was seemed contended (*sic.)* enough to be thought his (Shakespeare's) Son: he would tell them the story as above, in which way his mother had a very light report, whereby she was called a whore' " (Halliday, 128). The same tradition, again according to Aubrey, has it that Jane Davenant was " 'a very beautifull, & of a good witt and of conversation extremely agreeable' " (Halliday, 128). But, K.D. Sethna quashed away the candidature of Jane Davenant. Sethna wrote : "But Jane, according to verses once preserved at Warwick Castle, was 'a virtuous wife', and all the facts Chambers has collected about her are at variance with our chronology. Her vinter husband is not found at Oxford before 1602, and the Crown Tavern where Shakespeare is said by Aubrey to have lodged on his way each time between Stratford and London could not have come into John Davenant's possession prior to that year. Even the Cross Inn, a more fit place for lodging, was not in his hands before 1605. Either date is too late for the Dark Lady triangle. Nor have we evidence to think of the Tavern or the Inns continuing Shakespeare's relationship with Jane from an earlier period in London. She was a girl of the Shepherd family, from Durham, and John Davenant cannot be traced in London after 1589 and there is no sign of Jane's having been his wife before 1601" (Sethna, 115-16). Therefore, we cannot accept Jane Davenant as the Dark Lady.

Our last candidate is some 'Anastasia', suggested by K.D. Sethna *et al.* This is an Italian name. Sethna said that it might be wrong to search for the Dark Lady only within London, or even in the Continent, because in the Elizabethan age people from France, Spain, Germany, etc. as well as from Italy would come to London, chiefly for business purposes, and some of them settled there. Sethna wrote : "However, the Dark Lady need not have been an English-woman, as London had a lot of settled foreigners. Shakespeare's own landlord in the capital in 1604 was a French Huguenot. And undifferentiated immigrants from the Continent figure in certain official occasions. The Dark Lady could very well have been French, Italian, Spanish, Portuguese or South-German : her brunette colour would be best explained by such a nationality. 'Will' could be expected in both south and north Germany, but the largest likelihood is French or Italian origin for the Mistress" (Sethna, 151). But, how could the Dark Lady be addressed as 'Will', a form of male name? Referring to Sonnet 135, Sethna answered: "Shakespeare, twice (lines 6 and 8), without using a capital letter, speaks of 'my will' and again of 'One will of mine' (line 12) and uses too the phrase 'will in others'. The capitalised 'Will's who are the Dark Lady's lovers — two in the opinion of most commentators and three in that of some — may be held to match these uncapitalised references. But what then of the locutions : 'thy sweet will', and 'will' implied by 'thine'? May we not match them with something referring to the Dark Lady's own name?" (Sethna, 150).

Sethna suggested that 'Will' might have been derived from Italian 'Guilelma'. The Italian faminine form of English 'William' is 'Guglielma'; and perhaps, 'Guglielma' was anglicised into 'Gulielma'. That is, an Italian woman in England could be 'Guglielma' or 'Gulielma' or 'Willima', or simply 'Willa'; and Shakespeare further reduced 'Willa' or 'Will' (as the feminine form of the English 'William'). Sethna *et al* said that the Dark Lady was an Italian woman who had two names — 'Guglielma' or 'Williama' and 'Anastasia'. Sethna wrote : "The pre-eminence of 'Anastasia' may be caught also from an historical fact. It had a special prestige at the time. Ivan the Terrible of Muscovy, who was crowned the 1st Tsar of Russia on January 16, 1547, selected on February 3 in the same year Anastasia Zakharina Koshkina of the Romanov family to be his wife from among the virgins gathered from all the corners of the land. This celebrated Anastasia died in 1560. Her name would naturally get tagged, especially on the year's royalty....she was an uncommon commoner of London. Shakespeare must have met her when *Romeo and Juliet* was being written — possibly in 1597 or, since the early phase of the acquaintance is dramatised now, perhaps even in 1596. She kept him at arm's length and rendered him miserable. Like Rosaline in the play, she was not yet a palpable part of the drama of his life" (Sethna, 154-55). 'Anastasia's candidature is not very strong. Firstly, because it is very difficult to believe that 'Guglielma' became 'Will' in the Sonnets through a number of transformations and reductions. Secondly, we do not know very much, so as to satisfy ourselves, about the features and bio-data of the woman called 'Anastasia', so that we may tally her with the Dark Lady of the Sonnets.

Before we conclude this chapter, let us consider yet another woman for the office of the Dark Lady : Emilia Bassano Lanier, another Italian woman. Her case was produced by Dr. Rowse who found her name and her suitability to be the Dark Lady in the unpublished and voluminous notebooks of Simon Forman (1552-1611), an 'astrologer and physician of London in Shakespeare's day.' According to Forman, Emilia Bassano Lanier was the illegitimate daughter of Margaret Johnson by Battista Bassanio, a musician of Queen Elizabeth's Court. She was beautiful but brunette, and was the 'paramour' of the Lord Chamberlain. When she had been carrying, she was given in marriage to William Lanier, a minstrel. Forman believed that the 'Will' of the Sonnets 134 and 135 referred to William Lanier. Sethna wrote : "From Forman's diary we learn that she was a coquette and soon had him (Shakespeare) on the rack of an infatuation which she fed and starved by turns. Rowse seems in her all the ingredients which went into the heady mixture that was the Dark Lady, including the latter's musical ability. His conclusion is : Shakespeare who joined the Lord Chamberlain's Company of Players in 1594 came into touch with this fascinating Italianate woman and became her lover. In Rowse's picture the Sonnet-affair was already a thing of the past when Forman fell a victim to her wiles'' (Sethna, 159). But Emilia's case was not acceptable to Sethna. Because, Sethna wrote : ''Forman who unearthed so many facts, or what seemed so, about Emilia never provides the faintest allusion to any rapport between her and Shakespeare. ''Further, there is a chronological detail which is refractory to a Shakespeare-Emilia set-up. The year in which Emilia was with child by the Lord Chamberlain and was consequently discarded by him was 1593. This puts quite a substantial gap between the link we might surmise for her with theatreland and the entry in 1594 of Shakespeare in the Lord Chamberlain's Company — most probably in October. Besides, preoccupation with a child, over and above a regular husband thrust upon her, would be in the way of a free-love life. Any contact with Lord Herbert, even a passing acquaintance with him, is, of course, still more inprobable. It is true that he came into touch with the family of the same Lord Chamberlain : there were preliminaries of his betrothal to Elizabeth, daughter of the Lord Chamberlain's brother George Carey, but these took place as late as 1595'' (Sethna, 160).

Now where do we stand regarding the identity of the Fair Youth or of Mr. W.H. and that of the Dark Lady? The obvious answer is : over uncertainty. Regarding the Dark Lady, at least, Ivor Brown rightly said : ''We shall never know, it seems, who the Dark Lady was''(Brown, 196). But, is it very essential to know the identity of the Fair Youth and that of the Dark Lady to understand and appreciate the Sonnet? Harold c. Goddard's answer is very straightforward: ''A deluge of ink has descended over the *Sonnets,* until they are hardly visible....identification of them (of the Fair Youth and of the Dark Lady) are of only archaeological or at best biographical interest. That there was a 'real' Mr. W.H. and a 'real' Dark Lady I am as little inclined to doubt as that there was a 'real' Beatrice in Dante's life. But these persons may have resembled what they gave birth to about as much as an acorn resembles an oak. Of how little account they are to us! 'The soul knows no persons.' So, while their originals remain unknown, Shakespeare, though few seem to notice, tells us precisely who they were — poetically. Which is all that matters'' (Goddard, II, 7).

❐

IX

Are the Sonnets Autobiographical?

There has been a long debate, and it is still continuing, over the point of the presence of the author in his works — over the point, that is, whether creative works can be absolutely objective or not. In other words, the question is : can the artist completely hide himself behind his works? Let alone such a long debate, we can narrow down the scope of the debate and re-frame the question thus : Can sonnets, worth the term, be non-autobiographical? Without entering into yet another debate, we may, perhaps, say that contrary to narrative and dramtatic poems, sonnets tend to reveal in themselves their authors.

This generalisation is not absolute, for we have come across artificial and insincere sonnets too. For instance, some of Shakespeare's briefless lawyer-friends in London wrote artificial and insincere sonnets for private amusements. It is for this fact that some critics believe that Shakespeare himself also took sonnetry sportingly, following the suit of his lawyer-friends. They think that Shakespeare played with sonnetry without having any genuine emotion necessary for writing sonnets, while he, perhaps, felt bored or tired of writing plays in concatenation, as — and this we know for certain — Seneca wrote plays when he would become tired of his philosophical meditation. So the critics argue that it may be probable that Shakespeare is not present in the Sonnets, and that the emotions he expresses in them are not sincere; and, further, it is for this reason that "there is the theory, backed by comparison with other sonnet-sequences in his own and other languages, that Shkespeare was not autobiographical in these poems (the Sonnets), that they were largely an exercise on themes or a philosophical allegory" (Gittings, 90). Yvor Winters also suggested that Shakespeare did not take the sonnet tradition " 'with any real seriousness' " (Jones, 17). So how can the Sonnets be autobiographical?

This point of absence of Shakespeare in the Sonnets is in keeping, some critics say, with what Keats said about the poet's presence in his poetry. Keats wrote in *The Letters of John Keats* : " 'A Poet is the most unpoetical of anything in existence; because he has no Identity — he is continually informing and filling some other Body — the Sun, the Moon, the Sea and Men and Women who are creatures of impulse, are poetical and have about them an unchangeable attribute — the poet has none; no Identity — he is certainly unpoetical of all God's creatures' " (Wilson, xvi-xvii).

And yet the debate has been continuing to be. Wordsworth, who, by the by, was not very much impressed by the quality of the Sonnets, believed that the poems were autobiographical. In a sonnet on the sonnet-form, Wordsworth declared that "with this key/Shakespeare unlocked his heart". But Robert Browning was prompt to retort. At the beginning of the poem 'House' in his *Pacchiarotto,* Browning mocked at the belief that a sonnet reveals its author's personal particulars :

> Shall I sonnet-sing you about myself?
> Do I live in a house you would like to see?
> Is it scant of gear, has it store of pelf?
> 'Unlock my heart with a sonnet-key?'

And at the end of the poem, and referring to the belief of Wordsworth, Browning says:

> 'Hoity toity! A street to explore,
> Your house the exception! "*With this same key*
> *Skakespeare unlocked his heart,*" once more!'
> Did Shakespeare? If so, the less Shakespeare he!

But, perhaps, the question is not whether the Sonnets are autobiographical or not, because poetry can never be anonymous, 'fatherless', devoid of the laughs and tears of its author, but the question is how much autobiographical they are: the question is only one of degree, for no literary work can be absolutely non-autobiographical. But the term 'autobiography' in itself is opaque, for autobiography may be an objective chronological record of the events and vissicitudes of a person's life; and, again, it may also be the graphics of the tides and ebbs, undulations and various emotional nuances of a person's length of life, without any accurate reference to the time-sequence, documented by the person concerned. The latter is the psychological sort of autobiography; and John Kerrigan says that in the sense of a psychological autobiography, the Sonnets do not touch the mark of autobiography. Because, he says, the poet Shakespeare does not quite reveal himself in the Sonnets, and say 'This I am', — Shakespeare the man is always behind Shakespeare the poet, in the Sonnets. Kerrigan wrote : "The text is neither fictive nor confessional. Shakespeare stands behind the first person of his sequence as Sidney had stood behind Astrophil — sometimes near the poetic 'I', sometimes farther off, but never without some degree of rhetorical projection. The Sonnets are not autobiographical in a psychological mode" (Kerrigan, 11). Kerrigan further supported his contention by saying that "Autobiography hardly exists in sixteenth century England, and what there is, like Thomas Hoby's *Travail and Life,* relates deeds and opinions, not inward thought and emotion. It is not until the seventeenth century that the keeping of diaries and the framing of memoirs begin in earnest" (Kerrigan, 11).

On the other hand, M.M. Reese did not agree with Kerrigan. He said that the Sonnets are certainly autobiographical, only if we can read and understand them properly. He meant to say that the Sonnets are confessional because the poet consciously expressed his 'love, sex, friendship and much more besides' in the Sonnets. Reese believed that the Sonnets are the record of the 'story' of their author Shakespeare. He wrote: "If this story is a more or less literal account of events which actually happened to Shakespeare, it is autobiographical evidence of a sort which would compel us to believe that the pessimism of his tragic period, when love, sex, friendship and much more besides were censoriously called into account, was a personal confession. Again the decision will depend ultimately on individual feeling, but if this is an autobiography, it is one which has yet to be satisfactorily read" (Reese, 412).

So far we have not been able to decide if the Sonnets are autobiographical or not. But we should not ignore the fact that the Sonnets heavily correspond with at least some of the plays that were written during the period in which the Sonnets were written, principally with the two plays — *Love's Labour's Lost* and *Romeo and Juliet.* M.M. Reese very perceptibly wrote about the Sonnets: "These poems were not an isolated exercise, something to be viewed apart from his plays. They are relevant to the study of his development as a poet and dramatist, for he used them to make certain poetic experiments and to explore the themes which he would amplify on latter occasions" (Reese, 417). There is correspondence not only between the themes of the Sonnets and the themes of these plays, but also between the psychological make-up of the author of the Sonnets and that of the author of those plays. This is attested by Arthur Compton-Rickett who wrote : "Roughly speaking, the impression we have of Shakespeare the Man from the plays is confirmed by the Sonnets'' (Compton-Rickett, 132). Not only this, not only impression, in some of the plays Shakespeare himself peeps out : remember, for instance, Rosaline's description of Berowne in *Love's Labour's Lost* (II, i, 66-76). The description certainly dovetails with the general impress of Shakespeare that we may derive from all of his plays taken together, and from other sources gathered so far. Now, if the dramas — and dramas are the most objective of all artistic creations — do reveal Shakespeare, then can we not suppose that the Sonnets — and Sonnets are the most personal of artistic creations — are reflexions of the poet's personal traits consciously confessed by himself?

Further, it is now proved, almost beyond doubt, that Shakespeare had grown a fascination for a young man of beauty, status and parts. Be this man Pembroke or Southampton, Shakespeare had sort of Platonic love and his maddening fascination for beauty are certainly elements of his autobiography. The Dark Lady comprises a chapter of the life of Shakespeare. His approach-avoidance syndrome towards the Dark Lady, and his consequent heart-ache; his love-hate relation with the Fair Youth, *vis-a-vis* the Dark Lady, etc. are also autobiographical elements of Shakespeare, to be found in the Sonnets.

Now, let us go to the Sonnets themselves. First, the Sonnets of despair: Sonnets 5 (''I, whom fortune of such triumph bars''); 27 (''Weary with toil, I haste me to my bed,/The dear repose for limbs with travel tir'd''); 28 (''When day's oppression is not eas'd by night,/But day by night, and night by day, oppress'd''); 29 (''When, in disgrace with fortune and men's eyes,/I all along beweep my outcast state''); 30 (''I sigh the lack of many a thing I sought''); 32 (''Exceeded by the height of happier men''); etc. If these Sonnets were composed between 1592 and 1598 (and we think they were), then we can say that Shakespeare certainly revealed his state of mind in these sonnets. We know that it was the period when he was grudged by his fellow playwrights, principally by Robert Green. We know that, compared to them, Shakespeare had reasons to feel inferior and oppressed, for which reason his unbending spirit was always trying to cope with those fellow poets. Can we not say that this state of mind of Shakespeare was revealed in these Sonnets, making them, at least partially, autobiogrpahical?

Again, let us look at the Sonnet 111 where the poet bemoans his crest-fallen state, and protests against the public for the manner it has shown him:

O, for my sake do you with Fortune chide,
The guilty goddess of my harmful deeds,
That did not better for my life provide
Than public means which public manners breeds.
And almost thence my nature is subdu'd
To what it works in, like the dyer's hand:

Here also we find an inkling of the state of the mind of the poet during the time in which the Sonnets were written. In Sonnet 62, Shakespeare gives us a clue to estimate about his age: 'Painting my age with beauty of thy days.'' Here we should recall that tine Fair Youth was younger to the poet by a couple of years. This might be included in any biography of Shakespeare.

In Sonnet 77, the poet urges the Fair Youth to record his thoughts in a notebook, and in Sonnet 122, he apologises to the youth for losing a notebook (perhaps the same notebook). This is a very important point, for this may prove that the Sonnets, or some of them at the least, are related to the personal lives of the poet and the Fair Youth. Kerrigan wrote about these two Sonnets: ''Both sonnets have been urged to show that Shakespeare's sequence grew directly out of lived experience: for why should else would such trivial objects as notebooks turn up there?'' (Kerrigan, 343). Again, if we read correctly, in Sonnet 121 Shakespeare is confessing his sexual frailties: ''For why should other's false adulterate eyes/Give salutation to my sportive blood?'' Some critics are of the opinion that in Sonnet 136, the so-called 'Will Sonnet', Shakespeare is disclosing his name, for why otherwise should he repeat so many times the word 'will', and especially why should he conclude the Sonnet with the clause ''my name is *will*''? L.C. Knights also took notice of personal notes in the Sonnets. He wrote: '' 'In many of the Sonnets ostensibly concerned with a personal relationship we find there is something of far greater interest to Shakespeare than the compliments, complaints and pleas that provide the occasion of writing' '' (Jones, 95). Again, A.C. Ward is of the opinion that the Sonnets must be autobiographical: ''The intensity of emotion in the *Sonnets* leaves no room for doubt in most readers' minds that they relate to Shakespeare's personal experiences, and are not conventional poetic exercises. But what those experiences were is no more than allusively hinted, and it may well be that Shakespeare desired only to transmit the sensation of the experiences, not to give a riddling transcript of actual relationship or episodes'' (Ward, 215-16).

There is no dearth of supporters as well as opponents on either side of the debate over the question whether the Sonnets are autobiographical or not. Wordsworth was among the supporters. In 1815, in his *Essay, Supplementary to the Preface to* 'Lyrical Ballads', Wordsworth wrote about the Sonnets: " 'There is extant a small Volume of miscellaneous poems, in which Shakespeare expresses *his own feelings* in his own person' " (*italics mine*) (Jones, 42). And his friend S.T. Coleridge dittoed his opinion. Coleridge worte that " 'they (the Sonnets) will help to explain the mind of Shakespeare' " (Jones, 41). And William Hazlitt concurred with both Wordsworth and Coleridge. He wrote in 1817 that the Sonnets are " 'interesting as they relate to the state of the personal feelings of the author (Shakespeare)' " (Jones, 47). J.A. Noble, a critic, also clearly perceived the personal elements in the Sonnets. In his article 'The Sonnet in England' that appeared in *Contemporary Review,* vol. xxxviii (1880), Noble wrote: " 'And in his (Shakespeare's) poems, notably in these so-called Sonnets, which are the richest and completest of them, this unique personal note is as clearly discernible as in the noblest of the plays....' " (Jones, 50).

And yet M.M. Reese would not like to part with his 'theory' that the Sonnets are not autobiographical : "The *Sonnets* then tell us something of Shakespeare as an artist but little about him personally; they are of *greater* interest as poetry than as biographical documents, and it is unfortunate that their supposed value as a contribution to the story of Shakespeare's life has persuaded many to read them in the wrong way and for the wrong reasons. *They show him interested in the sort of things which always interested him,* and his deep seriousness permeates even the most lyrical passages" (*italics mine*) (Reese, 423). Here Reese admits that the Sonnets may be at least of some interest for the biography of Shakespeare; and that the Sonnets show some "*sort of things which always interested him* (Shakespeare)." If by biography or autobiography we do not merely mean an individual's dates and data, but also his likes and dislikes, interests and attentions, pleasures and pains, etc., then, perhaps, in the wider sense of the term 'autobiography' we can say that the Sonnets are certainly autobiographical.

Some critics have said that Shakespeare wrote only conventional sonnets in the conventional themes of love and related affections, and so we should not try to ferret out the author in the Sonnets. This charge cannot be accepted, because conventional or artificial sonnets cannot achieve the emotional intensity of genuine sonnets. "When, in disgrace with fortune and men's eyes,/I all along beweep my outcast stae,/....?

(Sonnet 29) — can any one write such verses by placing word after word, measuring feet after feet, and having an eye to rhyme-scheme, but without feeling any intense pain in his heart? This is not a solitary instance. True, the Sonnets betray variety of emotions and multitude and complexity of intensities of those of emotions, but no sonnets are there that are quite dry of emotions. This quality of the Sonnets should be a parameter of their genuineness. Writing about the 'Dark Lady Sonnets', G.W. Wilson discarded the view that the Sonnets are conventional or artificial. He wrote about the 'Dark Lady Sonnets': "Well, those to the Dark Lady are so strangely outspoken, so burdened with passion and paradox, with sin and sickness of soul, that they can hardly be considered in any normal sense conventional. No one would indulge in them for fun, to please himself; and we can scarcely suppose that they would have pleased the lady. They must be either true records or poetic fantasies possessing a high degree of personal validity" (Knight, 17).

Some commentators have claimed that we can well not only construct some of the physical features of the poet, but also list some important events of his life, from the Sonnets. They say that the poet (be he William Shakespeare, or Francis or Antony Bacon, or Walter Raleigh, or anybody, as the debate over the identity of 'William Shakespeare' is till now raging, although at a low key) was lame, as we understand from Sonnet 37 (line 3): "So I, made *lame* by Fortune's dearest spite". They also say that the poet was crook-backed: "And so my patent back again is swerving" (Sonnet 87, line 8); and "Join with the spite of Fortune, make me bow" (Sonnet 90, line 3); and "Speak of my lameness, and I straight will halt" (Sonnet 89, line 3). Some commentators believe that all these physical defects of Shakespeare were the result of "(a) a scuffle in which he was ambushed and beaten up, (b) an accident at the Fortune Theature ('Fortune's dearest spite'), (c) serving as soldier in the Low Countries, (d) fighting (in his role as Sir Walter Raleigh) at Cadiz in 1596" (Ingram, 88). Again, some also found evidences of the poet's changing of residence to Bath in Somerset, England, and to Wells, in Sonnets 26 ("Till whatsoever star that guides my moving"); 153 ("I, sick withal, the help of *bath* desir'd"); and 154 ("This brand she quenched in a cool *well* by"). Further, some commentators went even farther and said that Shakespeare went to Southern or Western Europe, as, they said, might be evident from Sonnet 33:

Full many a glorious morning have I seen
Flatter the mountain tops with sovereign eye,
Kissing with golden face the meadows green,
Gilding pale streams with heavenly alchemy,
Anon permit the basest clouds to ride
With ugly rack on his celestial face...

G. Sarrazin said that these lines " 'definitely indicate a long residence (of the poet) in a mountainous region, and that too in a land rich in sunlight' " (Ingram, 80). The description may point to some region in southern or western Europe. Now, all these probably, point to the autobiographical quality of the Sonnets, though very sparingly.

When we say that the Sonnets are autobiographical, we must not forget that of the 154 sonnets, about 94 are admittedly impersonal and only about 60 are debatably perseonal or autobiographical. At the point of our knowledge of Shakespearean, we should not make any hasty and conclusive comment about the supposed autobiographical quality of the Sonnets. Here, too, we may recall what Matthew Arnold said in a sonnet about Shakespeare: "Others abode our question. Thou art free./ We ask and ask: Thou smilest and art still,/Out-topping knowledge." And yet the search is on. As recently as in 1905, Lytton Strachey wrote about the search for the supposedly autobiographical elements in the Sonnets: " 'He is a bold man who sets out in quest of the key which shall unlock the mystery of Shakespeare's Sonnets. In that country the roads make heavy walking, and 'airy tongues that syllable men's name' lure the unwary traveller at every turn into paths already white with the bones of innumerable commentators. Yet the fascination of the search seems to outweigh its dangers, for each year adds to the number of these sanguine explorers, while it engulfs their predecessors in a deeper oblivion.' " (Jones, 52). And the search should continue, for, as T.S. Eliot said, "About anyone so great as Shakespeare, it is probable that we can never be right; and if we can never be right, it is better that we should from time to time change our way of being wrong" (Henri Fluchere, *Shakespeare,* trans. Guy Hamilton, London, etc., Longmans, Green and Co., 1953, the fly-leaf).

❐

X

Criticisms and Appreciations of the Sonnets

Till the beginning of the 19th century, there were few critical and appreciative approaches to the Sonnets. Francis Meres, in his 1598 edition of the Sonnets, was the first person to appreciate the poems. In his *Palladis Tamia* (1598), in which those Sonnets appeared, he wrote: " 'As the soul of Euphorbus was thought to live in Pythagoras: so the sweete wittie soul of *Ovid* lives in the mellifluous and honeytongued *Shakespeare,* witness his *Venus and Adonis,* his *Lucrece,* his sugred Sonnets among his private friends, &c.' " (Jones, 35). John Benson (d. 1667), in his 'Epistle to the Reader' of his 1640 edition of the Sonnets, wrote that the poems were " 'excellent and sweetely composed Poems' " in which 'you shall finde them *Seren,* cleere and eligantly plaine, such gentle straines as shall recreate and not perplex your braine, no intricacie or cloudly stuffe to puzzell intellect, but perfect eloquence; such as will raise your admiration to his (Shakespeare's) praise' " (Jones, 35).

In 1780, Edmund Malone, an Irish barrister who came to London and became a great Shakespeare scholar, added a volume, *Poems* (Shakespeare's Sonnets), to the multi-volume edition of Shakespeare's plays by George Steevens, another great Shakespeare scholar. In *Poems,* Malone appreciated the versification of the Sonnets: " 'I do not perceive that the versification of these pieces is less smooth and harmonious than that of Shakespeare's other compositions' " (Jones, 37).

All these are appreciations. We find criticisms of Shakespeare's sonnets firstly from George Steevens (1736-1800), as we have said, a great Shakespearean scholar like Capell and Malone. In 1766, he published *Twenty of the Plays of Shakespeare*; in 1773, ten volumes of Shakespeare's works; in 1778, Shakespeare's works, again in ten volumes; and in 1785, that still again in ten volumes. In 1790, Malone published Shakespeare's works in ten volumes, and this excited his jealousy, and he published Shakespeare's works in fifteen volumes in 1793. In this edition of Shakespeare's works, he commented on the Sonnets of Shakespeare: " 'Had Shakespeare produced no other works than these, his name would have reached us with as little celebrity as time has conferred on that of Thomas Watson, an older and much more elegant sonneteer' " (Jones, 37-38). It may be mentioned here that Steevens was certainly a great scholar of Elizabethan literature and Elizabethan stage, but he was not a great critic, and so his comments on the Sonnets may be taken only with a pinch of salt.

George Chalmers (1742-1825) was both an appreciator and a critic of the Sonnets. He was a Scottish antiquarian and writer, and published his *Apology for the Believers* in the 'Shakespeare-Papers' in 1797, where he had balanced comments, of course from his own point of view, on the Sonnets of Shakespeare: " 'Of those Amatory Verses (the Sonnets of Shakespeare), it may be truly said, that as a whole poem, which is often tied together by a very slight ligature, they have two of the worst faults, that can degrade any writing; they are obscure; and they are tedious. Spenser, who furnished the model of them, has his obscurities, and tediousness; but he has withal, more distinctness, in his topicks, and more facility, in his style: Shakespeare plainly endeavoured to go beyond the mark of his rivalry; but, in affecting the sublime, he sunk, by a natural cadence, into the unintelligible....Of such a poet, as Shakespeare, it may easily be conceived, that he has many happy phrases, and elegant lines, though they are generally darkened by conceit, and marred by affectation; with as many happy phrases, and elegant lines, Spenser has fewer conceits and less affectation;...Shakespeare, 'fancy's sweetest child', shows sometimes a manifest superiority in *imagination* over Spenser, when this wonderful poet is forming the same images. By an effort of his creative powers, Shakespeare appears to have carried away the palm, in this great quality of a true poet, from his rival, even when Spenser put forth his whole strength, in cultivating the same field' " (Jones, 38).

After George Chalmers, we do not hear of any important appreciations or criticisms of the Sonnets, till the Romantic period. At the beginning of the Romantic period, William Wordsworth very harshly criticised the Sonnets, particularly the 'Dark Lady Sonnets', but appreciated others, of course with reservations: " 'These sonnets beginning at cxxvii to his mistress, are worse than a puzzle-peg. They are abominably harsh, obscure, and worthless. The others are for the most part much better, have many fine lines (,) very fine lines and passages. They are also in many places warm with passion. Their chief faults — and heavy ones they are — are sameness, tediousness, quaintness, and elaborate obscurity' " (Jones, 41). This Wordsworth wrote about 1803, but he modified his stance in 1815 when he wrote about the Sonnets in his *Essays, Supplementary to the Preface to 'Lyrical Ballads'*: " '...in no part of the writings of this Poet (Shakespeare) is found, in an equal compass, a greater number of exquisite feelings felicitously expressed' " (Jones, 43).

Wordsworth's friend S.T.Coleridge differed from him in a big way. Coleridge was almost idolatrous regarding Shakespeare, and was an objector to Wordsworth's accusations about Shakespeare's Sonnets, Contrary to what Wordsworth said, he wrote: " 'I see no elaborate obscurity and very little quaintness — nor do I know any sonnets that will bear such frequent reperusal: so rich in metre, so full of thought and *exquisitest* diction' " (Jones, 42). In his *Table Talk* (14 May, 1833), Coleridge further wrote about the sonnets of Shakespeare : " 'These extraordinary sonnets form, in fact, a poem of so many stanzas of fourteen lines each; and, like the passion which inspired them, the sonnets are always the same, with a variety of expression, — continuous, if you regard the lover's soul — distinct, if you listen to him, as he heaves them sigh after sigh. "These sonnets, like the *Venus and Adonis*, and the *Rape of Lucrece*, are characterised by boundless fertility and laboured condensation of thought, with perfection of sweetness in rhythm and metre. These are the essentials in the budding of a great poet' " (Jones, 45).

John Keats, the most Shakespearean of poets, in a letter to John Hamilton Reynolds, wrote on 22 November, 1817, about the sonnets of Shakespeare: " 'One of the three Books I have with me is Shakespeare's Poems: I ne'er found so many beauties in the Sonnets — they seem to be full of fine things said unintentionally — in the intensity of working out conceits. Is it to be borne? Hark ye!

When lofty trees I see barren of leaves
　　Which erst from heat did canopy the herd,
And summer's green all girded up in sheaves,
　　Borne on the bier with white and bristly beard.

He has left nothing to say about nothing or anything: ....He overwhelms and genuine Love of Poesy with all manner of abuse, talking about —

a poet's rage
and stretched metre of an antique song' '' (Jones, 46).

Percy Byeshe Shelley's comment on the Sonnets can be had from his 'Note on the Hundred and Eleven Sonnets of Shakespeare' in *The Works of Percy Byeshe Shelley,* edited by Roger Ingpen and Walter E. Peck (1965), vol. vii, p. 152: " 'That famous passage in that pathetic sonnet in which, addressing a dear friend, he complains of his own situation as an actor, and says that his nature is (I quote from memory)

Subdued
To what it works in, like the dyer's hand.

Observe these images, how simple they are, and yet animated with what intense poetry and passion.' '' (Jones, 46-47).

William Hazlitt agrees with George Steevens and George Chalmers that Shakespeare's Sonnets fetched no admiration. In 1815, Hazlitt wrote about the Sonnets: '''It is not improbable, that if Shakespeare had written nothing but his Sonnets and smaller poems, he would, (...,) have been assigned to the class of cold, artificial writers, who had no genuine sense of nature or passion' '' (Jones, 47). But two years after, Hazlitt partially amended the above comment. He again wrote about the Sonnets in his *The Round Table and Characters of Shakespeare's Plays*: ''The subjects of them seems to be somewhat equivocal; but many of them are highly beautiful in themselves, and interesting as they relate to the state of personal feelings of the author....In all these, as well as in many others, there is a mild tone of sentiment, deep, mellow, and sustained, very different from the crudeness of his earlier poems'' (Hazlitt, 360-61). And yet Hazlitt complained that the Sonnets are ''overcharged and monotonous'' (Jones, 48).

Walter Savage Landor (1775-1864), a poet and stylist, also held an opinion similar to Hazlitt's. In his best known work, *Imaginary Conversation of Literary Men,* the imaginary characters Porson and Landor converse between them. Porson says that in the Sonnets of Shakespeare " 'there sometimes is a singular strength and intensity of thought, with little of that imagination which was afterward to raise him (Shakespeare) highest in the universe of poetry.' '' And to him Landor says: " '....A few of Milton's *Sonnets* are extremely bad: the rest are excellent. Among all Shakespeare's not a single one is very admirable, and a few sink very low. They are hot and pothery: there is much condensation, little delicacy; like raspberry jam without cream, without bread, to break its viscidity....' '' (Jones, 49).

Hazlitt and Landor had qualified appreciation about the Sonnets, but J.A. Noble, a critic, was all praise for the Sonnets. In his article 'The Sonnet in England' which appeared in *Contemporary Review,* xxxviii (1880), Noble said about the Sonnets : " 'There is the recognition of an unmistakable amplitude of treatment, a large utterance, and ensuing upon this a feeling of fellowship with a soul wealthy enough to disdain the smaller economics of the intellect. In these sonnets there is no sense of strain; we do not feel, as in reading Drummond, that the poet has touched his possibilities, but that even in his farthest reaches they are still long ahead of him. Even when the intellectual level attained by an author is not absolutely high, as it is here, there is always a felt charm in his work if it leave such an impression as this; a charm like that which belongs to the feats of some trained athlete who performs what seem muscular miracles with the graceful ease of effortless strength. "Coleridge has spoken of the 'condensation of thought' in these sonnets, Dyce of their 'profound thought', Archbishop Trench of their being 'double-shotted with thought'; but, if we mistake not, the thing which gives to them their specific gravity is not what is usually understood by thought, but what may rather be described as intellectualised emotion — that is, the incarnation of pure emotion, which is itself too rare and attenuated an essence to be adequately and at the same time sustainedly expressed, in a body of symbol or situation which is supplied by the intellect. The simple pouring out of passion is apt to become tiresome to all save the lover and the beloved; but in reading Shakespeare's Sonnets we are sensible of no such loss of gusto; the last is as piquant as the first; and this because the mere passion, which is in itself an ordinary thing — though the passion of a Titan must needs be Titanesque — is supplemented by the tremendous intellectual force which lies behind and beneath it, and bears it up as the foam-bell is borne on the bosom of the great sea....' " (Jones, 50-51).

Lytton Strachey, like Noble, was also an admirer of Shakespeare's sonnets. Again, G.K. Hunter was imbued by the Sonnets of Shakespeare. He said about the Sonnets: " 'The effect that is almost unique in Shakespeare is that of immediate contact with the suffering mind' " (Jones, 123). But in spite of all the approbations of some of the great critics, the sonnets of Shakespeare have not attracted as many admirers as his plays have been able to. Stefan George wrote about this and about the causes thereof: " 'Among the reasons why Shakespeare's Sonnets are still little esteemed by us, the most important, aside from the requirement of a very high understanding of verse, is an internal one:

that our custom regards all poetry as entirely 'romantic', but these quatorzains, though supreme poetry, are entirely 'unromantic', the external (reason) concerns the subject' " (Jones, 54).

In spite of all these various criticisms, in 1934, L.C. Knights said that "there is so little genuine criticism" about the Sonnets (Jones, 74). To Knights, the Sonnets dealing with the rival poets (Sonnets 78-86) are superior to the rest. Knights criticised the Sonnets thus: " 'It is not merely that the imagery is elaborated out of all proportion to any complexity of thought or feeling, the emotion is suspended whilst the conceit is developed, as it were, in its own right. Similarly the sound and movement of the verse, the alliteration, repetition and assonance, seem to exist as objects of attention in themselves rather than as the medium of a compulsive force working from within. Such emotion as is communicated is both vague and remote' " (Jones, 80-81). Knights, however, praised the Sonnets for their immediacy and precisions. He wrote: " 'In the Sonnets, as in the later plays, the imagery gives immediacy and precision, and it demands and fosters an alert attention' " (Jones, 91).

G.W. Knight believed that the 'story' of the Fair Youth and the Dark Lady were dubious, but he thinks that thereby the beauty of the Sonnets were not minimised. He wrote: "Whatever we think of the story, in so far as there is one, there flowers from its soil some of the world's greatest love-poetry. From this nettle-bed of vice, we pluck the flower, genius. Nor is the poetry itself anything but healthy: throughout there breaths an air of simplicity, honesty and purity, shirking nothing, and somehow finally establishing a spiritual principle of the kind which we naturally associate with the noblest literature" (Knight, 22). Like G.W. Knight, F.T. Prince also highly praised the Sonnets. Prince wrote: " 'Shakespeare's poetic sovereignty might be said to be enough to account for the pre-eminence of the Sonnets: they are the overflow of the life and mind of this genius, as Petrarch's were the overflow of *his* life and mind' " (Jones, 181). John Dover Wilson wrote about the appreciations of the Sonnets of Shakespeare by two great critics, in his book *The Sonnets:* J.W. Lever and C.S. Lewis. He wrote : " 'There is no parallel', writes J.W. Lever in a sensitive and learned book on *The Elizabethan Love Sonnet,* 'in the whole corpus of Renaissance poetry to Shakespeare's sustained exploration of the theme of friendship through more than 120 sonnets' " (Wilson, xiv). And Wilson wrote about the appreciation by C.S. Lews: "C.S. Lewis, the other critic (I must quote), proclaims the *Sonnets* not only as unique in the period of the

Renaissance but as the supreme love-poetry of the world'' (Wilson, xiv).

On the other hand, John Crowe Ransom criticised the structure of the Sonnets, in general. Ransom said: " 'Structurally, Shakespeare is a careless workman' " (Jones, 104). Ransom found metaphysical strains in the Sonnets: " 'He (Shakespeare) is upon occasion metaphysical enough, but not so metaphysical as Donne....' " (Jones, 105). Winifred M.T. Nowottny did not agree with Ransom, regarding the structural defects of the Sonnets; he rather praised the structure. In 1952, Nowottny wrote about the form of the Sonnets: " 'the *Sonnets* reveal Shakespeare's strong sense of form, and that it is with respect to their form that the peculiar feature or striking effects of individual sonnets may best be understood' " (Jones, 111). But, again, M.M. Reese would not agree with Nowottny: Reese thought that Shakespeare's faults in his sonnets were due to his erronous preference for the sonnet-form of Surrey over against the Italian or Petrarchan form. The form of Surrey was very widely followed by most of the Elizabethan sonneteers, and Shakespeare could not but join the band-wagon. Reese thought that this form had inherent weaknesses which Shakespeare was heir to. Let us quote Reese at some length: ''Although he adopted Petrarch's invariable break between the octave and the sestet, Shakespeare used Surrey's sonnet form of a progressive movement of quatrains, stating, repeating and illustrating the theme, which was then summarised in a final couplet. This form used seven rhymes, thus: *abab cdcd efef gg*. The Petrarchan sonnet had only four, or sometimes five, rhymes: the octave always went *abbaabba* and the sestet varied *cdcdcd* with the occasional introduction of a third rhyme. This was the form used by Wordsworth and by Milton, Milton dispensing with the break in sense between octave and sestet and making his poem an organic whole. The form chosen by Shakespeare lent itself to the Elizabethan enthusiasm for elaborate conceits: the necessary matter could be crammed into the first quatrain, or even into the first couplet, leaving two quatrains for the display of vituosity. It is perhaps for this reason that so few of the hundreds of Elizabethan sonnets, Shakespeare's included, attain the highest level: the chosen form was inimical to great poetry. It was inimical particularly to the two great characteristics of Shakespeare's dramatic verse, its intense concentration and the swift, unimpeded flow of its imagery. Concentration is inevitably diffused when the point is made in the opening lines and nothing remains but to elaborate it; and the self-enclosed movement of the quatrains would not allow the images to stream into one another and obliterate the pattern of the verse. Sonneteering was well enough for Shakespeare at a time when much of this dramatic verse was still static and he was content to stop its movement while he played with a seductive conceit until it died in its own too much. It was, too, an ideal form for the expression of feelings that were gentle rather than powerful, obligatory but not compulsive. It would never have served as a medium for passionate experience'' (Reese, 420-21). But even if we admit the constraints of the sonnet form Shakespeare used, yet we must say that the highly powerful poetic genius of Shakespeare could easily overcome the impediments of the sonnet form he had chosen.

However, to the appreciations of great critics, we may add that most of the Sonnets are evidently very dramatic in form. They are not addressed to some Fair Youth or some Dark Lady, but in them the poet is, as if, talking to a real person — a person of flesh and blood. Notice, for instance, Sonnet 26:

> Lord of my love, to whom in vassalage
> Thy merit hath my duty strongly knit,
> To thee I send this written embassage,
> To witness duty, not to show my wit :...

Such highly dramatic sonnets are certainly not very common. Again, most of the Sonnets are very lyrical. Witness, for instance, Sonnet 79:

> Whilst I alone did call upon thy aid,
> My verse alone had all thy gentle grace;
> But now my gracious numbers are decay'd,
> And my sick Muse doth give another place.

That Shakespeare was a great lyric poet can be seen also in the fact that he has as many as 66 songs in his 37 plays. And, lastly, Shakespeare must be appreciated for introducing so-far-not-employed themes of sonnets in his Sonnets, thereby enriching sonnets in general. Of course Milton and others, after him, employed variety of themes in sonnets, but, perhaps, Shakespeare was the pioneer in this regard. However, how far is Shakespeare Shakespeare for his sonnets? A.C. Ward very confidently answered: ''If Shakespeare had written nothing but his *Sonnets* he would still have a secure place among the great poets'' (Ward, vol. I, 215).

❐

XI
The Sonnets Explained

The 154 sonnets of Shakespeare can broadly be divided into two groups: the first 126 sonnets are addressed to some Fair Youth and the rest are addressed to some Dark Lady. In the first seventeen of the 126 'Fair Youth Sonnets', the poet persuades the Fair Youth to produce his own copies by marrying some fortunate girl, so that the charm of his beauty may be perpetuated. The theme of urging a beautiful youth to marry to multiply and thus perpetuate beauty was not new to Shakespeare, and, perhaps, he got the idea of writing a sonnet-sequence on this theme from Sir Philip Sidney's (1554-86) *Arcadia,* a pastoral-chivalric romance in prose and verse, which Sidney wrote for entertainment of his sister, the Countess of Pembroke. In *Arcadia,* which Sidney wrote in imitation of the Italian poet Jacopo Sannazaro's (1458-1530) pastoral romance *Arcadia,* Cecropia urges her niece Philoclea to marry and have multiple copies of her Ledaesque beauty. Cecropia tells her: "No, no, my dear niece, Nature, when you were first born, vowed you a woman, and as she made you child of a mother, so do your best to be the mother of a child. She gave you beauty to move love; she gave you wit to know love; she gave you an excellent body to reward love; which kind of liberal rewarding is crowned with an unspeakable felicity. For this, as it bindeth the receiver, so it makes happy the bestower. This doth not impoverish but enrich the giver. O, the comforts of comforts, to see your children grow up, in whom you are, as it were, eternised!" This theme of Sannazaro's *Arcadia* lived through Sidney's *Arcadia* and was reutilised by Shakespeare in his sequence of seventeen sonnets, *i.e.,* the first seventeen of the 154 sonnets.

Shakespeare must have been infatuated by this theme for long, for we find this same idea or theme recurring in his other works also. For instance, in *Venus and Adonis* (lines, 163-174) 'Sick-thoughted' Venus persuades the 'Rose-cheek'd' Adonis to make love to her thus:

'Torches are made to light, jewels to wear,
Dainties to taste, fresh beauty for the use,
Herbs for their smell, and sappy plant to bear:
Things growing to themselves are growth's abuse.
  Seeds spring from seeds, and beauty breedeth beauty;
  Thou wast begot — to get it is thy duty.
'Upon the earth's increase why shouldest thou feed,
Unless the earth with thy increase be fed?
By law of nature thou art bound to breed,
That thine may live when thou thyself art dead;
  And so in spite of death thou dost survive,
  In that thy likeness still is left alive.'

Again the same theme is to be found in *Romeo and Juliet* whose central theme is also love. But in this case, the persuasion to marry is not by a lady to another lady as in Sidney's *Arcadia,* or by a lady to a young man as in *Venus and Adonis,* but by a young man to a fair and young lady. In *Romeo and Juliet,* Romeo is in love with Rosaline (not yet with Juliet), the daughter of Prince Escalus. But Rosaline "will not stay the siege of loving terms,/Nor bide th' encounter of assailing eyes,/Not open her lap to saint-seducing gold" (I, i, 210-12). So Romeo is utterly dejected and tells Benvolio that she is thereby causing waste to the world (I, i, 216-18):

She hath, and in that sparing makes huge waste;
For beauty, starv'd with her severity,
Cuts beauty off from all posterity.

In those days, it was the custom to marry early, but the Fair Youth would not espouse a fair maid. The poet tells him that time will soon erase the beauty of his body, and then it will be a great loss to the world. Hence, the poet is urging him not to lead the life of an anchorite, but to marry and thus increase nature's store of beauty. This urge of the poet to persuade the Fair Youth to marry grew out of his love of the beauty which is resident in the person of the youth. And so, this love of the poet for the Fair Youth's beauty or the Fair Youth himself is non-carnal — it is a love of the beauty, of the spirit, not of the body — a kind of love that Plato describes in his *Symposium* where Diotima tells Socrates that "the beauties of the body are as nothing to beauties of the soul."

In the remaining sonnets of the Fair Youth Sonnets group, Shakespeare speaks of diverse matters — his journey away from the

Fair Youth, stealing away of the Dark Lady by the Fair Youth from the poet, his rival poet, and his diverse and complex emotional stresses consequent upcn all these, etc. — all of which, severally and collectively, revolve round his love for the Fair Youth. However, let us now try to understand these sonnets themselves.

1

From fairest creatures we desire increase,
That therby beauty's rose might never die,
But as the riper should by time decrease,
His tender heir might bear his memory:
But thou, contracted to thine own bright eyes,
Feedest thy light's flame with self-substantial fuel,
Making a famine where abundance lies,
Thyself thy foe, to thy sweet self too cruel.
Thou that art now the world's fresh ornament,
And only herald to the gaudy spring,
Within thy own bud buriest thy content,
And, tender churl, mak'st waste in niggarding.
  Pity the world, or else this glutton be,
  To eat the world's due, by the grave and thee.

The poet here says that all men desire that the world grow more and more beautiful through increase of beautiful things — beautiful flowers, beautiful animals, beautiful birds, and, to cap it all, beautiful human beings — so that the loveliness of beauty or beauty itself ('beauty's rose') may never vanish from the earth : "From fairest creatures we desire increase,/That thereby beauty's rose might never die". Perhaps, the poet, here, does not mean all sorts of human beauties or graces or aesthetic qualities, such as delicate manners, fineness of speech, sublimity of friendship, witticism, etc., but only the beauty of the form of human beings. Not that he does not wonder at the attributes of man. In *Hamlet,* the Prince of Denmark is awe-struck at the divine qualities or faculties and the admirable graces of man: "What a piece of work is a man! How noble in reason! how infinite in faculties! in form and moving, how express and admirable! in action, how like an angel! in apprehension, how like a god! the beauty of the world! the paragon of animals! If the Fair Youth of the Sonnets be the Earl of Pembroke, then it may be probable that when Shakespeare was writing these lines for Hamlet, the Prince of Denmark, he had in his mind's eye the model of the same Earl who was exquisitely beautiful.

The poet urges upon the Fair Youth to marry and produce children, so that when he will grow old ('riper') with the passage of time and consequently will of necessity decrease in beauty, his children ('tender heir') will be able to show to posterity or the coming generation copies ('memory') of the beauty he is now flaunting about: "But as the riper should by time decrease,/His tender heir might bear his memory". The poet is aware of the cruelty of Time that destroys everything in its passage. In Sonnets 63 and 64 also the poet is concerned about "time's injurious hand" (63) and "Time's fell hand" (64). It is for this reason — that Time will in course of its passage consume the Fair Youth's beauty — that the poet is persuading him to marry. But the Fair Youth is not interested in entering into a wed-lock with a girl: he is, like Narcissus, only interested in himself: "But thou, contracted to thine own bright eyes." The poet is, therefore, comparing the Fair Youth with a candle ('self-substantial fuel') whose light is consuming the body of the candle itself: "Feed'st thy light's flame with self-substantial fuel". And thus the youth is graudally and imperceptively creating a want of beauty ('famine'), though now he has an abundance of it: "Making a famine where abundance lies". It is for this reason that the poet says that the Fair Youth is his own enemy ('Thyself thy foe') and that he is cruel to himself: "Thyself thy foe, to thy sweet self too cruel."

The beauty of the Fair Youth, now, is like a 'fresh ornament' of the world, and is like the harbinger of the sweet and glittering ('gaudy') spring: "Thou that art now the world's fresh ornament,/And only herald to the gaudy spring". But the youth is quite insoucient about the importance of his own beauty: he is burying his own beauty within himself, and is not intent upon propagating it for the joy of the world. He is like a flower-bud that is stunting its own growth so that, instead of blosoming, it is withering into itself ('buriest thy content'): "Within thine own bud buriest thy content". Therefore, the poet feels offended, and in disgust calls the Fair Youth a niggard or an unwarrantedly thrifty or stingy person who does not like to spend or sow seeds for growing plants, *i.e.* does not like to marry and produce children from his own blood: "And, tender churl, mak'st waste in niggarding." As, yet, the Fair Youth does not give consent to marrying and procreating children, the poet, in the *envoi* (or envoy) of the sonnet, asks him to pity the world, for without the copies of his beautiful form, it will wax poor. If he does not marry and procreate, the poet would like him to devour whatever beauty the world now has to offer, by dying a celibate: "Pity the world, or else this glutton be,/To eat the world's due, by the grave and thee."

The word 'increase', in the sense in which it is used in this sonnet (line 1), can also be found in line 37 of Dryden's *Cymon and Iphigenia:* "The World when wast, he peopled with increase". The first two lines of this sonnet can be compared with lines 225-227 at *Twelfth Night,* I, v, where Viola-Cesario tells Olivia: "Lady, you are the cruell'st she alive,/If you lead these graces to the grave,/And leave the world no copy." Further, this Sonnet can also be compared with Milton's *Comus* where Comus, the son of Bacchus and Circe, tells the captivated chaste Lady:

> Beauty is Nature's coin; must not be hoarded,
> But must be current; and the good thereof
> Consists in mutual and partaken bliss,
> Unsavoury in th' enjoyment of itself.

2

When forty winters shall besiege thy brow,
And dig deep trenches in thy beauty's field,
Thy youth's proud livery, so gaz'd on now,
Will be a tatter'd weed, of small worth held:
They being ask'd where all thy beauty lies,
Where all the treasure of thy lusty days, —
To say within thine own deep-sinken eyes,
Were an all-eating shame and thriftless praise.
How much more praise deserv'd thy beauty's use,
If thou couldst answer — "This fair child of mine
Shall sum my count, and make my old excuse," —
Proving his beauty by succession thine!
This were to be new-made when thou art old,
And see thy blood warm when thou feel'st it cold.

Here the advice of the poet to the Fair Youth is the same as in the previous sonnet, here only the arguments are different. In the previous sonnet, the poet told him that if he did not leave behind copies of his beautiful form, the world would be the poorer for that, and in this sonnet the poet tells him that if he leaves behind him his progeny, only then his beauty will be perpetuated, and only then will the inevitable decay of his beauty will be enough compensated. If he procreates a child, only then can he say: "This fair child of mine/Shall sum my count, and make my old excuse." In this sense, the present sonnet is complementary to the previous one. The poet says that when the Fair Youth will attain the age of forty years or thereabout ('forty winters shall besiege thy brow'), then there will appear deep wrinkles ('trenches') in his beautiful face ('beauty's field'): "When forty winters shall besiege thy brow,/And dig deep trenches in thy beauty's field". Here the word 'forty' does not mean exactly forty, but a large number. John Dover Wilson commented on this word: " 'Used indefinitely to express a large number' (...). Shakespeare himself was about thirty when he wrote this" (Wilson, 94). It may be mentioned here that Shakespeare was fond of the numbers four, forty, forty-thousand, etc. For instance, in *Hamlet,* Hamlet tells his Queen-mother about his love for Ophelia: "I loved Ophelia: forty thousand brothers/Could not, with all their quantity of love,/Make up my sum" (V, i, 263-65). Again, Sir Andrew in *Twelfth Night* tells Olivia: "....I had rather than forty pounds I were at home."

The beauty of youth that the Fair Youth now feels proud of ('Thy youth's proud livery') and which people now admiringly look at ('gaz'd on now') will become like valueless ('of small worth') tattered ('totter'd') weed: "Thy youth's proud livery, so gaz'd on now,/Will be a totter'd weed of small worth held". The poet means to say that, like anything else, the beauty of the Fair Youth is also evanescent. At a future time (when he will be forty), one may ask the Fair Youth 'Where is all his beauty?' or 'Where are those days in which he would utilise his beauty in amorous enterprises or in Casanovasesque frolicks?' ('lusty days'): "They being ask'd where all thy beauty lies,/Where all the treasure of thy lusty days". Then if the Fair Youth answers that all that beauty and those amorous days are now there in his deeply shrunk ('sunken') eyes, then that will be an utter shame to him — shame that will, as if, eat up himself — ('all-eating shame') and that will be a sort of praise to his 'wasteful unprofitableness' or 'praise which will not profit' him ('thriftless praise'): "To say within thine own deep sunken eyes/Were an all-eating shame, and thriftless praise."

The poet repents because such praise is actually no praise at all. He, on the other hand, wonders that if the Fair Youth would procreate a child, then he could proudly say, pointing at his 'fair child' that that child is showing that the balance of his rights and wrongs in his doings is in his favour ('Shall sum my count'); and thereby his wrong doings would be ignored ('my old excuse'). By saying so the Fair Youth would be able to prove the worth of his beauty, once again, because he would then prove that his beauty is now inherited, or is inheritable, too: "How much more praise deserv'd thy beauty's use/If thou couldst answer: 'This fair child of mine/Shall sum my count, and make my old excuse', —/Proving his beauty by succession thine!"

In the concluding couplet, the poet tells the Fair Youth that his beauty will have to be renovated or refurbished ('This were to be new made'), when the Fair Youth will become old: "This were to be new made when thou art old". And, further, the poet tells him that he should feel the warmth of his blood, when it will become cold, in the warmth of the blood of his child: "And see thy blood warm when thou feel'st it cold." Kerrigan found a parallel to line 14 at *Henry V* (III, i, 18-19) where King Henry commands his soldiers thus: "On, on, you noblest English,/ Whose blood is fet from fathers of war-proof!"

3

Look in thy glass, and tell the face thou viewest
Now is the time that face should form another,
Whose fresh repair if now thou not renewest
Thou dost beguile the world, unbless some mother.
For where is she so fair whose unear'd womb
Disdain the tillage of thy bushandry?
Or who is he so fond will be the tomb
Of his self-love to stop posterity?
Thou art thy mother's glass, and she in thee
Calls back the lovely April of her prime;
So thou through windows of thine age shalt see
Despite of wrinkles this thy golden time.
    But if thou live remember'd not to be,
    Die single, and thine image dies with thee.

John Dover Wilson summarised the substance of this poem thus: "Just as your mother when looking at you can see herself as she was in the fresh beauty of her girlhood, so you, when womanlike you look in the glass to see how to keep your face in repair, will realize that the only way to do so is to hand on that face to your child, as your mother handed her lovely one to you — and what woman would refuse to become the mother of such a child or indeed what other man would so defeat his own interest as to deny posterity to himself? Die single, your loveliness dies with you and you choose to be forgotten" (Wilson, 95). The poet asks the Fair Youth to look at his image in a looking glass and tell that image ('the face thou viewest') that it is high time that that image should form its copy: "Look in thy glass, and tell the face thou viewest/Now is the time that face should form another". That image now is in fresh condition ('repair'), but if the Fair Youth does not renew it through reproduction, he will cozen ('beguile') the world, or make the world lose beautiful things, and he will deprive some girl of the benefit of maternity ('unless some mother'): "Whose fresh repair if now thou not renewest/Thou dost beguile the world, unbless some mother."

The poet says that there is no such fair girl who has not shared a bed with a man ('unear'd womb') and who will hate cohabitating with the Fair Youth ('tillage of thy husbandry'): "For where is she so fair whose unear'd womb/Disdains the tillage of thy husbandry?" John Kerrigan commented on lines 5-6: "Echoes a model letter in Erasmus's *De Conscribendis Epistolis* in which a young nobleman is urged to marry. Shakespeare apparently knew the epistle from Thomas Wilson's translation included in his *Art of Rhetoric* (1553): 'If that man be punished who little heedeth the maintenance of his tillage....what punishment is he worthy to suffer that refuseth to plough that land which, being tilled, yieldeth children' " (Kerrigan, 174). There is a parallel to the sense of the word 'unear'd' at *Antony and Cleopatra,* II,ii, 233: "He ploughed her, she cropped." The poet says that there is none who is so foolish ('fond') as to die loving only his own self (like Narcissus) and thus hand down nothing to posterity: "Or who is he so fond will be the tomb/Of his self-love to stop posterity?"

The poet tells the Fair Youth that he himself is the copy ('glass') of his mother, and that his mother recalls ('Calls back') the sweet days of her young age ('lovely April of her prime'): "thou art thy mother's glass, and she in thee/Calls back the lovely April of her prime". In *The Rape of Lucrece* also Shakespeare uses this simile: "in the child the father's image lies" (line 1753). Again, in the same poem (lines 1758-1759), after Lucrece's suicide, following her being raped by Sextus Tarquinius, her father laments: " 'Poor broken glass, I often did behold/ In thy sweet semblance my old age new born...". In the same way, the poet says, if the Fair Youth marries and procreates a child, he will be able to see ('shalt see') his present beauty and vitality ('this thy golden time') in the person of his child by his myopic eyes or 'eyes bleared by age', or with his hazy vision, though then the fair Youth will have furrows ('wrinkles') in his face: "So thou through windows of thine age shalt see/Despite of wrinkles this thy golden time." In line 11, the word 'windows' does not refer to the glass spoken of earlier, but to 'eyes bleared by old age'. The cue to this meaning can be found in the fact that "Elizabethan windows were much less trasparent than our own" (Kerrigan, 175).

But, contrarily, if the Fair Youth does not want to be commemorated ('remember'd not to be'), then the poet will hopelessly ask him to die a bachelor ('Die single'); and in that case, the poet further says, the beauty of the Fair Youth will also die for ever at the time of his death: "But if thou live remember'd not to be,/Die single, and thine image dies with thee." A parallel to the couplet may be found at *King Henry VI*, Part I, V, iv, 100: "Thy ignomy sleep with thee in the grave,/But not remember'd in thy epitaph."

4

Unthrifty loveliness, why dost thou spend
Upon thy self thy beauty's legacy?
Nature's bequest gives nothing, but doth lend,
And being frank she lends to those are free:
Then, beautious niggard, why dost thou abuse
The bounteous largess given thee to give?
Profitless usurer, why dost thou use
So great a sum of sums, yet canst not live?
For having traffic with thyself alone
thou of thyself thy sweet self dost deceive:
Then how when nature calls thee to be gone —
What acceptable audit canst thou leave?
Thy unus'd beauty must be tomb'd with thee,
Which used lives th' executor to be.

Kerrigan said that in the ten sonnets beginning from this one, there is the influence of Marlow's *Hero and Leadner* (1598). In the previous sonnet, the poet told the Fair Youth that his beauty was a legacy from his mother — beauty which the poet wishes he spends for furtherance of beauty through marriage and procreation. But the youth does otherwise: he unwisely spends his beauty, that he got from his mother, ('beauty's legacy') on himself, on his own person, to further his own beauty, like Narcissus. This is why the poet addresses him as 'Unthrifty loveliness' — lovely youth who spends without discrimination, drying up his store ('Unthrifty'). The poet asks him why he does so: "Unthrifty loveliness, who dost thou spend/Upon thy self thy beauty's legacy?" The poet says that nature never gives anything for ever, for good, but she only lends out. Nature's legacy ('bequest') can only be borrowed : "Nature's bequest gives nothing, but doth lend". And nature gives or lends only to those who are ready, or liberal ('free') enough, to lend to others. Nature herself is liberal ('frank') and so she expects that those who will borrow from her must be liberal to lend: "And being frank she lends to those are free".

If this be the state of affairs ('Then'), the poet asks the Fair Youth, why is he ('beauteous niggard') misusing his abundant store of beauty ('bounteous largess') that has been given to him for reinvesting ('to give') in furthering of it?: "Then, beauteous niggard, why dost thou abuse/The bounteous given thee to give?" The youth is enjoying the interest of his legacy ('usurer'), but by doing that he is really not getting any profit ('Profitless'). So the poet asks him why he utilises his great quantity of beauty ('sum of sums') on himself, or for himself, though by such utilisation he is getting no 'benefit from living, as the childless niggard does not': "Profitless usurer, why dost thou use/So great a sum of sums, yet canst not live?"

Being immured in himself, by being interested only in himself, and by utilising that legacy only on himself ('having traffic with thyself alone'), the youth is cozenning his own 'sweet self': "For having traffic with thyself alone/Thou of thyself thy sweet self dost deceive". The poet asks him, if he does not budge from his stand of not marrying, and if in due course of time nature bids him to leave his 'mortal coil', then what justifiable account of the legacy that he received from nature will he submit to her?: "Then how when nature calls thee to be gone —/ What acceptable audit canst thou leave?" The poet says that if things go like this, if the Fair Youth remains unresponsive to his persuasions, then the 'unus'd beauty' of the youth will only perish with his death. Contrarily, if the youth uses his beauty properly, that is if he transfers his beauty to his off-springs, then those off-springs would execute the legacy handed down to them by the youth, and, distantly, by nature herself: "Thy unus'd beauty must be tomb'd with thee,/Which used lives th' executor to be."

W.G. Ingram and Theodore Redpath, while commenting on this sonnet, said that many of Shakespeare's sonnets can be taken together into several bunches, like sonnets 1,2,4 and 6. They wrote: "The cumulative interlinked imagery of many groups in the *Sonnets* — one poem echoing the images of perhaps two or more preceding, while in its turn introducing a new image, itself echoed in those succeeding — is well illustrated here. The legacy of beauty to be held for the benefit of posterity, the contrast of capital put to profit or left idle, the account to be rendered, catch up themes from Sonnets 1 and 2, which will through their recombination here in terms of usury lead on to further development in Sonnet 6" (Ingram, 12).

5

Those hours that with gentle work did frame
The lovely gaze where every eye doth dwell
Will play the tyrants to the very same,
And that unfair which fairly doth excel:
For never-resting time leads summer on
To hideous winter and confounds him there,
Sap check'd with frost, and lusty leaves quite gone,
Beauty o'ersnow'd and bareness everywhere:
Then were not summer's distillation left
A liquid prisoner pent in walls of glass,
Beauty's effect with beauty were bereft,
Not it nor no remembrance what it was.
  But flowers distill'd, though they with winter meet,
  Leese but their show: their substance still lives sweet.

In this sonnet, time ('Those hours') is personified — time who will work upon the Fair Youth's beauty and destroy it. But this same time once gently moulded the beautiful shape of the Fair Youth who is an object of attraction to everyone: "Those hours that with gentle work did frame/The lovely gaze where every eye doth dwell". As the Fair Youth will grow old, his fair person which is now excellent will become 'unfair', that is, will be deprived of its excellence. The destructive power of time ('tyrants') is emphasised here, as also in sonnets 55 ('sluttish time'), 64 ('Time's fell hand'), and 65 ('who is spoil of beauty can forbid?'). Time relentlessly rolls the glittering summer forward to the frozening winter, when summer becomes, as if, non-plussed: "For never-resting time leads summer on/To hideous winter and confounds him there". When winter will come, the oozing out of sweet-scenting sap from tree-trunks will stop due to frost, and the trees will be denuded of their lively and amorously green leaves: "Sap check'd with frost, and lusty leaves quite gone". In the same way, when the winter of aging will come to the Fair Youth, his beauty will be covered by its snow and his beauty will not show anywhere in his person.

So it is better, before winter arrives, to collect by distillation, the sweet sap from the bark and preserve the liquid in a capped vial for future uses: "Then were not summer's distillation left/A liquid prisoner pent in walls of glass". Likewise, before the winter of aging comes, it is better to ciphon the essence of a beautiful person into the vials of his offsprings, for the survival of the beauty. But if this is not done, the enchanting power of beauty will be destroyed by the beauty of the Fair

Youth itself: "Beauty's effect with beauty were bereft". Ingram and Redpath paraphrase the 11th line of this sonnet thus: " 'The whole sensory impact and the fruit of beauty would be lost when the beauty itself faded.' " (Ingram, 14). Consequently, neither the original beauty nor the remembrance of it will remain in the world: "Nor it nor no remembrance what it was."

On the other hand, if the essence of the beauty is imprisoned in the offspring, that is, if the beauty finds newer habitat in the progeny, when the former container is worn out, then the essence of the beauty of the former container will continue to exist, albeit in a substitute or copied vial. To express this idea, the poet resorts to the simile of a flower. If the essence of a flower is distilled into the container of a vial, then though the flower may wither in winter and thus lose ('Leese') its beauty ('show'), its essence ('substance') will continue to be there: "But flowers distill'd, though they with winter meet,/Leese but their show: their substance still lives sweet." The envoy of this sonnet may be compared with the last three and a half lines of Sonnet 54:

Sweet roses do not so;
Of their sweet deaths are sweetest odours made:
And so of you, beautious and lovely youth,
When that shall vade, by verse distils your truth.

6

Then let not winter's ragged hand deface
In thee thy summer ere thou be distill'd:
Make sweet some vial; treassure thou some place
With beauty's treasure ere it be self kill'd:
That use is not forbidden usury
Which happies those that pay the willing loan —
That's for thyself to breed another thee,
Or ten times happier be it ten for one;
Ten times thyself were happier than thou art,
If ten of thine ten times refigur'd thee:
Then what could death do if thou shouldst depart
Leaving thee living in posterity?
Be not self-will'd, for thou art much too fair
To be death's conquest and make worms thine heir.

This sonnet continues and confirms the argument of the previous one. It is for this reason that the poet begins with the word 'Then'. The poet urges the Fair Youth not to let his beauty ('summer') be erased ('deface') by the rough ('ragged') hand of winter, *i.e.* by his old age, before his essence is percolated down ('distill'd) into his offsprings: "Then let not winter's ragg'd hand deface/In thee thy summer ere thou be distill'd". Shakespeare here means to say that the beauty of the youth can be perpetuated only through marriage and procreation of offsprings. So he persuades the youth to cohabit with some girl ('vial') and thus make her happy ('sweet') by treasuring his essence in her womb, before his beauty is destroyed by itself by being self-centred ('self-kill'd'). That is, the beauty of the youth will strangle itself ('self-kill'd) should it not perpetuate its existence through offsprings, and therefore, the poet urges upon treasuring his beauty in the womb of some mother: "Make sweet some vial; treasure thou some place/With beauty's treasure ere it be self-kill'd".

Usury does not generally get approbation, but there is at least one exception to the rule. Even if the Fair Youth illegally impregnates a woman, it will not be counted as usury, because in that case the woman will rather be happier by receiving the loan of his essence from him; and moreover, the woman will repay that loan willingly by producing offsprings: "That use is not forbidden usury/Which happies those that pay the willing loan —". It is for his own cause that he should procreate: "That's for thyself to breed another thee". If the youth thus multiplies himself into ten persons like him, people will be ten times happy; and even he himself will be ten times happy. Again, if each of his ten offsprings multiplies himself into further ten offsprings, then even death would not be able to erase the image of the Fair Youth from the earth, because he will then be living in his own progeny:

> Or ten times happier be it ten for one;
> Ten times thyself were happier than thou art,
> If ten of thine ten times refigur'd thee:
> Then what could death do if thou shouldst depart
> Leaving thee living in posterity?

It may be especially noticed that the poet here pleads for 'ten for ten'. This is, perhaps, because, as C.K. Pooler suggested, ten per cent was "the highest rate of interest allowed by the Henry VIII statute" (Ingram, 16). However, Ingram and Redpath wrote that the passage from line 5 to line 10 is a very difficult one, not well explained by commentators: "A difficult passage, surprisingly neglected by all commentators. A fair sense is made if Nature is taken as the usurer (...), and the borrower as the Friend (the Fair Youth) (...). The usury would not be inequitous if the rate of interest were a hundred or even a thousand per cent, for the borrower would be made happier in direct proportion. Ten children would make him ten times happier than one child would. Perhaps a still better sense, however, is given by taking 'use' as having its contemporary sexual meaning and as referring to the Friend's (the Fair Youth's) intercourse with a wife who would 'pay the willing loan' (bear him children)." (Ingram, 16). In line 7, Shakespeare persuaded the youth "to breed another thee". It may be noted here that Shakespeare at times uses the word 'breed' in the sense of 'interest'. For instance, in *The Merchant of Venice,* Antonio tells Shylock (I, ii, 128-29):

for when did friendhsip take
A *breed* for barren metal of his friend? —

In the envoi, the poet requests the Fair Youth not to be wayward and autocephalic, and thus follow what only he himself thinks fit. He is exquisitely beautiful, and therefore he should not be a victim to the inroad of death, and his beautiful person should not be eaten up by the meanest worms, after his death: "Be not self-will'd, for thou art much too fair/To be death's conquest and make worms thine heir." A parallel to the concluding couplet can be found at *Romeo and Juliet* (v, iii, 94-96):

Thou art not conquer'd, beauty's ensign yet
Is crimson in thy lips and in thy cheeks,
And death's pale flag is not advanced there.

7

Lo, in the orient when the gracious light
Lifts up his burning head, each under eye
Doth homage to his new-appearing sight,
Serving with looks his sacred majesty;
And having climb'd the steep-up heavenly hill,
Resembling strong youth in his middle age,
Yet mortal looks adore his beauty still,
Attending on his golden pilgrimage:
But when from highmost pitch, with weary car,
Like feeble age he reeleth from the day,
The eyes,' fore duteous, now converted are
From his low tract, and look another way:
So thou thyself out-going in thy noon,
Unlook'd on diest unless thou get a son.

This sonnet may be called an 'extended simile' because here the poet is simply comparing the Fair Youth with the sun, throughout the whole sonnet. In it, the poet says that when the sun rises in the east ('orient') with his majestic ('gracious') light and raises his fiery head, people offer their worship to his new appearance: "Lo, in the orient when the gracious light/Lifts up his burning head, each under eye/Doth homage to his new-appearing sight,/Serving with looks his sacred majesty". The sun is sacred and so everybody on earth ('each under eye') worships him. This same idea is also to be found at *Romeo and Juliet* (I, i, 116-17) where Benvolio tells Lady Montague: "Madam, an hour before the worshipped sun/Peer'd forth the golden windows of the east." Ingram and Redpath wrote about the first three lines: "Several editors refer (here) to the old superstition of worshipping the rising but not the setting sun. It is natural to ask whether the Elizabethans did not admire sunsets less than the Romantics were to do" (Ingram, 18). People look at the risen sun and admire it, and thus serve the 'sacred majesty' of the sun. Next, the sun rises still higher in the sky, and at a time reaches the apex of the firmament. The poet thinks that it is then the full youth of the sun, because it is then fully revealed: "And having climb'd the steep-up heavenly hill/Resembling strong youth in his middle age". The youth of the sun is the middle of his life. And when the sun is in its youth — full grown youth ('strong youth') — then the people admire the beauty of the sun who is on a pilgrimage from morning to dusk, in his car. But after that the sun becomes tired of its long journey, and so declines sharply from the highest point of the welkin, it, like a man, falls from his former youthful vitality, abruptly. And then those people no more admire that sun; they rather turn their eyes from the declining path of the sun to look somewhere else:

> Yet mortal looks adore his beauty still,
> Attending on his golden pilgrimage:
> But when from highmost pitch, with weary car,
> Like feeble age he reeleth from the day,
> The eyes ('fore duteous') now converted are
> From his low tract, and look another way:

People admire the sun only when it is in its youthful vitality. People ('mortal looks') then adore the beauty of the sun who is on his beautiful ('golden') journey ('pilgrimage'). But when the sun declines from the uppermost sky ('highmost pitch') due to its weariness, people ('The eyes') who previously admired it ('fore duteous') now turn their gaze away from the sun which has now come down to the lower sky ('low tract').

The poet is now comparing the aging Fair Youth with the journeying sun. The Fair Youth is now in his full youth ('in the noon') and so people are now admiring his beauty. But if he does not marry now, he will, on attaining senility, die like the dying sun, without being adored by anyone any more, for the lack of a son: "So thou thyself out-going in thy noon,/Unlook'd on diest unless thou get a son."

In this sonnet, there is a play with the two similar-sounding words: sun and son. Ingram and Redpath said that "The whole tenor of the sonnet suggests the conceit 'son/sun' " (Ingram, 18). In sonnets 5 and 6, the poet dwelt with summer and winter, but in this sonnet he is taking imagery from the sun. The phrase 'highmost pitch' at line 9 is a technical term used in hawking avocation. The first part of this sonnet can be compared with a part of Aaron's speech in *Titus Andronicus* (II, i, 5-8) :

As when the golden sun salutes the morn,
And having gilt the ocean with his beams,
Gallops the zodaic in his glistering coach
And overlooks the highest-peering hills,...

8

Music to hear, why hear'st thou music sadly?
Sweets with sweets war not, joy delights in joy:
Why lov'st thou that which thou receiv'st not gladly,
Or else receiv'st with pleasure thine annoy?
If the true concord of well-tuned sounds
By unions married do offend thine ear,
They do but sweetly chide thee, who confounds
In singleness the parts that thou shouldst bear:
Mark how one string, sweet husband to another,
Strikes each in each by mutual ordering,
Resembling sire, and child, and happy mother,
Who all in one one pleasing note do sing:
Whose speechless song, being many, seeming one,
Sings this to thee: 'Thou single wilt prove none'.

The argument of this sonnet is quite different from those of the previous ones. Further, the previous sonnets were dominated by the images and concepts of rose, light, winter, summer, glass, legacy, time, distillation of essence, usury, sun, etc., but the present sonnet is dominated by such images and concepts as music, sting, concord, etc. It may be noted here that there is also a reference to music in Sonnet 128: "How oft, when thou, my music, music play'st". This sonnet was, perhaps, inspired by a sentence in Sir Philip Sidney's *Arcadia:* "Then can one string make as good music as consort?" The argument of this sonnet is that in a musical instrument of several strings, if one string is struck, then it, in turn, strikes other srtings to create a harmonic that is so sweet to the ear; but if only one string produces sound, then that sound is not so sweet. The fair Youth is, as if, one string which alone cannot produce a sweet harmonic; and so the poet persuades him to strike another string, that is, to inspire a girl through marrying her.

The poet says that music is for hearing and for enjoying. And so he asks the Fair Youth why he is hearing the music sadly: "Music to hear, why hear'st thou music sadly? "In *The Merchant of Venice,* Jessica also does not like music: "I am never merry when I hear sweet music" (v, i. 69). The poet here in this sonnet means to say that the youth is hearing the sound of only a single cord, and so is deprived of the sweet music of several cords struck in unison. the note produced by a single cord is never sweet. When several cords are struck at a time, the mutually complementary sweet notes do not jar among themselves; rather they collectively become more inspiring, for then each note, as if, delights in the notes produced by the neighbouring cords: "Sweet with sweet war not, joy delights in joy." The poet asks the Fair Youth why he is listening to ('lov'st') his advice although he is not glad with that advice. The poet asks if the Fair Youth rather feels a sort of pleasure in being annoyed by the importunate advices of him: "Why lov'st thou that which thou receiv'st not gladly,/Or else receiv'st with pleasure thine annoy?" C.K. Pooler found inconsistency in these two lines, because one does not love that which he does not receive gladly, or one cannot get pleasure by being annoyed. However, according to Pooler, one may paraphrase these two lines thus: " 'If the harmonius agreement of notes in tune and in just musical relation is distasteful to you' " (Ingram, 20).

The poet tells the Fair Youth that if the sweet ('true') harmonic ('concord') of 'well-tuned sounds' which is produced by the union of several parts or cords ('By union married') then it is so because the harmonic mildly ('sweetly') oppugn ('chide') his singularity: "If the true concord of well-tuned sounds/By unions married do offend thine ear,/ They do but sweetly chide thee". The youth should not disengage the single notes from the orchestration, but he is doing just that, and thereby he is bewildering ('confounds') the several or single parts or notes of the orchestration. The poet tells him that he should rather be attentive to the harmonic ('that thou shouldst bear'): "who confounds/In singleness the parts that thou shouldst bear:". The poet asks the Fair Youth to notice how the different strings of a musical instrument is orderly arranged so that one string functions, as if, like a loving husband to the next string; and how each string, when struck, transfers its impact on to the next string, and so on, to produce a sweet orchestration of notes: ''Mark how one string, sweet husband to another,/Strikes each in each by mutual ordering''. The poet says that this phenomenon of a mutli-stringed musical isntrument can be compared with the familial concatenation (or orchestration) of births: father, mother, son. The family is a union of concordant units which, as if, produce a harmonius melody. The multiple members of one single family thus continue to sing eternally a single sweet song: ''Resembling sire, and child, and happy mother,/Who all in one one pleasing note do sing:''.

The song is not one but many, and yet those many songs convey a single message. What is the message of these unuttered or inaudible ('speechless') songs? The poet says that the songs mean to convey to the Fair Youth the truth that if he remains single, he will become a cypher ('none'): ''Whose speechless song, being many, seeming one,/ Sings this to thee: 'Thou single wilt prove none'.'' It may be noted here that the word 'none' in the last line is an antithesis of the word 'one' in the immediately preceding line.

9

Is it for fear to wet a widow's eye
That thou consum'st thyself in single life?
Ah! if thou issueless shalt hap to die,
The world will wail thee like a makeless wife;
The world will be thy widow and still weep
That thou no form of thee hast left behind,
When every private widow may keep
By children's eyes her husband's shape in mind:
Look, what an unthrift in the world doth spend
Shifts but his place, for still the world enjoys it;
But beauty's waste hath in the world an end,
And kept unus'd the user so destory it:
No love toward others in that bosom sits
That on himself such murderous shame commits.

John Dover Wilson very succinctly summarised the argument of this sonnet: ''If you excuse your remaining single, because you wish to spare a widow her tears, remember that at your death you will make the whole world a widow, one for ever lamenting that you left no child behind (....), when any individual widow has her husband's likeness alive in the children he gave her. When too an ordinary man wastes his wealth it goes into another man's pocket; but if you waste yourself the world's loss is absolute" (Wilson, 103). The poet asks the Fair Youth if the reason of his not consenting to marriage is that he is apprehensive ('fear') that if he marries then after his death his will-be wife will weep ('to wet a widow's eye') for him. He asks the youth whether this is the reason why he is leading the life of an anchorite — whether this is the reason why he is eating up himself ('consum'st thyself') living the life of a bachelor: "Is it for fear to wet a widow's eye/That thou consum'st thyself in single life?" If the youth dies without being survived by an issue, the whole world will mourn his death like a mateless ('makeless') wife, *i.e.* like a widow. Here the poet means to say that in the event of his death, without having an issue, the world itself will become a widow: "Ah if thou issueless shalt hap to die,/The world will wail thee like a makeless wife".

The poet compares the world with the not-yet-wedded wife of the Fair Youth, and says that should he die without leaving any issue behind, the world will weep not only for his death, but also because he will have left no copy of his, behind: "The world will be thy widow and still weep/That thou no form of thee hast left behind". It may be noted here that the alliterations in lines 4 and 5 are very appealing: world, will, wail, wife, world, will, widow, and weep. Generally, when a husband dies, his widow keeps in memory the features of her husband, and recalls those features by looking at her children who are the copies of her husband: "When every private widow well may keep/By children's eyes her husband's shape in mind". A widow is a private widow, says the poet; but if the youth dies, the whole world, or all the women of the world will be widowed, and so in the event of the death of the youth, there will be 'public' widowhood. The poet persuades the youth to understand ('Look') that when a wastrel ('unthrift') spends, then what he spends only changes place ('Shifts'), *i.e.* goes from one place to another, or from one pocket to another. He says that the world enjoys such changing of places of things. Here the poet means to say that the world is very lavish in spending in succession of generations, because it enjoys thus spending lavishly: "Look what an unthrift in the world doth spend/Shifts but his place, for still the world enjoys it". But the poet says that wasting of beauty is not possible for the world, since by wasting beauty, the world will come to an end: "But beauty's waste hath in the world an end". On the other hand, if anyone does not use ('kept unus'd') one's beauty, he is thereby destroying his beauty: "And kept unus'd the user. so destorys it''. In the concluding couplet, the poet says that not using one's beauty is an abject shame — a 'murderous shame' or a shameful murder. He says that one who is liable to such a shame has no love for any one : ''No love toward others in that bosom sits/That on himself such murderous shame commits.''

10

For shame deny that thou bear'st love to any,
Who for thyself art so unprovident!
Grant if thou wilt, thou art belov'd of many,
But that thou none lov'st is most evident:
For thou art so possess'd with murderous hate,
That 'gainst thyself thou stick'st not to conspire,
Seeking that beautious roof to ruinate
Which to repair should be thy chief desire:
Oh change thy thought, that I may change my mind!
Shall hate be fairer lodg'd than gentle love?
Be as thy presence is, gracious and kind,
Or to thyself at least kind-hearted prove:
    Make thee another self for love of me,
    That beauty still may live in thine or thee.

The first five lines of this sonnet may be taken to be complementary to the just preceding one, *i.e.*, sonnet 9. The words and phrases of this sonnet, such as, 'shame', 'murderous', and 'belov'd of many' are the echoes of the words 'shame', 'murderous' and 'love towards other's of the immediately preceding sonnet. John Dover Wilson wrote about this sonnet: ''In this sonnet the Poet speaks for the first time in his own perosn, begging W.H. to beget a child 'for love of me'. It also gives us another glimpse of W.H. himself in the petition:

> Be as thy presence is gracious and kind.

Further the whole sonnet is an acknowledgement of the fact that W.H. is determined not to marry,

> But that thou none lov'st is most evident,

and even that he hated women, although it is also evident that many women love him. D. (Edward Dowden, in his *The Sonnets of Shakespeare)* best brings out the general sense: 'The murderous shame' of 9.14 reappears in the 'For shame' and 'murderous hate' of 10 (Wilson, 104).

The poet tells the Fair Youth that if he says that he has love for some woman ('any'), it will be a shame to him, because actually he has no love for others; and so the poet declares that the Fair Youth is a miser ('unprovident') as regards love: "For shame thou deny thou bear'st love to any,/Who for thyself art so unprovident!" If the Fair Youth agrees to ('Grant') love, he will get so many women to love, because they too love him. But, the poet says, he loves no woman ('none'), and this is very clear ('most evident'): "Grant if thou wilt, thou art belov'd of many,/But that thou none lov'st is most evident". The Fair Youth is so much full of hatred ('murderous hate') that he does not refrain ('stick'st not') from planning ('conspire') destruction even on himself: "For thou art so possess'd with murderous hate,/That 'gainst thyself thou stick'st not to conspire". This sense is also to be found in the last line of Sonnet 9: "That on himself such murderous shame commits." The Fair Youth is seeking to destroy ('ruinate') his personal charm ('beautious roof') which it should be his principal aim to augment: "Seeking that beautious roof to ruinate,/Which to repair should be thy chief desire."

The poet tries to persuade the Fair Youth to change his attitude or mentality so that the poet also may change his attitude towards him, and a feeling of remorse, due to the Fair Youth's negative attitude towards marriage. But should the Fair Youth consent to marry and procreate, the poet will have all love for him: "Oh change thy thought, that I may change my mind!" The poet is in favour of love than hatred in the bosom of the youth. He therefore tells him that a heart full of hatred cannot be more attractive than a heart full of love. The poet asks him if his hatred that is there in his heart ('lodg'd') is better ('fairer') than a heart full of love which is gentle: "Shall hate be fairer lodg'd than gentle love?" The poet again implores him to be as 'gracious and kind' in heart as his personal charm is full of grace and kindness. If the Fair Youth, in no case, can be kind-hearted to others, the poet says, he should be kind-hearted at least to himself: "Be as thy presence is, gracious and kind,'/Or to thyself at least kind-hearted prove". The poet once again implores him to marry and beget a child ('Make thee another self') for the love the poet bears for him ('for love of me'). His argument for the marriage of the Fair Youth is that if the youth marries and begets a child, the beauty of the Fair Youth will continue either in his own person (till he is alive) or in the person of his progeny ('in thine or thee'): "Make thee another self for love of me,/That beauty still may live in thine or thee."

11

As fast as thou shalt wane so fast thou grow'st
In one of thine from that which thou departest,
And that fresh blood which youngly thou bestow'st
Thou mayst call thine when thou from youth convertest:
Herein lives wisdom, beauty, and increase;
Without this, folly, age, and cold decay:
If all were minded so, the times should cease,
And threescore year would make the world away.
Let those whom nature hath not made for store —
Harsh, featureless, and rude — barrenly perish:
Look, whom she best endow'd she gave the more;
Which bounteous gift thou shouldst in bounty cherish:
  She carv'd thee for her seal, and meant thereby
  Thou shouldst print more, not let that copy die.

If the Fair Youth marries and thus gets an issue, then though he may be waning rapidly with passage of years, yet, contrarily, he will be, in a sense, growing, in his issue ('In one of thine') (because that issue will concomitantly be growing with his decaying) — the issue from whom he will be departing (at the time of his death): "As fast as thou shalt wane so fast thou grow'st/In one of thine from that which thou departest". There is a covert conditional statement in the first two lines, and it is this: if the youth marries and gets an issue. Ingram and Redpath comment on the word 'departest': "Usually interpreted as 'leave behind', *i.e.* your youth. Thus, Tucker: 'You grow, in the person of one of yours begotten from that (prime) which you yourself are leaving.' This tortuous paraphrase heavily strains the construction with 'from' and 'departest'. Beeching seems nearer, taking 'departest' as 'separatest off', and 'that which thou departest' as 'a slip of thee'. 'Blood' (line 3), 'store' (line 9) and 'barrenly' (line 10), however, would seem to support Pooler's suggestion that the force of 'departest' is *seminal*. The sense of lines 1 and 2 would then be: 'Out of that seed which I am asking you to sow, you will grow, in a child of your making, as fast as you decline in yourself' " (Ingram, 26).

The sense of the first two lines is developed in the next two lines. The blood that the Fair Youth may transfer ('bestow'st') to his issue will ever remain his own, and so he may call the blood of his issue but his own blood. When in old age ('when thou from youth convertest'), he will have to leave this earth, but then he will, with satisfaction, be able to call the new blood his own blood: "And that fresh blood which youngly thou bestow'st/Thou mayst call thine when thou from youth convertest''. The poet says that one who follows this truth or ideal is wise, and he, by following this motto, augments the growth of beauty: ''Herein lives wisdom, beauty, and increase''. But if one does not understand this truth, he suffers from lack of understanding ('folly') and grows up with age or with the passage of years, and ultimately at some appointed time dies ('decay') worthlessly ('cold'): ''Without this, folly, age, and cold decay''. But, unfortunately, the Fair Youth will not yield to this argument and the poet's persuasion, and will remain anchored in his ego-centricity: he will not go for marriage. Frustrated, the poet reflects that if all men would hold such an attitude as the Fair Youth does, then 'there would be no more generations of men' ('the times should cease'). Becasue if men do away with the institution of marraige for sixty years ('threescore year') then there would be no more human beings in the world, and consequently, the world will be reduced to naught: ''If all were minded so, the times should cease,/And threescore year would make the world away.''

The poet says that those people who are recalcitrant ('Harsh'), ugly or devoid of physical beauty ('featureless') and are uncouth ('rude') — people whom nature has not created to perpetuate their existence ('not made for store') — may die ('perish') without leaving behind any issue ('barren'): ''Let those whom nature hath not made for store —/Harsh, featureless, and rude — barrenly perish''. The poet says that because they or their issues will not increase the beauty of the world. The poet draws the attention of the Fair Youth to the fact that nature gives beauty and all that very generously only to those whom she favours. She gives them gifts in excess ('bounteous gift') so that they may, in turn, bestow these to their progeny with a free hand and cheerfully. The youth also has received from nature's bounteous gift' in which he should be cheerful ('cherish') but only being himself bounteous or 'prolific': ''Look, whom she best endow'd she gave the more;/Which bounteous gift thou shouldst in bounty cherish''. Ingram and Redpath commented on the eleventh line thus: '' 'The best endowed creatures (those made for store) are also given by Nature the most generative vitality' '' (Ingram, 26). They interpreted the phrase 'Bounteous gift' as ''the gift of procreation'' (Ingram, 26). In the concluding coulpet, the poet tells the Fair Youth that nature made ('carv'd') him so exquisitely beautiful because she planned to use him as her seal of beauty, with which she would multiply copies or facsimiles ('print more') of his beauty in abundance, so that his beauty ('that copy') may not perish ('die'): ''She carv'd thee for her seal, and meant thereby/Thou shouldst print more, not let that copy die."

12

When I do count the clock that tells the time,
And see the brave day sunk in hideous night;
When I behold the violet past prime,
And sable curls o'er-silver'd all with white;
When lofty trees I see barren of leaves,
Which erst from heat did canopy the herd,
And summer's green all girded up in sheaves
Borne on the bier with white and bristly beard:
Then of thy beauty do I question make
That thou among the wastes of time must go,
Since sweets and beauties do themselves forsake,
And die as fast as they see others grow;
  And nothing 'gainst Time's scythe can make defence
  Save breed to brave him when he takes thee hence.

John Kerrigan said that this sonnet is "heavily influenced" (Kerrigan, 187) by Ovid's *Metamorphoses,* XV, 199-216. Shakespeare has a few sonnets (especially Sonnets 64 and 65) in which the concept of time or evanascence predominates, and in this sonnet he, for the first time, speaks of time. In all such sonnets, he meditates on the destructiveness of time. The present sonnet is, as if, the prologue to all such sonnets. In the first eight lines of this sonnet, the poet beautifully draws the images of the slow and imperceptible passage of time. The different images that he accumulates here present the stealthily slipping away of time: the clock chimes, the bright day enscones itself in the darkness of the night, the violet sheds the beauty of its young vitality ('prime') so that it does not die, the black curls of a youth's hair ('sable curls') turns grey ('o'er silver'd all with white'), and the high-rise ('lofty') trees become aged and shed off their green leaves — leaves which, before, spread themselves as a canopy over tired and resting people ('herd'). As time passes, the greenness of the inchoate summer is not to be found any more, because then the cultivators reap the corn and bind it into sheaves. And then these 'girded' sheaves are carried home on carts, like a corpse is carried on a bier — the corpse of an old man ('with white and bristly beard') whose beard is white due to aging, and whose hair is unkempt due to negligence. The poet says that there is no defence against the inroad of time, save only through one strategy: getting married and having issues. With all these instances, the poet tries to persuade the Fair Youth to get married.

The poet says that he sees the passage of time when he adds up ('count') the chimes of a clock, and when he perceives the bright ('brave') day sinking in the dark ('hideous') night: ''When I do count the clock that tells the time,/And see the brave day sunk in hideous night''. He also understands the passage of time when he sees a violet losing its freshness or excellence ('prime') in course of a short time, and when he sees pitch-dark curling hair turning very white — more white than silver is ('o'er-silver'd): ''When I behold the violet past prime,/And sable curls o'er-silver'd all with white''. He sees the passage of time also in the defoliation ('barren of leaves') of high-rise ('lofty') but old trees — trees that erstwhile in their young ages, seemed to be spreading canopies of leaves to shed people ('herd') off the scorching heat of the sun: ''When lofty trees I see barren of leaves,/Which erst from heat did canopy the herd''. And lastly, the poet sees the passage of time when he observes that the green corn of the early summer soon ripe and is cut and bound in sheaves ('girded up in sheaves'), and is then carried home on car like the corpse of an old man 'with white and bristly beard' is carried away on a bier to the grave: ''And summer's green all girded up in sheaves/ Borne on the bier with white and bristly beard''.

C.L. Finney said that Keats perhaps had in his mind the images of lines 5-8 of this sonnet when he wrote in *Grecian Urn*: ''Fair youth, beneath the trees, thou canst not leave/Thy song, nor ever can those trees be bare'' (Wilson, 107). Further, lines 7 and 8 of this sonnet can be compared with a part of Titania's speech in *A Midsummer Night's Dream*: ''The ox hath therefore stretch'd his yoke in vain,/The ploughman lost his sweat, and the green corn/Hath rotted ere his youth attain'd a beard'' (II, i, 93-95).

However, as everything grow and then die, the poet speculates ('question make') that the beauty of the Fair Youth will also vanish ('go') in course of time, like those ephemeral things, or his beauty will 'take place among things destroyed by Time' ('wastes of time'): ''Then of thy beauty do I question make/That thou among the wastes of time must go''. Because, the poet says, lovely and beautiful things ('sweets and beauties') are metamorphosed, or depart from their states of being lovely and beautiful ('forsake'). And they are destroyed (by time) as other lovely and beautiful things grow or come into being: ''Since sweets and beauties do themselves forsake,/And die as fast as they see others grow''. Lines 10 and 11 may be compared with the phrase 'beauty's waste' in sonnet 9 (line 11). In the *envoi,* the poet again emphasises the point that there is no force that can fight off the destructive onslaught of time ('nothing 'gainst Time's scythe'). But there is only one strategy for saving one's sweetness and beauty from the wreckage of time and that is getting married and having issues or copies of oneself. When time will in its course snatch oneself away, it will be these issues ('breed') who will accost time bravely ('brave him') in an attitude of defiance, for they will be able to carry on one's sweetness and beauty from generation to generation: "And nothing 'gainst Time's scythe can make defence/ Save breed to brave him when he takes hence."

13

Oh that you were your self! but, love, you are
No longer yours than you yourself here live;
Against this coming end you should prepare,
And your sweet semblance to some other give:
So should that beauty which you hold in lease
Find no determination; then you were
Your self again after yourself's decease,
When your sweet issue your sweet from should bear.
Who lets so fair a house fall to decay,
Which husbandry in honour might uphold
Against the stormy gusts of winter's day
And barren rage of death's eternal cold?
  Oh none but unthrifts, dear my love you know:
  You had a father, — let your son say so.

Ingram and Redpath have a general note on this sonnet which is very edifying: "Obscure at first sight through the apparently complex play on pronouns, this sonnet becomes clearer when the continuity of the image is apprehended. The 'you' of line 1 is either the body and its beauty, as opposed to the 'self' or soul, or is the composite of soul and body. If the bodily beauty (or the composite) and the soul were identical, the former, like the latter, would be immortal. Shakespeare embodies what he considers the actual relationship in the image of the eternal soul inhabiting a temporal house (cf. line 9). As long as the occupier remains heirless, this house is held on a lease determinable by death. Provident economy would not allow 'so fair a house' to fall into decay through age and inoccupancy; but by 'husbandry' (line 10, with an obvious play on the word) would produce an heir who would maintain the house both during the Friend's (the Fair Youth's) old age (line 11) and after his death (line 12)" (Ingram, 30).

The poet wishes that the Fair Youth becomes his own self or soul. He so wishes because, the poet says, the Fair Youth now does no longer seem to be sweet and beautiful, but, rather, seems to be reduced in beauty and sweetness: "Oh that you were your self! but, love, you are/No longer yours than you yourself here live". The Fair Youth has already grown a whit old and so he has shedded off some of his former charms. His beauty will wax reduced even further in the near future, and then he will be further removed from his true self — from his exquisitely beautiful self. So he advises him to arm himself against his sure and forthcoming death ('this coming end') by creating his facsimiles in his issues ('to some other give') to whom he will be able to transfer his beauty: "Against this coming end you should prepare,/And your sweet semblance to some other give". The youth got his beauty from his father (or mother) on lease, *i.e.* he has borrowed his father's beauty. Now, if, in turn, he gives this beauty to his progeny, again on lease, then the said beauty will not be bounded by time, or be destroyed by time (will not be ephemeral) but will be eternal ('Find no determination'): "So should that beauty which you hold in lease/Find no determination". Then even after his death, he will remain as if alive in his issues, because the issues will bear the ensign of his present beauty, in the future: "then you were/Your self again after yourself's decease,/When your sweet issue your sweet form should bear."

The poet compares the beautiful person of the youth with a delapidating but beautiful house. He asks if there is anybody who will let this fair but delapidating ('decay') house cave in, or to be destroyed. He says that this is a house that can be saved with 'husbandry', *i.e.* with "economy and good management" and can be reinstated in its former (not the present) dignity ('honour'): "Who lets so fair a house fall to decay,/Which husbandry in honour might uphold". The poet asks: who can save this fair but decaying house from the onslaught of time ('stormy gusts of winter's day'). This line may be compared with the concluding couplet of sonnet 5: "But flowers distill'd, though they with winter meet,/Leese but their show: their substance still lives sweet." Further, if the house of the beautiful person of the Fair Youth is thus guarded, then even the fruitless ('barren') ire ('rage') of the senseless ('cold') death will not be able to erase out his beauty from the earth: "Against the stormy gusts of winter's day/And barren rage of death's eternal cold?" The poet calls the rage of death 'barren' because death in that case will not be able to destroy the beauty of the Fair Youth. The poet concludes by saying that only the spendthrifts ('unthrifts), *i.e.*

only those who are ready to sow seeds to grow copies of his beauty will be able to protect that beautiful house: "Oh none but unthrifts, dear my love you know." Those who keep to themselves their seeds and do not spend those seeds for procreation of progenies are called by the poet thrifty or frugal. Such persons, he says, will not be able to perpetuate the beauty of the earth. On the other hand, those who are ready to spend their seeds for propagation of beauty are unthrifty ('unthrifts'), and only such persons can perpetuate beauty. Therefore, the poet urges the youth to be like those 'unthrifts'. The poet persuades the youth to understand that he himself had a father (who sowed seeds to procreate him); and so the youth also should have a son (by sowing seeds).

14

Not from the stars do I my judgement pluck,
And yet methinks I have astronomy —
But not to tell of good or evil luck,
Of plagues, of dearths, or season's quality:
Nor can I fortune to brief minutes tell,
Pointing to each his thunder, rain, and wind,
Or say with princes if it shall go well
By oft predict that I in heaven find:
But from thine eyes my knowledge I derive,
And, consult stars, in them I read such art
As truth and beauty shall together thrive
If from thy self to store thou wouldst convert:
  Or else of thee this I prognosticate:—
  Thy end is truth's and beauty's doom and date.

Shakespeare here tells the Fair Youth that he is not drawing conclusions ('pluck judgement') about the youth from the observation of the stars in the sky, though he has some knowledge of astrology ('astronomy'). Shakespeare means to say that he is acutally getting the knowledge of the future of the youth not from the observation of the stars of the sky, but from the observation of the youth's two eyes (which resemble the stars of the sky): "Not from the stars do I my judgement pluck/And yet methinks I have astronomy —". The poet says this again in line 9: "But from thine eyes my knowledge I derive". He says that he does not presage about anyone's good or bad lucks, or about plagues, famines ('dearths') or the harvest of the seasons ('seasons's quality'): "But not to tell of good or evil luck,/Of plagues, of dearths, or seasons' quality". The poet also cannot foretell ('fortune') about thunders, rains or storms ('wind') that may affect a person from time to time ('to brief minutes tell'): "Nor can I fortune to brief minute tell,/Pointing to each his thunder, rain, and wind". Of course, the poet predicts about the future of princes, from the indications he finds in the sky: he predicts if everything will go well with princes: "Or say with princes if it shall go well/By oft predict that I in heaven find". Ingram and Redpath wrote about the words 'oft' and 'predict': "There are seventeenth-century examples of 'oft' as an adjective; but this is the only recorded use of 'predict' as a noun" (Ingram, 32).

But the poet is not foretelling about the future of the youth from all such data; he is presaging depending rather on the data or insinuations that he observes in the two eyes of the Fair Youth. The eyes of the youth seem to be permanent stars ('constant stars') in the sky. What do these two eyes of the youth insinuate? The poet says that the two eyes portend that 'truth and beauty' can grow and persist to grow together ('together thrive') only if the youth turns ('convert') his mind from keeping hismelf within himself ('from thy self to store'), *i.e.* only if he moves away from his stand of not marrying and thus not procreating issues:

> But from thine eyes my knowledge I derive,
> And, constant stars, in them I read such art
> As truth and beauty shall together thrive
> If from thy self to store thou wouldst convert:

In the *envoi,* the poet simply repeats the foreboding ('art' in line 10 and 'prognosticate' in line 13) that he descries in the two eyes of the youth that if he dies without marrying, and so without any issue, both truth and beauty will cease to be ('doom and date'). The word 'date' here has been used, as we in modern times colloqually use it, to indicate final cessation. Thus, we say : " 'that's put a date to that' " (Ingram, 32). "Or else of thee this I prognosticate: —/Thy end is truth's and beauty's doom and date." It may not be a wild conjecture to think that John Keats might have been influenced by the two words 'truth' and 'beauty' of this sonnet (lines 11 and 14). It is interesting to note that, like Keats after him, Shakespeare also thought that truth and beauty are complementary as well as coeval: "As truth and beauty shall together thrive" (line 11). Lines 11 and 14 of this sonnet may be compared with Keats' line "Beauty is truth, truth beauty" in his 'Ode to a Grecian Urn'.

Line 9 of this sonnet may be compared with what Berowne says in *Love's Labour's Lost* :

From women's eyes this doctrine I derive:
They are the ground, the books, the academes,
From whence doth spring the true Promethean fire.

(IV, iii, 298-300)

or with what Berowne next says in the same speech:

From women's eyes this doctrine I derive:
They sparkle still the right Promethean fire;
They are the books, the arts, the academes,
That show, contain, and nourish all the world,

(IV, iii, 346-349)

15

When I consider every thing that grows
Hold in perfection but a little moment,
That this huge stage presenteth nought but shows
Whereon the stars in secret influence comment;
When I perceive that men as plants increase,
Cheered and check'd even by the selfsame sky,
Vaunt in their youthful sap, at height decrease,
And wear their brave state out of memory:
Then the conceit of this inconstant stay
Sets you most in youth before my sight,
Where wasteful time debateth with decay
To change your day of youth to sullied night;
And all in war with Time for love of you,
As he takes from you I engraft you new.

Everything that grows and develops ('Holds in perfection') is doomed to be evanascent, ephemeral: "When I consider every thing that grows/Holds in perfection but a little moment". The poet takes the world to be a stage (where plays are presented) which shows imaginary actions that mean nothing ('nought'): "That this huge stage presenteth nought but shows". This reminds us of Macbeth's ranting in *Macbeth* (V, v, 24-28) : "Life's but a walking shadow, a poor player,/That struts and frets his hour upon the stage,/And then is heard no more; it is a tale/Told by an idiot, full of sound and fury,/Signifying nothing." (Mark 'nought' in the sonnet and 'nothing' in the speech of Macbeth.) On this earthly stage (where worldly plays are staged) ('Whereon'), the stars from above secretly influence human actions by their comments: "Whereon the stars in secret influence comment". Ingram and Redpath wrote about this line (line 4): "Certainly Elizabethan audiences were given to 'commenting' during performances. They 'cheered and checked' as in line 6. Astrology held that the stars 'influenced' by their qualities and conjunctions human life and circumstance. This action, less noisy than the playhouse audience's, was known only by its effects. Some editors see a subtle contrast simultaneously distinguishing and binding together the rather disparate parts of this double metaphor: The audience comment audibly but do not influence the play's action, whereas the stars directly affect men's lives but are silent" (Ingram, 34).

Men grow and multiply like plants, and their growth and multiplication is controlled by those heavenly bodies — the stars: "When I perceive that men as plants increase,/Cheered and check'd even by the selfsame sky". Ingram and Redpath wrote about the two words 'Cheered' and 'check'd': "Both these terms have obviously a primary meaning relating to the 'plants' and the 'sky' (as = 'weather' or 'season'); a secondary meaning in reference back to the stars as occult 'influences'; and a tertiary in reference back yet again to the noisy playhouse audiences. Such multiple connotativeness is a feature of the style of the *Sonnets*" (Ingram, 34). Plants or trees, as if, swagger ('Vaunt') when they are young and full of abundant juice ('sap'), but when they grow up to their maximal height, they begin to decrease in shape and quantity, and also start wearing out, and, consequently, their showy splednour ('brave state') of former years is lost ('out of memory'): "Vaunt in their youthful sap, at height decrease,/And wear their brave state out of memory". Ingram and Redpath wrote about line 8: "It is possible that this line bears latent allusion to players' clothes. A decayed player (of the stage) continued to wear the finery (often originally handed over from noblemen's wardrobes) long after it had lost both gloss and fashion" (Ingram, 35).

When the poet thinks about the notion ('conceit') of the evanescence ('inconstant stay') of all these things, then the image of the young Fair Youth, in all his richness, appears before him: "Then the conceit of this inconstant stay/Sets you most rich in youth before my sight". And then time, that waste everything, and 'decay', that also wears out everything, conspire in unison ('debateth') to obfuscate the bright days of the youth and to bring in before him 'sullied' night — to bring for him gloomy darkness: "Where wasteful time debateth with decay/To change your day of youth to sullied night". But then the poet comes to his help and fights against the wasteful time and 'decay', to defend and protect the Fair Youth, *i.e.* to preserve the brightness of the Fair Youth's younger days. As old trees can be revived by grafting new and young branches onto them, so the poet grafts new verses (writes new verses) for the youth, so that he may continue to be as young as he was in his former days, *i.e.* in his young days: "And all in war with Time for love of you,/As he takes from you I engraft you new." Ingram and Redpath wrote about the concluding couplet: " 'As Time withers your features, I give you new life (by my verse). Old trees are revivified by inserting 'grafts' which, when they have taken, replace exhausted branches. Breeching and Fort among others note this as the first reference to the immortalizing power of the poet's verse (cf. sonnets 18 and 19)" (Ingram, 36).

16

But wherefore do not you a mightier way
Make war upon this bloody tyrant Time,
And fortify yourself in your decay
With means more blessed than my barren rhyme?
Now stand you on the top of happy hours,
And many maiden gardens, yet unset,
With virtuous wish would bear your living flowers,
Much liker than your painted counterfeit:
So should the lines of life that life repair
Which this (Time's pencil or my pupil pen)
Neither in inward worth nor outward fair
Can make you live yourself in eyes of men:
To give away yourself keeps your self still,
And you must live drawn by your own sweet skill.

In sonnet 15, the poet suggested that the beauty of the youth could be saved from the devastating onslaught of time by engrafting (writing) verses on the theme of the beauty of the Fair Youth, which in effect means waging a sort of war against time. The 'war with Time' of sonnet 15 is brought forward in the second line of this sonnet: "Make war upon this bloody tyrant Time". The poet asks the Fair Youth why the youth himself does not wage a more virulent war with this time and defend himself against the wasting ('decay') time: "But wherefore do not you a mightier way/Make war upon this bloody tyrant Time". If he does so, the youth will be richer and happier ('blessed') than if he is survived in the verses of the poet (suggested in sonnet 15). Because, howsoever potent his verses may be, the verses cannot procreate issues, while the beautiful youth can, and so the poet calls his verses infurtile ('barren rhyme'): "And fortify yourself in your decay/With means more blessed than by barren rhyme?"

Presently, the youth is the most happy because many beautiful ladies ('maiden gardens') who are not till date impregnated or 'sown with seed' ('yet unset') want to bear issues ('living flowers') of the youth — issues who will have more verisimilitude of him in them than any portrait ('painted counterfeit') of the Fair Youth: "Now stand you on the top of happy hours,/And many maiden gardens, yet unset,/With virtuous wish would bear your living flowers,/Much liker than your painted counterfeit." Ingram and Redpath said that the word 'virtuous', at line 7, means 'want to' or 'are eager to' and that it "may possibly also carry the secondary sense of fertility (The use of 'virtue' = 'power' is frequent in Shakespeare, cf. Lat. *virtus*) (Ingram, 38). The portraiture spoken of at line 8 ('painted counterfeit') may refer to the one drawn of the Earl of Southampton by Mirevelt in the early years of the Earl.

It is because the issues of the Fair Youth will bear more verisimilitude of the youth than his portraiture that the poet persuades him to beget issues in wedlock. The issues will continue the genealogy ('line of life') of the youth — genealogy that continually replaces old parts or members with new ones ('repair'). Ingram and Redpath presented a list of explanations of the phrase 'lines of life'. They wrote that it is a phrase "that has proved fertile of comment". The following list contains the most noteworthy interpretations with the names of their earliest and/or chief advocates:

(a) children (as 'living pictures') (Malone, who conjectured 'lives' for 'lines');

(b) lines drawn with a pencil — a portrait (Schmidt, Dowden, Empson);

(c) lineage, descendants (Dowden, Tyler, Beeching, Empson);

(d) wrinkles on the brow of age [Tyler, who later rejected it for (c), Empson];

(e) (from pamistry) marriage and procreation (Wyndham, Empson);

(f) form of personal appearance in the young men... or in his descendants (as one speaks of the lines of someone's figure) (Pooler, Empson);

(g) lines drawn with a pen in writing (Alden, Dowden, Empson);

(h) lines of verse ('the kind a sonnet has fourteen of') (Wyndham, Empson);

(i) lines of relationship in a genealogical table (Fort);

(j) space-time theorists describe such reality as they allow to a particle (Empson).

"It seems reasonable to hold with Professor Empson that there is a play here on several simultaneous connotations, and that the quality of the poem would be impaired if we confined our interpretation to a single association. But some selection and priorities would seem possible. We take it that 'lines of life' is the subject, and 'that' a demonstrative adjective, and that 'of life' bears the emphasis, and is intended to contrast the *living* portrait (the child) with the inanimate products of the 'pencil' or the 'pen'. This interpretation would seem to give highest priority to senses (a) and (c), and somewhat lower priority to (f), (e), and (i), in that order" (Ingram, 38-39).

The progeny of the Fair Youth would be better able to commemorate his beauty than anything else. The poet says that the portraiture of the Fair Youth drawn by Morevelt with a pencil ('Time's pencil'), or his obedient pen with which he composes verses ('my pupil pen') will not be able to perpetuate the youth's beauty more perfectly either with regard to his innate qualities of character ('inward worth') or with regard to his external beauty ('onward fair') than his progeny. For this reason the poet urges him to marry and get issues so that the youth may better be living in the eys of the public: "So should the lines of life that life repair/Which this (Time's pencil or my pupil pen)/Neither in inward worth nor outward fair/Can make you live yourself in eyes of men." The issues will be able to admirably perpetuate both the inward and the outward beauty of the Fair Youth, which nothing can similarly do. Therefore, the poet urges him to consent to wedlock, because only by propagating himself, *i.e.* by sowing his seeds in fair wombs ('To give away yourself'), he can remain immortal ('still'). If the Fair Youth wants to be immortal, *i.e.* wants to perpetuate his memory in any portraiture, then that portraiture must be drawn by himself with his own admirable skill ('sweet skill'), as a painter who paints with seeds and not with colours and brushes : "To give away yourself keeps your self still,/And you must live drawn by your own sweet skill." Ingram and Redpath wrote about the last line of this sonnet : "The plain sense seems to be: 'And the only way in which you can perpetuate yourself is to be your own painter and poet' " (Ingram, 40). Pooler said that the word 'pupil' at line 10 may mean 'immature and unskilled'.

17

Who will believe my verse in time to come?
If it were fill'd with your most high deserts —

Though yet heaven knows it is but a tomb
Which hides your life and shows not half your parts, —
If I could write the beauty of your eyes,
And in fresh numbers number all your graces,
The age to come would say: 'This poet lies;
Such heavenly touches ne'er touch'd earthly faces.'
So should my papers, yellow'd with their age,
Be scorn'd, like old men of less truth than tongue,
And your true rights be term'd a poet's rage
And stretched metre of an antique song:
But were some child of yours alive that time,
You should live twice — in it and in my rhyme.

We may remember that in sonnet 15, Shakespeare assured the Fair Youth that his 'perfection' will be immortalised in his verses which he (Shakespeare) will 'engraft' into the person of the youth. But in the very next sonnet, the poet's confidence turned into diffidence, for in it he said that his pupil pen' will not be as effective in this regard as the Fair Youth's 'sweet skill' of procreating issues. In the present sonnet, the poet is even more diffident: he doubts that anybody in the future will take his verses to be true ('believe'). He says that in the coming generation none will believe in the exquisite beauty of the Fair Youth about which he is speaking in his sonnets: ''Who will believe my verse in time to come?'' Even if the verses ('it') were filled with the praises ('deserts') of the beauty of the youth, yet the people of the coming ages would not believe in the verses. The poet admits that his verses are but a 'tomb' which only shrouds the beauty of the youth, and do not show even half of that beauty and the intellectual skills of the youth ('parts'): ''Though yet heaven knows it is but as a tomb/Which hides your life and shows not half your parts, —''. Even if the poet could portray ('write') all the charms in the eyes of the youth in his verses, and even if the poet could recount ('number') the Fair Youth's graces in lively ('fresh') verses ('numbers'), yet the coming age would not believe in his verses: ''If I could write the beauty of your eyes,/And in fresh numbers number all your graces''. The people of the coming ages then would rather say that the poet only lied ('This poet lies'). They would, moreover, say that such a beauty, or such a beautiful youth, could never have come down to earth from heaven: ''Such heavenly touches ne'er touch'd earthly faces''. The cause of this the poet explained earlier: the fact is that the beauty of the Fair Youth is not all expressed and is not perceivable because the verses of the poet is shrouding the youth, or his beauty, as if in a tomb. Therefore, even half the excellence ('parts') of the youth is not observable in the verses of the poet. In brief, the poet thinks that his verses can never immortalise the beauty of the Fair Youth.

The poet says that the pages, on which he will write verses in praise of the beauty of the youth, will, with passage of time, turn yellow (and dog-eared), *i.e.* the poet says that even the paper itself is not something permanent: "So should my papers, yellow'd with their age". People then will scoff at both the paper and the verses contained in it, as they scorn old men who talk much ('tongue') but seldom tell truths: "Be scorn'd, like old men of less truth than tongue". People then will not take the genuine praises ('true rights') of the youth translated into the verses to be true; they will rather think that all this effusion of praises are but the expression of the poet's wild imagination ('poet's rage') — they will think that all this is but the poet's '*furor poeticus*'. They will further think that the verses are " 'extravagances of a bygone poetical fashion' " (Ingram, 42): "And your true rights be term'd a poet's rage/And stretched metre of an antique song". On the contrary, if the Fair Youth begets a child through marriage, then at the future time, the youth will doubly live: firstly, he will live in the person of his child, and secondly, he will live also in the verses of the poet: "But were some child of yours alive that time,/You should live twice — in it and in my rhyme."

18

Shall I compare thee to a summer's day?
Thou art more lovely and more temperate:
Rough winds do shake the darling buds of May,
And summer's lease hath all too short a date:
Sometime too hot the eye of heaven shines,
And often is his gold complexion dimm'd,
And every fair from fair sometime declines,
By chance or nature's changing course untrimm'd:
But thy eternal summer shall not fade
Nor lose possession of that fair thou ow'st,
Nor shall Death brag thou wander'st in his shade,
When in eternal lines to time thou grow'st:
So long as men can breathe or eyes can see,
So long lives this, and this gives life to thee.

Ifor Brown is all praise for this sonnet, along with a few others. He wrote about the most beautiful sonnets of Shakespeare's sonnet-sequence: "A volume which contained only Nos. 18, 87, 94, 97, 98, 116 and 129 would stand on the peak of English poetry" (Brown, 193). In Sonnet 17, the poet was diffident as to the immortality of his verses, but in this sonnet, he is again very much confident that his verses are imperishable: "So long as men can breathe or eyes can see/So long live this." However, the poet compares the Fair Youth with a day of summer: "Shall I compare thee to a summer's day?" "Tucker suggests that 'day' is here used for 'season' rather than for a single day. The whole phrase could then be construed as a 'summertime'. This would make the progression of the imagery logically more compact. Line 4, with its reference to the length of summer's tenure, would appear less of a digression interposed between May's 'rough winds' (line 3) and the too hot or too cloudy weather of lines 5-6" (Ingram, 44). The poet says that the Fair Youth is more gentle or kind ('lovely') and more moderate ('temperate') than summer: "Thou art more lovely and more temperate". In May, *i.e.* in the season of summer, 'Rough winds' blow and pester the beautiful ('darling') buds of flowers: "Rough winds do shake the darling buds of May". A parallel to this line can be found in *Cymbeline* (I, iii, 36-37) where Imogen tells Pisanio: "And like the tyrannous breathing of the north/Shakes all our buds from growing." Further, the poet says that the tenure ('lease') of summer is very short: "And summer's lease hath all too short a date". In summer the sky ('eye of heaven') shines very hotly, and at times the beautiful clearness ('gold complexion') of the sky becomes overcast by clouds ('dimm'd): "Sometime too hot the eye of heaven shines,/And often is his gold complexion dimm'd". The face of summer is not always bright and attractive, because fair ladies lose ('decline') their fairness during summer. And due to chance happenings in summer ('chance') — such as, may be, storm, lightning, etc. — and due to changes in nature during summer-time, the complexion of summer is not attractive or beautiful ('untrimm'd'): "And every fair from fair declines,/By chance or nature's changing course untrimm'd".

But the summer of the Fair Youth's beauty is perpetual, unchanging and durable; it will never lose its slickness ('shall not fade'). The perpetual summer of the youth will never shed off its beauty — the beauty that the youth possesses ('ow'st'): "But thy eternal summer shall not fade/ Nor lose possession of that fair thou ow'st". Even death will not be able to be proud ('brag') thinking that he can cut off the thread of the youth's life, like Atropo, even though the youth be moving in the sphere of death ('wander'st in his shade'). This will be so because the poet will enshrine the beauty of the youth in his immortal verses ('eternal lines') — verses that will last as long as Time will last: "Nor shall Death brag thou wander'st in his shade,/When in eternal lines to time thou grow'st." The logic in the poet's argument is like this: being conjugated with the poet's eternal verses, the beauty of the youth will also be eternal. Ingram and Redpath wrote about the phrase 'to time thou grow'st': " 'to grow to' is to coalesce or become incorporate in, as a graft coalesces with its parent stock; *i.e.* as long as time lasts the Friend (the Fair Youth) will last" (Ingram, 44).

In the concluding couplet, the poet again says that his verses ('this') will last as long as men will live and perceive things ('men can breathe or eyes can see'); and that as the poet will canonise the Fair Youth in his immortal verses, the youth will receive an eternal lease of life in those verses: "So long as men can breathe or eyes can see,/So long lives this, and this gives life to thee." It may be pointed out here that in some of his sonnets, Shakespeare feels proud that his verses are immortal. Nevertheless we should not think that Shakespeare is immodest, for in his times many sonneteers also boasted like that. For instance, Michael Drayton (1563-1631) in his sonnet-sequence *Idea's Mirror* wrote thus in several places: "While thus my pen strives to eternize thee", "My name shall mount into eternity", "All that I see is to eternize thee", etc. Again, Samuel Daniel (1562/63-1619), in his sonnet-sequence *Delia* wrote such lines as "Thou mayest in after ages live esteemed,/Unburied in these lines" or "And these (verses) thy sacred virtues must protect/ Against the dark and time's consuming rage".

19

Devouring Time, blunt thou the lion's paws,
And make the earth devour her own sweet brood;
Pluck the keen teeth from the fierce tiger's jaws,
And burn the long-liv'd Phoenix in her blood;
Make glad and sorry seasons as thou fleets,
And do whate'er thou wilt, swift-footed Time,
To the wide world and all her fading sweets:
But I forbid thee one most heinous crime: —
Oh carve not with thy hours my love's fair brow,
Nor draw no lines there with thine antique pen;
Him in thy course untainted do allow
For beauty's pattern to succeeding men.
Yet do thy worst, old Time: despite thy wrong
My love shall in my verse ever live young.

The war on time that Shakespeare began in Sonnet 15, continues through Sonnet 19. He begins this sonnet even with an invective on time. He calls time 'Devouring time' — time that takes away ('blunt') the ferocity from the paws of a lion's feet. Time makes the earth destroy ('devour') all that grow out of her ('brood'): ''Devouring Time, blunt thou the lion's paws,/And make the earth devour her own sweet brood''. Ingram and Redpath explained the second line thus: '' 'And (as you habitually do) cause the earth to re-absorb the creatures which spring from her' ('sweet' suggests primarily flowers)'' (Ingram, 46). Time destroys the dreaded sharp teeth in the mouth of a tiger, *i.e.* as the tiger grows old, the teeth are either lost or become ineffective. Again, the legendary immortal bird Phoenix ('long-liv'd phoenix') that never dies for ever is proof against time's destruction. According to legend, the bird, after its death in a fire caused by itself, remains non-existent for a while and then rises again new-born from its own ashes. But the poet says that even such a bird is burnt out (by time) for ever even though it sustains life in itself ('in her blood'): ''Pluck the keen teeth from the fierce tiger's jaws,/And burn the long-liv'd phoenix in her blood''. And it is the fast moving ('swfit-footed') time that makes different seasons of the year either happy or mournful, as it passes ('fleets'): ''Make glad and sorry as thou fleets''. It is to be noted here that Shakespeare has oddly used a 's' after the verb 'fleet' in the 5th line. But Ingram and Redpath wrote that ''The second person singular in '— s' is historically a corrected form, common in First Folio (of Shakespeare's works) for verbs ending in '— t' or '— d' ''(Ingram, 46).

The poet cautions the 'swift-footed' time: he says that it may do whatever its sweet will prompts it to do over the whole world and against the world's decaying but beautiful things ('fading sweets'), but it must not commit ('forbid') one despicable ('heinous') crime: ''And do whate'er thou wilt, swift-footed Time,/To the wide world and all her fading sweets''. The crime the poet means here is time's furrowing out ('carve') the beautiful forehead of his beloved Fair Youth and drawing lines of care (on that forehead) with its grotesque or hoary tool ('antique pen'): ''Oh carve not with thy hours my love's fair brow,/Nor draw no lines there with thine antique pen''. The word 'antique', in different spellings, occurs in several places in Shakespeare's works. For instance, in *Richard II*, III, ii, 162 (''and there the antique sits''); in *Hamlet,* I, v, 172 (''an antic disposition''); and in *As You Like It,* II, iii, 57 (''the constant service of the antique world'').

The poet appeals to time to permit his beloved Fair Youth to run his course of life without being tainted, *i.e.* without his brow being drawn with lines of care ('untainted do allow'): "Him in thy course intainted do allow". The poet begs of time this favour so that the Fair Youth may devolve or hand down his beauty to his progeny or issues ('succeeding men'): "For beauty's pattern to succeeding men." In the *envoi,* the attitude of the poet changes abruptly: he throws his gauntlet before time and asks it to do — if it dares to do — all the uttermost wrongs it is capable of doing. He changes his attitude, because he knows that in spite of the onslaught of the devastating time ('thy worng'), his beloved will ever live young in his verses: "Yet do worst, old Time: despite thy wrong/My love shall in my verse ever live young."

20

A woman's face with nature's own hand painted
Hast thou, the master-mistress of my passion;
A woman's gentle heart, but not acquainted
With shifting change as if false women's fashion;
An eye more bright than theirs, less false in rolling,
Gilding the object whereupon it gazeth;
A man in hue all hues in his controlling,
Which steals men's eyes and women's soul amazeth:
And for a woman wert thou first created, —
Till nature as she wrought thee fell a-doting,
And by addition me of thee defeated,
By adding one thing to my purpose nothing.
  But since she prick'd thee out for women's pleasure,
  Mine be thy love and thy love's use their treasure.

In this sonnet the poet introduces, for the first time, the concept of womanly beauty, to explicate the exquisite beauty of the Fair Youth. It is said that beauty is essentially womanly or effeminate, *i.e.* beauty is the property of a woman, and not of a man; such that if a man happens to be extremely beautiful, he is supposed to be looking like a woman. It is for this reason that Milton, Shelley and such others who were extremely beautiful seemed womanly. The class-mates of Milton used to call him 'Lady of the Christ's' and the friends of Shelley used to call him a lady. In this sonnet the poet also means to say that the Fair Youth is so beautiful and attractive in his looks that he seems to be effeminate. The poet says that nature herself has moulded the youth in such a way that he is extremely beautiful, and so seems to have a woman's beautiful face. And that is why the youth is both the master of ladies and mistress of men ('master-mistress'): "A woman's face with nature's own hand painted/Hast thou the master-mistress of my passion". But the epithet 'master-mistress' has been variously interpreted by critics. Ingram and Redpath wrote about this: "Interpretation is multifarious and frequently subject to editor's theories of the Friend's (the Fair Youth's) identity and the poet's relation to him. Relevant notes (which are the exception) are offered by Mr. J.B. Leishman (*RES.* XV.94) and J.Q. Adams. The former writes: 'If, with Shakespeare's printer, we omit the hyphen, *Master Mistris* will mean 'supreme mistress'; if we insert the hyphen it will mean that the 'mistress' usually invoked by poets is in this case a man.' J.Q. Adams (*Life of William Shakespeare*, Houghton, Boston, and Constable, London, 1923) writes: 'Is not Sahkespeare here thinking of the numerous mistresses celebrated in sonnet cycles (as Delia, Laura, Diella, Stella, Phillis, etc.) and meaning to comment, favourably, on the fact that he is celebrating in his cycle of *man*?' " (Ingram, 48). But, perhaps, it would be better to avoid complications and interpret the epithet as meaning simply that the Fair Youth, though essentially a man, possesses, for all practical purposes, all the commendable qualities of a woman, including her Helenesque or Ledaesque beauty.

The Fair Youth has the passionate and gentle heart of a woman, but he is not as camelion-like ('shifting change') as a false woman is: there is no frequent change in his mood, as there is in a false woman: "A woman's gentle heart, but not acquainted/With shifting change as is false woman's fashion". The youth's eyes are brighter than those of a woman, but his eyes do not so much goggle in falsehood. His eyes are so bright and attractive that whenever he looks at an object, the object, as if, becomes laminated with gold foils ('Gilding'): "An eye more bright than theirs, less false in rolling,/Gilding the object whereupon it gazeth". The youth has an attractive form or figure ('hue' and he always controls all his gaits or liquid movements or changes of his form or figure. It should be noted here that during the time of Shakespeare, the word 'hue' meant 'form' or 'appearance', and not 'colour'. Ingram and Redpath wrote about the word 'hue': "The primary meaning of 'hue' till the middle of the seventeenth century was not 'colour' or 'complexion' but 'form', 'appearance' or 'species' " (Ingram, 49). Ingram and Redpath further wrote : "In interpreting the word here the form of the octave is significant. Each pair of the first six lines (of this sonnet) singles out one of the Friend's (the Fair Youth's) features — line 1 his 'woman's face', line 3 his 'woman's gentle heart', while line 5 wholly differentiates him from women by an eye brighter and less inconstant than theirs. To interpret the next comment (line 7) as a mere contradiction of line 1 would be to reduce this sequence to an absurdity. Instead, all these features which surpass those of woman are shown to be embodied in a manly form, which not only has at command all manliness, but epitomizes all the excellences ('hues') of both sexes. No wonder, then, that (line 8) he attracts the eyes of all men, and throws into confusion the souls of women'' (Ingram, 49-50). This interpretation of the word 'hue' is supported by Spenser's use of the same word with the same meaning. Spenser writes: ''He taught to initiate that Lady, trow,/Whose semblance she did carry under feigned *hue*'' (*Faerie Queene,* Bk I, Canto 1, stanza XXVI, line 9). However, the poet says that the shape or form of the body of the Fair Youth is so attractive and beautiful that men cannot but look attentively at it and women jealously and grudgingly stare at its beauty: ''A man in hue all hues in his controlling,/Which steals men's eyes and women's souls amazeth''.

The youth is so beautiful that it seems to the poet that the youth was moulded by nature herself at first in the shape of a woman: ''And for a woman wert thou first created, —''. While creating this beautiful Fair Youth, in the shape of a woman, nature herself became engrossed ('a-doting') in his beauty: ''Till nature as she wrought thee fell a-doting''. But, ultimately, nature changed her mind and changed the Fair Youth into a woman by adding 'one thing' (maybe, pudendum). As a consequence, the poet cannot love the Fair Youth as a woman, and so his object of getting a lady-love is frustrated ('defeated'): ''And by addition men of thee defeated''. As that 'one thing' was added to the youth, the 'purpose' of the poet came to a naught ('nothing'): ''By adding one thing to my purpose nothing.'' In the *envoi*, the poet says that although the Fair Youth has been ultimately changed into a man, yet his love may be directed to the poet, and the Fair Youth's 'use' of love, *i.e.*, his physical love may be directed to women: ''But since she prick'd thee for women's pleasure,/Mine be thy love and thy love's use their treasure.'' The poet says that nature has turned the youth from womanhood to manhood for the enjoyment ('pleasure') of the women-folk. So it is they who should get the physical love of the youth as their 'treasure', and the poet should receive only the Platonic love of the youth: ''But since she prick'd thee out for women's pleasure,/Mine be thy love and thy love's use their treasure.'' Ingram and Redpath wrote about the concluding lines of this sonnet: ''A realization of the equivoques here on 'one thing', 'to my purpose nothing', 'prick'd', and 'use' (...) is essentially to an understanding of this sonnet and of the poet's relationship to the Friend (the Fair Youth), but their detailed working except in the case of 'use' should be easy to grasp for these are familiar with modern bawdy and alert to innuendo'' (Ingram, 50). Accoding to Henry Brown, ''Sonnet 20 is the key to the whole series (of Shakespeare's sonnets)'' (Ralli, I, 484). Further, this sonnet is important for yet another reason. We are baffled about the identity of the mysterious Mr. W.H. One conjecture is that it is Willie Hughes. ''The name of Hughes appealed both the Butler and to Oscar Wilde, as well as to others, because of a punning line in the famous Sonnet 20'' (Brown, 186). The famous line referred to here is: ''A man in hue (hew) all hues (Hews/Hughes) in his controlling.''

21

So is it not with me as with that Muse,
Stirr'd by a painted beauty to his verse,
Who heaven itself for ornament doth use
And every fair with his fair doth rehearse,
Making a couplement of proud compare
With sun and moon, with earth and sea's rich gems,
With April's first-born flowers and all things rare
That heaven's air in this huge rondure hems.
Oh, let me true in love but truly write,
And then believe me my love is as fair
As any mother's child, though not so bright
As those gold candles fix'd in heaven's air:
Let them say more that like of hearsay well;
I will not praise that purpose not to sell.

Ingram and Redpath wrote a very profitable general introduction to this sonnet: ''Imitators of Petrarch employed nature symbolism and comaprisons extravagantly. Passages in this style occur in Shakespeare's poems (sonnets) and early poems. It also become in turn a convention to repudiate this convention, and to represent it as something the poet's sincerity rejected. Some commentators see in this sonnet such conventionality of the latter kind as warrants denial of Shakespeare's authorship. Others (*e.g.* Tucker), though not definitely impugning its authenticity, find its manner incompatible with the eulogistic style of its predecessors in the series, and some commentators (*e.g.* Pooler) would alter its position among the *Sonnets.* As to authorship, a rejection of this sonnet on the above grounds would involve rejection of a number of others, and for such a step there is no reliable evidence. As to sequence, though the sonnet does not differ appreciably in tone from its predecessors, it does not really differ in either structure, imagery, movement, or diction. Now, differences of tone do not necessarily break sequence; and in any case, it is highly questionable how far Shakespeare's *Sonnets* are to be regarded as forming a strict sequence, even throughout any group.'' There is a clear hint to the rival poet in this sonnet ('Muse', line 1), and it may be said that this sonnet begins the group of rival poet sonnets (see Sonnets 78, 83, 86).

However, though this sonnet begins with the word 'So', it is not the conclusion of any premises, because the word is to be taken in the Elizabethan sense of it, where it simply means 'as'. But Dowden, in his *Shakespeare's Sonnets,* said that Sonnet 20 might be taken as the premise of this present sonnet, and therefore the word 'so' might be taken also in its modern sense. In Sonnet 20, the poet told us that the Fair Youth was 'painted' by nature herself and so there was no artificiality, no poetic hyperbole, in the creation of nature (in the Fair Youth). On the other hand, in this sonnet, the poet seems to say that other poets (the rival poets), unlike himself, embellish the subject of their verses (possibly, the Fair Youth) with extreme hyperboles. Again, the word 'Muse' in the first line of this sonnet, means 'poet' and not some 'deity' of the fine arts. Therefore, we may explain the first two lines thus: the poet says that he is not like those poets who bounch in poetic inspiration when they are attracted by any artificial beauty, such as a painting ('painted beauty'): ''So is it not with me as with that Muse,/Stirr'd by a painted beauty to his verse.'' He says that such poets use all sorts of ornamentation in their verses, such that, if necessary, they make similes even with paradise ('heaven'), to beautify their compositions ('rehearse'): ''Who heaven itself for ornamentation doth use/And every fair with his fair doth rehearse''. Such poets, in their verses, compare or mention or enumerate ('rehearse') all the beautiful things ('every fair') in heaven and earth with their beautiful things ('his fair'), to embellish their poetry. For instance, they proudly ('proud') compare two ('couplement') things — the sun and the moon — with their subject of verses: ''Making a couplement of proud compare/With sun and moon''. They also compare their idols or objects of poetry with the precious stones ('rich gems') of the earth and the seas; with the prime flowers ('first-born') of April; and with all those rare things that belong to the sphere ('air') of the heaven, and which are mingled ('hem') by the inspiration of the heaven with this gigantic earth's roundness ('rondure'): ''with earth and sea's rich gems,/ With April's first-born flowers and all things rare/That heaven's air in this huge rondure hems.'' The word 'rondure', in the sense of 'roundness', is used by Shakespeare also in *King John* (II, i, 259): " 'Tis not the rondure of your old-fac'd walls".

The poet says that he is faithful in his love for the Fair Youth, and he appeals to all to let him faithfully compose ('wrote') verses about the youth: "Oh, let me true in love but truly write". He further appeals to all to believe that his beloved youth is no less fair than 'any mother's child', *i.e.*, less beautiful than any exquisitely beautiful man or woman. But, at the same time, he admits that the youth is not as bright as the bright and golden coloured ('gold') stars ('candles') of the sky: "And then believe me my love is as fair/As any mother's child, though not so bright/As those gold candles fix'd in heaven's air". Perhaps the poet is here satirising the compositions of the other (rival) poets who use hyperbolic comparisons. The 'gold candles', meaning stars, also occurs in *The Merchant of Venice* (V, i, 220), where Portia says: "For by these blessed candles of the night..."

In the concluding couplet, the poet emphasises his honesty in describing the features of the Fair Youth. He says that he will not over-estimate the worth of, or hyperbolise, the beauty of the youth ('purpose') to attract people ('sell') to that beauty: "I will not praise that purpose not to sell." The poet will refrain from doing so in spite of people's spreading the rumour or hearsay to the contrary, *i.e.* that the Fair Youth is not so beautiful. He resolves like this because he knows that people are 'hearsay-mongers', at least most of them are so: "Let them say more that like of hearsay well". The word 'sell', in the sense in which it appears here, also occurs in *Love's Labour's Lost* (IV, iii, 235-36) where Berowne tells King Ferdinand: "Fie, painted rhetoric ! O, she needs it not !/To things of sale a seller's praise belongs."

22

My glass shall not persuade me I am old
So long as youth and thou are of one date;
But when in the times furrows I behold
Then look I death my days should expiate:
For all the beauty that doth cover thee
Is but the seemly raiment of my heart,
Which in thy breast doth live, as thine in me, —
How can I then be elder than thou art?
Oh therefore, love, be of thyself so wary
As I not for myself but for thee will,
Bearing thy heart, which I will keep so chary
As tender nurse her babe from faring ill:

Presume not on thy heart when mine is slain;
Thou gav'st me thine not to give back again.

The poet says that when he looks at his face in a looking glass, it does not seem to him that he is an old man. He says that he cannot be old as long as the Fair Youth ('thou') and youthfulness ('youth') " 'last as long as each other' ('date' = determined end)" (Ingram, 54). The poet means to say that so long as the Fair Youth remains young, he cannot be old (because the youthful vitality and the beauty of the youth will continue to hold him in the buoyancy of life): "My glass shall not persuade me I am old/So long as youth and thou are of one date". But in the next two lines, the poet says that when he sees wrinkles ('time's furrows') in the brow of the Fair Youth — wrinkles that old age imprints on a man — then his thought about death comes to him, *i.e.*, he becomes apprehensive of his death: he thinks that his days are numbered, and that his life will soon come to an end ('expiate'): "But when in thee time's furrows I behold/Then look I death my days should expiate". In Shakespeare, the word 'expiate' means 'expired' or 'at an end' (*Chambers Twentieth Century Dictionary*). Ingram and Redpath wrote about the term 'expiate' and about the 4th line of this sonnet: "A puzzling use, and the only instance in Shakespeare of 'expiate' as a verb. The word itself was new in English at the time. (*OED* gives the first use as 1594). The only use of the verb at all resembling that in this line seems to involve some idea of (1) pacification, and (2) ending, *e.g.* Marlowe, *Dido,* V, ii: 'Die to expiate/The Grief that tires upon thine inward soul'; Tofte, *Honours Academy* (1610), 39: 'Nothing could appease and expiate this cankered rage'; T. Adams, *Lycanthropia* (1615), 29: 'Somewhat to expiate their savage fury'. With this kind of sense the line could mean: 'Then I expect (and perhaps even hope) that death will bring peace to my days by ending them.' Steeven's conjecture: ***expiate***, besides being ugly, neither has linguistic support nor makes good sense" (Ingram, 54).

The beautiful aspects of the Fair Youth that fold ('cover') him are, as if, the clothes ('raiment') of the heart of the poet. The heart of the poet resides within the breast of the youth as the heart of the youth subsists within the breast of the poet. And the clothes of beauty of the youth are very beautiful ('seemly') too: "For all the beauty that doth cover thee/Is but the seemly raiment of my heart,/Which in thy breast doth live, as thine in me, —". If all this be so, if both of them are thus entwined, then the poet cannot be senior to or older than ('elder') the youth: "How can I then be elder than thou art?" Therefore the peot appeals to the youth to be more careful ('wary') than himself not to be a victim of aging. Certainly the poet will also be careful about aging, but he will be careful not so much for himself as for the Fair Youth: "Oh therefore, love, be of thyself so wary/As I not for myself but for thee will". The poet will be so wary about the aging of the youth for he will bear the youth's heart within himself. The poet further says that he will be as careful ('chary') about the heart of the youth as a mother ('tender nurse') is careful about her baby ('babe'), so that the baby does not become ill ('faring ill'): "Bearing thy heart, which I will keep so chary/As tender nurse her babe from faring ill". And in the concluding couplet, the poet asks the Fair Youth not to claim ('presume') his (the youth's) heart (which is now within the breast of the poet) after the poet is dead ('slain'). Because the youth gave his heart away to the poet not to take that heart back to himself from the poet: "Presume not on thy heart when mine is slain;/Thou gav'st me thine not to give back again." Ingram and Redpath explained the phrase 'Presume not on' as " 'Do not count on being able to lay claim to' " (Ingram, 54).

23

As an unperfect actor on the stage,
Who with his fear is put besides his part,
Or some fierce thing replete with too much rage,
Whose strength's abundance weakens his own heart;
So I for fear of trust forget to say
The perfect ceremony of love's rite,
And in mine own love's strength seem to decay,
O'er-charg'd with burthen of mine own love's might:
Oh let my books be then the eloquence
And dumb presagers of my speaking breast,
Who plead for love and look for recompense
More than that tongue that more hath more express'd:
Oh learn to read what silent love hath writ;
To hear with eyes belongs to love's fine wit.

The poet is comparing himself with an imperfect ('unperfect') actor of a theatrical presentation — a genophobic actor who is nervous on the stage, and consequently forgets his speech ('part'): "As an unperfect actor on the stage,/Who with his fear is put besides his part". Again, the poet compares himself with a fierce man, who is full of rage, or is in temper tantrum, whose courage ('heart') is diminished due to his violent anger ('strength's abundance'): "Or some fierce thing replete with too much rage,/Whose strength's abundance weakens his own heart''. Both the persons — the actor and the person in temper tantrum — are ineffectual, for as the imperfect actor cannot deliver his speech well, so the person in extreme rage cannot well express his fury in words. The poet says that likewise overcome by his own passionate love, or by his fear that his beloved may not be able to understand the fierce love in his heart ('for fear of trust'), he (the poet) fails to express in words ('say') the appropriate emotions ('perfect ceremony') in love-making ('love's rite') : ''So I for fear of trust forget to say/The perfect ceremony of love's rite''. Further, like the man in full rage and the imperfect actor, the poet is so full of the heavy strain ('O'er-charg'd with burthen') of his own love that his love for the Fair Youth itself seems to be weakened ('decay'): ''And in mine own love's strength seem to decay,/O'er-charg'd with burthen of mine own love's might''.

As the poet cannot well express his love, so he rather desires that his verses ('books') be the sufficient testimony ('eloquence') of his love (for the Fair Youth): ''O let my books be then the eloquence''. Sewell (1725) conjectured that the word 'books' was actually as misprint of the word 'looks'. It is true that most modern editors follow Sewell. But John Kerrigan wrote about the word 'books': ''Not, as now, 'writings', 'printed and bound', but text on paper at any length (thus *Cymbeline* V. 4. 133, 'A book? O rare one!', of a single handwritten sheet). *Books* probably refers to the Sonnets themselves, forwarded to the youth, but those who favour the identification of the young man with Henry Wriothesley may be right in thinking them *Venus and Adonis* and *The Rape of Lucrece,* published in 1593 and 1594 and dedicated to Southampton'' (Kerrigan, 203). However, the poet desires that his veses be intuitive knowledge or fore-knowledge ('presagers') of the love within his breast that merely covertly and silently speaks ('speaking breast') about his love for the youth: ''And dumb presagers of my speaking breast''. His heart wants ('plead') love in return, and seeks ('look for') compensation or reward ('recompense') more than his tongue that is eloquent ('that more hath more express'd'): ''Who plead for love and look for recompense/More than that tongue that more hath more express'd.'' John Kerrigan explained ''look for recompense....express'd'' thus: ''seek greater rewards than that tongue which has spoken more grandly and more copiously (or often). The implication is that, whereas the *tongue* looks for material *recompense,* the poet's *books* seek that worthier prize, the young man's love. Though this text anticipates the later sonnets concerned with the rival poet(s), *that tongue* probably refers by synecdoche to the kind of imagined author identified in Sonnet 21 as *that Muse* (Kerrigan, 204). In the concluding couplet, the poet appeals to the Fair Youth to acquire the skill of deciphering ('learn to read') what his verbally unexpressed ('silent') love has written (in his verses or in his books). He tells him that thus hearing the appeals of heart by reading verses (that the heart has written) is possible only for the sensitive intelligence of one who is in love ('hear with eyes belongs to love's wit'): "Oh learn to read what silent love hath writ;/To hear with eyes belongs to love's fine wit."

24

Mine eye hath play'd the painter and hath steel'd
Thy beauty's form in table of my heart;
My body is the frame wherein 'tis held,
And persepctive it is best painter's art —
For through the painter must you see his skill
To find where your true image pictur'd lies,
Which in my bosom's shop hanging still,
That hath his windows glazed with thine eyes:
Now see what good turns eyes for eyes have done: —
Mine eyes have drawn thy shape, and thine for me
Are windows to my breast, wherethrough the sun
Delights to peep, the gaze therein on thee:
  Yet eyes this cunning want to grace their art, —
  They draw but what they see, know not the heart.

The poet's eye has been the painter ('play'd the painter') of the beauty of the Fair Youth, and he (the poet) has made the youth's painting or portraiture ('Thy beauty's form') on the pedestal ('table') of his heart, with a steel stylus ('steel'd): "Mine eye hath play'd the painter and hath steel'd/Thy beauty's form in table of my heart". Capell thought that the word 'steel'd' is a misprint of 'stelled' which means "an enclosure (usu. a ringwall) for sheltering sheep" (*Chambers Twentieth Century Dictionary*). One of the arguments of Capell for reading 'stelled' instead of 'steel'd' is that 'stelled' rhymes with 'held' of the third line better than 'steel'd'. And John Kerrigan agreed with Capell. Kerrigan said that " 'steel'd' is a possible reading if taken to mean 'engraved with steel tool' or 'inscribed with a stylus' (the imperfect rhyme with *held* is not an insuperable difficulty); but *painter* tells strongly against it" (Kerrigan, 204).

However, the poet says that the painting of the youth is held by the frame of his body. The poet has painted the beauty of the youth from the 'perspective' ('seen through the appropriate optical glass') of his heart (which is full of love of him). Therefore, if the youth wants to judge ('see') the painter's (the poet's) art ('skill'), then he must look through the heart of the poet — the heart on which the true picture of the youth is drawn: "For through the painter must you see his skill/To find where your true image pictur'd lies". Shakespeare here means to say that "his heart's image of the Friend (the Fair Youth) is a perfect portrait, though to realize this we must see it through the poet's eye" (Ingram, 63). The beautiful painting or portraiture of the youth is still suspended in the shop of the poet's bosom, and the windows of that shop are glossed ('glazed') with the brightness of the youth's eyes: "Which in my bosom's shop is hanging still,/That hath his windows glazed with thine eyes". Kerrigan wrote about the 8th line: "The *windows* of the peot's *bosom* (his eyes) are glossed over by the young man's, because as the poet looks into his friend's *eyes* those *eyes* can be seen reflected across the surface of his own; which must mean that the young man's *eyes* are as well-depicted in the *windows* of the *bosom* as behind them (in the *true image* displayed in the shop)" (Kerrigan, 205-206). Such a position of the poet's eyes *vis-a-vis* the eyes of the youth has brought immense mututal favour ('good turns') between them: "Now see what good turns eyes for eyes have done". The poet's eyes have schematised the beautiful form of the youth: "My eyes have drawn thy shape". And the eyes of the youth are but the slots through which the heart ('breast') of the poet can be observed: "and thine for me/Are windows to my breast". And through those slots of the youth's eyes, sun-beams enter to see (the image of) the youth with delight: where through the sun/Delights to peep, to gaze therein on thee". Nevertheless, the poet says, eyes do not possess that skill ('eyes this cunning want') with which these can 'give grace to' the beauty ('art') of the image of the youth. For the eyes only see what they see, *i.e.* the eyes see only the beauty of the image of the youth — only the physical beauty of the youth; and they cannot understand the love written within the heart: "Yet eyes this cunning want to grace their art, —/They draw but what they see, know not the heart." Kerrigan wrote that the last line meant "that the poet cannot judge whether the youth loves him as he does the youth. But the possibility of duplicity, of the youth deceiving the poet (confirmed later), (*i.e.* in the sonnets following this one), may also register" (Kerrigan, 206).

25

Let those who are in favour with their stars
Of public honour and proud titles boast,

Whilst I, whom fortune of such triumph bars,
Unlook'd for joy in that I honour most.
Great princes' favourites their fair leaves spread
But as the marigold at the sun's eye,
And in themselves their pride lies buried,
For at a frown they in their glory die.
The painful warrior famoused for might,
After a thousand victories once foil'd,
Is from the book of honour rased quite,
And all the rest forget for which he toil'd:
  Then happy I that love and am belov'd,
  Where I may not remove nor be remov'd.

In his *The Round Table and Characters of Shakespeare's Plays*, William Hazlitt captioned this sonnet as 'Constancy'. In this sonnet, for the first time, Shakespeare seems to be happy that his love for the youth is requitted, and it is in this sonnet that the poet, for the first time, expresses his dejection due to his dark fortune (''I, whom fortune of such triumph bars''). The poet says that there are many people who are enjoying the favour of their fortunes ('stars'). They are honoured by the public, and they are proud of their appellations given by the people: ''Let those who are in favour with their stars/Of public honour and proud titles boast''. On the other hand, he says, he is denied such honours by fortune ('whom fortune of such triumph bars'). He cannot have joy by having that thing which he values ('honour') most, because that joy is beyond his reach ('Unlook'd for joy'): ''Whilst I, whom fortune of such triumph bars,/Unlook'd for joy in that I honour most.'' Ingram and Redpath said that the phrase 'Unlook'd for' means ''Probably 'beyond expectation' rather than 'unnoticed' (in the sense of 'obscure'). The latter, redundant meaning fails to further the movement of the thought culminating in the final couplet'' (Ingram, 64).

Those who enjoy the favours of great princes or other dignitaries ('Great princes' favourites') flaunt their ostentations ('their fair leaves spread'), but their ostentations are smoothered in their very flaunting. They are like marigolds which expose their ostentation or ostentatious beauty to the scorching rays of the sun ('frown') and consequently, their ostentation or pride soon die (due to the hot sun), and they lie buried within themselves: ''But as marigold at the sun's eye,/And in themselves their pride lies buried,/For at a frown they in their glory die.'' By marigold, the poet is, perhaps, meaning garden marigold or *calendula officinalis* that, like the sun-flower, looks always to the sun, and changes its position as the sun courses through the sky. Again, the poet says, soldiers who suffer so much pain fighting wars, and thus achieve fame ('famoused') for their might of pushing back enemies and nullifying their winning, for a thousand times ('a thousand victories once foil'd') are at first enshrined in the 'book of honour'. But afterwards, their names are erased ('rased') from the 'book of honour', and people then forget their (legendary) bravery ('toil'd'): "The painful warrior famoused for might,/After a thousand victories once foil'd,/Is from the book of honour rased quite,/And all the rest forgot for which he toil'd". Most modern editors read 'razed' instead of 'rased'. In the concluding couplet, the poet says that if this be the case, then he must say that he is happy, because he both loves (the Fair Youth) and is loved (by him). The ostentatious beauty of the marigold and soldier's exploits may be forgotten, but neither the poet will forget the Fair Youth, or cast away ('remove') the Fair Youth from his (the poets) favour, nor will the poet himself be forgotten by the youth, or be cast away by the youth from his favour: "Then happy I that love and am belov'd,/Where I may not remove nor be remov'd."

26

Lord of my love, to whom in vassalage
Thy merit hath my duty strongly knit,
To thee I send this written ambassage
To witness duty, not to shew my wit, —
Duty so great, which wit so poor as mine
May make seem bare, in wanting words to shew it,
But that I hope some good conceit of thine
In thy soul's thought all naked will bestow it,
Till whatsoever star that guides my moving
Points on me graciously with fair aspect,
And puts apparel on my totter'd loving
To show me worthy of their sweet respect:
Then may I dare to boast how I do love thee, —
Till then not show my head where thou mayst prove me.

The sonnets 1 — 25 were published in a volume with this sonnet as an *envoi.* Editors and critics have found resemblance between this sonnet and the Dedication of *The Rape of Lucrece* to the Right Honourable Henry Wriothesley, Earl of Southampton, and Baron of Titchfield: "The love I dedicate to your Lordship is without end: whereof this Pamphlet without beginning is but a superfluous *Moity.* The warrant I have of your Honourable disposition, not the worth of my untutored Lines makes it assured of acceptance. What I have done is yours, what I have to doe is yours, being part in all I have, devoted yours. Were my worth greater my duety would shew greater, meane time, as it is, it is bound to your Lordship; To whom I wish long life still lengthened with all happinesse. — Your Lordship's in all duety. — William Shakespeare.''

However, the poet addresses the Fair Youth as 'the Lord of his love' and calls himself a subject ('vassalage') of the Lord. He tells his Lord that his verses, as his duty directed him, have appropriately ('strongly') portrayed or enshrined ('knit') his (the Lord'd) external and internal beauties ('merit'): ''Lord of my love, to whom in vassalage/Thy merit hath my duty strongly knit''. The verses which are, as if, the ambassador ('ambassage') of the poet, are being sent to the Fair Youth as a token ('witness') of his faithful duty to the Lord, and not to flaunt his skill of writing verses ('wit'): ''To thee I send this written ambasage/ To witness duty, not to shew my wit, —''. The poet says that his duty to the Fair Youth is so great that his poor skill in versification ('wit so poor') will only prove inefficient or worthless ('bare') if he tries to portray all his beauties, because he lacks in appropriate words for expressing these beauties or beautiful aspects ('wanting words to show it'): ''Duty so great, which wit so poor as mine/May make seem bare, in wanting words to shew it.''

But the poet hopes that some good and natural ('naked'), fancy ('conceit') which reside within the soul of the Fair Youth will show the required favour ('it') to the verses: ''But that I hope some good conceit of thine/In thy soul's thought all naked will bestow it''. The poet wishes that such favour be bestowed on him by the Fair Youth, until his fate that controls his activities ('Till whatsoever star that guides my moving') be generous ('Points on me graciously') and show a smiling face ('fair aspect') to him. Until, the poet further says, his fate bestows better clothes ('apparel') on his love (or on the Fair Youth) which is now in tattered clothes ('totter'd'), and thus make his love attractive, so that the poet's 'great duty and poor wit' may seem acceptable, so that, in other words, the poet may prove himself worthy of portraying in his verses the beautiful and attractive aspects ('sweet respects') of the Fair Youth: ''Till whatsoever star that guides my moving,/points on me graciously with fair aspect,/And puts on my totter'd loving/To show me worthy of their sweet respect''. Ingram and Redpath said that according to Professor Sisson, 'their' in line 12 should be read as 'thy'. But Ingram and Redpath further wrote: ''While agreeing with Sisson that 'their sweet respect' is the Friend (the Fair Youth), we take 'their' to refer to the poet's great duty and poor wit (cf. line 5), rather than to his duty, star, and loving'' (Ingram, 66). It may be mentioned here that in the Elizabethan period, sometimes 'their' would be used for 'thy'. However, in the concluding couplet, the poet says that if the Fair Youth really catches at a fancy ('conceit') and if his fate bestows added attractions to his seemingly shabby love ('totter'd loving'), then he can be proud of his love for the Fair Youth: ''Then may I dare to boast how I do love thee, —''. But before that, that is before the poet's love (of the youth) is fortified with the youth's favour and the clothes ('apparel') of his guiding star is bestowed on the youth, appeals the poet to the Fair Youth not to see or count the poet's reasons ('not show my head') to prove how much the poet loves the Fair Youth: ''Till then not show my head where thou mayst prove me.''

The word 'show' at line 14 means 'see' or 'count', and so the phrase 'Till then not show my head' means 'till then do not see or count my head or reasons'. Again, the word 'prove' at the same line means 'bring to the test', and so the phrase 'mayst prove me' means 'may bring me to the test' (to test how much the poet loves the Fair Youth).

27

Weary with toil I haste me to my bed,
The dear repose of limbs with travel tir'd;
But then begins a journey in my head
To work my mind when body's work's expir'd:
For then my thoughts, from far where I abide,
Intend a zealous pilgrimage to thee,
And keep my drooping eyelids open wide,
Looking on darkness which the blind do see:
Save that my soul's imaginary sight
Presents their shadow to my sightless view,
Which like a jewel hung in ghastly night
Makes black night beauteous and her old face new.
  Lo, thus by day my limbs, by night my mind,
  For thee, and for myself, no quiet find.

The poet hastens to bed after strenuous journey, or after his day's hard works, to relax his body ('repose'), which he earnestly so long desired ('dear'). But though his body's works are over ('expir'd'), then his mind begins to work ('To work my mind'): ''Weary with toil, I haste me to my bed,/The dear repose for limbs with travel tir'd''. There is a pun here between the words 'travel' (journey) and 'travail' (toil). When the work of the body ceases, the mind begins to work, because then the mind does not remain where the poet takes rest ('abide'), but goes far away ('from far where I abide') and wants to undertake a holy journey with intense enthusiasm ('zealous') to visit the Fair Youth: "But then begins a journey in my head/To work my mind when body's work's expir'd:/For then my thoughts, from far where I abide,/Intend a zealous pilgrimage to thee". The poet then feels drowsy ('drooping eyelids') due to tiredness which is, again, due to his body's hard work, and yet he keeps his eyes wide open, and then he sees deep darkness that only blind persons see: "And keep my drooping eyelids open wide,/Looking on darkness which the blind do see".

The poet then loses his physical sight, but the sight of his imagination ('soul's imaginary sight') remains in order, and that sight brings before the sightless poet schema or image of thought about the Fair Youth: "Save that my soul's imaginary sight/Presents their shadow to my sightless view". Ingram and Redpath explained the word 'shadow' as " 'the insubstantial image (of you) engendered by my thoughts (line 5)' " (Ingram, 68). The schema of thought about, or the insubstantial image of, the Fair Youth remains suspended like a jewel against the back-drop of a fearful ('ghastly') night ('ghastly, because of the pitch-black darkness of the night). The jewel remaining thus suspended rather beautifies the dark night and transforms the haggard-looking ('old') night into a fresh and beautiful one: "Which like a jewel hung in ghastly night/Makes black night beauteous and her old face new." Therefore the poet says that during the day his body ('limbs') and during the night his mind remains restless ('no quiet') — both for the Fair Youth and also for himself (because his consciousness of the youth cannot be separated from his self-consciousness): "Lo, thus by day my limbs, by night my mind,/For thee, and for myself, no quiet find." Lines 11 and 12 of this sonnet may be compared with what Romeo says about Juliet in *Romeo and Juliet* (I, v, 43-44): "It seems she hangs upon the cheek of night/As a rich jewel in an Ethiop's ear— ".

28

How can I then return in happy plight
That am debarr'd the benefit of rest,
When day's oppression is not eas'd by night,
But day by night and night by day oppress'd,
And each, though enemies to other's reign,
Do in consent shake hands to torture me,
The one by toil, the other to complain

How far I toil, still farther off from thee?
I tell the day to please him thou art bright
And do'st him grace when clouds do blot the heaven;
So flatter I the swart-complexion'd night
When sparkling stars twire not thou gild'st the even:
  But day doth daily draw my sorrows longer,
  And night doth nightly make grief's length seem stronger.

In both Sonnet 27 and Sonnet 28, the images of day and night play a prominent part, and therefore the two sonnets may be calld 'paired sonnets' or 'companion sonnets'. Another reason of calling them 'paired sonnets' or 'companion sonnets' is that the same theme is present in both of them. In this sonnet, the poet says that he can never take rest ('am debarr'd the benefit of rest'), because the strain of his day's work is not removed or minimised ('eas'd') by taking rest at night. Rather his days are oppressed or disturbed ('oppress'd') by his thoughts (about the Fair Youth, perhaps) at night, as his thoughts at night are oppressed or disturbed by his toil at day time. The poet means to say that he cannot do physical works well during the day time as he feels tired of thinking too much at night; and, again, he cannot think clearly at night as he is tired of doing hard physical works during day. And, therefore, he cannot go to, or think clearly about ('return'), the Fair Youth with a happy mood ('happy plight'): "How can I then return in happy plight/ That am debarr'd the benefit of rest,/When day's oppression is not eas'd by night,/But day by night and night by day oppress'd". The day and the night are rivals to each other ('enemies to either's rein'); but, nevertheless, they oppress the poet in collusion ('in consent shake hands'). The day ('The one') oppresses the poet by making him do hard work in the day time, and the night oppresses him by making him complain against himself for not toiling as much as he should do ('complain/How far I toil'). And therefore the poet is gradually moving away from the Fair Youth ('still farther off from thee'): "And each, though enemies to other's reign,/Do in consent shake hands to torture me,/The one by toil, the other to complain/How far I toil, still farther off from thee?"

To assuage or propitiate ('to please') the day (so that it may not be angry against, or be draconian towards, the poet), the poet flatters the day by saying that it is dazzlingly brilliant ('bright'); and even when clouds cover up the sun ('clouds blot the heaven'), the poet tells the day that it is beautiful ('grace'): "I tell the day to please him thou art bright/And do'st him grace when clouds do blot the the heaven". In the same way, and with the same purpose, the poet flatters the balck-coloured ('swart-complexion'd') night by saying that even when bright stars do not twinkle ('twire') in the sky, she [the night] beautifies ('gild'st') the evening ('even'): "So flatter I the swart-complexion'd night/When sparkling stars twire not thou gild'st the even:". Ingram and Redpath wrote about the word 'gild'st' that most modern editors read the word as it appears here. But in the quarto edition, the word was 'guil'st'; but the "only possible meaning for *guil'st* would be 'beguil'st', which would parallel 'flatter' (line 11), but the real parallel is with 'do'st...grace' (line 10)." However, in the two concluding lines, the poet says that the day is continually ('daily') lengthening his sorrows, and the night is continually deepening ('stronger') his sorrows. That is always — during day-time as well as during night-time — the sorrows of the poet (due to his going away from the Fair Youth, *i.e.* due to the gradual blurring of the memory of the poet about the youth) are getting prolonged and deepened: "But day doth daily draw my sorrows longer,/And night doth nightly make grief's length seem stronger." The alliterations in line 13 ('day doth daily draw') and in line 14 ('night doth nightly') are very sweet and attractive.

29

When in disgrace with Fortune and men's eyes,
I all alone beweep my outcast state,
And trouble deaf heaven with my bootless cries,
And look upon myself and curse my fate —
Wishing me like to one more rich in hope,
Featur'd like him, like him with friends possess'd,
Desiring this man's art and that man's scope,
With what I most enjoy contented least;
Yet in these thoughts myself almost despising
Haply I think on thee, and then my state,
Like to the lark at break of day arising
From sullen earth, sings hymns at heaven's gate:
For thy sweet love remember'd such wealth brings
That then I scorn to change my state with kings.

In his *The Round Table and Characters of Shakespeare's Plays,* William Hazlitt entitled this sonnet as 'Love's Consolation'. In this sonnet, for the first time, Shakespeare overtly expresses his worldly misfortunes: his straitened pecuniary plight and his feeling of social ostracism. This sonnet was written, perhaps, at the time when the poet suffered literary humiliations at the hands of some Univeristy Wits, particularly at the hands of Robert Greene who satirised the poet in his

Groatsworth of Wit thus: ''An upstart crow, beautified with our feathers....'' However, the poet says that sometimes he weeps lonely for his neglected plight ('outcast state') when he feels humiliated for his down-trodden and pityful state of existence due to his fortune ('in disgrace with Fortune'), and when he is humiliated by men: ''When, in disgrace with Fortune and men's eyes,/I all alone beweep my outcast state,''. Then he disturbs the unheeding ('deaf') God ('heaven') with his desperate cries, in vain ('bootless cries'). Thus frustrated thrice (by Fortune, men, and God who does not respond to his appeal), the poet then looks within himself, and holds just only himself responsible ('curse my fate') for his despicable condition: ''And trouble deaf heaven with my bootless cries,/And look upon myself and curse my fate —''. Ingram and Redpath wrote about the word 'Fortune' with a capital 'F': ''The capital is commonly removed by editors, thus reducing the personification to a mere abstraction.'' (Ingram, 72).

In his misfortunate condition, then, the poet wishes himself to be like that person who is more hopeful or aspirant than himself ('like to one more rich in hope'), or wishes to be as beautiful in person, or in bodily aspects, as that person (who is more hopeful than himself) ('Featur'd like him'), and also wishes to have a number of friends ('with friends possess'd') like that very person: ''Wishing me like one more rich in hope,/Featur'd like him, like him with friends possess'd,''. In lines 5 and 6, the poet is not speaking of three several persons, but of one person who is 'rich in hope', well 'Featur'd' and is always surrounded by a gang of friends. This perhaps, refers to the Fair Youth (either the Earl of Pembroke or the Earl of Southampton, both of whom possessed these three qualities). In his oneiric or wool-gathering thoughts, the poet then wishes to possess the skill or learning, or both, of one who has got all these things ('Desiring this man's art'), or wishes to get that opportunity of advancement that some one possesses ('that man's scope'). All this while, the poet feels that whatever he possesses, in whatever degree (hope, beauty, art and scope) ('what I most enjoy') can hardly give him peace ('contented least'): ''Desiring this man's art and that man's scope,/With what I most enjoy contented least;''.

But, though thus full of sorrows and self-despisal ('myself almost despising'), while he accidentally or fortunately ('haply') muses on the Fair Youth, then even in his despicable plight, he sings praises to God ('sings hymns at heaven's gate') like a lark. The poet means to say that then he feels happy even with the modicum of favour that the high heaven has bestowed upon him, and so he thanks the heaven. He says that then he feels that his night of adversity is over and so he sings in praise of God, like the lark that breaks the torpor of the night at break of day, and flies from the moribund ('sullen') earth to the sky (as if in hope) and sing happy songs: "Yet in these thoughts myself almost despising/Haply I think on thee, and then my state,/Like to the lark at break of day arising/From sullen earth, sings hymns at heaven's gate:". At that while, the poet becomes extremely happy, because then the remembrance or memory of the Fair Youth's sweet love brings so much of longed for things ('wealth') to him that he would then despise ('scorn') to swap his present state of existence even with those of monarchs: "For thy sweet love remember'd such wealth brings/That then I scorn to change my state with kings." Lines 11 and 12 of this sonnet may be compared with the first two lines of the Song that Muscians sing in *Cymbeline* (II, iii, 19-20): "Hark, hark! the lark at heaven's gate sings,/ And Phoebus 'gins arise". And the same imagery can also be found in Lyly's *Campaspe* (V, i): "How at heaven's gates she [the lark] claps her wings'/The morne not waking till she sings."

30

When to the sessions of sweet silent thought
I summon up remembrance of things past,
I sigh the lack of many a thing I sought,
And with old woes new wail my dear times waste:
Then can I drown an eye, unus'd to flow,
For precious friends hid in death's dateless night,
And weep afresh love's long since cancell'd woe,
And moan the expense of many a vanish'd sight:
Then can I grieve at grievances foregone,
And heavily from woe to woe tell o'er
The sad account of fore-bemoaned moan,
Which I new pay as if not paid before.
But if the while I think on thee, dear friend,
All losses are restor'd and sorrows end.

This sonnet brings forth the theme of the immediately preceding one, *i.e.* Sonnet 29, and so Sonnets 29 and 30 may be called 'companion sonnets'. In the earlier sonnet, *i.e.* in Sonnet 29, the poet was musing over his own present predicament, and in this sonnet, he is meditating over his past frustrations. One peculiarity of this sonnet is that in it the poet heavily resorts to legal terms and images, such as ***session, summon up, dateless, cancell'd*** etc. The terms 'sessions' and 'summon up' have direct legal referentiality. For instance, we say that the court is in *session* and it has issued a *summon* to the culprit. In the first four lines of the sonnet, the poet tells us that when he sits ('sessions') (*i.e.* in a relaxed mood) to muse on some happy ('sweet') images or things ('thought'), then he recalls ('summon up') memories ('remembrance') of past things. And with the remembrance of the past sorrows, the poet, in the present moment, once again mourns ('new wail') for the precious ('dear') time he had vainly devoted for those things he fruitlessly aspired after; or the poet recalls memories of past things, and thereby adds new sorrows ('new wail') to his previous store of sorrows ('old woes'); or with his previous store of sorrows, the poet once again bemoans ('new wail') the loss of things destroyed ('waste') by time: "When to the session of sweet silent thought/I summon up remembrance of things past,/I sigh the lack of many a thing I sought,/And with old woes new wail my dear times waste:". Ingram and Redpath explained the phrase 'dear times waste' as "'time's grievous destruction of things dear' " (Ingram, 74). They also explained the first line of this sonnet thus: " 'When I sit alone and meditate on the past' " (Ingram, 74). They further compared the 'legal image' (cf. 'session') present in the first line with a part of Iago's speech in *Othello* (III, iii, 142-45): "Who has that breast so pure/But some uncleanly apprehensions/Keep leets and law-days, and in sessions sit/With meditations lawful?" (Ingram, 74).

The poet says that when he recalls his memories of past things, then his eyes become full of tears ('drown my eyes') — eyes that do not usually get moistened with tears ('unus'd to flow'). He weeps for his fast and important ('precious') friends who are now shrouded by the eternal night of death ('death's dateless night'). In the past, when his friends died, he wept. But now his mourning for those friends is a thing of the past, *i.e.* he does not mourn their deaths now ('long since cancell'd woe'). Nevertheless, when he recalls the memories of his past friends, he weeps once again ('afresh') for them. Further, when he recalls the things of the past, he recollects the loss ('expense') of many experiences (happy experiences) that are no more now ('many a vanish'd sight'): "Then can I drown an eye, unus'd to flow,/For precious friends hid in death's dateless night,/And weep afresh love's long since cancell'd woe,/And moan the expense of many a vanish'd sight:". John Kerrigan explained the phrase 'expense of many a sight' in three different ways: "(1) loss of many things once seen; (2) expenditure of many fruitless sighs; (3) cost of myself of frequent and fruitless sighs. Senses (2) and (3) both depend on *sight* as a variant form of 'sigh' in sixteenth-century English. Sense (3) should be read in the light of the 'blood-consuming sighs' and 'blood-drinking sighs' of 2, *Henry VI.* III. 2.61 and 63; the Elizabethans believed that sighing consumed the blood.'' (Kerrigan, 212). Further, Kerrigan wrote about the legal reference of the word 'cancell'd' in the phrase 'long since cancell'd woe': ''The *woe* is like a bond or legally recorded debt, *cancelled* ('paid off, annulled') long ago. Part of the thread of legal and financial imagery starts with *sessions* and *summon up,* continues with dateless (for bonds and leases reach fruition and expire at their 'date'), and concludes in lines 11-14 with *sad account, pay, paid,* and *losses*'' (Kerrigan, 212).

When the poet thus recalls the memories of the past, then he can mourn ('grieve') over his past sorrows ('grievance foregone'), and can give an inventory ('account') of the lamentations he had done before ('sad account of fore-bemoaned moan'), citing instances of his heavy sorrows one after another ('heavily from woe to woe tell o'er'): ''Then can I grieve at grievances foregone,/And heavily from woe to woe tell o'er/The sad account of fore-bemoaned moan,''. The poet then thinks that he is then paying the price of his fruitless aspirations, as if he had not paid it in the past: ''Which I new pay as if not paid before.'' The poet means to say that in the past he did not weep enough for his frustrations; and when he recalls the past things or experiences, he weeps again to shed the required amount of tears for those frustrations. In the last two lines of this sonnet, the poet says that even in such a pitiful plight of his, when he meditates on his 'dear friend', the Fair Youth, he feels that all the losses he incurred in the past are compensated, and consequently, his mourning ends: ''But if the while I think on thee, dear friend,/All losses are restor'd and sorrows end.'' Like in Sonnet 28, here also Shakespeare has produced sweet alliterations in the first two lines with the words: 'sessions', 'sweet', 'silent', and 'summon'.

31

Thy bosom is endeared with all hearts
Which I by lacking have supposed dead,
And there reigns love, and all love's loving parts,
And all those friends which I thought buried.
How many a holy and obsequious tear
Hath dear religious love stol'n from mine eye
As interest of the dead, which now appear
But things remov'd that hidden in thee lie!
Thou art the grave where buried love doth live,
Hung with the trophies of my lovers gone,
Who all their parts of me to thee did give, —

That due of many now is thine alone.
    Their images I lov'd I view in thee;
    And thou, all they, hast all the all of me.

John Kerrigan wrote about this sonnet: ''This poem explains how the *losses* of 30.14 (...) are not so much 'made up for' as *restored.* The sonnet is intimately linked with its predecessor in vocabulary (*lack/ lacking* at 30.3 and 31.2, for example), imagery (*interest* and *due,* 31.7 and 12, pick up the financial metaphors of 30), and the deployment of material (31.5-6 matches 30.5-6) as well as in its concern with the past. But the poem also has affinities with Sonnets 53, 98, and 99 and *A Lover's Complaint* 253-80, for it presents the beloved as the focus, the inclusive centre, of love and beauty. The difficult first quatrain announces this theme, and the sestet clarifies and extends it: since the youth contains all the human beauty that the poet has ever loved (line 13), the poet must give him all the love he has ever felt (lines 11-12). As the seat of such love (almost of Love itself), the young man seems to comprise *all they* (line 14) — all those friends previously lost to *death's dateless night* (30.6)'' (Kerrigan, 213).

In Sonnet 30, Shakespeare mourned for, among other things, the deaths of his dear friends. But in this poem he imaginately reclaims those friends and thinks that they are living within the 'bosom' of the Fair Youth, and thus he finds a sort of consolation. In the first two lines of this sonnet, the poet says that he thought that his friends were dead ('supposed dead') but he now finds that those friends have made the heart ('bosom') of the Fair Youth dear or precious ('endeared') [the dead friends are present in the youth's bosom and so the bosom has become precious]: ''Thy bosom is endeared with all hearts/Which I by lacking have supposed dead''. The poet means to say that all his dead friends loved the Fair Youth, and their love is even now present in the bosom or heart of the youth. And therefore the poet thinks that those *friends themselves* are living within the bosom of the youth — friends whom he supposed to have lost ('lacking'). Kerrigan wrote about the meaning of these two lines: ''Initially 'loved by the hearts of all men' and so 'richly adorned with the hearts of all men' (exploiting, like Sonnet 22, the convention that lovers' *hearts* reside in their beloved's bosom); then, with the turn into line 2, 'made precious by including all those loved people (assuming, as often in Shakespeare, the synecdochic equivalence of *hearts* of their owners), enriched with all those *friends* (compare 30.6 and 31.4' '' (Kerrigan, 213). The conceit 'endeared' which means 'made more precious' runs through the whole sonnet. The poet says that in the heart of the youth there rules the deity of love (Eros) or there is predominance of love ('there reigns love'), and in the heart of the youth there "all the parts of the poet's love which have been shared among those he has lost are now united in the Friend [the Fair Youth]" (Ingram, 76). There in the heart of the youth also subsist the friends of the poet whom the poet thought dead ('those friends which I thought buried'): "And there reigns love, and all love's loving parts,/And all those friends which I thought buried."

Next, the poet says that after the deaths of his friends, he had shed much tear reverentially mourning ('holy and obsequious tear') for them for whom he had precious ('dear') and deep ('religious') love: "How many a holy and obsequious tear/Hath dear religious love stol'n from mine eye". The poet says that his mourning for his dead friends was, as if, a duty for him ('obsequious'). According to Kerrigan, the word 'dear' means "tender, precious, heartfelt, grievous" and the word 'religious' means "assiduous, full of faith, reverent, pure" (Kerrigan, 213). The poet shed so much tear as he owed to his dead friends as their interest on the principal of their love for him. Here the word 'interest' is used in the commercial or financial sense of the word, and so it means 'return due to investor'. But now the poet thinks that those dead friends ('which') are not actually gone for ever, but are only transported away ('remov'd) from his view, and that those dead friends are now existing secretly ('hidden') in the heart of the Fair Youth: "As interest of the dead, which now appear/But things remov'd that hidden in thee lie!" As the poet shed tears for paying the interest on the principle of his friends' love for him, so he said in line 5 that the tear was 'obsequious' or duty-bound. The word 'obsequious', with the same sense, appears also at line 9 of Sonnet 125 ("No, let me be obsequious in thy heart") and in *Hamlet* (I, ii, 91-92): "In filial obligation, for some term/To do obsequious sorrow."

As in the heart or person or body of the Fair Youth the dead friends have ensconced themselves, after their deaths, the body of the youth has become a grave ('Thou art the grave'), and in that grave the dead friends are, as if, buried, though they are somehow still alive ('where buried love doth live'). Emblems and wreaths commemorating the dead friends' winning over love (for the poet and also, possibly, for the youth) ('trophies') are hanging over their grave which is but the person of the Fair Youth: "Thou art the grave where buried love doth live,/Hung with the trophies of my lovers gone". We find the use of the word 'trophies' also in *A Lover's Complaint* (line 218): " 'Lo, all these trophies of affections hot...' ". Kerrigan commented on line 10: "It was classical and classicizing renaissance practice to hang emblems and wreaths commemorating a dead man's successes in life over his grave (compare *Titus Andronicus* I, 1, 388-89, 'There lie thy bones, sweet Mutius, with thy friends,/Till we with trophies do adorn thy tomb', and *All's Well That Ends Well* II, 3, 137-38, 'on every grave/A lying trophy'). Here the poet says that the *trophies* of his dead *friends* (recording, presumably, their emotional triumphs over him) adorn the young man's *bosom*" (Kerrigan, 214). The dead friends ('Who') gave to the Fair Youth all their shares in the poet, *i.e.* all that they could claim from the poet: "Who all their parts of me to thee did give". Consequently, the shares or possessions ('due') of so many (persons or friends) are now the possession of only the Fair Youth: "That due of many now is thine alone."

In the concluding couplet, the poet says that he loves to see the projections or pictures ('images') of those friends in the person of the Fair Youth. And, lastly, he says that the youth has now become the summation of all those friends ('And thou, all they'). And because the poet (or his love) was, as if, disbursed amongst his dead friends who are now in the possession of the Fair Youth, the youth has in his possession all or everything the poet once possessed ('hast all the all of me'): "Their images I lov'd I view in thee;/And thou, all they, hast all the all of me." Kerrigan wrote about the last line or line 14: "...because he [the Fair Youth] 'is' the lost *friends*, the young man possesses *all the all* of the poet — *all* his 'everything', where 'everything' is not only 'all the friends I ever loved' and 'all the love I ever gave' but 'all that I am'. This climatic conceit, which catches up *all the all* of the poem (see lines 1, 3, 4, 11, 14), is clinched in wordplay: 'the all of all' is a stock tag (used, for example, at *Love's Labour's Lost* V, 1, 103) meaning 'summary conclusion', and *all the all* sums and concludes sonnet." (Kerrigan, 214-15). In this sonnet, there are two sweet alliterations in line 14: one, between 'thou' and 'they'; and the other, between 'all' and 'all'.

32

If thou survive my well-contented day,
When that churl Death my bones with dust shall cover,
And shalt by fortune once more re-survey
These poor rude lines of thy deceased lover,
Compare them with the bettering of time,
And though they be outstripp'd by every pen
Reserve them for my love, not for their rhyme,

Exceeded by the height of happier men.
Oh then vouchsafe me but this loving thought:
'Had my friend's Muse grown with this growing age,
A dearer birth than this his love had brought
To march in ranks of better equipage:
But since he died, and poets better prove,
Theirs for their style I'll read, his for his love'.

Ingram and Redpath wrote a general introduction to this sonnet which runs thus: "This is one of the sonnets (like 55) into which commentators have read the theory that Shakespeare regarded his plays as 'pot-boilers', and believed real literary fame and the regard of a patron must depend on the Sonnets. (....). C.H. Crandall (*Representative Sonnets*, 1890, 50) even found here a provision of the resurgence of the Petrarchan form over the Shakespearean, and considered that Shakespeare was writing his own excuse!" (Ingram, 78). In this sonnet, for the first time, Shakespeare speaks of his own death instead of the death of his dear friend, and about his low estimation of his own works. He asks his friend, the Fair Youth, to re-read ('re-survey') his verses of small worth ('poor rude lines') after his death ('thy deceased lover'), and if the youth then be living ('survive') and if the youth fortunately ('by fortune') comes across these verses (his verses). The poet will not shrink back from death — death that will cover up his body with earth ('my bones with dust shall cover') but he will welcome death as his rought, base and discourteous fellow ('churl'): "If thou survive my well-contented day,/When that churl Death my bones with dust shall cover,/And shalt by fortune once more re-survey/These poor rude lines of thy deceased lover". Here, perhaps, the poet seems to be frustrated with life as is evident from the phrase 'well-contented day'. The day on which the poet will die will not be a sorrowful day but a happy day ('well-contented day'). Kerrigan explained the phrase 'my well-contented day' thus: "the day which I welcome (when I shall pay my debt to nature. 'To content' could mean 'to pay in full' " (Kerrigan, 215).

If the youth chances on the verses of the poet, the poet requests him to consider ('Compare') his verses against the literary progression or advancement of the (Elizabethan) time ('the bettering of the time'). It may be mentioned here that the Elizabethans were very conscious about their advancement in all fields, including the literary; and, further, they used to judge the worth of anything against the backdrop of their concept of progress. The poet says that while thus compared with the advancement of the age, *i.e.* with the compositions of all other poets of that age, it may be that the compositions of those poets will be judged worthier than the verses of the poet ('And though they be outstripp'd by every pen'). Nevertheless, the poet requests the Fair Youth to keep his verses in store ('Reserve them') for the poet's love of the youth, and not for the quality ('rhyme') of those verses, because the other poets who are more skilled ('happier') may have composed worthier verses, and consequently, the quality of his verses may be exceeded by the quality of the verses of those more skilled poets ('Exceeded by the height'): "Compare with the bettering of the time,/And though they be outstripp'd by every pen/Reserve them for my love, not for their rhyme,/Exceeded by the height of happier men."

The poet further asks or requests the Fair Youth to condescend to grant or approve ('vouchsafe') the happy ('loving') thought of the poet that the youth, in that future time will think that his [the youth's] friend's [the poet's] Muse of verses waxed finer, or his friend's poetic skill grew powerful, or rather more powerful, with the continuance of the progressive age (the Elizabethan age) ('this growing age'): "Oh then vouchsafe me but this loving thought:/'Had my friend's Muse grown with this growing age,". The poet requests the Fair Youth to deign to think that his [the youth's] friend [the poet] had written more precious poems ('dearer birth') than the age had seen: "A dearer birth than this his love had brought". The poet says that his more worthier verses have been, or will be, written owing to the youth's love for the poet ('this his love had brought'). In line 11, the word 'love' may mean both 'the poet' and 'the love of the youth for the poet'. But in either case, the general meaning is not disturbed. The verses of the poet would be able (or the youth is requested to think so) to take a place ('march in ranks') among all the better verses that are adorned with better decorations ('equipage'): "To march in ranks of better equipage:". At that future time, the poet will be a long-since-deceased versifier, and by that time, poets of more skill will come up and produce better verses ('poets better prove'). Nevertheless, the poet requests the youth to say that he [the youth] will be reading the other poets' verses but for their beauty ('Theirs for their style I'll read'), but he will be reading his [the poet's] verses because the poet loved him [the Fair Youth] ('his for his love'): "But since he died, and poets better prove,/Theirs for their style I'll read, his for his love'."

This sonnet may be compared with Sonnet 73 where also the poet shows his awareness of death. These two sonnets also share in common some images; for instances, that of death, of burial, etc. The meaning of the word 'contented' also appears in both the sonnets. Again, in this sonnet (lines 5-8) and in Sonnet 76, the poet shows his concern about the quality of his verses *vis-a-vis* those of other poets. The present sonnet contains two fine alliterations in the concluding couplet ('poet' and 'prove'; and 'his' and 'his') — a more or less common feature of Shakespearean concluding couplets.

33

Full many a glorious morning have I seen
Flatter the mountain tops with sovereign eye,
Kissing with golden face the meadows green,
Gilding pale streams with heavenly alchemy, —
Anon permit the basest clouds to ride
With ugly rack on his celestial face,
And from the forlorn world his visage hide,
Stealing useen to west with this disgrace:
Even so my sun one early morn did shine
With all triumphant splendour on my brow;
But out alack, he was but one hour mine —
The region cloud hath mask'd him from me now.
    Yet him for this my love no whit disdaineth:
    Suns of the world may stain, when heaven's sun staineth.

This sonnet begins the so-called 'estrangement' sonnets — sonnets in which a breach of friendship between the peot and the youth is dimly apparent. It distinguishes itself by its rich portrayal of nature imagery. The poet says that he has observed very many ('Full') bright ('glorious') mornings when the sun ('sovereign eye') caressed or cajoled the picks of mountains and kissed the green tracts ('meadows green') with its golden beams ('golden face'). The poet has seen the sun smoothly slid ('Glidding') over colourless ('pale') streams with its ethereal colour ('heavenly alchemy'): "Full many a glorious morning have I seen/Flatter the mountain tops with sovereign eye,/Kissing with golden face the meadows green,/Glidding pale streams with heavenly alchemy, ". Kerrigan has found parallels to the fourth line in *Venus and Adonis* and *King John*. (Kerrigan, 216). The liens 856-58 of *Venus and Adonis* read: "The sun ariseth in his majesty;/Who doth the world so gloriously behold/That cedar-tops and hills seem burnished gold". And in *King John* (III, i, 77-80), King Philip says:

To solemnize this day the glorious sun
Stays in his course and plays the alchemist,

Turning with splendour of his precious eye
The meagre cloddy earth to glittering gold.

But soon ('Anon') the bright sun allows base and black clouds to cover ('ride') the face of the sun ('his celestial face') with their despicable ('ugly') and damaging onslaught ('rack'): "Anon permit the basest clouds to ride/With ugly rack on his celestial face,". When the sun is so covered up, the world beneath becomes despondent ('forlorn') and the sun, as if, hides its face ('visage') from the outcast ('forlorn') earth, and stealthily ('Stealing') and imperceptively ('unseen') declines in the western sky bearing with it the disgrace it has suffered: "And from the forlorn world his visage hide,/Stealing unseen to west with this disgrace:".

The poet now compares the Fair Youth ('my sun') with the sun. He says that like the bright morning sun, the youth once in his early years ('one early morn') shone brightly, with all his 'glorious and exulting' fulguration ('all triumphant splendour') on the person ('on my brow') of the poet, as the sun threw its beams on the tops of mountains: "Even so my sun one early morn did shine/With all triumphant splendour on my brow;". But, unfortunately ('alack!'), the Fair Youth shone on him or belonged to him only for a short while ('but one hour mine'), and then the clouds of the upper sky ('region cloud') enveloped and curtained off ('mask'd') the youth from the poet: "But out alack, he was but one hour mine —/The region cloud hath mask'd him from me now." The word 'mask'd' (envelope or curtain) here may mean disaffection on the part of the youth as regards the poet, or it may refer to some other person who snatched away the favour of the youth from the poet. The poet says that in spite of all this, the poet ('my love') does not at all scoff even a little ('no whit') at the person ('him') who has taken away the Fair Youth from the possession of the poet: "Yet him for this my love no whit disdaineth:". The poet consoles himself by thinking that even the *heavenly* sun itself may be soiled or darkened ('stain') by the cloud, and so it is not unexpectable that the people of the world ('Suns of the world') will also be clouded or enveloped or 'mask'd'. Kerrigan explains the word 'staineth' thus: "The sun 'stains' when clouds cover it; but even when it shines freely it 'stains' in the now obsolete sense 'drains light away', for it takes lustre from other bright things." (Kerrigan, 217).

Some critics have conjectured that this sonnet was written about the time when Shakespeare wrote the First Part of *King Henry IV* in which play the poet depicted his hero much the same way in which he has delineated the Fair Youth in this sonnet. This is evident in the following lines of Prince of Wales in *King Henry IV*, Part I (I, ii, 190-96):

Yet herein will I imitate the *sun,*
Who doth permit the base contageous clouds
To smother up his beauty from the world,
That, when he please again to be himself,
Being wanted, he may be more wond'red at
By breaking through the foul and ugly mists
Of vapours that did seem to strangle him.

Parallels to the imagery of the sun and its being eclipsed by clouds and of the sun stealing away the lustre of objects may be found also in other places of Shakespeare's works. For instances:

i. in *Romeo and Juliet* where Romeo says (III, v, 9-10): "Night's candles are burnt out, and jocund day/Stands tip-toe on the misty mountain tops."
ii. in *A Midsummer Night's Dream* where Oberon says (III, ii, 391-93): "Even till the eastern gate, all fiery red,/Opening on Neptune with fair blessed beams,/Turns into yellow gold his salt green streams."
iii. in *King John* where King Philip says (III, i, 77-80): "To solemnize this day the glorious sun/Stay in his course and plays the alchemist,/Turning with splendour of his precious eye/The meagre cloddy earth to glittering gold."
iv. in *Venus and Adonis:*

The sun riseth in his majesty;
Who doth the world gloriously behold
That cedar-tops and hills seem burnish'd gold.

34

Why didst thou promise such a beauteous day,
And make me travel forth without my cloak,
To let base clouds o'ertake me in my way,
Hiding thy bravery in their rotten smoke?
'Tis not enough that through the cloud thou break
To dry the rain on my storm-beaten face,
For no man well of such a salve can speak
That heals the wound and cures not the disgrace:
Nor can thy shame give physic to my grief;
Though thou repent, yet I have still the loss:

> The offender's sorrow lends but weak relief
> To him that bears the strong offence's cross.
> Ah, but those tears are pearl which thy love sheds;
> And they are rich, and ransom all ill deeds.

Ingram and Redpath wrote a general note to this sonnet: "Story-hunters, by literal interpretation, have here detected specific events. Thus, Samuel Butler invented a waylaying and rough-handling of the poet that caused the 'lameness' he takes literally in 37.9 and 89.3, and F.G. Fleay (*A Biographical Chronicle of the English Drama,* 1559-1642, 2 vols., London, 1891, II, 216) interpreted line 2 as '(Make me) appear publicly as an author' " (Ingram, 82). However, this sonnet continues the argument of the immediately preceding one. In the earlier sonnet, the poet was aggrieved because the Fair Youth was "but one hour mine —", and here in this sonnet, he says that the youth caused him to grieve by not keeping his [the youth's] promise. In the first two lines, the poet says that his friend, the youth, promised that the poet would be able to walk through a bright ('beauteous') day, and so the poet did not take any protection against rain and storm ('make me travel forth without my cloak'): "Why didst thou promise such a beauteous day,/ And make me travel forth without my cloak,". This means that the youth vowed to be fair and friendly to the poet, and so the poet thought that he had nothing to fear.

But soon the situation changed: obnoxious rain ('base clouds') came and drenched ('o'ertake') the poet, and yet the Fair Youth did not come to his succour, *i.e.* did not show 'splendid friendliness' ('bravery') to the poet, but hid ('Hiding') his friendliness behind abject rain ('rotten smoke'): "To let base clouds o'ertake me in my way,/Hiding thy bravery in their rotten smoke?" Here the poet asks the youth why he [the poet] was thus betrayed by him. He may have realised the truth of the proverb: "Although the sun shines, leave not your cloak at home." Of course the Fair Youth has come to console the wounded heart ('storm-beaten face') of the poet and to wipe the tears from his eyes ('To dry the rain'), yet such rescuing or remedy ('salve') proffered by the youth to the poet does not console the poet (' 'Tis not enough'), because the scar left by the wound, after it is cured, is a mark of humiliation ('disgrace') in the eyes of the people. For the people will think that though the youth consoled the poet, yet it was only after he had hurt the heart of the poet. And so the poet says that such a succour ('salve') is not good in the eyes of the people ('no man well of such a salve can speak'): " 'Tis not enough that through the cloud thou break/To dry the rain on my storm-beaten face,/For no man well of such a salve speak/That heals the wound and cures not the disgrace:''. After wounding the heart of the poet, the Fair Youth may now feel ashamed ('thy shame') or he may feel sorry ('repent') for hurting the poet, but, the poet says, these will in no way either serve as an anodyne ('physic to my grief') or lessen the 'loss' of love of the poet: ''Nor can thy shame give physic to my grief;/Though thou repent, yet I have still the loss:''.

The poet now teaches the Fair Youth a generally practical truth. He tells him that one may offend some one and then repent for that offence ('offender's sorrow'), but that repentance can act as a relief or anodyne only minimally ('weak relief') to the person who suffered the heavy brunt of that offence ('cross'): ''The offender's sorrow lends but weak relief/To him that bears the strong offence's cross''. Nevertheless, as the poet sees the tears of repentance in the eyes of the Fair Youth, the beads of tears in the eyes of the youth appear to the poet to be as lovable, valuable and attractive as pearls ('but those tears are pearls'). And then, for the nonce, the poet thinks that those beads of tears are so invaluable ('rich') that those beads can adequately pay the price ('ransom') of the poet's wound in his heart: ''Ah, but those tears are pearls which thy love sheds;/And they are rich, and ransom all ill deeds.'' Kerrigan found a reference to the Bible in the 12th and the 14th lines of this sonnet. He wrote: ''The biblican resonance of line 12 (....) supports as hint of Christian imagery. As Christ died on the *cross* to *ransom* — the verb was commonly used — mankind from the effects of the fall and *all ill deeds,* so the young man's [the Fair Youth's] *tears* atone for his *ill deeds* against the poet'' (Kerrigan, 218). The idea of bearing a cross also occurs in *As You Like It* (II, iv, 10-12) where Touchstone tells Celia: ''For my part, I had rather *bear* with you than *bear* you; yet I should *bear no cross* if I did *bear* you; for I think you have no money in your purse.''

35

No more be griev'd at that which thou hast done:
Roses have thorns, and silver fountains mud,
Clouds and eclipses stain both moon and sun,
And loathsome canker lives in sweetest bud;
All men make faults, and even I in this,
Authorizing thy trespass with compare,
My self-corrupting salving thy amiss,
Excusing their sins more than their sins are:
For to thy sensual fault I bring in sense —

Thy adverse party is thy advocate —
And 'gainst myself a lawful plea commence:
Such civil war is in my love and hate
That I an accessary needs must be
To that sweet thief which sourly robs from me.

In this sonnet, the poet is making a *volte face* and is making good the accusations he made against the Fair Youth in lines 1-12 of the immediately preceding sonnet. This change of mood in him is caused by the remorse of the youth for doing wrong to the poet. In lines 1-4 of this sonnet, the poet is 'rationalising' for the wrongs done to him by the youth. And he persuades the youth not to grieve any more for the wrongs done by him, because, howsoever fair and beautiful one may be, he must have a quantum of wrong, or a tendency of doing wrongs to others, in him. This is only natural; this is only an inalienable quality of the creation. For instance, the poet says, the beautiful rose has its 'thorns'; the sparkling 'fountain' has its 'mud'; the beautiful moon and the firece sun sometimes get eclipsed; and, likewise, delicate and beautiful buds of flowers are infested with abominable ('loathsome') insects ('cankers'). Therefore, it is natural that a whit of evil must reside in the good, and a quantum of ugliness must be present in things beautiful: "No more be griev'd at that which thou hast done:/Roses have thorns, and silver fountains mud,/Clouds and eclipses stain both moon and sun,/And loathsome canker lives in sweetest bud;". The poet means to say that "not only that 'excellent things.'" (Kerrigan, 218). Similar images, as in lines 1-4, may be found in *The Rape of Lucrece* (lines 848-50): " 'Why shouldst the worm intrude the maiden bud?/Or hateful cuckoos hatch in sparrow's nests?/Or toads infect fair founts with venom mud?"

Not only the beautiful objects of nature harbour ugliness or flaws, but even in all human beings, there are flaws. The poet is thus justifying or excusing the wrongs done to him by the Fair Youth: "All men make faults". On the other hand, now the poet himself is feeling fuilty, because he is justifying ('Authorizing') a comparison ('this') between the youth's faults ('trespass') and the faults in nature: "even I in this,/Authorizing thy trespass with compare". The poet is further at fault because he is ignoring or slighting or minimising ('salving') the Fair Youth's offences ('amiss'), and thus, he says, he is himself doing corruption ('corrupting'): "My self corrupting salving thy amiss". Ingram and Redpath said that "This line, with its religious, medical, and legal associations, is pivotal in the poem" (Ingram, 84). The next line, *i.e.* line 8 is very confusing. Some critics and editors are of the opinion that the word 'their' which occurs twice in the line is a misprint of the word 'thy'. Kerrigan, who is a supporter of this view, explained this line thus: "As he [the poet] provides the young man [the Fair Youth] with comparisons potent enough to excuse him from sins worse than those he has actually committed, the poet makes faults not only by tolerating misconduct but by displaying the doting weakness which makes him overindulgent to his beloved, and by bringing sophistry (the *sense* of line 9) to the defence of *sensuality,* using a faculty which should know better than to absolve an instinctive amiss." (Kerrigan, 219): "Excusing their sins more than their sins are:". To me, here, the word 'their', perhaps, means the 'offences' of the youth: the poet is excusing the sins due to those offences; but he is more than excusing those offences, in the sense that he is supporting those sins, thinking them to be very natural for human beings.

However, the poet further accuses himself of arguing for, or justifying, with diverse arguments ('I bring in sense'), the Fair Youth's carnal corruption ('sensual fault'). The phrase 'sensual fault' may refer to the Fair Youth's physical relation with the Dark Lady. This is the cause of the poet's harbouring hatred ('adverse party') for the youth for whom, all at the same time, he has all love ('thy advocate'): "For to thy sensual fault I bring in sense —/Thy adverse party is thy advocate —". Consequently, the poet is ambivalent towards the youth (' 'gainst myself a lawful plea commence'). No doubt the poet now loves the youth, but he has enough arguments for hating him too. And there is a mental conflict or tension ('civil war') within himself regarding whether he will love the youth or whether he will hate him: "And 'gainst myself a lawful plea commence:/Such civil war is in my love and hate". The poet now pleads for the innocence ('advocate') of the youth, though, at the same time, he is inimical ('adverse') to him ('Thy adverse party is thy advocate'). The poet is, as if, legally defending ('lawful plea commence') the youth against the charge of corruption, though he has no intention of doing this.

In the concluding couplet, the poet says that both he and the youth are involved in corruption, and that the poet himself is, of necessity ('needs must be'), rather, an accomplice ('accessary') of the youth in the act of corruption (or being corrupted by the Dark Lady). And the poet calls the youth an affectionate burgler ('sweet thief'), because he has stealthily carried away ('robs') (the Dark Lady) from his possession, which is an act for which the poet is suffering pain ('sourly'): "That I an accessary needs must be/To that sweet thief which sourly robs from me.'' It may be mentioned here that it is in this sonnet that we hear about the Dark Lady and her association with the youth and the poet, for the first time. Besides this sonnet, though the 'Dark Lady Sonnets' begin from Sonnet 127, Sonnets 36, 40, 41 and 42 insinuate the relationships among the poet, the Fair Youth, and the Dark Lady.

36

Let me confess that we two must be twain
Although our undivided loves are one:
So shall those blots that do with me remain
Without thy help by me be borne alone.
In our two loves there is but one respect,
Though in our lives a separable spite,
Which though it alter not love's sole effect,
Yet doth it steal sweet hours from love's delight.
I may not evermore acknowlege thee,
Lest my bewailed guilt should do thee shame;
Nor thou with public kindness honour me,
Unless thou take that honour from thy name:
  But do not so; I love thee in such sort
  As, thou being mine, mine is thy good report.

This sonnet may be compared with Sonnet 96. Firstly, because the concluding couplet of this sonnet is the same as that of Sonnet 96; and secondly, because the theme of both the sonnets is the same: the poet loves in Fair Youth in spite of the youth's furtive relationship with the Dark Lady. As in the immediately preceding sonnet, the reference to the Dark Lady is also very covertly present here. However, in lines 1 and 2, the poet admits ('confess') that though he and the Fair Youth love the same object (the Dark Lady) and therefore they are two persons ('twain'), yet the love between himself and the youth is not cleaved into two halves, and therefore the love between them is one ('our undivided loves are one'): ''Let me confess that we two must be twain/Although our undivided loves are one:''. This means that as regards the love of the Dark Lady, the poet and the youth are certainly ('must be') two separate persons, but their mutual love is unitary ('our undivided loves are one'). Therefore ('So'), the poet is ready to 'bear alone' the disgrace ('those blots') without the help of the youth ('borne alone'): ''So shall those blots that do with me remain/Without thy help by me be borne alone.'' Ingram and Redpath wrote about the 'blots' refered to here: ''What these are is obscure. Pooler sees here a reference to the 'disgrace with fortune and men's eyes' of 29.1, and suspects that 36 has got out of sequence. This is possible, but no more. Adams suggests that the reference may be to 'the ''stain'' given the poet by the friend' (33.14, 35.3); but this depends on a misinterpretation of 'stain' (....)'' (Ingram, 86). Ingram and Redpath explained the word 'stain' as meaning 'growing dim' or 'loosing brightness'. Perhaps, the word 'blots' may be interpreted as meaning 'infamy'. If this be so, then we may say that in lines 3 and 4, the poet tells his friend, the Fair Youth, that he is ready to bear with the infamy with which he [the poet] has been besmeared — infamy, because his beloved Dark Lady has been shared by the Fair Youth.

As a consequence of this, there is animosity or jealousy ('spite') between the two contestants for the love of the Dark Lady ('one respect') — the poet and the youth. But this animosity or jealousy can be wiped off ('separable'). The word 'respect' may also refer to the animosity between the poet and the youth. We may explain line 6 also thus: the poet and the youth are currently separated from one another ('separable' meaning 'separating'). The poet says that though there is animosity between them regarding the Dark Lady, yet the animosity can be wiped off: ''In our two loves there is but one respect,/Though in our lives a separable spite,''. The poet says that this animosity or jealousy does not stand in the way of his love's only ('sole') property or object ('effect'). Perhaps this property or object is the Dark Lady. Nevertheless, the poet says, this animosity certainly lessens his enjoyment of love ('steal sweet hours'): ''Which, though it alter not love's sole effect,/Yet doth steal sweet hours from love's delight.'' The poet says that in the future ('not evermore') he may not deem ('acknowledge') the youth as his friend, because in that case the infamy or disgrace for which he is now repentant ('bewailed guilt') may tarnish him [the Fair Youth] as well, and thus make him ashamed: ''I may not evermore acknowledge thee,/Lest my bewailed guilt should do thee shame;''. The expression 'bewailed guilt' is difficult to explain. Ingram and Redpath wrote about the expression: ''We agree with Beeching that 'we have no clear light from any other passage in the Sonnets upon this expression', though there may be some connexion with the 'harmful deeds' of 111.2'' (Ingram, 86).

As the poet has besmeared himself with infamy ('guilt'), he says, the Fair Youth also would not show kindness or sympathy to him in public: ''Nor thou with public kindness honour me''. The youth can show kindness to the poet only by lowering ('take') his public stature: ''Unless thou take that honour from thy name:''. But the poet forbids the youth to do either of the two — smearing the 'guilt' of the poet on his personality and thus getting ashamed, and lowering his public image

('But do not so'). Contrarily, the poet tells the youth that he loves him so much ('I love thee in such sort') that, because he loves the youth ('thou being mine'), the youth's reputation ('good report') will be a precious possession of the poet: "But do not so; I love thee in such sort/As, thou being mine, mine is thy good report." It may be mentioned here that Sonnets 34, 35, and 36 betray the poet's complex mood: the under-current of his love-hate ambivalence.

37

As a decrepit father takes delight
To see his active child do deeds of youth,
So I, made lame by Fortune's dearest spite,
Take all my comfort of thy worth and truth;
For whether beauty, birth, or wealth, or wit,
Or any of these all, or all, or more,
Entitled in their parts, do crowned sit,
I make my love engrafted to this store:
So then I am not lame, poor, nor despis'd,
Whilst that this shadow doth such substance give
That I in thy abundance am suffic'd,
And by a part of all thy glory live:
    Look what is best, that best I wish in thee;
    This wish I have — then ten times happy me!

The poet here calls himself a *lame* man. The word 'lame' is very imporrant but very difficult to explain. Ingram and Redpath made an important comment on this word: "That William Shakespeare *alias* Francis or Anthony Bacon *alias* Walter Raleigh, not to mention his other names, was crook-backed (87.8 and 90.3), had a scar over his left eye, and was lame in the left leg (here and 89.3) as a result of (a) a scuffle in which he was ambushed and beaten up, (b) an accident at the Fortune Theatre ('Fortune's dearest spite'), (c) serving as a soldier in the Low Countries, (d) fighting in (in his role as Sir Walter Raleigh) at Cadis in 1596, has all been triumphantly proved from the sonnets; whence it has also been revealed that he once resided in Bath and in Wells (26, 153, 154) and in Southern Europe (33)" (Ingram, 88). We must not forget that all these are mere conjectures never proved beyond even the slightest doubt. And so whether the word 'lame' can be taken literally is certainly very doubtful. To me, it is, perhaps, better to take the word in its figurative sense.

However, in the first four lines, the poet compares himself with an infirm ('decrepit') father, and the Fair Youth with that father's youthful son; and says that as the infirm father enjoys seeing his able son perform acts needing strength ('do deeds of youth'), so he [the poet], who is also infirm ('lame'), delights ('comfort') in the worthiness and honesty ('truth') of the youth: "As a decrepit father takes delight/To see his active child do deeds of youth,/So I, made lame by Fortune's dearest spite,/Take all my comfort of thy worth and truth;". The poet is infirm due to the blow, in the shape or manner of bitterest or 'most grievous' ('dearest') criticism ('spite') of him in the Fortune Theatre, that he had to sustain ("made lame by Fortune's dearest spite"). He now delights in the view of the youth, because the youth is now crowned with every glory — beauty of person, glory of parentage, possession of wealth, sharpness of wit, and all such qualities. The youth has legal or justified claim ('Entitled') to these qualities which he now possesses ('crowned'). Ingram and Redpath read 'their parts' in line 7, instead of 'thy parts' which Kerrigan reads. The latter seems to be more correct. Further, Kerrigan explained line 7 thus: "having the right and title, sit throned like a king among your good qualities." (Kerrigan, 221). In addition to all these qualities, the poet is conjoining ('engrafting') his own love for the youth to the youth's treasure ('store') of all those ('I make my love engrafted to this store'): "For whether beauty, birth, or wealth, or wit,/ Or any of these all, or all, or more,/Entitled in their parts, do crowned sit,/I make my love engrafted to this store:".

And by doing so, the poet thinks that he is now no more infirm ('I am not lame'), or 'poor', or despicable ('despis'd'), because as the beloved friend, or subordiante ('shadow') of the newly and gorgeously enriched Fair Youth, he has added strength ('substance') to his decrepitude: "So then I am not lame, poor, nor despis'd,' Whilst that this shadow doth such substance give". Kerrigan explained the expression 'this shadow doth such substance give' thus: "A *shadow* is usually the product of a *substance,* and the former's inferiority to the latter was proverbial; but the young man's/the youth's/*shadow* (his image, made up of *worth and truth* and all the *store* of good *parts*) here gives 'tissue' and 'strength' (two Elizabethan sense of *substance*) to the *decrepit* poet" (Kerrigan, 221). Therefore the peot now feels that he is adequately 'supplied' or happy ('suffic'd') being in the sufficiency ('abundance') of the attributes of the youth: "That I in thy abundance am suffic'd". And thus the poet lives being a part-possessor of the triumphs of the youth: "And by a part of all thy glory live." In the *envoi,* the poet wishes the youth whatever is best, and wishing thus, the poet feels ten times more happy than before: "Look what is best, that best I wish in thee;/This wish I have — then ten times happy me!'' In the Elizabethan sense, 'look what' meant 'whatever', and so the poet wishes the youth whatever is best.

38

How can my Muse want subject to invent
While thou dost breathe that pour'st into my verse
Thine own sweet argument, too excellent
For ever vulgar paper to rehearse?
Oh, give thyself the thanks if aught in me
Worthy perusal stand against thy sight;
For who's so dumb that cannot write to thee,
When thou thyself dost give invention light?
Be thou the tenth Muse, ten times more in worth
Than those old nine which rhymers invocate;
And he that calls on thee, let him bring forth
Eternal numbers to outlive long date.
  If my slight Muse do please these curious days,
  The pain be mine, but thine shall be the praise.

The Fair Youth himself is ''an attractive literary theme'' ('Thine own sweet argument'), and he is lending ('pour'st') that marvellous ('too excellent') theme into the poetic composition of the poet that the poet is writing and re-writing ('rehearse') on base ('vulgar') pieces of paper. So the poet asks: can his 'creative faculty' ('Muse') lack in literary themes? The poet means to say that he is overwhelmed by the beauty of the youth so much so that he has a swarm of ideas to write poems on, and therefore, he has no need of newly creating ('invent') ideas or themes for his poetry: ''How can my Muse want subject to invent/While thou dost breathe that pour'st into my verse/Thine own sweet argument, too excellent/For every vulgar paper to rehearse?'' The poet asks the youth to thank himself [the youth] if the youth finds ('perusal') anything worthy in the verses ('in me'— this is a metonymy) that appears in his [the youth's] perspective ('stand against thy sight'): ''Oh, give thyself the thanks if aught in me/Worthy perusal stand against thy sight;''. Here the poet means to say that the beauty of the youth is certainly worth viewing and enjoying, but he is not certain if he [the poet] will be able to recreate that beauty in his verses. If the poet can create any beauty in his verses, he says, it is due to the beauty of the youth, for which only the youth deserves being praised or thanked, and not the poet.

None can remain silent or unresponsive ('dumb'), or help writing verses, if he has seen the beauty of the Fair Youth ('thee'): "For who's so dumb that cannot write to thee". Or, who can help writing verses when the Fair Youth himself stimulates (poetically) by lending inventive ('invention') inspiration ('light')?: "When thou thyself dost give invention light?" Kerrigan explained this line thus: "By being himself (that is, a *sweet argument* incarnate), the youth illuminates (like the sun) or lights the way (like a torchbearer) for, or else finds out or digs up (and thus brings to *light*), rhetorical *invention.* His mere being ensures that the poet has matter" (Kerrigan, 222). The poet wishes the Fair Youth be the tenth Muse, besides the accepted nine allegorical ('old') Muses to whom poets ('rhymers') supplicate and beg inspiration for writing verses ('invocate'). Further, he wishes that the youth becomes 'ten times' more worthy, as the tenth Muse, than those nine Muses: "Be thou the tenth Muse, ten times more in worth/Than those old nine which rhymers invocate;" The nine Muses are, according to Hesiod, the daughters of Zeus and Mnemosyne (or Memory). It is told that "after the defeat of the Titans the gods had asked Zeus to create divinities who were capable of celebrating the victory of the Olimpians. The master of the gods then went to Pieria, where he shared Mnemosyne's couch for nine consecutive nights. When her time had come Mnemosyne gave birth to nine daughters who formed the choir of the Muses." (*New Larousse Encyclopedia of Mythology,* Hamlyn, 199). The word 'invocation' ('invocate') reminds us of the famous invocation to the Muse in Milton's *Paradise Lost.* Shakespeare mocks at the tradition of the invocation in *Love's Labour's Lost* (V, ii, 405-07) where Berowne says:

> Taffeta phrases, silken terms precise,
> Three-pil'd hyperboles, spruce affectation,
> Figures pedantical —

The idea of making the beloved the tenth Muse appears also in Drayton's *Idea* where the poet wishes his patroness become the tenth Muse: "And my fair Muse one Muse into the nine/Makes everyone of these three nines a ten."

In lines 11 and 12, the poet wishes that if any poet invocates the Fair Youth ('he that calls on thee'), that poet may compose ('bring forth' — a term of obstetrics meaning 'giving birth to') immortal verses or notes ('numbers') which will outlast 'a far distant *date*' ('outlive long date'): "And he that calls on thee, let him bring forth/Eternal numbers to outlive long date." In the *envoi,* the poet tells the youth that if his ordinary ('slight') verses give delight to the readers of the present 'hypercritical' time ('these curious days'), then he will think that he [the poet] can claim only the toil or labour of composing the verses, but the praises of those verses will go to his friend, the Fair Youth ('thine shall be the praise'): "If my slight Muse do please these curious days,/The pain be mine, but thine shall be the praise." The poet is here using the word 'Muse' as a metonymy for the word 'verses'.

39

O' how thy worth with manners may I sing
When thou art all the better part of me?
What can mine own praise to mine own self bring?
And what is't but mine own when I praise thee?
Even for this let us divided live,
And our dear love lose name of single one,
That by this separation I may give
That due to thee which thou deserv'st alone.
O absence, what a torment wouldst thou prove,
Were it not thy sour leisure gave sweet leave
To entertain the time with thoughts of love,
Which time and thoughts so sweetly dost deceive,
And that thou teachest how to make one twain
By praising him here who doth hence remain!

In the previous sonnet, the poet announced that he would sing ('If my slight Muse do please these curious days,/The pain be mine') the praise of the Fair Youth, and here, in this sonnet, he is keeping his word. The poet calls the Fair Youth 'the better part of me' which means that the youth is, as if, his soul. Kerrigan surmised that Shakespeare might have taken this phrase ('the better part of me') from Ovid's *Metamorphoses* or from the proverbial saw: "A friend is one's second self". In the second sense the phrase occurs *mutatis mutandis* in Sonnets 42 ('my friend and I are one'); 62 [' 'Tis thee ('my self')]; and 133 ('my next self thou') (Kerrigan, 222). However, the poet wonders (or is afraid) whether he can properly ('with manners') sing about the worthiness of the Fair Youth, as the youth is the 'doppel-ganger' or alter ego of the poet ('the better part of me'): "O' how thy worth with manners may I sing/When thou art all the better part of me?"

In lines 3 and 4, the poet asks whether there is any meaning in his own praise ('mine own praise') of the Fair Youth who is, as if, his own self. He asks: can his praise of the young man be anything else than praising his own self, because the youth is none other than he himself, or, at least, his alter ego? He here means to say that it cannot be otherwise: "What can mine own praise to mine own self bring?/And what is't but mine own when I praise thee?" Kerrigan explained lines 3 and 4 thus: "where's the profit in praising myself, and what kind of praise is it if not self-praise when I praise you?" (Kerrigan, 223). To avoid this ('Even for this'), *i.e.* to avoid self-praising, the poet appeals to the youth to live in separation ('us divided live'): "Even for this let us divided live". So that the 'keenly felt' ('dear') love between them may not be taken to be 'narcissistic love' ('our dear love lose name of single one'), but may be taken as 'mutual love' or love between two separate persons: "And our dear love lose name of single one". If both of them remain thus separated ('by this separation'), only then the poet can proffer to the youth the praise which he really deserves — the praise which only he deserves ('which thou deserv'st alone'): "That by this separation I may give/That due to the thee which thou deserv'st alone."

If the two persons are really separated from each other, then the youth will be absent from the poet, and the absence will be something very painful ('torment') to the poet. It is to be noted here that the absence of the youth is personified by the poet: "O absence, what a torment wouldst thou prove". The time during which the youth will remain absent might be the time of bitter leisure ('sour leisure') to the poet; but actually this time will not be bitter, because the poet will fill ('entertain') that time with the memories ('thoughts') of his love for the youth, with the permission of that 'sour leisure': "Were it not thy sour leisure gave sweet leave/To entertain the time with thoughts of love,". Thus, the time of the youth's *absence* and the thoughts of the love of the youth during this time will beguile ('deceive') the poet of the *presence* of the youth: "Which time and thoughts so sweetly dost deceive". That is, during the absence of the youth, the poet will imaginatively feel the presence of the youth, and thus he will be beguiled. And thus being absent from the poet, the youth will teach (or teaches) the poet how their common and unitary or undivided 'self' can be sundered into two parts ('how to make one twain'): "And that thou teaches how to make one twain". In the last line, the poet says that their unitary self can be divided into two parts by writing verses in praise of the youth ('praising him'), remaining at the place where the poet is ('here'), while the youth lives ('remain') away from the poet's place ('hence'): "By praising him here who doth hence remain!" Kerrigan explained the expression 'to make ... remain' thus: "The straightforward conceit — that by writing laudatory verses about the young man the poet makes him present though absent and thus *one twain* — is accompanied by a return to the themes of lines 1-4; the poet and the young man are on an emotional level *one twain,* and the youth can be praised *here* though *hence* because, despite their physical separation, the young man is still the poet's *better part,* a piece of himself bound to be wherever he is'' (Kerrigan, 223).

40

Take all my loves, my love, yea, take them all:
What hast thou then more than thou hadst before?
No love, my love, that thou mayst true love call —
All mine was thine, before thou hadst this more.
Then if for my love thou my love receivest,
I cannot blame thee, for my love thou usest, —
But yet be blam'd, of thou this self deceivest
By wilful taste of what thy self refusest.
I do forgive thy robbery, gentle thief,
Although thou steal thee all my poverty:
And yet love knows it is a greater grief
To bear love's wrong than hate's known injury.
  Lascivious grace, in whom all ill well shows,
  Kill me with spites, yet we must not be foes.

This sonnet is very complex, as regards its meaning. Ingram and Redpath wrote about this sonnet: ''The full meaning of this sonnet is particularly dependent on ambiguities.'' (Ingram, 94). Perhaps, this sonnet is linked with Sonnets 41 and 42; and these three sonnets have the common reference to the Dark Lady, as is evident from lines 9 and 10 of this sonnet, and from, the word 'Lascivious' in line 13 of this sonnet (the Fair Youth is lascivious with the Dark Lady). However, Kerrigan introduced this sonnet with the comment: ''Whatever *ill deeds* lie behind, or are imagined in, Sonnets 34-6, the trachery described here and in the two poems resembles so closely the poet's betrayal by the Dark Lady and his youthful friend — discussed in several sonnets between 133 and 152 — that it is usually assumed that the two situations are one'' (Kerrigan, 224).

In the first two lines of this sonnet, the poet appeals to the Fair Youth to receive all the loves of the poet, and thus enrich ('more') his former possessions of love ('hadst before'). He then asks the youth to tell him what he [the youth] now has added to his former possessions: ''Take all my loves, my love, yea, take them all:/What hast thou then more than thou hadst before?'' The poet himself answers this question. He says that the youth has actually added nothing to his former possession, because what he has added is not 'true love', for all the loves of the poet were already possessed by the youth before ('All mine was thine before'), and so actually nothing was added ('more'): ''No love, my love, that thou mayst true love call —/All mine was thine, before thou hadst this more.'' Kerrigan explained lines 3 and 4 thus: ''Since the young man already enjoyed the poet's *love,* any extra *love* which he now takes can only be false'' (Kerrigan, 224).

If the youth earlier had taken away all the love of the poet for the youth, out of his love for the poet ('Then if for my love thou my love receivest'), then the poet cannot accuse the youth ('cannot blame thee') for any wrong done to him [the poet], because the youth certainly uses that taken-away love of the poet for the sake of the love for the poet ('for my love thou usest'): ''Then if for my love thou my love receivest,/ I cannot blame thee, for my love thou usest, —''. But immediately afterwards the poet says that the youth is to be accused if he deceives the poet ('this self') by voluntarily enjoying ('wilful taste of') that which he [the youth] himself detastes ('refusest'): ''But yet be blam'd, if thou this self deceivest/By wilful taste of what thy self refusest.'' Here is, perhaps, a reference to the seduction (?) of the Dark Lady by the Fair Youth, behind the back of the poet. However, nevertheless, the poet exonerates the youth ('gentle thief') very affectionately ('gentle') of the charge of forcibly occupying the possession [the Dark Lady] of the poet ('thy robbery'). No, the poet is even ready not to mind anything even if the youth stealthily takes away everything, and thus makes him poor ('poverty') — everything that belongs to the poet: ''I do forgive thy robbery, gentle thief,/Although thou steal thee all my poverty:''.

And, all the same, the poet is aggrieved and says that only one in love can apprehend or understand his grief. Because only one in love can understand that the pain due to a beloved's fault ('wrong') is more intense than that due to the hurt ('injury') caused by hatred which is only natural or known to everybody ('known'): ''And yet love knows it is a greater grief/To bear love's worng than hate's known injury.'' In the *envoi,* the poet is vitriolic and sweet, all at the same time. He calls the youth lustful beauty or charm ('Lascivious grace'). (Lustful, because the youth has frequent physical relation with the Dark Lady.) The poet now sees all evils in that lustful youth ('in whom all ill well shows'). Yet the poet is in fulsome love with the youth. So much so that even if the youth kills the poet ('Kill me') with his outrages ('spite'), the poet says, they [the youth and the poet] will not be enemies to each other ('yet we must not be foes'): "Lascivious grace, in whom all ill well shows,/Kill me with spites, yet we must not be foes." The expression 'Lascivious grace' is an oxymoron, *i.e.* a figure of speech in which two terms of contradictory meanings occur to give the combined meaning a special effect.

41

Those pretty wrongs that liberty commits
When I am sometimes absent from thy heart
Thy beauty and thy years full well befits,
For still temptation follows where thou art:
Gentle thou art, and therefore to be won;
Beauteous thou art, therefore to be assail'd;
And when a woman woos what woman's son
Will sourly leave her till he have prevail'd?
Ay me! but yet thou mightst my seat forbear,
And chide thy beauty and thy straying youth
Who lead thee in their riot even there
Where thou art forc'd to break a twofold truth, —
  Hers, by thy beauty tempting her to thee:
  Thine, by thy beauty being false to me.

This sonnet begins with another oxymoron ('pretty wrongs') that refers to the previous oxymoron at line 13 of the immediately preceding sonnet ('Lascivious grace'). The wrongs done to the poet by the Fair Youth are attractive or slight ('pretty wrongs'), because the poet is fond of him. The youth commits these wrongs when he behaves like a libertine ('liberty commits'), during the times when the poet remains away from the love of the youth ('absent from thy heart'): "Those pretty wrongs that liberty commits/When I am sometime absent from thy heart". The wrongs the youth commits from time to time are the wrongs of his illegitimate carnal relationship with the Dark Lady. The poet, next, says that the exquisite beauty and the young age of the Fair youth are very conducive to such relations ('full well befits'): "Thy beauty and thy years full well befits". Because where his beauty and his youth are present ('where thou art'), women are always ('still') tempted ('temptation'): "For still temptation follows where thou art:".

The Fair Youth is well-behaved ('Gentle'), and so women will be intent on winning him. Again, because he is beautiful, so he is to be seduced ('assail'd') (by women): "Gentle thou art, and therefore to won;/ Beauteous thou art, therefore to be assail'd;". Kerrigan wrote about line 5 that it is "Echoing and wittily inverting the commonplace 'She is a woman and therefore to be won (used by Shakespeare at, for instance, I *Henry VI* V.3.79 and *Titus Andronicus* II. 183-84). Perhaps the woman, it is implied, was to some extent wooed and won. As at 40.9, *gentle* involves both tenderness (which makes the young man winnable) and good birth (which makes him a prize worth winning).'' (Kerrigan, 225). The poet says that when a woman proposes ('woos') to a man ('woman's son'), then he cannot bitterly reject that woman ('sourly leave her'), before enjoying love with her ('till he have prevail'd): ''And when a woman woos what woman's son/Will sourly leave her till he have prevail'd?''

The poet is aggrieved at the usurpation of the Dark Lady by the youth ('Ay me!'), and he says that the youth could deny himself [the youth] ('forbear') the place that belonged to the poet ('my seat'). That is the youth could keep away from the Dark Lady: ''Ah me! but yet thou mightiest my seat forbear,''. The youth could also scold or rebuke his beauty and his wayward or vagabond ('straying') youthfulness which ('Who') being predominating or uncontrolled or reckless ('in their riot') pushed him [the youth] to the Dark Lady ('there/Where'). And going to the Dark Lady, the youth was compelled to break his honesty, or he became negligent to his duty ('truth') which is twofold: ''And chide thy beauty and thy straying youth/Who lead thee in their riot even there/ Where thou art forc'd to break a twofold truth,—''. What this twofold truth is we do not know for certain, but, perhaps, it is the honesty or duty of the youth to the poet, and the honesty or duty of the Dark Lady to the poet. The meaning of the twofold duty may be clear to some extent from the *envoi* where the poet says that the youth belongs to the Dark Lady ('Hers'), and the Dark Lady belongs to the youth ('Thine'). With his beauty, the youth tempted the Dark Lady to himself, and thus he became her possession. Again, the beautiful youth, being dishonest or insincere to the poet, drew the Dark Lady into his fold : ''Hers, by thy beauty tempting her thee:/Thine, by thy beauty false to me.''

42

That thou hast her, it is not all my grief;
And yet it may be said I lov'd her dearly:
That she hath thee is of my wailing chief,
A loss in love that touches me more nearly.
Loving offenders, thus I will excuse ye: —
Thou dost love her because thou know'st I love her;
And for my sake even so doth she abuse me,
Suffering my friend for my sake to approve her.
If I lose thee my loss is my love's gain;

And losing her, my friend hath found that loss:
Both find each other, and I lose both twain;
And both for my sake lay on me this cross.
But her's the joy: my friend and I are one.
— Sweet flattery! then she loves but me alone!

Kerrigan introduced this sonnet thus: "In Sonnet 40 the poet accuses the youth of the trachery yet absolves him from the offence (...). In 41 the critical note is more pronounced (....), but the still contrives to excuse the friend by blaming the *beauty* and *youth* which led him on (lines 9-12). Here, in Sonnet 42, the anxieties are resolved as the poet manages to admit the youth's duplicity while demonstrating to himself that the offence has effectively not been committed (and, interestingly, that he and his friend are closer than the friend and the mistress)." (Kerrigan, 225). However, the poet says that the Fair Youth now has possessed the Dark Lady ('her') is not his only sorrow ('not all my grief'). Nevertheless, the poet may say that he loved the lady very passionately ('dearly'): "That thou hast her, it is not all my grief;/And yet it may be said I lov' her dearly:". The poet's main cause of sorrow ('my wailing chief') is that the Dark Lady now has the Fair Youth in her possession, and this the poet counts as his 'loss in love' which affects ('touches') him greatly ('more nearly'): "That she hath thee is of my wailing chief,/ A loss in love that touches me more nearly."

Therefore, both the Dark Lady and the Fair Youth who earlier loved the poet ('Loving') are guilty; and yet the poet is ready to absolve the youth of his offence ('I will excuse ye'). The poet says that the youth loves the lady because he knows that the poet loves her: "Loving offenders, thus I will excuse ye:—/Thou dost love her because thou know'st I love her;". The poet believes that the Dark Lady mis-uses him [the poet] or uses him badly ('abuse') in this way ('even so') (by taking in her fold the youth instead of himself); but that she does for the poet's own sake: "And for my sake even so doth she abuse me". The Dark Lady thus puts herself to test ('approve') by having relation ('Suffering') with the youth, instead of himself (perhaps to test if she can love the youth more than the poet). And this, again, she does for the sake of himself [the poet] : "Suffering my friend for my sake to approve her." The poet says that the Dark Lady swapped or exchanged the poet for the youth only to test her love for the poet.

Now, if the youth is permanently possessed by the Dark Lady, then certainly it will be a deprivation ('loss') to the poet; but, on the other hand, it will be a profit ('gain') to the Dark Lady, correspondly: the loss to the poet is the gain to the lady ('my love's gain'): "If I lose thee my loss is my love's gain". Again, the Dark Lady may be lost to the poet ('losing her'); but, in that case, the lady's love is gained or recovered by the youth ('my friend hath found that loss'): "And losing her, my friend hath found that loss". In lines 9 and 10, the poet means to say that when the youth is lost to him, he [the youth] is a gain to the Dark Lady; and, likewise, when the Dark Lady is lost to the poet, she is a gain to the youth. Next, the poet says that thus being away from him, the youth and the lady come closer to each other ('Both find each other'); and consequently, the poet is deprived of both of them ('and I lose both twain'). And thus both of them mount a painful burden (of lost love) on the poet ('lay on me this cross'). But the poet thinks that they have done so only for the cause of himself ('both for my sake'): "Both find each other, and I lose both twain;/And both for my sake lay on me this cross."

Such a situation should be painful; but, contrarily, the poet is feeling happy, because he knows that he and his Fair Youth are not two separate persons, but are one person: "But here's joy: my friend and I are one." The poet means to say that as he and his friend are but one person, so even if the Dark Lady loves the youth, she indirectly loves but himself [the poet]. Therefore, it can be said that the Dark Lady loves none else but only the poet himself ('then she loves but me alone!'). But the poet knows that here he is only flattering himself, and, yet, such flattering is sweet to him: "— Sweet flattery! then she loves but me alone!"

43

When most I wink, then do mine eyes best see,
For all the day they view things unrespected;
But when I sleep, in dreams they look on thee,
And, darkly bright, are bright in dark directed;
Then thou whose shadow shadows doth make bright,
How would thy shadow's form form happy show
To the clear day with thy much clearer light,
When to unseeing eyes thy shade shines so!
How would, I say, mine eyes be blessed made
By looking on thee in the living day,
When in dead night thy fair imperfect shade
Through heavy sleep on sightless eyes doth stay!
All days are nights to see till I see thee,
And nights bright days when dreams do show thee me.

The poet says that when he closes his eyes ('wink') very tightly ('most'), then his eyes can see the best. The eyes see best when closed, because, the poet says, during day-time (when the eyes are open) the eyes see things without appropriate attention ('unrespected'): "When most I wink, then do mine eyes best see,/For all the day they view things unrespected". John Kerrigan made a very important comment on these two lines: "Playfully developing the proverb 'Although I wink, I am not blind'. The implication of this saw is moral, with *wink* meaning, in our idiom, 'turn a blind eye'. Hence, Macbeth's 'Let not light see my black and deep desires./The eye wink at the hand' (I.4.52-3). The sonnet thus develops its interest in night, sight, and sleep (already explored in Sonnets 27 and 28) from a line suggestive of the theme of the three preceding poems: the poet's ignoring faults in the friend. Setting aside its moral sense, *wink* means 'close the eye', as in modern English, but also 'nod off' (we still 'take forty winks'), 'sleep'. *Best see* is most immediately 'see most clearly'; but 'see the best there is to see (the youth)' can be discerned on rereading the sonnet" (Kerrigan, 226-27).

But, when the poet goes to bed and sees dreams, then his eyes ('they') see the Fair Youth ('look on thee'). The poet means to say that because in the day-time his eyes do not see attentively, so they cannot see the youth. But at night when the eyes are closed, the eyes see brightly (can see clearly the youth in dreams): the eyes, as if, become bright, though in darkness ('darkly bright'). The bright eyes are pointed towards darkness ('bright in dark directed'): "But when I sleep, in dreams they look on thee,/And darkly bright are bright in dark directed". John Kerrigan wrote about the expression 'bright in dark directed': "Interpretation depends on *bright*: it can be adjectival (the *bright* eyes are *directed* by night though wondering by day), adverbial (the eyes look 'cunningly' in darkness), or part of an adverbial compound, 'bright-in-dark' (which usually anticipates line 5)" (Kerrigan, 227).

However, when the poet directs his closed or blind eyes towards darkness (dreams), then the image ('shadow') of the youth brightens the darkness ('shadows'): "Then thou whose shadow shadows doth make bright". The poet wonders how beautiful ('happy') a spectacle ('show') the image of the youth ('thy shadow's form') will create! : "How would thy shadow's form form happy show". The newly created image will look wonderful when shown to the bright ('clear') day which will look much brighter ('clearer') because of the brightness of the youth's beauty: "To the clear day with thy much clearer light". And then the image of the youth will dazzle the closed ('unseeing') eyes of the poet!:

"When the unseeing eyes thy shade shines so!" The poet further wonders how much blessed his eyes would be by seeing the (image of the) youth in that bright ('living') day (*i.e.* when the darkenss of the night, his eyes being closed, will be glowing with the brightness of the image of the youth): "By looking on thee in the living day". His eyes will be blessed when in the 'lifeless' ('dead') night the 'imperfect' (because the image can never be equal to the original) but beautiful image ('shade') of the youth will remain before the closed eyes of the poet during his deep ('heavy') sleep: "When in dead night thy fair imperfect shade/ Through heavy sleep on sightless eyes doth stay!" The poet concludes by saying that to him all (bright) days seem to be (dark) nights, if he cannot see the Fair Youth: "All days are nights to see till I see thee". But, on the contrary, all nights seem to him to be 'bright days' if he can see the image of the youth in his dreams: "All nights bright days when dreams do show thee me."

Some of the images and expressions of this sonnet also occur in *The Two Genglemen of Verona* (III, i, 174-81) where Valentine in her soliloquy says:

> What *light is light,* if Silvia be not seen?
> What joy is joy, if Silvia be not by?
> Unless it be to think that she is by,
> And feed upon the *shadow of perfection.*
> Except I be by Silvia *in the night,*
> There is no music in the nightingale;
> Unless *I look on* Silvia *in the day,*
> There is *no day* for me *to look upon.*

44

> If the dull substance of my flesh were thought,
> Injurious distance should not stop my way;
> For then despite of space I would be brought
> From limits far remote where thou dost stay:
> No matter then although my foot did stand
> Upon the farthest earth remov'd from thee;
> For nimble thought can jump both sea and land
> As soon as think the place where he would be.
> But ah, thought kills me that I am not thought,
> To leap large lengths of miles when thou art gone,
> But that, so much of earth and water wrought,
> I must attend Time's leisure with my moan;

Receiving naught, by elements so slow,
But heavy tears — badges of either's woe!

John Kerrigan wrote about this sonnet: "Though clearly linked with sonent 43, this poem is paired explicitly with 45, and both are twinned with 50 and 51. At *Henry V* III. 7.11-78, in the Dauphin's eulogy on his horse, ideas rehearsed in these four sonnets (space, time, travel, the four elements) recur most interestingly...." (Kerrigan, 228). However, in the first two lines of this sonnet, the poet imagines that if the heavy ('dull') elements ('substance') of his body ('flesh') would have been (the insubstantial) thought, then the cruel or malicious ('injurious') long space ('distance') between himself and the Fair Youth would not be able to block his way ('stop my way') of meeting with the youth: "If the dull substance of my flesh were thought,/Injurious distance should not stop my way;". In lines 3 and 4, the poet explains the reason. He says that then, in spite of the long separating distance, he would be able to go there ('I would be brought') where the youth lives ('where thou dost stay'), from a very far place ('From limits far remote'): "For then despite of space I would be brought/From limits far remote where thou dost stay:". The long distance would not be a matter of hindrance (to the poet's meeting the youth) even though the poet would be standing on a place ('my foot did stand') upon the earth, which would be most far from the place where the youth is: "No matter then although my foot did stand/Upon the farthest earth remov'd from thee;". Because, as soon as the thought of the poet (thought is here personified) — and thought is very swift ('nimble') — would think of the place where the Fair Youth is, it (the thought) would jump or skip over the seas and the large expanse of land (to meet the youth): "For nimble thought can jump both sea and land/As soon as think the place where he would be." The jumping over 'sea and land' in line 7 of this sonnet can be compared with a part of the Prologue (Chorus's speech) in King *Henry V:* "Carry them here and there, jumping o'er times".

But the poet is dejected ('But ah'), because of the thought that he is not thought (personified): "thought kills me that I am not thought". So it is not possible for the poet to jump over several miles of terrain and reach the place where the Fair Youth is, or has gone away: "To leap large lengths of miles when thou art gone". This is so, because the poet is moulded ('wrought') with a considerable quantity of, or mostly with, ('much') earth and water; and for this reason, he is so gross that he has to wait and suffer pain ('moan') for a long time ('attend Time's leisure') : "But that, so much of earth and water wrought,/I must attend Time's leisure with my moan”. Kerrigan wrote about the expression ‘so much of earth and water wrought’: “*so much of earth and water wrought* being so thoroughly compounded of *earth and water.* Here and in Sonnet 45 Shakespeare relies on the old division of matter into four elements: *earth and water,* heavy, slow, and base; *air* and *fire,* light, quick, and noble. Ovid relates the four thus:

> This endless world contains therein I say
> Four substances of which all things are gendered.
> Of these four,
> The earth and water for their mass and weight are
> sunken lower.
> The other couple, air and fire, the purer of the twain,
> Mount up, and naught can keep them down.
> (*Metamorphoses* XV. 239-43. Golding's translation).

It is probably signficant that the poet is separated from the young man by the very elements of which he is *wrought* (the *sea and land,* line 7)” (Kerrigan, 228-29). The expression ‘so much of earth and water wrought’ also refers us to *King Henry V* where the Dauphin says: “...he is pure air and fire; and the dull elements of earth and water never appear in him....” (III, vii, 22-23).

In the *envoi,* the poet says that he is getting nothing (‘Receiving naught’) (from the youth) due to such heavy elements within himself (the earth and water) — elements which are not capable of moving fast (‘slow’). And so he is shedding sorrowful (‘heavy’) tears which are the signs (‘badges’) of the two elements' (‘either's’) sorrow (‘either's woe’): “Receiving naught, by elements so slow,/But heavy tears — badges of either's woe!” According to Kerrigan, “The *tears* represent *earth* by being *heavy* and *water* by being wet.” (Kerrigan, 229).

45

The other two — slight air and purging fire —
Are both with thee wherever I abide;
The first my thought, the other my desire,
These present-absent with swift motion slide;
So when these quicker elements are gone
In tender embassy of love to thee,
My life, being made of four, with two alone
Sinks down to death, oppress'd with melancholy:
Until life's composition be recur'd
By those swift messengers return'd from thee,

Who even but now come back again assur'd
Of thy fair health, recounting it to me:
  This told, I joy, but then no longer glad
  I send them back again, and straight grow sad.

This sonnet is to be linked with Sonnet 44 where the poet spoke of two of his four elements: earth and water. In this sonnet, he speaks of the other two elements: air and fire. That this sonnet is the continuation of the previous one is evident from the three beginning words of this sonnet: 'The other two'. These two elements are the 'insubstantial' air and the 'purifying' fire. They are always engaged with the Fair Youth ('both with thee'), wherever the poet may be living ('abide'). The first element, *i.e.* the air, is the thought, and the second element, *i.e.* the fire, is the desire, of the poet. These two — the air and fire, or the thought and the desire — have the fastest valency ('swift motion') with which they move ('slide') from the poet to the youth and back again, and so on. Their movements are so fast that they seem to be both present at and absent from the same place ('present-absent with swift motion slide'): "The other two — slight air and purging fire /Are both with thee wherever I abide;/The first my thought, the other my desire,/These present-absent with swift motion slide;".

When two fast-moving ('quicker') elements leave the poet in order to bear the message ('tender embassy') of love from him to the Fair Youth, the life of the poet, which is made of all the four elements, remains with only two elements (the earth and the water, the two other elements, being gone). And the life of the poet sinks down (under the heavy weight of the water and the earth) being "weighted down with brooding despondency" ('oppress'd with melancholy'), so much so that he feels that he is going to die ('Sinks down to death'): "So when these quicker elements are gone/In tender embassy of love to thee,/My life, being made of four, with two alone/Sinks down to death, oppress'd with melancholy:". The poet remains in this state till his life's four elements are restored to him ('life's composition be recur'd') with those two fast-moving elements (air and fire) that bore the message of love ('swift messenger's) returning to the poet from the Fair Youth: "Until life's composition be recur'd/By those swift messengers return'd from thee,". Those two fast-moving elements then come back from the Fair Youth being certain ('assur'd') of the good health of the youth, and they break that news of the youth's good health to the poet: "Who even but now come back again assur'd/Of thy fair health, recounting it to me:". And when the two elements tell the poet about the good health of the youth, the poet becomes happy ('I joy'). But, then, immediately afterwards, the poet does not remain glad ('no longer glad') (because, the poet again becomes anxious about the health of the youth), and therefore, send them (the air and the fire) back again to the youth, (to get the news of the youth's good health), and consequently the poet once again suffers from despair: "This told, I joy, but then no longer glad/I send them back again, and straight grow sad."

46

Mine eye and heart are at a mortal war
How to divide the conquest of thy sight;
Mine eye my heart thy picture's sight would bar, —
Mine heart, mine eye the freedom of that right:
My heart doth plead that thou in him dost lie —
A closet never pierc'd with crystal eyes;
But the defendant doth that plea deny,
And says in him thy fair appearance lies.
To 'cide this title is impanelled
A quest of thoughts, all tenants to the heart,
And by their verdict is determined
The clear eye's moiety and the dear heart's part,
    As thus: mine eye's due is thy outward part,
    And my heart's right thy inward love of heart.

Kerrigan introduced this sonnet thus: "Sonnets 46 and 47 rehearse and resolve a conflict, conventional in renaissance poetry, between the *eye* and the *heart* — apparently in the light of a portrait of the friend. As at *A Lover's Complaint* 134-40, where the picture of a lovely youth attracts similar devotion, the problem of outward show and inward life arises: should the grounds of love be beauty (pleasing to the *eye*) or moral character (satisfying mind and *heart)*?" (Kerrigan, 230). G.K. Hunter agreed with Kerrigan and said that Sonnet XLVI deals with the traditional theme of a war between the heart and eye; a more common place treatment of the same theme may be seen in Thomas Watson's *Tears of Fancy (Tears of Fancy,* XX) (Jones, 124-25):

My hart accus'd mine eies and was offended,
Vowing the cause was in mine eies aspiring:
Mine eies affirmd my hart might well amend it,
If he at first had banisht loues desiring.
Hart said that loue did enter at the eies,
And from the eies descended to the hart:

Eies said that in the hart did sparkes arise,
Which kindled flame that wrought the inward smart,
Hart said eies tears might sonn haue quencht that fl[ame]
Eies said....[etc.].

In the first two lines of this sonnet, the poet says that his eyes and his heart are engaged in a fatal ('mortal') battle over the issue of sharing the booty or spoils proceeding from the conquering of the beauty of the Fair Youth ('conquest of thy sight'): "Mine eye and heart are at a mortal war/How to divide the conquest of thy sight;". His eyes would not allow ('bar') his heart to have a view of the image ('picture') of the Fair Youth; and his heart would not allow his eyes to have the 'liberty to excuse the right (of seeing)" (Kerrigan, 230) of seeing the beauty of the youth: "Mine eye my heart thy picture's sight would bar, —/Mine heart, mine eye the freedom of that right:". The poet's heart claims ('plead') that the Fair Youth resides ('lie') within it : "My heart doth plead that thou in him dost lie—". The poet says that his heart is such an impervious room or cabinet ('closet') where even very clear or penetrating ('crystal') eyes cannot glance ('pierc'd'): "A closet never pierc'd with crystal eyes;". (The heart is here, as if, accusing the eyes of wrongful possession of the youth.) But the eyes are defending themselves ('defendant') against the charge, or are negating the argument of the heart ('doth that plea deny'): "But the defendant doth that plea deny". The eyes tell the heart that the beautiful complexion, or the beautiful mien, of the youth ('fair appearance') is due to ('lies') themselves ('him'): "And says in him thy fair appearance lies."

To decide upon a judgement or to assize (' 'cide'), regarding the controversy between the eyes and the heart on the question of the propriety ('title') as to the youth, a case has been entered in the registration book of the court ('impanell'd'): "To 'cide this title is impanelled". Critics and editors are not unanimous as to the correctness of the word ' 'cide', here. Some say that the proper reading should be ' 'cide' or 'decide'; and some are of the opinion that the word actually should be 'size' or 'assize'. In any case, the word must be a legal term, because before we came to this word, we had already come across a number of legal terms, in this sonnet, for instance, 'bar', 'right', 'plead', 'defendant' and 'plea'. But Kerrigan differs. He says: "It is possible that Q's 'side' should not be modernized in this way but interpreted as a very meaning 'assign to one or other side in a dispute'." (Kerrigan, 230-31). The case of dispute has been registered in the book of the court for the judgement or decision ('quest') of jurymen, over several arguments ('thoughts') — Jurymen who are inclined or obedient ('tenants') to the heart of the poet: "A quest of thoughts, all tenants to the heart;". Kerrigan wrote about the expression 'thoughts, all tenants to the heart': "The jury has been 'packed; to the advantage of the *heart*. The *heart* is often presented as a rational, or at least thinking, organ in Shakespeare; compare 69.2" (Kerrigan, 231). And according to the judgment ('verdict') of the thoughts of the jurymen, it is decided ('determined') that the lesser part or share ('moiety') [of the image or beauty of the youth, or the youth himself] will go to the keen ('clear') eyes of the poet; and the greater part of the youth will go to the poet's affectionate ('dear') heart: "And by their verdict is determined/The clear eye's moiety and the dear heart's part,". And as is already decided by the jurymen ('As thus'), the external beauty of the youth ('thy outward part') will go ('due') to the eyes of the poet, and the love within the heart of the youth will go to ('right') the heart of the poet: "As thus: mine eye's due is thy outward part,/And my heart's right thy inward love of heart." It may be mentioned that this sonnet contains the greatest number of legal terms, among all the sonnets. The legal terms of this sonnet are: *bar, right, plead, defendant, plea, title, impanelled, tenants, verdict,* etc.

47

Betwixt mine eye and heart a league is took,
And each doth good turns now unto the other:
When that mine eye is famish'd for a look,
Or heart in love with sighs himself doth smother,
With my love's picture then my eye doth feast,
And to the painted banquet bids my heart;
Another time mine eye is my heart's guest
And in his thoughts of love doth share a part.
So, either by thy picture or my love,
Thyself, away, art present still with me:
For thou not farther than my thoughts canst move
And am still with them and they with thee;
Or if they sleep, thy picture in my sight
Awakes my heart to heart's and eye's delight.

In Sonnet 46, we have seen that the poet's eye and heart were contending with each other, over the possession of the Fair Youth; but, in this sonnet, we find that they have made a truce, and now they are in a bond of mutual help. This is evident from the every first line of this sonnet: "Betwixt mine eye and heart a league is took". Now the two have become ('turns') good to each other: "And each doth good turns now unto the other''. Now, when the poet's eye starves ('famish'd) for want of the sight ('look') of the Fair Youth, or when the heart of the poet, which is in love of the youth, suffocates or stifles itself with sighs (because the youth is not near), the eye of the poet helps or entertains his heart. The eye arranges a feast with the pictures or images of the youth, and invites ('bids') the heart to that feast ('banquet') of those pictures or images ('painted'): ''When that mine eye is famish'd for a look,/Or heart in love with sighs himself doth smother,/With my love's picture then my eye doth feast,/And to the painted banquet bids my heart;''. Dowden has found a parallel to line 3 of this sonnet in *The Comedy of Errors* (II, i, 88), where Adriana says: ''His company must do his minions grace,/Whilst I at home starve for a look. However, again, when ('Another time') the heart invites the eye ('mine eye is my heart's guest') to a feast of a different kind in that feast arranged by the heart, the eye shares the heart's thoughts of love of the youth: ''Another time mine eye is my heart's guest/And in his thoughts of love share a part.''

The eye as well as the heart belongs to the poet himself. Therefore, if his eye creates the pictures or his heart creates the thoughts of the youth, then, though the youth may remain at a far off place ('away'), the youth (vicariously) is present by, or before, the poet: ''So, either by thy picture or my love,/Thyself away, art present still with me:''. This is possible, because the youth is not at so far as place as cannot be reached by his (the poet's) thought: ''For thou not farther than my thoughts canst move''. The poet is still with those thoughts (of the youth) — thoughts that belong to his heart — and those thoughts are about ('with') the youth ('thee'): ''And I am still with them and they with thee''. And ('Or') if the thoughts of the poet's heart ('they') fall to sleep (and become unaware of the youth), then the image of the youth which dwells in the eye ('sight') of the poet will arouse ('Awake') the poet's sleeping heart: ''Or if they sleep, thy picture in my sight/Awake my heart''. And when the heart is thus aroused, it is a joy to both the heart and the eye of the poet: ''to heart's and eye's delight.''

It may be mentioned here that war and truce between eye and heart was a very favourite topic for sonneteering, during the Elizabethan period, and even before that period. In Italy, Francesco Petrarh (1304-74) utilised this theme in his *Canzoniere*, and particularly in his Sonnets 55 and 99. Pierre de Ronsard (1524-85), the French poet, used this theme in his *Ode*. In England, Watson, Drayton, Barne, Constable and other poets also utilised this popular theme.

48

How careful was I when I took my way
Each trifle under truest bars to thrust,
That to my use it might unused stay
From hands of falsehood, in sure wards of trust!
But thou, to whom my jewels trifles are,
Most worthy comfort, now my greatest grief —
Thou best of dearest and mine only care
Art left the prey of every vulgar thief.
Thee have I not lock'd up in any chest
Save — where thou art not, though I feel thou art —
Within the gentle closure of my breast,
From whence at pleasure thou mayst come and part:
  And even thence thou wilt be stol'n, I fear,
  For truth proves thievish for a prize so dear.

The poet was very wary or chary when he went on a journey ('took my way'): "How careful was I, when I took my way". We do not know whether the poet wrote this sonnet while on a journey, or after it, or no. However, this sonnet may be linked with Sonnet 50 wherein also the poet spoke of his journey: "How heavy do I jouney on the way". While on his journey, the poet ensconced or hid ('thrust') even ordinary ('trifle') things in a very firm ('truest') place ('bars'): "Each trifle under truest bars to thrust". He did this thinking that those things would remain only for his own use ('to my use'), without being used by any other person ('unused stay'): "That to my use it might unused stay". He thought that those things would remain away from dishonest persons or thieves ('hands of falsehood'), but under the vigilant guards ('sure wards') of honest persons ('trust'): "From hands of falsehood, in sure wards of trust!" (But to the poet's utter surprise, this did not occur.) The Fair Youth is more valuable to the poet than jewels: to the poet, compared with the youth, jewels are as valueless as trifling things ('to whom my jewels trifles are'). To the poet, the youth was a thing of most valuable ('worthy') comfort; but now the youth has become the cause of the poet's extreme sorrow:'But thou, to whom my jewels trifles are,/ Most worthy comfort, now my greatest grief —". Because the youth who was the formemost of the poet's dear ones, and who was the poet's only thing to take care of, is now a thing of forey or a thing for looting ('prey') to all dishonest person ('vulgar thief'): "Thou best of dearest and mine only care/Art left the prey of every vulgar thief."

The poet has not locked up the youth in any other safety vault ('chest'), except ('Save') in the affectionate or soft ('gentle') enclosure or niche of his heart ('breast') where the youth is not actually present, but, yet, the poet feels the youth's presence there: "Thee have I not lock'd up in any chest/Save—where thou are not, though I feel thou art—/Within the gentle closure of my breast,". Line 11 may be compared with line 782 of *Venus and Adonis*: "Into the quiet closure of my breast". From that soft niche of the poet's heart, the youth can, at will ('at pleasure'), get out; and into which the youth can enter at his will: "From whence at pleasure thou mayst come and part:". The poet is afraid even from that soft niche of his heart ('even thence'), the Fair Youth may be stolen: "And even thence thou wilt be stol'n, I fear,". For, the poet says, even honest people ('truth') become ('proves') thieves for so valuable a thing as the youth is ('for a prize so dear'): "For truth proves thievish for a prize so dear." A parallel to this line may be found in line 724 of *Venus and Adonis:* "Rich preys make true-men thieves". Further, this was a proverb during the time of Shakespeare.

49

Against that time (if ever that time come)
When I shall see thee frown on my defects,
Whenas thy love hath cast his utmost sum,
Call'd to that audit by advis'd respects:
Against that time when thou shalt strangely pass,
And scarcely greet me with that sun thine eye;
When love converted from the thing it was
Shall reasons find of settled gravity:
Against that time do I ensconce me here
Within the knowledge of mine own desert,
And this my hand against myself uprear
To guard the lawful reasons on thy part.
To leave poor me thou hast the strength of laws,
Since why to love I can allege no cause.

The poet is preparing himself ('Against') for that particular time, if that time really ('ever') comes, when the poet will find that the Fair Youth is disgusted with, or angry for ('frown') the defects in the poet: "Against that time (if ever that time come)/ When I shall see thee frown on my defects,". Here the word 'Against' means 'in preparation for' as it does in *The Taming of the Shrew* (II, i, 307): "To buy apparel 'gainst the wedding day." The poet is preparing for that time when ('Whenas') the love of the youth for the poet will sum up its profits and losses:

''Whenas thy love hath cast his utmost sum''. Kerrigan wrote about this line: ''*Whenas thy love hath cast his utmost sum* when your love for me has made its final reckoning (thus closing the account. The image is, with cold irony, derived from commerce, but a phrase taken from dicing, 'at last cast', meaning 'in extremity, near ruin', informs *cast his utmost*)'' (Kerrigan, 232). The poet is preparing himself for that time when the love of the youth for the poet (love, here, is personified) will call the poet for hearing or auditting ('audit') the final reckoning (of the poet's love for the youth) after 'well-informed reflection or careful heed'' (Kerrigan, 232) ('by advis'd respects'): ''Call'd to that audit by advis'd respects''.

The poet is preparing for ('Against') that time when the youth will pass by him, but will hardly wish him [the poet] good, or congratulate him ('great') with the youth's eyes which are like the sun of the heaven: ''Against that time when thou shalt strangely pass/And scarcely greet me with that sun thine eye;''. Again, the poet is preparing for the time when love, which changed ('converted') from what it had been ('from the thing it was'), will see logic or rationality and that will make it grave: ''When love converted from the thing it was/Shall reasons find of settled gravity:''. The poet here means to say that now the youth no more loves him with intense emotion, or irrationally, or for wrong reasons; and so the youth now behaves wantonly or whimsically. However, in order to prepare himself for that time, the poet is taking shelter, or fortifying himself ('ensconce') at the place at which he is living: ''Against that time do I ensconce me here''. The poet is taking shelter within the knowledge of his own barren tract or waste land, or within his own isolation ('desert'), and the poet himself is raising his arms as if to take oath to testify, or to produce witness, against himself: ''Within the knowledge of my own desert,/And this my hand against myself uprear''. ''The poet is like a witness who swears (with raised *hand)* to testify against himself, and (especially in the light of *guard,* line 12) like a soldier who threaten himself with his own hand'' (Kerrigan, 233). The poet is testifying against himself to protect or support ('guard') the Fair Youth's legal arguments ('lawful reasons'): ''To guard the lawful reasons on thy part.'' He says that the youth has lawful reasons or points for rejecting ('leave') the wretched ('poor') poet: ''To leave poor me thou hast the strength of laws,''. On the other hand, the poet cannot offer ('allege') any reason ('cause') why he is to love the Fair Youth: ''Since why to love I can allege no cause.'' Kerrigan commented on the expression 'no cause' in line 14: ''But one has only to think of Cordelia's 'No cause, no cause' (*King Lear* IV. 7.75) to grasp how sharply Shakespeare condemns the youth in the poet's so painfully excusing him. Having asked, with Cordelia, Is love to be calculated? (lines 3-4), the poet now implies, "But who can *allege* a *cause* why I or anyone should be loved?" (Kerrigan, 233).

50

How heavy do I journey on the way,
When what I seek (my weary travel's end)
Doth teach that ease and that repose to say:
'Thus far the miles are measur'd from thy friend.'
The beast that bears me, tired with my woe,
Plods dully on to bear that weight in me,
As if by some instinct the wretch did know
His rider lov'd not speed being made from thee:
The bloody spur cannot provoke him on
That sometimes anger thrusts into his hide,
Which heavily he answears with a groan
More sharp to me than spurring to his side;
For that same groan doth put this in my mind: —
My grief lies onward and my joy behind.

This sonnet may be tagged with Sonnet 48, for in both the sonnets, the poet is speaking of his journey. In fact, in Sonnets 44, 48, 50 and 51, Shakespeare is speaking of distancing, or going away, from the Fair Youth, Both Sidney and Shakespeare "drew on a convention of indivisibility in good horsemanship" which may also be found in *A Lover's Complaint* (line 107): " 'That horse his mettle from his rider takes;...'" The poet is travelling with a heart full of sorrow ('heavy'): "How heavy do I journey on the way,". At the end of his fatiguing journey, comfort ('ease') and rest ('repose') — the two things that the poet is yearning after — tell him ('teach') only that he is now so many miles away from the Fair Youth: "When what I seek (my weary travel's end)/ Doth teach that ease and that repose to say:/'Thus far the miles are measur'd from thy friend.' " Ingram and Redpath explained lines 1-4 thus: " 'How disconsolate I travel onwards, when what I'm looking forward to, the end of each weary day's journey, only teaches that comfort and rest (which I am seeking) to tell me that all I have done is to travel farther away from my friend.' " (Ingram, 116). And Kerrigan wrote about lines 2-4: "*When what ...friend* when what I'm looking for, the goal and conclusion of my exhausting journey (the alternative sense of Q's 'trauel', that is 'toil', contributes here), only instructs the comfort and rest that I win at my *travel's end* to tell me that I am so many miles away from my *friend.* (Here, and throughout the sonnet, abstractions are subtly personified.) It is possible that the *travel's end* comes each day at dusk, and that the poet laments nightly that he has journeyed farther from the young man'' (Kerrigan, 234).

The horse ('beast') on which the poet is riding is tired of bearing the (heavy) sorrow ('woe') of the poet: ''The beast that bears me, tired with my woe,''. The horse is running heavily or laboriously ('Plods') and uninspiredly or unwillingly ('dully') to carry the burden of the sorrow of the poet: ''Plods dully on to bear that weight in me,''. The poet imagines ('As if') that the poor horse ('wretch') instinctively understood that his rider (the poet) did not like ('lov'd not') the speed with which he is carrying him (the poet) away from the Fair Youth ('being made from thee'): ''As if by some instinct the wretch did know/His rider lov'd not speed being made from thee:''. Sometimes the poet becomes infuriated by the slow motion of the horse, and then he pricks ('thrusts') the cruel ('bloody') spur ('anger') into the hide of the horse; but, yet, the horse ('him') is not stimulated ('provoked') to move faster: ''The bloody spur cannot provoke him on/That sometimes anger thrusts into his hide,''. When the horse is spurred, it responds ('answers') with heavy groaning: ''Which heavily he answers with a groan''. And that groaning of the horse is more painful ('sharp') to the poet than the working of the spur on the flank of the horse is to the horse: ''More sharp to me than spurring to his side''. Because that very groaning of the horse ('that same groan') tells the poet's mind ('put this in my mind') that his (the horse's) sorrow lies in the future or on the way yet to be covered ('onward'); but his (the poet's) happiness had been in the past or on the way he (the poet) has already covered ('behind'): ''For that same groan doth put this in my mind: —/My grief lies onward and my joy behind.''

51

Thus can my love excuse the slow offence
Of my dull bearer when from thee I speed:
From where thou art why should I haste me thence?
Till I return, of posting is no need.
Oh what excuse will my poor beast then find
When swift extremity can seem but slow?
Then should I spur though mounted on the wind;
In winged speed no motion shall I know:
Then can no horse with my desire keep pace;
Therefore desire, of perfect'st love being made,

Shall neigh — no dull flesh in his fiery race:
But love, for love, thus shall excuse my jade: —
'Since from thee going he went wilful slow,
Towards thee I'll run and give him leave to go.'

That this sonnet continues the argument of the immediately preceding one is evident from the very first word of this sonnet: 'Thus'. So bearing forward the sense of the previous sonnet, we can assume that the poet's love for the youth (or the poet himself) is excusing the offence of moving slowly ('slow offence') of his horse ('dull bearer'), because the poet is himself suffering when he is going away from the Fair Youth. However, in the first two lines, the poet says that the youth ('my love') can excuse the fault ('offence') of the slow movement of the wearied horse ('dull bearer') on which he is riding and going away from the youth ('from thee I speed'), because the poet himself is suffering while going away from the youth: "Thus can I my love excuse the slow offence/Of my dull bearer when from thee I speed:". The poet questions himself why he should go away speedily ('haste') from the place where the Fair Youth is: "From where thou art why should I haste me thence?" The poet is heavy-hearted, and so he says that till he comes back to the youth, there is no necessity of the horse going speedily ('posting'): "Till I return, of posting is no need."

While returning to the youth, even the extreme speed ('swift extremity') of the horse may seem to the poet to be slow motion. He raises the question: then what excuse for its slow motion will the wretched horse ('poor beast') be able to produce before himself? "Oh what excuse will my poor beast then find/When swift extremity can seem but slow?" Then, *i.e.* while returning to the Fair Youth, the poet will stir up ('spur') the seemingly slow-moving horse, though actually the horse will be moving with extremest speed, so that it would seem that the poet mounted not on a horse but on the fastest wind: "Then should I spur though mounted on the wind". The horse will be running so fast that it will seem that the horse is flying through the air (like the fastest bird) ('winged speed'), and it would seem to the poet that he is not moving at all: "In winged speed no motion shall I know". While returning to the Fair Youth, the poet will wish ('desire') to meet the youth the soonest. Such a desire of his will be so much so that no horse will be able to run as fast as the poet will wish: "Then can no horse with my desire keep pace;". For this reason, the wish of the poet (to meet the youth the soonest) which is made of, or which grew out of, his deepest love ('perfect'st' love') for the youth, will make horse-like noise ('neigh'):

"Therefore desire, of perfect'st love being made,/Shall neigh". Kerrigan commented on this expression thus: "the poet's *desire* is here imagined making a horse-like noise to match the human sound made by the horse in the corresponding line of the previous sonnet. (Compare the stallion in *Venus and Adonis*, which 'neighs' with sexual desire at lines 265 and 307.)" (Kerrigan, 235). The wish or desire of the poet then will seem to be (itself) a horse ('his') which has a 'proud lineage' or 'spirited breeding' ('fiery race'), and so it will not be a jaded horse ('no dull flesh'): "no dull flesh in his fiery race:". [Comapred to the 'desire-horse' of the poet, his real horse will seem to be a jaded horse.] But the love of the poet will not mind anything ('excuse') though the real horse be a jaded or a weak horse, for its (love's) own sake: "But love, for love, thus shall excuse my jade: —".

The poet says that when the horse was going away from the Fair Youth, it willingly went slowly: " 'Since from thee going he went wilful slow',". Therefore, the poet will himself run towards the youth (may be mentally), and will let the horse go where it wishes to: "Towards thee I'll run and give him leave to go." Kerrigan wrote about the last line of this sonnet: "In his eager *desire* the poet will dash home even faster than the horse carrying him (and horses that go *wilful slow* are likely to be leaving their stables and inclined to retrace their tracks with corresponding speed). *Give him leave* suggests a distinctly dismissive 'give him permission' as well as an unreined freedom to gallop; *to go,* playfully contrasted with *from thee going* in line 13, means 'to walk' as well as 'to move' (*desire* is so swift that it makes the horse's homeward gallop seem a plod" (Kerrigan, 235-36).

52

So am I as the rich whose blessed key
Can bring him to his sweet up-locked treasure,
The which he will not every hour survey,
For blunting the fine point of seldom pleasure.
Therefore are feasts so solemn and so rare,
Since, seldom coming, in the long year set
Like stones of worth they thinly placed are,
Or captain jewels in the carcanet.
So is the time that keeps you as my chest,
Or as the wardrobe which the robe doth hide,
To make some special instant special blest
By new unfolding his imprison'd pride.

Blessed are you whose worthiness gives scope
Being had, to triumph; being lack'd, to hope.

The poet thinks himself to be one who is rich as well as happy ('blessed'), with a key that can open before him dear treasure which he kept in safety ('up-locked'): "So am I as the rich whose blessed key/ Can bring him to his up-locked treasure,". The rich man, with whom the poet compares himself, does not enjoy looking at his treasure often ('every hour'), because that will diminish ('blunting the fine point') the enjoyment of looking at the treasure very rarely or at long intervals ('seldom'): "The which he will not every hour survey,/For blunting the fine point of seldom pleasure." [The intensity of pleasure to be derived from a thing diminishes if the thing is enjoyed oftener.] It is for this reason that feast-days come at long intervals, and this makes feast-days so excellent and distinct ('so solemn and so rare'). The word 'solemn' is used here in the sense of 'infrequent'. Because ('Since') such days come rarely in the whole year, they are placed ('set') sparsely like precious stones ('Like stones of worth') throughout the year. And such rare and intensely enjoyable days are like the chief ('captain') jewels in a stone-set or jewelled necklace ('carcanet'): "Therefore are feasts so solemn and so rare,/Since seldom coming, in the long year set/Like stones of worth they thinly placed are,/Or captain jewels in the carcanet." The argument in lines 3 and 4 again occurs in Sonnet 102 (line 12): "And sweets grown common lose their dear delight."

The poet now compares Time with the chest that keeps the Fair Youth in safety: "So is the time that keeps you as my chest". Kerrigan wrote about this line: "After an initial parallel with *the rich* of line 1, *the time* becomes *as a chest* (that is, 'like a chest'), containing the youth. It is the poet who resembles *the rich*, having access to *a chest* which holds the friend as *treasure*. The primary impact of *the time* lingers, however, into lines 11 and 12, where it contributes markedly." (Kerrigan, 236). The Time keeps the youth in safety like a wardrobe that keeps clothes hidden, so that when at some special moments the splendour of the treasure ('imprisoned pride') will be opened, it will be of special enjoyment: "Or as the wardrobe which the robe doth hide,/ To make some special instant special blest/By new unfolding his imprison'd pride." The lines 7-12 of this sonnet may be compared with a part of King's speech in *King Henry IV,* Part I (III, ii, 55-59):

Thus did I keep my person fresh and new,
My presence, like a robe pontifical,
Ne'er seen but wond'red at, and so my state,

Seldom but sumptuous, show'd like a feast
And won by rareness such solemnity.

In the *envoi,* the poet tells the Fair Youth that he [the youth] is a blessed one, because he is like one who, if he can get the opportunity ('scope') of witnessing his worth or value (the poet here is refering to the exquisite beauty of the youth), then he will be in 'exultant joy': "Blessed are you whose worthiness gives scope/Being had, to triumph". And, if he does not have ('lack'd') that scope, he will desire ('hope') to get such an opportunity: "being lack'd, to hope."

53

What is your substance, whereof are you made,
That millions of strange shadows on you tend?
Since every one hath, every one, one shade,
And you, but one, can every shadow lend:
Describe Adonis, and the counterfeit
Is poorly imitated after you;
On Helen's cheek all art of beauty set,
And you in Grecian tires are painted new.
Speak to the spring and foison fo the year,—
The one doth shadow of your beauty show,
The other as your bounty doth appear;
And you in every blessed shape we know.
In all external grace you have some part,
But you like none, none you, for constant heart.

Ingram and Redpath's general note to this poem reads thus: This sonnet exemplifies one of the ways in which Shakespeare lays under contribution the philosophical vocabulary of the time (here 'substance', 'shadows', 'shade'), without exploiting it with philosophical strictness or system" (Ingram, 122). And Kerrigan introduced this sonnet thus: "The poem enlivens, and deepens towards philosophical profundity (....), a sonneteering commonplace: that the beloved comprises all worldly beauty. Shakespeare satirised the same topic in a poem of Orlando's, at *As You Like It* III. 2.121-50. Explaining how Rosalind became 'The quintessence of every sprite/Heaven would in little show' (that is, the type of all lesser beauties), the lover writes, in lines intringuingly close to Sonnet 53:

Therefore Heaven Nature charged
The one body should be filled
With all graces wide-enlarged.
Nature presently distilled

Helen's cheek, but not her heart,
    Cleopatra's majesty
Atalanta's better part,
    Sad Lucretia's modesty.
Thus Rosalind of many parts
    By heavenly synod was devised,
Of many faces, eyes, and hearts,
    To have the touches dearest prized.
Heaven would that she these gifts should have,
    And I to live and die her slave.''

(*Kerrigan*, 237).

We have seen that in Sonnets 50 and 51, the poet was speaking about his subdued sorrow caused by the absence of the Fair Youth from his proximity. As the youth is now absent, the poet cannot enjoy the youth's energising beauty. The poet, therefore, tries to find joy in surrogates of the youth's beauty. In this sonnet, he finds two substitutes: Adonis and Helen — one male and the other female. But in neither of the two does he find the beauty of the youth — nay, even not a substitute of it. However, the poet asks the Fair Youth what his (the youth's) essential staff or nature is (with which he has been moulded) ('substance'): ''What is your substance, whereof are you made''. Kerrigan's comment on this line is very important, because it throws light on the meaning of the whole of this sonnet. Kerrigan wrote: ''The opposition deftly invoked at 37.10 here becomes the basis of a poem. As a result, its Platonic potential is realized. *Substance* is popularly the 'stuff of an object', but context requires 'essential nature', and the mild paradox posed by the conflicting senses answers the Platonic requirement that the 'form' or 'idea' (the 'quintessence' of Orlando's panegyric) be both abstracted from and more essentially real than its replicas or *shadows*'' (Kerrigan, 237). The poet asks this question because he wonders that millions of exotic or queer ('strange') copies or aspects ('shadows') are emanating or fulgarating from his person. The poet cannot comprehend this peculiar phenomenon of the Fair Youth: ''That millions of strange shadows on you tend?'' This is clear from lines 3 and 4 where the poet says that by the law of the world, any single phenomenon of the world has only one copy ('shade'), but though the Fair Youth is also a single and unitary thing or phenomenon, yet he can create varieties of numerous copies or aspects ('can every shadow lend') of himself: ''Since every one hath, every one, one shade,/ And you, but one, can every shadow lend:''.

One may describe the beautiful Adonis, but that description ('counterfeit') which is an imitation will but badly ('poorly') reflect the original which is the Fair Youth: "Describe Adonis, and the counterfeit/ Is poorly imitated after you". The poet here wants to say that the Fair Youth is more beautiful than Adonis. Again, Helen's face ('cheek') may contain 'all art of beauty', but the Fair Youth ('you'), in attires or apparel ('tires') of Greece, is insuperable: "On Helen's cheek all art of beauty set,/ And you in Grecian tires are painted new." The poet means to say that however beautiful Adonis and Helen may be, they cannot compare with the Fair Youth in beauty. Adonis is a mythological character wooed by Venus, as Ovid tells us in his *Metamorphoses.* Helen was the beautiful daughter of Leda by Zeus, for whom the battle of Troy ensued. Adonis is present in Shakespeare's *Venus and Adonis,* and Helen is present in his *Troilus and Cressida.* Kerrigan explained lines 7 and 8 in two different ways: "(1) concentrate on all the arts which deal with beauty on reproducing the beauty of Helen's cheek and what results is a picture of you [the Fair Youth] in Grecian head-dress; (2) paint Helen's cheek with artful cosmetics and the result will be a copy of you in Grecian head-dress. Sense (1), which stresses the difficulty art has in reproducing Helen's beauty, makes Helen worth comparing with the young man; but (2) reminds us how far short of him [the Fair Youth] she nevertheless falls. *New* means 'afresh, once again', but its commoner sense 'recent, novel' registers through paradox in the context of that old work of beauty, *Helen's cheek.* The young man contains the best of what has been as well as the best that the present world's *shadows* can contribute" (Kerrigan, 238).

The poet says that we may compare the Fair Youth with spring, the best and the most beautiful time of the year; and with the rich harvest ('foison') of the year. But then the spring ('one') will only counterfeit or imitate badly ('shadow') the beauty of the youth: "The one doth shadow of your beauty show,". And the rich harvest ('other') will only seem to be a counterfeit or limitation of the magnanimity of the Fair Youth: "The other as your bounty doth appear;". But the poet says that the Fair Youth appears in every beautiful thing, or in everything that is endowed ('blessed') with beautiful form: "And you in every blessed shape we know." The poet further says that in all the beautiful ('grace') things of the observable ('external') world, there is some part of the beauty of the Fair Youth: "In all external grace you have some part,". Ingram and Redpath said that this line does not mean " 'you share in every external beauty', but 'every external beauty partakes of you' "

(Ingram, 123). And yet, the poet says, the Fair Youth is not similar to any one of the beautiful things of the external world ('But you like none'); nor any one of the beautiful things is like him ('none you'). Because none of these beautiful things has a non-vacillating or constant heart like the youth ('for constant heart'): "But you like none, none you, for constant heart."

54

Oh how much more doth beauty beauteous seem
By that sweet ornament which truth doeth give!
The rose looks fair, but fairer we it deem
For that sweet odour which doth in it live.
The canker blooms have full as deep a dye
As the perfumed tincture of the roses,
Hang on such throne and play as want only
When summer's breath their masked buds discloses:
But for their virtue only is their show
They live unwoo'd and unrespected fade—
Die to themselves. Sweet roses do not so;
Of their sweet deaths are sweetest odours made:
  And so of you, beauteous and lovely youth,
  When that shall vade, by verse distils your truth.

We may recall that in the Sonnets 15-19, Shakespeare assured the Fair Youth that he would abide in the poet's verses even after death. The poet returns to this same assurance in this sonnet. There is yet another point to be noted here. In Sonnet 53, the poet spoke of the external beauty ('external grace') of the youth, but here in this sonnet, he is also speaking of the truthfulness of the youth — truthfulness that has enhanced the beauty of the youth. However, Kerrigan introduced this sonnet thus: "In Sonnets 15-19 the poet had raised, rejected, and then happily embraced the idea that his verse could make the young man live after death, providing child-like substitutes for children. Here he returns to the theme. Alluding to the rose and perfume imagery of Sonnets 5 and 6, he suggests that verse, not children or woman's wombs, will best contain the youth's distilled self" (Kerrigan, 239).

However, the poet wonders that beautiful things look much more beautiful ('beauteous') if those things are adorned with the beautifying articles ('ornament') that truth can offer, or if those beautiful things be also truthful, or if they are vested with the additional quality of being true: "Oh how much more doth beauty beauteous seem/By that sweet ornament which truth doth give!" The rose is beautiful, no doubt; but we think it to be more beautiful ('but fairer we it deem') because ('For') of its sweet scent: "The rose looks fair, but fairer we it deem/For that sweet odour which doth in it live." The blooms of the dog-rose, which have no perfume ('canker blooms') are as deeply coloured ('deep a dye') as the sweetly pigmented ('perfumed tincture') roses. The flowers of dog-rose (like the perfumed roses) remain suspended ('Hang') from thorny branches and swing sportively this way and that ('play as wantonly') in the breeze in the summer ('summer's breath') when they come out of their concealment in their buds or mask-like buds: "The canker blooms have full as deep a dye/As the perfumed tincture of the roses,/ Hang on such thorns and play as wantonly/When summer's breath their masked buds discloses:'. It should be clear that the truth the poet alludes to in line 2, means honesty or constancy or fidelity. The poet means to say that if the beloved is both beautiful and honest, then he or she looks more beautiful than when he or she is beautiful but lacks in fidelity.

However, the poet says that the perfumeless flowers of dog-rose have no other commendable quality or virtue other than their external beauty ('show'): "But for their virtue only is their show". Therefore, they are not loved by anybody ('unwoo'd'), and they die or dry up ('fade') without anybody's heed being paid to them ('unrespected'): "They live unwoo'd, and unrespected fade". In short they die without being appreciated by anybody or without attracting anybody — they die or wither unknown: "Die to themselves." But the sweetly perfumed roses do not die like the perfumeless dog-roses: "Sweet roses do not so:". For when the roses die, *i.e.* are squeezed, sweetest perfume is generated out of them, and so, the deaths of the roses are in a sense sweet ('sweet deaths'): "Of their sweet deaths are sweetest odours made:". Kerrigan wrote about this line: "The roses are crushed and made into scent. Given the bawdy overtones of *deaths* ('to die' could mean 'achieve orgasm'), it is probable that the sexual imagery of Sonnets 5 and 6 is invoked here, with the roses' *deaths* in aromatic pain recalling the fertilization of a woman's womb (*Make sweet some* vial, 6.3) — only for the poet wrest the emblame another way, and make his text a *vial*" (Kerrigan, 240). What is true of the perfumed roses is also true of the Fair Youth ('And so of you') who is a beautiful and lovable or attractive young man. The poet tells the youth in the last line of this poem that when his (the youth's) beauty ('that') shall fade ('vade': from the Latin root *vadere*) away, the essence, or beauty and fidelity ('truth') of the youth will be dripping ('distils') from the verses of the poet himself:

"And so of you, beauteous and lovely youth,/When that shall vade, by verse distils your truth." This sonnet, as a whole, may be compred with what Theseus tells Hermina in *A Midsummer Night's Dream* (I, i, 76-78): "But earthlier happy is the rose distill'd/Than that which withering on the virgin thorn/Grows, lives, and dies, in single blessedness."

55

Not marble, nor the gilded monuments
Of princes shall outlive this powerful rhyme;
But you shall shine more bright in these contents
Than unswept stone besmear'd with sluttish time.
When wasteful war shall statues overturn,
And broils root out the work of masonry,
Nor Mars his sword nor war's quick fire shall burn
The living record of your memory.
'Gainst death and all oblivious enmity
Shall you pace forth: your praise shall still find room
Even if the eyes of all posterity
That wear this world out to the ending doom.
So, till the judgment that yourself arise,
You live in this, and dwell in lovers' eyes.

The sonnet continues the argument of Sonnet 54: the poet assures the Fair Youth that he [the youth] will remain immortal in his poems. But all at the same time, this sonnet can be linked with Sonnets 12, 15, 16, 17, 18, 19, 60, 63, 64, and 65, in all of which the concept of Time predominates. Kerrigan presumes that Shakespeare may be indebted to Horace and Ovid for the present sonnet. Horace wrote in his *Odes* III.30.1-5):

More durable than bronze, higher than Pharaoh's
Pyramids is the monuments of I have made,
A shape that angry wind or hungry rain
Cannot demolish, nor the innumerable
Ranks of the years that march in centuries.

And Ovid in his *Metamorphoses* wrote:

Let come that fatal hour
Which (saving of this brittle flesh) hath over me no power,
And at his pleasure make an end of mine uncertain time.
Yet shall the better part of me assured be to climb
Aloft above the starry sky.

(*Kerrigan*, 240-241).

As a general note to this poem, Ingram and Redpath wrote: "Definance of Time, and the boast of the immortality verse can confer, have been a frequent theme of poets since Classical times, and we find it in the French and English sonneteers alike" (Ingram, 128). However, in the first two lines of this sonnet, the poet boastingly says that neither stones nor gilded tombs ('monuments') of princes will last longer than his powerful verses ('rhyme'): "Not marble, nor the gilded monuments/ Of princes shall outlive this powerful rhyme;". But the Fair Youth ('you') will shine more brightly than the stones or tombs, in the elements of this sonnet (or in the sonnet-sequence of the post) ('in these contents'). Because the stones are not cleaned by sweeping ('unswept'), *i.e.* are neglected, and are besmeared with the slovenliness or lewdness or whorishness ('sluttish') of time: "But you shall shine more bright in these contents/Than unswept stone besmear'd with sluttish time." Kerrigan wrote about the expression 'Than unswept stone': "The phrase makes good sense as the completion of *you shall shine more bright: you* makes *stone* a memorial statue over a tomb; *unswept,* and the notion of writing *contents,* suggests a *stone* set in a dirty church floor, its inscription obliterated by rushes and muddy feet. Yet the proximity of *in these contents* simultaneously turns the phrase into an elipsis lacking 'in': 'than in the grubby stone of a tomb (the dirt of which will sully your reputation)'." (Kerrigan, 242). The first four lines of this sonnet may be compared with the following four lines of *The Rape of Lucrece* (lines 944-947):

> To ruinate proud buildings with thy hours,
> And smear with dust their glitt'ring golden tow'rs;
> To fill with worm-holes stately monuments,
> To feed oblivion with decay of things....

The poet says that devastating and meaningless ('wasteful') battles will, in the future, pull down magnificient statues, and skirmishes ('broils') will destroy architectures ('masonry'): "When wasteful war shall statues overturn,/And broils root out the work of masonry,". But then the sword of the god of war, Mars, or the fast-spreading or fierce fire of war will not be able to destroy ('burn') the always-fresh ('living') register ('record') of the memory of the Fair Youth: "Nor Mars his sword nor war's quick fire shall burn/The living record of your memory." The Fair Youth will, the poet says, continue to be living, or walk along (in the verses of the poet), against death, and against all envious forces that lead things to oblivion:" 'Gainst death and all-oblivious enmity/Shall you pace forth". And, consequently, future generations ('in the eyes of all posterity') will remember the praise of the youth ('your praise still find room') — posterity "that will last until the world arrives at the doomsday which will end it." (Kerrigan, 242): " 'Gainst death and all oblivious enmity/Shall you pace forth: your praise shall still find room/ Even in the eyes of all posterity/That wear this world out to the ending doom." [At the doomsday, even the Fair Youth will die. But after that, on the Day of Judgment, he will again rise up.] In the *envoi*, the poet tells the youth that till the Day of Judgment, when he will arise as a living person, he will be living in this poem (or in the sonnet-sequence of the poet), and that he [the youth] will be living in the eyes of his lovers and beloveds during all the while.

56

Sweet love, renew thy force; be it not said
Thy edge should blunter be than appetite,
Which but to-day by feeding is allay'd,
Tomorrow sharpen's in his former might:
So, love, be thou; although to-day thou fill
Thy hungry eyes even till thy wink with fulness,
Tomorrow see again, and do not kill
The spirit of love with a perpetual dulness:
Let this sad interim like the ocean be
Which parts the shore where two contracted new
Come daily to the banks, that when they see
Return of love more blest may be the view:
As call it winter, which being full of care
Makes summer's welcome, thrice more wish'd, more rare.

The general note of Ingram and Redpath on this sonnet is very important: "Does this sonnet refer to (1) a physical absence, (2) an estrangement, or (3) a period of apathy? Consideration of the sonnet itself suggests (3) without supporting or contradicting (1) and (2). Sonnet 57 specifically mentions absence, but an editor challenging Q's order could not use that fact to support (1) here. If there is absence, it is the Friend [the Fair Youth] and not the poet who is away, in contrast to the poet's in 50-53. In any case, whether or not we take the *Sonnets* to be in detailed sequence autobiographical, there is no indication in those earlier 'sonnets of travel' that the poet felt his affection weakened by absence; but lines 1-8 clearly imply a touch of 'love's sad satiety'. Sonnet 58, which seems to imply an estrangement, might support (2), though this is inconclusive." (Ingram, 132).

Here in this sonnet, the poet is not addressing the Fair Youth himself, but rather a substitute of the youth — the poet's love for the youth, or, may be, their mutual love. Here the poet is personifying the love. Ingram and Redpath wrote about the expression 'Sweet love': "Not the Friend, but the feeling felt, either by both Friend and poet, or by the poet (not by the Friend alone (see lines 5-8). The feeling is almost personified: but to capitalise would misleadingly suggest the God of Love." (Ingram, 132). So, 'Sweet love' means the poet's affection for the Fair Youth, and not the youth himself. The poet asks the love to strengthen its bond between them: "Sweet love, renew thy force". The poet asks the love to do so, so that people may not say that the intensity ('edge') of it is less ('blunter') than its desire ('appetite'): "be it not said/Thy edge should blunter be than appetite,". The poet admits that today the intensity of love has diminished ('allay'd), because it has enjoyed what it desired ('by feeding'): "Which but to-day by feeding is allay'd". Nevertheless, the poet is confident that the love will again be intensified ('sharpen'd') in the future, and then it will gain its former intensity ('might'): "To-morrow sharpen'd in his former might:". The poet means to say that today the youth may be satisfied with love or satiated with love, and so remain absent from him; but soon he will again feel the urge for the love of the poet. Therefore, the youth should not remain indifferent to the poet, because he has been cloyed with love.

The poet urges the love (personified) to be true to itself, *i.e.* to be what it actually is: "So, love, be thou". He says that though today the love has filled up its fasting ('hungry') eyes (with the objects of love), and the eyes have become cloyed — so much so that the eyes tend to close ('wink') — yet he requests the love to open its eyes to see its love-objects in the future ('Tomorrow see again'), and not to reject, or do away with, the spirit (of love) with eternal indifference to love-objects ('with a perpetual dulness'): "So, love, be thou; although today thou fill/Thy hungry eyes even till they wink with fulness,/Tomorrow see again, and do not kill/The spirit of love with a perpetual dulness:". The love (personified) is away from the poet who requests the love (or the Fair Youth) to deem the distance beween them two ('interim') — the distance which is the cause of the poet's pain or sorrow — to be a wide ocean which bifurcates an expanse of land into two banks of it (the banks are separated from each other, but yet they are connected by water): "Let this sad interm like the ocean be/Which parts the shore". And on that two banks or shores of that ocean, the 'two newly bethrothed' ('two contracted new') lovers daily come: "Let this sad interim like the ocean be/Which parts the shore where two contracted new/ Come daily to the banks''. And when the tow lovers see that love has come back to them again ('Return of love'), their perception produces more happiness ('more blest may be the view'): ''that when they see/ Return of love, more blest may be the view;''.

Lines 9-12 are very difficult and obscure. Ingram and Redpath wrote about these four lines: ''Commentators have justifiably found the image obscure. The situation is similar to that of Hero and Leander, on whom Marlowe's poem was written before 1593. In our view 'shore' may well mean 'land' in general, which the seas divide. Moreover, the term 'return of love' would seem less appropriate to the return of either lover than to the arrival of some manifestation each awaits of the flow of feeling (cf. 45). The arrival would perhaps be comparable to the arrival of a mail-boat eagerly awaited by the lovers on their respective 'banks' (*i.e.* 'shores', in the narrower sense) (Ingram, 132). And this is what Kerrigan wrote about the same four lines: ''The quatrain has caused critical difficulties, partly because its metaphorical basis has been misunderstood — when *this sad interim* 'this unfortunate and miserable intermission in loving') is compared to *the ocean,* a temporal gap becomes spatial — and partly because the implications of *Let* have been overlooked. The poet is not saying that an *interim* compares easily with *an ocean.* He is saying: 'let us interpret our estrangement as though it were an *ocean* parting recently betrothed lovers (*two contracted new*), and then we might start to anticipate love's renewal (*Return of love* suggesting both the reciprocation of affection and the recovery of love lost) as such lovers do they come to the shore each day to look for a known sail'.'' (Kerrigan, 243).

In the concluding couplet, the poet says that as it (the separation of two lovers) is appropriately called winter ('As call it winter'), it (the winter) is full of anxieties and sorrows ('care'). But as winter is full of anxieties and sorrows, it makes the summer welcome, more enjoyable: ''As call it winter, which being full of care/Makes summer's welcome, thrice more wish'd, more rare.'' The poet says that the winter makes the summer a thing to be triplely wished for, and as the winter is oppressive, summer seems to be a rare season: ''thrice more wish'd more rare.'' The poet here means to say that the absence of the love (personified) is like a winter to him, and so it makes its [the love's] presence to be an extremely wished-for thing.

57

Being your salve, what should I do but tend
Upon the hours and times of your desire?
I have no precious time at all to spend,
Nor services to do, till you require:
Nor dare I chide the world-without-end hour
Whilst I, my sovereign, watch the clock for you,
Nor think the bitterness of absence sour
When you have bid your servant once adieu:
Nor dare I question with my jealous thought
Where you may be, or your affairs suppose,
But like a sad slave stay and think of nought
Save where you are how happy you make those.
So true a fool is love that in your will,
Though you do anything, he thinks no ill.

The poet deems himself to be a slave of the Fair Youth, and so he [the poet] has no control over himself. He [the poet] can only wait upon ('tend') the moments when the youth will desire (this thing or that from the poet): "Being your slave, what should I do but tend/Upon the hours and times of your desire?" The poet thinks that only the time when he engages himself in the services of the youth is valuable ('precious'), but, he says, he does not find any such time: "I have no precious time at all to spend." He thinks that only the services he discharges as per the requirement of the youth, are valuable; but, he says, he cannot offer such services to the youth: "Nor services to do, till you require:". The poet cannot even rebuke the useless time spent in waiting upon the Fair Youth — time that seems to the poet to be endless ('the world-without-end hour'): Nor dare I chide the world-without-end hour". Kerrigan wrote about the expression 'chide the world-without-end hour': "castigate the seemingly endless hour. An idea so odd that the reader is prompted to take the words as an ellipsis for what the poet cannot bring himself to say: 'chastise you, my friend, for the apparently endless hour (which you make, or have made, me wait)'." (Kerrigan, 244).

As the poet is the slave, so the Fair Youth, dialectically, is the master ('sovereign'). The slave does not like to wait upon his master and pass time impatiently ('watch the clock for you'): "Whilst I, my sovereign, watch the clock for you". 'watch the clock' is a proverb which means 'impatience making time pass slowly'. The term 'world-without-end' can be found also in *Love's Labour's Lost* (V, ii, 776-

777) where the Princess of France says: ''A time, methinks, too short/ To make a world-without-end bargain in.'' Again, the poet does not dare to think that the 'bitterness' caused by the absence of the youth is 'sour', because the youth himself bade farewell to the poet: ''Nor think the bitterness of absence sour/When you have bid your servant once adieu:'' Kerrigan wrote about the seventh line: : ''Ironic self-awareness here becomes more pronounced. The line effectively declares: 'and persuade myself that the *bitterness* (of your absence from me) is not sour'.'' (Kerrigan, 244). Still again, the poet says that he cannot jealously ask the Fair Youth where he is now abiding or living, or what his business ('affairs') intends ('suppose') to do: ''Nor dare I question with my jealous thought/Where you may be, or your affairs suppose,''. There may be a hint here as to the questionable relation of the youth with the Dark Lady.

As he cannot do any one of the several alternatives (stated above), the poet is remaining where he is ('stay') like a sorrowful servant, and is thinking only about vacuity or nothingness ('think of nought'); excepting ('Save') that he is thinking about the probable place of the youth's existence, and about how much happy he [the youth] is making those that are around him: ''But, like a sad slave, stay and think of nought/Save where you are how happy you make those.'' In the concluding couplet, the poet is discerning a verisimilitude between a fool and a person who is in love ('So true a fool is love'). And this is why though the youth may have done some wrong to the poet willingly ('that in your will/Though you do anything'), the poet, who is also in love, will not desire any harm to the youth ('he thinks no ill'): ''So true a fool is love that in your will,/Though you do anything, he thinks no ill.''

In the Quarto edition of the Sonnets, the word 'will' in line 13 was printed with a capital W. From this fact some critics assume that the word 'Will' (with a capital W) may secretively refer to William Shakespeare. Such punnings or cabbalistic references to William Shakespeare also occur in Sonnets 135 and 136. In Sonnet 135, Will provocatively appears at least 7 times, and in Sonnet 136, 3 times. But other critics reject this plea. Ingram and Redpath, for instance, wrote about the concluding couplet of this sonnet: ''The lines could mean: 'Love is so loyal (and real) a fool that, in your William Shakespeare, he (love) can....' Since, however, we do not regard such a meaning as primary, we do not retain Q's capital W.'' (Ingram, 134). Likewise, Kerrigan wrote: ''Q prints a capital W, but an allusion to Will [iam Shakespeare] seems unlikely'' (Kerrigan, 245).

58

That God forbid that made me first your slave
I should in thought control your times of pleasure,
Or at your hand the account of hours to crave,
Being your vassal bound to stay your leisure!
Oh let me suffer — being at your beck —
The imprison'd absence of your liberty,
And patience-tame, to sufferance bide each check
Without accusing you of injury!
Be where you list, your charter is so strong
That you yourself may privilege your time
To what you will, to you it doth belong
Yourself to pardon of self-doing crime:
I am to wait, though waiting so be hell, —
Not blame your pleasure, be it ill or well.

This sonnet is a continuation of the previous one. As in Sonnet 57, here also the poet is deeming himself to be a slave of the Fair Youth! He implores to god (probably, love deified) who first made him the slave of the youth, to forbid him to mentally control the times of the youth's pleasure: "That god forbid that made me first your slave/I should in thought control your times to pleasure,". Here 'pleasure' may mean the youth's physical relation with the Dark Lady, or with other women. The poet prays to god to forbid him eagerly desiring the time which is in the hand of the youth, *i.e.* the time that the youth can spare ('at your hand the account of hours'). Because he (the poet) is his (the youth's) servant or ministrant, and for the reason of that he is compelled ('bound') to wait ('stay') for his (the youth's) pleasure: "Or at your hand the account of hours to crave,/Being your vassal bound to stay your leisure!" The poet is ready to suffer willingly (for the absence or the coldness of the youth), because he is serving under the order ('beck') of the youth: "Oh let me suffer— being at your beck—". He (the poet) is suffering, because he feels himself isolated, estranged or ostracised ('imprison'd') due to the coldness of love, or due to the absence, of the youth, which, again, is due to the libertinism ('liberty') of the youth: "The imprison'd absence of your liberty,". The poet has all forbearance and is uncomplaining ('patience-tame') in the face of all suffering; and he is ready to swallow all vituperations ('check'). And he will not arrogate the youth for any harm ('injury') done to him: "And patience-tame, to sufferance bide each check/Without accusing you of injury!" Lines 7 and 8 may be compared with the following two lines of Troilus in *Troilus and Cressida* (I, i, 27-28): "Patience herself, what goddess e'er she be,/ Doth lesser blench at suff'rance that I do."

The poet wishes the youth to be where he likes ('list') to be. He says that the 'acknowledged right' ('charter') of the youth is so powerful that he (the youth) may employ his time according to his will ('privilege'), in whatever way he chooses: "Be where you list, your charter is so strong/That you yourself may privilege your time/To what you will,". To the youth also belongs the privilege of excusing ('pardon') any offence done by himself ('self-doing crime'): "to you it doth belong/ Yourself to pardon of self-doing crime." The poet has only to wait, even though this waiting may be oppressive ('hell') to him: "I am to wait, though waiting so be hell. —". Such an idea is also present in Sonnet 120 (line 6): "As I by yours, you've pass'd a hell of time". Again, this is also present in *The Rape of Lucrece* (lines 1287-88): "And that deep torture may be call'd a hell,/ When more is felt than one hath power to tell." However, the poet will not criticise ('blame') the enjoyment or diversions of the youth, whether it be commendable or not ('be it ill or well'): "Not blame your pleasure, be it ill or well."

59

If there be nothing new, but that which is
Hath been before, how are our brains beguil'd,
Which labouring for invention bear amiss
The second burthen of a former child !
Oh that record could with a backward look
Even of five hundred course of the sun
Show me your image in some antique book
Since mind at first in character was done! —
That I might see what the old world could say
To this composed wonder of your frame,
Whether we are mended, or whe'er better they,
Or whether revolution be the same.
Oh sure I am the wits of former days
To subjects worse have given admiring praise.

Ingram and Redpath wrote a long general note to this poem: "The idea that at intervals the course of the world exactly repeats itself occurs frequently in ancient speculation. In the West it was elaborated most fully by some of the Pythagoreans and Stoics. Eudemus, the pupil of Aristotle, writes: 'If we are to believe the Pythagoreans, exactly the same conditions will be repeated, and I with this little rod in my hand shall come some day again, be addressing you in my class sitting round me precisely as you sit now, and everything in like manner will recur precisely as before.'.... Astronomically the Great Year was the period (variously reckoned) after which all the heavenly bodies were supposed to return to their original positions. To those who believed in stellar influence on human affairs this would naturally seem to cause a corresponding recurrence in human affairs. The periods assigned to the Great Year included 540 years and 600 years as well as far logner periods. On these smaller estimates, if a cycle were in measurable distance of its end, a regression of five hundred years (....) would put the world back into a previous cycle'' (Ingram, 138). The same idea is present in Marcus Aurelius's philosophy, where the savant says: ''there is nothing new under the sun.'' Frederick Nietzsche also believed in the same natural law: he believed in 'the eternal recurrence of the same'. Shakespeare utilises this idea of recurrence in this sonnet.

He says that there is nothing novel in this world; everything that is here now, had been here before: ''If there is nothing new, but that which is/Hath been before''. Therefore, the poet wonders how foolishly ('beguil'd') we employ our intellect ('brain') in the unsuccessful ('amiss') endeavour of searching out ('invention') some new thing, instead of old ones ('second burthen of a former child'): 'how are our brains beugil'd,/ Which labouring for invention bear amiss/The second burthen of a former child!'' The poet believes with wonder that if he could look back at the memory ('record') of a time five hundered years ago, then he could see the same appearence or beauty ('image') of the Fair Youth as it is to-day, in some old book (of the history of the world): ''Oh that record could with a backward look/Even of five hundred courses of the sun/Show me your image in some antique book''. Here the word 'record' means some imagined written account as at *Hamlet* (I, v, 98-99) where Hanlet says: ''Yea, from the table of my memory/I'll wipe away all trival fond records''; and also at *Twelfth Night* (V, i, 238) where Sebastian says: ''O, that record is lively in my soul!'' Kerrigan wrote about the expression 'five hundred courses of the sun': ''Alluding to the ancient belief that the heavens move in 540, 600, 12,960, 36,000 or 49,000 annual cycles. The poet here speculates that 600 years ago, when the heavens last held their present astrological configuration, someone resembling the young man [the Fair Youth] lived and was written about. (The word *hundrado* in Old Norse originally meant 120. In English it has usually been applied to the decimal hundred, but traces of the older usage have lingered, and Shakespeare here invokes the 'great' and 'long' hundred of six score.)'' (Kerrigan, 247). The peot here is referring to the 'recorded time', *i.e.* the time when human consciousness ('mind') first expressed itself in written alphabets ('character'): "Since mind at first in character was done!—".

The poet desires to see the old, primeaval, or originary beauty of the Fair Youth ('That I might see') to know how that old image of the youth would compare with the symmetrical ('composed') beauty ('wonder') of the youth's present generation or birth: "That I might see what the old world could say/To this composed wonder of your frame." Then the poet could discern if the present human beings (or the poet and the youth) have improved upon their former generations ('Whether we are mended'), or if the former generations were better than the present generation; or whether the recreations or re-generations ('revolution') have remained all the same: "Whether we are mended, or whe'er better they,/Or whether revolution be the same." Kerrigan commented on line 11: "The poet's speculation here ranges beyond recurrence to the old ideas (often associated with Lucretius and Ovid respectively) of continual human progress and constant decline." (Kerrigan, 248). The poet is sure (like Ovid) that the men of intellect of old days ('wits of former days') certainly thought that future generations ('subjects'), who are really worse, would be better, and therefore admired and praised the would-be generations: "Oh sure I am the wits of former days/To subjects worse have given admiring praise." Ingram and Redpath thought that the concluding couplet was perhaps "an intentionally ironic understatement; otherwise the ending would be inaffably banal." (Ingram, 139).

60

Like as the waves make towards the pebbled shore,
So do our minutes hasten to their end;
Each changing place with that which goes before
In sequent toil all forwards do contend.
Nativity, once in the main of light,
Crawls to maturity, wherewith being crown'd,
Crooked eclipses 'gainst his glory fight,
And Time that gave doth now his gift confound.
Time doth transfix the flourish set on youth,
And delves the parallels in beauty's brow,
Feeds on the rarities of nature's truth;
And nothing stands but for his scythe to mow.
  And yet to times in hope my verse shall stand,
  Praising thy worth, despite his cruel hand.

This sonnet reverts to the theme of Sonnets 15, 17, 18, 19 and 55, in all of which the poet assured the Fair Youth that he (the youth) will continue to live till the end of eternity, being engraved within the compass of his (the poet's) verses, in spite of the inroads of the cruel time upon him (the youth). In this sonnet the poet first compares the respiteless and fast passing away of time ('minutes hasten') with the racing of waves to the sea's shingled shore: "Like as the waves make towards the pebbled shore,/So do our minutes hasten to their end;". Every ('Each') succeeding minute takes the place of the preceding minute, and in this way each moment ('minutes') strives ('contend') to move forward and reach its destination: "Each changing place with that which goes before,/In sequent toil all forwards do contend." Kerrigan thought that the first four lines of this sonnet might have been inspired by a passage of Ovid's *Metamorphoses* (XV, 178-185) which in Golding's translation reads like this:

> Things ebb and flow, and every shape is made to pass away.
> The time itself continually is fleeting like a brook.
> For neither brook nor lightsome time can tarry still. But look
> As every wave drives other forth, and that that comes behind
> Both thrusteth and is thrust itself: Even so the times by kind
> Do fly and follow both at once, and evermore renew.
> For that that was before is left, and straight there doth ensue
> Another that was never erst."

The newly born baby who for the first time sees the broad day-light or the "broad expanse" ('main') of light, gradually moves ('crawls') to manhood ('maturity'): "Nativity, once in the main of light,/Crawls to maturity". Ingram and Redpath had this is to say about the term 'Nativity': "Shakespeare frequently uses abstract for concrete. So 'Nativity' here means, first, 'new-born infant', and leads to one association of 'Crawls' (line 6). But as it has also the astrological sense of the movement of birth in relation to the conjunction of planets and their position in the twelve Houses, the imagery next moves from the sea to the heavens, from the element of water to that of light, and so on to the sun (see line 7)." (Ingram, 140). Growing to maturity, the baby is crowned with achievements ('crown'd'). But then malignant and pernicious ('Crooked') misfortunes ('eclipses') fight against the achievements of the grown up man:" wherewith being crown'd,/Crooked eclipses 'gainst his glory fight,".

It was Time that bestowed upon man all his crowning glory, but once man is in the possession of all his glory, Time now destroys ('confound') these achievements bestowed upon him by Time itself—Time now destroys its own gifts: "And Time that gave doth now his gift confound." Time now stops or destroys or 'pierce through' all the embellishments ('flourish') of man — all the embellishments that Time itself conferred on him, in his (man's) youth: "Time doth transfix the flourish set on youth;". Time also creates furrows or wrinkles ('delves the parallels') in the forehead of the beautiful youth (by plunging him into diverse cares): "And delves the parallels in beauty's brow,". Kerrigan wrote about the word 'parallels': "Shakespeare meant *parallels* to suggest 'lines of latitude'; at *Twelfth Night* (III. 2.74-6), Malvolio is said to 'smile his face into more lines than is the new map with the augmentation of the Indies.' At all events, the *parallels* recall the *waves* of lines 1-4, moving up the beach is insidous ranks, and, like wrinkles, auguring death." (Kerrigan, 249). Lastly, Time eats up or destroys all the filigree delicacies of beauty ('rarities') in man (in his youth), that is expressive of nature's integrity ('truth'). And so nothing there is but waits ('stands') for Time which will destroy everything with its iron hand which resembles the scythe of the farmer with which he mows corn ('scythe to mow'): "Feeds on the rarities of nature's truth;/ And nothing stands but for his scythe to mow."

Nevertheless, in the concluding couplet, the poet hopes that his poems will continue to remain ('my verse shall stand'), despite the inroads of Time, — poems that are full of the praises of the Fair Youth: "And yet to time in hope my verse shall stand,/Praising thy worth, despite his cruel hand." It may be mentioned here, once again, that according to some critics, Shakespeare took to sonneteering light-heartedly. That they are wrong is evident from this sonnet as well as from such other sonnets where Shakespeare shows his confidence that his verses will continue to remain despite the ravages of time.

61

Is it thy will thy image should keep open
My heavy eyelids to the weary night?
Dost thou desire my slumbers should be broken,
While shadows like to thee do mock my sight?
Is it thy spirit that thou send'st from thee
So far from home into my deeds to pry,
To find out shames and idle hours in me,
The scope and tenour of thy jealousy?
Oh no! thy love though much is not so great;
It is my love that keeps mine eye awake —

Mine own true love that doth my rest defeat,
To play the watchman ever for thy sake: 12
For thee watch I, whilst thou dost wake elsewhere,
From me far off, with others all too near.

The poet enquires of the Fair Youth if it is his (the youth's) will that his imaginary picture ('image') will not let the poet sleep, and will keep his (the poet's) drowsy ('heavy') eyes wide open at night, even though he is tired ('weary night'): "Is it thy will thy image should keep open/ My heavy eyelids to the weary night?" The poet wants to know from the youth whether he (the youth) wishes that his (the poet's) sleep should be interrupted ('broken') by the youth's self-same images ('shadows') deriding, or scoffing derisively at, him (the poet) ('mock'): "Dost thou desire my slumbers should be broken,/While shadows like to thee do mock my sight?" Perhaps the poet here apprehends that the image of the youth may deride him for his deplorable plight which is due to his unrequited love of the youth. The youth is far away from the poet ('home'), and the poet wants to know if the youth sends his spirit to ghost from that far-away place to examine the activities of the poet with curiosity ('pry'): "Is it thy spirit that thou send'st from thee/So far from home into my deeds to pry," Does the youth send his spirit to see the poet's shameful deeds and his hours of inaction? The poet thinks that these two (the poet's shameful deeds and his hours of inaction) are the aim and purpose, or the chief concern, of the youth's suspicion ('jealousy'): "To find out shames and idle hours in me,/The scope and tenor of thy jealousy?" Perhaps, here the youth is not so much suspicious of the poet, as the poet is of the youth.

Upto line 8, the poet was charging the Fair Youth of suspicion, of keeping him awake, or examining his deeds with curiosity, etc. But from line 9 onwards, he is retracting ('Oh no!'), because he says that though the youth's love for him is much, yet it is not so great that the youth may be suspicious of him. Therefore, it is the poet's love for the youth itself that is actually keeping him sleepless: "Oh no! thy love though much is not so great;/It is my love that keeps mine eye awake —". The poet says that it is his own and honest ('true') love for the Fair Youth that does not allow him ('defeat') to take rest: "Mine own true love that doth my rest defeat". This line (line 11) may be compared with the lines at *Othello,* IV, ii, 160-61, where Desdemona tells Iago: "Unkindness may do much;/ And his unkindness may defeat my life". It is the poet's honest love that is always serving as the watchman (not to let the poet fall asleep) for the cause of the youth: "To play the watchman ever for thy sake:".

In the *envoi,* the poet says that it is not his love, but he himself, who is keeping vigil ('watch'), being at his own place, for the sake of the Fair Youth, while the youth, who is at a far place, is passing sleepless nights ('wake') with persons who are very near to him (physically and emotionally): "For thee watch I, whilst thou dost wake elsewhere,/From me far off, with others all too near." Kerrigan commented on the expression 'with others all too near': "A jealous reference to the poet's rival(s) and/or, in the light of 40-42, his mistress (*near* him emotionally when physically *near* the friend).

62

Sin of self-love possesseth all mine eye,
And all my soul, and all my every part;
And for this sin there is no rememdy,
It is so grounded inward in my heart. 4
Methinks no face so gracious is as mine,
No shape so true, no truth of such account,
And for myself mine own worth do define
As I all other in all worths surmount. 8
But when my glass shews me my self indeed,
Beated and chopp'd with tann'd antiquity,
Mine own self-love quite contrary I read —
Self so self-loving were iniquity: 12
'Tis thee (my self) that for myself I praise,
Painting my age with beauty of thy days.

The poet says that he is sinning because he is loving his own self. This self-love of the poet has taken possession of his vision ('eye'), his soul, and every part of his person — in short, his whole being: "Sin of self-love possesseth all mine eye,/And all my soul, and all my every part". Ingram and Redpath commented on the term 'self-love': "The 'self-love' is not just selfishness, but conceit, with the features (hence 'eye', line 1) and 'worth' (hence 'soul', line 2) of the 'self'. This 'self' throughout the octave, is made to seem to be the poet; but the sestet refutes this, and reveals that the true 'self' the poet loves is the Friend [the Fair Youth]." (Ingram, 144). The youth is the *döppelganger* or alter ego of the poet, and so to love the youth is to love the poet himself. The logic here is that if self-love is sinful, then loving the youth, who is the alter ego, is also sinful. This sin of self-love is so ingrained in the heart of the poet that there is no way before the poet to absolve himself of this sin: "And for this sin there is no remedy,/It is so ingrained inward in my heart." The poet thinks that there is none more lovely or charming ('gracious') than himself: "Methinks no face so gracious is as mine". Here 'gracious' does not actually mean 'lovely' or 'charming', but the state of being free from 'sins'. The poet claims to be free from the sin of self-love (or loving the youth), and so he thinks that he is gracious. This is consequent upon the poet's belief that loving his beloved [the Fair Youth] cannot be sinful. The poet is also constant in his love, and possesses integrity of character ('true') more than anybody else ('No shape'); and his constancy and integrity is of utmost value. Such constancy and integrity are not to be found in any one else ('no truth of such account'): "No shape so true, no truth of such account,". The poet has a very high opinion about himself: he estimates ('define') his value or 'worth' (regarding his love of the youth and his own constancy and integrity) to be so high that he thinks that he will exceed all other persons in all parameters of value: "And for myself mine own worth to define/As I all other in all worths surmount."

Nevertheless, when the poet looks at his own self in the mirror of his own self, *i.e.* when he introspects ('But when my glass shews me myself indeed'), he finds his self as defeated by adversities ('beaten') and furrowed ('chopp'd') by black and dreary history ('tann'd antiquity'): "But when my glass shews me myself indeed,/Beated and chopp'd with tann'd antiquity,". Line 10 may be compared with line 1452 of *The Rape of Lucrece*: "Her cheeks with chaps and wrinkles were disguised". However, when the poet gets such a view of his own-self through introspection, he forms a diametrically opposite ('contrary') opinion about his self-love: "Mine own self-love quite contrary I read —". Then he thinks that it is unjust ('inquity') that the self should love itself so much: "Self so self-loving were iniquity:". Kerrigan interpreted this line thus: "it would be wicked for the self to be so conceited." (Kerrigan, 252). The poet concludes by saying that it is his friend, the Fair Youth, who is his alter ego ('myself') whom the poet is actually praising, and that he is doing for himself (the poet):" 'Tis thee (myself) that for myself I praise,". It may be mentioned here that in this 13th line, the problem of self-love *versus* love of the Fair Youth is resolved. Here the poet is explicitly saying that the youth is equivalent to the self of the poet:" 'Tis thee (myself)". He thinks himself to be aged ('age'), and so he is refurbishing ('painting') his own appearance with the young beauty ('beauty of thy days') of the youth: "Painting my age with beauty of thy days." This line may be compared with line 240 of the third scene of Act IV of *Love's Labour's Lost* where Berowne says: "Beauty doth varnish age, as if new-born".

63

Against my love shall be as I am now,
With Time's injurious hand crush'd had o'erworn;
When hours have drain'd his blood and fill'd his brow
With lines and wrinkles; when his youthful morn
Hath travail'd on to age's steepy night,
And all those beauties whereof now he's kind
Are vanishing or vanish'd out of sight,
Stealing away the treasure of his spring:
For such a time do I now fortify
Aginst confounding age's cruel knife,
That he shall never cut from memory
My sweet love's beauty, though my lover's life:
  His beauty shall in these black lines be seen,
  And they shall live, and he in them still green.

The potentiality of the verses of the poet of eternalising the memory of the Fair Youth is once again demonstrated here, as it was done in Sonnets 15, 17-19, 55 and 60. The poet says that he shall be prepared for the defence ('Against') of the Fair Youth in the future, as he is now: "Against my love shall be as I am now". Kerrigan interpreted the expression 'Against my love' as meaning "In preparation for the time when my beloved". (Kerrigan, 252). And Ingram and Redpath interpreted the word 'Against' as meaning "in preparation for the time when...." (Ingram, 148). The poet will keep himself prepared against the harmful ('injurious') hand (because it destroys everything) of Time that will pound into dust or wear out the youth: "With Time's injurious hand crush'd and o'erworn". He will prepare himself for the time when Time ('hours') will have taken the vitality of the youth (drain'd his blood'), and will have engraved furrows of care across the forehead of the youth: "When hours have drain'd his blood and fill'd his brow/ With lines and wrinkles". The poet will keep him armed against the time when the youth will have left far behind the freshness ('morn') of his young age, and will have reached the sharply declining age of senility ('age's steepy night'): "when his youthful morn/Hath travail'd on to age's steepy night,". This one and a half line may be compared with line 16 and 17 of scene iv of Act IV of *King Richard III* where Queen Margaret says: "Hover about her; say that right for right/Hath dimm'd your infant morn to aged night." However, at that time for which the poet is waiting, the youth will no more remain the paragon of all beautiful things (as he is now), but all his beautiful aspects will either be diminishing or will already have vanished beyond recognition (‘out of sight’): “And all those beauties whereof now he is king/Are vanishing or vanish’d out of sight,”. And at that time, Time will surreptitiously take away all the store of the Fair Youth’s ‘charms and physical graces’ (‘spring’): “Stealing away the treasure of his spring:”.

The poet is repeating that he is preparing himself for that time (‘such a time’), and against Time’s (‘age’s’) destroying (‘confounding’) and cruel isntrument (‘knife’): “For such a time do I now fortify/Against confounding age’s cruel knife,”. The poet is so preparing himself so that (‘That’) Time (‘he’) will never be able to send to oblivion (‘cut from memory’) the Fair Youth’s beauty (‘My sweet love’s beauty’), even though Time will snatch away the life of the youth (‘love’): “That he shall never cut from memory/My sweet love’s beauty, though my love’s life:”. The poet concludes by saying that the youth will remain in his verses written in black ink (‘black lines’) — verses that will be read and estimated in the future: “His beauty shall in these black lines be seen,”. The poet is confident that his verses (‘they’) will continue to exist (even after the deaths of the poet and the Fair Youth), and that the youth will remain enshrined in these verses, as fresh (‘green’) as he (the youth) is now: “And they shall live, and he in them still green.”

64

When I have seen by Time’s fell hand defac’d
The rich proud cost of outworn buried age;
When sometime lofty towers I see down raz’d,
And brass eternal slave to mortal rage;
When I have seen the hungry ocean gain
Advantage on the kingdom of the shore,
And the firm soil win of the watery main,
Increasing store with loss and loss with store:
When I have been such interchange of state,
Or state itself confounded to decay,
Ruin hath taught me thus to ruminate —
That time will come and take my love away.
This thought is as a death, which cannot choose
But weep to have that which it fears to lose.

In this and in the next sonnet, the poet is heavily complaining against the ravages of time. In this poem, he says that he has seen Time’s destructive and deadly (‘fell’) hand devastating (‘defac’d’) the splendid ('rich') and valuable or precious things to be proud of — things that belonged to an old ('outworn') and forgotten age: "When I have seen by Time's fell hand defac'd/The rich proud cost of outworn buried age;". The poet means to say that Time has destroyed the mementoes of ancient times — mementoes that once were very costly, and were things of pride to the ancient citizens. The poet has several cases ('sometime') of high-rise monuments worn out and destroyed in course of time, and he has seen that even things of such hard and durable metals as brass are always liable ('eternal slave') to be destroyed by the corrosive inroads of Time ('mortal rage'): "When sometime lofty towers I see raz'd,/ And brass eternal slave to mortal rage;". the poet has also seen that aggressive ('hungry') ocean intrudes into its shore ('gain/Advantage') and thereby uproots kingdoms standing on the shore: "When I have seen the hungry ocean gain/Advantage on the kingdom of the shore,". He has also seen, contrarily, that the shore ('firm soil') plays the aggressive role and intrudes into the ocean ('watery main'): "And the firm soil win of the watery main,".

Kerrigan wrote about lines 5-7: "Some argue that the movement of the tides up and down the shore is evoked here (compare 60.1); but the *hungry ocean* and *firm soil* too decisive for such a gentle to and fro. The sea brings down cliffs and devours fields, while the land asserts itself in the main, putting out spurs, laying down salt-marsh, and so forth. Shakespeare's source — Ovid's *Metamorphoses* XV. 261-4 — confirms this:

> Even so have places oftentimes exchanged their estate.
> For I have seen it sea which was substantial ground alate [formerly],
> Again where sea was, I have seen the same become dry land,
> And shells and scales of seafish far have lain from any strand,
> And in the tops of mountains high old anchor have been found.
>
> (Golding's transalations.)"
>
> (Kerrigan, 254)

Thus the poet has seen how the store of one place increases with loss of store at another place, and *vice versa* (as in the case of the shore and the ocean): "Increasing store with loss and loss with store:". This line does not mean that the store is increased with the loss of the same store, or the loss is increased with additions.

However, the poet has seen such changings of states of things ('interchange') (as ocean becoming expanse of land, and land becoming expanse of water): "When I have seen interchange of state,". He has also seen ('Or') state of a thing being liable (confounded') to destruction or wearing off: "Or state itself confounded to decay,". Lines 5-10 may be compared with *2 Henry IV*, III, i, where King says (45-53):

O God! that one might read the book of fate,
And see the revolution of the times
Make monuments, and the continent,
Weary of solid firmness, melt itself
Into the sea; and other times to see
The beachy girdle of the ocean
Too wide for Neptune's hips; how chances mock,
And changes fill the cup of alternation
With divers liquors !

Such observances of ruins due to Time have caused the poet to meditate ('ruminate') on the fact that sometime Time will come to snatch away also his beloved Fair Youth from him: "Ruin hath taught me to ruminate —/That Time will come and take my love away." The poet says that such a meditation is equivalent to death to him: "This thought is as a death". He further says that when he so meditates, he cannot but ('cannot choose') weep and pine to have near him the Fair Youth ('that'), although at the same time he becomes afraid or apprehensive that (like those monuments that have been destroyed by Time) he may also have to lose the Fair Youth: "which cannot choose/ But weep to have that which it fears to lose."

65

Since brass, nor stone, nor earth, nor boundless sea,
But sad mortality o'ersways their power,
How with this rage shall beauty hold a plea,
Whose action is no stronger than a flower?
Oh how shall summer's honey breath hold out
Against the wreckful siege of battering days,
When rocks impregnable are not so stout
Nor gates of steel so strong but time decays?
Oh fearful meditation! where, alack,
Shall Time's best jewel from Time's chest lie hid?
Or what strong hand can hold his swift foot back?
Or who his spoil of beauty can forbid?

Oh none, unless this miracle have might —
That in black ink my love still shine bright.

Grievous destruction or mortality ('sad mortality') is like a monarch that overrules ('o'ersways') such strong things as are made of brass or stone, or such things as the earth and the sea: "Since brass, nor stone, nor earth, nor boundless sea,/ But sad mortality o'ersways their power,". If this be so ('Since', line 1), *i.e.* if destruction which is like a king be so insolent or outrageous ('this rage'), then beauty cannot prevail upon or persuade ('hold a plea') destruction not to be outrageous, because beauty has no more strength than that of a flower: "How with this rage shall beauty hold a plea,/Whose action is no stronger than a flower?" Time ('days') is holding a siege over all things, howsoever strong they may be, with the intention of destroying them ('wreckful'), and with that intention is pounding ('battering') them always: "the wreckful siege of battering days,". If this be so, then beautiful, sweet-smelling and fragile things of summer days ('summer's honey breath') (like flowers) will not be able to continue to exist ('hold out'), in spite of ('Against') the marauding Time: "Oh how shall summer's honey breath hold out/ Against the wreckful siege of battering days,". Kerrigan found references of the word 'honey' (in line 5 of this sonnet) in *Venus and Adonis, Titus Andronicus,* and in Marlowe's *Hero and Leander*. In *Venus and Adonis,* the word appears in line 452: "Which to his speech did honey passage yield". In *Titus Andronicus,* Marcus says (II, iv, 21-25): "Why dost not speak to me?/Alas, a crimson river of warm blood,/Like to a bubbling fountain stirr'd with wind,/Doth rise and fall between thy rosed lips,/ Coming and going with thy honey breath." And Marlowe in his *Hero and Leander* (Sestiad I, 21-24) wrote:

Many would praise the sweet smell as she passed,
When 'twas the odour which her breath forth cast;
And there for honey bees have sought in vain,
And beat from thence, have lighted there again.

How can soft beauty be everlasting against the battering of Time, when invincible ('impregnable') rocks and steel-made gates are not strong enough against the destruction (decay') of that Time? "When rocks impregnable are not so stout/Nor gates of steel so strong but time decays?" When the poet thinks over all these things, he becomes apprehensive ('fearful meditation'). The poet, while thinking over these things, is afraid principally because such thoughts lead him to the inevitable conclusion that his beloved Fair Youth also will be destroyed by the cruel hand of Time. Therefore, woebegone ('alack'), he wonders where the youth, who is the most precious thing of the creation ('Time's best jewel') can be ensconced or hidden ('lie hid'), so that he does not have to enter into a coffin, or into Time's 'jewel-case' ('Time's chest'): "Oh fearful meditation! where, alack,/ Shall Time's best jewel from Time's chest lie hid?" Kerrigan wrote about these two lines: "The young man is a beautiful gem lent to the world by Time; and Time will be sure to reclaim him, locking him up in his jewel-case (suggesting a coffin), wherever he hides. The words compare interestingly with 52.9)" (Kerrigan, 256).

The devastating of Time is very quick in movement ('swift foot'). The poet says that none is so strong who will be able to buttonhole ('hold') Time: "Or what strong hand can hold his swift foot back?" The poet answers his own question and says that none will be able to stop ('forbid') Time's spoiling the beautiful things (including the Fair Youth) of the world: "Or who his spoil of beauty can forbid?" The poet repeats: none can do all these: "Oh none". He says that only in his verses, written in black ink, can the Fair Youth ('my love') live eternally and brightly ('shine bright'), in spite ('still') of the aggressive destruction of Time: "That in black ink my love may still shine bright." The poet calls his verse a supernatural phenomenon ('miracle'), because nothing other than his verse can stall the inroads of Time, and so he says that only his verse is capable ('might') of supernaturally saving the Fair Youth from the fell hands of Time: "unless this miracle have might —".

66

Tir'd with all these for restful death I cry, —
As to behold Desert a beggar born,
And needy Nothing trimm'd in jollity,
And purest Fair unhappily forsworn,
And gilded Honour shamefully misplac'd,
And maiden Virtue rudely strumpeted,
And right Perfection wrongfully disgrac'd,
And strength by limping Sway disabled,
And Art made tongue-tied by Authority,
And Folly, Doctor-like, controlling Skill,
And simple Truth miscall'd Simplicity,
And captive Good attending captain Ill:
Tir'd with all these, from these would I be gone —
Save that, to die, I leave my love alone.

Kerrigan has very correctly compared this sonnet with "Hamlet's famous soliloquy 'to be, or not to be' (III.1.56-90), where the Prince describes 'Th' oppressor's wrong, the proud man's contumely' and analogous evils, and Lucrece's eloquent complaing against Opportunity (*The Rape of Lucrece* 848-924)'' (Kerrigan, 256). However, the poet is wearied by his observations of many painful facts that he will spell out later on ('all these'), and therefore he is crying for absolute rest in his death: ''Tir'd with all these for restful death I cry, —''. All these painful observations are the following. Firstly, the poet was born as a poor person, and nevertheless, he finds help from nowhere ('behold Desert'): ''As to behold Desert a beggar born''. Secondly, he has seen worthless persons ('needy Nothing') full of ('trimm'd') mirth ('jollity'): ''And needy Nothing trimm'd in jollity,''. Ingram and Redpath's comment on the expression 'needy Nothing': ''A personification of 'worthless creatures of no gifts or qualities'. There is no implication of social pity extended to the 'worthy poor'. The antithesis here is to 'Desert' (line 2). 'Nothing' as applied to persons is a strong term in Elizabethan English. (Cloten is 'that harsh, noble, simple nothing', Cymb. III. iv. 135; and to Hamlet Claudius is 'a thing ....of no thing' (*Ham*. IV. ii. 30-32)'' (Ingram, 154). The relevant passage in *Cymbeline* referred to by Ingram and Redpath is :

Imgen. No court, no father, nor no more ado
With that harsh, noble, simple nothing—
That Cloten, whose love-suit hath been to me
As fearful as a siege.

And that of *Hamlet* :

Hamlet. The body is with the king, but the king not with the body. The king is a thing—

Guildenstern. A thing, my lord!

Hamlet. Of nothing. Bring me to him. Hide fox, and all after.

It is clear from these two excerpts that the term 'nothing', in the Elizabethan age, often meant a person.

Thirdly, another of the poet's painful observation is that sometimes absolutely faithful persons ('purest Faith') are left painfully in the lurch: ''And purest Faith unhappily forsworn''. Fourthly, at times high ('gilded') honour is shamelessly conferred on undeserving persons ('misplac'd'): ''And gilded Honour shamelessly misplac'd''. Fifthly, chastity of maidens is sometimes violated ('strumpeted'): ''And maiden Vritue rudely strumpeted,''. Sixthly, genuinely perfect persons are sometimes slighted unlawfully or rudely: ''And right Perfection wrongly disgrac'd,''.

Seventhly, strong persons — strong, because honest and right — are degarded ('disabled') by persons who are in power, though they are 'weak and uncertain': "And strength by limping Sway disabled,". Eighthly, learning and science, or learned persons, ('Art') are suppressed ('tongue-tied') by (unrefined) persons in power ('Authority'): "And Art made tongue-tied by Authority,". Ninthly, unintelligent persons or simpletons ('folly'), assuming the air of intelligent persons ('Doctor-like') control intelligent persons ('Skill'): "And Folly, Doctor-like, controlling Skill,". Tenthly, 'straightforward honesty' and 'plain fact' ('simple truth') are wrongly thought to be ('miscall'd') stupidity or naivete ('Simplicity'): "And simple Truth miscall'd Simplicity,". Eleventhly, the poet has seen ill to be dominating ('captain Ill') over good which has become ill's, as if, prisoner-of-war ('captive'), and is serving the ill ('attending'): "And captain Good attending captain Ill:".

Ingram and Redpath wrote about lines 9 and 10: "Learning and science are silenced by those in authority, and stupid ignorance, giving itself the air of an expert, controls and directs the real technicians. 'A number of commentators have either seen or conjectured a reference here to censorhsip difficulties of the players; but we regard the point as inconclusive" (Ingram, 154). Nevertheless, we may say that there may be some allusions in this sonnet to the anomaly in the ideal social order or hierarchy during the Elizabethan period, by some of which the poet himself might have been painfully affected. To take only a single example, we may refer ourselves to the 'To be, or not to be' soliloquy of Hamlet, which some critics agree to be at least marginally autobiographical. Mark at least these expressions of the soliloquy: "The slings and arrows of outrageous fortune'; 'sea of troubles'; 'The heart-ache and the thousand natural shocks'; and

> For who would bear the whips and scorns of time,
> Th' oppressor's wrong, the proud man's contumely,
> The pangs of despis'd love, the law's delay,
> The insolence of office, and the spurns
> That patient merit of th' unworthy takes,
> ....
> ....Who would these fardels bear,
> To grunt and sweat under a weary life,...

However, in the 13th line, the poet is repeating what he said in the very first line: he says that all these experiences of his have made him tired, and therefore (to take rest) he would like to go away from all these, or from this world: 'Tir'd with all these, from these would I be gone —''. When the poet says that his experiences of all these have made him tired, he, perhaps, means to say that these have made him dejected. Now, the poet would certainly desire to die, but he stops short of so desiring, because he knows that if he dies, he will have to leave behind the Fair Youth all alone: ''Save that, to die, I leave my love alone.'' It may be noted here that this sonnet is so full of self-pitying lamentation.

67

Ah, wherefore with infection should he live
And with his presence grace impiety,
That sin by him advantage should achieve
And lace itself with his society?
Why should false painting imitate his cheek
And steal dead seeming of his living hue?
Why should poor beauty indirectly seek
Roses of shadow since his rose is true?
Why should he live, now Nature bankrupt is —
Beggar'd of blood to blush through lively veins,
For she hath no exchequer now but his,
And proud of many, lives upon his gains?
Oh him she stores, to show what wealth she had
In days long since, before these last so bad.

Kerrigan's introduction to this sonnet is very important: ''In its reference to the friend [the Fair Youth] as *he*, this poem — especially in the wake of 66, with its self-pitying lament — marks a crucial stage in the poet's account of the youth. It uniquely anticipates (if 5, resolved by 6, is expected) the issues of 94, as 69 — within a group which arguably extends from this sonnet to 70 — anticipates, particularly in lines 9-12, that poem, with its third-person (but, further, impersonal) account.'' (Kerrigan, 257). However, the poet does not want that the Fair Youth ('he') lives in this 'corrupt and vicious' ('infection') world, and that he [the Fair Youth] should, by living in such an abject world, a world full of immorality, adorn, or should give a face-lift to, this world which lacks in morality or religiosity ('impiety'): ''Ah, wherefore with infection should he live/And with his presence grace impiety,''. The poet does not like that this sinful world ('sin') should gain some illusory upliftment (with the presence of the youth) ('advantage'), and that this sinful world should make friend with the youth ('his society'), or keep ('lace') company ('society') with him: ''That sin by him advantage should achieve,/And lace itself with his society?'' Such beautiful application of the word 'lace' is also to be found in *Macbeth* (II, iii, 111) where Macbeth says of Ducan's gory corpse: "His silver skin lac'd with his golden blood". Kerrigan's comment on the first four lines of this sonnet is, perhaps edifying: "The young man is ostensively the innocent victim of *sin,* which uses him as a front to conceal its ugliness; but the youth's moral shortcomings are emphasized so strongly in earlier sonents that it is difficult to ignore an ironic undertow: 'Oh, why should he be allowed to live, corrupted as he is, only to make impiety look gracious through his charm so that sin profits from his loose loveliness, becoming his bosom friend?' " (Kerrigan, 257-58).

The poet asks why ('wherefore', line 1) should this corrupted world make a false copy ('painting') of the liveliness of the youth ('cheek') by surreptitiously taking away false ('dead') pictures ('seeming') of the living complexion ('living hue') of the youth?: "Why should false painting imitate his cheek/And steal dead seeming of his living hue?" Kerrigan explained these two lines (lines 5 and 6) thus: "why should cosmetics be applied to other cheeks to make them look like his, taking a lifeless appearance from (or 'copying the mere appearance of') his living *hue* ('complexion, colour, form, air, being', that cluster of senses exploited at 20.7)? The old theory that *painting* refers to portraiture is hardly plausible; more persuasive is the suggestion that poetic 'depiction' is touched on (compare the cosmetic imagery of Sonnets 82 and 83)" (Kerrigan, 258).

The poet again asks why should those who lack in perfect beauty ('poor beauty') indirectly (because they want to copy) want to get the imitation of beauty ('Roses') from the perfect ('true') beauty of the youth: "Why should poor beauty indirectly seek/Roses of shadow since his rose is true?" The nature of the world is now devoid ('bankrupt') of all instances of beauty ('now Nature bankrupt is —"). Now nature has no ('Beggar'd of') blood, that signifies life, so she can shine ('blush') through her veins, which are supposed to contain blood to the brain. Therefore,why should the Fair Youth live in this pale and dead and ugly world: "Why should he live, now Nature bankrupt is—/ Beggar'd of blood to blush through lively veins,". Because, nature has no store of beauty ('exchequer'); she has only the Fair Youth's store of beauty to draw upon: "For she hath no exchequer now but his," Once this nature could boast of many instances of beauty: "And proud of many". But now she lives only upon drawing ('gains') beauty from him: "lives upon his gains?" Moreover, nature now is pointing to the beauty of the youth, to show how much of collection of instances of beauty she once had in her treasury ('store'): "On him she stores, to show what wealth she had". That is now a bygone time when she had such a huge store of instances of beauty: "In days long since". But now (since then), at least, ('before these last') nature is suffering from abject poverty ('so bad') of beauty: "before these last so bad." Kerrigan wrote about the expression 'In days long since': "In lines 9-12, the blame had almost been the young man's for bankrupting *Nature;* but now it seems that Time, that familiar Shakespearean enemy, has deprived *Nature* and her progeny of ***beauty***, leaving only the young man as a relic of the better past (perhaps, as 68.1 and 9-10 suggest, as good and long gone as the golden age)" (Kerrigan, 259).

68

Thus is his cheek the map of days outworn
When beauty lived and died as flowers do now,
Before these bastard signs of fair were borne,
Or durst inhabit on a living brow:
Before the golden tresses of the dead,
The right of sepulchres, were shorn away
To live a second life on second head:
Ere beauty's dead fleece made another gay.
In him those holy antique hours are seen
Without all ornament, it self and true,
Making no summer of antoher's green,
　And him as for a map doth Nature store,
　To show false Art what beauty was of yore.

This sonnet is a continuation of the previous one, as regards the theme of the two sonnets. That this sonnet is a continuation of the previous one is clear from the first word of the first line of this sonnet: 'Thus'. In the previous sonnet, the poet said that nature once bestored upon the Fair Youth all her beauty; but now she is drawing beauty from him (the youth). In the present sonnet, the poet says that it is for this reason that ('Thus') the beautiful cheek of the Fair Youth has become creasy or wrinkled, and the wrinkled cheek indicates ('map') that the cheek is very old ('days outworn'): "Thus is his cheek the map of days outworn". The poet means to say that because of nature's drawing beauty from the youth, the youth is now lacking in freshness. The cheek now bears only the signs ('map') of its past beauty. In the past, beauty showed itself in that cheek ('beauty lived'), but afterwards that beauty faded away ('died'), as beautiful flowers soon fade away — a fact that the poet even at present ('now') observes: "When beauty lived and died as flowers do now,''. In the times past ('Before') these abject or adulterated ('bastard') signs or the wrinkles of beauty ('fair') were not present in the cheek ('borne'), and those abject signs did not dare to subsist ('durst inhabit') in the beautiful and fresh ('living') forehead of the youth: ''Before these bastard signs of fair were borne,/Or durst inhabit on a living brow:''. Kerrigan wrote about the expression 'bastard signs of fair':. ''Those marks and features which seem to signify beauty in modern faces and forms are illegitimate (base as well as ill-founded and false) because they derive from other faces and forms than the ones they garnish'' (Kerrigan, 259). It may be noted that, perhaps, Shakespeare did not like toiletry or cosmetics as is evident from the expression 'bastard signs' of this sonnet, and from the expression 'false painting' of Sonnet 67.

The poet is speaking of a time (regarding the beauty of the youth) when beautiful locks of hair ('golden tresses') of one who was dead — locks that rightly belonged to tombs ('sepulchres') — would not be cut off and worn as periwigs ('To live a second life') by another person ('on second head'): ''Before the golden tresses of the dead,/The right of sepulchres, were shorn away,/To live a second life on second head:'' The locks of hair naturally goes to the tomb, but now people cut off the locks of hair of the dead, and wear those locks as periwigs to show that they are not old, though actually they are so. The poet here is speaking of the artificial beauty of contemporary times. The poet is repeating this idea in the next line. He says that he is speaking of the time when the beautiful hairs of a deceased person ('dead fleece') was not put on by another person to make himself joyous: ''Ere beauty's dead fleece made another gay.''

The poet can see in the Fair Youth ('him') all the sacred or blessed ('holy') beauty and graces of the ancient times ('antique hours'), without the accompaniment of furbishing decorations or ornamentations: ''In him those holy antique hours are seen/Without all ornament''. The youth is not changed by any ornamentation, and therefore his beauty is natural ('it self') and perfect ('true'): ''it self and true,''. The youth is not beautified ('summer') with another person's colour or cosmetics ('green') (like people put on other's hair as periwigs): ''Making no summer of another's green,''. Kerrigan wrote about line 11: ''Attention here shifts from the *cheek* as a *map* to the *cheek* itself, unadorned by cosmetics, set under the young man's own hair, not another's'' (Kerrigan, 260). The youth is not forcibly taking anything ('Robbing') from any dead person ('old') (compare lines 4-8) to refurbish or beautify himself afresh ('new'): "Robbing no old to dress his beauty new:". The poet concludes by saying that nature is keeping the youth in store to use him as a specimen or instance ('map') to show surrogate or imitative ('false') art (personified) what actually beauty in the ancient time ('yore') looked like: "And him as for a map doth Nature store,/To show false Art what beauty was of yore." The poet means to say that the natural beauty of the Fair Youth is comparable with the paragon of beautiful things of the ancient world.

69

Those parts of thee that the world's eye doth view
Want nothing that the thought of hearts can mend;
All tongues (the voice of souls) give thee that due,
Uttering bare truth, even so as foes commend:
Thine outward thus with outward praise is crown'd;
But those same tongues that give thee so thine own
In other accents do this praise confound
By seeing farther than the eye hath shown:
They look into the beauty of thy mind,
And that, in guess, they measure by thy deeds;
Then, churls, their thoughts, although their eyes were kind,
To thy fair flower add rank smell of weeds.
But why thy odour matcheth not thy show,
The soil is this — that thou dost common grow.

The beautiful aspects of the Fair Youth ('thee') that people can outwardly perceive ('the world's eye doth view') lack in nothing ('Want nothing') that can affectioantely or sympathetically be ignored or corrected ('that the thought of hearts can mend'): "Those parts of thee that the world's eye doth view/Want nothing that the thought of hearts can mend;". The poet means to say that the youth lacks in no aspects of beauty. Everyone duly praise the youth from the core of his soul: "All tongues (the voice of souls) give thee that due,". Line 3 may be compared with lines 82 and 83 of sc.i of Act III of *Titus Andronicus:* "O, that delightful engine of her thoughts/That blabb'd them with such pleasing eloquence". By doing so, everyone tells only the truth and nothing but the truth ('Uttering bare truth'). Even those people who are the youth's enemies, likewise, recommend his beauty to others ('even so as foes commend'): "Uttering bare truth, even so as foes commend:". In this way, the outward beauty of the Fair Youth is adorned ('crown'd') with the praise of unfamiliar ('outward') people; or, in this way, people's praise of this outward beauty rewards ('crown'd') his outward beauty:

"Thine outward thus with outward praise is crown'd;". But those same persons who praise his outward beauty which he can claim ('those same tongues that give thee so thine own'), belie or refute ('confound') those praises 'using quite other language' or saying different things at other times or at different places ('In other accents'): "But those same tongues that give thee so thine own/In other accents do this praise confound". Because those people lie to see beauty not only in the body (of the youth), which of course their eyes have seen, but also elsewhere ('seeing farther than the eye hath shown'). That is these people pry ('look') into the mind of the Fair Youth to see if beauty subsist there as well: "By seeing farther than the eye hath shown:/They look into the beauty of thy mind,". These people guessingly or intuitively estimate the extent of the beauty of the youth's mind ('that') from an account of his deeds ('they measure by thy deeds'): "And that, in guess, they measure by thy deeds;". Their eye-estimation is certainly sympathetic (because they see the youth's outward beauty quite correctly): "although their eyes were kind". But they think of the Fair Youth rustically, or with the thoughts of a rustic ('churls'): "Then, churls, their thoughts". Ingram and Redpath interpreted line 11 thus: " 'Then, unlike their eyes, which rightly reported you handsome, and looked kindly, their nasty minds interpret your actions churlishly' " (Ingram, 160). In this way, those people add to the beauty of the youth ('thy fair flower') downright notority which can be compared with the bad smell of weeds ('rank smell of weeds'): "To thy fair flower add the rank smell of weeds." Kerrigan commented on this line: "Here, as often in Shakespeare, *flower* means 'finest part' (compare 'the flower of chivalry') as well as 'blossom, bloom' (used, as in line 2 of the previous sonnet, to image beauty). The friend's [the Fair Youth's] *outward* is said to be his *flower* (both implications), his *mind* and moral character are found *rank* as *weeds* (quibblingly, only the natural organic sense of *flower* is answered)" (Kerrigan, 261).

In the *envoi,* the poet asks the Fair Youth why his moral character ('odour') is not befitting ('matcheth') his outward beauty ('thy show'): "But why thy odour matcheth not thy show,". And the poet answers the question himself. He says that it is because the youth has got his blemish or vulgarity ('soil') which is due to his descending down to the common rank of people (from his high social status) or due to his growing common, among whom such vulgarity is common: "The soil is this — that thou dost common grow." Ingram and Redpath wrote that the word 'soil' "was in current use between the fourteenth and early sixteenth centuries *as a verb* meaning 'to resolve, explain, answer (a question)'.'' If we accept this meaning of the word 'soil', then we may explain the expression 'The soil is this' as meaning 'The answer to this question is that'.

70

That thou art blam'd shall not be thy defect,
For slander's mark was ever yet the fair:
The ornament of beauty is suspect—
A crow that flies in heaven's sweetest air.
So thou be good, slander doth but approve
Thy worth the greater, being woo'd of time;
For canker vice the sweetest buds doth love,
And thou present'st a pure unstained prime:
Thou hast pass'd by the ambush of young days
Either not assail'd, or victor being charg'd;
Yet this thy praise cannot be so thy praise
To tie up envy, evermore enlarg'd:
    If some suspect of ill mask'd not thy show
    Then thou alone kingdoms of hearts shouldst owe.

Ingram and Redpath wrote a general note on this sonnet, which is very important: ''The apparent inconsistancy between the portrayal of the Friend's [the Fair Youth's] character here and that in other sonnets (*e.g.* 23-25) has led some commentators to hold that different young men are addressed in different sonnets....but we should perhaps pass the opinion that such conclusions are especially hazardous where poems expressing divergent attitudes may well have been written at widely separated dates'' (Ingram, 162). However, in the previous sonnet, the poet said that the people were critical of the Fair Youth, and in this sonnet, he is defending the youth. The poet says that people may blame the youth, but that will not be counted as a blemish on his (the youth's) character, because ('For') slandering always takes the beautiful ('fair') as its object of attacking ('mark'): ''That thou art blam'd shall not be thy defect,/For slander's mark was ever yet the fair:''. The poet says that suspicion ('suspect') is as if a decoration ('ornament') (rather than a flaw) of beautiful things: ''The ornament of beauty is suspect —''. The poet is comparing suspicion with the black and malicious bird, crow, which can fly into the sweet air of the sky with which the Fair Youth is compared here: ''A crow that flies in heaven's sweetest air.'' He wants to say that though bad birds fly into the sweet sky, yet the sky is not tainted thereby.

Therefore, the poet says that the youth ('thou') is good (in spite of the slandering), and that the slandering is rather proving ('approve') the worth of the youth the more ('the greater'): "so thou be good, slander doth but approve/Thy worth the greater". This is so because in spite of the attempt of the present time's bid to seduce him, the youth is remaining good and blameless : "being woo'd of time". Kerrigan explained the expression 'being woo'd of time' thus: "since you [the youth] are seductively tempted by the (corrupt) present day (but do not succumb, remaining *good*)" (Kerrigan, 262). Because, the canker, which is the vice or evil of a flower ('bud') also loves the sweet flower: "For canker vice the sweetest buds doth love,". And the fair Youth ('thou') shows ('present'st') a pure and unadulterated youth ('unstainted prime'): "And thou present'st a pure unstainted prime:". The poet here wants to say that though canker harms flowers, yet they love the flowers (otherwise they would not stay on those flowers), in the same way, though the people slander the Fair Youth, yet they certainly love him.

The poet says that the youth has successfully avoided ('pass'd') the dangers of distraction and moral turpitude ('ambush') of his youthful age: "Thou hast passed by the ambush of young days". The Fair Youth, at that time, either was not seduced ('assail'd') or, if he fell a victim of seduction ('charg'd'), he came out victorious, *i.e.* he could successfully escape the attempts at seduction: "Either not assail'd, or victor being charg'd;". Nevertheless, this praise of the youth by the poet (that the youth had a blameless young age, or that he could successfully avoid all seductions) is not actually the praise of the youth ('cannot be so thy praise'), says the poet. Because, this praise cannot leash or butt or control the jealousy (of the people) ('to tie up envy') — jealousy which is always growing ('evermore enlarg'd'): "Yet this thy praise cannot be so thy praise/To tie up envy, evermore enlarg'd:". The poet concludes by telling the youth that if his beauty ('show') is not covered ('mask'd') by some suspicion of misdeeds ('suspect of ill') done by him, then the entire population of the nation ('kingdoms') should remain heartily grateful ('owe') to the him [the Fair Youth] alone: "If some suspect of ill mask'd not thy show/Then thou along kingdoms of hearts shouldst owe." Kerrigan explained the *envoi* thus: "if a hint or suspcion of badness did not disguise your true appearance, entire nations would be in thrall to you" (Kerrigan, 262).

71

No longer mourn for me when I am dead
Than you shall hear the surly sullen bell

Give warning to the world that I am fled
From this vile world with vildest worms to dwell:
Nay, if you read this line, remember not
The hand that writ it, for I love you so
That I in your sweet thoughts would be forgot
If thinking on me then should make you woe.
Oh if, I say, you look upon this verse
When I perhaps compounded am with clay,
Do not so much as my poor name rehearse,
But let your love even with my life decay;
  Lest the wise world should look into your moan,
  And mock you with me after I am gone.

The poet requests the Fair Youth not to mourn for him, after he is dead, any longer than the mournful sound of a passing bell ('surly sullen bell') lasts: ''No longer mourn for me when I am dead/Than you shall hear the surly sullen bell''. The poet asks him to announce to the world his demise ('fled') when he will leave behind this loathsome ('vile') world to let loathsome ('vildest'; some commentators read 'vilest') worms to live in: ''Give warning to the world that I am fled/ From this vile world with vildest worms to dwell:''. The poet also asks the youth not to recall or remember (him) who wrote this verse (or these verses) ('this line'), should the youth read the verse (or these verses): ''Nay, if you read this line, remember not/The hand that writ it''. Because, the poet loves the youth so much so that if the youth recalls him (the poet) and then weeps for him (the poet), then the youth will forget him (the poet): ''for I love you so/That I in your sweet thoughts would be forgot/If thinking on me then should make you woe.'' The poet means to say that after his death the youth may recall his memory, and that will be sweet memory ('sweet thoughts'); but immediately afterwards the youth will weep for him, and then the youth will drown his memory in his tears, and will forget him. It is for this reason that the poet asks the youth not to recall his memory. Again, the poet asks the youth, if he [the youth] reads ('look upon') his poems, when the poet is deceased ('compounded am with clay'), the youth must not even recall ('rehearse') the poor or unlucky name of the poet: ''Oh if, I say, you look upon this verse/ When I perhaps compounded am with clay,/Do not so much as my poor name rehearse,''. On the contrary, the poet requests the youth to let his (the youth's) love for the poet to die ('decay') just with the death of the poet: ''But let your love even with my life decay;''. The poet wishes that all his memory be wiped away from the world, or, at least from the mind of the youth. Because, the poet says, if, after his (the poet's) death, the youth mourns ('moan') over his death, then the heartless or practically tuned ('wise', used mockingly) people would enquire into his (the youth's) mourning, and would be jesting with, or taunting at, the youth and the poet ('with me'): "Lest the wise world should look into your moan,/And mock you with me after I am gone."

72

Oh, lest the world should task you to recite
What merit lived in me that you should love,
After my death, dear love, forget me quite,
For you in me can nothing worthy prove,
Unless you would devise some virtuous lie
To do more for me than mine own desert,
And hang more praise upon deceased I
Than niggard truth would willingly impart:
Oh, lest your true love may seem false in this,
That you for love speak well of me untrue,
My name be buried where my body is
And live no more to shame nor me nor you:
For I am sham'd by that which I bring forth,
And so should you, to love things nothing worth.

This sonnet is clearly a continuation of the previous one. Here the poet again asks the youth to forget him after his death, and tells the youth why the world will mock at the youth when he will be remembering the deceased poet. In the first four lines of this sonnet, the poet asks the Fair Youth to forget him completely after his (the poet's) death. Because, the poet says, otherwise, people ('the world') will ask the youth to tell ('task you to recite') them for what merits in the poet, the youth loved him, and then the youth will not be able to tell them anything, for actually there is no worth in the poet ('nothing worthy prove'): "Oh, lest the world should task you to recite/What merit lived in me that you should love,/After my death, dear love, forget me quite,/ For you in me can nothing worthy prove, —". If thus asked by the people, then the youth can only invent ('devise') some 'morally credible' falsehood (lie that will prove that the poet is morally upright, or lie that is commendable because it is being told for the beloved's benefit): "Unless you would devise some virtuous lie". Telling such lies will be telling something which the poet does not deserve being told ('than mine own desert'). And that will be equivalent to showering ('hang') more praise (than the poet deserves) on the deceased poet: "To do more for me than mine own desert,/And hang more praise upon deceased I''. Such lies will never be told ('impart') voluntarily ('willingly') by the abject ('niggard', because heartless, unfriendly) truth (personified): ''Than niggard truth will willingly impart:''. Kerrigan wrote about the expression 'hang, more praise upon deceased I': ''The image of a mob hung with trophies (...) the parallel which comes first to mind is *Much Ado About Nothing* V.3, where Claudio reads Hero's *praise* from an epitaph hung *upon* her tomb (see V.1.271-2)'' (Kerrigan, 264).

After the death of the poet, the youth may be speaking untruth about the poet by speaking well of the poet, because the youth loves the poet: ''That you for love speak well of me untrue,''. The youth will be doing so so that his true love for the poet may not seem to be false love: ''Oh, lest your true love may seem false in this,''. Kerrigan explained at some length the expression 'lest your true love may seem false': ''The primary sense, 'in case your constant affection should seem inconstant', turns on a quibble, *false* meaning 'dishonest' as well as 'inconstant', and the playful paradox is that the dishonesty which would make the friend *false* and therefore 'inconstant' would be perpetrated because of the constancy which would make him loyal to the poet, *true* or *false*. On a secondary level, the words suggest 'in case your faithful beloved (me the poet) should appear to be misrepresented (falsified, however favouarbly)' '' (Kerrigan, 264).

The poet wishes that his memory ('name') should vanish ('buried') with his dead body being entombed: ''My name be buried where my body is''. He does not wish that his memory continue to live and thereby remain as a thing of shame for himself and for the youth: ''And live no more to shame nor me nor you:''. The poet feels ashamed for his creations or for his works ('that which I bring forth'): ''For I am sham'd by that which I bring forth,''. He says that, likewise, the youth also should feel ashamed ('so should you'), because the youth loves something (the poet) which is of no worth: ''And so should you, to love things nothing worth.'' Ingram and Redpath wrote about line 13: ''Variously explained as referring to (1) a sense that his poems were, or were thought, bad poetry; (2) as sense that all his work was, or was thought, poor work; (3) the social stigma of being a writer for the public playhouse. (3) seems to us the most likely interpretation'' (Ingram, 166).

73

That time of year thou mayst in me behold
When yellow leaves, or none, or few, do hang
Upon those boughs which shake against the cold,

Bare ruin'd choirs where late the sweet birds sang:
In me thou see'st the twilight of such day
As after sunset fadeth in the west,
Which by and by black night doth take away,
Death's second self that seals up all in rest:
In me thou see'st the glowing of such fire
That on the ashes of his youth doth lie
As the death bed whereon it must expire,
Consum'd with that which it was nourish'd by:
  This thou perceiv'st, which makes thy love more strong
  To love that well which thou must leave ere long.

In Sonnets 71 (line 1, 'when I am dead'), 72 (line 3, 'After my death'); 73 (lines 8, 'Death's second self that seals up all in rest'), and 74 (lines 1-2, 'when that fell arrest/Without all bail shall carry me away'), the poet is intensely conscious about his death, and consequently, these sonnets are all full of melancholy strains. However, in this sonnet, the poet tells the Fair Youth that he can see the winter, or the fag end, of the poet's life in himself (in the poet). The poet here compares his state with winter when leaves of trees become yellow, or trees shed off all their leaves ('or none'), or only a few leaves ('or few') hang on the boughs of trees which, seeming to be old, as if shake in the cold winter: "That time of year thou mayst in me behold/When yellow leaves, or none, or few, do hang/Upon those boughs which shake against the cold,". Line 2 may be compared with a line and a half of Macbeth in *Macbeth* (V, iii, 22-23): "My way of life/Is fall'n into the sear, the yellow leaf". And line 3 of this sonnet may be compared with the following lines of Belarius in *Cymbeline* (III, iii, 60-64):

Then was I as a tree
Whose boughs did bend with fruit; but in one night
A storm, or robbery, call it what you will,
Shook down my mellow hangings, nay, my leaves,
And left me bare to weather.

The poet says that formerly ('late'), in the boughs of the trees, beautiful and melifluous birds sang in a choir, but now there is no birds on the boughs ('Bare'), and so there is no chorus of songs ('ruin'd choirs'): "Bare ruin'd choirs where late the sweet birds sang:". Kerrigan explained the expression 'where late the sweet birds sang' at some length: "The *sweet birds* which *sang* in summer, and are now silent, are like choirboys (...) because they sing in piping treble voices in chorus and because choir-boys look rather like birds when dressed in fluttering, ruffed plumage. Whether a further parallel can be drawn in doubtful, but if, as has often been suggested, the *choirs* of line 4 are monastic churches, sacked and *ruined* at the dissolution, the absent birds would be like pre-Reformation choristers, who sang formerly but not now. (The difficulty with such a reading is that, while *late* can mean 'formerly', it is usually applied to some recent event — which the dissolution by no means was when the Sonnets were written.)'' (Kerrigan, 265-66).

In lines 1-4, the poet compared his state with defoliated trees mournfully standing in winter, and now he is comparing himself with dusk — the border-state between day and night. He tells the Fair Youth that he (the youth) can see in him (the poet) the pale evening ('twilight') of a day when the sun has just gone down the western horizon — the evening that is soon ('by and by') enveloped ('taken away') by the darkness of night: ''In me thou see'st the twilight of such day/As after sunset fadeth in the west,/Which by and by black night doth take away,''. Line 6 may be compred with line 4 of T.S. Eliot's *Prelude* I: ''The burnt-out ends of smoky days.'' The poet says that then night which is almost self-same death, or eternal sleep, ('Death's second self') closes up ('seals up') all eyes, for rest: ''Death's second self that seals up all in rest:''. The poet here means to say that he is on the verge of being carried away by death which gives us eternal rest. Here we may remember what Hamlet told us in his 'To be, or not to be' soliloquy: ''To die, to sleep;/.../.../ When we have suffled off this mortal coil,/ Must give us pause.'' Kerrigan wrote about the expression 'seals up all in rest': ''There are three threads of imagery entangled here: *night* is like a coffin in which the day's life is sealed; *night* resembles a letter writer, bringing the day to completion by folding it up and sealing it, or a testator, sealing a will on his *death-bed*; *night* closes all eyes, like the falconer who 'seals' or 'stitches up' the eyes of his hawk (compare *Macbeth* III. 2. 46-7, 'Come, seeling night/scarf up the tender eye of pitiful day')'' (Kerrigan, 266).

The poet is now comparing his state with a fire which is about to be extinguished. He tells the youth that the youth sees in him (the poet) the glow or spark of a fire that is burning ('doth lie') in the deposit of ashes that the fire itself reduced something to by burning, previously ('youth'): ''In me thou see'st the glowing of such fire/That on the ashes of his youth doth lie''. The fire was previously nourished by the fuel ('that') which has now become ash — the death-bed of that fire — by which the same fire ultimately becomes eaten up: ''as the death-bed whereon it must expire,/Consum'd with that which it was nourish'd by:". The poet tells the Fair Youth that he (the youth) must have understood ('perceiv'st') the fact of the fire and the fuel ('This') And this understanding is making the love of the youth for life ('that', line 14) more deep and strong — the life that the Fair Youth ('thou') will certainly depart from in the near future: "This thou perceiv'st, which makes thy love more strong/To love that well which thou must leave ere long." It may seem arbitrary to interpret the word 'that' at line 14 as 'life', but that this is the correct meaning of the word will be clear from the first two lines of the next sonnet: "But be contented when that fell arrest/Without all bail shall carry me away:".

74

But be contented when that fell arrest
Without all bail shall carry me away:
My life hath in this line some interest
Which for memorial still with thee shall stay.
When thou reviewest this, thou dost review
The very part was consecrate to thee:
The earth can have but earth, which is his due;
My spirit is thine, the better part of me:
So then thou hast but lost the dregs of life,
The prey of worms, my body being dead,
The coward conquest of a wretch's knife,
Too base of thee to be remembered:
The worth of that is that which it contains,
And that is this, and this with thee remains.

Kerrigan's general note to this sonnet runs thus: "As the argument proceeds through Sonnets 73 and 74 it becomes increasingly Christian in tenor. The Ovidian association between man and the seasons which informs 73.1-4 (...) gives way, after the *Bare ruined choir* are introduced to echoes of Job 17. 11-13:

> My days are past, and my counsels and thoughts of my heart are vanished away, changing the night into day, and the light approaching into darkness. Though I tarry never so much, yet the grave is my house, and I have made my bed in the dark" (Kerrigan, 266).

Kerrigan further said that the Elizabethan burial service, particularly the Book of Common Prayer, has influence on the 7th line of this sonnet. The Book of Common Prayer contains such expressions as " 'earth to earth, ashes to ashes, dust to dust' ". Nevertheless, Kerrigan said: "And yet the sonnet by no means orthodox in its treatment of the flesh, the spirit, and immortality, harnesses Christian *contemptus mundi,* it might be said, for its own secular ends." (Kerrigan, 267).

However, the haunting concept of death is still lingering with the poet; and yet, the poet believes in the immortality of his sonnets. In the previous sonnet, he announced to the Fair Youth about his (the poet's) approaching death. And in this sonnet the poet asks him to remain happy ('contented') in spite of his (the poet's) harmful or horrible death ('that fell arrest') taking him (the poet) away ('carry me away') without letting him go ('Without all bail'): "But be contented when that fell arrest/Without all bail shall carry me away:". The word 'arrest', in line 1, may be compared with the same word in *Hamlet* at V, ii, 328-29 where Hamlet tells his mother: "Had I but time, as this fell sergeant Death/Is strict in his arrest, O, I could tell you—". The poet says that his life, which can be compared with an estate, has some yield ('interest') to derive from ('in') his poems or sonnets (either this sonnet, or, more correctly, all his sonnets) ('this line'), and this benefit or yield will continue to remain along with the youth (who is enshrined in the sonnets), even after his (the poet's) death, as a memorial of him (the poet): "My life hath in this line some interest/Which for memorial still with thee shall stay." When the Fair Youth will re-read ('reviewest') this sonnet (or sonnets) of the poet, then he will understand that the spirit (see line 8), or the essence, or the essential part, of the poet ('The very part') was sacred or honest ('consecrate') to the youth: "When thou reviewest this, thou dost review/The very part was consecrate to thee:"

The poet tells the youth that his body is made of earth, and so after his death, the earth will get only the earth-element of him (which is due to the earth); but the spiritual element of him will be earmarked for the youth — the spiritual element which makes the better part of the poet: "The earth can have but earth, which is his due;/My spirit is thine, the better part of me:". So, after the physical death of the poet ('my body being dead'), the youth will lose only the earthen part of the poet, which is but the worthless part of him ('the dregs of life') that is fated to be eaten by the sub-terranian worms: "So then thou hast but lost the dregs of life,/The prey of worms, my body being dead,".

The death of the body of the poet is a booty ('conquest') of the cowardly wretch which is the worm which tears to pieces ('knife') the body: "The coward conquest of a wretch's knife,". This line is very confusing and difficult to explain. Ingram and Redpath wrote about this line:

"Several problems arise:

(1) Who is the 'wretch'?

(2) Is it the 'body', or the 'wretch', or his action that is cowardly? (The last seems impossible on grammatical grounds.)

(3) Does 'conquest' mean (a) what is overcome (victim), or (b) what is acquired (booty, or, just possibly, 'legal possession gained otherwise than by inheritance', cf. 6.14 and 46.2)?" (Ingram, 170).

Various answers to these questions have been produced by commentators. However, the explanation of this line (line 11) given by Kerrigan seems tenable: "Perhaps the body is a *coward* because it timorously gives up its life to something as slight as a *knife,* more likely the *wretch* with the *knife* makes a *coward* (acting as adjective) *conquest* when it stealthily assassinates the body." (Kerrigan, 268). Therefore the body of the poet is something very lowly ('Too base'), and so it does not deserve to be remembered by the Fair Youth ('thee').

In the concluding couplet, the poet tells the youth that the value of his body ('worth of that') is the spirit, or the love of the poet for the youth ('that') which the body ('it') envelopes or preserves ('contains'): "The worth of that is that which it contains,". And that spirit of the poet, or the love of the poet for the youth ('that'), remains ('is') in this sonnet (or in all the sonnets of the poet) ('this'); and again, this sonnet will remain with the Fair Youth ('thee'): "And that is this, and this with thee remains." Dowden said that this sonnet seemed to him to be an *envoi* to all the preceding sonnets, *i.e*. Sonnets 1-73.

75

So are you to my thoughts as food to life,
Or as sweet season'd showers are to the ground;
And for the peace of you I hold such strife
As 'twixt a miser and his wealth is found, —
Now proud as an enjoyer, and anon
Doubting the filching age will steal his treasure;
Now counting best to be with you alone,
Then better'd that the world may see my pleasure;
Sometime all full with feasting on your sight,
And by and by clean starved for look;

Possessing or pursuing no delight
Save what is had or must from you be took:
    Thus do I pine and surfeit day by day,
    Or gluttoning on all, or all away.

As told earlier, according to Dowden, this sonnet, perhaps, begins a new set or sequence of sonnets. However, the poet tells the Fair Youth that he (the youth) is as essential to the thought of the poet, as food is to his (the poet's) life: "So are you to my thoughts as food to life,". The poet means to say that he cannot think without the Fair Youth. The youth is to the poet like 'gentle and temperate'('sweet') showers of rain of the rainy seaon or of the spring time ('season'd') when the thirsty earth desires water: "Or as sweet season'd showers are to the ground;". The miser always strives to hold within his possession the wealth he has amassed. Therefore there is, as if, a battle ('strife') between the miser and his possession (Here we may imagine that the possession of the miser wants to fly away from him, but the miser strives to keep the wealth under his control, and hence there is a struggle or strife between them.). In the same way, the poet (compared to the miser) wants to possess the happiness ('peace') cosequent to his friendship with, or love for, the youth. But that happiness, as if, does not yield to the poet, and so he is struggling ('strife') for that happiness: "And for the peace of you I hold such strife/As 'twixt a miser and his wealth is found, —". The expression 'for the peace of you' is not clear. Ingram and Redpath suggest five possible meanings: (1) " 'as a result of the peace and contentment I find in your friendship' "; (2) "in order to achieve the tranquil enjoyment of your friendship"; (3) "in order to resovle the issue of how best to enjoy your friendship in tranquil security"; (4) "instead of the peace which I ought to find in your friendship"; and (5) "in order to achieve undisputed possession of your friendship" (Ingram, 174).

From the fifth line to the last line of this sonnet, the poet shows his vacillation. He says that at one time ('Now') he supposes himself to be exulted ('proud') for possessing ('enjoyer') everything of the Fair Youth, but the next moment ('anon'), he is afraid that the pilfering age will thieve the possession ('treasure') of the youth: "Now proud as an enjoyer, and anon/Doubting the filching age will steal his treasure;" Here, there may be an allusion to the poet's rivals (rival poets) in his friendship with the Fair Youth. At one time the poet thinks that he is the happiest man ('best') being the companion or friend of the youth in secrecy ('alone'), but the next moment the poet thinks that it would be better if the poet would see that he and the youth are in company, *i.e.* if their cordial relation ('pleasure') would be observed by the public: "Now counting best to be with you alone,/Then better'd that the world may see my pleasure;". Kerrigan explained line 8 thus: "then thinking it even better (*counting* the *best* to have been *bettered*) that people can see (with a hint of 'when people see') me enjoying your company (or just 'you, who give me, indeed are, *my pleasure*')." (Kerrigan, 268-69).

At some time, the poet enjoys ('feasting') the beauty of the youth ('your sight') to his heart's utmost satisfaction ('all full'), but soon ('by and by') the poet begins starving quite ('clean') for want of the sight of the youth: "Sometime all full with feasting on your sight,/And by and by clean starved for a look;". Thus the poet either possesses the beauty of the youth (and thus becomes full of mirth) or he lacks in mirth ('pursuing no delight') excepting only that enjoyment which the poet has already had ('Save what is had'), and excepting that enjoyment which the poet must snatch away from the youth ('or must from you be took'): "possessing or pursuing no delight/Save what is had or must from you be took:". In this way, the poet is either getting his full enjoyment ('surfeit') or is hankering after such enjoyment ('do I pine'), day in and day out ('day by day'): "Thus do I pine and surfeit day by day," Or in other words, the poet is " 'Either feasting myself on every delight, or finding the table of my pleasure empty'." (Ingram, 174): "Or gluttoning on all, or all away'."

76

Why is my verse so barren of new pride,
So far from variation or quick change?
Why with the time do I not glance aside
To new-found methods and to compounds strange?
Why write I still all one, ever the same,
And keep invention in a noted weed,
That every word doth almost tell my name,
Shewing their birth and where they did proceed?
Oh know, sweet love, I always write of you,
And you and love are still my argument;
So all my best is dressing old words new,
Spending again what is already spent:
For as the sun is daily new and old,
So is my love still telling what is told.

Shakespeare sometimes became frustrated and self-critical about his own verses, particularly when his verses were put by his rivals under pungent criticisms, or rather when these were unjustifiably attacked by them. This is clear at least in Sonnets 32 (lines 5-8) and 76 (lines 1-2). In this sonnet, the poet is self-accusative: he asks himself why his verses lack ('barren') in unique ('new') material and formal elements which he can be proud of? He asks himself why his verses do not contain 'nimbleness of expression and variety in argument' ('variation')?: "Why is my verse so barren of new pride,/So far from variation or quick change?" It may be noted here that according to the poet, 'nimbleness of expression and variety in argument' are the two marks of good rhetoric. The poet asks himself why he does not, with the change of time and mode of poetry, look elsewhere ('aside') for new-fangled styles ('methods') and peculiarly compounded words (to adorn his verse)?: "Why with the time do I not glance aside/To new-found methods and to compounds strange?" Kerrigan wrote about the expression 'compounds strange': "exotic compound words (of the kind used by modish poets like Marston and Joseph Hall). Because composite drugs and poisons were called *compounds* as against 'simples', the refined extract from single sources — Shakespeare can suggest that fashionable diction resembles odd and probably dangerous substances" (Kerrigan, 269-70). The poet means to say that the time has changed and with it the mode of poetry, but he is unable to change the mode or style of his poetry, by using the new fashion in poetry-writing, and by using peculiar compound words, as his contemporary poets do.

The poet asks himself why he writes verses in the same and unaltered style ('all one'), and why his poems are always the same poem, without any variation or change in them ('ever the same'): "Why write I still all one, ever the same,". he asks himself why he does not dress or adorn his new written poems ('invention') in famous or attractive ('noted') garments ('weed') (of language, style, etc.): "And keep convention in a noted weed,". If he could do all these, then every word of his verses would bear his impress or individuality; and every word of his verses would show people from where (from the poet) they have issued forth, and what effect they would produce in the minds of the people: "That every word doth almost tell my name,/Shewing their birth and where they did proceed?" Kerrigan explained the expression 'where they did proceed' thus: "(1) where they issued from whence they came; (2) where they graduated from. The idea of (2) is that, having been born in the poet, *every word* is educated there and issues into poetry rather like a young man who, having taken a degree, begins to make his way in the world. Compare the quibble 'proceeding' at *Love's Labour's Lost* I, 1.95." (Kerrigan, 270).

In the octave, the poet was self-critical, but in the sestet, he justifies his action — his old mode of writing verses using single (and not compounded) or simple words. He frankly tells the Fair Youth that he (the poet) always writes verses about him (the youth), and that the only argument in all his verses is, even today, the youth ('you') and his (the poet's) love for the youth: "Oh know, sweet love, I always write of you,/And you and love are still my argument;". Therefore, the poet says, the best he can do ('all my best') is only to clothe or arrange old or often-used (or simple, and not compounded words) words in a new fashion ('new'): "So all my best is dressing old words new,". Again, all that the poet can do is that he can use ('spending') only those words that have been used ('spent'), once more: "Spending again what is already spent:".

In the concluding couplet, the poet is comparing his love for the youth with the sun. The sun is new and old both on the same day. It has actually got no newness, because we see the same sun daily. Nevertheless, we can say that each day we see a new sun, because it appears each day after each night, during which time the sun remains unobservable. Therefore, the sun is both old and new. Again, the sun, though it apparently changes through the day and the night, shows each day the same brilliance. In the same way, the poet's love for the youth is nothing new because it is an old love (or eternal love). Yet, whenever the poet writes his verses on his love, the love seems to be new. That is, when the poet tells about his love, he is only re-telling about it: "For as the sun is daily new and old,/So is my love still telling what is old." Kerrigan wrote about line 13: "If *old words* new registers as an apology for mediocrity (because he cannot write about new material and in hew fashion — SKS), *new and old* are here linked by the sun's blaze of glory. The poet's love is as predictable — yet as dazzlingly beautiful as the sun. If he lacks orginality, that is only a consequence of his being inviolably true." (Kerrigan, 280). Again, Kerrigan wrote about the expression 'telling what is told': "The financial-for-literary imagery of line 12 turns into wordplay: saying things *already* said, the poet 'once more counts over the coinage of love' (compare the *counting* of the *miser* in Sonnet 75.)" (Kerrigan, 270-71).

77

Thy glass will shew thee how thy beauties wear,
Thy dial how thy precious minutes waste,
The vacant leaves thy mind's imprint will bear,
And of this book learning mayst thou taste:

The wrinkles which thy glass will truly show
Of mouthed graves will give thee memory;
Thou by thy dial's shady stealth mayst know
Time's thievish progress to eternity;
Look what thy memory cannot contain
Commit to these waste blanks, and thou shalt find
Those children nurs'd, deliver'd from thy brain,
To take a new acquaintance of thy mind.
These offices so oft as thou wilt look
Shall profit thee and much enrich thy book.

According to Ivor Brown, this is a poor sonnet. Brown said: "It is a poor, limping sonnet and might very well have been written by someone seeking to sustain the idiom of the sonnet correspondence but lacking the full power to do so" (Brown, 189). However, Ingram and Redpath wrote a general note on this sonnet: "Steeven's suggestion that this sonnet 'was designed to accompany a present of a book consisting of blank paper' seems almost certainly right. Such a gift would, both in Shakespeare's and in Steeven's time, be a much less unusual and more valuable gift than today, and examples still come into the antique market. Whether the mirror and sundial also formed part of the gift must remain uncertain, though 'thy glass' and 'thy dial' do somewhat suggest the view that they did not." (Ingram, 178). In the previous sonnet Shakespeare told his friend, the Fair Youth, that time had been passing non-stop from moment to moment, to reach the 'last syllable' of eternity, and that with the passage of time, his non-pareil beauty must fade away. Therefore the poet had been writing verses (or sonnets) to immortalise the youth. But here, in this sonnet, he says that he will not write verses, but he will, instead, ask the youth to write verses and then read those verses afterwards to see how time passed between his writing verses and reading them. That is, the poet asks the youth to see for himself the continual mutability of the world.

The poet tells the Fair Youth that if he looks into a mirror then he (the youth) will see how his beauty has been fading ('wear'): "Thy glass will shew thee how thy beauties wear,". He, again, tells the youth that the 'sundial' (not watch) will show him how he is wasting, or passing in vain, his valuable time ('precious minutes'): "Thy dial how thy precious minutes waste,". Kerrigan wrote about the 'dial' in line 2: "The *shady stealth* of line 7 defines the *dial* as the face of a 'sundial' rather than some other kind of timepiece. Why *dial* instead of 'sundial'? Presumably Shakespeare used the part for the whole to parallel line 1 more precisely: both the *glass,* showing the young man's face, and the *dial* (the 'face' of the timepiece register the progress of time'' (Kerrigan, 271).

The poet asks the youth to write verses himself on the blank pages ('vacant leaves') of the book that the poet presented him, and thus the pages will contain ('bear') the impression of the youth's mind: ''The vacant leaves thy mind's imprint will bear,''. Afterwards, the youth (if he actually writes verses on these pages) may read, and thereby enjoy ('taste') the verses ('learning') that he will write in that book: ''And of this book this learning mayst thou taste:''. The mirror ('glass') will perfectly ('truly') show the youth the furrows or lines of age in his face, and thus will remind him ('give thee memory') of the gaping and ever-ready-to-receive ('mouthed') grave (which will soon devour him): ''The wrinkes which thy glass will truly show/Of mouthed graves will give thee memory;''. Again, if the youth observes the stealthy, and therefore underhand or dishonest, ('shady') movement or progess of his sundial, then he may understand that Time is imperceptively ('thievish') proceeding towards the end of eternity: ''Thou by thy dial's shady stealth may know/Time's thievish progress to eternity;''.

The poet asks the youth to find out ('Look') what (events, things, love, etc.) his memory cannot preserve in it (that is whatever he may forget): ''Look what thy memory cannot contain''. He asks the youth to write down ('Commit') all these things in those blank and useless ('waste') pages of the book (that the poet presents the youth with): ''Commit to these waste blanks''. If the youth thus writes down those things that are now in his mind, then we will see that those things which are like his issues or progeny ('children') and whom he so long nursed (in the womb of his mind or brain), and now has delivered them from his mind or brain (by writing them down in those pages) are looking like different things with which the youth himself now has to be acquainted afresh: ''Those children nurs'd, deliver'd from thy brain,/To take a new acquanitance of thy mind.'' Kerrigan explained the portion of this sonnet 'shalt find....thy mind.' thus: ''will find those ideas of yours matured (like children past nursing) and ready to be newly acquainted (as though new acquaintances) with your mind'' (Kerrigan, 271). The poet enjoins that all these (looking in the mirror, looking at the sundial, and writing down his thoughts and memories on the blank pages of the book) will be the duties ('offices') of the Fair Youth, which the youth will have to discharge frequently ('so oft'): ''These offices so oft as thou wilt look''. And if the youth honestly performs all these duties, then he will be gainer ('profit thee'), and further, whatever he will write down in those blank pages, keeping in view this injunction, will greatly enrich the book (which the poet is presenting to the youth): "Shall profit thee and much enrich thy book."

78

So oft have I invok'd thee for my Muse
And found such fair assistance in my verse
As every alien pen hath got my use
And under thee their poesy disperse.
Thine eyes, that taught the dumb on high to sing
And heavy ignorance aloft to fly,
Have added feathers to the learned wing,
And given grace a double majesty.
Yet be most proud of that which I compile,
Whose influence is thine and born of thee:
In other's works thou dost but mend the style,
And arts with thy sweet graces graced be.
 But thou art all my art, and dost advance
 As high as learning my rude ignorance.

This is the first of the several sonnets in which Shakespeare wittingly or unwittingly spoke about his rival poets. Of course there was a clear hint to the rival poet in Sonnet 21, but actually this present sonnet unfolds the 'rival poet sonnet-sequence'. We do not know who his rival poet (or poets) had been, in spite of the several details found in Sonnet 86. Guesses are many: Marlowe, Jonson, Chapman, Tuberville and others. There are also guesses that the rival poet is imaginary. But Kerrigan wrote: "...while it seems unlikely that the antagonist was merely invented (wrought from the concerns of the sequence), he is, in the development of its anxieties, a 'wonderous necessary man', and, as a being projected by the verse, subordiante in interest, at every point, to the poetic issues raised by his existence" (Kerrigan, 272). Further, what is the cause of the rivalry or mutual jealousy we do not know. Maybe the cause is this that in spite of not being much educated, in the academic sense, Shakespeare wrote verses which outdistanced the verses of the academically educated poet (or poets), in poetic quality.

However, the poet tells the Fair Youth that he (the poet) regards him as his goddess of poetic inspiration (Muse), and so he has often prayed to him for poetic inspiration ('invoked'), as great poets, before writing epopes, pray for inspiration from the Muse. He says that as an answer to his prayer, he has got much good ('fair') help in the shape of inspiration from him (the youth), while writing verses : So oft have I invok'd thee for my Muse/And found such fair assistance in my verse''. The poet has got as much help from the youth as his rival poet ('alien pen') has received from him (the poet) (by, maybe, stealing or imitating his imagery, style, etc.): ''And every alien pen hath got my use''. The rival poet has written verses ('their poesy') which have been distributed or circulated ('disperse') under the patronage or auspices of the youth ('under thee'): ''And under thee their poesy disperse.''. The brilliant eyes of the youth have inspired even those who are dumb to sing in pitched or treble voice ('on high to sing'), and those who are extremely ('heavy') ignorant to rise high up in their poetic imagination ('aloft to fly'): ''Thine eyes, that taught the dumb on high to sing/And heavy ignorance aloft to fly,''. The charming eyes, or the beauty, of the youth has given extra-ornamentation or fame ('feathers') to the fame of the (academically) educated and rival writer ('learned wing'), and also added extra brilliance and charm ('grace') to, and thus doubled the prominance ('majesty') of, the writer: ''Have added feathers to the learned's wing,/ And given grace a double majesty.'' Kerrigan wrote about the expression 'added feathers to the learned's wing': ''A metaphor from falconry. The poet's *learned* rivals have been imped (given extra wing feathers) by their master, and now they fly even higher than they did.'' (Kerrigan, 272). Further, Kerrigan wrote about the expression 'given grace a double majesty': ''doubled the glorious superiority of already excellent wits'' (Kerrigan, 272).

But the poet asks the Fair Youth to pride highly only on the verses which he himself composes ('compile') — verses that have been inspired by ('influence'), and were written on the theme of the youth ('born of thee'): ''Yet be most proud of that which I compile,/Whose influence is thine and born of thee:''. Kerrigan wrote about the expressions 'Whose influence is thine' and 'born of thee': ''whose nature is determined by you. The *influence* is astrological. Presumably the image was prompted by the educative *eyes* of line 5; here, as at 14.10, the *eyes* become stars, *born of thee* is your child. The poet's verses are the intellectual offspring of the young man; ....'' (Kerrigan, 273). In those rival poets's works ('In others' works'), the youth or his beauty changes for bettter ('mend') the style of the verses; and the poetic beauty ('arts') in their verses is graced by the elegance of the Fair Youth: ''In other's works thou dost but mend the style,/And arts with thy sweet graces graced be.'' But to the poet, the youth is the reification or embodiment of all the arts, and the youth enhances the skill of the poet so much so ('As high as') that his gross ('rude') ignorance can compare with the erudition ('learning') of his rival poets: "But thou art all my art, and dost advance/As high as learning my rude ignorance."

79

Whilst I alone did call upon thy aid,
My verse alone had all thy gentle grace;
But now my gracious numbers are decay'd,
And my sick muse doth give another place.
I grant, sweet love, thy lovely argument
Deserves the travail of a worthier pen;
Yet what of thee thy poet doth invent
He robs thee of, and pays it thee again:
He lends thee virtue, and he stole that word
From thy behaviour; beauty doth he give,
And found it in thy cheek: he can afford
No praise to thee but what in thee doth live.
Then thank him not for that which he doth say,
Since what he owes thee thou thyself dost pay.

The 'rival-poet sonnet sequence' consists of this sonnet, the previous one, and the next one. In this sonnet, the poet says that when only he met, or received, ('did call upon') the favour ('aid') of the Fair Youth, only then his verses contained the modest or affable grace ('gentle grace') of the youth: "Whilst I alone did call upon thy aid,/My verse alone had all thy gentle grace;". Ingram and Redpath wrote about the expression 'had all thy gentle grace': "A gentle pun, involving at least the senses (1) 'was fully possessed of the same elegance as that of your person and character'; (2) 'gave full expression to your excellence'; and, not least, (3) reveived the whole of your favour'." (Ingram, 182). But now, the verses ('numbers') of the poet, which formerly were graceful, have fallen from their elegance, or have declined in quality: "But now my gracious numbers are decay'd,". The guardian spirit of poetry ('Muse') of the poet has become sick, *i.e.* the spirit now no more inspires the poet. And, further, the Muse now has admitted another poet, in lieu of the present poet, for her favour ('doth give another place'): "And my sick Muse doth give another place."

Therefore, the poet admits to the youth that his (the youth's) beauty ('lovely argument') should be ('Deserves') the theme or object of the labour ('travail') of another poet who is more skilled than himself ('worthier pen'): "I grant, sweet love, thy lovely argument/Deserves the travail of a worthier pen;". Nonetheless, this is also true that the 'worthier' (and rival) poet re-presents or re-paints those aspects of the beauty of the youth that this poet (Shakespeare) first discovered; and so, the 'worthier' poet actually robs those aspects of the beauty of the youth (actually, robs this poet of his credit of showing the beautiful aspects of the youth, for the first time), and uses these in his (the other poet's) verses. And the other poet then presents his verses ('invent') to the Fair Youth ('pays it thee again'): "Yet what of thee thy poet invent/ He robs thee of, and pays it thee again:". The 'worthier' poet ascribes ('lends') to the youth qualities or excellences ('virtue'), but, all at the same time he withheld ('stole') that word, virtue, from the manner or bearing of the youth: "He lends thee virtue, and stole that word/From thy behaviour". The poet, perhaps, means to say that the other poet or the rival poet ascribes virtue to the youth from outside, with the help of his imagination, and cannot see that virtue present in the youth, and so actually steals the youth's virtue which is present in his manner.

The 'worthier' or 'rival' poet certainly speaks of the beauty of the youth ('beauty doth he give'), as that poet found that beauty in the person ('cheek') of the youth: "beauty doth he give,/And found it in thy cheek". Therefore, the 'worthier' or 'rival' poet cannot praise the youth more than he deserves — he can only praise the beauty which is present in the youth (really), and no more ('can afford/ No praise'): "he can afford/No praise to thee but what in thee doth live." That is, the other poet cannot exaggerate the beauty of the youth in his verses, and thus praise his beauty. Therefore, the present poet asks the youth not to express gratitude ('thank') to that other poet for what he has written in his verses in his (the youth's) praise, because what that other poet gives ('owes') the youth through his verses, is actually what the youth gives him (the other poet) by being an object of beauty, and so also as an inspirer of verse: "Then thank not for that which he doth say,/Since what he owes thee thou thyself dost pay."

80

Oh how I faint when I of you do write,
Knowing a better spirit doth use your name,
And in the praise thereof spends all his might,
To make me tongue-tied speaking of your fame!
But since your worth, wide as the ocean is,
The humble as the produest sail doth bear,
My saucy bark, inferior far to his,
On your broad main doth wilfully appear.
Your shallowest help will hold me up afloat,

Whilst he upon your soundless deep doth ride;
Or, being wreck'd, I am/a worthless boat,
He of tall building and of goodly pride:
  Then if he thrive and I be cast away
  The worst was this: — my love was my decay.

Gittings wrote about this sonnet: "Sonnet 80 is the first to take a slightly different tone. In the extended sea-image we have noticed, Shakespeare develops the idea of 'your worth (wide as the Ocean is)' to include both himself as a 'sawsie barke' and the rival as a tall proud ship. For the first time he addresses the rival as 'a better spirit' but we are not made seriously to feel that the rival is a better *poet*" (Gittings, 102). The 'rival poet sonnet-sequence' continues till this poem. Here also the poet shows his jealousy. He says that he loses heart or languishes ('faint') when he composes verses ('write') on the theme of the Fair Youth, because he knows that a worthier poet ('better spirit') also writes verses on the theme of the youth: "Oh how I faint when I of you do write,/Knowing a better spirit doth use your name,". That rival poet uses all his poetic skill ('might') in praising the youth, so much so that this poet (Shakespeare) fails to compose verses ('tongue-tied') on the fame of the youth: "And in the praise thereof spends all his might,/To make me tongue-tied speaking of your fame!" The worth of the youth is as boundless ('wide') as the ocean; and the poet is like an inferior ('humble') and impertinent ('saucy') boat ('bark') which is inferior to the (great) vessel of the other or rival poet who has the strongest and widest ('proudest') sail or vessel: "But since your worth, wide as the ocean is,/The humble as the proudest sail doth bear,/My saucy bark, inferior to his,". Nevertheless, the inferior vessel, which is the poet, willingly floats itself onto the wide ocean ('broad main') of the youth: "On your broad main doth wilfully appear."

The poet says that even the slightest ('shallowest') help of the youth will keep the poet's inferior boat floating on the vast ocean, side by side ('Whilst') the mighty vessel of the other or the rival poet, that courses through ('ride') the high-rise waves of the unfathomable ('soundless') (because too deep) ocean which is the Fair Youth: "Your shallowest help will hold me up afloat,/Whilst he upon your soundless deep doth ride;". If the boat of the poet is destroyed ('wreck'd') on the ocean (which is the youth), then the poet will think that his boat is an unworthy boat: "Or, being wreck'd, I am a worthless boat,". And then the poet will also think that the vessel of the other or the rival poet ('he') is of 'sturdy and imposing construction', and so the other poet can certainly be proud of his vessel ('goodly pride'): "He of tall building and of goodly pride:". Kerrigan commented on lines 4-12: "The extended image of seas and shipwreck recalls Nestor's speech on valour at *Troilus and Cressida* I.3.33-45, where the large 'strong-ribbed bark' again comes out well and the 'saucy boat' badly — fleeing to harbour 'Or made a toast for Neptune' when the sea gets rough" (Kerrigan, 274). The poet concludes by saying that if this actually happens, *i.e.* if the other or the rival poet ('he') continues to be successful ('thrive') in taking possession of the Fair Youth, and if, on the other hand, this present poet is rejected ('cast away') by him (the youth), then the present poet will think that he had already done ('was') something worst beforehand ('The worst was this'): "Then if he thrives and I be cast away/The worst was this". The present poet then will think that his love for the Fair Youth in the past ('was') is the cause of his ruin ('decay'): "my love was my decay."

81

Or I shall live your epitaph to make,
Or you survive when I in earth am rotten,
From hence your memory death cannot take,
Although in me each part will be forgotten:
Your name from hence immortal life shall have,
Though I, once gone, to all the world must die;
The earth can yield me but a common grave,
When you entombed in men's eyes shall lie:
Your monument shall be my gentle verse,
Which eyes not yet created shall o'er-read;
And tongues to be your being shall rehearse
When all the breathers of this world are dead:
  You still shall live — such virtue hath my pen —
  Where breath most breathes, even in the mouths of men.

In the last three sonnets, Shakespeare had been despairing for his imaginary inability to cope with the rival poet in writing better verses. But in this sonnet, he regains his aplomb and confidence; he says that his verses are immortal, and that the Fair Youth will also be immortal being enshrined in his verses. In this sonnet, the poet suggests two possible future alternatives: 'Or'. It may be that the poet will outlive the Fair Youth, and write the latter's tombstone inscription ('epitaph'): "Or I shall live your epitaph to make,". Or, it may be that the Fair Youth will continue to live ('survive') when the poet will be rotting in his grave: "Or you survive when I in earth am rotten,". The poet says that, in any case, death will not be able to send the memory of the youth to oblivion, by snatching his memory away from the verses of the poet ('hence'), even though everything ('in me each part') (each member of the body of the poet, or each aspect of his, or the poet) will be forgotten by the people: ''From hence your memory death cannot take,/Although in me each part will be forgotten.''

Though the poet will one day go away from this world ('once gone'), and though he must die, *i.e.* must be dead to the people of the world (because his reputation will be forgotten by the people) ('to all the world must die'), the name or reputation of the youth will be immortal through these verses ('from hence'): ''Your name from hence immortal life shall have,/Though I, once gone, to all the world must die;''. When the poet will die, the world ('earth') will provide him with ('yield') only a simple or ordinary grave; but the youth will, after his death, remain ('lie') in the grave ('entombed') of men's eyes, *i.e.* will remain in the memory of the people: ''the earth can yield me but a common grave,/When you entombed in men's eyes shall lie:''. Kerrigan wrote about the expression 'entombed in men's eyes': ''Evoking one of those fine renaissance tombs on which the dead lie, at eye level, in effigy, bust, or family group. If the friend [the Fair Youth] of this sonnet is the well-born youth addressed in Sonnets 1-19, such a tomb would be his due, and the turn into line 9 would imply 'Despite this, *your* real *monument* ....', drawing on the priorities established in such sonnets as 55'' (Kerrigan, 275).

The poet says that his modest ('gentle') verses will be the sepulchre or memorial stone on the grave of the youth; and the new generation of people ('eyes not yet created') will find more value ('o'er-read') in these verses, or in the 'monument' of his verses: ''Your monument shall be my gentle verse,/Which eyes not yet created shall o'er-read;''. When all the inhabitants or people ('breathers') of this world will be dead, then all their souls will recount ('rehearse') these verses of the poet to be as immortal as the youth will be ('to be your being'): ''And all tongues to be your being shall rehearse/When all the breathers of this world are dead:''. The expression 'breathers of this world' may be compared with what Messenger says in *Antony and Cleopatra* (III, ii, 20-21): ''She shows a body rather than a life,/A statue than a breather.''

However, the poet says that the youth must continue to live in his verses, because his pen with which he will write those verses is skilful or strong ('such virtue hath my pen'): ''You still shall live — such virute hath my pen —''. And in his verses ('Where') life ('breath') lives most lively ('breaths'), not only at other places, but even when people rehearse his verses ('even in the mouths of men'): "Where breath most breathes, even in the mouths of men."

82

I grant thou wert not married to my Muse,
And therefore mayst without attaint o'erlook
The dedicated words which writers use
Of their fair subject, blessing every book:
Thou art as fair in knowledge as in hue,
Finding thy worth a limit past my praise,
And therefore art enforc'd to seek anew
Some fresher stamp of the time-bettering days:
And do so, love; yet when they have devis'd
What strained touches rhetoric can lend,
Thou, truly fair, wert truly sympathiz'd
In true plain words by thy true-telling friend;
And their gross painting might be better us'd
Where cheeks need blood — in thee it is abus'd.

Gittings said that "It is not until Sonnet 32 that Shakespeare begins to attack the rival. He accuses him of the fault common to all Elizabethan poets — overwriting, 'Periergia, or Overlabour', as we saw Puttenham calling it" (Gittings, 102). The truth of this observation may be found especially in lines 13 and 14 of this sonnet. The poet admits ('I grant') that his verses ('Muse') have not done justice ('married') to the Fair Youth, *i.e.* the verses of the poet are not appropriate to the beauty of the youth, and so the youth may ignore ('o'erlook') his verses without being dishonoured ('attaint') by his verses: "Igrant thou wert not married to my Muse,/And therefore mayst without attaint o'erlook". The youth may ignore all the words that writers of sonnets use about their fair and virtuous subjects (lovers or beloveds) and thus make their sonnet-sequences ('book') blessed: "The dedicated words which writers use/ Of their fair subject, blessing every book:" The Fair Youth is both fair in complexion ('hue') and wise ('fair in knoweldge'). Therefore the youth's worth (beauty and wisdom) is so much that poet's praise is never equal to the worth of the youth: "Thou art as fair in knowledge as in hue,/ Finding thy worth a limit past my praise,". Kerrigan wrote about the expression 'Finding thy worth past my praise': "in deciding that your merit forms a region beyond the reach of my praise, when you discover that your merits extends to a boundary beyond the range of my praise" (Kerrigan, 276). Therefore, the youth is compelled to find out afresh ('enforc'd to seek anew') some new and more worthy poet, or impression ('stamp') of the "days which have brought such improvements (in the arts. Compare *the battering of the time* 32.5.)." (Kerrigan, 276): "And therefore art enforc'd to seek anew/Some fresher stamp of the time-battering days:".

The poet asks or requests the youth to do just this: "And do so, love". When worthier poets of better times ('time-battering days') will use laborious means of poetic style ('strained touches') of the Fair Youth, only then the really beautiful youth will be sympathetically or accurately depicted ('truly sympathised') by those realistic ('true-telling') poets ('friend') who will only use accurate but simple or non-artificial words: "yet when they have devis'd/What strained touches rhetoric can lend,/Thou, truly fair, wert truly sympathized/In true plain words by thy true-telling friend;". Line 11 may be compared with lines 1112 and 1113 of *The Rape of Lucrece* : "True sorrow then is fellingly suffic'd/ When with like semblance it is sympathiz'd". But one caution is to be served. Those time-bettering poets may use crimson colours heavily on the cheek of the Fair Youth, wherever it is necessary ('Where cheeks need blood'), or wherever they think it necessary, to improve the colour of the youth's cheek: "And their gross painting might be better us'd/ Where cheek need blood". But the present poet says that if they do so, they will actually be abusing the youth's natural crimson colour: "in thee it is abus'd." The poet here means to say that the Fair Youth is naturally a paragon of beautiful things. And so, if the other poets try to add more beauty to the youth, they will only mar the brilliance of his beauty.

83

I never saw that you did painting need,
And therefore to your fair no painting set;
I found — or thought I found — you did exceed
The barren tender of a poet's debt:
And therefore have I slept in your report,
That you yourself being extant well might show
How far a modern quill doth come too short,
Speaking of worth, what worth in you doth grow.
This silence for my sin you did impute,
Which shall be most my glory, being dumb;
For I impair not beauty, being mute,
When others would give life and bring a tomb.
  There lives more life in one of your fair eyes
  Than both your poets can in praise devise.

This sonnet is a continuation of the previous one, and is also a 'rival poet sonnet' (mark line 12). The argument of the previous sonnet was that the Fair Youth is more beautiful than the poet himself, or the rival poet(s) could picture his beauty in his or in their verses. And in this sonnet, the poet says that he did not think that the beauty of the youth required an embellishment ('painting'), and so did not add any ornamentation to his beauty ('fair') (in his verses): "I never saw that you did painting need,/And therefore to your fair no painting set;". The poet found, or thought, that he discovered that the beauty of the youth was more ('exceed') than the worthless ('barren') beauty portrayal in verse wrought by a poet and proffered ('tender') to the youth as a repayment of the borrowing ('debt') of the poet from the youth: "I found — or thought I found — you did exceed/The barren tender of a poet's debt:". Kerrigan wrote about the expression 'barren tender of a poet's debt': "sterile and worthless tribute which a poet is obliged to *tender* you (in return for patronage or just because your beauty required praise. Comapre the obligation at 79.14). *Barren* only confirms the insufficiency of *tender,* a word which implied in the period 'mere promise, only an offer'; at *Hamlet* I.3.105-7, Polonius tells Ophelia: 'Think yourself a baby/That you have ta'en these tenders for true pay/ Which are not sterling' " (Kerrigan, 277). However, because the poet thought that the youth's beauty exceeded all imitations and adornments of the poet, he stayed unconcerned about what other poet did write about the beauty of the youth — he slept being sure of the youth's reputation: "And therefore have I slept in your report,". The poet thought that as the youth is living ('extant'), he might prove ('show') with his beauty the inordinate inefficiency ('too short') of the ordinary ('modern') poets ('quill') in depicting his beauty: "That you yourself being extant well might show/How far a modern quill doth come too short,". The inordinate inefficiency will show itself when the poets will speak about the value of the youth, or about the value that is increasing in him: "Speaking of worth, what worth in you doth grow."

While the other poets are composing verses on the theme of the beauty of the youth, the present poet (Shakespeare) is keeping silent, which the poet thinks to be a sin on his part, and which is, he thinks, due to the youth himself ('you did impute'): "This silence for my sin you did impute,". But the poet takes this sin to be rather his (the poet's) glory — sin that is due to his (the poet's) remaining silent ('being dumb'): "Which shall be most my glory, being dumb;". This is so, because remaining silent, *i.e.* not composing verses in praise of the youth, the poet is not diminishing the beauty of the youth, thereby (but if he would be composing verses, then he might be diminishing the beauty, because, he thinks, his verses are not so efficient): "For I impair not beauty, being mute,". On the other hand, the other poets ('others') are giving expression ('life') to the youth's beauty, but, in actuality, they are destroying ('bring a tomb') that beauty: "When others would give life and bring a tomb." Line 12 may be compared with lines 1-4 of Sonnet 17. The poet concludes by saying that even a single and beautiful ('fair') eye of the youth is full of more vivacity and liveliness ('life') than the two ('both') rival poets can create ('devise') in writing poems in praise of the youth: "There lives more life in one of your fair eyes/ Than both your poets can in praise devise."

84

Who is it that says most which can say more
Than this rich praise, — that you alone are you,
In whose confine immured is the store
Which should example where your equal grew?
Lean penury within that pen doth dwell
that to his subject lends not some small glory;
But he that writes of you, if he can tell
That you are you, so dignifies his story:
Let him but copy what in you is writ,
Not making worse what nature made so clear,
And such a counterpart shall fame his wit,
Making his style admired everywhere.
You to your beauteous blessings add a curse,
Being fond on praise, which makes your praises worse.

The poet tells the Fair Youth that there is none (or nothing) (other than himself) who can make extravagant eulogies of the youth ('that says most') more than this sonnet (or these sonnets) which is full of profuse praises of the youth: "Who is it that says most which can say more/Than this rich praise". He says that none can praise the youth the most by saying that the youth is non-pareil in beauty, that no one can compare himself with the youth, and so the youth is uncomparable ('alone'): "that you alone are you,". In the person of the youth ('confine') is walled up ('immured') the abundance ('store') of beauty: "In whose confine immured is the store". And this storehouse of beauty can supply examples or instances of beautiful things which can act as models of things that want to grow up to be as beautiful as the Fair Youth: "Which should example where your equal grew?" Ingram and Redpath explained line 4 thus: "The sense would be that the only stock from which one could learn under what conditions a person of the Friend's (the Fair Youth's) excellence could develop is to be found in the Friend himself." (Ingram, 192). The poet becomes deductive in lines 5 and 6. He says that if one does not apply limited ('small') praise to his theme ('subject') or does not adorn his theme with moderate ornamentation, then he will find his extreme poverty ('Lean penury') in writing about his theme: "Lean penury within that pen doth dwell/That to his subject lends not some small glory;". On the other hand, if a poet writes about the youth and represents him as he is, *i.e.* if his representation is true to the youth, then his verses ('story') will be invested with honour ('dignifies'): "But if he that writes of you, if he can tell/That you are you, so dignifies his story:".

The present poet advises that poet (who likes to write, or compose verses, about the Fair Youth) to simply duplicate ('copy') the beauty that is present ('writ') in the youth. That poet should not invent anything and thereby make the bright and pure beauty of the youth, bestowed by nature, inferior ('worse') in his verses: "Let him but copy what in you is writ,/Not making worse what nature made so clear,". That unidentified poet is a rival ('counterpart') of this present poet (Shakespeare). If that rival poet composes verses on the youth as per the directions given before, then his poetic genius ('wit') thereby will be famous, and his poetic style will be respected by persons at all places: "And such a counterpart shall fame his wit,/Making his style admired everywhere." In the *envoi*, the poet changes his argument. He here warns the youth because the youth is very desirous of being praised, which is blasphemous ('curse') to himself. The poet says that the youth has already the blessings of God, of being beautiful ('beauteous blessing'), but if, even then, he is covetous of praises, then he is simply adding blasphemy to himself, which actually will convert his fame into notoriety ('make your praises worse'): "You to your beauteous belessings add a curse,/ Being fond of praise, which makes your praise worse."

85

My tongue-tied Muse in manners holds her still,
While comments of your praise richly compil'd
Reserve their character with golden quill
And precious phrase by all the Muses fil'd.
I think good thoughts, whilst others write good words,
And like unletter'd clerk still cry 'Amen'
To every hymn that able spirit affords

In polish'd form of well-refined pen.
Hearing you praise'd I say, 'Tis so, 'tis true',
And to the most of praise add something more;
But that is in my thought, whose love to you,
Though words come hindmost, holds his rank before.
Then others for the breath of words respect:
Me for my dumb thoughts, speaking in effect.

The poet laments that while the rival poets are elaborately writing ('richly compil'd') about the praise of the Fair Youth, the guardian spirit of his poetic genius, Muse, is keeping quiet ('in manners hold her still') and is remaining dumb ('tongue-tied'): "My tongue-tied Muse in manners hold her still,/While comments of your praise richly compil'd". The rival poets are storing or piling up ('Reserve') their writing ('character') which are done with their precious ('golden') quill: "Reserve their character with golden quill". Ingram and Redpath were of the opinion that the word 'Reserve' should be amended as 'Preserve', and that by the word 'character' Shakespeare always meant 'writing'. (Ingram, 194). The writings of the rival poets have been filled with attractive and worthy styles and phrases ('precious phrase') by the Muses themselves: "And precious phrases by all the Muses fil'd." While the rival poets are writing good verses ('words') about the Fair Youth, the present poet is only thinking well ('good thoughts') of the youth. The present poet is ejaculating 'be it so' ('Amen') hearing each and every poem ('hymn') that has been composed by the worthy poets ('able spirit'). The poet thinks himself to be an illiterate ('unletter'd') parish clerk: "I think good thoughts, whilst others write good words,/ And like unletter'd clerk still cry 'Amen'/To every hymn that able spirit affords/In polish'd form of well-refin'd pen." Kerrigan wrote about line 8: "in the smooth and shapely style which flows from a thoroughly cultivated writer. Or *pen* may be, like *quill,* a metonymy for writing rather than a writer: 'in the smooth and shapely style (and perhaps 'the elegantly shaped lettering', for calligraphy was taken very seriously) of thoroughly civilized writing " (Kerrigan, 280).

When the present poet reads ('Hearing') the verses by the other poets, praising the Fair Youth, he approves their praises ('Tis so, It is true'); and even though they praise the youth very highly ('to the most of praise'), the present poet praises him even more than that ('add something more'): "Hearing you prais'd I say, ' 'Tis so, 'tis ture',/And to the most of praise add something more;". The praise of the youth is always present in the mind of the poet ('But that is in my thought'). The poet's love for him ('whose love to you') is foremost in the poet ('holds his rank before'), though the poet's words come gingerly afterwards to express that love ('Though words come hindmost'): "But that is in my thought, whose love to you,/Though words come hindmost, holds his rank before." Ingram and Redpath explained lines 11 and 12 thus: "The inferiority of Shakespeare's words assigns them a rank behind those of other poets, but his love for the Friend sustains the claim of his thought to rank before theirs" (Ingram, 195). Therefore, the present poet advises the youth to pay attention to ('respect') the other poets only for the beauty of their verses ('others for breath of words'), and to pay attention to himself (the poet) for his silent thoughts about the youth ('Me for my dumb thoughts') — because the poet is, in his silent thinking, really speaking (or writing verses) effectively, in praise of the beauty of the youth: "Then others for the breath of words respect:/Me for my dumb thoughts, speaking in effect."

86

Was it the proud full sail of his verse,
Bound for the prize of all-too-precious you,
That did my ripe thoughts in my brain inhearse,
Making their tomb the womb wherein they grew?
Was it his spirit, by spirits taught to write
Above a mortal pitch, that struck me dead?
No, neither he, nor his compeers by night
Giving him aid, my verse astonished:
He, nor that affable familiar ghost
Which nightly gulls him with intelligence,
As victors of my silence cannot boast, —
I was not sick of any fear from thence:
But when your countenance fill'd up his line,
Then lack'd matter; that enfebbl'd mine.

This is the last sonnet of the 'rival poet sonnet-sequence'. Critics have analysed especially this sonnet to identify the rival poet. John Dover Wilson said that on scrutinising this sonnet, we might guess that George Chapman was the rival poet. He wrote: "A strong case for the identification was cogently set forth a century ago by William Minto, supported by Dowden in 1881, and still further strengthened in 1952 by the arguments of J.A.K. Thomson" (Wilson, 189). Kerrigan wrote that "Chapman would seem a strong candidate" (Kerrigan, 280). He further wrote about this sonnet: "In its imagery the poet recalls Sonnet 80 (Compare, for example, 86.1 with 80.6 and 12), but its argument connects with Sonnet 85'' (Kerrigan, 280). The allusions of this sonnet are very difficult to follow. Kerrigan wrote about this difficulty: ''Perhaps the chief problem in interpreting the poem, and pondering the nature of its reference, is the degree of credence to be attached to the paranormal implications of *spirits* and *familiar ghost* and the degree of literalness allowed *compeers*. Are these lofty ironic ways of describing literary derivativeness, or the depiction of a particular author's erudite and self-regarding superstition?'' (Kerrigan, 281).

However, the poet asks the Fair Youth whether the splendourous ('proud') and arrogant ('full sail of') poems of the rival poet, which are written to win the favour ('prize') of the very precious Fair Youth ('you') have defeated and buried ('inhearse') his (the poet's) mature ('ripe') thoughts about him (the youth): ''Was it the proud full sail of his great verse,/Bound for the prize of all-too-precious you,/That did my ripe thoughts in my brain inhearse,''. The poet asks the youth if the verses of the rival poet have made the brain of the poet, which was the source ('womb') of the poet's verses, the burial ground ('tomb') of the verses of the poet: ''Making their tomb the womb wherein they grew?'' The poet asks the youth whether it was the vigorous and sprightly temperament ('spirit') to write immortal ('Above mortal pitch') verses, that has conclusively defeated his (the poet's) poetic spirit or skill ('struck me dead'): ''Was it his spirit, by spirits taught to write/Above a mortal pitch, that struck me dead?'' (Shakespeare here plays on the word 'spirit'.)

The poet rejects all these as untrue. He says that neither the rival poet ('he') nor his associates ('compeers') who helped the rival poet, by lending books ('Giving him aid') which the rival poet read burning mid-night oil ('night') and profitted himself thereby, are the cause of the defeat of his (the present poet's) verses ('my verse astonished'). He says that neither the rival poet nor some other unknown but great poet ('familiar ghost') who is easily approachable ('affable') and whose composition the rival poet read night after night and was influenced thereby ('Which nightly gulls him') and from whom the rival poet derived poetic skill ('intelligence'), can be proud of defeating the present poet, and thus of making him forsake writing poetry: ''he, nor that affable familiar ghost/Which nightly gulls him with intelligence,/As victors of my silence cannot boast, —''. The present poet was not afraid ('sick of any fear') of that unknown poet, or his influence over the rival poet ('thence'): ''I was not sick of any fear from thence:''. But the present poet was flaberghasted, awe-struck, and vacant-minded ('lack'd I matter') only when he found that the rival poet's verses contained the description ('countenance') of the Fair Youth ('your'): "But when your countenance fill'd up his line,/Then lack'd I matter". He says that only the presence of the Fair Youth in the rival poet's verses ('that') made him (the present poet) lose his poetic skill and inspiration: "that enfeebl'd mine." Kerrigan found the word 'countenance' bearing different connotations at various places of Shakespeare's works. He wrote: "*countenance* (1) face and feature ('Clear up, fair Queen, that cloudy countenance', *Titus Andronicus* I. 1.263), manner and bearing ('Lift up your countenance', says Florizel to the downcast Perdita at *The Winter's Tale* IV.4.49), pleasing appearance ('the evil which is here wrapped up/In countenance', *Measure for Measure* V. 1. 117-18); (2) regard and approval (' [a sponze] that soaks up the King's countenance, his rewards, his authorities', *Hamlet* IV. 2. 15-16), patronage, favour, and protection (thus, at *2 Henry IV* V.1.33-4 and 38-9, Davy asks Justice Shallow 'to countenance William Visor of Woncot against Clement Perkes o' th' Hill', insisting that 'a knave should have some countenance at his friend's request')." (Kerrigan, 282-83).

87

Farewell — thou art too dear for my possessing,
And like enough thou know'st thy estimate:
The charter of thy worth gives thee releasing;
My bonds in thee are all determinate.
For how do I hold thee but by thy granting?
And for that riches where is my deserving?
The cause of this fair gift in me is wanting,
And so my patent back again is swerving.
Thy self thou gav'st, thy own worth then not knowing;
Or me, to whom thou gav'st it, else mistaking:
So thy great gift, upon misprision growing,
Comes home again on better judgment making.
Thus have I had thee as a dream doth flatter—
In sleep a king, but waking on such matter.

This sonnet begins what John Dover Wilson called the 'Farewell Sonnet Sequence' that ends with Sonnet 126. Of course, according to Wilson, Sonnet 49 can be added to this sequence. This sonnet has a peculiarity, for it contains double rhymes throughout, excepting the concluding couplet. Again, Kerrigan noted, all the rhymes are feminine except the words 'estimate' and 'determinate'. This sonnet shows the extremity of coldness of relationship between the poet and the Fair Youth, The poet understands that he can never possess the youth, and so bids farewell to him: "Farewell". He tells the youth flatly that he (the youth) is too precious ('dear') for the poet to possess, and that the youth understands full well his own value ('estimate'): "Thou art too dear for my possessing,/And like enough thou know'st thy estimate". The list or inventory ('charter') of the youth's attractive attributes ('worth') gives him freedom from the poet (*i.e.* he is not dependent on the poet's praises): "The charter of thy worth gives thee releasing;". According to Ingram and Redpath, the word 'releasing' means "exemptions from legal obligations", which, in effect, means freedom. As the youth, for all his worths, is enjoying freedom, the poet presumes that all his bonds or connections with the youth is terminated ('determinate') (de + terminate): "My bonds in thee are all determinate." The poet so presumes because he cannot possess the youth with his (the youth's) consent ('granting'); and consequently, the poet does not deserve to possess the riches that are the worths of the youth: "For how do I hold thee but by thy granting?/And for that riches where is my deserving?" There is nothing in the poet ('wanting') that may procure, or may be the means of achieving, ('cause') the worths of the youth, which are, as if, good gifts for the poet: "The cause of this fair gift in me is wanting,". This is the reason why the 'right of ownership' ('patent') of the poet (over the riches of the youth) is again going back ('back again is swerving') to the youth himself — the 'right of ownership' that the poet so long enjoyed: "And so my patent back is swerving."

The youth gave his self to, or surrendered himself to, the poet, because he (the youth) then did not understand his own worth. Or, it might be that the poet, to whom his (the youth's) worth was proffered or presented, misjudged or overestimated ('mistaking') the amount of that worth: "Thy self thou gav'st, thy own worth then not knowing;/Or me, to whom thou gav'st it, else mistaking:". Consequently ('So'), the immense value ('great gift') that the poet applied to the worth of the youth grew on the error ('misprision' = not precise) of judgment of the poet: "So thy great gift, upon misprision growing,". But afterwards the poet made better consideration of the value of the youth's worth ('better judgment making'), and, as a result, the overestimated value of the youth's worth was reduced to its proper proportion ('Comes home again'): "Comes home again on better judgment making."

The poet says that in this way he possessed the Fair Youth: he thought that he possessed the youth, but it was all mere oneric pride of possession, because he foolishly felt complemented. The poet thus thought himself to be, as if, a king in his dream ('sleep'), but when he woke up from his sleep, he found that all that he saw in his dream, was but illusion ('no such matter'): "Thus I had thee as a dream doth flatter —/" In sleep a king, but waking no such matter." A parallel to the expression 'as a dream doth flatter' may be found at *Romeo and Juliet* (V. i, 1-2): "If I may trust the flattering truth of sleep,/My dreams presage some joyful news at hand".

88

When thou shalt be dispos'd to set me light,
And place my merit in the eye of scorn,
Upon thy side against myself I'll fight,
And prove thee virtuous, though thou art forsworn.
With my own weakness being best acquainted,
Upon thy part I can set down a story
Of faults conceal'd wherein I am attainted,
That thou in losing me shall win much glory:
And I by this will be a gainer too—
For bending all my loving thoughts on thee
The injuries that to my self I do,
Doing thee vantage, double vantage me.
  Such is my love, to thee I so belong,
  That for thy right myself will bear ali wrong.

According to Kerrigan, this sonnet is in "many ways a recapitulation of Sonnet 49." (Kerrigan, 284). This sonnet has also some similarities with Sonnet 35. In the preceding sonnet, the poet parted company with the youth and bade farewell to him, and yet the poet has no animosity for the youth. Contrarily, he has all sympathy for, and feels deeply attracted to, the youth. The poet says, in this sonnet, that even if the Fair Youth is inclined ('dispos'd') to undervaluate him ('to set me light'), and even if the youth ridicules or hates or deprecates ('scorn') the commendable (poetic) qualities of the poet ('merit'), yet the poet will not be offended thereby; but will, on the other hand, support the youth ('thy side'), and thus discount his own merits ('myself I'll fight'): "When thou shalt be dispos'd to set me light,/And place my merits in the eye of scorn,/Upon thy side against myself I'll fight,". Thus, though the youth is now renounced upon oath ('forsworn') by the poet, yet the poet will attest the virtues or worths of the youth: "And prove thee virtuous, though thou art forsworn." The expression 'eye of scorn' may be compared with lines 55 and 56 of *Othello,* IV, ii,: "The fixed figure for the time of scorn/To point his slow unmoving finger at!—". Again, the expression 'against myself' of this sonent (line 3) may be compared with

Sonnet 149 (lines 1 and 2): "Canst thou, O cruel, say I love thee not,/ When I against myself with thee partake?"

Being very much aware ('acquainted') with his own defects ('weakness'), the poet can fabricate a case ('story') in favour of the youth ('Upon thy part'): "With mine own weakness being best acquainted,/ Upon thy part I can set down a story". In that fabricated case ('story'), the defects ('faults') of the youth will be avoided or hidden ('conceal'd'), and, on the other hand, the poet himself will be dishonoured ('attainted'): "Of faults conceal'd wherein I am attainted, —". The poet will do all these so that ('That'), though the youth will then be estranged from the poet ('losing me'), the youth will be much glorified: "That thou in losing me shall win much glory:". And though the poet will glorify the youth at the cost of his own defamation, yet, the poet says, he (the poet) will be profitted thereby ('gainer'): "And I by this will be a gainer too —". Because ('For') the harms ('injuries') that the poet will cause to himself by concentrating ('bending') all his thoughts of love upon the Fair Youth ('thee'), and thus giving advantage or benefit ('vantage') to the youth, will procure twice the advantage or profit that he is at present enjoying: "For bending all my loving thoughts on thee/The injuries that to my self I do,/Doing the vantage, double vantage me." The poet is so much in love with the youth, and he is so much attracted ('belong') to him, that the poet is ready to own ('bear') all wrongs for the sake of the youth's righteousness or virtuousness ('thy right'): "Such is my love, to thee I so belong,/That for thy right myself will bear all wrong."

89

Say that thou didst forsake me for some fault,
And I will comment upon that offence;
Speak of my lameness, and I straight will halt,
Against my reasons making no defence:
Thou canst not, love, disgrace me half so ill,
To set a form upon desired change,
As I'll myself disgrace, knowing thy will:
I will acquaintance strangle and look strange,
Be absent from thy walks, and in my tongue
Thy sweet beloved name no more shall dwell,
Lest I, too much profane, should do it wrong
And haply of our old acquaintance tell:
For thee, against my self I'll vow debate,
For I must ne'er love him whom thou dost hate.

The poet continues to dote on the Fair Youth. He tells the youth that if he (the youth) says or supposes that he rejected or deserted the poet for some offence ('fault') of the poet, then the poet will 'discourse at large upon', or add more to ('comment'), the offences of the poet: "Say that thou didst forsake me for some fault,/And I will comment upon that offence;". Again, if the youth says that the poet is wanting in something ('lameness'), then the poet will not argue with him, but will instantly stop ('straight will halt') arguing with the youth; and the poet will not try to defend himself against the arguments ('reasons') put forth by the youth: "Speak of my lameness, and I straight will halt,/ Against thy reasons making no defence:". But the poet is confident that the youth cannot dishonour ('disgrace') him even to half of the poet's disadvantage ('half so ill'), and thus 'give shape and order' ('To set a form upon') on the poet to have changed him (the poet) according to his (the youth's) will ('desired change'): "Thou canst not, love, disgrace me half so ill,/To set a form upon desired change,". A parallel to line 6 may be found at *A Midsummer Night's Dream*, I, i, 232-33: "Things base and vile, holding no quantity,/Love can transpose to form and dignity." The poet says that he will be disgraced by the dishonouring of the youth, because the poet himself will heap disgraces upon himself, as, he knows, it is the will of the youth: "As I'll myself disgrace, knowing thy will:".

Then the poet will forcefully cut off or stifle ('strangle') all his relations ('acquaintance') with the Fair Youth, and then he will seem to be an unknown person ('look strange') to the youth: "I will acquaintance strangle and look strange,". Then the poet will keep himself away from the paths ('absent from thy walks') of the youth, and the poet will never utter with his tongue the sweet name of the Fair Youth: "Be absent from thy walks, and in my tongue/Thy sweet beloved name no more shall dwell." Thus, the poet will constrain or control himself, for otherwise ('Lest') he (the poet) who is himself so much blasphemed, may anyway do some wrong to the youth, or inadvertantly ('haply') may tell to somebody about his former relations ('old acquaintance') with the youth: "Lest I, too much profane, should do it wrong/And haply of our old acquaintance tell:". The poet will promise ('vow') that he will wage a war ('debate') against himself and for the youth ('For thee'), because he will never love somebody whom the youth hates: "For thee, against my self I'll vow debate,/For I must ne'er love him whom thou dost hate." According to G.K. Hunter, this is a very dramatic poem. Hunter wrote: " 'Sonnet LXXXIX is presented as a 'still' form of a love-drama, a picture in which the gestures not only make up a present harmony, but hint (with subtle economy of means, which reveals the dramatist) at a psychological background, so that a powerful reaction is built up, as if to a history of love' '' (Jones, 122).

90

Then hate me when thou wilt, — if ever, now—
Now, while the world is bent my deeds to cross,
Join with the spite of Fortune, make me bow,
And do not drop in for an after-loss:
Ah do not, when my heart hath 'scap'd this sorrow,
Come in the rearward of a conquer'd woe;
Give not a windy night a rainy morrow,
To linger out a purpos'd overthrow.
If thou wilt leave me, do not leave me last,
When other petty griefs have done their spite,
But in the onset come: so shall I taste
At first the very worst of Fortune's might; —
  And other strains of woe, which now seem woe,
  Compar'd with loss of thee will not seem so.

In this sonnet, Shakespeare gives vent to his pent up 'woe' — a word that appears thrice in the poem. The self-critical strain of the previous sonnet flows through this sonnet. In line 14 of the previous sonnet, the poet said that he would not love a person whom the Fair Youth hates. But here, in this sonnet, he aks the youth to despise himself ('me') whenever the youth will choose to; and, further, if the youth really chooses to hate the poet, then the poet asks the youth to despise him just at the instant: ''Then hate me when thou wilt, — if ever, now —''. The poet asks him to despise him (the poet) at this moment, and not to come before him ('drop in') at some later time and see the final disaster or defeat ('after-loss') of the poet: ''And do not drop in for an after-loss:'' He asks the youth to despise himself even at this moment when the world is pre-empting to thwart or obfuscate the works of the poet ('bent my deeds to cross'), and when the world is working as an accomplice with Fortune's hatred for the poet to make him lie low, or to make him suffer from inferiority ('bow'): ''Now, while the world is bent my deeds to cross,/Join with the spite of Fortune, make me bow,''. Kerrigan found the phrase 'drop in' at *Antony and Cleoptra,* II, xiii, 158-62 (Kerrigan, 286):

Ah dear, if I be so,
From my cold heart let heaven engender hail,

And poison it in the source, and the first stone
Drop in my neck: as it determines, so
Dissolve my life!

The poet asks the youth not to come to him when the poet's heart has escaped from, or come out of, his (present) sorrow, and not to come as an additional source of sorrow issuing from behind ('in the rearward') after the poet has already defeated or overcome ('conquer'd') his front-ranking or present sorrow: "Ah do not, when my heart hath 'scap'd this sorrow,/Come in the rearward of a conquer'd woe;". The expression 'the rearward of a conquer'd woe' may be compared with lines 125-27 of sc. 1 of Act IV of *Much Ado About Nothing*: "Thought I thy spirits were stronger than thy shames,/Myself would, on the rearward of reproaches,/Strike at thy life." The poet asks him not to make the morrow full of tears that fall like rain ('rainy') — morrow that follows the night which was full painful sighs that blows like wind ('windy'): "Give not a windy night a rainy morrow,". The poet asks the youth not to do all these, because then the purposeful obliteration or obfuscation or rejection ('overthrow') of the poet by the youth will be prolongated ('linger') thereby: "To linger out a purpos'd overthrow." The word 'linger' with this connotation may be found at *Midsummer Night's Dream* (I, i, 4): " 'she lingers my desires'."

If the Fair Youth at all wants to reject ('leave') him (the poet), the poet would pray to him not to leave him (the poet) at the last moment (to give the most extreme grief) — moment before which the poet will suffer other lesser sorrows' stings ('spite'): "If thou wilt leave me, do not leave me last,/When other petty griefs have done their spite,". But the poet prays to the youth to come to him just at the beginning ('in the onset') of his mourning, so that the poet can suffer ('taste') at the first instant the extreme sorrows owing to his estranged Forutne's strongest hatred ('Fortune's might'): "But in the onset come: so shall I taste/At first the very worst of Fortune's might;—". Further, the poet asks the youth to leave him in extreme grief, if the youth will at all do so, before the poet suffers yet other clutch of sorrows ('other strains of woe') — sorrows that at the present moment seem to be sorrows, but will not seem to be sorrows ('will not seem so'), if compared with the extreme sorrow caused by the loss of the Fair Youth ('thee'): "And other strains of woe, which now seem woe,/Compar'd with loss of thee will not seem so." A parallel to line 13 may be found at *Much Ado About Nothing* (V, i, 11-12) where Leonato tells Antonio: "Measure his woe the length and breadth of mine,/And let it answer every strain for strain".

91

Some glory in their birth, some in their skill,
Some in their wealth, some in their body's force,
Some in their garments — though new-fangled ill,—
Some in their hawks and hounds, some in their horse:
And every humour hath his adjunct pleasure
Wherein it finds a joy above the rest;
But these particulars are not my measure:
All these I better in one general best.
Thy love is better than high birth to me,
Richer than wealth, prouder than garments' cost,
Of more delight than hawks or horses be;
And having thee of all men's pride I boast:
Wretched in this alone, that thou mayst take
All this away and me most wretched make.

Keller wrote that this sonnet was most probably inspired by the Ode of Horace to Maecenas. But John Dover Wilson said that Book i of Xenophon's *Memorabilia* might be the source of this sonnet. In *Memorabilia,* Socrates, the great philosopher, says:

Some delight in good horses or dogs or birds;
I delight even more in good friends.

These two lines may be compared with the first four lines of this sonnet. Again, the first four lines of this sonnet may be compared with what Malvolio reads from a letter at *Twelfth Night* (II, v, 32): " 'Some are born great, some achieve greatness, and some have greatness thrust upon 'em'."

However, in the first four lines of this sonnet, the poet tells the Fair Youth that some people are proud of their high birth; some of their 'knowledge and intelligence' ('skill'); some of their great mass of wealth; some of their muscular strength ('body's force'); some of their accoutriments ('garments'), though the dresses have become outmoded ('new-fangled ill'); some of their exhibits of hawks and hounds; and some of their presentable horses. These different people have, therefore, various prides or different humours of prides, and they have their corresponding ('adjunct') pleasures wherefrom these people derive different joys, more than the rest of the people: "And every humour hath his adjunct pleasure/Wherein it finds a joy above the rest;".

But the poet tells the youth that all these pleasures ('particulars') cannot satisfy him ('are not my measure'). To the poet, one other pleasure, which is his best pleasure — general or over-all pleasure — will supersede all these pleasures: “But these particulars are not my measure:/All these I better in one general best.” To the poet, the love of the Fair Youth is better than birth in the upper crust of the society. The love is more valuable (‘Richer’) than material wealth, and more to be proud of than precious accoutriments (‘garments’ cost’): “Thy love is better than high birth to me,/Richer than wealth, prouder than garments’ cost,”. Dowden found a parallel to line line 10 at *Cymbeline,* III, iii, 23-24: “Richer than doing nothing for a bribe,/Prouder than rustling in unpaid-for silk”. The love of the youth is of more enjoyment than domesticated hawks and trained horses. And, therefore, by possessing the Fair Youth, or the love of him, the poet can be the most proud among all the people: “Of more delight than hawks or horses be;/ And having thee of all men's pride I boast:”. Nevertheless, the poet thinks himself wretched in one respect only (‘in this alone’) that the Fair Youth (‘thou’) may take away this love (‘this’) for which the poet boasts, and thus make him wretched that he had not formerly been: “Wretched in this alone, that thou mayst take/All this away and me most wretched make.”

92

But do thy worst to steal thyself away,
For term of life thou art assured mine;
And life no longer than thy love will stay,
For it depends upon that love of thine:
Then need I not to fear the worst of wrongs,
When in the least of them my life hath end;
I see a better state to me belongs
Than that which on thy humour doth depend:
Thou canst not vex me with inconstant mind,
Since that my life on thy revolt doth lie.
Oh what a happy title do I find—
Happy to have thy love, happy to die!
  But what's so blessed fair that fears no bolt?
  Thou mayst be false and yet I know it not.

The argument of the preceding sonnet continues in this sonnet. Ingram and Redpath observed that three sonnets begin with the word ‘But’, Sonnets 16,74 and 92, and this indicates that this present sonnet has some link with the two other preceding sonnets (Ingram, 210). But there is no special skein passing through these three sonnets, besides the common link that is natural in a sonnet-sequence. However, the poet tells the youth, in this sonnet, to take himself (the youth) away ('steal'), even at the worst cost, if need arises, and if he wills so, because the poet is certain that for the length of his (the poet's) life, the youth belongs to him ('assured mine'): "But do thy worst to steal thyself away,/For term of life thou are assured mine;". Kerrigan compared the term 'assured' of the second line with the same word at *King John* II, i, 533-35:

King Philip. It likes us well. Young princes, close your hands.

Austria. And your lips too — for I am well assured
That I did so when I was first assured.

Kerrigan said that 'assured' was often used (in the Elizabethan age) to mean 'betrothed'. (Kerrigan, 288). The poet says that he will not live for longer period of time than that during which he will enjoy the love of the Fair Youth, because his (the poet's) life ('it') depends on the love of the youth: "And life no longer than thy love will stay,/For it depends upon that love of thine:". The poet is not afraid of 'the worst of wrongs', because he is certain that his life will end in the least harmful of wrongs (which is taking away of the love of the Fair Youth from the poet, or the cessation of love between them): "Then need I not fear the worst of wrongs,/When in the least of them my life hath end;".

The poet, rather, realises that he is at a vantage point, or in a better state, than if he had been dependent on the whim or mood ('humour') of the youth: "I see a better state to me belongs/Than that which on thy humour doth depend:". Because (as the youth is in love with the poet), the youth cannot be inconstant or unfaithful to the poet, and thus make him anxious ('vex') from time to time: "Thou canst not vex me with inconstant mind,". Again, the youth cannot be inconstant because (he knows that) the life of the poet depends on the reversal or change ('revolt') of the love of the youth for the poet, *i.e.* the moment the youth will, if it at all occurs, cease to love the poet, the poet will die: "Since that my life on thy revolt doth lie." Line 10 may be compared with what Malcolm says at *Macbeth,* V, iv, 10-14:

'Tis his main hope;
For where there is advantage to be given,
Both more and less have given him the revolt;
And none serve with him but constrained things,
Whose hearts are absent too.

The poet is beyond any shred of doubt that the youth will never part his love with him (the poet), and so the poet joyfully wonders to realise that he has the proprietorship (of the love of the youth, or of the youth himself): "Oh what a happy title do I find —". He is wonderfully happy because he has got the love of the youth ('thy love'), and if he dies, yet he will be happy because he has enjoyed the love of the youth: "Oh what a happy title do I find—/Happy to have thy love, happy to die!"

The poet is not only happy, but he also thinks that his present condition or state or situation is free from faults ('fair'), and is, therefore, full of bliss. But he knows that nothing can be absolutely free from faults, and be absolutely blissful, such that it does not give rise to apprehensions ('fears') of changes in that situation or state, or of harbouring defects ('blot'): "But what's so blessed fair that fears no blot?" Ingram and Redpath explained line 13 thus: " 'But what beautiful time (here the splendid situation) is so fortunate as not to run the danger of being sullied?' " (Ingram, 210). And Kerrigan wrote about the same line: "This seems to refer to the *title,* poet's situation in life and love, until, in line 14, the *blot* sticks to the young man" (Kerrigan, 289). Furhter, line 13 may be compared with what Iago says at *Othello,* III, iii, 142-45:

Who has that breast so pure
But some uncleanly apprehensions
Keep leets and law-days, and in sessions sit
With meditations lawful?

As the blessed and fair thing can also turn to be having faults, the poet apprehends that the Fair Youth also may turn to be unfair and cursed: "Thou mayst be false". Nevertheless, the peot has some consolation in that he is not yet aware ('know it not') of the faults of the Fair Youth: "and yet I know it not." Ingram and Redpath wrote about the concluding couplet: "The couplet expresses a pang of awareness of a possibility hitherto blissfully uncontemplated. On the surface is merely hypothetical, 'mayst' bearing a future meaning, and 'yet' the sense 'nevertheless'. But subtly underlying this may be a darker hint, for 'mayst' could be taken as present, and 'yet', as meaning 'as yet', as frequently in Shakespeare" (Ingram, 210). And Kerrigan agreed with them, particularly regarding the last line: "Though the line's primary reference involves fear for the future ('you may one day be false, and I nevertheless not know it'), *mayst* allows a darker and more immediate threat, which *yet* supports ('you may be being false and I as yet not know of it')" (Kerrigan, 289).

93

So shall I live supposing thou art true
Like a deceived husband; so love's face
May still seem love to me, though alter'd new,—
Thy looks with me, thy heart in other place:
For there can live no hatred in thine eye,
Therefore in that I cannot know thy change;
In many's looks the false heart's history
I writ in moods and frowns and wrinkles strange:
But heaven in thy creation did decree
That in thy face sweet love should ever dwell,—
Whate'er thy thoughts or thy heart's workings be
They looks should nothing thence but sweetness tell.
    How like Eve's apple doth thy beauty grow
    If thy sweet virtue answer not thy show!

This sonnet is also clearly a continuation of the previous one. In the previous sonnet, the poet said that the Fair Youth might be unfaithful to him, but the poet is not aware of it: "Thou may be false and yet I know it not." And at the beginning of the present sonnet, he says that for that reason ('So'), he will take the Fair Youth to be faithful ('true'): "So shall I live supposing thou art ture". But the poet is aware that that would amount to cuckoldry on his part: "Like a deceived husband". He will suppose the youth to be true so that the love between them, though it may be tainted ('though alter'd new'), may seem to be perfect love: "so love's face/ May still seem love to me, though alter'd new, —". By the expression 'alter'd new', the poet means to say that the love of the youth has altered or changed, *i.e.* the youth's love now is no more with the poet, but with somebody else. This is clear from thc next line (line 4) where the poet says that though the youth or his appearance ('looks') remains with the poet, the youth's affection is bent towards somebody else: "Thy looks with me, thy heart in other place:".

The poet cannot discover, or cannot believe that there can be, any sign of hatred in the eye of the youth for the poet, and so the poet cannot apprehend any change in the youth: "For there can live no hatred in thine eye,/Therefore in that I cannot know thy change;". In many person's appearances or visages, the account of their hypocrisy ('false heart's history') is evident ('writ') from their particular moods, frowns and uncommon ('strange') lines ('wrinkles'): "In many's looks the false heart's history/Is writ in moods and frowns and wirnkles strange:". But when the heaven (or God) created the Fair Youth, it ordered that (even if the youth be false), his face or appearance would only show marks of 'sweet love': "But heaven in thy creation did decree/ That in thy face sweet love should ever dwell,—". The poet tells the Fair Youth that whatever may be the thoughts and feelings ('workings') in the heart of the youth, the appearance of the youth should only be sweet, or should show sweetness ('sweetness tell'): "Whate'er thy thoughts or thy heart's workings be/Thy looks should nothing thence but sweetness tell." A parallel to lines 11 and 12 may be found at *Macbeth,* I, iv, 12-13, where Duncan says: "There's no art/To find the mind's construction in the face". And again at *Macbeth,* I, vii, 82, where Macbeth says: "False face must hide what the false heart doth know." Kerrigan found another parallel to the expression 'heart's workings' at *Love's Labour's Lost,* IV, i, 33: "working of the heart" (Kerrigan, 290).

In the concluding couplet, the poet compares the enhancement or increase of the beauty of the Fair Youth with the apple of Eve as narrated in Genesis, if the beautiful appearance ('show') of the youth does not complement ('answer') his expected 'sweet virtue': "How like Eve's apple doth thy beauty grow/If thy sweet virtue answer not thy show!" Kerrigan wrote about the last two lines: "Compare Genesis 3.6 (on the beauty of the fatal tree) and, more immediately, the proverb, also used at *The Merchant of Venice* I.3.98-99, 'An apple may be fair without and bad within'." (Kerrigan, 290). The two lines referred to by Kerrigan (above) of *The Merchant of Venice* are: "A goodly apple rotten at the heart,/Oh, what a goodly outside falsehood hath!" The apple of the mythological Eve is brilliant to look at, but within itself, it is obnoxious and harmful. So the poet says that if the youth is not morally good, then the brilliance of his outward beauty will not be different from that apple of Eve.

94

They that have power to hurt and will do none,
That do not do the thing they most do show,
Who moving others are themselves as stone,
Unmoved, cold; and to temptation slow—
They rightly do inherit heaven's graces,
And husband nature's riches from expense;
They are the lords and owners of their faces,
Others but stewards of their excellence.
The summer's flower is to the summer sweet,
Though to itself it only live and die;

But if that flower with base infection meet,
The basest weed outbraves his dignity:
  For sweetest things turn sourest by their deeds;
  Lilies that fester smell far worse than weeds.

This sonnet reads like a sermon on the ideality of man, or, maybe, on the practical dealings of a social man or a man in society. Curiously enough, the first five lines of this sonnet preach almost the injunctions of the *Karmayoga* of the *Gita.* Ingram and Redpath wrote about this sonnet: "One of the chief difficulties of this somewhat elusive poem is to determine how far the portrait of the type of men described is intended as laudatory. Some commentators take it as an ideal portrait, others as highly critical one. We feel that it is an ambivalent one, expressing admiration but also implying, particularly in lines 3 and 4, and possibly also in line 7, certain reservations. The virtue described is, in any case, a passive or negative one...."We would suggest the following paraphrase: 'Those who (by their personality, or their physical, social or spiritual qualities) have the power to harm others, and yet have no desire to do so — who in fact do not do what they most look as if they could: who affect other strongly but themselves remain, like stone, unaffected, cold in disposition and slow to succumb to temptation — such people do indeed inherit from heaven all sorts of graces, and they do not squander irresponsibly these gifts of nature: they are truly the masters of the appearance they present to the world, while others are merely the stewards of qualities richly bestowed on (1) the 'lords and owners' (line 7), or (2) themselves (....). A flower that blooms in summer gives out its sweetness to the summer even though it blooms alone and dies alone (unpollinated and bearing no fruit) (*i.e.* it is nevertheless a positive addition to the summer's total worth); *but* (and here lies a warning), if that flower is attacked by disease and corruption, then the coarsest weed (in its rank vigour) makes a finer show than the (now ruined) dignity of the flower. "(Remember), the sweetest things, when their vital force is perverted into wrong activity, become the sourest. Rotting lilies stink far worse than weeds (Corruption of the best is ever the worst corruption)" (Ingram, 214).

However, in the first five lines, the poet says that those people are blessed by the heaven, or are the favourites of the heaven, who do not harm others, in spite of having the power to do so ('will do none'): who do not do dangerous things ('the thing') that their appearance show they can do ('do show'); who move others emotionally, but maintain their aplomb ('are themselves as stone'); who are not emotionally affected and who remain detached ('cold'); and who are seldom attracted by temptation. The poet (ironically?) says that such persons receive the favour ('graces') of the heaven: "They rightly do inherit heaven's graces,". Such people carefully protect nature's gifts ('riches') from being wasted — they spend only economically ('husband') nature's gifts: "And husband nature's riches from expense;". By nature's riches', Kerrigan meant 'beauty and charm' (Kerrigan, 291). The poet says that these people have complete control over the expressions of their features ('lords and owners'), while others have only limited control over the beautiful expressions ('excellence') of their features: "They are the lords and owners of their faces,/Others but stewards of their excellence." (Does the poet mean by the expression 'lords and owners' hypocrates?) The peot says that the flowers that bloom in the summer is attractive in the summer days, even though the flower blooms and dies alone ('to itself'): "The summer's flower is to the summer sweet,/Though to itself it only live and die;". Kerrigan said that in these two lines, the poet "suggests the sterility of glamour" (Kerrigan, 292). But, perhaps, the poet also means to say that beauty should remain pure, and should not let it be adulterated, though that beauty is not appreciated by anybody: the flower of the summer should not be adulterated by any other season. This sense can be dovetailed into the next two lines where the poet says that if the flower of summer is contaminated with impurity ('infection meet'), then even the rank ('basest') weed will seem to exceed ('outbrave') the flower, in dignity: "But if that flower with base infection meet,/The basest weed outbraves his dignity:". Because, even sweet things become ('turn') most abject ('sourest') things, if those sweet things cause untoward effects ('deeds') on man. For instance, lilies which are very sweet become far worse things ('smell far worse') than abject weeds, if those lilies cause vexations ('fester'): "For sweetest things turn sourest by their deeds;/Lilies that fester smell far worse than weeds." Kerrigan said that a parallel to line 14 occurs in *Edward III* which is often attributed to Shakespeare: " 'The lily is fair in show but foul in smell'." (Kerrigan, 293).

95

How sweet and lovely dost thou make the shame
Which like a canker in the fragrant rose
Doth spot the beauty of thy budding name!
Oh, in what sweets dost thou thy sins enclose !
That tongue that tells the story of thy days,
Making lascivious comments on thy sport,

Cannot dispraise, but in a kind of praise,
Naming thy name, blesses an ill report.
Oh, what a mansion have those vices got
Which for their habitation chose out thee!—
Where beauty's veil doth cover every blot
And all things turns to fair that eyes can see.
Take heed, dear heart, of this large privilege:
The hardest knife ill us'd doth lose his edge.

In the previous sonnet, the poet innuendoed to the faults of the Fair Youth, and now in this sonnet, he speaks of the fault of the youth quite explicitly. In the previous sonnet, he said that that fault would mar the beauty of the youth; but, in this sonnet, he excuses the faults, and further says that, instead of subtracting the beauty of the youth, the faults will rather enhance it. The poet wonders how the youth is converting his shame, due to his faults, into something 'sweet and lovely': "How sweet and lovely dost thou make the shame". The faults are looking like 'beauty spots' on the increasing fame ('budding name') of the youth, as a canker seems to be a 'beauty spot' on the sweet-smelling rose: "Which like a canker in the fragrant rose/Doth spot the beauty of the budding name!" Therefore, the poet wonders how dexteriously the youth coats or covers ('enclose') his faults ('sins') with his beautiful aspects ('sweets'): "Oh, in what sweets dost thou thy sins enclose!"

Even the man ('tongue') who speaks of, or narrates, the youth's activities ('the story of thy days'), and while doing so, makes wanton or stray ('lascivious') comments on the evil or immoral activities of the youth, cannot despise or dishonour ('dispraise') him (the youth): "That tongue that tells the story of thy days,/Making lascivous comments on thy sport,/Cannot dispraise". Because, that man by calling the youth bad names ('Naming thy name'), in a way ('in a kind'), actually praises the youth, and approves or glorifies ('blesses') his (the man's) bad report of the youth's evil deeds: "but in a kind of praise,/Naming thy name, blesses an ill report." The poet wonders that the vices or faults of the youth have got a very precious or great or kingly house ('mansion') to dwell in ('habitation') in the person of the youth: "Oh, what a mansion have those vices got/Which for their habitation chose out thee!—". In that kingly house ('Where') the veil of beauty or the brilliance of beauty ('beauty's veil') shrouds all the vices or moral faults ('blot') of a person, and in that kingly house, everything, which is not beautiful, becomes expressly beautiful ('turns to fair') to the eyes of everyone ('that eyes can see'): "Where beauty's veil doth cover every blot/And all things turns to fair that eyes can see." It is a great ('large') privilege on the part of the youth that his faults are shrouded or coated by the brilliance of his beauty. But the poet cautions the youth about this privilege of his. He tells the youth that even a very hard knife will become blunted ('lose his edge') if it is used badly: "Take heed, dear heart, of this large privilege:/The hardest knife ill us'd doth lose his edge." The poet means to say that if the youth misuses his great privilege of covering his faults or vices with the brilliance of his beauty, this privilege will soon wither away.

96

Some say thy fault is youth, some wantonness;
Some say thy grace is youth and gentle sport;
Both grace and faults are lov'd of more and less,—
Thou mak'st faults graces that to thee resort.
As on the finger of a throned queen
The basest jewel will be well esteem'd,
So are those errors that in thee are seen
To truths translated and for true things deem'd.
How many lambs might the stern wolf betray
If like a lamb he could his looks translate!
How many gazers mightest thou lead away
If thou wouldst use the strength of all thy state!
But do not so: I love thee in such sort
As, thou being mine, mine is thy good report.

Some people say that the faults or vices of the youth are due to his young age; and some say that these are due to his frivolity, or even due to his lechery ('wantonness'). On the other hand, some are of the opinion that the youth is graced by his tender age ('youth', line 2) and his aristocratic ('gentle', line 2) frivolity or lechery ('sport'): "Some say thy fault is youth, some wantonness;/Some thy grace is youth and gentle sport;". Thus both the grace and the faults of the youth are loved by the people of the higher social stratum ('of more') as well as those of the lower social stratum ('less'), *i.e.* both by the people who have 'more' wealth and by the people who have 'less' wealth: "Both grace and faults are lov'd of more and less,—". The Fair Youth turns vices into virtues ('graces') — vices that take shelter in him ('to thee resort'): "Thou mak'st faults graces that to thee resort." Ingram and Redpath explained the first four lines thus: " 'Some people say that the trouble with you (the Fair Youth) is just that you are young, but others think there is more to it, and say that you are naturally frivolous (or 'lascivous' (....). Other people more indulgently say that your very attraction lies in your youth and your being a playboy (or 'in the sexual freedom, allowable to the high-born, which you indulge in'). But whether they find these qualities attractive or blameworthy everybody likes them; for all blemishes that come your way you turn into attractions' '' (Ingram, 220).

The poet draws a parallel to the faults turning into virtues in the youth. He says that the most base jewel will also be looked at as a precious thing if it is worn on the finger by a queen. In the same way, the faults or vices ('error') of the youth are metamorphosed or changed ('translated') into virtues ('truths') in the personality of the Fair Youth, and are then estim'd ('deem'd') as virtuous ('true') things: ''As on the finger of a throned queen/The basest jewel will be well estim'd,/ So are those errors that in thee are seen/To truths translated and for ture things deem'd.'' Kerrigan wrote about the word 'translated': ''The usual word for metamorphosis, as, famously, at *A Midsummer Night's Dream* III. 1. 112-13, 'Bliss thee, Bottom! Bliss thee! Thou art translated!' '' (Kerrigan, 296). The poet says that if a grim and cruel wolf could transform ('translate') itself into the shape of a lamb, then it could deceive a great number of lambs: ''How many lambs might the stern wolf betray/If like a lamb he could his looks translate!'' In the same way, if the Fair Youth would use all the strength ('force') of his beauty, fame, eminence, skill, glamour, etc. ('of all thy state'), then he could command ('lead away') the respect or admiration of a great number of his viewers or those people who look at his beauty with wonder ('gazers'): ''How many gazers mightest thou lead away/If thou wouldest use the strength of all thy state!'' But the poet forbids him to do so (to use all his forces of beauty, fame, etc.), because the poet loves him in such a way (or, the poet is so fond of him) that as the youth belongs to the poet, he (the poet) will only publish well ('good report') of the youth, *i.e.* the poet will only circulate the praises of the youth: ''But do not so: I love thee in such sort/As, thou being mine, mine is thy good report.''

97

How like a winter hath my absence been
From thee, the pleasure of the fleeting year!
What freezings have I felt, what dark days seen!—
What old December's bareness everywhere!
And yet this time remov'd was summer's time,—
The teeming autumn big with rich increase

Bearing the wanton burthen of the prime,
Like widow'd wombs after their lord's decease;
Yet this abundant issue seem'd to me
But hope of orphans, and unfather'd fruit;
For summer and his pleasures wait on thee,
And thou away the very birds are mute:
  Or if they sing, 'tis with so dull a cheer
  That leaves look pale, dreading the winter's near.

Ingram and Redpath wrote a general note on this poem: "This splendid sonnet does not too readily reveal all its secrets. The general tone is immediately evident; but the precise sense of the second and third quatrains presents difficulties: (1) the exact nature of the relation intended between the seasons; (2) the mood or tone of line 8; (3) the significance of 'Yet' (line 9); (4) the meaning of line 10." (Ingram, 222). The Fair Youth was, perhaps, physically absent from the poet who bemoans the absence and compares it with the winter. The youth is the sum-total of all enjoyments of the passing ('fleeting') year to the poet: "How like a winter hath my absence been/From thee, the pleasure of the fleeting year!" Kerrigan explained the expression 'thee, the pleasure of the fleeting year' in two different ways, but said that they are compatible to each other: "Probably 'you, the sum of what is delightful in the swift-passing year'; but perhaps 'you, who delight the year as it swiftly passes'. The two interpretations are not quite incompatible" (Kerrigan, 297). The poet has felt extremely cold ('freezing' and seen extreme darkness in those days, or has seen joyless days, due to his absence from the Fair Youth: "What freezing have I felt, what dark days seen!—". He has also observed everywhere the barenness (defoliation and infertility in the nature, and lack of prosperity elsewhere, etc.) of a cold ('old') December (December is old, because it is cold, and also because it comes latest.): "What old December's bareness everywhere!"

The time of absence (of the poet from the youth) ('remov'd') was the time of summer: "And yet this time remov'd was summer's time,—". But actually the time is not summer, but autumn. Kerrigan wrote about the expression 'summer's time': "Not, quibblingly, 'summer-time' but the 'time when summer laboured to bear offspring' (that is, early autumn); compare *The Winter's Tale* II.2.25, where Emilia says that Hermione is 'something before her time delivered'." (Kerirgan, 298). It was the full autumn that was pregnant ('big') with issues or abundance of life ('with rich increase'), and it was, therefore, carrying the extreme weight ('burthen') of the issues which she (the autumn) conceived in her early days ('prime'): "The teeming autumn big with rich increase/Bearing the wanton burthen of the prime,". The autumn was bearing the weight of her issues like widows who carry the weight of their children in their wombs, after the deaths of their husbands ('lords' decease'): "Like widow'd wombs after their lords' decease:".

The poet was not quite happy with the prosperity ('abundant') of the nature all around him, for he knew that the prosperity or the richness of the autumn would be enjoyed by none, *i.e.* there would be none to look at that richness and be happy, like a father who takes care of his issues and is happy with his issues ('unfather'd fruit'), and unsequently, the richness will be like orphans: "Yet this abundant issue seem'd to me/But hopes of orphans, and unfather'd fruit;". This was so, because the summer and its pleasures cannot be enjoyed without the Fair Youth ('wait on thee'). But the poet is away from the youth and so he thinks that this absence of the youth is the cause of the birds remaining silent and not singing songs: "For summer and his pleasures wait on thee,/ And thou away the very birds are mute:". Or, if the birds at all sing, the poet says, then they sing only uninspiringly ('with so dull a cheer'). And the uninspiring songs make the leaves of trees wan, because, it seems, the leaves become apprehensive ('dreading') that winter is not far away ('near'): "Or if they sing, 'tis with so dull a cheer/That leaves look pale, dreading the winter's near."

The time-scheme of this sonnet seems to be difficult to follow. Ingram and Redpath wrote about the time-scheme: "The time-scheme of the sonnet seems to be as follows: At whatever season Shakespeare may have written the poem, its 'poetical moment' is in the autumn. The months of separation have been like winter to the poet (lines 1-4), though by the calendar they should have been summer, as the actual coming of autumn with its bumper crops has proved (lines 5-8). Lines 9-10 take us back to the period of dejected separation; and there we remain for the rest of the poem, since the present tense of the remaining lines (11-14) is a neutral or definite one, describing what is *always* the case when the Friend is absent" (Ingram, 223).

98

From you have I been absent in the spring,
When proud-pied April, dress'd in all his trim,
Hath put a spirit of youth in every thing,
That heavy Saturn laugh' and leapt with him.
Yet nor the lays of birds, nor the sweet smell
Of different flowers in odour and in hue,

Could make me any summer's story tell,
Or from their proud lap pluck them where they grew:
Nor did I wonder at the lily's white,
Nor praise the deep vermilion in the rose;
They were but sweet, but figures of delight
Drawn after you, you pattern of all those.
  Yet seem'd it winter still; and, you away,
  As with your shadow I with these did play.

The theme of the previous sonnet continues in this one. In the former sonnet, the time of separation was summer, but here it is spring: “From you have I been absent in the spring,”. The month is April, the month which is proud of its colours (seen in nature) and is clothed in fine-shaped flowers, foliation, etc. (‘dress'd in all his trim'): “When proud-pied April, dress'd in all his trim,”. The April has conferred (‘put') youthful joviality (‘spirit of youth') in all things, such that even the sombre (‘heavy') Saturn is smiling and has become frolicksome along with the April: “Hath put a spirit of youth in every thing,/That heavy Saturn laugh'd and leapt with him.”

But all these are not pleasing to the poet. Neither the songs (‘lays') of birds, nor the sweet-smelling flowers of various scents and colours (‘hue') would be able to make the poet speak or write anything about (‘tell') the beauty of the summer: “Yet nor the lays of birds, nor the sweet smell/Of different flowers in odour and in hue,/Could make me any summer's story tell,”. Kerrigan found two parallels to the expression ‘summer's story tell': “‘A sad tale's best for winter', says Mamillius at *The Winter's Tale* II. 1.25. *Cymbeline* III.4.11-14 ; also seems relevant:

> Why tender'st thou that paper to me with
> A look untender? If't be summer news,
> Smile to't before; if winterly, thou need'st
> But keep that count'nance still.
>
> (Kerrigan, 299)

The poet has no proclivity to gather those flowers from the rich (‘proud') green field (‘lap') in which those flowers have grown: “Or from their proud lap pluck them where they grew:”. The word ‘lap' may be compared with the same word that occurs at *Richard II* (V.2. 47) : “ ‘the green lap of the new-coming spring' ” (Kerrigan, 299).

The poet has no penchant for enjoying with awe the perfect whiteness of the lily or the brilliant red colour (‘vermilion') of the petals of a rose: “Nor did I wonder at the lily's white,/Nor praise the deep vermilion in the rose;''. The flowers were, no doubt, sweet, but their beautiful configuration ('figures'), that is an object of delight, had been borrowed from the Fair Youth ('you'), and the form ('pattern') of the flowers was but replica of the form of the youth: ''They were but sweet, but figures of delight/Drawn after you, you pattern of all those.'' In spite of all these nice things, it seemed to the poet then that the time of the year was not summer, but the fag end of winter: ''Yet seem'd it winter still''. And the poet merely played (absent-mindedly) with the flowers ('these'), as if the poet was playing with the shadows of the Fair Youth: ''and, you away,/As with your shadow I with these did play.'' The poet here means to say that the beautiful and sweet flowers are but the shadows of the Fair Youth, and so in the absence of the youth he reluctantly played with the flowers.

99

The forward violet thus did I chide:
'Sweet thief, whence didst thou steal thy sweet that smells,
If not from my love's breath? The purple pride
Which on thy soft cheek for complexion dwells
In my love's veins thou hast too grossly dyed.'
The lily I condemned for thy hand,
And buds of marjoram had stol'n thy hair;
The roses fearfully on thorns did stand—
One blushing shame, another white despair;
A third, nor red nor white, had stol'n of both,
And to his robbery had annex'd thy breath,
But for his theft in pride of all his growth
A vengeful canker ate him up to death.
More flowers I noted, yet I none could see
But sweet or colour it had stol'n from thee.

This is a peculiar sonnet in that it has 15 lines instead of 14. Ingram and Redpath wrote about this: ''The only fifteen-line sonnet in the collection. Instances occur, however, in other Elizabethan collections. No line here can be removed without damage to the sense of syntax, though in point of rhyme alone line 1 or line 5 is the extra line.'' (Ingram, 226). The sonnet is also distinctive for its 'stray iambic pentameter'. In this sonnet, the poet dwells at length on the message of line 12 of the immediately preceding sonnet: ''Drawn after you, you pattern of all those.'' In the previous sonnet, the poet said that the beautiful flowers of summer drew their brilliance from the Fair Youth. In the first five lines of this sonnet, therefore, the poet scolds them — the flowers. He first rebukes the impudent ('forward') violet. Calling the violet a filcher ('thief'), the poet tells it that it could not thieve its sweet smell from anywhere but from the breath of the Fair Youth. The purple colour, that is the point of the violet to be proud of, subsists ('dwells') or the cheek of the flower and thus gives the flower its hue ('complexion'). This same colour runs through the blood of the veins of the Fair Youth. But the violet has taken away that colour from the youth, and has coloured ('dyed') itself very heavily ('grossly') with this colour. Kerrigan found a parallel to lines 2-5 at *Venus and Adonis,* 1165-70 (Kerrigan, 301):

> By this the boy that by her side lay killed
> Was melted like a vapour from her sight,
> And in his blood that on the ground lay spilled
> A purple flow'r sprung up, check'red with white,
>   Resembling well his pale cheeks, and the blood
>   Which in round drops upon their whiteness stood.

Line 1 may be compared with lines 935 and 936 of *Venus and Adonis*: "his breath and beauty set/Gloss on the rose, smell to the violet?"

The poet looked down upon ('condemned') the lily and chose, instead, the beautiful hand of the youth. He says that the buds of marjoram, a labiate armoatic plant, have beautified themselves with the hair of the youth: "The lily I condemned for thy hand,/ And buds of marjoram had stol'n thy hair". The roses were afraid that they might no more be loved by people, and so instinctively or reflexively stood on their thorns, as the hairs stand on end when one is afraid. One rose blushed in shame another become pale ('white') despairing that it might not attract people any more: "The roses fearfully on thorns did stand—/ One blushing shame, and another white despair;". The third rose is neither perfectly red nor perfectly white — it is damask. And this rose has stolen partially the red colour and partially the white colour (the former from the blood and the latter from the skin) of the Fair Youth: "A third, nor red nor white, had stol'n of both,". The poet says that the third rose has not really stolen these two colours, but has possessed ('annex'd') these colours by comitting robbery. Further, the third rose has also appropriated ('annex'd') the life or spirit ('breath') of the Fair Youth: "And to his robbery had annex'd thy breath,". Yet the third rose could not prosper by such robbery or theft. Because, a canker became revengeful for the robbery of the third rose and for the rose's taking pride, or becoming proud, for its prosperity ('growth') (in beauty). And consequently the canker had eaten up the rose, and thus brought in the death of the third rose: "But for his theft in pride of all his growth/A vengeful canker ate up to death.'' The poet concludes by telling the Fair Youth that he (the poet) has observed many other flowers, but he has not seen a single flower which has not robbed the youth ('stol'n from thee') of his sweetness and colour: ''More flowers I noted, yet none could see/But sweet or colour it had stol'n from thee.''

100

Where art thou, Muse, that thou forget'st so long
To speak of that which gives thee all thy might?
Spend'st thou thy fury on some worthless song,
Darkening thy power to lend base subjects light?
Return, forgetful Muse, and straingth redeem
In gentle numbers time so idly spent;
Sing to the ear that doth thy lays esteem
And gives thy pen both skill and argument.
Rise, resty Muse, my love's sweet face survey,
If time have any wrinkle graven there, —
If any, be a satire to decay
And make Time's spoils despised everywhere:
Give my love fame faster than Time wastes life;
So thou prevent'st his scythe and crooked knife.

Kerrigan said that in ''the next four sonnets the poet elegantly blames, and excuses, himself for neglecting the friend in verse.'' (Kerrigan, 302). John Dover Wilson believed that this sonnet was, probably, written after a cessation of sonnet-writing, during which time Shakespeare engaged himself in writing plays. At the time of writing this sonnet, perhaps, a repprochement grew over again between the poet and the Fair Youth. Shakespeare now '' is no logner the elder deeply concerned for a boy's [the Fair Youth's] conduct; he now seems to look up for help and guidance'' (Wilson, 209). However, the poet addresses the Muse (of poetry) and asks her to tell him where she had so long been (for the period of time while Shakespeare had been writing only plays and no sonnets). He tells her that due to her absence he has forgotten to sing ('speak') of the Fair Youth ('that') who gave her all her skill ('might') of singing or composing songs or sonnets: ''Where art thou, Muse, that thou forget'st so long/To speak of that which gives thee all thy might?'' The poet asks her (the Muse) whether she expends her poetic rage or inspiration ('fury') on the composition of some bad songs (about some mean person), and thereby diminishes or clouds or attenuates her poetic skill, so that she can give ('lend') light to, or enlighten, some mean ('base') person or thing: "Spend'st thou thy fury on some worthless song,/Darkening thy power to lend base subjects light?"

The poet supplicates to the Muse, who is prone to amnesia, for persuading her to come back to her former state, and straightaway compensate ('redeem') for the time which she whiled away ('idly spent'), and did not compose any song, by once again singing mild ('gentle') songs ('numbers'): "Return, forgetful Muse, and straight redeem/In gentle numbers time so idly spent;". The poet urges upon her to sing or write verses ('lay') only for that person ('the ear') who respects ('esteem') her song or verses, and who gives her verses ('pen') beauty and good subject-matter ('argument'): "Sing to the ear that doth thy lays esteem/And gives thy pen both skill and argument." He implores the idle ('resty') Muse to rise up for works and observe the sweet face of the Fair Youth, to see if Time has created ('graven') furrows ('wrinkles') on that face: if the youth has worn himself out with the passage of time: "Rise, resty Muse, my love's sweet face survey,/If Time have any wrinkle graven there,—". The word 'resty' may also be found at *Cymbeline,* III, vi, 33-35: "weariness/Can snore upon the flint, when resty sloth/Find the down pillow hard." And also at Sidney's *Astrophel and Stella,* 80,12: "And no spare can his resty race renew."

If there are any such wrinkles ('If any'), the poet tells the Muse, then let her satirise on the aging ('decay') of the Fair Youth (because, the poet says, such a beautiful youth should not be spoiled by Time): "If any, be a satire to decay". He asks the Muse, further, to condemn ('despised') the destructiveness ('spoils') of Time at all places: "And make Time's spoils despised everywhere". On the other hand, the poet prays to the Muse to endow the youth ('my love') with fame sooner ('faster') than Time can consume his (the youth's) life, *i.e.* to give fame before the death of the youth. Thus, the Muse can placate ('prevent') the workings of Time's ('his') destructive sickle ('scythe') and bending ('crooked') knife, *i.e.* Time's destructiveness: "Give my love fame faster than Time wastes life;/ So thou prevent'st his scythe and crooked knife."

101

O truant Muse, what shall be thy amends
For thy neglect of truth in beauty dyed?
Both truth and beauty on my love depends:
So dost thou too, and therein dignified.
Make answer, Muse: wilt thou not haply say,
'Truth needs no colour with his colour fix'd,
Beauty no pencil beauty's truth lay,

But best is best if never intermix'd'?
Because he needs no praise wilt thou be dumb?
Excuse not silence so, for it lies in thee
To make him much outlive a gilded tomb
And to be prais'd of ages yet to be.
  Then do thy office, Muse (I teach thee how): —
  To make him seem long hence as he shows now.

In Sonnets 100, 101 and 103, Shakespeare concerns himself with the Muse. In the former two, he addresses the Muse and accuses her directly, but in 103 he accuses her obliquely. In Sonnet 101, he asks her what will be the compensation ('amends') of her negligence of the 'moral integrity' ('truth') coupled with beauty ('beauty dyed') of the Fair Youth: ''O truant Muse, what shall be thy amends/For thy neglect of truth in beauty dyed?'' Here the poet expresses his belief that moral perfection ('truth') and physical beauty are co-extensive. The poet says that both truth and beauty are present in the Fair Youth ('my love'), as these are also present in the Muse, and that by these two components she is dignified: ''Both truth and beauty on my love depends:/So dost thou too, and therein dignified.'' It may be noted here that Shakespeare has employed the two nouns 'truth' and 'beauty' as a singular noun (mark 'depends'). This may remind us of the Keatsian expression ''Beauty is truth, truth beauty' in his ''Ode on a Gracian Urn'. Further, line 3 may well be compared with line 11 of Sonnet 14: ''As truth and beauty shall together thrive''.

The poet importunes to the Muse to say ('answer') whether she would not happily ('haply') say that having its own natural colour ('his own colour fix'd'), Truth needs not borrow further colour; and that one who is naturally beautiful, needs not paint ('lay') oneself (in the eye-brow, etc.) with dying pencils, to beautify oneself; and that a thing that is naturally the most beautiful is such ('best is best') even though nothing is added to it ('intermix'd'): ''Make answer, Muse: wilt thou not haply say,/'Truth needs no colour with his colour fix'd,/ Beauty no pencil beauty's truth to lay,/But best is best if never intermix'd?'' The word 'colour' has yet another meaning than 'pigment': 'colour' also means 'excuse'. If line 6 is read keeping this meaning of the word in mind, then the meaning of line 6 will be: moral perfection needs no excuse (or reason) as it has got its own excuse. Kerrigan wrote about the meaning of the word 'colour': ''*Colour* includes 'excusing' and 'disguise' ('Why hunt I then for colour or excuses', 'Under what colour he commits this ill', *The Rape of Lucrece* 267 and 476) and 'deceiving rhetoric' (the metaphor was commonplace). Quibblingly, Shakespeare exploits a secondary, literal notion: *colour* as pigment, used for make up and portraiture'' (Kerrigan, 304).

In spite of the pote's pertinacy, the Muse remains silent. The poet then asks her whether it is because a beautiful thing ('he') (here the Fair Youth) needs no praise that she is keeping silent ('dumb'): ''Because he needs no praise wilt thou be dumb?'' If this be the reason of the Muse's silence, if she remains silent because the Fair Youth, being an object of beauty, does no need praise, then the poet will ask her not to remain silent, and further, not to pardon ('Excuse') herself, or her own silence due to that reason ('so'). Because ('for') it is the responsibility of the Muse ('it lies in thee') to make the Fair Youth ('him') live much longer ('outlive') than a gold-gilt sepulchral monument ('gilded tomb'): ''Excuse not silence so, for it lies in thee/To make him much outlive a gilded tomb''. The poet tells her that it is her charge to make the youth praise (she should praise him) throughout the future ages: ''And to be prais'd of ages yet to be.'' As all this be so ('Then'), the poet asks the Muse to discharge her duties ('do thy office'), and, in subdued voice, tells her that he will teach her how to discharge her duties: ''Then do thy office, Muse (I teach thee how);—''. In the last line, the poet explains that duty or charge of the Muse. He says that it is to make the Fair Youth live long from now on ('hence'), as it now appears from his qualities that the youth will live long: ''To make him seem long hence as he shows now.''

102

My love is strengthen'd, though more weak in seeming;
I love not less, though less the show appear:
That love is merchandiz'd whose rich esteeming
The owner's tongue doth publish everywhere.
Our love was new, and then but in the spring,
When I was wont to greet it with my lays;
As Philomel in summer's front doth sing,
And stops her pipe in growth of riper days:
Not that the summer is less pleasant now
Than when her mournful hymn did hush the night,
But that wild music burthens every bough,
And sweets grown common lose their dear delight.
Therefore like her I sometime hold my tongue;
Because I would not dull you with my song.

The poet tells the Fair Youth that though his love for him (the youth) seems to have become lighter or shallower ('more weak'), it has actually deepened. The poet now does not love him less; only the outward expression of his love shows the love to be weaker: "My love is strengthen'd, though more weak in seeming;/I love not less, though less the show appear". The poet says that his love is not a merchandise or a thing to be sold and so he does not need advertising his love. He says that only that love is like a merchandise, the very good qualities ('rich esteeming') of which its proprietor orally ('tongue') advertises ('publish') everywhere: "That love is merchandiz'd whose rich esteeming/The owner's tongue doth publish everywhere." Lines 3 and 4 may be compared with the following lines at *Love's Labour's Lost,* I, ii, 13-16, where Princess of France tells Boyet:

my beauty, though but mean,
Needs not the painted flourish of your praise.
Beauty is bought by judgment of the eye,
Not utt'red by base sale of chapmen's tongues;

However, the poet tells the youth that they fell in new love at the time of spring during which time or season it was the habit of the poet (the poet was wont to) receive ('greet') that love with the presentation of his songs ('lays'): "Our love was new, and then but in the spring,/When I was wont to greet it with my lays;". He sang those songs like the legendary bird Philomel at the beginning ('front') of the summer, and he would stop singing those songs ('stop her pipe'), again like Philomel, as the summer would wane, and autumn would then make the fruits ripe ('in growth of riper days'): "As Philomel in summer's front doth sing,/ And stops her pipe in growth of riper days". Philomel or Philomela is a legendary character. She is the daughter of Pandion. Tereus, the husband of her sister, Procne, fell in love with, and raped, her (Philomel). Philomel threatened Tereus by saying that she would publish the rape. Tereus then cut off her tongue to prevent the fact of rape from being published. However, she was later on changed into a nightingle and since then she sings in the spring. Line 7 of this sonnet has a parallel at *The Winter's Tale,* IV, iv, 1-3, where Florizel tells Perdita: "These your unusual weeds to each part of you/Do give a life — no shepherdess, but Flora/Peering in April's front."

The poet says that the summer is not less pleasant than the autumn when at night the loud songs of nightingales subdued the songs of the little birds which were less loud ('did hush the night'): "Not that the summer is less pleasant now/Than when her mournful hymns did hush the night,''. The only difference between the autumn and the summer is that in the autumn only few birds (nightingales) sang, while in the summer, every bird sings, and therefore, songs have become very common. The poet says that in the summer, birds sing on every bough, and so the summation of the songs seems to be noise ('wild music'). Every bough is thus burdened ('burthens') with songs. The poet also says that if a thing that is sweet becomes a common thing, then that sweet thing loses its sweetness ('dear delight'): ''But that wild music burthens every bough,/And sweets grown common lose their dear delight.'' Here the poet means to say that formerly only he himself (like the nightingale) would compose verses ('sing songs) in praise of the Fair Youth, but now many a poet are writing verses like him. Consequently, the praise of the youth has become common and commonplace. It is for this reason that the poet sometimes stops writing verses in praise of the youth, or stops singing songs in praise of him, like the nightingale which sometimes refrains from singing songs ('sometimes hold my tongue'). He does so, so that the youth may not become bored ('dull') with the songs, or with the verses, written by him in praise of the youth: ''Therefore like her I sometimes hold my tongue;/Because I would not dull you with my song.''

103

Alack, what poverty my Muse brings forth,
That having such a scope to show her pride
The argument all bare is of more worth
Than when it hath my added praise beside!
Oh, blame me not if I no more can write!
Look in your glass, and there appears a face
That over-goes my blunt invention quite,
Dulling my lines and doing me disgrace.
Were it not sinful then, striving to mend,
To mar the subject that before was well?
For to no other pass my verses tend
Than of your graces and your gifts to tell:
And more, much more, than in my verse can sit
Your own glass shows you when you look in it.

The theme of the previous sonnet continues in this sonnet: the poet mourns over his loss of poetic metier and *élan,* but at the same time he redeems this loss by thinking that this is rather investing for the Fair Youth. In this sonnet, he thinks it to be a bad luck for him that the Muse has brought forth for him the poverty of poetic metier and *élan*, when such a proper subject-matter of poetic composition as the Fair Youth ('such a scope') lies before the Muse to show her the pride of composing verses: "Alack, what poverty my Muse brings forth,/That having such a scope to show her pride". Line 1 of this sonnet has a parallel at line 5 of Sonnet 84: "Lean penury within that pen doth dwell". However, yet, the poet condones his poverty thinking that the subject-matter of his poetry ('argument'), *i.e.* the youth, will be of more virtues ('more worth') when it (the youth) is not praised by him or by anybody else ('all bare'), than when he praises ('added praise') the subject-matter, or the youth: "The argument all bare is of more worth/Than when it hath my added praise beside!" Lines 3 and 4 may be compared with what Duke of Albany tells Goneril at *King Lear,* I, iv, 347: "Striving to better, oft we mar what's well."

The poet forbids the youth not to censure ('blame') him if he (the poet) cannot write any more verse in his (the youth's) praise: "Oh, blame me not if I no more can write!" He asks the youth to look into his mirror ('glass') where he will find a replica of his own face ('a face') which face far exceeds ('over-goes') in beauty the ordinary verses ('blunt invention') of his (the poet's). While reflected in the mirror, the face of the youth will make the verses of the poet dull ('Dulling my lines') and will also put shame ('disgrace') on the poet: "That over-goes my blunt invention quite,/Dulling my lines and doing me disgrace." If this is so, and so it is says the poet, then it would be wrong ('sinful') on the part of the poet to try to correct ('mend') his wrong versification, because by thus correcting his wrong versification, the poet will only put injury ('mar') into the beauty of the Fair Youth ('subject') — the beauty of the youth is far better than the beauty the verses of the poet will present: "Were it not sinful then, striving to mend,/To mar the subject that before was well?" Because, the poet says, the object ('pass') of his verses is nothing else than telling about, or making an inventory of, the graces and virtues ('gifts') of the Fair Youth: "For to no other pass my verses tend/Than of your graces and your gifts to tell:". Nevertheless, the poet admits, his verses cannot show the youth more of his graces and virtues than the mirror ('glass') of the youth, when he will look into it and see his image in it, will show, because in his (the poet's) verses, only much lesser number of his graces and virtues inhere ('sit'): "And more, much more, than in my verse can sit/Your own glass shows you when you look in it."

104

To me fair friend, you never can be old,
For as you were when first your eye I eyed
Such seems your beauty still: three winters cold
Have from the forests shook three summers' pride,
Three beauteous springs to yellow autumn turn'd
In process of the seasons have I seen,
Three April perfumes in three hot Junes burn'd,
Since first I saw you fresh which yet are green.
Ah yet doth beauty like a dial hand
Steal from his figure and no pace perceiv'd,
So your sweet hue, which methinks still doth stand,
Hath motion, and mine eye may be deceiv'd,
For fear of which hear this, thou age unbred:
Ere you were born was beauty's summer dead.

According to John Dover Wilson, this sonnet is misplaced in the present (accepted) sequence of the sonnets of Shakespeare. Wilson wrote: "This sonnet was written immediately after 99 and is linked stylistically with the group 97-99 which it should follow." (Wilson, 212). Ingram and Redpath said that this sonnet "has played a large part in the controversy on the dating of the *Sonnets*" (Ingram, 236). Wilson further wrote about the dating and occasion of this sonnet: "I conclude that it was composed for Herbert's 20th birthday, 8 April 1600, and that the 'three years' it speaks of fix the date of the first meeting of the friends at 8 April 1597, *viz.* Herbert's 17th birthday —" (Wilson, 212). However, this is one of the most beautiful sonnets of Shakespeare, with all its beautiful images culled from the seasons.

The poet tells the youth that he (the youth) can never become old in his eye, because the youth is still as beautiful (after three years) as he had been when the poet first saw his eyes ('your eye I eyed'): "To me, fair friend, you never can be old,/For as you were when first your eye I eyed/Such seems your beauty still". During the period between the first and the second meetings between the youth and the poet, three winters and three summers have elapsed. The chill of these three winters has shaken off the beauty (the verdure) of the forest, of which the three summers had been proud of ('shook three summers' pride'), and during the same period, the green leaves of the spring have turned yellow in the seasons of autumn: "three winters cold/Have from the forests shook three summers' pride,/Three beauteous springs to yellow autumn turn'd". Line 4 may be compared with what Capulet tells County Paris at

Romeo and Juliet, I,ii, 10: ''Let two more summers wither in their pride''. In the concatenation ('process') of the seasons, the poet has seen three springs in three Aprils, with their sweet-scenting flowers ('perfumes') to have been charred ('burn'd') in the scorching summers of Junes: ''In process of the seasons have I seen,/Three April perfumes in three hot Junes burn'd,''. All this the poet as seen after his first meeting with the Fair Youth ('you') who then had been as young ('fresh') as he is now (fresh, 'green'): ''Since first I saw you fresh which yet are green.''

But, all the same, the poet is painfully ('Ah') aware that the beauty of the Fair Youth is imperceptibly ('no pace perceiv'd') moving or going away from him ('Steal from his figure'), like the hand of a clock ('a dial hand') moves round its centre while the movement cannot be observed: ''Ah yet doth beauty like a dial hand/Steal from his figure and no pace peceiv'd,''. A parallel to the expression may be found at line 7 of Sonnet 77: ''Thou by thy dial's shady stealth mayst know''. Likewise, the attractive ('sweet') complexion ('hue') of the youth is also changing ('motion') for the worse, though the poet thinks that it is unchangeable ('still doth stand'), and so the poet thinks that his observation of the unchangeableness of the complexion may be false ('mine eye may be deceiv'd,—''): ''So your sweet hue, which methinks still doth stand,'/ Hath motion, and mine eye may be deceiv'd,—''. The poet is apprehensive of all this, and so he tells the future or oncoming ('unbred) age or generation (personified) ('thou age') that before it will have come into being ('Ere you were born'), 'the golden time of Beauty' ('beauty's summer') will have died: ''For fear of which hear this, thou age unbred:/ Ere you were born was beauty's summer dead.'' The poet here means to say that with the death of the Fair Youth, the golden age of beauty will cease to be, so that the future generations will not be able to estimate what perfect beauty (that the youth now possesses) is.

105

Let not my love be call'd idolatry,
Nor my beloved as an idol show,
Since all alike my songs and praises be
To one, of one, still such, and ever so.
Kind is my love today, tomorrow kind,
Still constant in a wondrous excellence:
Therefore my verse, to constancy confin'd,
One thing expressing, leaves out difference.
'Fair, kind, and true' is all my argument—

'Fair, kind, and true' varying to other words;
And in this change is my invention spent—
Three themes in one, which wondrous scope affords. 12
Fair, kind, and true have often liv'd alone,
Which three till now never kept seat in one.

Kerrigan wrote a general introduction to this sonnet: ''The poet's persona is strongly registered here, since the sonnet draws its strength from the weakness of its argument. The 'I' projected by *my verse* is read or heard defending — with such obvious sophistry that assumes some excess is being concealed — his devotion to the youth. He tries to refute the charge of idolatry by demonstrating that his *love* is monotheistic — indeed, trinitarian, like orthodox Christianity — and directed at someone whose unique blend of beauty, generosity, and truth is almost miraculous; but although polytheism was, for most Elizabethan readers, ineluctably idolatrous, *idolatry* is not necessarily polytheistic, and the tone of the sestet — the manner of the poet's defence of *love* — supports a suggestion that he thinks his friend is a worldly god, an *idol.* At the same time, the sonnet is not particularly complex. Almost bare of metaphor, with a chaste rhetorical 'colour' scheme, it exemplifies in verbal terms the flatness of *constancy*'' (Kerrigan, 309-10).

The poet says that his love for the Fair Youth should not be called worshipping of images ('idolatry'), and no one should say that his object of love ('beloved') seems to be an image of worhsip: ''Let not my love be call'd idolatry,/Nor my beloved as an idol show,''. Because ('Since') all the songs and the praises of the poet — all in the same manner ('all alike') — are addressed to the same Fair Youth ('To one'), and the songs and praises are about the same youth ('of one'). These songs and praises have continued to be so to the present moment ('still such'), and will continue to be so in the future ('ever so'): ''Since all alike my songs and praises be/To one, of one, still such, and ever so.'' Unfortunately it is not clear here whether by the word 'Since' Shakespeare means to submit arguments in defence of his not being an idolater, or to prove that he is really an idolater. Ingram and Redpath wrote: ''The crux is, as Pooler suggests, whether this is the reason for the accusation or the beginning of a defence against it. We think the former. To say that the 'songs and praises' are all addressed to one person and in the same strain would be a poor counter to an accusation of idolatry!'' (Ingram, 238). However, the love of the poet for the youth is generous ('kind') at present, and it will continue to be so in the future. It is also even now ('Still') invariable and wonderful and excellent: "Kind is my love today, tomorrow kind,/Still constant in a wonderous excellence:". It is for this reason that the verses of the poet are also constant ('to constancy confin'd'), *i.e.* the subject-matter of these verses is the same and invariable thing: the beauty of the Fair Youth. And the verses, consequently, express only one idea, the beauty of the youth, and at the same time exclude ('leaves out') other literary themes ('difference'): "Therefore my verse, to constancy confin'd,/One thing expressing, leaves out difference." Kerrigan wrote about the expression 'leaves out difference': "The poet means 'ignores other literary subjects' and 'needs not record diversity (because you are so *constant*)'; but 'fails to mention disagreements (between us)' and 'excludes changes of mood (in you)' must also register. The poet's idolatrous self-deception is subtly exposed; you cannot *leave out* what isn't there" (Kerrigan, 310).

The argument of the verses of the poet is that the Fair Youth is beautiful, generous, and honest ('Fair, kind, and true'), and the poet expresses these concepts, as applied in the case of the youth, in other different words also: " 'Fair, kind, and true' is all my argument—/'Fair, kind, and true' varying to other words;". The expression 'Fair, kind, and true' that occurs in lines 9 and 10, may be compared with what Lorenzo tells Gratiano at *The Merchant of Venice,* II, vi, 52-57 :

> Beshrew me, but I love her heartily,
> For she is wise, if I can judge of her,
> And fair she is, if that mine eyes be true,
> And true she is, as she hath prov'd herself;
> And therefore, like herself, wise, fair, and true,
> Shall she be placed in my constant soul.

Kerrigan wrote about the same expression: "*Fair* suggests beauty, justice, and kindness; *kind,* generosity, gentleness, affection, naturalness; *true,* natural integrity, spontaneous honesty, constancy, true rather than feigned beauty" (Kerrigan, 311). However, the poet says that only to vary the three words — fair, kind, and true — or to express the three concepts in diverse words ('this change'), he composes verses, *i.e.* spends his time and energy in the composition of his verses ('my invention'): "And in this change is my invention spent —". These are the three themes or topics of his verses fairness, kindness, and honesty, all of which are available in just one thing, *i.e.* the Fair Youth. And a wonderful (literary) opportunity ('scope') has given the poet these three themes: "Three themes in one, which wonderous scope affords." Yes, the poet says, these three themes or qualities have often been found separately ('alone') in different persons ('often liv'd alone'), but these three things have never occupied the same person ('never kept seat in one'): "Fair, kind, and true have often liv'd alone,/Which three till now never kept seat in one."

106

When in the chronicle of wasted time
I see descriptions of the fairest weights,
And beauty making beautiful old rhyme
In praise of ladies dead and lovely knights,
Then in the blazon of sweet beauty's best—
Of hand, of foot, of lip, of eye, of brow—
I see their antique pen would have express'd
Even such a beauty as you master now:
So all their praises are but prophecies
Of this our time, all you prefiguring;
And for they look'd but with divining eyes
They had not skill enough your worth to sing:
  For we which now behold these present days
  Have eyes to wonder, but lack tongues to praise.

In the first six lines of this sonnet, the poet says that when he reads or hears the history ('chronicle') of the ruined age ('wasted time') or of the age that is past now, he finds there descriptions of very beautiful men and women ('weights'). He also learns, there in the history of the past time, that at that time beautiful men and women inspired ('making') poets to write beautiful verses ('rhyme') praising beautiful ladies who were then dead, and praising beautiful ('lovely') knights who were then the objects of 'rich and precise description' ('blazon'), and praising the best of beautiful men and women. While describing beauty, poets would then resort to the beauty of their hands, feet, lips, eyes and brows. The poet can imagine ('see') that those ancient poets ('antique pen') would have described ('express'd) also the beauty that the Fair Youth now possesses ('master'): "I see their antique pen would have express'd/ Even such a beauty as you master now:".

Therefore ('So'), the poet says that all the praises of the ancient and dead poets were only prognostications ('prophecies') (to the effect that a greater beauty would come thereafter) of the present time ('this our time'), and that the beauty of the Fair Youth ('you') appeared beforehand ('prefiguring') in the verses of those ancient poets (who praised beauty): "So all their praises are but prophecies/Of our time, all you prefiguring;''. Those poets certainly could correctly see ('with divining eyes') what true beauty is, but they lacked in the poetic dexterity of writing verses to express or describe the beauty of the Fair Youth ('your worth'): ''And for they look'd but with divining eyes/They had not skill enough your worth to sing:''. Similarly ('For'), the poet and his coevals can witness, and wonder at, the beauty of the Fair Youth ('Have eyes to wonder'), but they also have no poetic skill ('lack tongues') to write verses praising that beauty: ''For we which now behold these present days/Have eyes to wonder, but lack tongues to praise.''

107

Not mine own fears, nor the prophetic soul
Of the wide world dreaming on things to come
Can yet the lease of my true love control,
Suppos'd as forfeit to a confin'd doom.
The mortal moon hath her eclipse endur'd,
And the sad augurs mock their own presage;
Incertainties now crown themselves assur'd,
And peace proclaims olives of endless age.
Now with the drops of this most balmy time
My love looks fresh; and Death to me subscribes,
Since spite of him I'll live in this poor rhyme
While he insults o'er dull and speechless tribes:
  And thou in this shalt find thy monument
  When tyrants' crests and tombs of brass are spent.

Kerrigan wrote about this poem: ''As in Sonnet 106, the survival of poetry through time and the character of prophecies about the present occupy the poet. Here, however, the present events are realized so vividly that they can be read as topical allusions. As a result, the poem has played a crucial role in attempts to date the Sonnets — and rightly (...).'' (Kerrigan, 313). Wilson wrote that this sonnet is ''The most difficult of the sonnets'' (Wilson, 215). However, in the first four lines of this sonnet, the poet says that he has his own personal fears, and, besides, all the poeple of the whole ('wide') world are prophetically imagining ('dreaming') the shape of the (foreboding) events in the future ('things to come'). But all these can have no effect ('control') on '' 'the period for which my deep and constant love (for my friend) is to last' '' ('the lease of my true love') — love which is thought fated ('confin'd') to be doomed or confirmed to be spoiled. Kerrigan wrote about 'prophetic soul/Of the wide world': ''Imagining the soul, as often in Shakespeare, a seat of intuition and premonition ('O my prophetic soul' cries Hamlet at I.5.40).

Here *soul* represents the collective consciousness of the world at large (the *world* of men and women, not of earth and its objects), fearful for the future'' (Kerrigan, 319).

Queen Elizabeth ('The mortal moon') has sustained the attack by the Spanish Armada (1588) ('eclipse endur'd'): ''The mortal moon hath her eclipse endur'd''. Opinions differ as to the meaning of the expression 'mortal moon'. Ingram and Redpath enlisted some of the different interpretations of the expression (Ingram, 244):

a. the Spanish Armada, 1588 (Butler, Hotson);
b. the Queen's Grand Climacteric, 1595-96 (Harrison);
c. the Queen's illness in 1599-1600 (Chambers);
d. Essex's rebellion, 1601 (Tyler);
e. the Queen's death, 1603 (*e.g.* Masey, Minto, Lee, Beeching);
f. a lunar eclipse, *e.g.* in 1595 (O.F. Emerson);
g. an eclipse of the Queen's favour (Conrad).

All these and many others may be the referent of the expression 'mortal moon', but, perhaps, the most plausible referent is Queen Elizabeth's fear of the Spanish Armada, because all the people of Britain got apprehensive of the Armada during the reign of the Queen Elizabeth, and this referent dovetails with the meaning of the expression 'wide world' (line 2). However, the apprehension fizzled out, and the worried ('sad') augurers, who prognosticated a doom on the reign of the Queen at that time, have to ridicule their own predictions ('presage') which proved to be null: ''And the sad augurs mock their own presage''.

As the Queen has come out of her troubled time, or as the foreboding days have passed, the uncertainties ('Incertainties') are now all over, and so the uncertainties are now, as if, crowned (with glories) and thus have become certainties ('assur'd'). Now the dove of peace has settled down in the state, and the dove of peace has prophesied ('proclaims') that the state will win victories (in every sphere) ('olives') ever in the future ('endless age'): ''Incertainties now crown themselves assur'd,/ And peace proclaims olives of endless age.'' We are not very clear about the 'Incertainties' and how these were resolved. Kerrigan wrote about these: ''These *Incertainties* — since we are now talking about the general forebodings of line 7 — were only resolved at the coronation of James VI of Scotland, the successor that Elizabeth named on her deathbed. He came to power with an ease which was as widely welcomed as it was found surprising — the general fear of unrest simultaneously rallying people behind this 'heir' and astonishing them that the transition should be so smooth'' (Kerrigan, 315). However, lines 5-8 of this sonnet may be compared with lines 509-510 of *Venus and Adonis*: ''That the star-gazers, having writ on death,/May say the plague is banish'd by thy breath.'' Ingram and Redpath wrote about line 8: ''The tremendous effect of this line has been long and widely recognized. As with many typically Shakespearean lines, however, the statement it makes is, in fact, a simple and not particularly remarkable one: 'We can now hope for perpetual peace' '' (Ingram, 246).

As the mist of the uncertainties and the accompanying apprehensions of the previous time are now gone, the present time seems to the poet to be very comfortable and soothing ('balmy time'), and the moments ('drops') of this comfortable time are freshening the beauty ('look') of the Fair Youth: ''Now with the drops of this most balmy time/My love looks fresh''. Ingram and Redpath wrote about the expression: 'Now with the drops of this most balmy time/My love looks fresh': ''The image is of reinvigorating plants. The happiness of the poet's love revives as plants do when moisture follows a drought. 'Balmy' in Elizabethan English contains both the element of 'sap' and that of healing or refreshment. The rise of the 'sap' would be promoted by the 'drops' (of rain or dew), and the word 'balmy' itself would readily follow from the word 'drops' by independent verbal association.'' (Ingram, 247). The moribund Fair Youth has come back to life, and so death has been subdued, and thus death has been compelled to pay obeisance to the poet ('Death to me subscribes'). Because ('Since'), though death will humble ('insults') the witless and inarticulate ('speechless') multitude ('tribes') of lesser poets by taking them away, the present poet, in spite of the death ('in spite of him') will remain immortal in his humble ('poor') (Shakespeare says this courtiously) verses: ''and Death to me subscribes,/ Since spite of him I'll live in this poor rhyme''. Perhaps, it is only in this sonnet that Shakespeare expresses his belief in his own immortality in his sonnets ('I'll live in this poor rhyme'), though in several of his sonnets, he was confident of the immortality of the Fair Youth. Of course, he also speaks of the immortality of the youth, in his verses, in this sonnet ('And thou in this shalt find thy monument'). Lastly, in the concluding couplet, the poet assures the youth that this sonnet (or, rather, the sonnet-sequence of Shakespeare) will be his (the youth's) enduring sepulchral monument, while the flaunted might ('crests') and sepulchral monuments ('tombs') of warrior-tyrants, though they may be made of hard metals like brass, will be consumed by time ('spent'): "And thou in this shalt find thy monument/When tyrants' crests and tombs of brass are spent."

108

What's in the brain that ink may character
Which hath not figur'd to thee my true spirit?
What's new to speak, what now to register,
That may express my love or thy dear merit? 4
Nothing, sweet boy; but yet like prayers divine
I must each day say o'er the very same,
Counting no old thing old, — thou mine, I thine—
Even as when first I hallow'd thy fair name. 8
So that eternal love in love's fresh case
Weighs not the dust and injury of age,
Nor gives to necessary wrinkles place;
But makes antiquity for aye his page, 12
Finding the first conceit of love there bred
Where time and outward form would show it dead.

The poet asks the fair Youth to tell him if there is anything in his (the poet's) mind ('brain') which he may write about ('character') with ink. The poet again asks him if there is anything in his mind that has not represented ('figur'd') to him (Fair Youth) his (the poet's) constant ('true') love ('spirit') of him (the youth): "What's in the brain that ink may character/Which hath not figur'd to thee my true spirit?" The poet asks the youth if there is anything of him which has not been written about, or anything that needs to be recorded ('register') in his verse, anything that may either express the poet's love for the youth or may express the rare or lovable ('dear') qualities ('merit') of his (of the youth): "What's new to speak, what now to register,/That may express my love or thy dear merit?" Answering his own questions, the poet says that there is no such thing: "Nothing, sweet boy". And, yet, as one prays to God ('prayers divine') and in the course of one's daily prayers reiterates the same thing over and over again, the poet must repeat the same thing daily ('say o'er the very same'), and what the poet will repeat is that the Fair Youth is his, and that he belongs to the Fair Youth ('thou mine, I thine'). In thus reiterating the same thing, the poet will not think that he is saying, again and again, the same old thing: "thou mine, I thine —". ('Counting no old thing old'). And there will be no change in tone or pitch or emotion in the poet when he will be repeating that thing, but when he will say the same thing in the future, his utterance will sound as fresh as when he first uttered the thing, to sanctify ('hallow'd') the

Fair Youth's. beautiful name: ''but yet like prayers divine/I must each day say o'er the very same,/Counting no old thing old, — thou mine, I thine —/Even as when first I hallow'd thy fair name.'' The poet sanctified or hallowed the name of the youth with the intention that ('So that') the perpetual or constant love (of the poet for the youth) ('eternal love'), which is an instance of pure love ('love's fresh case'), may not be adulterated or obliterated or suppressed or weighed down ('Weighs'), by the corruption, hypocrisy, etc. ('dust') and by the sufference ('injury') of the people of this age: ''So that eternal love in love's fresh case/ Weighs not the dust and injury of age,''. The poet hallowed the youth's name so that the 'dust and injury' may not make the youth worried and thus form furrows on his brow ('wrinkles'): ''Nor gives to necessary wrinkes place;'' And so that, contrarily or rather ('But'), the youth may make Time ('antiquity') his proper ('aye') servant ('page'): ''But makes antiquity for aye his page,''. The poet here means to say that he is sanctifying the name or beauty of the youth so that the youth may not be aging, or may not become old.

When the poet first loved the youth, then ('there') the first idea ('conceit') was born, and then, or at that moment, ('Where'), Time and physical beauty ('outward form') became meaningless or ineffectual ('dead'): ''Finding the first conceit of love there bred/Where time and outward form would show it dead.'' The poet here says that when he, for the first time, loved the youth, it was then that Love itself came down to earth for the first time, and at that moment it seemed to him that Time stopped its journey, and he realised that physical beauty has no business in the celestial birth of love.

109

Oh never say that I was false of heart,
Though absence seem'd my flame to qualify!
As easy might I from my self depart
As from my soul, which in thy breast doth lie; —
That is my home of love: if I have rang'd,
Like him that travels I return again,
Just to the time, not with the time exchang'd,
So that myself bring water for my stain.
Never believe, though in my nature reign'd
All frailties that besiege all kinds of blood,
That it could so preposterously be stain'd
To leave for nothing all thy sum of good —

For nothing this wide universe I call,
Save thou my rose: in it thou art my all.

In this sonnet, the poet is returning to the theme of absence about which he spoke in Sonnets 97 and 98. There he mourned the absence only, but in this sonnet he says that he has returned from his furlough, and that the absence has not in any way been able to abate his passion for the Fair Youth. He appeals to the youth not to believe that his (the poet's) absence signified the falsity of his love for him (the youth), although it might seem to him (the youth) that the absence indicated reduction ('qualify') in his passion ('flame'): "Oh never say that I was false of heart,/Though absence seem'd my flame to qualify!" The poet says that he can go away ('depart') from the soul that is acutally there within the heart ('breast') of the youth as easily as he can go away from his own self. He equates his soul with the Fair Youth, and his self with his (the youth's) personality: "As easy might I from my self depart/As from my soul, which in thy breast doth lie; —". The heart of the youth ('That') is the abode of the love of the poet: "That is my home of love". If the poet so long wandered away ('rang'd') from home, *i.e.* from the heart of the youth, like travellers, then, even like the travellers, he has now returned to the heart of the youth: "if I have rang'd,/Like him that travels I return again,". The poet has returned punctually ('Just to the time'), and he has not changed ('exchang'd') the appointed time of his return journey, *i.e.* he has not prolonged the period of his absence. He had done this so that he could bring solace ('water') for his own pain ('stain'), or so that he could shed tears ('water') with which he could wash away his offence ('stain'), of remaining absent from the youth: "Just to the time, not with the time exchang'd,/So that myself bring water for my stain."

The poet owns that all sorts of immoral tendencies are active in his nature — immoral tendencies that are present in, and control ('besiege'), all kinds of human beings ('all kinds of blood'). Nevertheless, he solicits the Fair Youth on to believe that all these immoral tendenceis or immoralities ('it') that the poet is bearing ('sustain'd') unnaturally or unwillingly ('preposterously') can make the totality of the good qualities of the youth ('all thy sum of good') worthless or valueless: "Never believe, though in my nature reign'd/All frailties that besiege all kinds of blood,/That it could so preposterously be sustain'd/To leave for nothing all thy sum of good —". Kerrigan wrote about the word 'preposterously': "Shakespeare found the word newly coined and free of its modern implication of risibility" (Kerrigan, 323). The poet would call, or think, this immense ('wide') universe a 'big nothing' ('For nothing') but for the fact ('Save') that the Fair Youth who seems to the poet to be a rose, residing in it. And in this universe ('it'), the Fair Youth is everything for the poet: "For nothing this wide universe I call,/Save thou my rose: in it thou art my all."

110

Alas, 'Tis ture, I have gone here and there
And made myself a motley to the view,
Gor'd mine own thoughts, sold cheap what is a most dear,
Made old offences of affections new:
Most true it is that I have look'd on truth
Askance and strangely: but, by all above,
These blenches gave my heart another youth,
And worse essays prov'd thee my best of love.
Now all is done, have what shall have no end:
Mine appetite I never more will grind
On newer proof to try an older friend —
A god in love, to whom I confin'd.
Then give me welcome, next my heaven the best,
Even to thy pure and most most loving breast.

It is only in this sonnet that Shakespeare calls the Fair Youth his 'friend' (line 11). In his headnote to this sonnet, Kerrigan wrote: "Though the poet confesses in earlier sonnets to verbal deficiencies, and to the fault of excusing the friend's faults, and though he hints at some estrangement in Sonnets 100-103 and 109, this is the first sonnet in which he roundly accuses himself of emotional betrayal" (Kerrigan, 323). The poet admits his inconstancy ('I have gone here and there'), and that he has, thus showing affections to other persons, become like a parti-coloured cloth ('motley') in the view of people, and that he is sorry for all this ('Alas'): "Alas, 'tis true, I have gone here and there/ And made myself a motley to the view,". He has bored or pierced or censured ('Gor'd') his own thoughts, and sold the very valuable love of the Fair Youth ('What is most dear') at a cheap price: "Gor'd mine own thoughts, sold cheap what is most dear,". The poet here means to say that there had been a time when he neglected the most valuable love of the youth and became attracted by the cheap love of some other persons. Further, by having passions elsewhere, the poet created more instances of his inconstancy in addition to his earlier instances of inconstancies ('old offences'): "Made old offences of affections new:".

The poet also admits that it is true that he looked upon truth 'with disdainful surprise and reserve' ('Askance and strangely'), *i.e.* he had not been constant to his first love (which is the truth): "Most true it is that I have look'd upon truth/Askance and strangely". He swears by heaven ('by all above') that these goings away, or these inconstancies ('blenches'), reinvigorated his heart for more passion of love ('gave my heart another youth'): "but, by all above,/These blenches gave my heart another youth". And with his experiences ('essays') of new loves which are worse (compared with his former and true love for the Fair Youth), it had been proved that the youth ('thee') is the best of his beloveds: "And worse essays prov'd thee my best of love."

Now the poet has parted company with all those new beloveds: "Now all is done". Therefore he offers the youth all over again his love ('what') that shall never cease to be: "have what shall have no end:". He will never again whet ('grind') his passion of love ('appetite'), *i.e.* he will no more go to other persons for love, and thereby intensify his passion of love. And he will not assay the quality of his love for the Fair Youth ('older friend') with is new love's quality ('newer proof'). The poet now regards the youth as a god with whom he is in love, and as a god only to whom he is inalienably conjoined ('confin'd'): "Mine appetite I never more will grind/On newer proof to try an older friend —/ A god in love, to whom I am confin'd." Therefore, the poet prays to the youth to heartily accept him (the poet) ('give me welcome'): "Then give me welcome". The poet now regards the youth or his love as the second best thing after heaven which is the first best thing — the youth is the most desirable thing only after the heaven: "Then give me welcome, next my heaven the best". The poet requests the youth to accept him (the poet) within his (the youth's) very very passionate heart: "Even to thy pure and most most loving breast." It may be noted here that this sonnet peculiarly contains a number of comparisons and superlatives: 'most dear', 'most true', 'worse essays', 'best of love', 'newer proof', 'older friend', and 'the best'.

111

Oh, for my sake do you with Fortune chide,
The guilty goddess of my harmful deeds,
That did not better for my life provide
Than public means which public manners greeds
Thence comes it that my name receives a brand,
And almost thence my nature is subdu'd
To what it works in, like dyer's hand.

> Pity me then, and wish I were renew'd;
> Whilst like a willing patient I will drink
> Potions of eisel 'gainst my strong infection —
> No bitterness that I will bitter think,
> Nor double penance to correct correction:
>   Pity me then, dear friend, and I assure ye
>   Even that your pity is enough to cure me.

Ingram and Redpath wrote a very informative general note on this sonnet: "Malone saw here a lament by Shakespeare at being reduced to the necessity of appearing on the stage, or writing for the theatre, and many other commentators have shared his opinion. There have, however, been dissestients. Bell, in particular (ed. 1855), taxes Malone with failing to explain why Shakespeare should say that his connexion with the theatre, from which he derived all his honours, had fixed a brand on his name. Malone's view seems plausable for us, espically in view of lines 3-4 and 6-7. Bell's objection does not seem cogent, for why should not Shakespeare complain at the disadvantages of his profession and at the low value set on it by society at the time; especially since, at the time when he wrote the *Sonnets,* it may not have brought him much honour?" (Ingram, 256).

The poet implores the Fair Youth to rebuke ('chide') the goddess of fortune who is guilty of harming him (the poet), or is responsible for his (the poet's) wrongful deeds ('my harmful deeds'), for his (the poet's) own sake: "Oh, for my sake do you with Fortune chide,/The guilty goddess of my harmful deeds,". Here the poet means to say that either the goddess harmed him, or she instigated him to do wrongful deeds. The goddess of fortune ('That'), the poet complains, did not provide him with better provisions or honours; she has provided him only with the means enough for common people ('public means') — means that are only customarily necessary, or means that are required for living according to public manners ('public manners breed'): "That did not better for my life provide/Then public means which public manners breeds." Kerrigan explained the expression 'public means' thus: "a livelihood won in public (by means of acting and presenting composed plays. *Means* operates twice, as a 'way' and as an 'income'. By extension, 'a career dependent on public approval if not indeed sheer vulgar acclaim')" (Kerrigan, 325). And Kerrigan explained the expression 'which public manners breeds' thus: (1) which makes one familiar with all and sundry (and thus prone to wander here and there

(110.1) in love; (2) which encourages vulgar display and unfeelingly superficial charm'' (Kerrigan, 325).

The poet says that it was because of the guilty deeds of the goddess of fortune ('Thence') that his name was branded: ''Thence comes it that my name receives a brand,''. How the poet's name was branded we do not know. Perhaps the word 'brand' here means 'to dishonour' — and so we may understand that the poet means to say that his name was stigmatised or he was dishonoured. Kerrigan wrote about the expression 'my name receives a brand': ''Criminals were sometimes branded (Ben Jonson, for example, received a brand on his thumb in 1598 for killing the actor Gabriel Spencer in a duel). So the poet's reputation is dishonoured'. It is possible that Shakespeare means to allude to the Roman practice of marking with *notae* names of citizens guilty of immorality where they appeared on census lists.'' (Kerrigan, 325-26). However, the poet further says that it is also almost for the guilty deeds of the goddess of fortune ('thence') that his writing of plays or poetic quality ('nature') was suppressed or adversely criticised ('subdu'd') for the language or style or rhetoric of those plays — things with which the plays ('it') embellished ('To what it works in') themselves, as the dyer embellishes or beautifies clothes with colour ('like the dyer's hand'): ''And almost thence my nature is subdu'd/To what it works in, like the dyer's hand.'' Perhaps, here the poet says that it was due to the wrongful goddess that his plays were severely and adversely criticised as regards their language, style, rhetoric etc., and thus the plays were brought to the unfavourable notice of the public (and consequently, the poet has to live meanly with only 'public means').

For all this, the poet asks the Fair Youth to feel grief or sorrow for him ('Pity me then'), and he wishes that he might be reformed or corrected ('wish I were renew'd'), (and that he might get back his former *élan* for writing plays and composing verses after shaking off his sloth and dejection that accrued to him, consequent upon the goddess' misdeeds done to him and the bitterly adverse criticism of him from some quarters): ''Pity me then, and wish I were renew'd''. The poet is ready to drink a 'concoction of vinegar' ('Potions of eisel') willingly like a patient, to be cured of his serious diseases ('infection'): ''Whilst like a willing patient I will drink/Potions of eisel 'gainst my strong infection—''. Kerrigan wrote that ''concoction of vinegar' is ''Often used '*gainst'* ('as a cure for') the plague; but employed, too, for removing stubborn stains (for cleaning *the dyer's hand*)'' (Kerrigan, 326). Ingram and Redpath further said that ''The great French physician Pare included oxymel (vinegar and honey) among his prescriptions for the plague'' (Ingram, 256). To cure himself, the poet will not deem even bitter potions to be bitter or two-fold penance to be tortuous ('bitter'), if these be administered for his right ('correct') correcting measures ('correction'): ''No bitterness that I will bitter think,/Nor double penance to correct correction''. In the concluding couplet, the poet again implores the Fair Youth ('dear friend') to pity him (the poet), and at the same time gives assurance to the youth ('ye') that just the pity of the youth for the poet will be medicine enough for curing the poet of disease (of dejection, inferiority-complex, etc.): ''Pity me then, dear friend, and I assure ye/ Even that your pity is enough to cure me.''

112

Your love and pity doth the impression fill
Which vulgar scandal stamp'd upon my brow;
For what care I who calls me well or ill,
So you o'er-green my bad, my good allow?
You are my all-the-world, and I must strive
To know my shame and praises from your tongue—
None else to me nor I to none alive
That my steel'd sense or changes right or wrong.
In so profound abysm I throw all care
Of other's voices that my adder's sense
To critic and to flatterer stopped are.
Mark how with my neglect I do dispense:
  You are so strongly in my purpose bred
  That all the world besides methinks they are dead.

The thought of the previous sonnet continues here; the poet continues to muse over the acrimony of his adversaries. However, he tells the Fair Youth that his (the youth's) love and pity for him (the poet) covers up ('fill') the hollow scar ('impression') that was created by the mean branding ('vulgar scandal') of his honour ('brow'): ''Your love and pity doth the impression fill/Which vulgar scandal stamp'd upon my brow;''. Because ('For'), as he now enjoys the love and pity of the youth, the poet does not care for either the praise or the disgrace of him by the people. And so the love and pity to the youth conceal the poet's misdeeds or his blemishes ('o'er-green my bad'), and publish or exposes ('allow') his good qualities: ''For what care I who calls me well or ill,/So you o'er-green my bad, my good allow?'' The poet means to say that as the Fair Youth conceals the bad qualities or aspects of the poet, and publishes his good qualities, he (the poet) does not care for either the praise or the censure of him by the people. Kerrigan explained the expression 'o'er-green my bad' thus: "The friend covers the poet's *bad* (mostly his 'disgrace', but partly the 'evil doing' which earned it) with fresh *love and pity,* rather as green ivy grows over dead trees and ugly ruins, or, if *o'er-green* (which seems to be Shakespeare's coinage) is read in strict accordance with *fill,* by inlaying greenery to conceal an unsightly blemish (as, for instance, when a damaged lawn is patched with fresh turf). (Kerrigan, 326-27). And Kerrigan wrote about the expression 'my good allow': "The friend recognizes what is *good* in the disgraced poet. Arguably, the phrase cannot be entirely detached from *o'er-green my bad so that, once allow* registers in the sense 'concede that I have, approve', *o'er-green* starts to mean 'gloss over, regard as attractive (in your own mind, whatever the *world* says)':" (Kerrigan, 327).

The poet says that the Fair Youth is as good as, or equivalent to, all the world; or the poet says that he values only the opinion of the Fair Youth, and of none else of the rest of the world. And so the poet must try to know about his (the poet's) disgraces and graces ('shames and praises') from the youth himself ('from your tongue'): "You are my all-the-world, and I must strive/To know my shames and praises from your tongue —". In the whole world, there is nobody who exists for the poet (save the Fair Youth), and there is nobody for whom the poet exists (save the Fair Youth); and there is nobody who can veer the hardened ('steel'd') sensibility (of the poet) either towards right deeds or towards wrong deeds; "None else to me nor I to none alive/That my steel'd sense or changes right or wrong." The poet means to say that the buffets of the bitterest and indiscriminate criticisms of him by the vulgar people have hardened his mentality, so that now such criticisms in the future will not be able to alter him, or to alter his course of actions.

The poet has thrown all his cares and concerns about those censures of the vulgar persons ('others' voices') into the deepest pit ('profound abyss'). And, therefore, the poet has turned his deaf ear to the critics as well as to the flatterers. Now the poet is as deaf as a snake ('adder's sense') to the critics and the flatterers, and so his cares have ceased to be ('stopped are'): "In so profound abyss I throw all care/Of others' voices that my adder's sense/To critic and to flatterer stopped are." The poet, therefore, asks the Fair Youth to see how negligently he (the poet) brushes aside ('dispense') those criticisms and flattery, or the good and bad opinions of the vulgar persons: "Mark how with my neglect I do dispense". Line 12 has a parallel at *The Rape of Lucrece,* line 1070: "And with my trespass never will dispense". The poet concludes by telling the youth that he (the youth) is so strongly present ('bred') in the motive of the poet that to him (the poet) all the world, save the youth ('besides'), seems to be meaningless ('dead'): "You are so strongly in my purpose bred/That all the world besides methinks they are dead."

113

Since I left you, mine eye is in my mind,
And that which governs me to go about
Doth part his function and is partly blind—
Seems seeing, but effectually is out:
For it no form delivers to the heart
Of bird, of flower, or shape which it doth latch;
Of his quick objects hath the mind no part,
Nor his own vision holds what it doth catch:
For if it see the rud'st or gentlest sight,
The most sweet favour, or deformed'st creature,
The mountain, or the sea, the day, or night,
The crow, or dove, it shapes them to your feature:
  Incapable of more, replete with you,
  My most true mind thus maketh mine eye untrue.

This sonnet has reference of Sonnets 109 and 110, where the poet asked the Fair Youth not to construe his (the poet's) absence from him as lack of love for him. Here, in this sonnet, he dwells further on this theme and pleads for excusing his absence. He says that from the moment he went away from him (the youth), he (the poet) took his eyes within the inner regard of his mind ('my eye in my mind'), so that his soul or vision ('that') which sees through the eyes ('that which governs me') ceased its functions of observing; and therefore, the eyes have become blind (to external things or objects). It now seems that the soul had been seeing, but actually it had partially stopped functioning ('but effectually is out'): "Since I left you, mine eye is in my mind,/ And that which governs me to go about/Doth part his function and is partly blind—/Seems seeing, but effectually is out". Kerrigan wrote about the lines quoted above: "The poet regards the world through what Hamlet calls the 'mind's eye' (I.2.185), through visionary fancy, because he is in love. As Helena observes at *A Midsummer Night's Dream* I.1.234, 'Love looks not with the eyes, but with the mind'." (Kerrigan, 328). And regarding lines 2-4, Kerrigan wrote: "one *eye* is turned within and the other out, making the poet a combination of stylized seer and Cyclops. (The conceit merely carries to an extreme Claudius' 'one Auspicious, and one Dropping eye' at Folio *Hamlet* I.2.11.)'' (Kerrigan, 328). The ''Cyclops were storm genii, as their names indicate: Brontes, thunder: Steropes, lightning; Arges, thunderbolt.'' (*New Larouses Encyclopedia of Mythology*, 89). Kerrigan found a parallel to the word 'out' in line 4 of this sonnet at *Love's Labour's Lost*, IV, i, 134: ''Wide o' the bow hand! I' faith, your hand is out'' (Kerrigan, 328).

The poet says that now the soul or vision ('it') cannot carry any contour or form, — beautiful or no — to the heart — any contour, of bird or flower or anything — which the soul or vision catches at ('doth latch'). Here the poet, perhaps, means to say that as his eye is now turned inwards into his mind, whatever he now perceives, is not attended by his heart, *i.e.* his passion is now indifferent to whatever he sees. Whatever his soul perceives, or whatever he sees in his vision in quick succession, is not received by his mind ('the mind hath no part'). Again, whatever his eyes ('it') catch at or perceive is not sustained by his fancy ('vision'): ''For it no form delivers to the heart/Of bird, of flower, or shape which it doth latch,/Of his quick objects hath the mind no part,/Nor his own vision holds what it doth catch:''. In these lines, the poet means to say that he now does not view things as they are, but sees them with his dissuatude, or with his imaginative eye. This is clear from lines 9-12. The use of the word 'latch' may be found at *Macbeth*, IV, iii, 193-95, where Ross says: ''But I have words/That would be howl'd out in the desert air,/Where hearing should not latch them.''

That such transformation of actual sight into the sight of imagination is true is attested by what the poet says in lines 9-12. He says that when his soul or vision ('it') sees the most unwelcome ('rud'st') sight or the most affable ('gentlest') sight, or the most sweet appearance ('favour'), or the most deformed creature, or any mountain, or the sea, or the day, or the night, or any crow, or any dove, — anything whatsoever — his soul or vision transforms all these things into the (beautiful) shape of the Fair Youth ('your feature'): ''For if it see the rud'st or gentlest sight,/The most sweet favour, or deformed'st creature,/The mountain, or the sea, the day, or night,/The crow, or dove, it shapes them to your feature:''. The poet cannot think of anything beyond the Fair Youth ('Incapable of more'), because he is satiated ('replete') with the youth. Therefore, his (the poet's) honest mind falsifies what his eyes offer him as true, *i.e.* his mind does not believe (that anyone else than the Fair Youth also can be fair, honest, etc.) what he sees with his own eyes (that there are other persons who are as beautiful as the Fair Youth):

"Incapable of more, replete with you,/My most true mind thus maketh mine eye untrue."

114

Or whether doth my mind, being crown'd with you,
Drinks up the monarch's plague, this flattery,
Or whether shall I say mine eye saith true,
And that your love taught it this alchemy,
To make of monsters and things indigest
Such cherubins as your sweet self resemble,
Creating every bad a perfect best
As fast as objects to his beams assemble?
Oh, 'tis the first ! 'tis flattery in my seeing,
And my great mind most kingly drinks it up:
Mine eye well knows what with his gust is 'greeing,
And to his palate doth prepare the cup.
  If it be poison'd, 'tis the lesser sin
  That mine eye loves it and doth first begin.

The argument of Sonnet 113 continues here. In the preceding sonnet, Shakespeare told the Fair Youth that his (the poet's) eyes do not report to his (the poet's) mind correctly about objects. And in this sonnet, he asks the youth why his (the poet's) eyes give him (the poet) false perception of objects. He tells the youth that the cause may be his (the poet's) being crowned with the love of the youth ('being crown'd with you'), and consequently, his being charmed ('Drink up') by the idea that he (the poet) is being flattered by the love of the youth, like a king is flattered by a buffoon ('monarch's plague'): "Or whether doth my mind, being crown'd with you,/Drink up the monarch's plague, this flattery,". The poet further tells the youth that, alternatively, the cause may be this that his (the poet's) eyes reported to his mind correctly about objects ('mine eye saith true'), but his love for the youth transformed ('alchemy') the correct perceptions into incorrect perceptions: "Or whether shall I say mine eye saith true,/And that your love taught it this alchemy." The poet compares the Fair Youth with beautiful cherubins — cherubins which can digest ('indigest') ugly monsters and things, or rather, cherubins which can transforms ugly and shapeless things into beautiful things. The poet says that his mind transforms what it receives through his eyes because he wants the youth to be metamorphosed into cherubins: "To make of monsters and things indigest/Such cherubins as your sweet self resemble,". Thus, the mind of the poet transmogrifies all bad (ugly, unsavoury, dishonest etc.) things into most welcome things, as soon as ('as fast') those bad things are reflected ('assemble') in the sparkling eyes of his mind ('his beams'): “Creating every bad a perfect best/As fast as objects to his beams assemble?” The poet means to say that the eyes of the youth have Midas-like quality, such that whenever any unsavoury thing is reflected in those eyes, that thing is instantaneously beautified.

No, the poet says, what he sees at first (before the intervention of his mind which falsifies his perception, because of its being bemused by the Fair Youth) is correct (' 'tis the first'). And so, what he sees with his eyes in collusion with his mind, is false ('flattery'): “Oh, 'tis the first! — 'tis flattery in my seeing,”. Line 9 has a parallel at *Twelfth Night*, I, vi, 292-93), where Olivia, after falling in love with Cesario, says: “I do I know not what, and fear to find/Mine eye too great a flatterer for my mind.” And, the poet says, whatever sight his eyes fetches for his mind is consumed like wine by his majestic and all-powerful mind (so that even if any sight be unwelcome, it is consumed by the mind and thus converted, as if alchemically, into welcome or becoming sight): “And my great mind most kingly drinks it up:”. However, it is also true that the eyes of the poet knows well what is delicious or tasteful ('gust is 'greeing') to his mind ('his'): “Mine eye well knows what with his gust is 'greeing,”. And, accordingly, the eyes of the poet catches only those sights ('prepare the cup') which are delicious or attractive to the 'palate' of his mind: “And to his palate doth prepare the cup.” The poet concludes by saying that such distortions ('poison'd') of actual perceptions of the eyes by the mind may seem to be a grave wrong ('sin'), but it is actually a lesser wrong. And the mind of the poet loves to distort things like this ('it'), and it is the poet's own eyes that first start distorting the perceptions: “If it be poison'd. 'tis the lesser sin/ That mine eye loves it and doth first begin.”

115

Those lines that I before have writ do lie,
Even those that said I could not love you dearer:
Yet then my judgment knew no reason why
My most full flame should afterwards burn clearer.
But reckoning Time, whose milion'd accidents
Creep in 'twixt vows, and change decrees of kings,
Tan sacred beauty, blunt the sharp'st intents,
Divert strong minds to the course of altering things,—
Alas! why, fearing of Time's tyranny,

Might I not then say, 'Now I love you best',
When I was certain o'er incertainty,
Crowning the present, doubting of the rest?
  Love is a babe: then might I not say so,
  To give full growth to that which still doth grow.

Commetators frequently compare this sonnet with John Donne's poem 'Love's Growth', because the style of argumentation in both the poems is almost the same, though the arguments are different. The poem 'Love's Growth' begins thus:

I scarce beleeve my love to be so pure
  As I had thought it was,
  Because it doth endure
Vicissitudes, and season, as the grasse;
Me thinks I lyed all winter, when I swore,
My love was infinite, if spring make it more.

The theme of Time appears again in this sonnet. In this poem, the poet tells the Fair Youth that what he (the poet) wrote ('writ') in his verses was not true ('do lie'). Even those lines of his poems in which he said that he could not love the youth more ('dearer') than what he is doing now (because the poet loved him the most) were false: "Those lines that I before have writ do lie,/Even those that said I could not love you dearer". He then did not understand ('my judgment') why his full passion ('flame') should be the most intense ('burn clearer') only at a later date ('afterwards'): "Yet then my judgment knew no reason why/ My most full flame should afterwards burn clearer." The poet vowed to love the youth the most; but Time stood in his way of loving him. Time produces millions of accidents or unpredictable incidents which gradually intrude ('creep in') between ("twixt') two vows; forces even kings to change or revise their royal orders ('decrees'); blackens by burning the fair-complexioned beautiful women; throws cold blankets on one's strongest motives ('blunt the sharp'st intents'); and forces even the strong-willed persons to alter their course of actions, according as situations change ('to the course of altering things'): "whose million'd accidents/Creep in 'twixt vows, and change decrees of kings,/Tan sacred beauty, blunt the sharp'st intents,/Divert strong minds to the course of altering things,—". The poet remembers that Time can do all these things: "But reckoning Time". He feels frustrated and dejected ('Alas!') and is afraid of the tyrannical attitude of Time: "Alas! why, fearing of Time's tyranny,".

Recounting all these fierce whimsicalities of Time and its tyrannical dispensations, the poet tells the youth that he (the poet) may, perhaps, say that at present he loves the youth the most: "Might I not then say, 'Now I love you best' ". He says that it is now that he is sure ('certain') about his love for the youth, in spite of all uncertainties ('incertainties') due to the whimsicalities of Time. He, therefore, deems the present moment to be the best moment ('Crowning the present') for loving the youth; and he has all doubts about all other moments ('doubting of the rest'): "When I was certain o'er incertainty,/Crowning the present, doubting of the rest?" The love of the poet for the youth is green, fresh, young, and so is like a baby ('Love is a babe') like Cupid the god of love who is depicted as a young boy. And this baby is growing up, *i.e.* the love of the poet for the Fair Youth is increasing ('doth grow'). Therefore, the poet can certainly say that at the present time he loves the youth the most ('then might I not say so'). And the poet is saying this so that this love may grow up, — love which is actually growing: "Love is a babe: then might I not say so,/To give full growth to that which still doth grow."

116

Let me not to the marriage of true minds
Admit impediments: love is not love
Which alters when it alternation finds,
Or bends with the remover to remove.
Oh no! it is an ever-fixed mark
That looks on tempests and is never shaken;
It is the star to every wandering bark,
Whose worth's unknown, although his height be taken.
Love's not Time's fool, though rosy lips and cheeks
Within his bending sickle's compass come;
Love alters not with his brief hours and weeks,
But bears it out even to the edge of doom.
If this be error and upon me prov'd,
I never writ, nor no man ever lov'd.

Ingram and Redpath's general note to this sonnet is important: "In general terms it could, perhaps, be said that the poem is probably neither a plea to the Friend [the Fair Youth] to be faithful, nor an apologia for the poet's own conduct, nor a defence against suspicions of his infidelity, but a meditative attempt to define perfect love" (Ingram, 268). The poet prays that there may be no proclamation of banns ('Admit impediments') to the union ('marriage') of the minds of two lovers (the poet and the youth): ''Let me not to the marriage of true minds/Admit impediments''. Ingram and Redpath wrote about the word 'impediments': ''Alluding to the wording of the banns of marriage (and cf. the marriage service in the book of Common Prayer): 'If any of you know cause, or just impediment, why these two persons should not be joined together in holy matrimony, ye are to declare it' '' (Ingram, 268). The poet says that that love is not perfect or true love which changes when there is scope of infidelity, *i.e.* when any one of the two in love-lock finds alternative love-objects: ''love is not lvoe/Which alters when it alternation finds''. Again that love is not true love in which when one partner strays away ('remover'), the other partner also tends ('bends') to stray away ('remove'): ''Or bends with the remover to remove.'' A parallel to the expression 'love is not love/Which alters when it alteration finds' may be found at *King Lear*, I,i, 238-40 where King of France tells Lord of Burgandy: ''Love's not love/When it is mingled with regards that stands/Aloof from th' entire point.''

The poet says that true love never changes ('Oh no!'). He says that love is like a strongly constituted light-house ('ever-fixed mark') that is not shaken by tempests, or is even not afraid when it looks at tempests: ''Oh no! it is an everfixed mark/That looks on tempests and is not shaken''. Kerrigan wrote about the expresison 'ever-fixed mark': ''Presumably the kind of light-house or beacon referred to at *Coriolanus* V, 3. 74-5: 'a great sea-mark, standing every flaw/And saving those that eye thee!'' (Kerrigan, 333). Lover ('It') is like a pole star that guides boats that course through high seas: ''It is the star to every wandering bark,''. Kerrigan wrote about the term 'star': ''It is natural to think of the pole star, and (because of *everfixed* in line 5) of Caesar's boast at *Julius Caesar* III.1.60-62: 'But I am constant as the northern star,/Of whose true-fixed and resting quality/There is no fellow in the firmament' '' (Kerrigan, 333). The value of the pole star with which love is compared here cannot be known, but its height can be known ('taken'), and in the same way, the value of love cannot be estimated though its depth can be measured; ''Whose worth's unknown although his height be taken.''

The poet says that love is not a buffoon or a laughing stock of Time, *i.e.* love does not change faces with changes in Time. Though one may be approached by ladies with their damask lips and cheeks, and though one may possess those ladies, as a harvester harvests corns with his sickle easily (''Within his bending sickle's compass come'), yet one in love will not try to possess those ladies, and change one's (former) love-objects, and thus behave like a buffoon: ''Love's not

Time's fool, though rosy lips and cheeks/Within his bending sickle's compass come;''. The concept of 'bending sickle' may be found also at *King Lear*, II, i, 44-45, where Edmund says: ''I told him the revenging gods/'Gainst parricides did all the thunder bend''; and at *I Henry IV*, V,v, 35-36: ''You, son John, and my cousin Westmorland,/Towards York shall bend you with your dearest speed''. Kerrigan wrote about 'sickle' and 'love': ''The *sickle* seems to encompass the sonnet's *rosy lips and cheeks,* with cruel conviction, as we read. *Love's* antagonism to *Time* is marked here, too; for *love* never *bends* (line 4), though Time's *sickle* does'' (Kerrigan, 334). Further, the expression 'Time's fool' occurs also in Sonnet 124 (at line 13): ''To this I witness call the fools of time''; and also at *I Henry*, IV, iv, 80, where Hotspur says: ''But thoughts, the slaves of life, and life, time's fool''.

The poet says that true love does not change during the brief period of time in which it continues to be ('brief hours and weeks'). Love is short, because life itself is short. However, true love, on the contrary, continues to be even to the biblical Day of Judgment: ''Love alters not with his brief hours and weeks,/But bears it out even to the edge of doom.'' The poet concludes by saying that if what he has written be false ('If this be error'), and if this be (legally) proved against him ('upon me prov'd'), then he will think that he has written nothing ('never writ'), and that no one has so far loved truly ('ever lov'd'): ''If this be error and upon me prov'd,/I never writ, nor no man ever lov'd.'' Here, by using negation, the poet is establishing affirmation: he means to say that he has loved the Fair Youth perfectly, honestly, and absolutely.

117

Accuse me thus: that I have scanted all
Wherein I should your great deserts repay;
Forgot upon your dearest love to call,
Whereto all bonds to tie me day by day;
That I have frequent been with unknown minds
And given to time your own dear-purchas'd right;
That I have hoisted sail to all the winds
Which should transport me farthest from your sight:
Book both my wilfulness and errors down,
And on just proof surmise accumulate;
Bring me within the level of your frown,
But shoot not at me in your waken'd hate:
  Since my appeal says I did strive to prove
  The constancy and virtue of your love.

Kerrigan wrote about this sonnet: "Although Sonnet 117 is quite different in tone from 116, it discusses some of the same subjects (constancy, removing, proof, measure, worth), it shares at least two metaphors (of navigation and the legal proof of love), and it echoes some of its predecessor's diction (*minds* and *unknown* at 116.1 and 8 become the *unknown minds* of 117.5, and *error* at 116.13 becomes *errors* at 117.9, while the rhyme words of both final couplets are close)" (Kerrigan, 335). However, the poet advises the Fair Youth, like a lawyer, to indict ('accuse') him (the poet) for being utterly negligent ('scanted') in giving the Fair Youth back everything according to the absolute ('great') rights ('desert') of the youth: "Accuse me thus: that I have scanted all/Wherein I should your great deserts repay". The poet admits that he had forgotten to visit the love (personified) of the youth ('upon your dearest love to call') — the love with which ('Whereto') the poet was being bound with more and more ties ('all bonds'), day after day: "Forgot upon your dearest love to call,/Whereto all bonds to tie me day by day".

The poet also owns that he had frequently been with some unfamiliar persons ('unknown minds'), and thus wasted time ('given to time') — time that was bought legally or rightfully by your love ('your dear-purchas'd right'): "That I have frequent been with unknown minds/ And given to time your own dear-purchas'd right." Ingram and Redpath explained line 6 thus: " 'And given to the passing hour that attention which is yours by right because you have paid for it the high price of giving me your love" (Ingram, 270). The poet also admits that he had strayed away from the Fair Youth by freely moving towards every other person, like a ship moves in all directions by raising the sails to winds of all directions. And thus he (the poet) was carried away to the farthest point from the youth ('from your sight'): "That I have hoisted sail to all the winds/Which should transport me farthest from your sight." Ingram and Redpath explained lines 7 and 8 thus: " 'I have yielded to every distraction which was most likely to isolate me from you (both spatially and spiritually)' " (Ingram, 270).

The poet counts or records ('Book') both his cases of wantonness and his faults or perversities ('errors'), and form opinion about himself ('surmise accumulate') only on dependable and correct evidences ('just proof'): "Book both my wilfulness and errors down,/And on just proof surmise accumulate". The peot asks the youth to be angry with, or threaten, him (the poet), *i.e.* to bring him within the compass of his (the youth's) anger or threat: "Bring me within the level of your frown."

Kerrigan wrote about the word 'level' "range and aim (as when Leontes complains that Polixenes is "quite beyond mine arm, out of the blank/ And level of my brain, plot-proof', *The Winter's Tale* II.3.)" (Kerrigan, 336). Nevertheless, the poet forbids the Fair Youth to kill ('shoot') him (the poet) in his (the youth's) intensified ('waken'd') hatred: "But shoot not at me in your waken'd hate." and as a plea or appeal for his forbiddance, the poet says that he strove to establish the fact that he was constant and strong or honest ('virtue': the Latin 'vitrus' means 'strong') in his love for the youth, or the youth was constant and strong or honest in his love for the poet: "Since my appeal says I did strive to prove/The constancy and virtue of your love."

118

Like as, to make our appetites more keen,
With eager compounds we our palate urge;
As to prevent our maladies unseen
We sicken to shun sickness when we purge:
Even so, being full of your ne'er cloying sweetness,
To bitter sauces did I frame my feeding;
And, sick of welfare, found a kind of meetness
To be diseas'd ere that there was true needing.
Thus policy in love, to anticipate
The ills that were not, grew to faults assur'd,
And brought to medicine a healthful state
Which, rank of goodness, would by ill be cur'd:
But thence I learn, and find the lesson true,
Drugs poison him that so fell sick of you.

Ingram and Redpath, in their general note on this sonnet, wrote: "As Mrs. Winifred Nowothny rightly observes (*The Language Poets Use,* Athlone Press, London, 1962), this is a much more 'contrived' sonnet than 119." (Ingram, 272). However, the poet says that to make his and the Fair Youth's passion of love ('our appetities') intensified ('more keen'), they are stimulating their emotion ('palate') with 'pungent concoctions': "Like as, to make our appetites more keen,/With eager compounds we our palate urge". Kerrigan thought that the word 'appetite' has 'sexual implications' as at 56.2 (Kerrigan, 336). The word 'eager' has a parallel use at *Hamlet,* I, iv, 2: "It is a nipping and eager air." And also at *Hamlet,* I, v, 68-69: "And with a sudden vigour it doth posset/And curd, like eager droppings into milk". To forestall any unobservable impediments ('prevent our maladies unseen') in their mutual love, they are adopting protective measures which entail weakening of their passion — measures which diffuse their emotion ('sicken to shun sickness when we purge'): "As to prevent our maladies unseen/We sicken to shun sickness when we purge". The poet here is adopting a simile from medical science. Kerrigan wrote about line 4: "Laxatives of sickening strength were frequently prescribed by doctors to guard against disease" (Kerrigan, 336).

Again, for the same reason ('Even so'), in spite of being full of the sweet love of the Fair Youth — love that, the poet says, never cloys any one — the poet added to his consumption of love ('frame my feeding') some bitter-sweet experiences ('bitter sauces'): "Even so, being full of your ne'er cloying sweetness,/To bitter sauces did I frame my feeding". The poet, perhaps, means to say that to perpetrate their love, he had been seeking love with flirting women ('sauces'). His love for the youth was like meat, sweet and tasteful. But to enhance the welcome taste of the meat, he added to it the sour sauce. The poet is here justifying his wantonness of love, and his straying away from the love of the youth. Further, the poet says that he was, as if, tired or bored ('sick') of the love of the Fair Youth ('welfare'), and, therefore, thought it good or fit ('meetness') to be sick ('diseas'd') before there was actual need to be sick or diseased ('needing'): "And, sick of welfare, found a kind of meetness/To be diseas'd ere that there was true needing." The poet here means to say that he was surfeited with the love of the youth, such that he might be averse to his (the youth's) love; and to come out of this possible condition, he went away from him (temporarily) and made love elsewhere. But he admits that this his policy in his love-affairs — *i.e.* expecting ('anticipate') bad imaginary ('were not') consequences (that he would become sick or averse to that love) — ultimately proved certainly ('assur'd') defective or faulty: "Thus policy in love, to anticipate/The ills that were not, grew to faults assur'd". And this defective policy led his healthy state to an unhealthy state that needed the administration of medicine: "And brought to medicine a healthful state". The poet thought that that condition of his, which was sickened by, or fell ill due to, the extreme ('rank') love or excellence or virtue ('goodness') of the Fair Youth, would be cured by ill or unwelcome behaviour (*i.e.* by his unfaithful love-affairs elsewhere): "Which rank of goodness, would by ill be cur'd". The word 'rank' may be found also at *2 King Henry IV*, IV, i, 63-64, where Archbishop says: "But rather show awhile like fearful war/To diet rank minds sick of happiness."

In the concluding couplet, the poet says that from that ill experiences (*i.e.* his wanton loves) he has learnt the truth and found a true lesson that whoever will fall sick of the love of the Fair Youth, will be killed or poisoned by the same medicine which he may take to cure himself of that sickness (of being surfeited or cloyed by the love of the youth): "But thence I learn, and find the lesson true,/Drugs poison him that so fell sick of you." Kerrigan wrote about the expression 'Drugs poison', in his commentary on *A Lover's Complaint*: "Shakespeare's interest in the ambivalence of drugs, and in the Platonic idea of the *Pharmakon* (that which is interchangeably 'poison' and 'medicine'), can be followed from the philtres of *Romeo and Juliet* to those of *Cymbeline*." (Kerrigan, 422).

119

What potions have I drunk of Siren tears
Distill'd from limbecks foul as hell within,
Applying fears to hopes and hopes to fears,
Still losing when I saw myself to win!
What wretched errors hath my heart committed
Whilst it hath thought itself so blessed never!
How have mine eyes out of their spheres been fitted
In the distraction of this madding fever!
Oh, benefit of ill! now I find true
That better is by evil still made better,
And ruin'd love when it is built anew
Grows fairer than at first, more strong, far greater:
    So I return rebuk'd to my content,
    And gain by ills thrice more than I have spent.

In this sonnet, the poet expresses his sorrow and repentence for his staying away from the Fair Youth, and for his wanton love-affairs elsewhere. He has now come back into the fold of the youth, and feels overjoyed at his renewed love. He says that he has taken the tears of the mythical bird Siren as medicine ('potions'). The medicine (of which we have heard in Sonent 118, and which is the poet's wanton love) seems to be pure, unadulterated, like liquid distilled in an alembic ('limbeck'), but within it seeming purity, there is rank impurity ('foul as hell within'): "What potions have I drunk of Siren tears/Distill'd from limbecks foul as hell within". The Siren is a mythical bird to which divinity is attributed. "The name Siren derives from a Greek root meaning 'to bind or attach' and clearly alludes to the role of Sirens played in mythology. One is inclined, however, to consider them as divinities who symbolised the souls of the dead. They would thus be funerary genii, avid for blood and hostile to the living. With their bird's body and woman's head, they recall the human-headed Egyptian hawk who also incarnated the souls of the dead. The Sirens were invoked at the moment of death, and their images are frequently found on tombs. Legend, however, has retained nothing of this conception of them, and depicts the Sirens only as malevolent monsters of the sea.'' (*Larousse Encyclopedia of Mythology*, 147-48).

However, when the poet was straying away from the Fair Youth, he added fears to his hopes, and hopes to his fears (to possess new objects of love), and yet ('Still') he failed ('losing') when he thought he would be winner: ''Applying fears to hopes and hopes to fears,/Still losing when I saw myself to win!'' During that period of time, he committed grave blunders ('wretched errors') by thinking himself as fortunate ('blessed') as he had never been: ''What wretched errors hath my heart committed/Whilst it hath thought itself so blessed never!'' During that time he suffered from 'fitful fever' while his two eye-balls were rolling in fits or convulsions ('fitted') in their sockets ('spheres'), due to the confusion or commotion of the fever: ''How have mine eyes out of their spheres been fitted/In the distraction of this madding fever!'' Line 7 may be compared with what Ghost says at *Hamlet,* I, v, 17: ''Make thy two eyes, like stars, start from their spheres''. And the expression 'madding fever' has a parallel at *Macbeth,* III, ii, 22-23, where Macbeth tells Lady Macbeth: ''Duncan is in his grave;/After life's fitful fever he sleeps well.''

The poet wonders at the benefit that can be derived from ill. He says that he has now understood that it is true that even that which is better can be improved by the aid of ill: ''Oh, benefit of ill! now I find true/That better is by evil still made better''. The poet, perhaps, means to say that his wanton love-affairs, when he was away from the youth, have proved helpful to his love of the youth, and have improved it (for now he has come to realise the proper value of the love of the youth, which formerly he could not do). The poet says that broken ('ruin'd) love, when it is renewed, becomes more enjoyable ('fairer') than before, and when renewed, it becomes stronger in bond, and deeper in feeling or passion, (as has been the case of his love for the Fair Youth): ''And ruin'd love when it is built anew/Grows fairer than at first, more strong, far greater''. It is for this reason that the poet is returning to the passionate fold of the youth, and being rebuked or scolded by the youth, he feels rather contented. And he now understands that he has gained love from the youth three times what he earlier received from him, and that this is due to the wrong ('ill') done by him in the shape of making wanton loves, or spending love ('spent') elsewhere: "So I return rebuk'd to my content,/And gain by ills thrice more than I have spent."

120

That you were once unkind befriends me now,
And for that sorrow which I then did feel
Needs must I under my transgression bow,
Unless my nerves were brass or hammer'd steel:
For if you were by my unkindness shaken
As I by yours, you have pass'd a hell of time;
And I, a tyrant, have no leisure taken
To weigh how once I suffer'd in your crime.
Oh, that our night of woe might have remember'd
My deepest sense how hard true sorrow hits,
And soon to you as you to me then tender'd
The humble salve which wounded bosoms fits!
But that your trespass now becomes a fee:
Mine ransoms yours, and yours must ransom me.

That the Fair Youth once betrayed the poet is clear from this sonnet, though the poet, in some earlier sonnets, innuendoed to this. In sonnets 113-119, we knew that the poet himself was unfaithful to the youth; and here in this sonnet, for the first time, he (the poet) says that he himself was betrayed by the youth. Ingram and Redpath very correctly paraphrased the whole of this sonnet thus: "The sonnet could perhaps be paraphrased roughly as follows: 'The fact that you [the youth] were once unkind to me [the poet] serves me a friendly turn; for were I not now able to recall the anguish I then felt, I should be quite beaten down under the sense of the wrong I have done you, unless my fibre were as tough as brass or hammered steel. For if you have been shaken by my unkindness as I was then by yours, you have gone through a hellish time; and I, tyrant-like, have given no leisure to considering how I once suffered from your offence to me (and so how you must now have suffered from mine).

" 'Would that that time of anguish we then suffered might have put me in mind in my deepest feelings how sharply real sorrow hurts, and so might indirectly (through impelling me to act) have offered to you now, with the same promptness as you then did to me, the salve of apology and humility which is apt for wounded hearts! But the wrong you did me then now becomes the ransom-money for my offence; for my injury to you expiates yours to me, and you must in turn allow yours to expiate mine' " (Ingram, 276).

The poet tells the Fair Youth that the fact that the youth once betrayed ('unkind') him is now acting as a friend to him (the poet), or is proving beneficial ('befriends') to him (the poet): "That you were once unkind befriends me now". And the poet must forget or subdue ('bow') the sorrow he suffered then (for that betrayal) recalling his (the poet's) own betrayal of the youth at another previous time ('transgression'), if the nerves of the poet is not as insensitive as brass or beaten ('hammer'd') steel: "And for that sorrow which I then did feel/ Needs must I under my transgression bow,/Unless my nerves were brass or hammer'd steel". The poet is ready to forget the unkindness or betrayal of the youth because ('For') the youth was as much perturbed ('shaken') by the betrayal ('unkindness') of the poet as the poet himself has been, and because the youth passed a hellish time during the betrayal of the poet: "For if you were by my unkindness shaken/As I by yours, you have pass'd a hell of time". A parallel to line 6 may be found at *Othello,* III, iii, 173-174, where Iago says: "But, O, what damned minutes tells he o'er/Who dotes, yet doubts, suspects, yet strongly loves!" However, for this reason, the poet calls himself a persecutor or tyrant ('I, a tyrant'), and says that he actually had no time or opportunity ('leisure') to estimate ('weigh') the quantity of his sufferance due to the betrayal of the youth ('your crime'): "And I, a tyrant have no leisure taken/To weigh how once I suffer'd in your crime." It may be noted here that the poet is condoning the crime of the youth for two reasons: (1) the poet is guilty of the same offence, and (2) he could not estimate the quantity of his sufferance due to the youth's betrayal, and so, naturally, the poet could not feel quite well the impact of the crime of the youth against him.

The poet wishes that their (his and the youth's) gloomy time of sufferance from betrayal ('our night of woe') remembered the pain owing to deepest sense of unbearable ('hard') true sorrow: "Oh, that our night of woe might have remember'd/My deepest sense how hard true sorrow hits". Line 9 may be compared with line 481 of *Venus and Adonis:* "The night of sorrow now is turn'd to day." The poet further wishes that soon they both will offer ('tender'd') appropriate ('fits') and humble medicine ('salve') or 'salving humility', one to the other, for the hurt or wounded hearts ('bosoms') of both of them. That is, he wishes that each of them will beg humble apology to the other for his own betrayal to the other, soon. But in the concluding couplet, the poet says that all that will not be required to be done. Because, the poet now thinks that the betrayal ('trespass') by the youth is ('becomes') a payment or recompense ('fee') of the betrayal by the poet: "But that your trespass now becomes a fee". That is, the betrayal by the poet 'provides recompense for' ('ransoms') the betrayal by the youth ('yours'), and, therefore, the betrayal by the youth ('yours') must provide recompense for that by the poet: "Mine ransoms yours, and yours must ransom me." The last line of this sonnet may be compared with the final line of Sonnet 34: "And they are rich, and ransom all ill deeds." Not only this, lines 10-14 of this sonnet, curiously, contains many of the words and images of Sonnet 34 (lines 7-14), such as 'salve', 'wound', 'sorrow', 'trespass', etc.

121

'Tis better to be vile than vile esteem'd,
When not to be receives reproach of being,
And the just pleasure lost which is so deem'd
Not by our feeling but by other's seeing.
For why should others' false adulterate eyes
Give salutation to my sportive blood?
Or on my frailties why are frailer spies,
Which in their wills count bad what I think good?
No: I am that I am, and they that level
At my abuses reckon up their own;
I may be straight though they themselves be bevel;
By their rank thoughts my deeds must not be shown,—
Unless this general evil they maintain:
All men are bad and in their badness reign.

The poet says that it is better to be actually contemptible than not being acutally contemptible but at the same time thought ('esteem'd') by people to be contemptible: " 'Tis better to be vile than vile esteem'd". He says, in other words, that it is better to be contemptible when one, not being contemptible ('not to be') has to bear with ('receives') the upbraiding or blame ('reproach') for being so: "When not to be receives reproach of being". He says that it is better to be vile when the legitimate ('just') pleasure of his love for the Fair Youth is lost — the pleasure that people deem to be vile ('which is so deem'd'), but which the poet and the youth do not think to be vile ('Not by our feeling'), but only other people see ('others' seeing') this pleasure to be vile: "and the just pleasure lost which is so deem'd/Not by our feeling but by other's seeing." Ingram and Redpath found two possible interpretations of lines 3-4: "(1) 'And the legitimate pleasure (in some comparatively innocent affair) is destroyed by the reproach that it is vile, though this is only the opinion of those looking on, and not what our own experience tells us'; (2) 'And one hasn't had the fun, which other people would consider legitimate in such cases, though we should not do so ourselves'. 'So' in (1) would refer to 'vile', and in (2) to 'just pleasure'. It is hard to decide between the two interpretations'' (Ingram, 278).

The poet says that all this is so because the other people are winking or are exchanging 'knowing' looks among themselves, or are implicating them (the poet and the youth), tongue in cheek, for their illegitimate relationship. He says that other people's opinions are corrupted, and so are false ('other's false adulterate eyes') — people who thus implicate ('Give salutation') corruption to the poet's playful relationship ('sportive blood') with the Fair Youth: ''For why should others' false adulterate eyes/Give salutation to my sportive blood?'' Ingram and Redpath explained lines 5-6 thus: '''Why, just because I have a certain sexual vitality, should other people's shifty corrupted eyes greet it with knowing glances (or, 'hail it as vicious like themselves')?'' (Ingram, 278). The word 'blood' in line 6 may have a sexual connotation, and so line 6 may be compared with line 162 of *A Lover's Complaint:* '' 'Nor gives it satisfaction to our blood'.'' The poet asks why those other persons who are loose-charactered, or are more full of vices ('frailer') than he himself and who are spying on his (the poet's) vices ('frailties'), are willingly counting or thinking as his immodest ('bad') behaviour which he himself thinks to be modest ('good')?: ''Or on my frailties why are frailer spies,/Which in their wills count bad what I think good?''

The poet does not admit other people's accusations, and asserts that he is certainly less corrupted and less perverse than those other people: ''No: I am that I am''. Kerrigan wrote about the expression 'I am that I am': ''God's words to Moses at Exodus 3.14, used ruefully, as though 'I'm not God, but I'm less flawed than some think'. Asserting his integrity, the poet puts himself as far from Iago (that arch-misconstruer of others's affairs) as possible: 'I am not what I am' (*Othello* I.1.66). Compare *you alone are you* at 84.2'' (Kerrigan, 342). The poet further says that those people who take aim at, or aim their gun of accusation or censuring ('they that level') at, his frailties ('abuses') are actually counting ('reckon up') their own frailties: ''and they that level/At my abuses reckon up their own''. Kerrigan found a parallel use of the word 'level' at *The Merchant of Venice,* I, ii, 35-36, where Portia tells her maid: ''according to my description level at my affection'' (while describing the characters of her wooers); and at *Romeo and Juliet,* III, iii, 103: ''deadly level of a gun'' (Kerrigan, 342). The poet claims that he can be above frailties, and can be honest and virtuous (if he wishes) even if those people ('they themselves') may be crooked ('bevel'): "I may be straight though they themselves be bevel". He demands that his behaviour or actions ('deeds') in no case be judged ('shown') by the contemptible ('rank') thinking of those people: "By their rank thoughts my deeds must not be shown,—". The poet says all this only conditionally. He says that those people can judge his actions only if they hold up or accept ('maintain') this general evil as the fact that all men are frail ('bad'), and live ('reign') in or with their frailties: "Unless this general evil they maintain:/All men are bad and in their badness reign."

122

Thy gift, thy tables, are within my brain
Full character'd with lasting memory,
Which shall above that idle rank remain
Beyond all date even to eternity, —
Or at least so long as brain and heart
Have faculty by nature to subsist;
Till each to raz'd oblivion yield his part
Of thee, thy record never can be miss'd.
That poor retention could not so much hold,
Nor need I tallies thy dear love to score;
Therefore to give them from me was I bold,
To trust those tables that receive thee more.
To keep an adjunct to remember these
Were to import forgetfulness in me.

According to Ivor Brown, "It is a poor limping Sonnet and might very well have been written by someone seeking to sustain the idiom of the Sonnet correspondence but lacking the full power to do so" (Brown, 189). Kerrigan wrote as an introduction to this poem: "the poet apologizes for giving away — or excuses himself for losing (thus *missed,* line 8) — a notebook apparently inscribed with the friend's [the Fair Youth's] writings. In Sonnet 77 the poet urges the young man to record his thoughts in a blank notebook sent, it seems, with the poem; some critics believe that this notebook, filled in and returned to the poet, is the one discussed in 122. Both sonnets have been urged to show that Shakespeare's sequence grew directly out of lived experience: for why else would such trivial objects as notebooks turn up there?" (Kerrigan, 343). However, the poet tells the Fair Youth that the gifts or presentation, *i.e.* the notebooks ('tables') that the youth sent to him (the poet), are remaining within the memory (of the poet) as fully recorded ('Full character'd'), and so will last long in his (the poet's) memory: "Thy gift, thy tables, are within my brain/Full character'd with lasting memory,". Line 1 may be compared with lines 97-98 at *Hamlet,* I, v, where Hamlet, addressing the absent Ghost, says: "Remember thee!/Yea, from the table of my memory". The gift, *i.e.* the notebook, shall remain in the mind of the poet while other useless ('idle') and abject ('rank') things will be forgotten; and that gift will remain in the mind of the poet even upto eternity, and will not be dated or destroyed or erased ('Beyond all date'): "Which shall above that idle rank remain/Beyond all date even to eternity,—".

The poet shows his doubt about so much of longevity of the memory of the gift. He says that if the memory does not last upto eternity, it will last, at least, so long as his brain and heart (the physiological brain and his love for the youth) will continue to remain in tact ('subsist'), naturally ('by nature'), with their faculties of remembrance and love, respectively: "Or at the least so long as brain and heart/Have faculty by nature to subsist". Until the brain and the heart, each of them severally, go to ('yield') oblivion — oblivion that destroys ('raz'd') everything — the memory of the youth ('thy') cannot be erased ('miss'd'): "Till each to raz'd oblivion yield his part/Of thee, thy record never can be miss'd."

The poet calls the notebook a 'poor retention' because the notebook could not record all the memories of the youth: its recording capacity was limited: "That poor retention could not so much hold". The poet, therefore, does not require that notebook. He also does not require tallies or counting devices to count ('score') the precious ('dear') love of the youth: "Nor need I tallies thy dear love to score". Kerrigan wrote about this line: "The notebook is scornfully compared to *tallies,* sticks notched (*scored*) with records of debt. Judging from 2 *Henry VI,* IV.7. 31-33, where the rebel Jack Cade speaks strongly in their favour, the 'score and tally' were regarded as basely rustic devices" (Kerrigan, 344). It is for this reason ('Therefore') that the poet took the liberty ('I was bold') of rejecting the notebook and the gifts that the youth gave the poet (as means of remembering him, *i.e.* the youth). And, instead, the poet trusts the tables of his own memory that will be able to receive more impressions of the Fair Youth ('that revive thee more') (and will also be able to retain those impressions more) than the gifts and the notebook: "Therefore to give them from me was I bold,/To trust those tables that receive thee more." The poet tells the youth that if he (the poet) takes the help of an assistant ('adjunct'), like the gifts and the notebook, to remember the youth, it will simply amount to introducing the negative faculty of forgetting things (about the youth) ('import forgetfulness') in his (the poet's) mind ('in me'): "to keep an adjunct to remember thee/Were to import forgetfulness in me."

123

No, Time, thou shalt not boast that I do change:
Thy pyramids built up with newer might
To me are nothing novel, nothing strange, —
They are but dressings of a former sight.
Our dates are brief, and therefore we admire
What thou dost foist upon us that is old,
And rather make them born to our desire
Than think that we before have heard them told.
Thy registers and thee I both defy,
Not wondering at the present nor the past;
For thy records and what we see doth lie,
Made more or less by thy continual haste.
This I do vow and this shall ever be:—
I will be true despite thy scythe and thee.

Like some other sonnets, this sonnet is used by commentators for dating the Sonnets. This Sonnet may suggest Shakespeare's belief in Platonism, particularly his belief in Plato's theory of immortality of the soul and reincarnation (*vide* lines 4-8 of this sonnet). In this sonnet, the poet does not address the Fair Youth, as usual in other sonnets, but he addresses Time. The poet challenges Time and says that Time will not be able to be proud ('boast') for being able to change the state of the poet, that is, Time will not be able to make the poet old: "No, Time, thou shalt not boast that I do change". It is true that Time has constructed high-rise buildings at the present time — buildings that can be compared with the Egyptian pyramids — with more ('newer') strength in those buildings. Kerrigan wrote about the word 'pyramid': "It has been suggested that Shakespeare had particular structures in mind — the Egyptian obelisks set up in Rome during the late 1580s by Pope Sixtus V, certain triumphal monuments erected in 1603 for the coronation of James I — but it seems more likely that the word was used because it suggested, in Jacobean English, a whole range of inspiring contemporary buildings (lofty spire and steeples, pinnacles, conical roofs) without losing its roots in Egyptian antiquity, and thus the past (lines 3-4). [The point is worth emphasizing. When Cleopatra, who ought to know about Egyptian *pyramids*, declares, 'make/My country's high pyramids my gibbet' (V.2.60-61), she is clearly thinking of something steeper than the *pyramids* by the Nile. Dowden's gloss is apt in its grand indefinition: 'all that Time piles up....all his new stupendous erections']'' (Kerrigan, 345).

However, the poet tells Time that all these high-rise and mighty buildings are not in any way ('nothing') new or strange to him. These mighty buildings are to the poet only re-erections or refurbishings ('dressings') of former buildings ('or former sight'): ''To me are nothing novel, nothing strange,—/they are but dressings of a former sight.'' We, no doubt, admire whatever Time shows us as new, by subterfuges or tricks ('foist'), but this we do because our lives are short in span ('Our dates are brief'): ''Our dates are brief, and therefore we admire/ What thou dost foist upon us that is old''. The poet means to say that as we live in this world for a short period of time, we cannot understand that what we admire as new and mighty buildings are actually reconstructions of old buildings. The poet further says that we rather wilfully ('desire') believe those buildings to be new, with the help of our imagination; but, in actuality, in our previous generations, we had heard about (or saw) those buildings: ''And rather make them born to our desire/Than think that we before have heard them told.'' If we interpret these lines (lines 5-8), then we may presume that Shakespeare believed in the Platonic theory of immortality and transmigration of the soul. But neither Ingram and Redpath nor Kerrigan interpreted these lines from the angle of immortality and transmigration of the soul. Kerrigan, for instance, interpreted the expression 'make them born to our desire' thus: ''(1) construe them as the product of our own conceptions, imagine them to be invented by us; (2) make them new in wanting them (assuming that because we want them they are as new to the world as new-*born* babies)'' (Kerrigan, 345). Ingram and Redpath as well as Kerrigan interpreted the expression 'we before have heard them told' as meaning that we have heard (the poet says) that those high-rise buildings were actually new, but later on found that the newness of those buildings was the creation of our imagination.

Howsoever that may be, the poet flouts ('defy') both all the records ('registers') of Time and Time itself ('thee'); and he does not get awe-struck ('wonder') at the present chevisance of Time or its past achievements, in the form of, say, high-rise and strong buildings: ''Thy registers and thee I both defy,/Not wondering at the present nor the past''. The poet flouts or challenges Time because, he says, the records of Time (the buildings, etc.) and other things that the poet and his contemporary people see at the present time ('what we see') are deceptive ('doth lie'). All these are not being properly judged by the poet and his coevals: sometimes they overvalue those things, and sometimes they undervalue them ('Made more or less'). And this is so because Time runs very fast, and continually at that ('thy continual haste'): "For thy records and what we see doth lie,/Made more or less by thy continual haste." The poet means to say that as Time passes very fast, so our lives are very short, and consequently, we cannot make proper evaluation of things. In the concluding couplet, the poet swears ('vow') that in spite of man's dearth of time to judge things properly, and in spite of Time's profession of destroying things ('thy scythe'), and, further, in spite of Time's will to do so for ever ('and thee'), he (the poet) shall remain faithful to his love, or the Fair Youth ('will be true'): "This I do vow and this shall ever be:—/I will be true despite thy scythe and thee."

124

If my dear love were but the child of state,
It might for Fortune's bastard be unfather'd,
As subject to Time's love or to Time's hate,
Weeds among weeds or flowers with flowers gather'd.
No, it was builded far from accident;
It suffers not in smiling pomp, nor falls
Under the blow of thralled discontent
Whereto the inviting time our fashion calls;
It fears not policy, that heretic
Which works on leases of short-number'd hours:
But all alone stands hugely politic,
That it nor grows with heat nor drowns with showers.
To this I witness call the fools of time,
Which die for goodness, who have liv'd for crime.

Kerrigan's comment on the whole of this sonnet is very edifying: "A sonnet of beautiful complexity, drawing many of its images and concens from 116. *Love* is here, lived and inward, its monumental status resting on groundedness. In this last group of poems to the youth — beginning perhaps with the sestet of 119 (...) — writing yields in strength to emotion, verbs of making are given over (so that *render*, for instance, is, after *no art* in 125.11-12, *Nature's* at 126.12), and sonneteering becomes less sufficient (its form indeed breaking down with 126)." (Kerrigan, 346). However, the poet expresses his love for the Fair Youth with profound emotion and says that if the youth would merely be the offspring to the circumstances (in which he was born and brought up, and in which he lives) ('state'), then he (the youth) would be called a capricious offspring or issue of Fortune, having no father ('unfather'd'), and so he would be called a bastard: "If my dear love were but the child of state,/It might for Fortune's bastard be unfather'd". Kerrigan wrote about the expression 'but the child of state': "Only the produce of circumstance. There may be a glance at the state of the young man, his 'high rank' and 'wealthy grandeur' (the connexion between this sonnet and the next....the poet says his love is not the mere product of deference and social climbing" (Kerrigan, 346).

If the Fair Youth would have been the product ('child') of his high social stratum, then the youth would be controlled ('subject to') by impermanent love ('Time's love'), and by impermanent reproach ('Time's hate'), *i.e.* sometimes he would be loved by the poet or other persons, and sometimes he would be hated by them: "As subject to Time's love or to Time's hate". According to Kerrigan, the next line indicates "mature style at its best, in verse as resistant to paraphrase as it is near perfection" (Kerrigan, 347). However, in the next line (line 4), the poet says that had the youth been the product of his high social circumstance only, then he would be as abject or ordinary a youth as any other youth ('Weeds among weeds'), and people would choose him as they choose flowers, *i.e.* they would find no singularity in him, as people do not distinguish different flowers from each other when they go out to gather flowers: "Weeds among weeds or flowers with flowers gather'd."

The poet negates such a possibility. He says that the Fair Youth did not grow up ('builded') by chance caprice ('accident'). The poet, perhaps, means to say that the youth was born in high society, and he did not grow up like any other individual of that society, to become an ordinary youth. This is evident from the fact that the youth ('It') does not degenerate ('suffers') when he is entertained by favour-extending ('smiling') men of the high society ('pomp'): "It suffers not in smiling pomp". Again, the youth does not have to be the object ('nor falls') of muffled or controlled or unexpressed ('thralled') hatred or vexations ('discontent') of the people — hatred or vexations that are the fashion or custom of the day, to which people are attracted ('inviting'): "nor falls/Under the blow of thralled discontent/Whereto the inviting time our fashion calls". Kerrigan wrote about the eighth line: "towards which the seductive present day beckons *our fashion* ('our behaviours, our *mores*' or 'men of our ilk, men like us'). Melancholy *discontent* was in vogue during the late 1590s and early 1600s; Shakespeare anatomizes it in his characterization of Jaques in *As You Like It*'' (Kerrigan, 347).

The Fair Youth or his love ('It') is not afraid of any expediency ('policy') whatsoever: ''It fears no policy''. He is a fellow of false principles ('that heretic') who 'acts according to short-term view (whereas love fixes its mind on the permanent)'' (Ingram, 284) ('Which works on leases of short-number'd hours'): ''It fears not policy, that heretic/Which works on leases of short-number'd hours''. The word 'heretic' may also be found at *Romeo and Juliet,* I, ii, 91: ''Transparent heretics, be burnt for liars!'' The poet says that either the Fair Youth or his love stands absolutely ('hugely') independent, and as the only prudent ('politic') thing: ''But all alone stands hugely politic''. And, therefore, the Fair Youth or his love does not undergo changes: does not improve with favourable and passionate appeal ('heat'), and does not degenerate or get reduced ('drowns') by sorrow ('showers'): ''That it nor grows with heat nor drowns with showers.''

The poet calls the time-servers — those who change as their time changes ('the fools of time') — for bearing evidence or witness of what the poet so far claimed ('To this'), *i.e.* of the fact that the Fair Youth is not the product of his circumstance or of his high birth: ''To this I witness call the fools of time''. The poet calls the time-servers to witness or see those people who committed crimes during their active lives ('who have lived for crime') but prayed to the heaven in their death-beds for salvation ('Which die for goodness'): ''To this I witness call the fools of time,/Which die for goodness, who have liv'd for crime.'' Commentators have tried to identify such people, but perhaps in vain. Ingram and Redpath wrote about such people: ''Various allusions have been suggested, *e.g.* to Jesuit conspirators, to the Gunpowder Plot, to Essex and his followers, to Foxe's Marlyrs; but the evidence for any of these is far too tenuous to carry conviction'' (Ingram, 285).

125

Were it aught to me I bore the canopy,
With my extern the outward honouring,
Or laid great bases for eternity
Which proves more short than waste or ruining?
Have I not seen dwellers on form and favour
Lose all and more by paying too much rent,
For compound sweet forgoing simple savour—
Pitiful thrivers in their gazing spent?
No, let me be obsequious in thy heart,

And take you my oblation, poor but free, —
Which is not mix'd with seconds, knows no art
But mutual render, only me for thee.
Hence, thou suborn'd informer! a true soul
When most impeach'd stands least in thy control.

John Dover Wilson wrote about this poem: ''This like 121 replies to real or simulated scandal-mongers (....). D. [Edward Dowden (ed), *The Sonnets of Shakespeare,* 1891] associated it with 124: 'There Sh. [Shakespeare] asserted that his love was not subject to Time, as friendship founded in self-interest are; here he asserts that it is not founded on beauty of person, and therefore cannot pass away with the decay of such beauty. It is pure love for love.' And B. [H.C. Beeching (ed.), *The Sonnet of Shakespeare,* 1904] thus sums up the argument: 'The poet is repudiating charges laid against him by the (imagined) 'informer' of line 13. The charges are of caring too much for his friend's beauty, and laying upon that a basis for eternity. To which he replies in the second quatrain that so far from his being the case his own experience of others has shown him that such conduct leads only to disaster'.'' (Wilson, 239). Kerrigan introduced this sonnet thus: ''The poet responds to the criticism of an onlooker (perhaps one of those described in Sonnet 121), who has apparently suggested that his *love* is just *the child of state* (124.1), by insisting that he recognizes the vanity of pomp and circumstance and has been impressed in the past by the folly of those seduced by appearances'' (Kerrigan, 348).

However, the poet ''is repudiating the informer's (line 11) suggestion that in honouring the Friend [the Fair Youth] he is aiming at acquiring reputation for himself'' (Ingram, 286). He means to say that he is honouring the Fair Youth for nothing in return. He says that if honouring the youth would be of any gain ('Were it aught to me'), then he would certainly hold the embroidered awning ('canopy'), that are held over great dignitaries, over his head till now (but he does not like to hold it over his head): ''Were it aught to me I bore the canopy''. Kerrigan wrote about the first line: ''Perhaps the poet is saying that, although he once carried the *canopy,* the privilege means nothing to him (suppling the ellipsis before *I bore* with 'that'); but it seems more likely that he is insisting that he is so wary of display that even the privilege of carrying the *canopy* would mean nothing to him if it came his way (reading 'if' before *I bore*'' (Kerrigan, 349). Further, if the poet would honour (or love) the youth for some gain, then he would honour the outward aspects of the youth ('outward honouring') with his own outward pomp ('my extern'): "With my extern the outward honouring." Perhaps the poet here means to say that in that case he would enhance the dignity of the youth in the eyes of the public by enhancing his own external pomp: if the poet himself would make himself gorgeous, his friend, the Fair Youth, indirectly would also be elevated in the public eye.

The poet further says that if he would desire any gain for his honouring the youth, then, alternatively ('Or'), he would make a great and strong concrete monumental structure for the youth that would be expected to last upto eternity ('laid great bases for eternity'), but that concrete monumental structure " 'paradoxically, turns out to be briefer than the time required to run through an estate by extravagance'." (Ingram, 286): "Or laid great bases for eternity/Which proves more short than waste or ruining?" The poet, perhaps, means to say that he was never fascinated by the pomp and grandeur of the youth, and was never attracted thereby. The poet says that he has seen that those people who 'make much (or too much) of beauty in form and face" (Wilson, 239), *i.e.* those people who are attracted more by the beauty of form and face ('favour') of their beloveds ('dwellers on form and favour') ultimately lose all attractions and all that ('Lose all and more') for their beloveds, because of their too much attention to that beauty of form and face, and so gets their taste of beauty cloyed ('by paying too much rent'): "Have I not seen dwellers on form and favour/Lose all and more by paying too much rent,". Such people are after the twin fascinations ('compound sweet') of the beauty of form, and the beauty of face; and they (foolishly) reject the single taste ('simple savour') of love — pure and simple. The poet calls such people pitiably prosperous ('Pitiful thrivers'), because they spend their energy and all that only on their perceptual enjoyment ('in their gazing spent'): "For compound sweet forgoing simple savour—/ Pitiful thrivers in their gazing spent?"

The poet is averse to such people and to such sort of love-making ('No'). He begs to the Fair Youth to let him show his (the poet's) humble devotion to him (the youth) ('let me be obsequious in thy heart'). That is, the poet only wants to take a place in the heart of the youth. He also prays to the youth to accept his (the poet's) love, as gods accept the offerings ('oblation') of devotees. He tells the youth that his love may be lacking in ostentation ('poor'), but it is not encumbered with, or adulterated by, anything ('free'): "No, let me be obsequious in thy heart,/ And take thou my oblation, poor but free,—". He reiterates that his love is unalloyed by any other things ('not mix'd with seconds'), and that his love does not contain any concoction or ostentation, or craftiness ('art').

He asks the youth to exchange love with him mutually ('mutual render'). The poet begs to the youth to take only him (the poet) as his beloved ('only me for thee'): "Which is not mix'd with seconds, knows no art/ But mutual render, only me for thee."

In the concluding couplet, the poet ruefully and bluntly calls the informer (who informed the poet about the hearsay that the poet loved the youth for some gain — honour, favour, etc.) a bribed or false ('suborn'd') informer. He tells the informer that one with pure love may be strongly accused ('most impeach'd'), but falsity cannot win over ('control') true love or true soul ('stands least in thy control'): "Hence, thou suborn'd informer! a true soul/When most impeach's stands least in thy control." Lines 13-14 may be compared with lines 655-658 of *Venus and Adonis:* " 'This sour informer, this bate-breeding spy,/This canker that eats up Love's tender spring,/This carry-tale, dissentious Jealousy,/That sometimes true news, sometimes false doth bring."

126

O thou my lovely boy, who in thy power
Dost hold Time's fickle glass, his sickle hour;
Who hast by waning grown, and therein show'st
Thy lovers withering as thy sweet self grow'st;
If Nature, sovereign mistress over wrack,
As thou goest onwards, still will pluck thee back,
She keeps thee to this purpose, that her skill
May Time disgrace and wretched minutes kill.
Yet fear her, O thou minion of her pleasure!
She may detain but not still keep her treasure:
Her audit, though delay'd, answer'd must be,
And her quietus is to render thee.

Wilson wrote about this sonnet: "Unquestionably written as an Envoy to the sonnet series addressed to the Friend [the Fair Youth] ...It carries on and rounds off the theme of the conflict between Love and Time which is that of its immediate predecessors" (Wilson, 240). This sonnet differs from all the rest 153 sonnets in at least two regards: firstly, it does not contain 14 lines, as was usual for a sonnet, but only 12 lines; and secondly, it consists of only 6 rhymed couplets. But we should keep in mind that "Many Elizabethan' sonnets' varied in length and structure from what is now considered a 'sonnet'. The great majority were, however, of fourteen lines" (Ingram, 288). Some may think that the poem is incomplete because it contains only 12 lines, but Ingram and Redpath said that "the poem (such as it is) forms a complete whole" (Ingram, 288).

However, the poet addresses the Fair Youth as 'lovely boy' and says that the youth holds within his power or control the passage of Time though stealthy, inconstant or changing ('fickle'); and controls the destructive or cutting (like a 'sickle') hour: "O thou my lovely boy, who in thy power/Dost hold Time's fickle glass, his sickle hour". The 'lovely boy' or the Fair Youth has grown in beauty or attractiveness with his ageing ('waning') — the more he is growing in age, the more he is becoming beautiful. On the other hand, as the youth is growing in beauty, his lovers, as if, by contrast, are losing their beauty ('withering'); and this the youth is showing as his lovely ('sweet') self is growing in beauty and attractiveness: "Who hast by waning grown, and therein show'st/The lovers withering as thy sweet self grow'st".

The poet tells the youth that even if he (the youth) progressively decays in beauty as he ages ('As thou goest onwards'), Nature, who presides over ('sovereign mistress') the destruction ('wrack') of Time, will, neverthless, give the youth back all his former or present beauty ('still will pluck thee back'): "If Nature, sovereign mistress over wrack,/ As thou goest onwards, still will pluck thee back". The poet says that Nature has her own motive in doing so: in bringing the youth back to his former glory of beauty. The purpose is this that by refurbishing the beauty of the youth, Nature will prove her skill of disgracing Time, and thus of killing the helpless ('wretched') minutes contained in Time: "She keeps thee to this purpose, that her skill/May Time disgrace and wretched minutes kill." The poet means to say that Time always erases beauty and destroys things, but Nature has the skill of staying this erasing of beauty and destroying of things. Time, naturally, will erase the beauty of the youth, but if Nature prevents Time's erasing of the beauty of the youth, then Time will be disgraced, humiliated, and the moments will be made ineffectual thereby, too.

Nevertheless, the poet advises the Fair Youth to beware of Nature ('her'), though the youth is the most loveable object ('minion') of the pleasure of Nature. Because, the poet tells him, Nature may (temporarily) stop ('detain') the maul-marauding of Time, but she (Nature) will certainly not permanently keep or hold the youth as unchangeable, even though the youth is a treasure-trove to Nature: "Yet fear her, O thou minion of her pleasure!/She may detain but not still keep her treasure". The poet means to say Nature herself may help the youth halt, or the youth may himself naturally halt, the ravages of Time, as he will continue to grow with age, but the same Nature will some day let Time hold his (Time's) sway over the youth. That is, as the youth will grow in age, someday he will certainly lose his beauty. The poet says that Nature must someday summon the account ('audit'), though delayedly, and she must be provided with the account, *i.e.* her questions must be answered. And this is her responsibility to oversee the account, *i.e.* to see that the youth, like all others, has lost his beauty, by order of her. Only then can she be discharged from her responsibility and be quiet ('quietus') — only by making ('render') the youth shorn of all his beauty, can Nature be quiet: "Her audit, though delay'd answer'd must be,/And her quietus is to render thee." The word 'quietus' immediately transports us to Hamlet's soliloquy: "When he himself might his quietus make/With a bare bodkin?" (*Hamlet,* III, i, 75-76).

THE DARK LADY SONNETS

127

In the old age black was not counted fair,
Or if it were it bore not beauty's name;
But now is black beauty's successive heir,
And beauty slander'd with a bastard shame:
For since each hand hath put on Nature's power,
Fairing the foul with Art's false borrow'd face,
Sweet Beauty hath no name, no holy bower,
But is profan'd, if not lives in disgrace.
Therefore my mistress' eyes are raven black,
Her brow so suited, and the mourners seem
At such who not born fair no beauty lack,
Slandering creation with a false esteem:
Yet so they mourn becoming of their woe,
That every tongue says beauty should look so.

This is first of the sonnets in the sonnet-sequence devoted to the so-called Dark Lady (Sonnets 127-152). With Sonnet 127, we turn attention from the Fair Youth, and address it to the Dark Lady. Whether the Dark Lady was an imaginary being, or there was really a woman having verisimilitude with the Dark Lady, we do not know for certain. Though before this sonnet, the poet did not say anything explicitly about his favourite mistress, the Dark Lady, yet we have had some innuendoes about the betrayal of the poet by the Dark Lady, in collusion with the Fair Youth, in Sonnets 40, 41 and 42. We are not certain if the sequence of the Dark Lady sonnet group is correct and faithful to the original sequence. Ingram and Redpath wrote about this: ''On the order within the group, however, very little agreement has been expressed, but no really satisfactory rearrangement has been proposed. ''Some critics suggest that a number of the sonnets of this group refer to the same events as sonnets 33-42, where the poet complains of the wrong done him by the Friend [the Fair Youth]'' (Ingram, 290).

However, in this sonnet, the poet says that formerly persons with black complexion were not considered to be beautiful; or, if they were admired for their charms, yet they were not called beautiful persons ('bore not beauty's name'): ''In the old age black was not counted fair,/ Or if it were it bore not beauty's name''. But now people think of beauty in different terms: now black complexion is being considred as a component of beauty, *i.e.* black complexion is being considered as the legitimate successor ('successive heir') of Beauty. On the other hand, what was formerly considered as Beauty is now being caluminated, defamed ('slanderd') as the illegitimate offspring ('bastard') of Beauty, and therefore, the former Beauty is thus being put to shame: ''But now is black beauty's successive heir,/And beauty slander'd with a bastard shame''. Lines 3-4 may be compared with lines 244-49 at *Love's Labour's Lost,* IV, iii, where Berowne says:

Is ebony like her? O wood divine !
A wife of such wood were felicity.
O, who can give an oath? Where is a book?
That I may swear beauty doth beauty lack,
If that she learn not of her eye to look.
No face is fair that is not full so black.

However, in the sonnet, the poet says so because formerly ('For since') everybody ('each hand') took possession of the power of Nature, — Nature that is entitled to preside over Beauty, — by using cosmetics to blanch them or to make them look fair. And thus people would convert what was actually ugly ('foul') into seeming beauty ('fairing foul'), with the aid of false cosmetic art; and so, thus they would, as if, borrow a different and beautiful face: ''For since each hand hath put on Nature's power,/Fairing the foul with Art's false borrow'd face,''.

The poet says that fair complexion or blondness ('Sweet Beauty') itself now has no reputation ('no name'), and it is now not held in reverence ('holy bower'). Rather, now fair complexion or blondness is held in disreputation ('profan'd') and in disgrace: "Sweet Beauty hath no name, no holy bower,/But is profan'd, if not lives in disgrace." Kerrigan found a parallel to the expression 'Sweet Beauty hath no name' at *Coriolanus,* V, i,12-15: "he forbade all names:/He was a kind of nothing, titleless,/Till he had forged himself a name i' th' fire/Of burning Rome'". Ingram and Redpath explained lines 7 and 8 thus: " 'Fresh and natural blonde beauty is held neither in repute nor in reverence, but either its appearance is profanely assumed or it is utterly discredited' " (Ingram, 290). It is for this reason that the poet claims that his mistress, the Dark Lady, is beautiful, because she has a pair of raven-black eyes, and her brow is also as black as suits the black eyes: "Therefore my mistress' eyes are raven black,/Her brow so suited". And the eyes and the brow ('they') of the Dark Lady seem to be mourning over the despicable plight of those people who ('such who') were not born with fair complexion, or were not born as blonde, but use cosmetics to show themselves as blonde, and thus show that they do not lack in beauty ('not born fair no beauty lack'): "and they mourners seem/At such who not born fair no beauty lack,". The poet says that such people are thus indirectly discrediting and defaming ('slandering') Nature's creation with their false idea that they can improve upon Nature's creation, and in this way they can show respect ('esteem') to Nature: "Slandering creation with a false esteem". The poet concludes by saying that when the eyes and the brow ('they') mourn, they (the eyes and the brow) become more beautiful, for their sorrow ('becoming of their woe'). And so ('That') everybody ('every tongue') says that every beautiful person should have such a pair of mournful eyes and sorrowful brow ('beauty should look so'): "Yet so they mourn becoming of their woe,/That every tongue says beauty should look so."

128

How oft, when thou, my music, music play'st
Upon that blessed wood whose motion sounds
With thy sweet figners, when thou gently sway'st
The wiry concord that mine ear confounds,
Do I envy those jacks that nimble leap
To kiss the tender inward of thy hand,
Whilst my poor lips, which should that harvest reap,
At the wood's boldness by thee blushing stand!
To be so tickled they would change their state
And situation with those dancing chips
O'er whom thy fingers walk with gentle gait,

Making dead wood more blest than living lips.
Since saucy jacks so happy are in this,
Give them thy fingers, me thy lips to kiss.

Kerrigan's introduction to this sonnet is very edifying: ''Apparently the ingenius elaboration of a conceit so well-worn by the end of the 1590's that Jonson mocked it in *Every Man Out of His Humour* (1599), making the 'Neat, spruce, affecting Courtier' Fastidius Brisk say of his mistress Saviolina, as she plays the viola da gamba: 'You see the subject of her sweet fingers, there?... Oh, she tickles it so, that ....she makes it laugh most divinely ....I'll tell you a good jest now, and yourself shall say it's a good one: I have wished myself to be that instrument, I think, a thousand times, and not so few, by heaven' (III, 9. 101-6). Shakespeare approaches lines 3-6 in a more serious context at *Titus Andronicus* II.4.44-7: 'O, had the mosnter seen those lily hands/ Tremble like aspen leaves upon a lute/And made the silken strings delight to kiss them/He would not have touched them for his life!' '' (Kerrigan, 355). However, this sonnet may have made innuendoes to the possible carnal love of the poet for the Dark Lady, at least at line 14: ''Give them thy fingers, me thy lips to kiss.''

The poet relates that his mistress, whom he affectionately calls 'my music', frequently plays on her violin or such wooden musical instruments, and then the movements of the wooden keys, which the poet supposes to be blessed because of the touches of his mistress' fingers ('blessed wood'), create sounds in unison with the fingers of his mistress: ''How oft, when thou, my music, music play'st/Upon that blessed wood whose motion sounds/With thy sweet fingers''. And when the mistress lightly governs or controls ('gently sway'st'), the orchestration, or the harmonius unity of sounds ('concord'), of the different sounds that come out of the strings ('wiry'), the ear of the poet or the poet himself becomes awe-struck ('confounds'): ''when thou gently sway'st/The wiry concord that mine ear confounds''. At that time, the poet becomes jealous ('envy') of the vertical elevators of the keys of the musical instrument ('jacks') that nimbly jumps up successively, as if to kiss the soft palm of the mistress' hand ('inward of thy hand': ''Do I envy those jacks that nimble leap/To kiss the tender inward of thy hand''. And, at the same time, the lips of the poet, which should beget the favour ('harvest') of the Dark Lady (rather, the touch of her lips), becomes red in angry jealousy ('blushing stand'), beside the Lady ('by thee'), as these (the lips of the poet) witness those wooden jacks' boldness in leaping up to kiss the palm of the Lady.

Then the poet becomes astonished at all these things: "Whilst my poor lips, which should that harvest reap,/At the wood's boldness by thee blushing stand!"

The poet says that to get the light and pleasant touches ('tickled') of the Lady's fingers, the jacks ('they') would jump up and down ('change their state') and change their positions ('situations') with those leaping wooden keys ('dancing chips'), over which keys the Lady's fingers moved ('walk') to and fro in nimble gait ('gentle gait'): "To be so tickled they would change their state/And situation with those dancing chips/O'er whom thy fingers walk with gentle gait." And the nimble touches of the fingers of the Lady would, as if, make those keys, made of dead wood, more blessed than the living lips of the poet: "Making dead wood more blest than living lips." The poet implores to the Lady to extend the favour of her fingers to those wooden pert or lascivious keys which feel so happy in that favour ('this'), and to extend her lips to the poet for kissing: "Since saucy jacks so happy are in this,/Give them thy fingers, me thy lips to kiss."

129

The expense of spirit in a waste of shame
Is lust in action; and till action, lust
Is perjur'd, murderous, bloody, full of blame,
Savage, extreme, rude, cruel, not to trust;
Enjoy'd no sooner but despised straight;
Past reason hated, as a swallow'd bait
On purpose laid to make the taker mad,—
Mad in pursuit, and in possession so;
Had, having, and in quest to have, extreme;
A bliss in proof; and prov'd, a very woe;
Before, a joy propos'd; behind a dream.
All this the world well knows; yet none knows well
To shun the heaven that leads men to this hell.

Kerrigan's headnote to this sonnet is very important: "Of the 154 sonnets in Q [the Quarto edition of Shakespeare's sonnets], only 94 compares with this in impersonal profundity, in its illumination of the sequence by means of indirect because general statement. While 94 moves steadily, however, undercutting itself by the recoil of one clause or line upon another, 129 is rapid, almost frenetic, is its pursuits of lust, satiety, and despair" (Kerrigan, 356). The lust spoken of in this sonnet, can be compared with the lust to be found at *The Rape of Lucrece* (lines

674-76): "For light and lust are deadly enemies;/Shame folded up in blind concealing night,/When most unseen, then most doth tyrannise"; and, again at *Venus and Adonis* (lines 799-804):

Love comforteth like sunshine after rain,
But Lust's effect is tempest after sun;
Love's gentle spring doth always fresh remain:
Lust's winter comes ere summer half be done.
  Love surfeits not: Lust like a glutton dies.
  Love is all truth: Lust full of forged lies.

However, the poet begins this sonnet with a definition of lust. He says that lust ('lust in action') means spending vital physical energy ('expense of spirit') in wasteful and obscene ('of shame') activities: "The expense of spirit in a waste of shame/Is lust in action". The poet next heaps up a number of vituperations on lust. He says that until lust is satisfied through dissipation of the store of physical amorous energy, it (the lust or the person with lust) swears falsely ('perjur'd'), it can commit murder, it can do bloody actions, and it is full of guilt ('blame'). It is, till its satisfaction, uncivilised, extreme, brutal, cruel, and it cannot be trusted: "and till action, lust/Is perjur'd, murderous, bloody, full of blame,/Savage, extreme, rude, cruel, not to trust". No sooner lust is satisfied or gratified than it is despised straightaway, and it makes one hunt for objects for its gratification beyond the region permitted by rationality. But as soon as lust is gratified, one despises one's lust itself beyond the limit endorsed by one's rationality: "Past reason hunted; and no sooner had,/Past reason hated". Lust is like an object or thing of temptation ('bait') which is purposefully laid before one, and as soon a as one deglutinates the bait or falls into the trap of temptation ('taker'), one goes out of one's senses or rationality: "as a swallow'd bait/On purpose laid to make the taker mad,—". Kerrigan found two passages, one in *Macbeth* and another in *Measure for Measure*, as parallels to the expression 'a swallow'd bait/On purpose laid to make the taker mad'. He wrote: "Two passages in the plays are illuminating: *Macbeth* I.3.83-84, where Banquo asks the protagonist 'have we eaten on the insane root/That takes the reason prisoner?', and *Measure for Measure* I.2. 127-29, where Claudio explains to Lucio his lapse into mild sexual irregularity: 'Our natures do pursue,/Like rats that ravin down their proper bane,/A thristy evil, and when we drink we die' " (Kerrigan, 358). The poet says that when one falls into the grip of lust, one becomes mad in one's pursuit of gratifying that lust; and if the object for gratifying the lust is possessed, then also one remains mad. One is always mad ('extreme') whether one once had the object for gratifying the lust ('Had'), or now is possessing that object ('having'), or now is in the search ('quest') of getting such an object: "Mad in pursuit, and in possession so;/Had, having, and in quest to have, extreme."

Lust seems to be very enjoyable ('bliss') when it is being tasted or gratified ('in proof'). But once it has been tasted, it proves to be a great source of sorrow ('woe'). Before it is gratified, or when it is in the process or prospect of being gratified ('Before'), it is the source of anticipated enjoyment ('a joy propos'd'), but after gratification, the gratification itself seems to be all but a fiction — one then feels that the gratification was but fictitious ('dream'): "A bliss in proof; and prov'd, a very woe;/Before, a joy propos'd; behind, a dream." These two lines may be compared with lines 211-12 of *The Rape of Lucrece* where Tarquin repents: " 'What win I if I gain the thing I seek?/A dream, a breath, a froth of fleeting joy....' ". The poet concludes his aspersions on lust by saying that all people know all this very well. But, he says, no one knows well the fact that it is better to avoid ('shun') the gratification of lust that gives one extreme physical pleasure ('heaven') — the gratification that pushes one to the experience of extreme mental pain or the experience of torment: "All this the world well knows; yet none knows well/To shun the heaven that leads men to this hell."

130

My mistress' eyes are nothing like the sun;
Coral is far more red than her lips' red;
If snow be white, why then her breasts are dun;
If hairs be wires, black grow on her head:
I have seen roses damask'd, red and white,
But no such roses see I in her cheeks;
And in some perfumes is there more delight
Than in the breath that from my mistress reeks:
I love to hear her speak, yet well I know
That music hath a far more pleasing sound;
I grant I never saw a goddess go,—
My mistress when she walks treads on the ground.
  And yet by heaven I think my love as rare
  As any she belied with false compare.

According to Beaty and Matchett, this is an instance of what they call anti-sonnet. To them, an anti-sonnet is a sonnet "which attempts freshness through denying the usual images, as in Shakespeare's 'Sonnet 130' " (Beaty, 329). Sonents generally eulgogises the features of the beloved, but, contrarily, anti-sonnets deny the attractive features in the beloved. But, nonetheless, it must be admitted that even the anti-sonnet in the end eulogises the beloved, and expresses the fascination of the poet for the beloved. However, in their general note to this sonnet, Ingram and Redpath wrote: "This sonnet is not a denigration of the attractions of the poet's mistress, or even an admission that she had not the conventional beauties and graces. It is a satirical repudiation of false comparisons current in contemporary poetry ['complements of proud (but false) compare']. The poet is affirming by implication the physical reality of the woman. In line 3, for example, he is not saying that his mistress' breasts are 'dun', but denying that the colour of snow would be appropriate to her breasts, and, perhaps, by implication, to those of any desirable woman, since 'any she' would be 'belied with' that 'false compare'." (Ingram, 298). The sonnet is full of paradoxical statements. Lucas suggested that "behind Shakespeare's paradoxical praises of the Dark Lady, there lies a love-hate for her 'black deeds' that makes him willing, under the flattering caresses, to wound sadistically" (Ingram, 298). Further, this sonnet may remind us of some of the sonnets in Thomas Watson's *Hekatompathia* (1582), in which also the poet describes the attractions of his lady-love in detail. See for intance, the following poem (Kerrigan, 19-20):

Hark you that list to hear what saint I serve:
Her yellow locks exceed the beaten gold;
Her sparkling eyes in heaven a place deserve;
Her forehead high and fair of comely mould;
  Her words are music all of silver sound;
  Her wit so sharp as like can scarce be found:
Each eyebrow hangs like Iris in the skies;
Her Eagle's nose is straight of stately frame;
On either cheek a Rose and Lily lies;
Her breath is sweet perfume, or holy flame;
  Her lips more red than any coral stone;
  Her neck more white than aged swans that moan;
Her breast transparent is, like crystal rock;
Her fingers long, fit for Apollo's lute;
Her slipper such as Momus dare not mock;
Her virtues all so great as make me mute:
  What other parts she hath I need not say,
  Whose face alone is cause of my decay.

The poet says that his mistress' eyes (the eyes of the Dark Lady) are not as bright, or burning, as the sun; and her lips are less red than the coral: "My mistress' eyes are nothing like the sun;/Coral is far more red than her lips' red". Line 1 may be compared with line 7 of Daniel's *Delia,* 37: "thine eye's bright sun"; and with line 6 of Shakespeare's Sonnet 49: "And scarcely greet me with that sun thine eye". And line 2 of the present sonnet may be compared with line 2 of Linche's *Diella,* 31: "sweet lips of coral hue but silken softness". We may also find parallels to line 2 at *Venus and Adonis* (line 542: 'sweet coral mouth'), and at *The Rape of Lucrece* (line 420: 'coral lips').

The breasts of the Dark Lady are greyish brown ('dun') and not as white as snow, as fair women are supposed to possess. And the hair that grow on her head are like black wires, and not like golden wires that are generally held in admiration: "If snow be white, why then her breasts are dun;/If hair be wires, black wires grow on her head". Kerrigan wrote about these two lines: "The conventional *mistress* of Elizabethan love poetry had blond tresses (....), frequently compared to *wires* or drawn gold, the kind of precious thread used in fine embroidered cloth" (Kerrigan, 359). Line 4 may be compared with lines 290-91 of the 4th Sestiad of Marlow'es *Hero and Leander*: "For her aspect: her tresses were of wire,/Knit like a net, where hearts all set on fire". However, the poet further says that the cheeks of the Lady are also not conventionally red ('damask'd') and white, so that they may be compared with red and white roses that the poet has seen: "I have seen roses damask'd, red and white,/But no such roses see I in her cheeks". It may be noted here that from what we have been able to understand of the Lady's complexion, we can say that she was not of unifrom complexion, but she had different colours in different parts of her skin. And we have also seen that it was in vogue during the time of Shakespeare to describe lady-love as white or blonde all over her body. But Ingram and Redpath wrote about this point: "Such a variegation of hue in a woman's complexion was highly esteemed in Elizabethan court circles, where an even complexion would have been considered dull. In consonance with the whole drift of the sonnet Shakespeare is saying, in effect, that he will not praise his mistress as bearing conventional colouring" (Ingram, 300).

The poet further says that the scent of the breath of the Lady that is being exhaled ('reek') from her mouth, is also not as pleasing ('delight') as the scent of some essences ('perfumes'): "And in some perfumes is there more delight/Than in the breath that form my mistress reeks:".

Again, her speech is not so pleasing, though the poet loves to hear her speak. He says that he knows well that her voice is not as pleasing as the sound of music: "I love to hear her speak, yet well I know/That music hath a far more pleasing sound". These two lines may be compared with line 11 of Sydney's *Astrophil and Stella*, 100: "While sobbed out words a perfect music give". The poet says that he admits ('grant') that whenever he has seen the Dark Lady walking, it had never come to his mind that he had been seeing a goddess (the Dark Lady could not be compared with a goddess, as the poet wished to), *i.e.* to the poet, the Lady could not be compared with a goddess. Rather, when she walks, the poet thinks that she is walking like any other woman who walks on the ground — and not in the heaven or over the ground like a goddess ('treads on the ground'): "I grant I never saw a goddess go,—/My mistress when she walks treads on the ground." But, the Dark Lady's lacking in all these conventional faminine attractions has never come in the way of the poet's loving her. The poet swears by heaven and thinks that his love for the Lady ('my love') is as rare and precious as any other true love ('As any'), and that she does not admit ('belied') of any comparison with any other lady, because such comparison will be false ('false compare'), or if she be compared with any other lady then that lady will be said to have false beauty: "And yet by heaven I think my love as rare/As any she belied with false compare."

131

Thou art as tyrannous, so as thou art,
As those whose beauties proudly make them cruel;
For well thou know'st to my dear doting heart
Thou art the fairest and most precious jewel.
Yet in good faith some say that thee behold
Thy face hath not the power to make love groan:
To say they err I dare not be so bold,
Although I swear it to myself alone.
And to be sure that is not false I swear,
A thousand groans but thinking on thy face
One on another's neck to witness bear
Thy black is fairest in my judgment's place.
    In nothing art thou black save in thy deeds,
    And thence this slander as I think proceeds.

This sonnet may be clubbed together with Sonnet 130, because the themes of the two sonnets are the same. In both the sonnets, the poet says that his lady-love, the Dark Lady, is black, but, yet, he is very fond of her. In this sonnet, the poet tells the Lady that she is as tyrannical and curel, as she really is ('as thou art'), as those women whose beauty makes them both proud and cruel: "Thou art as tyrannous, so as thou art,/As those whose beauties proudly make them cruel". Because, the poet says the Lady ('thou') knows well that she is the most beautiful and the most valuable ornament or stone ('precious jewel') to him (the poet) who foolishly and externally as well as excessively loves ('doting') ('to my dear doting heart'): "For well thou know'st to my dear doting heart/Thou art the fairest and most precious jewel." Nevertheless, the poet says honestly ('in good faith') that some people who ('that') sees her ('the behold') say that her ('Thy') mien ('face') has not the power of beauty to make one pine ('groan') for her love: "Yet in good faith some say that thee behold/Thy face hath not the power to make love groan". The poet cannot be as bold as to say that such people ('they') are wrong ('err') in their depreciation of the Lady. He can only adjure that depreciation ('it') only to himself in soliloquy ('to myself alone') and not to anybody else: "To say they err I dare not be so bold,/ Although I swear it myself alone."

To make certain what he said earlier ('that') that that the Dark Lady is the most beautiful and the most valuable woman to him (line 4) is not false, the poet is again swearing: "And to be sure that is not false I swear". Of course many many people are protesting ('groans') to what the poet says (that the Lady is the most beautiful and precious woman): "A thousand groans". But meditating ('thinking') several times on the beauty of the face of the Dark Lady, or on several aspects of her in quick succession ('One on another's neck'), the poet is bearing witness of the fact that in his opinion or evaluation, the black complexion of the Dark Lady is the fairest of all : "but thinking on thy face/One on another's neck do witness bear/Thy black is fairest in my judgment's place." The poet concludes by saying that though her complexion is really black, she does not seem to him to be ugly or black. But she is ugly or black only in her deeds, *i.e.* the poet notices only her immoral deeds to be black. And he says that the slanderings of her, in vogue, are due only to her immoral deeds ('thence'), and not to her black complexion or to anything else.

132

Thine eyes I love, and they, as pitying me,—
Knowing thy heart torment me with disdain —
Have put on black, and loving mourners be,
Looking with pretty ruth upon my pain.

And truly not the morning sun of heaven
Better becomes the grey cheeks of the east,
Nor that full star that ushers in the even
Doth half that glory to the sober west
As those two mourning eyes become thy face.
Oh, let it then as well beseem thy heart
To mourn for me, since mourning doth thee grace,
And suit thy pity like in every part.
Then will I swear Beauty herself is black,
And all they foul that thy complexion lack.

According to John Dover Wilson, this is the sixth of the 'Poet, Friend and Mistress' series of Shakespeare's sonnets. Here the mistress of the poet, the Dark Lady, is mourning for the poet, "though she disdain him in her heart. Light badinage" (Wilson, 249). However, the poet says that he loves the eyes of the Dark Lady, and that her eyes ('they') seem to him (the poet) to be pitying him ('and they, as pitying me'). Those eyes are putting on black colour — the colour of mourning — because the heart of the Lady is hating ('disdain') the poet, and by doing so is tormenting him: "Thine eyes I love, and they, as pitying me,—/ Knowing thy heart torment me with disdain—/Have put on black". Those eyes are mourning because they love the poet ('loving mourners be') as well as hate him. It is painful to the poet that the heart of the Lady hates him ('my pain'). But, in spite of this, her eyes are looking at the painful condition of the poet with proper or sufficient or charming ('pretty') pity ('ruth'): "and loving mourners be,/Looking with pretty ruth upon my pain." The eyes of the Lady are certainly not like the bright sun of the morning, but are, rather, like ('better becomes') the cloudy sky ('grey cheeks') of the eastern horizon lighted by the morning sun: "And truly not the morning sun of heaven/Better becomes the grey cheeks of the east". Again, the eyes are not like the clear ('full') star, Hesperus, that brings in ('ushers') the evening ('even'), and spreads soft ('sober') glow ('glory') over the western sky in the evening — glow that is of half the intensity of the sun ('half that glory'). The poet thinks that such a pair of mourning eyes are befitting ('become') to the sad face of the Lady: "Nor that full star that ushers in the even/Doth half that glory to the sober west/As those two mourning eyes become they face." Here, the poet means to say that those two sad eyes are rather adding to the beauty of the face of the Dark Lady.

Therefore, the poet wishes that her heart may also put on black or mourning ('it'), *i.e.* her heart may also mourn for him, because mourning makes her more graceful ('doth thee grace'): "Oh, let it then as well beseem thy heart/To mourn for me, since mourning doth thee grace." The poet asks her to clothe or decorate ('suit') her pity (or blackness) with her mourning, in both the parts of her body equally ('like') (or alike) — the eyes and the heart: "And suit thy pity like in every part." In the concluding couplet, the poet says that if black can beautify, or if mourning (the symbol of mourning is black) can enhance beauty, then he will vow ('swear') that the goddess of beauty ('Beauty') herself must be black in complexion. Not only this, the poet, contrarily, says that those people who are not black, *i.e.* who are blonde (those people or, rather, those women, who are not of the same complexion as belongs to the Lady), must be ugly or detestable ('foul'): "Then will I swear Beauty herself is black,/And all they foul that thy complexion lack."

133

Beshrew that heart that makes my heart to groan
For that deep wound it gives my friend and me!
Is't not enough to torture me alone,
But slave to slavery my sweet'st friend must be?
Me from myself thy cruel eye hath taken,
And my next self thou harder hast engross'd:
Of him, my self, and thee I am forsaken,—
A torment thrice threefold, thus to be cross'd.
Prison my heart in thy steel bosom's ward,
But then my friend's heart let my poor heart bail;
Whoe'er keeps me, let my heart be his guard:
Thou canst not then use rigour in my jail.
 And yet thou wilt; for I, being pent in thee,
 Perforce am thine, and all that is in me.

According to John Dover Wilson, Sonnets 131-136 and 143-144 are sonnets of the eternal triangle — of the triangular relation that exists among one woman and her two lovers, or among one man and his two beloveds. In all these sonnets, the triangle exists among the poet, his friend, and the Dark Lady. This is evident from the first two lines of this sonnet. The poet asks the Lady to curse ('Beshrew') her own heart ('that heart') that makes his own heart cry in pain ('groan'), because her heart has deeply wounded both himself and his friend, the Fair Youth: "Beshrew that heart that makes my heart to groan/For that deep wound it gives my friend and me!" The poet asks the Dark Lady whether she is not satisfied with torturing only himself ('alone'), and whether she also definitely needs to make his sweet friend, the Fair

Youth, a slave to herself, or a slave to slavery under herself: "Is't not enough to torture me alone,/But slave to slavery my sweetest friend must be?"

The next four lines 5-8 show a very complex relation among the poet, the Fair Youth, and the Dark Lady. Ingram and Redpath beautifully showed the relations, with the help of a diagram which will help us understand the whole sonnet better, particularly the quatrain of lines 5-8. The diagram is as follows (Ingram, 306):

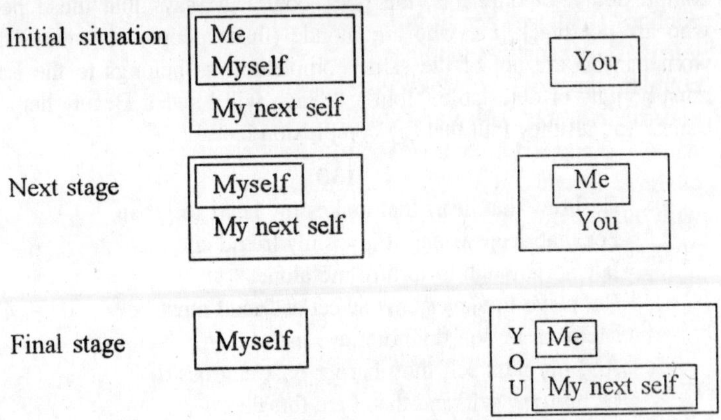

The diagram may become clear to us if we take 'My next self' for the Fair Youth; 'Myself' for the subjectivity of the poet; 'Me' for the objectively of the poet; and 'You' for the Dark Lady.

However, the poet says that his objective self ('Me') has known ('taken') about the cruelty of the Dark Lady ('cruel eye') from his subjective experience ('myself'). The poet, perhaps, means to say that from his own experience of the cruelty of the Lady, he (the objective self of the poet) has come to know the cruelty of the Lady, and this has made him engrossed or degraded. And the Lady has made his friend, the Fair Youth ('my next self'), fascinated ('engross'd'), or degraded or gross ('engross'd') much more than the poet himself: "Me from myself thy cruel eye hath taken,/And my next self harder hast engross'd". The poet says that now he is deprived of both his friend, the Fair Youth ('my self') and the Lady ('thee'). And so his mental pain or torture ('tourment') has been multiplied nine times ('thrice threefold'), which the poet wants to overcome or cross over ('to be corss'd'): "Of him, myself, and thee I am forsaken,—/A torment thrice threefold, thus to be cross'd."

The poet urges the Dark Lady to incarcerate his heart in the closet ('ward') of her ('thy') steel-framed breast. But at the same time he prays to her to let his poor or unworthy heart throw away ('bail') the heart of his friend, the Fair Youth: "Prison my heart in thy steel bosom's ward,/ But then my friend's heart let my poor heart bail". Whoever keeps the poet ('me') within the confine of his heart, will get his unworthy or unfortunate ('poor') heart as his security ('guard'). And if the Lady keeps the heart of the poet within her heart, she will not be able to be hard or unbearable ('hard') with the poet who will then reside within the confines ('jail') of her heart: "Whoe'er keeps me, let my heart be his guard:/Thou canst not then use rigour in my jail." But, in the concluding couplet, the poet controverts what he has just said. He says that, nevertheless, the Dark Lady will be rigorous to the poet ('And yet thou wilt'). To support his conviction, the poet says that he will then remain confined ('pent') in the bosom of the Lady, and therefore, he will be willy-nilly hers, and, further, whatever there is in the poet, will be possessed by the Dark Lady: "And yet thou wilt; for I being pent up in thee,/Perforce am thine, and all that is in me."

134

So, now I have confess'd that he is thine,
And I myself am mortgag'd to thy will,
My self I'll forfeit, so that other mine
Thou wilt restore to be my comfort still.
But thou wilt not, nor he will not be free;
For thou art covetous, and he is kind;
He learn'd but surety-like to write for me
Under that bond that him as fast doth bind.
The statute of thy beauty thou wilt take,
Thou usurer, that putt'st forth all to use,
And sue a friend came debtor for my sake;
So him I lose through my unkind abuse.
  Him have I lost; thou hast both him and me:
  He pays the whole, and yet am I not free.

The octave of this sonnet has an alternative punctuation which is as follows (Ingram, 309):

So, now I have confess'd that he is thine;
And I myself mortgag'd to thy will:
My self I'll forfeit, so that other mine
Thou wilt restore to be my comfort still.

But thou wilt not; nor he will not be free.
For thou art covetous, and he is kind,—
He learn'd but surety-like to write for me
Under that bond that him as fast doth bind. 8

This sonnet is full of legal terms, such as 'mortgag'd', 'forfeit', 'will', 'surety-like', 'statute' 'debtor', etc. From the very first line of this sonnet, it is clear that this sonnet is linked with the immediately preceding one. The poet says that he has ownd ('confess'd') that the Fair Youth ('he') belongs to the Dark Lady ('thine'). And, at the same time, the poet is also in possession (mortgag'd') of the Lady ('to thy will'): "So, now I have confess'd that he is thine,/And I myself am mortgag'd to thy will,". He says that he will pay himself as a penalty ('forfeit') to the Lady. He will do so so that his friend, the Fair Youth ('other mine') may be restored to the Lady, and that will be his comfort for ever ('still'), or even if the youth belongs to the Lady, still that will be the comfort of the poet: "My self I'll forfeit, so that other mine/Thou wilt restore to be my comfort still."

Nevertheless, the poet says, the Dark Lady will not be independent of her lovers, or will not be able to get rid of their clutches ('thou wilt not'). In the same way, the Fair Youth ('he') will also not be able to release himself from her clutch. Because, the poet says, the Lady is covetous, and the Fair Youth ('he') is sympathetic, or very prompt to respond to amorous invitations ('kind'): "But thou wilt not, nor he will not be free;/For thou art covetous, and he is kind". Kerrigan explained the next two lines thus: "The young man was persuaded to underwrite the *bond* which committed the poet to the lady, but it turned out that the *bond* to which he set his pen committed him as well as the poet. The suggestion (supported by line 11) is that the young man, sent to recommend the poet's love to the lady, fell in love with the lady on his own account." (Kerrigan, 364): "He learn'd but surety-like to write for me/Under that bond that him as fast doth bind."

The attractive beauty of the Dark Lady will legally ('statute') take due forfeiture stipulated by the bond which the youth underwrote and which made the poet the legal property of the Lady: "The statute of thy beauty thou wilt take." Kerrigan explained this line thus: "You will exact the full forfeiture stipulated by the bond, to which seizure, indeed, your beauty entitles you. The poet and the friend both stand in the lady's power" (Kerrigan, 364). Therefore, the poet calls the Lady usurer. She also lends out everything ('putt'st forth') on interest (or profit): "Thou usurer, that putt'st forth all to use." Ingram and Redpath wrote about the expression 'that putt'st forth all to use': "she [the Dark Lady] will give nothing except for interest. There is also an evident amatory innuendo in 'use' " (Ingram, 309). And now the Fair Youth ('a friend') has become a debtor to the Dark Lady, for the sake of the poet. For this reason ('So'), the poet has to lose, or part with, the Fair Youth, for the poet's misuse of his friend, the Fair Youth: "And sue a friend came debtor for my sake;/So him I lose through my unkind abuse." And consequently, the poet has lost the Fair Youth ('Him'), and the Dark Lady has got both the poet and the Fair Youth ('him'). The Fair Youth is now giving the Lady whatever is due to her, fully ('He pays the whole'), but nevertheless, the poet himself cannot get release from her clutch: "Him have I lost; thou hast both him and me:/He pays the whole, and yet am I not free."

135

Whoever hath her wish, thou hast thy *Will,*
And *Will* to boot, and *Will* in overplus:
More than enough am I that vex thee still,
To thy sweet will making addition thus.
Wilt thou whose will is large and spacious
Not vouchsafe to hide my will in thine?
Shall will in others seem right gracious,
And in my will no fair acceptance shine?
The sea all water, yet receives rain still,
And in abundance addeth to his store:
So thou being rich in *Will* add to thy *Will*
One will of mine to make thy large *Will* more.
Let 'No', unkind, no fair beseechers kill;
Think all but one, and me in that one *Will.*

This sonnet is appropriately called 'Will Sonnet', for there are as many as thirteen 'wills' in this poem. In it Shakespeare punned on the word 'Will', as Donne, later on, did on 'Donne', 'Anne' and 'Undone'. In the next sonnet also 'will' is profusely used: six times. And so the next sonnet may also be called, for convenience at least, 'Will Sonnet'. In this sonnet (Sonnet 135), the word 'will' is deliberately used in at least six senses. Kerrigan wrote about this: "Here and in the following poem Shakespeare quibbles compulsively on six senses of *will* (examples appended): (1) what is wanted (*thou hast thy Will* 135.1); (2) lust, carnal desire (*thou being rich in Will* 135.11); (3) shall (*Will will fulfil the treasure of thy love* 136.5); (4) penis (*hide my will* 135.6); (5) vagina (*thy sweet will* 135.4); (6) William (my name is Will 136.14)'' (Kerrigan, 365). In the Quarto edition of the Sonnets (1609), more than half of the 'wills' of this sonnet and of the next sonnet (Sonnets 135 and 136) were italicised From this fact, some scholars guess that the word suggests the authorship of William Shakespeare of this sonnet-sequence.

However, in this sonnet, the poet tells the Dark Lady that if other women have their individual desires ('wish'), then she has her William Shakespeare ('*Will*'). The poet means to say that as other women have their individual lovers, so the Dark Lady has William Shakespeare as her lover. Further, the Lady has her William Shakespeare ('*Will*') in addition to ('to boot') other persons, and so she has William Shakespeare as a surplus ('overplus'): ''Whoever hath her wish, thou hast thy *Will*,/ And Will to boot, and *Will* in overplus''. And because the poet (William Shakespeare) is in excess ('More than enough'), so he (the poet) annoys, agitates (may be with sexual undertows) ('vex') the Lady constantly ('still'). And thus the poet brings grist to the (sexual) mill of the Lady ('will') in addition to other persons' titillation (sexual): ''More than enough am I that vex thee still,/To thy sweet will making addition thus.'' The poet asks the Lady, whose amorous licentiousness is too much ('whose will is large and spacious'), if once she will swear or guarantee ('vouchsafe') that she will grant or admit ('hide') the poet's will or desire (or pudendum) in her will or desire (or cunt): ''Wilt thou whose will is large and spacious/Not once vouchsafe to hide my will in thine?'' Will the Lady deem only other persons' will ('will in others') to be absolutely kind and favourable ('gracious'), and will she not, therefore, accept the will (pudendum) of the poet as beautiful and shining?: ''Shall will in others seem right gracious,/And in my will no fair acceptance shine?''

The poet, next, persuades the Lady to grant his amorous appeal, in addition to other persons' appeals that have already been granted by her. He asks her to be more magnanimous, and so present before her the exmaple of the sea. He says that the sea is full of water, and yet, it receives rain-water: the sea which is already in abundance of water, adds to its store of water the rain-water: ''The sea, all water, yet receives rain still,/And in abundance addeth to his store''. Lines 9-10 may be compared and contrasted with lines 96-100 at *Twelfth Night*, II, iv, where Duke says about women's love and about his love:

> Alas, their love may be call'd appetite —
> No motion of the liver, but the palate —

That suffers surfeit, cloyment, and revolt;
But mine is all as hungry as the sea,
And can digest as much.

The poet thus persuades the Dark Lady to become more rich by accepting himself (William Shakespeare) (*'Will')* in her amorous circle of favourites, and, in addition to himself or his love ('*Will*') his will (may be his pudendum), so that her already great ('large') William Shakespeare ('*Will*') may become greater ('more'): "So thou being rich in *Will* add to thy *Will*/One will of mine to make thy large *Will* more." Lastly, the poet once again appeals to the Lady not to say 'No' — 'No' which is an unkind word — to honest implorers' ('beseechers') plea, and thus frustrate ('kill') them (implorers like the poet himself): "Let, 'No', unkind, no fair beseechers kill;". He also appeals to her to take into account all her lovers as a whole, or as a composite lover ('Think all but one'), and to include himself in that composite lover ('me in that') — composite lover which will actually amount simply to the single person, William Shakespeare (*'Will'):* "Think all but one, and me in that one *Will.*" Both Ingram and Redpath, and Kerrigan said that the last word of this sonnet, '*Will*', includes all the available sense of the word as are in this sonnet.

136

If thy soul check thee that I come so near,
Swear to thy blind soul that I was thy *Will,*
And will, thy soul knows, is admitted there;
Thus far for love my love-suit, sweet, fulfil.
Will will fulfil the treasure of thy love,—
Ay, fill it with wills, and my will one.
In things of great receipt with ease we prove
Among a number one is reckon'd none:
Then in the number let me pass untold,
Though in thy store's account I one must be;
For nothing hold me, so it please thee hold
That no-thing me a some-thing, sweet, to thee,
    Make but my name thy love, and love that still,—
    And then thou lov'st me, for my name is *Will.*

As told earlier, this sonnet also may be called a 'Will Sonnet'. Here the poet asks the Dark Lady to avouch ('Swear') to her ignorant or heedless ('blind') soul that the poet was none else than her favourite William Shakespeare ('*Will*'). The poet asks her to swear thus if her soul constrains her from responding to the approach of the poet, whenever he becomes forthright, or comes (or goes) near her body ('come so near'): "If thy soul check thee I come so near,/Swear to thy blind soul that I was thy *Will,*". The soul of the Lady knows that there is a 'will' in it ('admitted there') for the acceptance of the poet (in her bed). And so far, the Dark Lady, who is the sweet beloved ('my love-suit, sweet') fulfils the desire of the poet, for love of him: "And will, thy soul knows, is admitted there;/Thus far for love my love-suit, sweet, fulfil." The poet says that he himself, or William Shakespeare, ('Will') wilfully plenish the treasure of her love. He asks her to fill her treasure of love fully with the wills or amorous approaches of all persons ('fill it full with wills'), but he requests her to include his own will also: "*Will* will fulfil the treasure of thy love,—/Ay, fill it full with wills, and my will one." Line 6 may be compared with line 14 of the previous sonnet: "think all but one, and me in that one *Will.*" If the receipt or collection is of a great number of things ('things of great receipt'), then we can easily prove that among a great number of things ('Among a number'), if one extra thing is added, it means that, as if, nothing is added ('one is reckon'd none'): "In things of great receipt with ease we prove/Among a number one is reckon'd none:". The poet means to say that the Lady has a great number of paramours, and so, if he himself is included among them, then it will make no difference in any way. The expression 'one is reckon'd none' may be compared with the expression 'One is no number' at Marlowe's *Hero and Leander,* Sestiad I, line 255.

As one extra thing makes no difference in a number of things, so the poet requests the Dark Lady to keep him ('let me pass') as one paramour among a number of her paramours ('in the number'), and he requests her to keep him thus unnoticed or secretly ('untold'). But, all the same, he demands that he must remain in the inventory or account or list of her lovers, as one more lover or paramour: "Then in the number let me pass untold,/Though in thy store's account I one must be;". The poet further requests the Dark Lady not to think, or take, ('hold') him as worthless ('nothing'). And so he also requests her to take ('hold') that supposedly worthless ('no-thing') as something of worth ('some-thing'), and thus take him to herself (to her bosom): "For nothing hold me, so it please thee hold/That no-thing me a some-thing, sweet, to these,". Lastly, the poet prays to the Lady to make his name or, rather, himself, her beloved; and to love that name, or rather, himself, always ('still'). And only then will the poet think that the Lady actually loves him, because his name is *Will* or William Shakespeare: "Make but my name thy love, and love that still,—/And then thou lov'st me, for my name is *Will.*"

Kerrigan wrote about the expression 'my name is Will' (line 14): "And at the very point where the poetry seems autobiographically explicit, we are closest to the commonplace. Here is the fifty-first riddle in *The Book of Merry Riddles* (1629):

My lover's will
I am content for to fulfil;
Within this rhyme his name is framed;
Tell me then how he is named?

Solution: His name is William; for in the first line is *will*, and in the beginning of the second line is *I am*, and then put them together, and it maketh *William*.... Certainly, the echo of 'will ... fulfil' in lines 4-6 of 136 suggests that Shakespeare knew the puzzle, while the popularity of the book — several times reprinted — supports the idea that he might have expected early readers to recognize at least the genre to which his self-revelation belonged" (Kerrigan, 368).

137

Thou blind fool, Love, what dost thou to mine eyes,
That they behold, and see not what they see?
They know what beauty is, see where it lies,
Yet what the best is take the worst to be.
If eyes corrupt by over-partial looks
Be anchor'd in the bay where all men ride,
Why of eyes' falsehood hast thou forged hooks;
Whereto the judgment of my heart is tied?
Why should my heart think that a several plot
Which my heart knows the wide world's common place?
Or mine eyes, seeing this, say this is not,
To put fair truth so foul a face?
In things right true my heart and eyes have err'd,
And to this false plague are they now transferr'd.

This sonnet may be compared with Sonnets 113 and 114. Here the poet addresses Love or the god of love, Cupid, as a blind fool, and demands of him to tell him (the poet) what he (the god of love) has done to his (the poet's) eyes, so that the eyes now only stare at ('behold') objects, but cannot recognise anything ('see not what they see'): "Thou blind fool, Love, what dost thou to mine eyes,/That they behold, and see not what they see?" No doubt, his eyes know what real beauty is, and where the real beauty exists, nevertheless ('Yet'), they take, or think, the most beautiful thing ('best') to be the most ugly thing ('worst'):

"They know what beauty is, see where it lies,/ Yet what the best is take the worst to be." The poet asks Love, or Cupid, if its, or his, eyes are somehow corrupted (so that they cannot see what real beauty is) for incorrect observation ('over-partial looks'), or corrupted for seeing, or being fixed on ('Be anchor'd'), only the sexual organ ('bay') where all men reside ('ride'): "If eyes corrupt by over-partial looks/Be anchor'd in the bay where all men ride," Kerrigan wrote about the expression 'anchor'd in the bay where all men ride': "A standard image (compare *Cymbeline* V.5. 393, where Posthumus 'anchors upon Imogen', or *Antony and Cleopatra* I.5. 31-33, where Cleopatra claims that 'great Pompey/Would stand and make his eyes grow in my brow;/There would he anchor his aspect') turned to bawdy uses" (Kerrigan, 368). The poet asks the god of love, Cupid, why he has pierced ('forged') hook into the deceptiveness of his eyes, — hook on which his judgment depends: "Why of eyes' falsehood hast thou forged hooks/Whereto the judgment of my heart is tied?" The poet means to say that the god of love has taken possession of the deceptiveness of his (the poet's) eyes for his (the god's) own amorous objective, such that now the poet cannot judge independently.

The poet, again, questions the god of love why the patch of private land ('a several plot') of which his heart knows that it (the plot of land) belongs to it (the heart) has now become a common or public place for the people of the whole world ('wide world's common place'): "Why should my heart think that a several plot/Which my heart knows the wide world's common place?" Lines 9-10 may be compared with lines 222-23 at *Love's Labour's Lost,* II, i, where Katherine tells Boyet: "Not so, gentle beast;/My lips are no common, though several they be." The poet further asks why his eyes, even knowing ('seeing') all this to be so, say that all this is not so ('say this is not'). And the eyes deny all this to make the appearance good, though under that good appearance, the reality is foul or ugly ('upon so foul a face'): "Or mine eyes, seeing this, say this is not,/To put fair truth upon so foul a face?" The poet means to say that though his eyes well know that the Dark Lady is foul, yet they see her to be wearing an honest and attractive mien; and that this is due to the fact that the god of love has corrupted his eyes. To conclude, the poet says that his heart and his eyes have committed error in recognising true and faithful ('right true') things; and, consequently, now the heart and the eyes have been shifted ('transferr'd') to this dishonest and abject thing ('this false plague') (which is the Dark Lady): "In things right true my heart and eyes have err'd,/And to this false plague are they now transferr'd.'' Kerrigan wrote about the concluding couplet: ''This is the poet's answer to his accumulated questions, though it registers as a cry of despair. His *heart* and *eyes* have made mistakes *In* judging *things right true* ('chaste cunts' and 'honest women' as well as 'true acts and statements'), and love has enforced a deranged fixation on the Dark Lady as a punishment (*to the false plague....now transferred* meaning both 'transformed into this self-deceiving disease, this affliction of misinterpretation' and 'shifted to this *untrue* woman, this fever of mine')'' (Kerrigan, 369).

138

When my love swears that she is made of truth
I do believe her, though I know she lies,
That she might think me some untutor'd youth
Unlearned in the world's false subtleties.
Thus vainly thinking that she thinks me young,
Although she knows my days are past the best,
Simply I credit her false-speaking tongue:
On both sides thus is simple truth suppress'd.
But wherefore says she not she is unjust?
And wherefore say not I that I am old?
Oh, love's best habit is in seeming trust,
And age in love loves not to have years told.
  Therefore I lie with her, and she with me,
  And in our faults by lies we flatter'd be.

This sonnet and sonnet 144 were first printed by William Jaggard in *The Passionate Pilgrim,* in 1599, before these two sonnets appeared in the Quarto edition of Shakespeare's complete sonnet-sequence. In this sonnet, Shakespeare confesses that the love between himself and the Dark Lady is false and seeming. He says that when his lady-love swears that she is quite honest ('is made of truth'), then he believes (or, rather, he shows that he believes) her to be honest, although he knows that she is telling lies: ''When my love swears that she is made of truth/I do believe her, though I know she lies,''. These two lines may be compared with poem no. 7 of *The Passionate Pilgrim:* ''Her lips to mine how often hath she joined,/Between each kiss her oaths of true love swearing!'...Yet, in the midst of all her pure protestings,/Her faith, her oaths, her tears, and all, were jestings.'' But why does the poet do so: why, in spite of knowing her falsehood, does he believe her? The poet says that he does so so that the Lady might think him to be an uncouth ('untutor'd') young man (of very young age), and so that she might take him to be a youth who is not schooled ('Unlearned') in the subtle falsities of the world (and so that she might therefore love him dearly): ''That she might think me some untutor'd youth/Unlearned in the world's false subtleties.'' But though the poet seems to believe willingly the words of the Lady, to prove before her that he is a young man with unsophisticated mind, he does so fruitlessly. Because, the poet says, he is vainly thinking that she is taking him for a young man, because ('Although') the Lady knows that the best days of the poet are gone, *i.e.* the young days to the poet are past ('my days or past the best'): ''Thus, vainly thinking that she thinks me young,/Although she knows my days are past the best,''.

But the poet is not dejected thereby, because, he says, he is deliberately or unconditionally ('Simply') believing ('credit') what the Lady swears about, or says ('credit her false-speaking tongue'). So the simple matter stands thus: both the Lady and the poet are telling lies, by suppressing the truth: ''Simply I credit her false-speaking tongue:/On both sides thus is simple truth suppress'd.'' But the poet questions his own self why the Lady does not admit ('say') that she is false ('unjust'), and likewise, he asks himself why he does not tell her that he is not young but old: ''But wherefore says she not she is unjust?/And wherefore say not I that I am old?'' He answers his own questions with a truism. He dejectedly says that in love lovers in most cases ('best habit') do have superficial faith or seeming faith in each other, and that lovers do not like ('love not') to speak about their actual age (that is, they like to hide their actual age): ''Oh, love's best habit is in seeming trust,/And age in love loves not to have years told.'' And, it is for this reason that the poet tells lies to the Lady, as she does to him. Thus both of them are at faults, or are in falsehood, because both of them tell lies. However, thereby (by their telling lies to each other), they both are exulted or appreciated excessively ('flatter'd be'): ''Therefore I lie with her, and she with me,/And in our faults by lies we flatter'd be.'' The poet means to say that when he falsely tells the Lady that he is young, the Lady adulates him more, and so he is exulted or flattered. In the same way, when the Lady suppresses her old age, the poet becomes gladdened and flatters her more and more. In this way, both of them are mutually flattered.

139

Oh call not me to justify the wrong
That thy unkindness lays upon my heart!
Wound me not with thine eye but with thy tongue;

Use power with power and slay me not by art:
Tell me thou lov'st elsewhere; but in my sight,
Dear heart, forbear to glance thine eye aside —
What need'st thou wound with cunning, when thy might
Is more than my o'erpress'd defence can bide?
Let me excuse thee: 'Ah, my love well knows
Her pretty looks have been mine enemies;
And therefore from my face she turns my foes,
That they elsewhere might dart their injuries'.
Yet do not so; but since I am near slain,
Kill me outright with looks, and rid my pain.

Kerrigan wrote about this sonnet: ''Initially resisting convention — to *justify* a mistress' *wrong* was standard sonneteering strategy — the poet succumbs to its pressure in the sestet (with a lapse into the appropriate idiom), only to conclude with an image which, despite its commonplace origins, is so violent that it carries a more than conventional weight'' (Kerrigan, 370). However, the poet tells the Dark Lady not to ask him, or not to request him, to excuse ('justify') the wrongs done to him (by her) ('upon my heart') by being unkind to him : ''Oh call not me to justify the wrong/That thy unkindness lays upon my heart !'' The poet requests her not to hurt him ('Wound me') by turning away from him and thereby not noticing him ('with thine eye'). But, the poet says, if she must wound him, she may vituperate him to her satisfaction ('but with thy tongue'). She may use all her power ('power with power') bluntly or directly or naively; but he forbids her not to hurt ('slay') him with cunning ('art') : ''Wound me not with thine eye but with thy tongue;/ Use power with power and slay me not by art :''. She may even tell him that she loves other person or persons ('thou lov'st elsewhere'), but the poet requests her, whenever she will be near him ('in my sight'), to suffer the pain ('forbear') of retractng her look, or veering her look, from that person, or those persons ('to glance thine eye aside') : ''Tell me thou lov'st elsehwere; but in my sight,/Dear heart, forbear to glance thine eye aside—''. The poet cannot find any reason, or need ('What need'st thou'), for her wounding him craftily ('with cunning'). Because, the poet says, she has enough might to inflict more pain on him than his already oppressed defence can resist ('o'erpress'd defence can bide') : ''What need'st thou wound with cunning, when thy might/Is more than my o'erpress'd defence can bide?''

In the sestet, the poet justifies the wrongs done to him by the Lady, though in the very first line of this poem he refused to do so. He tells her that he will excuse the harm done him by the Lady : "Let me excuse thee". And he excuses her by saying that the Lady ('my love') knows well that her beautiful face, or the beauty of her whole body ('pretty looks') is the enemy of the poet. By calling her beauty his enemy, the poet means to say that it is for that beautiful face, or the beauty of her whole body, that he fell in love with her, and consequently, underwent unbearable mental tortures because she proved to be unfaithful to him. Nevertheless, the Lady is doing a good service to the poet by turning her face away, for, by turning her face away from the poet, she is actually turning his enemies out. And thus the poet is relieved of his enemies who now may harm ('dart their injuries') other persons ('elsewhere'), instead of the poet : "Ah, my love well knows/Her pretty looks have been mine enemies;/And therefore from face she turns my foes,/That they elsewhere might dart their injuries'." But in the concluding couplet, the poet makes a *volte face*. He prays to her not to do so : not to turn her face, or looks, away from him. He says he is almost killed by the wrongs (dishonesties) done to him by her ('I am near slain'), and he is suffering pain for being half-killed. Therefore, he requests her to jugulate him completely and immediately ('outright') with her looks, or with her fierce eyes — eyes that look like those of Medusa —, and thereby put an end to his suffering ('rid my pain') : "Yet do not so; but since I am near slain,/Kill me outright with looks, and rid my pain." Kerrigan wrote about line 14 : "Though the likely source for this is *Astrophil and Stella* 48, 'Soul's joy, bend not those morning stars from me' (with its final line 'A kind of grace it is to slay with speed'), it evokes a host of Elizabethan love poems in which the mistress' eye is like Medusa's or the basilisk's" (Kerrigan, 371). The particular lines in *Astrophil and Stella* that Kerrigan referred to here are lines 13 and 14 of the poem : "Dear killer, spare not thy cruel shot;/A kind of grace it is to slay with speed."

140

By wise as thou art cruel : do not press
My tonuge-tied patience with too much disdain;
Lest sorrow lend me words, and words express
The manner of my pity-wanting pain.
If I might teach thee wit, better it were,
Though not to love, yet, love, to tell me so;—
As testy sick men, when their deaths be near,
No news but health from their physicians know.
For if I should despair, I should grow mad,

And in my madness might speak ill of thee.
Now this ill-wresting world is grown so bad
Mad slanderers by mad ears believed be :
  That I may not be so, nor thou belied,
  Bear thine eyes straight though thy proud heart go wide.

The poet asks the Dark Lady to be as wise as she is cruel, or asks her to qualify her cruelty with her wisdom. He asks her not to tax ('press') his unprotesting ('tongue-tied') forbearance ('patience') with too much hatred ('disdain'): "Be wise as thou art cruel: do not press/My tongue-tied patience with too much disdain;". The poet tells her all this, because, otherwise, his over-much of sorrow may burst out into words (or cries), and those words may tell, or specify the kind ('manner'), of his pain — pain that lacks in pity from anyone: "Lest sorrow lend me words and words express/The manner of my pity-wanting pain." Line 3 may make one recall lines 209-210 of *Macbeth*, Iv, iii; "The grief that does not speak/Whispers the o'er-fraught heart and bids it break." The poet tells the Lady that it would be better if he could instruct her in the lesson of wisdom ('wit'). And the wisdom to be taught is that she should at least tell him that she loves him ('love, to tell me so'), though she may not love him: "If I might teach thee wit, better it were,/Though not to love, yet, love, to tell me so; —".

The poet compares his condition with that of a fretful or fitful ('testy') sick man who is on the verge of death. Such people will not hear anything but only the news that their condition is good ('healthy'), from their physicians: "As testy sick men, when their deaths be near,/No news but health from their physicians know." He says this because ('For') if he knows that he has no hope of recovery, *i.e.* if he knows that he will never get back the love of the Dark Lady ('if I should despair'), he may grow mad, and in his mental derangement ('madness'), he may perchance speak ill of her: "For if I should despair, I should grow mad,/And in my madness might speak ill of thee." And, the poet says, at the present time, the world is turning everything to badness ('ill-wresting world'), so that the world has grown very ('so') bad. And, as a result, those, who are maliciously defaming others ('slanderers') like madcaps, may be believed by some other madcaps to be speaking the truth: "Now this ill-wresting world is grown so bad/Mad slanderers by mad ears believed be:". But the poet wants neither to be a mad slanderer nor a mad believer (one who believes without any rhyme or reason whatsoever): "That I may not be so". He also wishes that the Lady be not slandered ('belied'): "nor thou belied,". Therefore, he asks the Lady to be aiming at the truth straight ('Bear thine eyes straight'), although her heart, which is proud of her beauty ('thy proud heart'), may be false in offering love to diverse persons ('go wide'): ''Bear thine eyes straight though thy proud heart go wide.'' Ingram and Redpath wrote about the last line: ''It seems likely that there is an image from archery here. The difficulty is to see its exact working'' (Ingram, 322).

141

In faith, I do not love thee with mine eyes,
For they in thee a thousand errors note;
But 'tis my heart that loves what they despise,
Who in despite of view is pleas'd to dote:
Nor are mine ears with thy tongue's tune delighted,
Nor tender feeling to base touches prone;
Nor taste nor smell desire to be invited
To any sensual feast with thee alone.
But my five wits nor my five senses can
Dissuade one foolish heart from serving thee,
Who leaves unsway'd the likeness of a man,
Thy proud heart's slave and vassal wretch to be:
  Only my plague thus far I count my gain,
  That she that makes me sim awards me pain.

The poet frankly tells the Dark Lady that he does not observe her with his eyes (he does not observe her beautiful physical features) and then loves her, being attracted by her physical beauty; because, in that case, he would find ('note') a thousand faults in her features, or would find a thousand instances of her dishonesties (if he would observe her behaviour with his eyes): ''In faith, I do not love thee with mine eyes,/ For they in thee a thousand errors note;''. Line 1 may be compared with the song at *The Merchant of Venice,* III, ii, 63-69:

Tell me where is fancy bred,
Or in the heart or in the head,
How begot, how nourish'd?
  Reply, reply.
It is engend'red in the eyes,
With gazing fed; and fancy dies
In the cradle where it lies.

The poet says that it is rather his heart that loves the Lady whom his eyes ('they') hate or look down upon. And, that heart ('Who'), in spite of the negative attitude of the eyes to the Lady ('in despite of view'), gladly dotes on the Lady: ''But, 'tis my heart that loves what they desptie,/Who in despite of view is pleas'd to dote:''. Save his heart, all the sense organs of the poet is averse to the Lady. The poet says that his ears are not delighted at the conversation of the Lady ('thy tongue's tune'), and his delicate touch-sensing organ, or his skin, is not inclined ('prone') to touch the Lady, because it (the skin) thinks that she is a base object: ''Nor are mine ears with thy tongue's tune delighted,/ Nor tender feeling to base touches prone;''. Again, his tongue ('taste') and nose ('smell') are also not interested in enjoying ('feast') their appropriate sensations severally ('alone'), on the body of the Lady: ''Nor taste nor smell desire to be invited/To any sensual feast with thee alone.'' Line 8 may be compared with lines 445-450 of *Venus and Adonis*:

'But, O, what banquet wert thou to the taste,
Being nurse and feeder of the other four!
Would they not wish the feast might ever last,
And bid Suspicion double-lock the door,
  Lest Jealousy, that sour unwelcome guest,
  Should by his stealing in disturb the feast?

LIne 8 may also be compared with lines 309-15 at *Love's Labour's Lost,* IV, iii :

It adds a precious seeing to the eye:
A lover's eyes will gaze an eagle blind.
A lover's ear will hear the lowest sound
When the suspicious head of theft is stopped.
Love's feeling is more soft and sensible
Than are the tender horns of cockled snails.
Love'st tongue proves dainty Bacchus gross in taste...

In spite of the indifference of his five sense organs, the heart of the poet is still interested in the Dark Lady. The poet says that his five sense organs ('wits') and his five kind of sensations have been unable to dissuade his native, simple, and easily gullible heart from serving or loving the Dark Lady: ''But my five wits nor my five senses can/ Dissuade one foolish heart from serving thee,''. Kerrigan wrote about line 9: ''A standard division of the intellectual powers — 'four of his five wits went halting off', *Much Ado About Nothing* I. 1.61, 'Bless thy five wits', *King Lear* III.4.55 — constructed by analogy with the *five senses* (...) and usually reckoned thus: common wit, imagination, fantasy, estimation, memory'' (Kerrigan, 373). The heart ('Who') is not controlled or governed by anything ('unsway'd'). And this heart, when it has fallen in love with the Lady, put off its manly quality ('likeness of a man'), like the husk of a grain, and then becomes a slave of the proud heart of the Dark Lady — becomes a wretched vassal of her heart: "Who leaves unsway'd the likeness of a man,/Thy proud heart's slave and vassal wretch to be:". In spite of all this, the poet thinks that he is at the vantage point. He says that the contention or disagreement between his senses and his heart is certainly disturbing ('plague'); but, nevertheless, he counts this disturbance as his benefit ('gain'). Because, though the Lady makes the poet commit moral wrongs or faults ('sin'), yet she, thereby, gives him pain — pain that the poet happily enjoys: "Only my plague thus far I count my gain,/That she that makes me sin awards me pain." Ingram and Redpath wrote about lines 13 and 14: "It seems probable that these lines are not usually well understood. It might appear, on the surface, that there could be little advantage in the seductress making the poet suffer for his 'sin' with her. But Samuel Butler, alone among commentators reveal real point in the lines. He paraphrases: 'I shall suffer less for my sin hereafter, for I get some of the punishment coincidently with the offence' " (Ingram, 324-25).

142

Love is my sin, and thy dear virtue hate —
Hate of my sin, grounded on sinful loving:
Oh, but with mine compare thou thine own state
And thou shalt find it merits not reproving;
Or if it do, not from those lips of thine,
That have profan'd their scarlet ornaments
And seal'd false bonds of love as oft as mine —
Robb'd others' beds' revenues of their rents.
Be it lawful I love thee as thou lov'st those
Whom thine eyes woo as mine importune thee:
Root pity in thy heart, that when it grows
Thy pity may deserve to pitied be.
If thou dost seek to have what thou dost hide,
By self-example mayst thou be denied!

According to Dover Wilson, this sonnet, in a manner, explains Sonnet 141, "since it clearly paints the situation underlying both sonnets" (Wilson, 259). The poet's sin is due to his loving the Dark Lady; and the precious virtue of the Dark Lady is her hate — hate for the poet's sin which is, again, due to his loving her immorally ('sinful'): "Love is my sin, and thy dear virtue hate—./ Hate of my sin, grounded on sinful loving:". Line 1 is chiastic, *i.e.* the two parts of the line, on either side of the caesura, are parallels to each other by contarst: 'Love is my sin' and 'thy dear virtue hate'. The poet has sinned; nevertheless, he appeals to her not to reprimand him ('merits not reproving'). He tells her that if she compares her condition with that of his, then she will find that he does not deserve reprobation from her: "Oh, but with mine compare thou thine own state/And thou shalt find it merits not reproving;". And, yet, if the poet really deserves reprobation ('if it do'), the poet appeals to her not to vituperate him with those lips of her, that have desanctified ('profan'd') their (beautiful) red-brown colour ('ornaments'), and like his own lips ('as mine'), have impressed ('seal'd') false indentures ('bonds') of love, often: "Or if it do, not from those lips of thine,/That have profan'd their scarlet ornaments/And seal'd false bonds of love as oft as mine —". The scarlet-coloured lips of the Lady were once sacred, but she has made indentures of false love with her lips, and thus have desanctified those lips. She has done so as frequently as the poet himself has done so. Lines 5-7 may be compared with lines 511-12 of *Venus and Adonis*: "'Pure lips, sweet seals in my soft lips imprinted,/What bargains may I make, still to be sealing?" Again, lines 6-7 may be compared with line 7 of *The Two Gentlemen of Verona,* II, ii: "seal the bargain with a holy kiss"; and with lines 114-15 of *Romeo and Juliet,* V, iii: "seal with a righteous kiss/A dateless bargain". However, those lips of the Lady thus have usurped ('Robb'd') the benefit or pleasure (of love) of other persons ('others' beds' revenues of their rents'): "Robb'd others' beds' revenues of their rents." The poet here clearly innuendoes to the promiscuousness of the Dark Lady.

The poet wishes that his love for her be deemed moral ('lawful'), (because he loves her). He says that he loves her as much as she loves those persons whom she wooes with her eyes, as the poet's eyes insistently wooes her: "Be it lawful I love thee as thou lov'st those/Whom thine eyes woo as mine importune thee:". The poet appeals to her to plant ('Root') pity in her heart, *i.e.* to fill her heart with pity, so that when her heart is filled up with pity ('when it grows'), it will itself deserve to be pitied: "Root pity in thy heart, that when it grows/Thy pity may deserve to pittied be." Kerrigan wrote about the word 'pity': "the pité of the troubadours and their descendants; emotional grace and sexaul favour, not just sympathy" (Kerrigan, 374). In line 12, the poet, perhaps, means to say that if the Lady fills her heart fully with pity for the poet, then people will pity her for her loving as worthless or destitute a person as the poet himself. In the concluding couplet, the poet tells the Lady that if she inwardly wants to have pity ('to have what') that she outwardly wants to hide, then, following her example ('By self-example'), people also may hide their pity, and so she may be denied pity: "If thou dost seek to have what thou dost hide,/ By self-example mayst thou be denied!"

143

Lo, as a careful housewife runs to catch
One of her feather'd creatures broke away,
Sets down her babe and makes all swift dispatch
In pursuit of the thing she would have stay:
Whilst her neglected child holds her in chase,
Cries to catch her whose busy care is bent
To follow that which flies before her face,
Not prizing her poor infant's discontent:
So run'st thou after that which flies from thee,
Whislt I thy babe chase afar behind;—
But if thou catch thy hope, turn back to me
And play the mother's part, — kiss me, be kind:
So will I pray that thou mayst have thy *Will,*
If thou turn back and my loud crying still.

This sonnet may also be called a 'Will Sonnet' (see line 13). This is a peculiar sonnet in that in it the poet compares himself with a baby and the Dark Lady with its mother. From this we may presume that Shakespeare's relation with the Dark Lady was a complicated one: the relation was not as simple as that between two profligate lovers, but, may be, like that between a baby and its mother. However, in this sonnet, the poet produces three parallels: (1) the Dark Lady and a housewife; (2) other people that the Lady loves and the 'feather'd creatures'; and (3) the poet and a baby. He tells the Lady that she is running after other persons (for love), as a housewife runs to catch fowls, or one of her fowls ('feather'd creatures') that have come out of their cage, very carefully: "Lo, as a housewife runs to catch/One of her feather'd creatures broke away," Kerrigan wrote about the expression 'One of her feather'd cratures': "The poet's rival is charged, obliquely, with feathered foppery. He resembles that 'plume of feathers' Don Armado (*Love's Labour's Lost* IV.1.95) and Ostricke (compare Ostrich) of the second Quarto of *Hamlet,* the absurd courtier with the fashionable hat. Feathered headgear was modish in the 1590s and 1600s" (Kerrigan, 374). The housewife sets down her baby from her lap and swiftly runs ('makes all swift dispatch') after that thing (*i.e.*, the Lady's lovers) (pursuit') which she would like to track down and keep with her ('would have stay'): "Sets down her babe and makes all swift dispatch/ In pursuit of the thing she would have stay:". When the housewife begins her chasing the fowl, after neglectfully putting her baby down, the baby holds her back (or her clothes) in an effort of constraining her chasing. The baby cries aloud so as to restrain her ('catch her') who is the while carefully pursuing to catch hold of the fowl that is flying away even in front of her ('flies before her face'). But in spite of all this, the housewife runs away, not caring ('Not prizing') the wretched baby's pains ('discontents'): "Whilst her neglected child holds her chase,/Cries to catch her whose care is bent/To follow that which flies before her face,/ Not prizing her poor infant's discontent:".

The poet tells the Lady that, in the same way, she is running after those 'feather'd creatures', or after her foppish lovers, who are actually ('flies') away from her. And during that while when she runs after her foppish lovers, the poet, who deems himself to be her baby ('Whilst I thy babe'), runs after her to catch her, but cannot overtake her, and remains far behind her ('afar behind'): "So run'st thou after that which flies from thee,/Whilst I thy babe chase thee afar behind;—". But if the Dark Lady has already caught or possessed her paramour like a fowl ('catch thy hope'), then the poet will ask her to look back again at him, take him in her lap like a mother ('play the mother's part'), and kiss him and be kind to him: "But if thou catch thy hope, turn back to me/And play the mother's part,— kiss me, be kind:". If the Lady does accordingly ('So'), *i.e.* if she comes back to him while he is crying loudly (in pain), then ('So'), the poet will pray that she may fulfil her wish, or will ('thou mayst have thy *Will*'), or she may possess himself (William Shakespeare) (*'Will')*: "So will I pray that thou mayst have thy *Will,*/If thou turn back and my loud crying still." Ingram and Redpath commented on lines 13-14: "Three persons are involved in the sonnet, and the poet is willing that the woman should have her other love ('the feather'd creatures') provided she will give him (the 'neglected child') satisfaction too" (Ingram, 328).

144

Two loves I have, of comfort and despair,
Which like two spirits do suggest me still:
The better angel is a man right fair,
The worser spirit a woman colour'd ill.
To win me soon to hell, my female evil
Tempteth my better angel from my side,
And would corrupt my saint to be a devil,

Wooing his purity with her foul pride.
And whether that my angel be turn'd fiend
Suspect I may, yet not directly tell;
But being both from me, both to each friend,
I guess one angel in another's hell:
  Yet this shall I ne'er know, but live in doubt
  Till my bad angel fire my good one out.

We may recall here what we said earlier that Sonnets 138 and 144 were printed by William Jaggard in *The Passionate Pilgrim* in 1599. Here the poet almost clearly speaks about his association with the Fair Youth and the Dark Lady, and about the tangle of tensions resulting therefrom. It may be noted here that this poem is not addressed to anyone (like all other sonnets), but it is, rather, a monologue. The poet says that he has two beloveds ('loves'), one of whom brings comfort or happiness to him, and the other despair or sorrow. These two beloveds always ('still') tempt or control ('suggest') the poet like two presiding angels or ghosts ('spirits'): "Two loves I have, of comfort and despair,/ Which like two spirits do suggest me still:". One of these spirits is good and the other is bad. The better spirit is like an angel, and it is beautiful (*i.e.* the Fair Youth); and the worse spirit is a black-complexioned woman, or a brunette ('colour'd ill') (*i.e.* the Dark Lady): "The better angel is a man right fair,/The worser spirit a woman colour'd ill." The evil woman, *i.e.* the Dark Lady, tempts the good Fair Youth away from the poet, to lead him to destruction and misery ('hell'). The bad woman tempts ('Wooing') the pure or honest and good Fair Youth with her immoral physical fascination ('foul pride'), and thus corrupts the saintly youth to become a devil: "To win me soon too hell, my female evil/Tempteth my better angel from my side,/And would corrupt my saint to be a devil,/Wooing his purity with her foul pride." Line 8 may remind us of lines 7 and 8 of Sonnet 41: "And when a woman woos what woman's son/Will sourly leave her till she have prevail'd?"

But the poet is not sure if the angelic Fair Youth will yield to the temptation of the Dark Lady, and turn into a fiend or not: he is only apprehensive of it ('Suspect I may'), but cannot say this definitely ('not directly tell'): "And whether that my angel be turn'd fiend/Suspect I may, yet not directly tell;". He can say this much that both the Dark Lady and the Fair Youth are now estranged from himself ('being both from me'), and are friends to each other. And, therefore, the poet presumes ('guess') that the angelic Fair Youth ('one angel') is now in the hellish possession of the Dark Lady ('in another's hell'): "But being both from me, both to each friend,/I guess one angel in another's hell:''. Here the word 'hell' may mean 'the female sexual organ'. Line 12 may be compared with lines 124-129 at *King Lear,* IV, vi: ''Down from the waist they are centaurs,/Though women all above;/But to the girdle do the gods inherit,/Beneath is all the fiends';/There's hell, there's darkness, there is the sulpherous pit—/Burning, scalding, stench, consumption.''

But, in the concluding couplet, the poet says that he will never be certain about what he has just now said (that the youth is in the 'hell' of the Lady) ('Yet this shall I ne'er know'), and that the poet will continue to be in doubt (about the physical relationship of the two persons). The poet will remain in this condition of doubt until the Dark Lady ('bad angel') infects the Fair Youth ('good one') with venereal disease ('fire my good one out'), and destroys him (the youth): ''Yet this shall I ne'er know, but live in doubt/Till my bad angel fire my good one out.'' Ingram and Redpath wrote about the last line: ''Evidently a gross insult to the woman, though veiled under the innocent meaning of 'casting off'. The underlying sense is that the poet will not know whether the Friend [the Fair Youth] has slept with the woman [the Dark Lady], until he sees whether he [the Fair Youth] has contracted venereal disease ('Fire out' was common usage for 'infect with a venereal disease')'' (Ingram, 332).

145

Those lips that Love's own hand did make
Breath'd forth the sound that said 'I hate'
To me that languish'd for her sake:
But when she saw my woeful state,
Straight in her heart did mercy come
Chiding that tongue that ever sweet
Was us'd in giving gentle doom,
And taught it thus anew to greet:
'I hate' she alter'd with an end
That follow'd it as gentle day
Doth follow night, who like a fiend
From heaven to hell is flown away:
'I hate' from hate away she threw,
And sav'd my life, saying — 'Not you'.

Shakespeare's authorship of this sonnet, some commentators argue, is doubtful. However, Kerrigan made some important observations on this sonnet: ''That the sonnet uses *you* instead of the *thou* general in the Dark Lady series, and octosyllabics rather than pentameters (....), supports the notion that 145 is a piece of juvenalia flanked by mature writing. Was it included for sentimental reasons? Did it find its way into Shakespeare's manuscript by mistake? Was it inserted by a scribe, by Thorpe, or by someone at Eld's printing shop? More than any other sonnet, 145 casts doubt on the authority and order of Q. [Quarto edition]. Yet even here — it cannot be too strongly said — thematic links with what preceds and follows the poem in Q are evident: *fiend, heaven,* and *hell* in lines 11-12 help it blend into context'' (Kerrigan, 376). This sonnet is a trifling poem, no doubt, and this is another cause of doubting Shakespeare's authorship of this poem. The words 'hate away' in line 14, some commentators opine, may refer to the surname of 'Shakespeare's Stratford wife'.'' (Kerrigan, 376). This poem is not addressed to anybody.

However, the poet exults the beautiful lips of the Dark Lady. He says that those lips were made by the goddess of love herself ('Love'). But those beautiful lips uttered the words 'I hate': ''Those lips that Love's own hand did make/Breath'd forth the sound that said 'I hate'.'' The poet means to say that the Lady told him that she hated him. But, contrarily, the poet was getting depressed ('languish'd') for long, waiting to possess her: ''To me that languish'd for her sake:'' But as soon as the Lady saw the sorrowful plight of the poet, mercy settled on her heart: ''But when she saw my woeful state,/Straight in her heart did mercy come''. Mercy (personified) then scolded the tongue of the Lady — the tongue that was always sweet, and was accustomed to pass mild sentences or judgments ('gentle doom') on the poet — and taught the tongue afresh how to invite the poet well ('greet'): ''Chiding that tongue that ever sweet/Was us'd in giving gentle doom,/And taught it thus anew to greet:''.

That mercy ('she') changed the meaning of the sentence, or the two words, 'I hate', by adding to it some other words ('alter'd with an end'). And those additional words followed the sentence 'I hate' ('it') as a beautiful ('gentle') day follows a dark and oppressive night. And, consequently, the sentence, 'I hate' ('who') was flown away like a fiend by those additional words, from heaven to hell: '' 'I hate' she utter'd with an end/That follow'd it as gentle day/Doth follow night, who like a fiend/From heaven to hell is flown away:''. Kerrigan found a parallel to lines 10-11 at *Hamlet* I, iii, 79-80, where Polonius says: ''And it must follow, as the night the day,/Thou canst not then be false to any man''. The Dark Lady threw away the sentence 'I hate' from her hatred ('hate') and thus saved the life of the poet. She now said that she no more hated the poet ('Not you'): " 'I hate' from hate away she threw,/ And sav'd my life, saying — 'Not you'.''

146

Poor soul, the centre of my sinful earth,
[Foil'd by] these rebel powers that thee array,
Why dost thou pine within and suffer dearth,
Painting thy outward walls so costly gay?
Why so large cost, having so short lease,
Dost thou upon thy fading mansion spend?
Shall worms, inheritors of this excess,
Eat up thy charge? Is this thy body's end?
Then, soul, live thou upon thy servant's loss,
And let that pine to aggravate thy store;
Buy terms divine in selling hours of dross;
Within be fed, without be rich no more:
So shalt thou feed on Death, that feeds on men,
And Death once dead there's no more dying then.

This sonnet has no reference to the Dark Lady, though it is included in the 'Dark Lady Sonnets'. Commentators have dealt at some length on this sonnet. They say that this sonnet might have been influenced by a long line of poems presenting dialogues between Soul and Body, by Sidney's famous sonnet 'Leave me, O Love, which reachest but to dust'; by the dexterously serious style of the young John Donne; and, most immediately, by a weak poem in Bartholomew Griffin's *Fidessa* (1596):

Well may my soul, immortal and divine,
That is imprisoned in a lump of clay,
Breathe out laments until this body pine,
That from her takes her pleasures all away.
Pine then, thou loathed prison of my life!
Untoward subject of the last aggrievance!
O, let me die! Mortality is rife!...

Here, in this present sonnet, the poet compares his body with earth and his soul with the centre of that earth which is, he says, sinful or immoral. Addressing his wretched ('Poor') soul, the poet tells it that it has been defeated ('Foil'd') by its own rebellious powers or passions that have been arranged into battle-formation against itself (and against itself): "Poor soul, the centre of my sinful earth,/[Foil'd by] these rebel powers that thee array". These two lines have been frequently amended by commentators in various ways. Some commentators have expressed the opinion that the exact meaning to these two lines is not clear. However, these two lines may be compared with lines 1 and 2 at *Romeo and Juliet,* II, i, where Romeo says: "Can I go forward when my heart is here?/Turn back, dull earth, and find thy centre out." The poet further asks his soul why it is pining within itself, or inwardly, and suffering from want or privation ('dearth'), although it (the soul) is showing ('Painting') a very gaudy ('costly') and hilarious ('gay') externality: "Why dost thou pine within and suffer dearth,/Painting thy outward walls so costly gay?"

The poet, again, asks his soul why it is spending so huge an amount of money ('so large cost') in his dilapidating ('fading') mansion which is his body which the soul is enjoying on lease, knowing full well that the time period of the lease is very short: "Why so large cost, having so short a lease,/Dost thou upon thy fading mansion spend?" Will not worms soon eat up the body which the soul is now enjoying on trust ('charge')? The worms, therefore, may be called the heirs ('inheritors') of the body. And the body is some sort of superfluity or extravagance ('excess') to the soul, because the body is not something essential to the soul, but is something accidental. Here, the Platonic influence on the poet is quite evident. The poet tells his soul that this is the fate of the body (that it shall be eaten up by worms): "Shall worms, inheritors of this excess,/Eat up thy charge? Is this thy body's end?"

If this be the state of affairs ('Then'), the poet will ask his soul to continue to live on the decay of the body ('thy servant's loss'), and to let the body ('that') mourn over its decay ('pine'), so that it (the soul) may increase ('aggravate') its possessions ('store'): "Then, soul, live thou upon thy servant's loss,/And let that pine to aggravate thy store;". The poet, perhaps, means to say that the soul can grow only if the body decays. He asks his soul to swap or exchange ('selling') the length of the life of the body, which is something worthless ('dross'), with the length of the life of the soul which is divine ('terms divine'). Or, in other words, the poet asks his soul to buy the length of the life of the divine soul with the sell-proceeds of the length of the worthless life of the body: "Buy terms divine in selling hours of dross;". He further asks his soul to grow within itself (to grow divinely, or in divinity) or inwardly ('Within be fed'), and not to grow gaudy ('rich') in the external features of the body, any more: ''Within be fed, without be rich no more''. If the soul of the poet does accordingly, only then can it benefits from dying, or from its Death ('feed on Death') — Death that lives on killing men. And if the soul can consume Death and thus kill it ('Death once dead'), then there will be no more death: ''So shalt thou feed on Death, that feeds on men,/And Death once dead there's no more dying then.'' The poet means to say that if the soul grows well then even if the body dies, it will not die — it will be able to conquer Death, or it will survive the death of the body.

147

My love is as a fever, longing still
For that which longer nurseth the disease,
Feeding on that which doth preserve the ill,
The uncertain sickly appetite to please.
My reason, the physician to my love,
Angry that his prescriptions are not kept,
Hath left me, and I desperate now approve
Desire is death, which physic did except.
Past cure I am now, reason is past care,
And frantic mad with evermore unrest;
My thoughts and my discourse as madmen's are,
At random from the truth, vainly express'd:
For I have sworn thee fair, and thought thee bright,
Who art as black as hell, as dark as night.

This sonnet has connection with the previous one, in the sense that in the former, the poet exhorted his soul to grow on the decay of the body, but in this sonnet, he says that the body is still dominating his soul. Further, with this sonnet, we go back to the theme of Sonnets 118 and 119 where the poet spoke of his physical love for the Lady. In this sonnet, the poet says that his love for the Lady is like fever, because his love pines for, or aspires after, ('longing') that very thing which is the cause, or which prolongs ('longer nurseth'), that fever (of running after the Dark Lady) ('disease'): ''My love is as a fever, longing still/For that which longer nurseth the disease,''. The underlying meaning of these two lines is that the poet is now fretfully enjoying physical love with the Lady, but he cannot be satisfied with such enjoyment, for the more he enjoys, the more he feels hungry for such enjoyment. Therefore, he says that his fever is devouring ('feeding') that which increases or aggravates the fever, and that thereby his fever, or his urge for enjoying physical love, is trying to satisfy ('please') his hunger ('appetite') which is unhealthy, or harmful to health, ('sickly') and which is capricious or intermittant (now, the urge is satisfied, and then it increases): "Feeding on that which doth preserve the ill,/The uncertain sickly appetite to please." The poet calls his rationality ('reason') the controller or physician of his love. He says that as he (the poet) does not abide by the recipes ('prescriptions') of the physician, the physician becomes angry with him (the poet), and so the physician (the rationality of the poet) has almost parted with him ('Half left me'): "My reason, the physician to my love,/Angry that his prescriptions are not kept,/Half left me". The poet means to say that his rationality fails to control or leash his urge for enjoying physical love with the Dark Lady. Line 5 may be compared with lines 5-7 at *The Merry Wives of Windsor*, II, i : "Ask me no reason why I love you; for though Love use Reason for his physician, he admits him not for his counsellor."

Now, the poet has become desperate, and now he realises by experience ('approve') that such urge for physical love ('Desire') is nothing but death — death that his physician rationality, or the medical skill of the physician ('physic') forbids him to resort to ('did except'): "and I desperate now approve/Desire is death, which physic did except." Now the condition of the poet is such that he cannot come round from his disease ('Past cure'), and therefore, it is of no help for him to care for reason or rationality, his physician ('reason is past care'). He is now frantically mad, and is extremely ('evermore') restless: "Past cure I am now reason is past care,/And frantic mad with evermore unrest;". His thoughts and his arguments ('discourse') are now like those who are mad, because his thoughts and discourses are far from or wide of, the point ('At random'). And whatever, now, he expresses is ineffectual or ineffective, or rather, whenever he expresses, he does so ineffectually or ineffectively ('vainly'): "My thoughts and my discoruse as madmen's are,/At random from the truth, vainly express'd." The poet says that what he is saying is far from truth, and this is so because he is feverishly desiring the physical love of the Dark Lady. But what is it that he says and what is it that is far from truth? The poet answers this question in the concluding couplet. He says that it is this that he has said on oath ('have sworn') that the Lady ('thee') is beautiful ('fair'), and that he has thought her to be bright too, although, in reality, she is "as black as hell", *i.e.* she is as immoral as the inhabitants of hell, and her character is as dark or dishonest ('dark') as night which inspires immoral and dishonest activities: "For I have sworn thee fair, and thought thee bright,/ Who art as black as hell, as dark as night."

148

Oh me! what eyes hath love put in my head,
Which have no correspondence with true sight?
Or if they have, where is my judgment fled,
That censures falsely what they see aright?
If that be fair whereon my false eyes dote,
What means the world to say it is not so?
If it be not, then love doth well denote
Love's eye is not so true as all men's: No;
How can it? Oh, how can love's eye be true,
That is so vex'd watching and with tears?
No marvel then though I mistake my view—
The sun itself sees not till heaven clears.
O cunning love! with tears thou keep'st me blind,
Lest eyes, well seeing, thy foul faults should find.

This sonnet continues the argument of the previous one. In Sonnet 147, the poet said that he called the Dark Lady fair, though actually she was not so; and here in Sonnet 148, he gives the *raison de 'etre*: he says that as his eyes are, himself being in love, tired with watching (the beauty of the beloved) and full of tears (for not getting as much love from her as he expects, may be), so he cannot perceive the Dark Lady truly. The present sonnet may also be compared with Sonnets 113 and 114, in both of which the poet complains about his troubles with sight. In the present sonnet, he ruefully complains that Love has put in his forehead such a pair of eyes as cannot perceive correctly ('have no correspondence with true sight'): ''Oh me! what eyes hath love put in my head,/Which have no correspondence with true sight?'' Alternatively, he says that if the eyes can see perfectly, his power of judgment, or his rationality, has left him ('judgment fled'). The poet says this because, he says, his rationality now cannot rightly monitor or guide or amend or censure ('censures falsely') what his eyes see truly ('aright'): ''Or if they have, where is my judgment fled,/That censures falsely what they see aright?''

The poet says if the Lady ('that') seems to be beautiful to his eyes which do not see correctly ('false eyes'), and, if consequently he foolishly loves her ('dote'), then it does not matter that the people of the whole world say that what the eyes see is not correct ('is not so'): ''If that be fair whereon my false eyes dote,/What means the world to say it is not so?'' If what his eyes see is not really beautiful ('If it be not'), then the poet will think that Love very well marks the point, or proves the point ('denote') that the eyes of one who is in love do not see as correctly as the eyes of other people who are not in love: "If it be not, then love doth well denote/Love's eye is not so true as all men's". The poet emphasises the point that the eyes of one in love cannot see as correctly as the eyes of other people who are not in love: "No". The poet asks: how can the two categories of eyes be the same? And he answers that the eyes of one in love cannot see correctly ('how can love's eye be true') because the eyes of one in love are troubled with constant observation of the love-object ('watching') and with weeping ('tears'): "How can it? Oh, how can love's eye be true,/That is so vex'd with watching and with tears?"

The poet says that it is not astonishing ('No marvel'), therefore, that he (who is in love) is not perceiving things correctly ('I mistake my view'). He, as told earlier, cannot see correctly, because his eyes are full of tears. He now compares his eyes with cloudy sky, and himself with the sun. The sun cannot see clearly if the sky ('heaven') remains cloudy. Likewise, the eyes of the poet are also cloudy (for his tears), and so he cannot see clearly: "No marvel then though I mistake my view—/The sun itself sees not till heaven clears." In the concluding couplet, the poet accuses the goddess of love for his (the poet's) being unable to see things correctly. He says that the goddess of love is very crafty ('cunning'), because she keeps his eyes blind, or veiled, with tears. She does so, because otherwise ('Lest') his eyes would be able to see things well ('seeing well'), and would, consequently, be able to see the grave aesthetic and moral defects ('foul faults') of the Dark Lady ('thy'): "O cunning love! with tears thou keep'st me blind,/Lest eyes, well seeing, thy foul faults should find."

149

Canst thou, O cruel, say I love thee not,
When I against myself with thee partake?
Do I not think on thee, when I forgot
Am of myself, all tyrant, for thy sake?
Who hateth thee that I do call my friend?
On whom frown'st thou that I do fawn upon?
Nay, if thou lour'st on me, do I not spend
Revenge upon myself with present moan?
What merit do I in myself respect
That is so proud thy service to despise,
When all my best doth worship thy defect,
Commanded by the motion of thine eyes?

But, love, hate on; for now I know thy mind:
Those that can see thou lov'st — and I am blind.

This sonnet bears the implication of the last line of the previous one. In this sonnet, we find the poet divided into two selves — one self loving the Dark Lady, and the other holding himself back from loving her. The poet addresses the Dark Lady as a cruel woman, and asks her if she can say that he (the poet) does not love her, when one half of his self is taking side with her, or one half of his self is loving ('partake') her, in spite of the protestation of the other half of his self: ''Canst thou, O cruel, say I love thee not,/When I against myself with thee partake?'' He tells her that he always thinks on her, ignoring ('forgot') the other self of his, or the other half of his self ('Am of myself') which restrains him from loving her, like a tyrant; and that he loves her for her own sake: ''Do I not think on thee, when I forgot/Am of myself, all tyrant, for thy self?'' Does the poet call him who hates the Dark Lady his friend? The answer is 'no'. Kerrigan said that line 5 is an echo of Psalm 139.21: '''Do not I hate them, O God, that hate thee'.'' However, the poet again asks her: does he (the poet) flatter ('fawn') the person on whom she shows her anger ('frown'st')? Again, the answer is 'no': ''On whom frown'st thou that I do fawn upon?'' He further asks her: does he not take revenge upon himself by bringing upon himself immediate suffering or lamentation ('present moan') whenever the Dark Lady ('thou') shows him a gloomy and threatening appearance ('lour'st')?: ''Nay, if thou lour'st on me, do I not spend/Revenge upon myself with present moan?''

The poet asks the Lady what merit in himself he does respect, which merit is proud enough to despise any service to her? And the obvious answer of the poet is: there is no such merit. He says that there can be no such merit in him that hates to serve her, because ('When') all the best merits or efforts of the poet adulate or respect ('worship') even her aesthetic and moral faults ('defect'), being commended by the attraction or glancing ('motion') of her beautiful eyes: ''What merit do I in himself respect/That is so proud thy service to despise,/When all my best doth worhsip thy defect,/Commended by the motion of thine eyes?'' Kerrigan found parallels to the use of the word 'motion' at line 12 of this sonnet at *The Merry Wives of Windsor,* III, ii, 31-32 ('He gives for folly motion and advantage'), and at *King John,* IV, ii, 255 ('The dreadful motion of a murderous thought'). (Kerrigan, 382). However, in the concluding couplet, the poet asks the Lady to continue to hate him, because he has now understood the workings of her mind, or what she has decided ('I know thy mind'). He says that the Lady loves only those persons who ('Those that') see her beauty as it really is ('can see'), but he himself cannot see her beauty as it really is, because, being uncritical about her, he is blind: "But, love, hate on; for now I know thy mind:/Those that can see thou lov'st — and I am blind." Kerrigan explained line 14 thus: "The lady loves those who see and admire her, but the poet so admires that he cannot really see (compare Sonnet 148); he is, because uncritical, *blind* (as at 148.13), and (in her mind at least) to that extent unlovable. The psychology of shallow loving" (Kerrigan, 382).

150

Oh, from what power hast thou this powerful night
With insufficiency my heart to sway,
To make me give the lie to my true sight
And swear that brightness doth not grace the day? 4
Whence hast thou this becoming of things ill,
That in the very refuse of thy deeds
There is such strength and warrantise of skill
That in my mind thy worst all best exceeds? 8
Who taught thee how to make me love thee more
The more I hear and see just cause of hate?
Oh, though I love what others do abhor,
With others thou shouldst not abhor my state! 12
If thy unworthiness rais'd love in me,
More worthy I to be belov'd of thee.

The poet asks the Dark Lady from what suspernatural or mysterious source ('what power') she has derived her vigorous or potent power with which she controls ('sway') his heart, though not completely or absolutely ('With insufficiency'): "Oh, from what power hast thou this powerful might/With insufficiency my heart to sway," With that power (derived power), the Lady compels the poet not to believe ('give the lie') what he correctly sees ('true sight'). Further, with that derived power, the Lady makes the poet say on oath ('swear') that the day is not lovely or graceful ('grace') though it is bright (rather, that day is lovely which has insufficient or defective light, or which is dark, like the Dark Lady): "To make me the lie to my true sight/And swear that brightness doth not grace the day?" Kerrigan explained line 4 thus: "The sufficiency of the lady seems so beautiful to the poet that he rejects everything fair, thinking only blackness an ornament to the day. Perhaps he even thinks, perversely, that since the day is lovely it must be dark, not bright." (Kerrigan, 383).

The poet asks the Lady from where she has received the power to make ugly things ('things ill') look beautiful ('becoming'), so that even in the most abominable ('refuse') of her activities, there is so much ('such') strength and assurance ('warrantise') of skill that, to the mind of the poet, even the worst aspects of her person, or her worst activities, seem to surpass ('exceed') all that is good, in valuation or estimation: "Whence hast thou this becoming of things ill,/That in the very refuse of thy deeds/There is such strength and warrantise of skill/That in my mind thy worst all best exceeds?" Line 5 may be compared with lines 242-44 at *Antony and Cleopatra,* II,ii, where Enobarbus tells about Cleopatra: "for vilest things/Become themselves in her, that the holy priests/Bless her when she is riggish."

The poet asks the Dark Lady to tell him who taught her how to make him love her the more, the more he hears about her aesthetic and moral faults, and so he finds just cause of hating her: "Who taught thee how to make me love thee more/The more I hear and see just cause of hate?" He appeals to the Lady not to despise ('abhor') his despicable plight, along with those persons who despise her whom he loves: "Oh, thou I love what others do abhor,/With others thou shouldst not abhor my state!" The poet says that it is her unworthiness of being loved that actually caused him to love her. And if this be so, then he claims to be more worthy to be loved by her, or he demands her love the more (because it is only he who loves her in spite of all her unworthiness): "If thy unworthiness rais'd love in me,/More worthy I to be belov'd of thee." Kerrigan explained the concluding couplet as follows: "Beneath the poet's claim that he deserves to be loved because he loves even the lady's faults lurks the insulting insinuation that by loving someone so unworthy as the lady the poet has shown himself unworthy enough to be worthy [of] her love" (Kerrigan, 383).

151

Love is too young to know what conscience is,—
Yet who knows not conscience is born of love?
Then, gentle cheater, urge not my amiss,
Lest guilty of my faults thy sweet self prove:
For, thou betraying me, I do betray
My nobler part to my gross body's treason;
My soul doth tell my body that he may
Triumph in love: flesh stays no farther reason,
But rising at thy name doth point out thee
As his triumph prize. Proud of this pride,

He is contented thy poor drudge to be,
To stand in thy affairs, fall by thy side.
  No want of conscience hold it that I call
  Her 'love' for whose dear love I rise and fall.

This sonnet, particularly, is full of puns or double meanings. The poet says that love (personified) is not mature enough so that it has moral sense ('conscience'): "Love is too young to know what conscience is,—". The poet means to say that love or, rather, physical intercourse, cannot be mutually congruent. Kerrigan said that the Latin proverb "*Penis erectus non habet conscientiam*" (if the penis is erected, one cannot have moral scruple) was prevalent in the Elizabethan period (Kerrigan, 383). Shakespeare, perhaps, means to say the same thing. He says that knowledge of the female sexual organ ('conscience') follows only love-affairs: "Yet who knows not conscience is born of love?" In the first two lines of this sonnet, Shakespeare puns on the word 'conscience'. In line 1, the word means 'moral sense', but in line 2, the word means 'conscience' or 'cunt-knowledge' (the French word 'con' means cunt or female sexual organ). Love cannot have conscience and love is naturally followed by 'conscience', and so the poet appeals to the Dark Lady, whom he calls 'gentle cheater', not to be interested in, or not to urge herself to be interested in, his moral faults ('my amiss'), because ('Lest') in that case, the sweet self of the Dark Lady will prove himself guilty of moral aberrations ('faults'): "Then, gentle cheater, urge not my amiss,/Lest guilty of my faults thy sweet self prove:". The poet, again, urges her not to be interested in his moral faults, bacause ('For') if she reveals ('betraying') his faults, then it will be clear that he has cheated ('betray') his prue and nobler part of his passion, or of his self, into the sexual enjoyment of his physical body which his pure self proscribes ('gross body's treason'): "For thou betraying me, I do betray/ My nobler part to my gross body's treason;".

The poet says that his soul tells his body that it (the body) may be triumphant in the affairs of (pure) love; but his body ('flesh') would not hear ('stays') any argument or talk ('reason') of his soul: "My soul doth tell my body that he may/Triumph in love: flesh stays no further reason,". Kerrigan wrote about the expression 'stays no further reason': "doesn't stop to argue, doesn't linger to hear more justification for its action. No doubt the *soul* means one thing by love, while the *body* and its *flesh* jump to quite another conclusion." (Kerrigan, 384). Rather ('But'), when the body of the poet hears the name of the Lady ('rising at thy name'), it bends itself, or inclines, to the Lady ('doth point out thee'), and thinks of her as its prize of victory ('triumphant prize'): ''But rising at thy name doth point out thee/As his triumphant prize''. Line 9 bears sexual implication, too. When his body finds the Lady, its sexual organ becomes entumesced and pointed, and takes the Lady as its object to win over. His body, or rather his sexual organ, thus (being entumesced) becomes proud; but at the same time, it is satisfied ('contented') to be a poor drudge or slave for the physical satisfaction of the Lady: ''Proud of this pride,/He is contented thy poor drudge to be,''. The sexual organ is then ready to serve the Lady in her physical enjoyment ('stand in thy affair'), and is ready to fall vanquished, like a soldier in a battle, after the physical affair with the Lady is over: ''To stand in thy affairs, fall by thy side.'' The words 'stand' and 'fall' overtly bear sexual implications. However, yet the poet says that when he calls the Lady his lady-love, there is no lack of moral sense ('conscience') in what he says, because it is for her precious ('dear') love that he feels elated ('rise'), or depressed ('fall'): ''No want of conscience hold it that I call/Her 'love' for whose dear love I rise and fall.''

152

In loving thee thou know'st I am forsworn;
But thou art twice forsworn to me love swearing,—
In act thy bed-vow broke, and new faith torn
In vowing new hate after new love bearing.
But why of two oaths' breach do I accuse thee,
When I break twenty? I am perjur'd most:
For all my vows are oaths but to misuse thee,
And all my honest faith in thee is lost.
For I have sworn deep oaths of thy deep kindness—
Oaths of thy love, thy truth, thy constancy;
And to enlighten thee gave eyes to blindness,
Or made them swear against the thing they see:
For I have sworn thee fair,— more perjur'd eye,
To swear against the truth so foul a lie!

This is a very complicated sonnet, for it is not clear how many parties are involved here. Ingram and Redpath wrote: ''Commentators have differed as to how many parties are involved. Wyndham mentions four — the woman, her husband, the Friend, and the poet — leaving unmentioned the question whether line 1 refers to the poet's own marriage-vow. Other commentators, *e.g.* Beeching, Pooler, and Tucker, hold that the Friend is not referred to. It seems to us impossible to decide the point from the lines alone'' (Ingram, 350). The poet tells the

Dark Lady that she knows that when he loves her, he bresks faith (with another woman) ('forsworn'): "In loving thee thou know'st I am forsworn;". According to Kerrigan, the poet means forswearing his love of his friend, the Fair Youth; but according to other commentators, the poet means forswearing his avowed love to Anne Hathaway, the poet's wife. But, the poet says, when she (the Dark Lady) swears love to him (the poet), then she is breaking her vow ('forsworn') of love twice (once, may be, with her husband; and secondly, with the Fair Youth): "But thou art twice forsworn to me love swearing,—". In her activities or behaviour, the Lady has broken her nuptial vow ('bed-vow'), and she has broken her new and subsequent faith to another person when she vowed to hate that person ('vowing new hate'), and, further, when, at the same time, she bore love for (the third and) new person ('after new love bearing): "In act thy bed-vow broke, and new faith torn/In vowing new hate after new love bearing." The sequence of the Lady's loves and hates is such: firstly, she broke vow with her husband ('bed-vow'); secondly, she vowed faith to another person; thirdly, she vowed to hate the second candidate; and fourthly, she loved a third candidate. The second and the third candidates may be the Fair Youth and the poet, respectively.

The Lady has thus broken vows twice ('two oaths' breach'). But the poet would not accuse her still then, because he himself has broken oaths twenty times ('break twenty') and, therefore, he is the greatest forswearer ('perjur'd most'): "But why of two oaths' breach do I accuse thee,/When I break twenty? I am perjur'd most:". Because, he says, he has vowed so many times only to deceive or slander or mistreat ('misuse') the Dark Lady. The poet says that he has lost all honest faith in her, or in loving her he has lost his integrity: "For all my vows are oaths but to misuse thee,/And all my honest faith in thee is lost." Ingram and Redpath interpreted line 8 thus: " 'In my realtionship with you I have entirely lost my integrity' " (Ingram, 352). Because, the poet says, he has sworn profoundly ('sworn deep oaths') that the Lady is full of profound kindness, that she is full of (honest) love, that she is true, and that she is constant (all these are said ironically): "For I have sworn deep oaths of thy kindness—/Oaths of thy love, thy constancy;". Further, to exult her the most ('to enlighten thee'), the poet has made himself blind, or has turned himself ignorant ('gave eyes to blindness'). Or, he has made his eyes swear that they do not see what they see ('swear against the thing they see'), *i.e.* he has made his eyes not to see the aesthetic and moral faults of the Lady, in order to make her seem (falsely) illuminated: "And to enlighten thee gave eyes to blindness,/ Or made them swear against the thing they see:". The poet has done all these because ('For') he has avowedly said that the Lady is beautiful and honest ('fair'). And in doing this, he has made his eyes swear falsely ('more perjur'd eye'), because he has made his eyes to swear a great and foul lie, and that he did against the truth: "For I have sworn thee fair,— more perjur'd eye,/To swear against the truth so foul a lie!"

153

Cupid laid by his brand and fell asleep.
A maid of Dian's this advantage found,
And his love-kindling fire did quickly steep
In a cold valley-fountain of that ground;
Which borrow'd from this holy fire of Love
A dateless lively heat, still to endure,
And grew a seething bath which men yet prove
Against strange maladies a sovereign cure.
But at my mistress' eye Love's brand new fir'd,
The boy for trial needs would touch my breast.
I, sick withal, the help of bath desir'd,
And thither hied, a sad distemper'd guest;
But found no cure: the bath for my help lies
Where Cupid got new fire — my mistress' eyes.

This sonnet and the next one dwell on almsot the same theme or conceit which "is to be found in many other poems, ranging from an epigram by the fifth-century Byzantine Marianus Scholasticus (...) to various poems in different langauges (*e.g.* Latin, Italian, French) published in the sixteenth century and even later" (Ingram, 354). Kerrigan wrote a long headnote to this poem (as well as one to Sonnet 154). He wrote (Kerrigan, 387): "When Shakespeare penned this poem and Sonnet 154, he was elaborating a conceit already at least a thousand years old. The Greek Anthology records a six-line epigram by Marianus Scholasticus, a fifth-century Byzantine poet, which has been translated thus:

> Beneath these plane trees, detained by gentle slumber, Love slept, having put his torch in the care of the Nymphs; but the Nymphs said one to another: 'Why wait? Would that together with this we could quench the fire in the hearts of men.' But the torch set fire even to the water, and with hot water thenceforth the Love-Nymphs fill the bath."

However, the poet narrates the story of the love-god Cupid and Dian's maid. Cupid laid by his side his torch ('brand'), and fell asleep. At this hour a maid of Dian or Diana took his opportunity ('advantage found'): "Cupid laid by his brand and fell asleep./A maid of Dian's this advantage found,". Here the brand or torch of Cupid represents or symbolises passion, particularly the passion of love. Dian or Diana is the moon-goddess who hunts and who is the queen of chastity. Diana has a train of chaste nymphs. When Cupid stealthily remained in this state, the maid of Diana took away the torch of Cupid — torch that can ignite love in human hearts ('love-kindling fire'). The maid then fast ('quickly') immersed ('steep') that burning torch in the cold water of a fountain or jet of water which was there in a valley of that region ('of that ground'): "And his love-kindling fire did quickly steep/In a cold valley-fountain of that ground;". As a result, the valley ('Which') received perennial ('dateless') heat or wormth from that sacred fire of Love resident in the torch; and the valley was to keep that resplendant ('lively') heat eternally ('still'): "Which borrow'd from this holy fire of Love/A dateless lively heat, still to endure,". And, consequently, the valley turned into a bath-tub or bath-sink with very hot water ('seething bath'). And then, from that time till today ('yet') people have proved (by demonstration) that the valley or, rather, the hot water of the valley, is a very effective medicine ('sovereign cure') for curing diverse unknown diseases ('maladies'): "And grew a seething bath which men yet prove/ Against strange maladies a sovereign cure." Line 8 may be compared with line 916 of *Venus and Adonis* : " 'Gainst venom'd sores the only sovereign plaster".

Next, the poet says that the torch of love ignited, once more, the eyes of his mistress, the Dark Lady. And now the god of love, Cupid ('The boy': Cupid is always represented as a boy) wanted to see if the heart of the poet can also be fired with his torch. And so he would like to touch the breast of the poet to try ('trial') if it could be enkindled: "But at my mistress' eye Love's brand new fir'd,/The boy for trial needs would touch my breast." The poet was also ('withal') indisposed (*i.e.* suffering from maladies), and therefore he wished to be cured of his indisposition, with the help of bathing (in the valley where the water was warmed with the fire of love, or with the torch of Cupid). He, therefore, hurried, or made a bee-line to that place ('hither hied'), as a sorrowful and unhappy ('sad distemper'd') new commer ('guest'): "I sick withal, the help of bath desir'd,/And thither hied, a sad distemper'd guest;". But there the poet was not cured. So he thinks that the bath that he needs for curing himself of his disease (of melancholy) is not to be had in the said valley of love-fired water, but at that place where the god of love enkindled new fire (of love), *i.e.* in the eyes of his mistress, the Dark Lady: "But found no cure: the bath for my help lies/Where Cupid got new fire — my mistress' eyes."

154

The little Love-god lying once asleep
Laid by his side his heart-inflaming brand,
Whilst many nymphs that vow'd chaste life to keep
Came tripping by; but in her maiden hand
The fairest votary took up that fire
Which many legions of true hearts had warm'd,
And so the General of hot desire
Was sleeping by a virgin hand disarm'd.
This brand she quenched in a cool well by,
Which from Love's fire took heat perpetual,
Growing a bath and healthful remedy
For men diseas'd. But, I, my mistress' thrall,
  Came there for cure; and this by that I prove:
  Love's fire heats water, water cools not love.

According to Dante Gabriel Rossetti, this sonnet and the previous one may be deemed to form the Epilogue to the sonnet-sequence from Sonnet 127 to 152. The theme or conceit of this present sonnet, as told earlier, is the same as in Sonnet 153; and further, the source of this sonnet is, perhaps, the same poem which is the source of the immediately preceding one. Curiously, it is not clear why a great poet that Shakespeare was wrote two sonnets on the identical theme, in almost the same form. However, the poet narrates that once the young god of love had been lying asleep laying beside him his heart-burning torch of love ('heart-flaming brand'): "The little Love-god lying once asleep/Laid by his side his heart-flaming brand,". At that time, many nymphs, who vowed that they would keep themsleves chaste, came there prancingly or skippingly, or, as if dancing ('tripping'): "Whilst many nymphs that vow'd chaste life to keep/Came tripping by". But though the nymphs vowed to keep their lives chaste, the most beautiful of them, who also vowed ('votary') in that way, took up in her hand that flaming torch of love ('that fire') — the torch that was warmed by a great number ('legion') of true lovers ('true hearts'): "but in her maiden hand/The fairest votary took up that fire/Which many legions of true hearts had warm'd,". The god of love ('the General of hot desire') was thus disarmed, *i.e.* his armour of the flaming torch was taken away by a spinster nymph ('by a virgin hand'), while the god of love was sleeping: "And so the General of hot desire/Was sleeping by a virgin hand disarm'd."

The most beautiful nymph, who was nearby ('by'), then dipped ('quenched') the flaming torch of love ('brand') in a well of cool water, and, consequently, the heat of the torch was transferred to the cool water of the well, and so the water of the well became perpetually hot: "This brand she quenched in a cool well by,/Which from Love's fire took heat perpetual,". And thus, further, the water of the well became a medicinal element (like Spa), such that if one takes bath in that well, one would be cured of diseases, and become healthy once again: "Growing a bath and healthful remedy/For men diseas'd". The poet, who is a slave ('thrall') of his mistress, the Dark Lady, has also come to that well (because he is also sick) to get his disease cured: "But, I, my mistress' thrall,/Come there for cure". But by taking bath in that well, the poet (who has, nevertheless, not been cured) has demonstrated the fact ('that') that such a bath is ineffectual in curing disease (*i.e.* hunger for love): he has proved that love's heat can only warm anybody, but nothing can cool the heat or passion of love: "and this by that I prove:/Love's fire heats water, water cools not love." Kerrigan said about line 14: "The wit of the line turns, in part, on the echo of the Song of Solomon 8.7: 'Her coals are coals of fire, and a very vehement flame (of the Lord): so that many waters are not able to quench love, neither may the streams drown it: Yea, if a man would give all the good of his house for love, he should count it nothing'." (Kerrigan, 388).

In the Quarto edition, this last sonnet is followed by the word FINIS in large capitals.

❒

Index of First Lines of the Sonnets

Bibliography

(Only the Titles Referred to in this Book)

Alpers, Paul J. (ed.), *Elizabethan Poetry,* Oxford University Press, 1967.

Andrews, W.T., *Critics of Shakespeare,* Universal Book Stall, New Delhi, 1973.

Artz, Frederick B., *Renaissance to Romaticism,* The University of Chicago Press, Chicago and London, 1975.

Beaty, Jerome and Matchett, William H., *Poetry: From Statement to Meaning,* Oxford University Press, 1965.

Brown, Ivor, *Shakespeare,* Collins, London, 1955.

Brown, John Russell and Harris, Bernard (General editors), *Elizabethan Poetry,* (Startford-Upon-Avon Studies-2), London, 1960.

Compton-Rickett, Arthur, *A History of English Literature,* Universal Book Stall, New Delhi, 1992.

Coleridge, Samuel Taylor, *Lectures on Shakespeare,* etc., J.M. Dent, London, 1951.

Cuddon, J.A., *A Dictionary of Literary Terms,* Penguin Books, 1979.

Daiches, David (ed.), *The Penguin Companion to Literature,* vol. I, Penguin Books, 1971.

Fripp, Edgar I., *Shakespeare: Man and Artist,* 2 vols., Oxford University Press, London, 1964.

Ford, Boris (ed.), *The Age of Shakespeare (The Penguin Guide to English Literature,* vol. 2), Penguin Books, 1973.

Gittings, Robert, *Shakespeare's Rival,* Heinemann, London, etc., 1960.

Goddard, Harold C., *The Meaning of Shakespeare,* vol. 2, Phoenix Books, Chicago and London, 1951.

Halliday, F.E., *A Shakespeare Companion,* Penguin Books, 1969.

Hazlitt, William, *The Round Table and Charcters of Shakespeare's Plays*, J.M. Dent and Sons, London, 1957.

Hamlyn, *New Larousse Encyclopedia of Mythology*, Paris, 1995.

Ingram, W.G. and Redpath, Theodore, *Shakespeare's Sonnets*, B.I. Publications, Bombay, etc., 1979.

Jones, Pater (ed.), *Shakespeare: The Sonnets (A Casebook)*, Macmillan, 1989.

Kerrigan, John, *William Shakespeare: The Sonnets and A Lover's Complaint*, Penguin Books, 1986.

Knight, G. Wilson, *The Mutual Flame*, Methuen, London, 1955.

Preminger, Alex (ed.), *Princeton Encyclopedia of Poetry and Poetics*, Macmillan, 1974.

Peacock, Ronald, *The Art of Drama*, Routledge & Kegan Paul, London, 1957.

Reese, M. M., *Shakespeare: His World and His Work*, Edward Arnold Ltd., London, 1958.

Raleigh, Walter, *Shakespeare*, Macmillan, London, 1953.

Ralli, Augustus, *A History of Shakespearian Criticism*, (2 vols.), The Humanities Press, New York, 1965.

Setna, K.D., *Two Loves and 'A Worthier Pen'*, Arnold-Heinemann, New Delhi, 1984.

Sampson, George, *The Concise Cambridge History of English Literature*, Cambridge University Press, 1970.

Thomson, J.A.K., *Classical Influence on English Poetry*, George Allen & Unwin, London, 1951.

Tennyson, G.B. (ed.), *A Carlyle Reader*, Modern Library College Edition, New York, 1964.

Wilson, John Dover (ed.), *The Works of Shakespeare: The Sonnets*, Cambridge University Press, 1969.

Ward, A.C., *Illustrated History of English Literature*, vol. I, Longmans, Green and Co., London, etc. (4th impression), 1958.

INDEX